T0281011

Lecture Notes in Computer Science   11774

More information about this series at http://www.springer.com/series/7410

Peter Schwabe · Nicolas Thériault (Eds.)

Progress in Cryptology – LATINCRYPT 2019

6th International Conference on Cryptology
and Information Security in Latin America
Santiago de Chile, Chile, October 2–4, 2019
Proceedings

 Springer

Editors
Peter Schwabe
Radboud University Nijmegen
Nijmegen, The Netherlands

Nicolas Thériault
Universidad de Santiago de Chile
Santiago, Chile

ISSN 0302-9743 ISSN 1611-3349 (electronic)
Lecture Notes in Computer Science
ISBN 978-3-030-30529-1 ISBN 978-3-030-30530-7 (eBook)
https://doi.org/10.1007/978-3-030-30530-7

LNCS Sublibrary: SL4 – Security and Cryptology

This Springer imprint is published by the registered company Springer Nature Switzerland AG
The registered company address is: Gewerbestrasse 11, 6330 Cham, Switzerland

Preface

This book constitutes the proceedings of the 6th International Conference on Cryptology and Information Security in Latin America, LATINCRYPT 2019, held in Santiago, Chile, during October 2–4, 2019. The main conference program was preceded by the Advanced School on Cryptology and Information Security in Latin America (ASCrypto), held during September 30 – October 1, 2019. LATINCRYPT 2019 was organized by the Departamento de Matemática y Ciencia de la Computación of the Universidad de Santiago de Chile, in cooperation with the International Association for Cryptologic Research (IACR). The general chair of the conference was Nicolas Thériault.

LATINCRYPT 2019 received 40 submissions. Each submission was assigned to at least three members of the Program Committee for review. Submissions co-authored by members of the Program Committee were assigned to at least five committee members. The reviewing process was challenging, owing to the large number of high-quality submissions, and we are deeply grateful to the committee members and external reviewers for their indefatigable work. Special thanks go out to the shepherds of this edition, who greatly helped us in making a better paper selection.

After careful deliberation, the Program Committee, which was chaired by Peter Schwabe and Nicolas Thériault, selected 18 submissions for presentation at the conference. In addition to these presentations, the program also included three invited talks by Gilles Barthe (Max-Planck Society, Germany, and IMDEA Software Institute, Spain), Sonia Belaïd (CryptoExperts, France), and Patrick Longa (Microsoft Research, USA).

The reviewing process was run using the WebSubRev software, written by Shai Halevi from IBM Research. We are grateful to him for releasing this software. Finally, we would like to thank our sponsors, namely, Bitmark and the United States Air Force Office of Scientific Research for their financial support, as well as all the people who contributed to the success of this conference. We are also indebted to the members of the LATINCRYPT Steering Committee for making this conference possible. We would also like to thank Springer for publishing these proceedings in the *Lecture Notes in Computer Science* series. It was a great honor to be Program Committee chairs for LATINCRYPT 2019 and we look forward to the next edition in the conference series.

October 2019

Peter Schwabe
Nicolas Thériault

Organization

General Chair

Nicolas Thériault   Universidad de Santiago de Chile, Chile

Program Chairs

Peter Schwabe   Radboud University, The Netherlands
Nicolas Thériault   Universidad de Santiago de Chile, Chile

Steering Committee

Michel Abdalla   CNRS and DI/ENS, PSL University, France
Diego Aranha   Aarhus University, Denmark, and Universidade
         Estadual de Campinas, Brazil
Paulo Barreto   University of Washington Tacoma, USA
Ricardo Dahab   Universidade Estadual de Campinas, Brazil
Alejandro Hevia   Universidad de Chile, Chile
Kristin Lauter   Microsoft Research, USA
Julio López   Universidade Estadual de Campinas, Brazil
Daniel Panario   Carleton University, Canada
Francisco   CINVESTAV-IPN, Mexico
    Rodríguez- Henríquez
Alfredo Viola   Universidad de la República, Uruguay

Program Committee

Rodrigo Abarzúa   Universidad de Santiago de Chile, Chile
Michel Abdalla   CNRS and DI/ENS, PSL University, France
Diego Aranha   Aarhus University, Denmark, and Universidade
         Estadual de Campinas, Brazil
Paulo Barreto   University of Washington Tacoma, USA
Billy Bob Brumley   Tampere University, Finland
Ricardo Dahab   Universidade Estadual de Campinas, Brazil
Luis J. Dominguez Perez   CIMAT Zacatecas, Mexico
Léo Ducas   CWI Amsterdam, The Netherlands
Orr Dunkelman   University of Haifa, Israel
Maria Eichlseder   Technische Universität Graz, Austria
Gina Gallegos-García   Instituto Politécnico Nacional, Mexico
Jeroen van de Graaf   Universidade Federal de Minas Gerais, Brazil
Benjamin Grégoire   Inria, France
Aurore Guillevic   Inria, France

Helena Handschuh	Rambus, USA
Alejandro Hevia	Universidad de Chile, Chile
Andreas Hülsing	Technische Universiteit Eindhoven, The Netherlands
Sorina Ionica	Université de Picardie Jules Verne, France
Michael Jacobson Jr.	University of Calgary, Canada
Tibor Jager	Universität Paderborn, Germany
Stefan Kölbl	Cybercrypt, Denmark
Tanja Lange	Technische Universiteit Eindhoven, The Netherlands
Julio López	Universidade Estadual de Campinas, Brazil
Michael Naehrig	Microsoft Research, USA
Anderson Nascimento	University of Washington Tacoma, USA
Daniel Panario	Carleton University, Canada
Thomas Pöppelmann	Infineon Technologies, Germany
Bart Preneel	Katholieke Universiteit Leuven, Belgium
Francisco Rodríguez- Henríquez	CINVESTAV-IPN, Mexico
Eyal Ronen	Tel Aviv University, Israel, and Katholieke Universiteit Leuven, Belgium
Simona Samardjiska	Radboud University, The Netherlands
Johanna Sepúlveda	Airbus Defense and Space, Germany
Benjamin Smith	Inria and École Polytechnique, France
Martijn Stam	Simula UiB, Norway
Rainer Steinwandt	Florida Atlantic University, USA
Yosuke Todo	NTT Secure Platform Laboratories, Japan
Alfredo Viola	Universidad de la República, Uruguay
Yuval Yarom	University of Adelaide, Data61, Australia

Additional Reviewers

Gualberto Aguilar-Torres
Alessandro Amadori
Kazumaro Aoki
Koen de Boer
Daniel Cervantes-Vázquez
Jesús-Javier Chi-Domínguez
Alain Couvreur
Alfonso F. De Abiega-L'Eglisse
Kevin A. Delgado-Vargas
John-Marc Desmarais
Georg Fuchsbauer
Mike Hamburg

Akinori Hosoyamada
Thais Bardini Idalino
Mario Larangeira
Sebastian Lindner
Jean Martina
Eduardo Moraes de Morais
Anton Mosunov
Ruben Niederhagen
Luis A. Rivera-Zamarripa
Olimpia Saucedo-Estrada
Elmar Tischhauser
Randy Yee

Contents

Signatures and Protocols

Implementation

Cryptanalysis

Quantum LLL with an Application to Mersenne Number Cryptosystems

Marcel Tiepelt[1(✉)] and Alan Szepieniec[2]

[1] Karlsruhe Institute of Technology, Karlsruhe, Germany
tiepelt@dev-null.de
[2] Nervos Foundation, Hangzhou, China
alan@nervos.org

Abstract. In this work we analyze the impact of translating the well-known LLL algorithm for lattice reduction into the quantum setting. We present the first (to the best of our knowledge) quantum circuit representation of a lattice reduction algorithm in the form of explicit quantum circuits implementing the textbook LLL algorithm. Our analysis identifies a set of challenges arising from constructing reversible lattice reduction as well as solutions to these challenges. We give a detailed resource estimate with the Toffoli gate count and the number of logical qubits as complexity metrics.

As an application of the previous, we attack Mersenne number cryptosystems by Groverizing an attack due to Beunardeau et al. that uses LLL as a subprocedure. While Grover's quantum algorithm promises a quadratic speedup over exhaustive search given access to a oracle that distinguishes solutions from non-solutions, we show that in our case, realizing the oracle comes at the cost of a large number of qubits. When an adversary translates the attack by Beunardeau et al. into the quantum setting, the overhead of the quantum LLL circuit may be as large as 2^{52} qubits for the text-book implementation and 2^{33} for a floating-point variant.

Keywords: LLL · Lattice reduction · Quantum circuit · Grover's algorithm · Mersenne number cryptosystems

1 Introduction

The famous lattice reduction procedure by Lenstra-Lenstra-Lovász (LLL) [13] was the first algorithm to solve high dimensional lattice problems provably in polynomial time. While its original application was in the factorization of polynomials, has since been applied to great effect in many branches of computer algebra, such as integer programming, Diophantine equations, and cryptanalysis. Recently, the National Institute for Standards and Technology (NIST) has

Part of this work was conducted at the Computer Security and Industrial Cryptography group (COSIC) at KU Leuven, Leuven, Belgium.

© Springer Nature Switzerland AG 2019
P. Schwabe and N. Thériault (Eds.): LATINCRYPT 2019, LNCS 11774, pp. 3–23, 2019.
https://doi.org/10.1007/978-3-030-30530-7_1

launched a project to standardize post-quantum cryptosystems. Out of 69 round 1 candidates 27 were based on the hardness of lattice problems. In round 2 14 of the 26 selected candidates are related to lattice problems. The LLL algorithm's application to cryptanalysis extends beyond attacks on lattice-based cryptosystems to other attacks that require shortest vector oracles, e.g., attacks on Mersenne number cryptosystems. Therefore, when analyzing post-quantum cryptosystems, it is natural to analyze lattice reduction procedures in a quantum context.

The original LLL algorithm was based on rational arithmetic and terminates after polynomial many steps as a function of the initial norms of the lattice basis and the lattice rank, i.e., $O(r^6 \log^3 \tilde{B})$ where r is the rank of the lattice and $\tilde{B}$ bound the maximal initial norm of a vector. Furthermore, it appears to perform better in practice than a rigorous analysis would suggest [17]. One can improve on the theoretical and practical run time by considering floating-point variants that approximate the rational numbers to a certain precision. The first floating-point LLL that would provably find a LLL-reduced basis was due to Schnorr [22] who implemented the coefficients of the intermediate Gram-Schmidt matrix as floating-point numbers with precision $O(r + \log \tilde{B})$. Additionally he introduced a new method to update the matrix in every iteration of the lattice reduction. The L^2 algorithm by Stehlé and Nguyen [16] is the only LLL variant which achieves a complexity quadratic in the bound of the initial norms, namely $O(r^5 \log^2 \tilde{B})$. The quadratic complexity results from approximating the coefficients of the Gram-Schmidt matrix using a precision of $1.6r + o(r)$ and performing a more efficient vector size-reduction. Nevertheless, both floating-point variants of the LLL algorithm do improve on the time spent for arithmetic operations during the lattice reduction, but retain the same upper bound on iterations of the main reduction loop. Furthermore, the underlying operations, such as the vector-size reduction remain equivalent to that of the original LLL algorithm.

Quantum Algorithms. With Shor's algorithm [21,24] most of the deployed public-key cryptosystems are rendered insecure in the context of large-scale quantum computers. The famous result gave rise to research on *post-quantum cryptosystems*, i.e., cryptography that can withstand quantum attacks. In contrast to Shor's famous algorithm, the equally famous result of Grover does not lead to a complete break of cryptosystems. Grover's algorithm [10] promises a quadratic improvement of exhaustive (key) searches, effectively halving the key length of schemes that aim to achieve the same security level. Grover's algorithm depends on the implementation of a function that captures the problem in question by identifying its solutions and distinguishing them from non-solutions.

Mersenne Prime Key Encapsulation. A public key encryption scheme on integer relations modulo a Mersenne number was first introduced by Aggarwal et al. [1] and a later refined thereof was developed and submitted to the NIST post-quantum competition by Aggarwal et al. and independently by Szepieniec [25]. The schemes build upon computation over the ring induced modulo a Mersenne prime using secret integers with low Hamming weight.

Shortly after the introduction of Mersenne number cryptosystems by Aggarwal et al. [1], researchers Beunardeau, Connolly, Géraud and Naccache [3] presented an attack with an exponential complexity in the Hamming weight of the sparse secret integers. The main idea of the attack is find the correct lattice representation that hides the sparse secrets as the shortest vector; a lattice reduction algorithm can then extract the secrets. The name reflects the strategy of repeatedly partitioning the sparse integers at random until lattice reduction succeeds in extracting the secret. The attack's complexity arises from the relatively small probability of randomly sampling a good partition.

Our Contribution. First, we present a quantum circuit representation of the textbook LLL algorithm. Particularly we explicitly present a range of subcircuits that appear in our representation and discuss how they impact the ancillary qubits. We identify a set of challenges arising from reversible lattice reduction and propose explicit quantum circuits to overcome these. Furthermore, we provide an in-depth complexity analysis of our proposed solution in the quantum setting. We analyze the number of ancillary qubits as well as the number of Toffoli gates needed. We compare the estimates to the memory requirements induced by a floating-point implementation and discuss the memory overhead for the general problem of a reversible lattice reduction. We show that, due to the need for reversibility of the lattice reduction, we need to allocate and maintain a large amount of qubits in every iteration to remember the reduction of the basis vectors. While our circuits are based on the rational textbook LLL we show that our results carry over to floating-point variants implementing the same arithmetic operations. Second, we use this quantum LLL algorithm to complete the analysis of a Groverization of the Slice-and-Dice attack on Mersenne number cryptosystems. As a result, a quantum Slice-and-Dice attack on Mersenne number cryptosystems using the LLL algorithm may have a quantum memory overhead as high as 2^{52} qubits.

Roadmap. Section 2 provides an overview of notions and definitions used for our implementation and analysis. We review the classical LLL algorithm which we used as a starting point for our implementation. Furthermore we give an overview of Mersenne number cryptography and explain the attack by Beunardeau et al. In Sect. 3 we present our quantum circuits for the LLL algorithm by giving a range of quantum component circuits needed to perform the lattice reduction. We estimate the resources needed to implement those constructions and suggest potential improvements. Section 4 shows how to combine Grover's algorithm with the attack by Beunardeau et al. using our quantum LLL circuit as a subroutine. We calculate the needed quantum resources when instantiating the crytosystems to achieve a 128-bit security level against quantum attack, as per the parameters suggested by Aggarwal et al. [1] and by Szepieniec [25].

2   Preliminaries

LLL Algorithm. The LLL algorithm is a well-known lattice reduction algorithm with many applications in cryptanalysis. Given a modular equation

$y \equiv \sum_i \alpha_i x_i \mod p$ with $\prod_i x_i < p$ the LLL algorithm is able to determine the unique solution in polynomial time [12]. The solution is determined by constructing a lattice of rank r represented by the canonical basis $(b_1, \dots, b_r)$. On input of the basis matrix, the lattice reduction procedure computes a reduced basis $\tilde{B}$ for a fixed approximation factor δ such that the Gram-Schmidt orthogonalized basis $\tilde{B}$ satisfies $||\tilde{b}_i^*||^2(\delta - \frac{1}{4}) \leq ||\tilde{b}_{i+1}^*||^2$ for all $1 \leq i \leq r$ [12, ch. 10]. In general the length of the shortest vector can be approximated with the Minkowski theorem as the first minimum of the lattice: $\lambda_1(\mathcal{L}) \leq \sqrt{\gamma_r}\det(\mathcal{L})^{\frac{1}{r}}$ where γ_r is Hermite's constant. Depending on the approximation factor δ and the difference in length between the first and the second minima of the lattice the shortest vector might not be found.

The algorithm first computes an orthogonal basis using the Gram-Schmidt procedure followed by an iterative approach examining each two subsequent vectors of the basis. Each iteration considers the plane spanned by the two vectors $b_i, \tilde{b}_{i+1}$ and attempts to reduce the vector $\tilde{b}_{i+1}$ by an integer multiple of the vector $\tilde{b}_i$. Then, if the two vectors fulfill the Lovász condition, $\delta||\tilde{b}_i^*||^2 \leq ||\tilde{b}_{i+1}^*||^2 + (\tilde{b}_{i+1}|\tilde{b}_i^*)/||\tilde{b}_i^*||^2$, the vector $\tilde{b}_{i+1}$ is size-reduced and projected onto the hyperplane spanned by all lesser vectors. If the ordering is not fulfilled, the vectors are swapped such that the vector b_{i+1} is compared to the lesser vectors in the following iterations. Intuitively the Lovász condition ensures that the vectors are approximately orthogonal and allows to reorder them if this is not the case. The LLL algorithm terminates as soon as each subsequent pair of basis vectors fulfills the Lovász condition and if they are ordered by length with respect to the approximation factor.

The pseudo-code in Algorithm 2.1 reflects the classical approach using *exact* values, implemented with rational numbers to compute the coefficients of the Gram-Schmidt matrix M.

Algorithm 2.1: LLL Algorithm

1: **Input: Basis** $B = (b_1, b_2, \dots, b_r)$
2: **Output: Reduced Basis** B^*
3: $B^*, M \leftarrow$ Gram-Schmidt orthogonalization(B)
4: $L_i \leftarrow$ Compute length of vectors b_i for $i \in \{1, 2, \dots, r\}$
5: $k \leftarrow 2$
6: **while** $k \leq r$ **do**
7:     Reduce b_k by $\lfloor m_{k,k-1} \rceil b_{k-1}$ and update M s.t. $B = MB^*$
8:     **if** Lovász condition holds on b_k and b_{k-1} **then**
9:         **for** $j = k - 2$ to 0 **do**
10:             Reduce b_k by $\lfloor m_{k,j} \rceil b_j$ and update M s.t. $B = MB^*$
11:         $k+ = 1$
12:     **else**
13:         Swap b_k and b_{k-1}
14:         Update length L_i, L_{i-1} and Gram-Schmidt matrix M to reflect swap
15:         $k \leftarrow max(2, k - 1)$

The complexity of the LLL algorithm is dominated by the main loop and further depends on the size of the numbers that being processed. The number of iterations of the main loop can be bounded by defining the potential of the lattice: $D = \prod_{i=0}^{r} ||b_i^*||^{2i}$ as shown by Nguyen and Valle [Thm 10][18]. Whenever the Lovàsz condition is not fulfilled two vectors are swapped and D decreases by a factor of δ. Since D is an integer larger than 0, the number of swaps is bounded by the logarithm of D, bound by $\tilde{B}^{2d}$, where $\tilde{B}$ is the maximum initial norm of the input vectors.

Withing the main loop the most expensive operation is to update the Gram-Schmidt matrix of size rd. Furthermore the rationals in the naive LLL algorithm have bit length at most $O(r \log \tilde{B})$. The operations within LLL on these numbers can be computed in at most square time. This results in an overall complexity of $O(r^5 d \log^3 \tilde{B})$ [18].

Schnorr [22] introduced a more efficient variant using floating-point approximations with precision $O(r + \log \tilde{B})$ for the coefficients of the Gram-Schmidt matrix. The approximation of the coefficients significantly reduces the computational effort of each loop iteration, resulting in a complexity of $O(r^4 \log \tilde{B}(r + \log \tilde{B})^2)$ operations.

The result was later improved by Nguyen and Stehlé [16] introducing the L^2 algorithm, the first provable lattice reduction algorithm with complexity quadratic in the norm of the input vectors. The L^2 algorithm adopts the approach to approximate the Gram-Schmidt coefficients using floating-point numbers and combines it with a provable floating-point procedure mimicking the Gram-Schmidt orthogonalization process. The algorithm is the best known result for a lattice reduction with a complexity of $O(r^5(r + \log \tilde{B}) \log \tilde{B})$.

Reversible Floating-Point Arithmetic. The use of floating-point representations in classical computing usually implies the loss of information due to rounding errors. Translating this inherently non-reversible process into an unitary operations requires preserving additional information, *e.g.*, the inputs of the initiating arithmetic operation. Bennett [11] showed how to translate any ordinary Turing machine running in time T and space S into a reversible Turing machine running in time $O(T^{1+\epsilon})$ and space $O(S \log T)$, making it clear that such an operation can be implemented on a quantum computer. While this gives a constructive approach for a reversible Turing machine it may not be clear how to translate this into an circuit. The first reversible floating-point adder meeting the requirements of industrial standards was introduced by Nachtigal et al. [14,15]. While the quantum gate-cost of their circuit was linear in the number of (qu)bits, the output also includes $O(n)$ garbage qubits. Nguyen and Meter [6] presented improved floating-point arithmetic circuits with only a constant number of garbage qubits. However, *both representations must preserve one of the inputs to allow reversibility.*

There is no widely adopted procedure to implement floating-point numbers in a quantum circuit. The classical approach with two registers containing mantissa and exponent seems to be a feasible scheme. However, one would need an extra register to keep track of a "remainder" which is discarded in classical computing. Another approach was introduced by Wiebe et al. [26] by implementing small rotations onto single qubits which allows to mimic and compute on mantissa and exponent. Due to the lack of standardized or widely adopted representation of floating-point arithmetic in the quantum setup we do not optimize nor establish any arithmetic circuits for floating-point operations.

Grover's Algorithm. We assume the reader to be familiar with the basic notions of quantum computation (a standard text is Nielsen and Chuang [19]). Grover's algorithm improves the search of an unordered data set with a quantum computer gaining a quadratic improvement [10] over an unstructured classical search. The algorithm employs a procedure that starts out with a superposition of all elements in the data set, such that each element is equally likely to be observed. A successive application of the *Grover iteration* improves the success probability of observing a target element as described below.

Let there be an unordered set of cardinality N containing M target elements. The goal is to extract any one of the targets. Consider $\mathcal{H}$ to be a Hilbert space which describes the state space of a quantum system. Furthermore assume the access to a black-box operator $\mathcal{U}_\mathcal{O} : \mathcal{H} \to \mathcal{H}$ which computes $|x, c\rangle \mapsto |x, c \oplus f(x)\rangle$ and implements the function f mapping target elements to 1 and non-target elements to 0. The operator therefore splits the state space into a direct sum of subspaces such that the *good* subspace for $f(x) = 1$ represents the target elements and the *bad* subspace for $f(x) = 0$ represents the non-target elements. Let ρ denote the initial success probability of observing a target element. Then Grover's algorithm requires $\rho^{-\frac{1}{2}}$ iterations until a target element is observed with high probability.

Mersenne Number Key Encapsulation. Mersenne number cryptosystems compute over the integer ring $\mathbb{Z}/p\mathbb{Z}$ where $p = 2^n - 1$ is a Mersenne number such that all integers have bit length at most n. The encapsulation schemes follow the idea of establishing a shared noisy one-time pad using a noisy Diffie-Hellman protocol. The later is embedded into a framework featuring de-randomization and re-encryption to achieve CCA security in the (quantum) random oracle model. Two sparse integers $a, b \in \mathbb{Z}/p\mathbb{Z}$ are chosen uniformly random with Hamming weight ω during the key generation. Together with an uniformly random $G \in \mathbb{Z}/p\mathbb{Z}$ and $H = aG + b \mod p$ they form the secret and the public key: $sk := (a, b), pk := (G, H)$. The schemes suggested by Aggarwal et al. [1] and by Szepieniec [25] are based on the *Mersenne low Hamming combination search problem (LHCS)*: given a tuple $(G, aG + b \mod p)$ with parameters as above, find the integers a and b. The problem is believed to be hard for classical as well as quantum computers.

Slice-and-Dice Attack. Beunardeau et al. [3] presented an attack on the LHCS Problem exploiting the uniqueness of the sparse solutions to the equation $H = aG + b \mod p$. The attack revolves around the idea of partitioning the binary expansion of unknown integers into intervals. The intervals are used to construct a lattice which is then reduced to find the shortest vectors. If the intervals are chosen "correctly", the constructed lattice hides the secrets a, b as shortest vectors: Consider the segmentation of a, b into partitions P_a, P_b. Since the two integers are sparse there are relatively few ones, such that there exists a partition

msb   lsb

Fig. 1. Partition of a sparse integer into intervals. The blocks represent the binary expansion, the black blocks as ones and the white blocks as zeros. Interpreting an interval as integer yields a small number, e.g., the first interval represents $2^3 = 8$. (Color figure online)

where each block represents a "small" number. Such a partitioning is depicted in Fig. 1. Each partition is uniquely defined by a set of starting positions $p_{a,i}, p_{b,j}$ inducing the partitioning into blocks.

The intention of the attack is to sample these starting positions and construct a lattice accordingly as in Eq. (1) such that there exists an exponential gap in terms of vectors' length between those representing the secrets and any other vectors of the lattice. De Boer et al. [4] show that this occurs if and only if all the ones of the secrets fall into a certain range of each interval.

$$\mathcal{L}_{a,b,H} = \left\{ (x_1, ..., x_k, y_1, ... y_l, z) \middle| \sum_i^k 2^{p_{a,i}} x_i G + \sum_j^l 2^{p_{b,j}} y_j \equiv H \mod p \right\} \quad (1)$$

For correctly sampled starting positions the shortest vector represents the secrets and can be extracted using a lattice reduction technique, *e.g.*, the LLL algorithm. In order to apply the LLL algorithm one needs the canonical representation of the lattice basis as matrix from the partitions P_a and P_b. Consider the case where the integers are partitioned into $k + l$ parts and let $\boldsymbol{\mathcal{I}}$ denote the $(k + l) \times (k + l)$ sized identity matrix. Then the matrix in Eq. (2) as a set of row vectors form a basis for the lattice $\mathcal{L}_{a,b,H}$. Each row vector represents an interval and is constructed to fulfill Eq. (1). After performing the lattice reduction with sampled partitions one needs to check the Hamming weight of the reduced basis vectors. If the Hamming weight of the shortest vectors equals the Hamming weight of the secrets, the attack was successful [3, Sect. 2].

Algorithm 2.2: Slice-and-Dice

1: **Input: Basis** H, G, p, ω
2: **Output:** a, b
3: **while** True **do**
4:     $P_a \leftarrow$ sample ω random intervals covering the range $(0, p)$
5:     $P_b \leftarrow$ sample ω random intervals covering the range $(0, p)$
6:     $B \leftarrow$ construct $\mathcal{L}_{a,b,H}(H, G, p, P_a, P_b)$
7:     $B^* \leftarrow LLL(B)$
8:     **if** $\exists b^* \in B^*$ s.t. $Ham(bin(b^*)) = 2 \cdot \omega$ **then**
9:         Return b^*

$$
\begin{pmatrix}
 & \begin{matrix} 0 \\ \vdots \\ 0 \end{matrix} & \begin{matrix} -2^{p_{a,1}}GH^{-1} \mod p \\ \vdots \\ -2^{p_{b,l}}H^{-1} \mod p \end{matrix} \\
\hline
0 \ldots 0 & 1 & -H \\
0 \ldots 0 & 0 & p
\end{pmatrix}
\tag{2}
$$

Algorithm 3.1: Conditioned Loop

$k \leftarrow 0$
while $k \leq r$ **do**
    ApplyTask(k)
    if *SomeCondition(k)* **then**
        $k \leftarrow k + 1$
    else
        $k \leftarrow k - 1$

---

3 Quantum Lattice Reduction Algorithm

The textbook description of the LLL algorithm by Joux [12, chap. 10] using rational numbers serves as a starting point for our implementation. We chose this variant over the more efficient approximate floating-point techniques due to the natural correspondence of implementing (quantum) arithmetic with rational numbers, in particular, the impossibility to *forget* rounding errors in the quantum setting: floating-point operations as in the classical sense require forgetting information, whereas fractional arithmetic does not. However, the results from our implementation of a conditioned loop and the uncomputation of the Gram-Schmidt matrix carry over to the floating-point variants. We use the following list of quantum registers throughout our implementation:

$|B\rangle$ The basis matrix spanning the lattice.
$|B^*\rangle$ The Gram-Schmidt orthogonalized basis.
$|L\rangle$ The lengths of the vectors in B.
$|M^{(k)}\rangle$ The Gram-Schmidt matrix M for each iteration k.
$|\mathcal{L}\rangle$ A single qubit containing the result of checking the Lovász condition
$|K\rangle$ The counter of the main loop.
$|ctl\rangle$ Generic control qubits.

Furthermore, we make use of the following subcircuits implementing basic arithmetic operations:

Addition $\mathcal{A} : |x, y, 0\rangle \mapsto |y, y, x + y\rangle$
Multiplication $\mathcal{M} : |x, y, 0\rangle \mapsto |x, y, x + y\rangle$
Division $\mathcal{D} : |x, y, 0\rangle \mapsto |r, y, \lfloor x/y \rfloor\rangle$, where r is the remainder of x/y

3.1   Quantum Designs

Conditional Loops. Conditioned *while*-loops are widely used in classical computing to execute a certain task based on the current state of a variable, which may or may not be modified within the loop. Consider the loop in Algorithm 3.1 that runs until the variable k reaches the value of r. The loop may or may not run for an infinite time depending on the outcome of the condition.

When translating this structure to a quantum circuit, k may be in superposition, say $|K\rangle$, representing multiple different values at the same time. The conditioned loop may require a different number of iterations of a task for each value represented by $|K\rangle$. However, the algorithm in Sect. 3.1 applies the loop to the register k in every iteration. Our quantum implementation in Circuit 2 controls the application of the loop task based on a lower and upper control qubit, checking if the counter $|K\rangle$ is within its valid limitation. In order to assure that the loop is applied often enough, one needs to find an upper bound on the number of iterations, and hence on the counter $|K\rangle$. The loop then consists of bound (K) many cycles where the task is applied if the counter is within its valid limits.

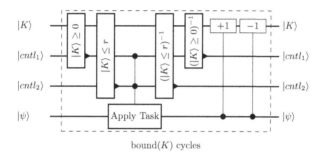

bound(K) cycles

Fig. 2. Conditioned quantum loop with lower and upper limit control qubits.

Therefore, our implementation of the quantum *while*-loop is a *for*-loop with some reasonable termination bound. The important takeaway here is that conditioned loops always have worst-case run time. In the particular case of the LLL algorithm the Line 6 of Algorithm 2.1 is such a construction.

Uncomputation. The copy-uncompute trick, first introduced by Bennett et al. [2], is a well known procedure to reset quantum memory to a known state. The purpose of resetting garbage qubits is to avoid unwanted interference when using subroutines in a larger circuit. Additionally, uncomputed qubits may be reused as ancillary qubits for following operations. The trick allows to design reversible operations where the number of "used" output qubits matches the number of "used" input qubits. For example, consider the following addition procedure where the register y is reset to a known state $|0\rangle$ such that $|y|$ many qubits can be reused after the operation:

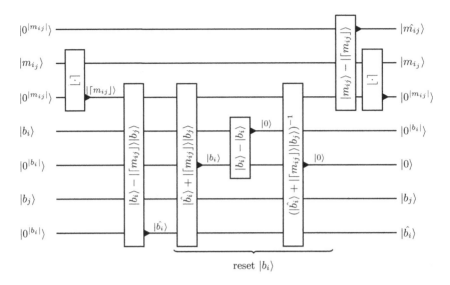

Fig. 3. Vector size-reduction and uncomputation of original vector b_i.

$$|x, y, 0^{max(|x|,|y|)+1}\rangle \mapsto |x, y, x + y\rangle \mapsto |x, 0^{|y|}, x + y\rangle \qquad (3)$$

However, not all operations within the LLL algorithm can be implemented in a way, that allows to reuse all input qubits in such generic way. Consider a function that computes a vector-size reduction: a vector $b_i \in B$ is length reduced by an integer multiple of some vector b_j by a factor of $\lceil m_{ij} \rfloor$. On a basic level the following operations are performed:

$$\lceil m_{ij} \rfloor \leftarrow \text{round}(m_{ij}) \qquad (4)$$

$$\hat{b}_i \leftarrow b_i - \lceil m_{ij} \rfloor b_j \qquad (5)$$

$$\hat{m}_{ij} \leftarrow m_{ij} - \lceil m_{ij} \rfloor \qquad (6)$$

In the classical case, the computation of the new value $\hat{m}_{ij}$ overriding the value m_{ij} results in the loss of the information required to recompute b_i from the size-reduced vector $\hat{b}_i$. In order to be able to reverse the size-reduction it is necessary to maintain addition information, mainly the old value m_{ij}. Translating this procedure into the quantum context results in Circuit 3: the size-reduced basis vector $|\hat{b}_i\rangle$ is computed from the (rounded) coefficient $|m_{ij}\rangle$ and some vector $|b_j\rangle$. Then the new Gram-Schmidt coefficient $|\hat{m}_{ij}\rangle$ is computed from $|m_{ij}\rangle$ and its rounded value. With the quantum registers $|m_{ij}\rangle$ and $|\hat{b}_i\rangle$ the value of the vector $|b_i\rangle$ can be first recomputed. This can then be used to reset the original quantum register $|b_i\rangle$ into a zero state, and then the value of $|b_i\rangle$ can be uncomputed. At last either the quantum register containing the rounded value $|\lceil m_{ij} \rfloor\rangle$ or the quantum register $|m_{ij}\rangle$ can be uncomputed. However, neither of them can be uncomputed with out the information contained in the other. Therefore, either $|m_{ij}\rangle$ or $|\lceil m_{ij} \rfloor\rangle$ have to be preserved when using reversible arithmetic operations.

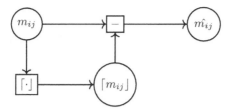

Fig. 4. Information flow when updating Gram-Schmidt matrix coefficients.

Algorithm 3.2: GSO Algorithm [12, Alg 10.3]

1: **Input: Basis** $B = (b_1, b_2, ..., b_r)$
2: **Output: Orthogonal basis** B^* **and transformation** M
3: **for** $i \leftarrow 1$ to r **do**
4:     $b_i^* \leftarrow b_i$
5:     **for** $j \leftarrow 1$ to $i - 1$ **do**
6:         $m_{i,j} \leftarrow \frac{(b_i | b_j^*)}{||b_j^*||^2}$
7:         $b_i^* \leftarrow b_i^* - m_{i,j} b_j^*$

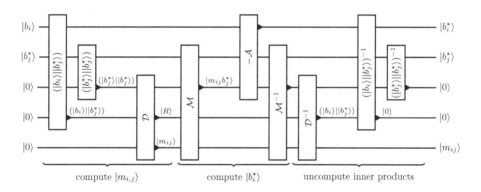

Fig. 5. Single iteration of the quantum Gram-Schmidt orthogonalization inner loop.

Figure 4 shows a dependency graph visualizing the operation in question. The directed edges depict the flow of information, whereas the rounded nodes represent quantum registers and the squared nodes represent the functions. In order to uncompute an input value of a function, one needs to preserve the output as well as the other inputs. Since the node $\lceil m_{ij} \rfloor$ is both input and output of a function it cannot be uncomputed while serving as information for uncomputation.

Overall, the size-reduction operator requires preserving the initial coefficient of the Gram-Schmidt matrix for reversibility. In the quantum case, this operation is applied in every iteration of the main loop in Line 6 of Algorithm 2.1.

3.2   Miscellaneous Circuits

Quantum Gram-Schmidt Orthogonalization. The circuit implementing a single iteration of the quantum Gram-Schmidt orthogonalization (QGSO) in Fig. 5 is based on the Pseudo-code 3.2 of the classical procedure by Joux [12].

Rounding to the Nearest Integer. The vector length reduction $b_i \leftarrow b_i - \lceil m_{ij} \rfloor b_j$ appearing in the LLL algorithm requires rounding the rational number $m_{ij} = m_n/m_d$ to the nearest integer. The rounding to the closest integer in positive direction is based on the decimal part. Therefore, we need to compute the division of m_n/m_d with some precision. In our example we choose a precision of 1 (qu)bit. The integer part is stored in register $|m_{0...n-1}\rangle$, the decimal part in register $|m.f\rangle$. The sign (qu)bit of the rational number is stored in the register $|m_s\rangle$. The rounded value equals the integer part plus or minus 1, depending on the decimal part and the sign (qu)bit as below:

$$m_s = 1 \wedge m.f = 1 \Leftrightarrow \lceil m \rceil = \lfloor m \rfloor - 1$$
$$m_s = 0 \wedge m.f = 1 \Leftrightarrow \lceil m \rceil = \lfloor m \rfloor + 1$$
$$m.f = 0 \Leftrightarrow \lceil m \rceil = \lfloor m \rfloor$$

We implement our vector size-reduction using the rounding operator in Fig. 6. The gate cost of the rounding circuit is $2\mathcal{D}_T + 3\mathcal{A}_T$ and referred to as $\mathcal{R}_T$.

max(2, k-1). Circuit 7 implements the $|K\rangle = max(2, |K\rangle - 1)$ operator that is required to conditionally decrement the counter in the second branch of the main loop.

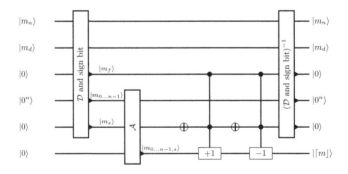

Fig. 6. Rounding to the nearest integer in positive direction.

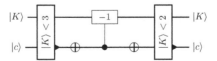

Fig. 7. Circuit implementing the operation $K := max(2, K - 1)$

LLL. Circuit 8 shows the LLL algorithm with the respective conditioned loops and the controls of the branching. In each cycle we cache coefficients of the Gram-Schmidt matrix in a new register $|M\rangle$ to preserve reversibility.

3.3 Resource Estimate

Gate Count. Toffoli gates are universal for quantum computing and can be constructed from the *Clifford+T* group, whereas the cost of such a gate depends mostly on the number of T-gates. Selinger [23] gives a construction of a Toffoli gate with T-depth of 1. Therefore, the Toffoli gate count is closely related to the full cost of a quantum circuit. In addition, Fowler, Mariantoni and Cleland [7] show that the number of logical qubits scales with the number of Toffoli gates. Consequently, we use the Toffoli gate count as a complexity metric in this work.

Let m be the (qu) bit-length of the numbers processed in the LLL algorithm. We use the Toffoli gate count of the following implementations of quantum circuits in our analysis:

- Curracaro [5] presented a quantum adder using $2m + O(1)$ Toffoli gates referred to as $\mathcal{A}_T$. Note that a subtraction can be implemented using the same gates.
- Gidney [9] achieves a multiplication circuit using windowing and table lookups in $O(m^2/\log n)$ Toffoli gates as $\mathcal{M}_T$.
- Rines and Chuang [20] propose a division circuit comprising $4m^2$ Toffoli gates as $\mathcal{D}_T$.

Let $r := rank(\mathcal{L})$ be the rank of the lattice such that there are r basis vectors: $(b_1, \ldots, b_r)$ with $b_i \in \mathbb{R}^d$. The frequently used inner product $(b_i | b_j)$ or $||b_j||^2$ can be constructed from $d \cdot \mathcal{M}_T \cdot \mathcal{A}_T$ Toffoli gates. We will refer to this count as $\mathcal{I}_T$. Note that the Toffoli gate depth is significantly lower when applying vector multiplication in parallel and enabling a tree like addition procedure.

QGSO. The quantum GSO consists of an outer loop iterating the r basis vectors and an inner loop iterating the respective lesser vectors. Each iteration consists of the computation of a coefficient of the Gram-Schmidt matrix by computing two inner products and a division, which intermediate result has to be uncomputed with total cost: $2(2\mathcal{I}_T + \mathcal{D}_T)$. Furthermore the vector $|b_i^*\rangle$ is computed with a scalar multiplication and a vector subtraction. The cost in Toffoli gates with uncomputation is: $2d(\mathcal{M}_T + \mathcal{A}_T)$. Overall the quantum GSO requires $\frac{r^2-r}{2}(4\mathcal{I}_T + 2\mathcal{D}_T + 2d(\mathcal{M}_T + \mathcal{A}_T))$ Toffoli gates.

Main Loop. The gate count of the main loop of the textbook LLL implementation is closely related to the worst-case analysis of the classical case.

The computation of the first branch consists of the computation of a length reduction for r vectors. Each reduction requires a rounding operator, the actual size-reduction and the computation of the new Gram-Schmidt coefficient $|m_{ij}\rangle$ with cost: $2\mathcal{R}_\mathcal{I} + 2d(\mathcal{M}_T + \mathcal{A}_T) + \mathcal{A}_T$. The remaining coefficients in the same row of the matrix are updated using $r(\mathcal{M}_T + \mathcal{A}_T)$ Toffoli gates. The first branch is dominated by the terms $(2rd + r^2)(\mathcal{M}_T + \mathcal{A}_T)$.

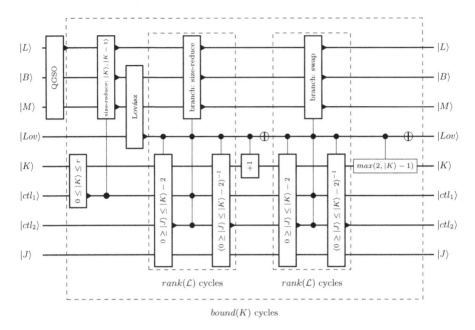

Fig. 8. Quantum circuit implementing the LLL algorithm where the *branch: size reduce* represents the size reduction if the Lovász holds and the *branch: swap* the respective other branch. Note that each cycle of the main loop requires additional qubits for the Gram-Schmidt matrix M.

The second branch consists of swapping the vectors and updating the Gram-Schmidt matrix accordingly with a Toffoli cost of $r(2(\mathcal{M}_T + \mathcal{A}_T))$. Uncomputation cost is negligible due to caching the matrix in every iteration. Both branches have to be applied subsequently.

The computation of the Lovász qubit and the initial length reduction is negligible and therefore omitted from the calculation. The number of cycles of the main loop can be bound using by the classical worst-case with $\text{bound}(K) := r^2 \log \tilde{B}$, e.g. by Nguyen [17], where $\tilde{B}$ bounds the norms of the input basis. Expressing the gate count with regards to the (qu)bit length m of the arithmetic operations the Toffoli gate count is in the order of:

$$O\left(2\log\tilde{B}\left(r^3 d + r^4\right)\left(\frac{m^2}{\log m} + 2m\right)\right) \tag{7}$$

Logical Qubits. The number of logical qubits is derived from representing the basis matrix $|B\rangle$ and the Gram-Schmidt matrix $|M\rangle$ with rd coefficients where each one has qubit length $m = r \log \tilde{B}$ for the textbook implementation. One requires to cache $r^2 \log \tilde{B}$ such matrices. Additionally our implementation requires $r^2 \log \tilde{B}$ for the counter $|K\rangle$, as well as $max(r, d) \cdot m$ ancillary qubits for arithmetic operations. The total number of qubits for a reversible LLL algorithm is thus:

$$r^4 d \log^2 \tilde{B} + r^2 \log \tilde{B} + max(d, r) \cdot m \qquad (8)$$

Physical Qubits. We note that the number of physical qubits to implement a fault tolerant circuit using an error correcting architecture is significantly higher.

3.4   Improvements

Intermediate Uncomputation. We propose a time/space trade-off to improve on the number of logical qubits required. During the course of the lattice reduction we suggest to independently run the (quantum) LLL circuit on intermediate lattice basis' and to recompute the Gram-Schmidt matrices. This allows to reset the cached matrices to a known value, i.e., a quantum register with a zero vector, and to reuse these qubits in the following operations.

The vector size-reduction takes as input the matrices $B^{(i)}$ and $M^{(i)}$ and outputs the reduced basis $B^{(i+1)}$ with updated Gram-Schmidt matrix $M^{(i+1)}$. With every such operation new memory to cache the matrix $M^{(i+1)}$ is required, while $B^{(i)}$ can be reset to a known state. Let $|M|$ be the number of qubits required to store the Gram-Schmidt matrix ($|B|$ respectively for the basis matrix). Then the following sequence is computed over the course of the main loop:

$$|B^{(i)}\rangle|M^{(i)}\rangle|0^{|B|}\rangle|0^{|M|}\rangle \xrightarrow{size-reduce} |0^{|B|}\rangle|M^{(i)}\rangle|B^{(i+1)}\rangle|M^{(i+1)}\rangle$$

$$|B^{(i+1)}\rangle|M^{(i+1)}\rangle|0^{|B|}\rangle|0^{|M|}\rangle \xrightarrow{size-reduce} |0^{|B|}\rangle|M^{(i+1)}\rangle|B^{(i+2)}\rangle|M^{(i+2)}\rangle$$

$$\cdots$$

$$|B^{(j-2)}\rangle|M^{(j-2)}\rangle|0^{|B|}\rangle|0^{|M|}\rangle \xrightarrow{size-reduce} |0^{|B|}\rangle|M^{(j-2)}\rangle|B^{(j-1)}\rangle|M^{(j-1)}\rangle$$

$$|B^{(j-1)}\rangle|M^{(j-1)}\rangle|0^{|B|}\rangle|0^{|M|}\rangle \xrightarrow{size-reduce} |0^{|B|}\rangle|M^{(j-1)}\rangle|B^{(j)}\rangle|M^{(j)}\rangle$$

Given the registers $|M^{(j-1)}\rangle|B^{(j)}\rangle|M^{(j)}\rangle$ it is impossible to reconstruct the matrices $|B^{(i)}\rangle|M^{(i)}\rangle$. However, the sequence was computed from the initial basis $|B^{(i)}\rangle$ and the Gram-Schmidt matrix $|M^{(i)}\rangle$, hence one can use the initial state to uncompute the sequence:

Forward Steps. Recompute $|M^{(i+1)}\rangle, |M^{(i+2)}\rangle, \ldots, |M^{(j-2)}\rangle, |M^{(j-1)}\rangle$.
Backwards Steps. Each Gram-Schmidt matrix can be used to uncompute its
   successor, e.g., $|M^{(j-2)}\rangle$ is used to uncompute $|M^{(j-1)}\rangle$.

By following this procedure, one can free all the quantum memory but the initial register $|M^{(i)}\rangle$ and the last cached state $|M^{(j)}\rangle$. The number of cached qubits in the sequence can been reduced from $(j+1) \cdot sizeOf(M)$ to $2 \cdot sizeOf(M)$ as in Fig. 9. The trade-off allows to reset $j \cdot sizeOf(M)$ many qubits using j iterations of the main loop and $j \cdot sizeOf(M)$ *temporary* ancillary qubits. Let bound(K) be the number of iterations of the main loop in our implementation and hence the number of cached Gram-Schmidt matrices. The trade-off is optimal for $j = (\text{bound}(K))^{\frac{1}{2}}$. This is equivalent to performing an uncomputation sequence every $(\text{bound}(K))^{\frac{1}{2}}$ iterations of the main loop.

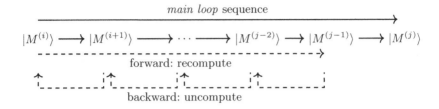

Fig. 9. Sequential uncomputation of Gram-Schmidt matrices

By applying this improvement the number of cached Gram-Schmidt matrices can be reduced by a square root to $r(\log \tilde{B})^{\frac{1}{2}}$ in our textbook implementation. The largest term from Eq. (8) on the number of logical qubits is now reduced to $r^3 d \log \tilde{B}(\log \tilde{B})^{\frac{1}{2}}$. The enhancement carries over to the naive floating point variant and the loop implementing the L^2 algorithm.

Floating-Point LLL. Our results regarding conditioned loops and the reversibility of reducing vectors by an integer multiple carry over to naive floating-point variants. In particular, the LLL algorithm shares certain computational methods with its provable floating point variants, such as the vector size-reduction by an integer multiple or the conditioned loop. The significant increase in efficiency is based on the representation and processing of the Gram-Schmidt coefficients. Applying our analysis on Schnorr's [22] variant results in the use of $\geq r^2 d \log \tilde{B}(\log \tilde{B})^{\frac{1}{2}}$ qubits. The L^2 algorithm due to Nguyen and Stehlé [16, Fig. 4] implements an equivalent vector length-reduction. It follows that the L^2 algorithm [16, Theorem 2] with a precision of $l = 1.6d + o(d)$ would require $\geq r^2 d \log \tilde{B}(1.6d + o(d))$ many qubits to preserve reversibility in the quantum setup. However, we did not analyze the L^2 algorithm in detail and do not claim that this is optimal.

Execution Parameters. The (classical) worst-case of the number of iterations can be improved by adjusting the parameter δ resulting in a loss of "quality" of the reduced basis with regards to the length of the reduced vectors. Nguyen and Stehlé [17] evaluate the running time of LLL for different domains, such as random knapsack problems, and suggest that the complexity is lower on average. We leave an analysis of specific problem instances as a future line of work. However, we do give an heuristic value for the Slice-and-Dice attack in the next section.

4   Quantum Slice-and-Dice

The combination of the Slice-and-Dice attack with Grover's algorithm utilizes our quantum representation of the LLL algorithm from the previous section as a subroutine. Given the public-key of a Mersenne number cryptosystem one starts out with a superposition of all possible partitions which in turn represent all possible starting positions of intervals. The lattice reduction subroutine

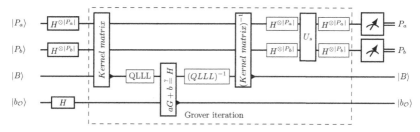

The U_S operator flips all states except 0

Fig. 10. Groverized Slice-and-Dice with a LLL oracle.

distinguishes those partitions that allow extraction of the secret sparse vectors using a lattice reduction, and those that do not allow said extraction. First, the subroutine computes the basis matrix, which is the direct translation of the classical case. Each partition is now represented by the superpositions $|P_a\rangle, |P_b\rangle$. The lattice reduction is performed and the "correct" partitions are identified. This procedure can be implemented using canonical modular operations to recompute the public key and comparing to the input. Afterwards the process has to be inverted to uncompute all operations. Figure 10 shows Grover's algorithm with our subroutine.

Identification of the Shortest Vector. The attack is successful if and only if the Grover oracle can successfully distinguish the sparse secret integers in the reduced basis from other short vectors. Then the oracle qubit has to be flipped according to the secret integers and respectively not-flipped by other short vectors. In the classical case, Beunardeau et al. identify the solutions by computing the sum of the Hamming weights of the resulting basis vectors. This is not sufficient in the quantum setting due to the existence of other vectors with low Hamming weight.

De Boer et al. [4] showed that the lattice contains vectors of the form $(0, \ldots, 0, 2^m, -1, 0, \ldots, 0)$ of length $(4^{|P_i|} + 1)^{\frac{1}{2}}$. Moreover, the authors bound the minimal size of the partition based on an approximation of the first minimum by Gama and Nguyen [8]: $\lambda_1(\mathcal{L}) \approx (n/2\pi e)^{\frac{1}{2}} \cdot 2^{\frac{n}{r}}$. Furthermore, De Boer et al. show that the lattice reduction is successful if the intervals have size at least $n/r + \Theta(n)$.

In the quantum case, the input basis is a superposition of all possible partitions. Therefore, there exists a lattice construction that contains a partition with small block size such that the vectors described by De Boer et al. are shorter than the vectors representing the secrets. Furthermore, these vectors have low Hamming weight and may thus be misidentified as solutions. Therefore, in the quantum setting, we recompute the public component $H' = a'G + b'$ for every basis vector and flip the oracle qubit on the outcome of the comparison with H.

Number of Grover Iterations. The number of iterations is determined by the initial success probability of measuring a correct partition. The success probability depends directly on the number of correct partitions and hence on the positions of the ones, therefore varies with every secret key that is attacked. De Boer et al. [4] analyze the probability that the bits of a secret key fall into the "correct" interval. The authors showed that the lattice reduction succeeds in identifying the secret if the average size of the intervals is $O(n/\omega + \log n)$. Based on an upper and lower bound for a valid size of the intervals they derive the probability to recover the secret key on input of a random lattice as $\frac{1}{2} - c(\frac{r}{\omega})^2 + o(1)$. Since the dimension of the lattice in the case of the quantum attack is fixed to $r = 2\omega$ the expected number of partitions allowing to recover the secrets is

$$\mathbf{E}[valid\ partitions] = \sum_{i=1}^{N} \left(\frac{1}{2} - 8c + o(1) \right)^{2\omega}. \tag{9}$$

In the setup of the quantum Slice-and-Dice attack the number N of all partitions is equal to the number of all possible starting positions: $N = n^{2\omega}$. The number of Grover iterations follows as

$$\left(\frac{N}{M} \right)^{\frac{1}{2}} = \left(\frac{n^{2\omega}}{n^{2\omega} \left(\frac{1}{2} - 8c + o(1) \right)^{2\omega}} \right)^{\frac{1}{2}} = \left(\frac{2}{1 - 8c + 2o(1)} \right)^{\omega}. \tag{10}$$

Bounding LLL Iterations. Consider a partition of the binary expansion of the public key integer $aG + b - H \mod p$ for the Slice-and-Dice attack into intervals. Each interval is represented by a single basis vector. De Boer et al. [4] bound the maximal size of the initial vectors for a successful attack as

$$\frac{n}{2\omega} \left(1 - \frac{r(r-1)\log\gamma}{2n} - \frac{r\log r}{2n} \right), where\ \gamma\ is\ Hermite's\ constant.$$

We suggest the following Heuristic 1 to bound the initial potential of a "correctly" partitioned public key and hence the required number of swap operations.

Heuristic 1 (Number of Swaps for a Correct Slice-and-Dice Lattice). *Let $\mathcal{L}$ be a lattice constructed from "correct" partitioning a public key $aG + b \equiv H \mod p$ of bit length at most n into ω parts. Then the LLL algorithm finds the shortest vectors after at most $n/2\omega$ swaps.*

Consider a register in superposition representing lattices constructed from partitions in superposition. The superposition represents lattices that hide the secrets and those that do not. After performing LLL iterations according to 1 the lattice representations hiding the secrets will be fully reduced. The other lattices might not be fully reduced yet. However, their basis vectors do not hide the secret vectors and are thus not relevant for flipping the oracle qubit. Therefore, one can bound the number of LLL iterations for the Slice-and-Dice attack according to Heuristic 1.

Instantiation. Consider the instantiation of a Mersenne number cryptosystem with the bit-length $n = 756839 \geq 2^{19}$ and Hamming weight $\omega = 128 = 2^7$ of the sparse integers. An implementation of the Groverized attack uses 2ω intervals where each interval represents a number in $\mathbb{Z}_n$. The quantum registers in superposition representing the partitions $|P_A\rangle, |P_B\rangle$ are can be implemented by $\geq 2^{27}$ qubits.

The oracle is constructed for a lattice of rank $2 \cdot (\omega+2) \geq 2\omega$ whereas the basis vectors are of equally many coefficients, hence $d \geq 2\omega$. The basis matrix contains $(2\omega + 2)^2 \geq 2\omega^2$ coefficients. Following the heuristic the necessary number of iterations of the main loop can be bounded by $2^{19}/2^8 = 2^{11}$. We base the estimate of the number of logical qubits on the largest term in Eq. 8 with application of the trade-off: $r(\log \tilde{B})^{\frac{1}{2}}m)$, where m is the (qu)bit length of the coefficients of the Gram-Schmidt matrix. The Toffoli gate count is based on Eq. 7.

Textbook Implementation. Considering only the largest term an implementation following our circuit representation requires a total of $r^3 d \log \tilde{B} (\log \tilde{B})^{\frac{1}{2}} \geq 2^{24} \cdot 2^8 \cdot 2^{11} \cdot 2^{\frac{19}{2}} \geq 2^{52}$ qubits to cache the Gram-Schmidt matrices. The number of Toffoli gates would be as high as $2^{85} + 2^{66}$.

Fp-LLL à la Schnorr. Implementing the coefficients of the Gram-Schmidt matrix as floating point numbers with precision $m = r + \log \tilde{B}$ the number of qubits is reduced to at least $2^{44} + 2^{33} \geq 2^{44}$. The number of Toffoli gates would be reduced to $2^{65} + 2^{54}$.

L^2. The L^2 algorithm can implement the attack in at most 2^{33} qubits and using at most 2^{55} Toffoli gates.

5   Conclusion

Our quantum circuit representation of the LLL algorithm suggests that quantum lattice reduction requires a large number of logical qubits. We do not claim optimality. The construction of reversible circuits that require less quantum memory as well as the detailed analysis of floating-point variants are lines of future work. The presented quantum design can be adapted to be used in similar reduction processes or to be used as subroutines, e.g., as a quantum shortest vector oracle. Another line of thought goes towards the evaluation of problem classes where the number of iterations of the main loop can be bounded tightly.

Our result challenges the idea that Grover's algorithm improves the attack complexity by a square root. Taking Grover's promise as given to evaluate the security of cryptosystems leads to a very pessimistic security estimates. In the case of the attack on Mersenne number cryptosystems an instantiation of the LLL algorithm as Grover's oracle requires a large amount of qubits as well as a large Toffoli gate count, throwing into question the practicality of the attack even in the context of large scale quantum computers.

Acknowledgements. The authors should like to thank the anonymous reviewers for their helpful feedback and suggestions. This work was supported in part by the Research Council KU Leuven: C16/15/058. In addition, this work was supported by the European Commission through the Horizon 2020 research and innovation programme under grant agreement H2020-DS-LEIT-2017-780108 FENTEC, by the Flemish Government through FWO SBO project SNIPPET S007619N and by the IF/C1 on Cryptanalysis of post-quantum cryptography. Alan Szepieniec was supported by a research grant of the Institute for the Promotion of Innovation through Science and Technology in Flanders (IWT-Vlaanderen), and is now supported by the Nervos Foundation.

References

1. Aggarwal, D., Joux, A., Prakash, A., Santha, M.: A new public-key cryptosystem via mersenne numbers. In: Shacham, H., Boldyreva, A. (eds.) CRYPTO 2018. LNCS, vol. 10993, pp. 459–482. Springer, Cham (2018). https://doi.org/10.1007/978-3-319-96878-0_16

2. Bennett, C.H., Bernstein, E., Brassard, G., Vazirani, U.: Strengths and weaknesses of quantum computing. SIAM J. Comput. **26**(5), 1510–1523 (1997). https://doi.org/10.1137/S0097539796300933

3. Beunardeau, M., Connolly, A., Géraud, R., Naccache, D.: On the hardness of the Mersenne low hamming ratio assumption. IACR Cryptology ePrint Arch. **2017**, 522 (2017)

4. de Boer, K., Ducas, L., Jeffery, S., de Wolf, R.: Attacks on the AJPS Mersenne-based cryptosystem. In: Lange, T., Steinwandt, R. (eds.) PQCrypto 2018. LNCS, vol. 10786, pp. 101–120. Springer, Cham (2018). https://doi.org/10.1007/978-3-319-79063-3_5

5. Cuccaro, S.A., Draper, T.G., Kutin, S.A., Moulton, D.P.: A new quantum ripple-carry addition circuit. arXiv. arXiv:quant-ph/0410184 (2004)

6. Duc Nguyen, T., Van Meter, R.: A space-efficient design for reversible floating point adder in quantum computing. ACM J. Emerg. Technol. Comput. Syst. **11**, 3 (2013). https://doi.org/10.1145/2629525

7. Fowler, A.G., Mariantoni, M., Martinis, J.M., Cleland, A.N.: Surface codes: towards practical large-scale quantum computation. Phys. Rev. A **86**, 032324 (2012). https://doi.org/10.1103/PhysRevA.86.032324

8. Gama, N., Nguyen, P.Q.: Predicting lattice reduction. In: Smart, N. (ed.) EUROCRYPT 2008. LNCS, vol. 4965, pp. 31–51. Springer, Heidelberg (2008). https://doi.org/10.1007/978-3-540-78967-3_3

9. Gidney, C.: Windowed quantum arithmetic. arXiv:1905.07682 (2019)

10. Grover, L.K.: A fast quantum mechanical algorithm for database search. In: ACM STOC, pp. 212–219. STOC 1996. ACM, New York (1996). https://doi.org/10.1145/237814.237866

11. Bennett, C.H.: Time/space trade-offs for reversible computation. SIAM J. Comput. **18**, 766–776 (1989). https://doi.org/10.1137/0218053

12. Joux, A.: Algorithmic Cryptanalysis, 1st edn. Chapman & Hall/CRC, Boca Raton (2009)

13. Lenstra, A.K., Lenstra, H.W., Lovász, L.: Factoring polynomials with rational coefficients. Math. Ann. **261**(4), 515–534 (1982). https://doi.org/10.1007/BF01457454

14. Nachtigal, M., Thapliyal, H., Ranganathan, N.: Design of a reversible single precision floating point multiplier based on operand decomposition. In: 10th IEEE International Conference on Nanotechnology, pp. 233–237 (August 2010). https://doi.org/10.1109/NANO.2010.5697746

15. Nachtigal, M., Thapliyal, H., Ranganathan, N.: Design of a reversible floating-point adder architecture. In: 2011 11th IEEE International Conference on Nanotechnology, pp. 451–456 (August 2011). https://doi.org/10.1109/NANO.2011.6144358

16. Nguên, P.Q., Stehlé, D.: Floating-point LLL revisited. In: Cramer, R. (ed.) EURO-CRYPT 2005. LNCS, vol. 3494, pp. 215–233. Springer, Heidelberg (2005). https://doi.org/10.1007/11426639_13
17. Nguyen, P.Q., Stehlé, D.: LLL on the average. In: Hess, F., Pauli, S., Pohst, M. (eds.) ANTS 2006. LNCS, vol. 4076, pp. 238–256. Springer, Heidelberg (2006). https://doi.org/10.1007/11792086_18
18. Nguyen, P.Q., Valle, B.: The LLL Algorithm: Survey and Applications, 1st edn. Springer, Berlin (2009). https://doi.org/10.1007/978-3-642-02295-1
19. Nielsen, M.A., Chuang, I.L.: Quantum Computation and Quantum Information, 10th edn. Cambridge University Press, New York (2011)
20. Rines, R., Chuang, I.: High performance quantum modular multipliers. arXiv arXiv:1801.01081 (2018)
21. Roetteler, M., Naehrig, M., Svore, K.M., Lauter, K.: Quantum resource esti-mates for computing elliptic curve discrete logarithms. In: Takagi, T., Peyrin, T. (eds.) ASIACRYPT 2017. LNCS, vol. 10625, pp. 241–270. Springer, Cham (2017). https://doi.org/10.1007/978-3-319-70697-9_9
22. Schnorr, C.P.: A more efficient algorithm for lattice basis reduction. J. Algorithms 9(1), 47–62 (1988). https://doi.org/10.1016/0196-6774(88)90004-1
23. Selinger, P.: Quantum circuits of t-depth one. Phys. Rev. A 87, 042302 (2013). https://doi.org/10.1103/PhysRevA.87.042302
24. Shor, P.W.: Algorithms for quantum computation: Discrete logarithms and fac-toring. In: FOCS, pp. 124–134. SFCS 1994. IEEE Computer Society, Washington, D.C. (1994). https://doi.org/10.1109/SFCS.1994.365700
25. Szepieniec, A.: Ramstake. NIST Submission (2017) https://csrc.nist.gov/Projects/Post-Quantum-Cryptography/Round-1-Submissions
26. Wiebe, N., Kliuchnikov, V.: Floating point representations in quantum circuit syn-thesis. New J. Phys. 15(9), 093041 (2013). https://doi.org/10.1088/1367-2630/15/9/093041

Breaking Randomized Mixed-Radix Scalar Multiplication Algorithms

Jérémie Detrey[1] and Laurent Imbert[2(✉)]

[1] LORIA, INRIA, CNRS, Université de Lorraine, Nancy, France
jeremie.detrey@loria.fr
[2] LIRMM, CNRS, Université de Montpellier, Montpellier, France
laurent.imbert@lirmm.fr

Abstract. In this paper we present a novel, powerful attack on a recently introduced randomized scalar multiplication algorithm based on covering systems of congruences. Our attack can recover the whole key with very few traces, even when those only provide partial information on the sequence of operations. In an attempt to solve the issues raised by the broken algorithm, we designed a constant-time version with no secret dependent branching nor memory access based on the so-called mixed-radix number system. We eventually present our conclusions regarding the use of mixed-radix representations as a randomization setting.

1 Introduction

After more than twenty years of research on side-channel attacks, it is now very clear that protections of cryptographic implementation are absolutely mandatory. The level and type of protections that need to be implemented depend on the security model. In the software model, one usually simply considers timing and cache attacks. In the more delicate hardware model, where the adversary can monitor power or electromagnetic emanation, insert faults, etc., extra contermeasures are required. This advanced model should also be seriously considered when writing software for a micro-controller, where the user has full access to the device and can therefore be the adversary. In this case, randomization is considered as the number-one countermeasure.

In the context of public-key algorithms, a not so frequent randomization strategy consists in randomizing the exponentiation or scalar multiplication algorithm itself. This can be achieved by taking random decisions in the course of the algorithm. In the elliptic curve setting, Oswald and Aigner proposed the use of randomized addition-subtraction chains [11]. Their solution was broken using the so-called hidden Markov Model (HMM) cryptanalysis by Karlof and Wagner [9]. Another randomization approach of the same kind was proposed by Ha and Moon [8]. Their solution based on Binary Signed Digit (BSD) recodings [4] was broken in [5]. Méloni and Hasan generalized the fractional w-NAF method by allowing random choices for the expansion digits [10].

The first contribution of this paper is a novel attack on a recently proposed approach based on covering systems on congruences (CSC) [7]. The threat model

© Springer Nature Switzerland AG 2019
P. Schwabe and N. Thériault (Eds.): LATINCRYPT 2019, LNCS 11774, pp. 24–39, 2019.
https://doi.org/10.1007/978-3-030-30530-7_2

that we consider simply assumes that the attacker can distinguish point doublings from point additions in an execution trace. Our attack only requires a few
traces to recover the whole key.

In a second part, we introduce a new randomized, yet constant-time algorithm which eludes the weaknesses of the original CSC-based approach under
the same threat model. Our algorithm uses the so-called mixed-radix number
system.

Finally, we sketch out some potential weaknesses of MRS-based randomization strategies in a more advanced threat model. Our conclusion is that mixed-
radix based algorithms might remain vulnerable to sophisticated attacks relying
on deep-learning and Coppersmith-like techniques.

2 Covering Systems of Congruences: Presentation and Weakness

In [7], Guerrini et al. use covering systems of congruences to randomize the scalar
multiplication algorithm. A covering system of congruences (CSC) is defined as a
set $S = \{(r_1, m_1), \ldots, (r_n, m_n)\} \subset \mathbb{Z} \times \mathbb{N}$ such that, for any integer x, there exists
at least one congruence $(r_i, m_i) \in S$ such that $x \equiv r_i \pmod{m_i}$. In other words,
S forms a covering of $\mathbb{Z}$, where each pair (r_i, m_i) represents the congruence class
$m_i\mathbb{Z} + r_i$.

Then, given a scalar k and a point $P \in E$, the authors randomize the computation of $[k]P$ by picking a random decomposition of k in the covering system
S: starting with $k_0 = k$, they recursively compute k_j as $(k_{j-1} - r_{i_j})/m_{i_j}$, for all
$j > 0$, where i_j is taken uniformly at random among all indices $i \in \{1, \ldots, n\}$
such that $k_{j-1} \equiv r_i \pmod{m_i}$. The algorithm terminates, as the resulting
sequence $(k_j)_{j \geq 0}$ is strictly decreasing (in absolute value) until it eventually
reaches $k_\ell = 0$. The sequence of congruences $\mathcal{R} = ((r_{i_1}, m_{i_1}), \ldots, (r_{i_\ell}, m_{i_\ell}))$ is
then a random decomposition of the scalar k in the covering system S, and
computing $[k]P = [k_0]P$ relies on the fact that, for any $0 < j \leq \ell$, $[k_{j-1}]P$ can
be computed recursively from $[k_j]P$ and P as $[k_{j-1}]P = [m_{i_j}]([k_j]P) + [r_{i_j}]P$,
starting from $[k_\ell]P = [0]P = \mathcal{O}$.

Although the algorithm does not run in constant-time and uses non-uniform
curve operations (i.e. doublings and additions reveal different patterns in an
execution trace), the authors of [7] claimed that their randomization is robust
against both simple and more advanced attacks.

In the next section we present a novel attack that can recover the secret
scalar k by observing only a few execution traces. Our threat model simply
assumes that the attacker can distinguish the pattern of a curve doubling from
that of an addition. This is a very common threat model that applies to a wide
variety of settings, from remote timing attacks to local power or EM observations.
Using this information, we are able to deduce critical data about the sequence
of congruences $\mathcal{R}$, which render the CSC-based randomization strategy totally
useless.

In the sequences of curve operations proposed by the authors in [7, Table 4], one can see that some sequences of operations are specific to only a few congruence classes. Indeed, even if the function $\mu : \mathcal{S} \to \{A, D\}^*$, which maps each congruence class (r_i, m_i) to the corresponding sequence of curve operations is not injective, this is not enough: as soon as μ maps a subset (and only this subset) $\mathcal{S}'$ of $\mathcal{S}$ to some patterns of operations, then it becomes possible to determine whether or not congruences in $\mathcal{S}'$ were used in a given decomposition $\mathcal{R}$ just by checking if these patterns appear in the corresponding trace. Furthermore, if $\mathcal{S}'$ does not form a covering of $\mathbb{Z}$, then this will reveal data on the secret scalar k, by eliminating all integers not covered by $\mathcal{S}'$. For instance, in [7, Table 4], one can see that k_j is odd if and only if the sequence of operations leading to the computation of $[k_j]P$ ends with an addition (A).

3   Full-Key Recovery Algorithm

Based on this observation, we present here an algorithm which recovers the secret scalar k by analyzing traces $\tau \in \{A, D\}^*$ corresponding to randomized scalar multiplications by k, for a given covering system $\mathcal{S}$ and a given function $\mu : \mathcal{S} \to \{A, D\}^*$ such as those described in [7].

To achieve this, the algorithm maintains, for each intercepted trace τ, a set $\mathcal{D}_\tau$ of *partially decoded traces*. Such a partially decoded trace is a triple $(\pi, r, m) \in \{A, D\}^* \times \mathbb{Z} \times \mathbb{N}$, such that π is a prefix of τ, and such that there exists a sequence $((r_{i_1}, m_{i_1}), \ldots, (r_{i_d}, m_{i_d}))$ of congruences of $\mathcal{S}$ which satisfies

$$\begin{cases} \tau = \pi \,\|\, \mu(r_{i_d}, m_{i_d}) \,\|\, \ldots \,\|\, \mu(r_{i_1}, m_{i_1}), \\ r = r_{i_d} m_{i_{d-1}} \ldots m_{i_1} + \cdots + r_{i_2} m_{i_1} + r_{i_1}, \text{ and} \\ m = m_{i_d} \ldots m_{i_1}, \end{cases}$$

where the operator $\|$ denotes the concatenation in $\{A, D\}^*$. In other words, each partially decoded trace in $(\pi, r, m) \in \mathcal{D}_\tau$ corresponds to a congruence class $m\mathbb{Z} + r$ whose elements all admit a decomposition in $\mathcal{S}$ starting with $((r_{i_1}, m_{i_1}), \ldots, (r_{i_d}, m_{i_d}))$, thus accounting for the operations observed in the final part of the trace τ, up to its prefix π which still remains to be decoded.

Therefore, for each trace τ, the algorithm will maintain the set $\mathcal{D}_\tau$ in such a way that there always exists a partially decoded trace $(\pi, r, m) \in \mathcal{D}_\tau$ so that $k \in m\mathbb{Z} + r$ or, equivalently, that $k \in \bigcup_{(\pi,r,m) \in \mathcal{D}_\tau} (m\mathbb{Z} + r)$.

When a trace τ is first acquired, $\mathcal{D}_\tau$ initially only contains the undecoded trace $(\tau, 0, 1)$. One can then repeatedly apply the decoding function δ to the elements of $\mathcal{D}_\tau$, where δ is defined as

$$\delta : (\pi, r, m) \mapsto \{(\pi', r_i m + r, m_i m) \mid (r_i, m_i) \in \mathcal{S} \text{ and } \pi = \pi' \,\|\, \mu(r_i, m_i)\}.$$

Note that fully decoding the trace τ (i.e., applying δ until the prefix π of each decoded trace in $\mathcal{D}_\tau$ is the empty string ϵ) is not directly possible, as the number of such traces grows exponentially with the length of τ. We thus need a way to keep this growth under control. This can be achieved by confronting intercepted traces together: given two traces τ and τ', if the congruence class $m\mathbb{Z} + r$ of a partially decoded trace $(\pi, r, m) \in \mathcal{D}_\tau$ is disjoint from the union of the congruence classes of the partially decoded traces of $\mathcal{D}_{\tau'}$, then $k \notin m\mathbb{Z} + r$ and (π, r, m) can be safely discarded from $\mathcal{D}_\tau$.

To this effect, the algorithm also maintains a set $\mathcal{H}$ of congruence classes such that for any combination of partially decoded traces

$$((\pi^{(1)}, r^{(1)}, m^{(1)}), \ldots, (\pi^{(t)}, r^{(t)}, m^{(t)})) \in \mathcal{D}_{\tau^{(1)}} \times \cdots \times \mathcal{D}_{\tau^{(t)}},$$

there exists a congruence class $(\hat{r}, \hat{m}) \in \mathcal{H}$ such that

$$\bigcap_{1 \leq i \leq t} (m^{(i)}\mathbb{Z} + r^{(i)}) \subset \hat{m}\mathbb{Z} + \hat{r}.$$

In the following, let $\mathcal{T} = \{\tau^{(1)}, \ldots, \tau^{(t)}\}$ denote the set of intercepted traces. The complete key recovery algorithm is described in Algorithm 1. Based on the ideas given above, it progressively decodes the intercepted traces, keeping only the partially decoded traces (π, r, m) which are compatible with $\mathcal{H}$, that is, such that $(m\mathbb{Z} + r) \cap \bigcup_{(\hat{r}, \hat{m}) \in \mathcal{H}} (\hat{m}\mathbb{Z} + \hat{r}) \neq \emptyset$. It then updates $\mathcal{H}$ by computing all pairwise intersections between partially decoded traces and elements of $\mathcal{H}$.

Note that the inclusion tests and intersections of congruence classes required by the algorithm can be computed efficiently. Indeed, for any two congruence classes $m\mathbb{Z} + r$ and $m'\mathbb{Z} + r'$:

- $m\mathbb{Z} + r \subset m'\mathbb{Z} + r'$ if and only if m' divides m and $r \equiv r' \pmod{m'}$;
- $(m\mathbb{Z} + r) \cap (m'\mathbb{Z} + r') \neq \emptyset$ if and only if $r \equiv r' \pmod{\gcd(m, m')}$;
- if $r \equiv r' \pmod{\gcd(m, m')}$, then $(m\mathbb{Z} + r) \cap (m'\mathbb{Z} + r') = \mathrm{lcm}(m, m')\mathbb{Z} + r''$, where r'', computed using the Chinese remainder theorem, is the unique integer in $\{0, \ldots, \mathrm{lcm}(m, m') - 1\}$ such that $r'' \equiv r \pmod{m}$ and $r'' \equiv r' \pmod{m'}$.

4   Implementation and Experimental Results

This key recovery algorithm was implemented in C. It can be downloaded at http://imbert.lirmm.net/cover-systems/ together with examples of covering systems of congruences from [7]. On covering systems such as u3c-48-24 presented in [7, Table 4], it retrieves a 256-bit secret scalar k in a few seconds using between 10 and 15 traces. Using larger covering systems (such as an exact 12-cover consisting of 3315 congruences, kindly provided by the authors), the algorithm takes only slightly longer, but requires the same amount of traces.

We have also tried our key recovery algorithm with an implementation function μ' which leaks slightly less data in the trace about the chosen congruences (r_{i_j}, m_{i_j}) in the random decomposition of the secret scalar k: μ' corresponds to an implementation of the scalar multiplication algorithm which, at each step, in order to compute $Q \leftarrow [m_{i_j}]Q + [r_{i_j}]P$, first computes $[m_{i_j}]Q$ and then adds the precomputed point $[r_{i_j}]P$. This way, in the observed addition/doubling traces,

---

Algorithm 1. Key recovery algorithm for the CSC-based scalar multiplication [7].

Input: A covering system $\mathcal{S} = \{(r_1, m_1), \ldots, (r_n, m_n)\}$, an implementation $\mu : \mathcal{S} \to \{A, D\}^*$, an oracle Ω generating multiplication traces by an unknown scalar k, and a decoding bound N (typically, $N = 256$).

Output: A small set $\mathcal{K}$ such that $k \in \mathcal{K}$.

  1: **function** PARTIALDECODE($\mathcal{D}$, $\mathcal{H}$)
  2:     **repeat**
  3:         $\mathcal{D}' \leftarrow \{(\pi, r, m) \in \mathcal{D} \mid |\pi| > 0 \text{ and } m \leq \max_{(\hat{r}, \hat{m}) \in \mathcal{H}} \hat{m}\}$
              ▷ *Select only the partially decoded traces we want to decode further.*
  4:         $\mathcal{D} \leftarrow \mathcal{D} \setminus \mathcal{D}'$
  5:         **for all** $(\pi, r, m) \in \mathcal{D}'$ **do**
  6:             $\mathcal{D} \leftarrow \mathcal{D} \cup \{(\pi', r', m') \in \delta(\pi, r, m) \mid \exists (\hat{r}, \hat{m}) \in \mathcal{H}, (m'\mathbb{Z} + r') \cap (\hat{m}\mathbb{Z} + \hat{r}) \neq \emptyset\}$
  7:     **until** $|\mathcal{D}| \geq N$ **or** $\mathcal{D}' = \emptyset$
  8:     **return** $\mathcal{D}$
  9: **end function**

10: $\mathcal{H} \leftarrow \{(0, 1)\}$; $\mathcal{T} \leftarrow \{\}$
11: **loop**
12:     $\tau_{\text{new}} \leftarrow \Omega()$; $\mathcal{T} \leftarrow \mathcal{T} \cup \{\tau_{\text{new}}\}$; $\mathcal{D}_{\tau_{\text{new}}} \leftarrow \{(\tau_{\text{new}}, 0, 1)\}$ ▷ *Intercept new trace.*
13:     **repeat**
14:         done $\leftarrow \top$
15:         **for all** $\tau \in \mathcal{T}$ **do**
16:             $\mathcal{D}_\tau \leftarrow \{(\pi, r, m) \in \mathcal{D}_\tau \mid \exists (\hat{r}, \hat{m}) \in \mathcal{H}, (m\mathbb{Z} + r) \cap (\hat{m}\mathbb{Z} + \hat{r}) \neq \emptyset\}$
              ▷ *Remove partially decoded traces which are incompatible with $\mathcal{H}$.*
17:             **if** $\mathcal{D}_\tau$ has changed after the previous step **or if** $\mathcal{D}_\tau = \{(\tau, 0, 1)\}$ **then**
18:                 $\mathcal{D}_\tau \leftarrow$ PARTIALDECODE($\mathcal{D}_\tau$, $\mathcal{H}$)   ▷ *Further decode trace τ.*
19:                 **if** $\forall (\pi, r, m) \in \mathcal{D}_\tau, |\pi| = 0$ **then**
20:                     **return** $\{r \mid (\pi, r, m) \in \mathcal{D}_\tau\}$
21:                 $\mathcal{H} \leftarrow \{(\hat{r}', \hat{m}') \mid \exists (\pi, r, m) \in \mathcal{D}_\tau \text{ and } \exists (\hat{r}, \hat{m}) \in \mathcal{H},$
                                $\hat{m}'\mathbb{Z} + \hat{r}' = (m\mathbb{Z} + r) \cap (\hat{m}\mathbb{Z} + \hat{r})\}$
              ▷ *Merge congruence classes from newly decoded traces into $\mathcal{H}$.*
22:                 $\mathcal{H} \leftarrow \{(\hat{r}, \hat{m}) \in \mathcal{H} \mid \nexists (\hat{r}', \hat{m}') \in \mathcal{H}, m \neq m' \text{ and } \hat{m}\mathbb{Z} + \hat{r} \subset \hat{m}'\mathbb{Z} + \hat{r}'\}$
              ▷ *Remove redundant congruence classes from $\mathcal{H}$.*
23:         **if** $\mathcal{H}$ has changed after the two previous steps **then**
24:             done $\leftarrow \bot$
25:     **until** done
26: **end loop**

$\mu'(r_{i_j}, m_{i_j})$ only reveals the chosen modulus m_{i_j}, but not the residue r_{i_j}. However, for the covering systems mentioned in [7], the knowledge of the m_{i_j}'s only is still enough to retrieve the key. Indeed, according to our experiments, the program will take up to an hour and will require between 20 and 40 traces, but will still completely recover the secret scalar k.

Of course, the less data leaked by the implementation about the chosen congruences (r_{i_j}, m_{i_j}) in the random decomposition of k, the harder it is for our algorithm to recover the key. Ideally, a covering system in which all the moduli

m_i of $\mathcal{S}$ would have the same bit-length, paired with a constant time implementation where the function μ would map all congruences $(r_i, m_i) \in \mathcal{S}$ to the same sequence of operations would render our key recovery algorithm totally useless. The question whether such an algorithm could be efficiently turned into a robust randomized implementation is addressed in the next section.

5   A Constant-Time Alternative

In order to fix the problems raised by our attack, we introduce an alternative scalar multiplication algorithm based on the so-called Mixed-Radix Number System (MRS) – a non-standard positional number system that uses multiple radices – that can be seen as a generalization of Guerrini et al.'s CSC-based approach.

5.1   The Mixed-Radix Number System

In any positional system, numbers are represented using an ordered sequence of numeral symbols, called digits. The contribution of each digit is given by its value scaled by the weight of its position expressed in the base (or radix) of the system. For example, in the conventional, radix-b number system, the contribution of a digit x_i at position i is equal to $x_i b^i$. The total value of the number x represented as $(x_k \ldots x_0)_b$ is the sum of the contributions assigned to each digit, i.e., $x = \sum_{i=0}^{k} x_i b^i$.

In the mixed-radix number system (MRS), the weight of each position is no longer expressed as a power of a constant radix. Instead, an MRS base is given by an ordered sequence $\mathcal{B} = (b_1, b_2, \ldots, b_n)$ of integer radices all greater than 1. The weight associated to position i is equal to the product of the first $i-1$ elements of that sequence. Hence, the value of the number represented by the sequence of $n+1$ digits $(x_1, x_2, \ldots, x_{n+1})$ is

$$x = x_1 + x_2 b_1 + x_3 b_1 b_2 + \cdots + x_{n+1} \prod_{j=1}^{n} b_j = \sum_{i=1}^{n+1} x_i \Pi_{\mathcal{B}}^{(i-1)}, \qquad (1)$$

where $\Pi_{\mathcal{B}}^{(k)}$ denotes the product of the first k elements of $\mathcal{B}$. By convention, we set $\Pi_{\mathcal{B}}^{(0)} = 1$ and for any $0 < k \leq n$, $\Pi_{\mathcal{B}}^{(k)} = b_1 b_2 \ldots b_k = \prod_{j=1}^{k} b_j$.

A number system is said to be *complete* if every integer can be represented. It is *unambiguous* if each integer admits a unique representation. The usual, radix-b number system with digits in $\{0, \ldots, b-1\}$ is complete and unambiguous. In the next Lemma, we recall a known result which shows that these properties may also hold for mixed-radix systems.

Lemma 1. *Let $\mathcal{B} = (b_1, \ldots, b_n)$ be a sequence of integer radices all greater than 1. Then, every integer $x \in \mathbb{N}$ can be uniquely written in the form of (1), where the "digits" x_i are integers satisfying $0 \leq x_i < b_i$, for $1 \leq i \leq n$, and $x_{n+1} \geq 0$. We say that the $(n+1)$-tuple $(x_1, \ldots, x_{n+1})$ is a mixed-radix representation of x in base $\mathcal{B}$, and we write $x = (x_1, \ldots, x_{n+1})_{\mathcal{B}}$.*

Proof. Let $x \in \mathbb{N}$. Starting from $t_1 = x$, one can construct the recursive sequence defined by $t_{i+1} = \lfloor t_i/b_i \rfloor = (t_i - x_i)/b_i$, with $x_i = t_i \bmod b_i$, for all $1 \le i \le n$, and then terminate the process by taking $x_{n+1} = t_{n+1}$. Using (1), one can then easily verify that $(x_1, \ldots, x_{n+1})$ is indeed a mixed-radix representation of x in base $\mathcal{B}$.

Suppose that there exist two distinct MRS representations $(x_1, \ldots, x_{n+1})_\mathcal{B}$ and $(x'_1, \ldots, x'_{n+1})_\mathcal{B}$ of x in base $\mathcal{B}$, with digits such that $0 \le x_i, x'_i < b_i$ for all $1 \le i \le n$, and $x_{n+1}, x'_{n+1} \ge 0$. Let i_0 be the smallest integer such that $x_{i_0} \ne x'_{i_0}$. Then, by (1), we have

$$0 = x - x = (x_{i_0} - x'_{i_0})\Pi_\mathcal{B}^{(i_0-1)} + (x_{i_0+1} - x'_{i_0+1})\Pi_\mathcal{B}^{(i_0)} + \cdots + (x_{n+1} - x'_{n+1})\Pi_\mathcal{B}^{(n)}.$$

- If $i_0 = n+1$, then this gives $(x_{n+1} - x'_{n+1})\Pi_\mathcal{B}^{(n)} = 0$ and, consequently, $x_{n+1} = x'_{n+1}$, which is a contradiction.
- Otherwise, dividing the previous equation by $\Pi_\mathcal{B}^{(i_0-1)}$ and considering it modulo b_{i_0}, we obtain $x_{i_0} - x'_{i_0} \equiv 0 \pmod{b_{i_0}}$. Since $0 \le x_{i_0}, x'_{i_0} < b_{i_0}$, then $x_{i_0} = x'_{i_0}$, which is also a contradiction.

Therefore, x has a unique MRS representation in base $\mathcal{B}$. □

Note that, following the proof of Lemma 1, if $(x_1, \ldots, x_{n+1})_\mathcal{B}$ is the MRS representation of a given non-negative integer x, the most significant digit x_{n+1} is equal to $\lfloor x/\Pi_\mathcal{B}^{(n)} \rfloor$.

5.2 A Deterministic MRS-Based Scalar Multiplication

The algorithm we present here performs a scalar multiplication using an MRS representation of the scalar: given an MRS base $\mathcal{B}$, a scalar k, and a point P on the curve, it first computes the MRS representation of k in base $\mathcal{B}$ then proceeds to computing the actual scalar multiplication in order to obtain $[k]P$.

Recall the algorithm for computing the MRS representation of a given integer k in base $\mathcal{B} = (b_1, \ldots, b_n)$, as sketched in the proof of Lemma 1: starting from $t_1 = k$, one iteratively computes $t_{i+1} = (t_i - k_i)/b_i$, where each digit k_i is given by $t_i \bmod b_i$, for i ranging from 1 to n. Finally, the most-significant digit k_{n+1} is directly given by t_{n+1}. Then, computing $[k]P$ from the MRS representation $(k_1, \ldots, k_{n+1})_\mathcal{B}$ of k is just a matter of taking this algorithm in reverse, remarking that $t_i = b_i t_{i+1} + k_i$ and that, given $T = [t_{i+1}]P$, one can thus compute $[t_i]P$ as $[b_i]T + [k_i]P$.

For the sake of the exposition, Algorithm 2 presented below is purely deterministic. Its randomization and the ensuing issues it raises will be addressed in the next sections.

In this algorithm, special attention should be paid so as not to reveal any information about the digits k_i representing the scalar k, both when computing each of them (line 3) and when evaluating $[b_i]T + [k_i]P$ (line 8). The former will be addressed in Sect. 5.5. For the latter, we use a regular double-scalar multiplication algorithm such as the one proposed by Bernstein [1]. For the same security reasons, we also use a constant-time Montgomery ladder when computing the scalar multiplication by the most-significant digits k_{n+1} on line 3.

Algorithm 2. Deterministic mixed-radix scalar multiplication algorithm.

Input: An MRS base $\mathcal{B} = (b_1, \ldots, b_n)$, a scalar $k \in \mathbb{N}$, and $P \in E$.
Output: $[k]P \in E$.

1: $t \leftarrow k$
2: **for** $i \leftarrow 1$ **to** n **do**   ▷ *Compute the MRS representation of k in base $\mathcal{B}$.*
3:    $k_i \leftarrow t \bmod b_i$
4:    $t \leftarrow (t - k_i)/b_i$
5: $k_{n+1} \leftarrow t$
6: $T \leftarrow [k_{n+1}]P$ ▷ *Computed using a Montgomery ladder.*
7: **for** $i \leftarrow n$ **downto** 1 **do**
8:    $T \leftarrow [b_i]T + [k_i]P$ ▷ *Computed using a regular double-scalar multiplication.*
9: **return** T

5.3 Regular Double-Scalar Multiplication

Given two points P and Q on an elliptic curve E, and two scalars a and $b \in \mathbb{N}$, the double-scalar multiplication is the operation which computes the point $[a]P + [b]Q$. In [12], Strauss was the first to suggest that this operation can be computed in at most $2\max(\log_2(a), \log_2(b))$ curve operations instead of $2(\log_2(a) + \log_2(b))$ if $[a]P$ and $[b]Q$ are evaluated independently. Unfortunately, Strauss' algorithm cannot be used when side-channel protection is required since the curve operations depend on the values of the scalars a and b.

In 2003, a regular double-scalar multiplication was published in a paper by Ciet and Joye [3]. Their algorithm uses secret-dependent memory accesses and might therefore be vulnerable to cache attacks. More problematically, the proposed algorithm is incorrect[1].

In a 2006 preprint [1], which was then published in [2], Bernstein proposed a regular two-dimensional ladder, inspired by the Montgomery ladder, and compatible with curves where only differential additions are supported. In order to compute $[a]P + [b]Q$ for any two non-negative scalars a and b, Bernstein's algorithm requires knowledge of the two points P and Q, along with their difference $P - Q$.

Here we present a slight modification of Bernstein's ladder where the input points are P, Q, and $P+Q$. Indeed, as can be seen in Algorithm 2, the proposed MRS scalar multiplication performs a sequence of double-scalar multiplications where the first point of an iteration is the result of the previous one, and where the second point is always the same. In this context, we decided to adapt Bernstein's two-dimensional ladder algorithm so as to return both $R = [a]P + [b]Q$ and $R + Q = [a]P + [b+1]Q$, at no extra cost, which then allows us to directly call the next double-scalar multiplication with input points R, Q, and $R + Q$.

---

[1] When $a_i = b_i = 0$, register R_1 is wrongly updated. A possible workaround would be to perform a dummy operation when both a_i and b_i are equal to zero (in [3, Fig. 3], add a fourth register R_4 and replace the instruction $R_b \leftarrow R_b + R_c$ with $R_{4b} \leftarrow R_b + R_c$) but the resulting algorithm would then be subject to fault attacks.

The proposed variant of this two-dimensional ladder is given in Algorithm 3. This algorithm maintains a loop invariant in which, just after iteration i (or, equivalently, just before iteration $i-1$), we have

$$\begin{cases} U = T + [\overline{a_i}]P + [\overline{b_i}]Q, \\ V = T + [a_i]P + [b_i]Q, \text{ and} \\ W = T + [a_i \oplus d_i]P + [b_i \oplus \overline{d_i}]Q, \end{cases}$$

with $T = [\lfloor a/2^i \rfloor]P + [\lfloor b/2^i \rfloor]Q$, and where $\overline{x}$ denotes the negation of bit x (i.e., $\overline{x} = 1 - x$), and $x \oplus y$ the XOR of bits x and y (i.e., $x \oplus y = (x+y) \bmod 2$). The bit sequence $(d_i)_{0 \le i \le n}$, computed on lines 3 to 7, corresponds to the quantity d defined recursively on page 9 of [1], with the initial value $d_0 = a \bmod 2 = a_0$ and

$$d_{i+1} = \begin{cases} 0 & \text{if } (a_i \oplus a_{i+1}, b_i \oplus b_{i+1}) = (0,1), \\ 1 & \text{if } (a_i \oplus a_{i+1}, b_i \oplus b_{i+1}) = (1,0), \\ d_i & \text{if } (a_i \oplus a_{i+1}, b_i \oplus b_{i+1}) = (0,0), \text{ and} \\ 1 - d_i & \text{if } (a_i \oplus a_{i+1}, b_i \oplus b_{i+1}) = (1,1). \end{cases}$$

Algorithm 3. Our variant of Bernstein's two-dimensional ladder [1].

Input: Scalars a and b such that $0 \le a, b < 2^n$, and points P, Q, and $D_+ = P+Q \in E$.
Output: $R = [a]P + [b]Q$ and $R + Q = [a]P + [b+1]Q \in E$.
1: $(a_n \dots a_0)_2 \leftarrow a$ ▷ $(n+1)$-bit binary expansion of a, with $a_n = 0$.
2: $(b_n \dots b_0)_2 \leftarrow b$ ▷ $(n+1)$-bit binary expansion of b, with $b_n = 0$.
3: $d_0 \leftarrow a_0$
4: **for** $i \leftarrow 0$ **to** $n-1$ **do**
5:      $\delta a_i \leftarrow a_i \oplus a_{i+1}$
6:      $\delta b_i \leftarrow b_i \oplus b_{i+1}$
7:      $d_{i+1} \leftarrow \left(\overline{(\delta a_i \oplus \delta b_i)} \cdot d_i \right) \oplus \delta a_i$ ▷ Computation of d, as in [1, p.9].

8: $D_- \leftarrow \mathbf{diffadd}(P, -Q, D_+)$ ▷ Compute $D_- = P - Q$.
9: $U \leftarrow D_+$; $V \leftarrow \mathcal{O}$; $W \leftarrow \mathbf{select}(P, Q, d_n)$ ▷ Initialization.
10: **for** $i \leftarrow n-1$ **downto** 0 **do**
11:      $T_0 \leftarrow \mathbf{select}(W, \mathbf{select}(U, V, \delta a_i), \delta a_i \oplus \delta b_i)$ ▷ Select operands.
12:      $T_1 \leftarrow \mathbf{select}(U, V, d_i \oplus d_{i+1})$
13:      $T_2 \leftarrow \mathbf{select}(D_-, D_+, a_{i+1} \oplus b_{i+1})$
14:      $T_3 \leftarrow \mathbf{select}(P, Q, d_i)$
15:      $U \leftarrow \mathbf{diffadd}(U, V, T_2)$ ▷ Update U, V, and W.
16:      $V \leftarrow [2]T_0$
17:      $W \leftarrow \mathbf{diffadd}(W, T_1, T_3)$
18: $\mathbf{cswap}(U, V, a_0)$
19: $\mathbf{cswap}(V, W, a_0 \oplus b_0)$
20: **return** V, W

Note that, as mentioned before, this algorithm supports curves with formulae for differential addition. This operation is denoted by **diffadd** in Algorithm 3: for any two points S and $T \in E$, **diffadd**$(S, T, S - T)$ computes the point

$S + T$. However, if a regular addition formulae is available on E, **diffadd** can be replaced by a normal point addition, and its third argument is not used. In that case, the computation of D_- on line 8, along with those of T_2 and T_3 on lines 13 and 14, respectively, can be ignored.

Note also that, on the very first iteration of the ladder, when $i = n - 1$, the first differential addition on line 15 is trivial, since $V = \mathcal{O}$. It can then safely be ignored as well. Consequently, putting it all together, this algorithm performs $2n$ differential additions (or $2n - 1$ regular additions, if differential additions are not available) and n doublings on E.

Finally, note that Algorithm 3 contains no secret-dependent conditional branching instruction or memory access, so as to avoid branch-prediction and cache attacks. For this purpose, the only secret-dependent conditional operations in the algorithm are selections and conditional swaps, denoted by **select** and **cswap**, respectively:

- The former is equivalent to a conditional operator: it returns its first or its second argument depending on whether its third one, a single bit, is 1 or 0, respectively. It can be implemented without conditional branching using arithmetic operations or bit-masking techniques. For instance, the operation $R \leftarrow \textbf{select}(X, Y, c)$ can be implemented as

$$R \leftarrow Y \oplus ((X \oplus Y) \times c),$$

  where $\oplus$ denotes the bitwise XOR.
- Similarly, the operation $\textbf{cswap}(X, Y, c)$, which swaps the values of X and Y if and only if c is 1, can be implemented as

$$\begin{aligned} M \quad &\leftarrow (X \oplus Y) \times c \\ (X, Y) &\leftarrow (X \oplus M, Y \oplus M). \end{aligned}$$

5.4 Randomizing the MRS-Based Scalar Multiplication

The MRS digits k_i and radices b_i processed by the deterministic MRS scalar multiplication introduced in Algorithm 2 exclusively depend on the MRS base $\mathcal{B}$ used to represent k. The basic idea of our randomized version is quite simple. We simply represent the secret scalar k using an MRS base $\mathcal{B}$ chosen uniformly at random prior to each scalar multiplication. This way, each call to the algorithm manipulates different values k_i and b_i, even if the same scalar k is used as input, hence producing different execution traces. This new algorithm can be somehow seen as a refinement and an improvement of the CSC-based algorithm proposed in [7].

As will be seen in the next section, some caution is required. In particular, the base $\mathcal{B}$ is randomly chosen among a predefined family $\mathcal{F}$ of fine-tuned MRS basis. And each base $\mathcal{B}$ from $\mathcal{F}$ should be able to represent scalars in a predetermined interval whose bounds are denoted $X_{\mathcal{F}}^{\min}$ and $X_{\mathcal{F}}^{\max}$. For completeness, we give the randomized version in Algorithm 4.

Algorithm 4. Randomized mixed-radix scalar multiplication algorithm.

Input: A family $\mathcal{F}$ of MRS bases, a scalar $k \in \{X_{\mathcal{F}}^{\min}, \ldots, X_{\mathcal{F}}^{\max} - 1\}$, and $P \in E$.
Output: $[k]P \in E$.

1: $\mathcal{B} = (b_1, \ldots, b_n) \xleftarrow{\$} \mathcal{F}$ ▷ *Choose an MRS base in $\mathcal{F}$ uniformly at random.*
2: $t \leftarrow k$
3: **for** $i \leftarrow 1$ **to** n **do** ▷ *Compute the MRS representation of k in base $\mathcal{B}$.*
4:     $k_i \leftarrow t \bmod b_i$
5:     $t \leftarrow (t - k_i)/b_i$
6: $k_{n+1} \leftarrow t$
7: $T \leftarrow [k_{n+1}]P$ ▷ *Computed using a Montgomery ladder.*
8: **for** $i \leftarrow n$ **downto** 1 **do**
9:     $T \leftarrow [b_i]T + [k_i]P$ ▷ *Computed using Bernstein's regular double ladder.*
10: **return** T

Even though the idea behind this randomization is quite simple, it raises several additional issues, mostly because the randomized algorithm should not reveal the randomly chosen MRS base $\mathcal{B}$. Namely, we need to find suitable families $\mathcal{F}$ of MRS bases such that the following requirements are fulfilled:

1. the range $\{X_{\mathcal{F}}^{\min}, \ldots, X_{\mathcal{F}}^{\max} - 1\}$ can accommodate any scalar k of relevance for the cryptosystem at hand;
2. $\mathcal{F}$ is large enough to ensure a sufficient amount of randomization;
3. one can securely pick $\mathcal{B} \in \mathcal{F}$ at random;
4. one can securely compute the MRS representation of k in base $\mathcal{B}$;
5. one can securely compute the scalar multiplication $[k]P$.

As already stated, is it essential that any implementation of Algorithm 4 runs in constant-time. This implies in particular that the conversion of k into its MRS form and the subsequent MRS-based scalar multiplication both run in constant-time.

5.5 Secure Mixed-Radix Decomposition

The **for** loop on lines 3 to 5 of Algorithm 4 computes the representation of the secret scalar k in the randomly selecter MRS basis $\mathcal{B}$ by iteratively computing residues and divisions by the radices b_i. Obviously, special care has to be paid here to perform this scalar decomposition so as not to reveal any information on k by side channels, but we should also ensure that no data is leaked about the radices b_i as well.

As will be seen in Sect. 5.6, our family of MRS bases consists of n-tuples of radices taken from a predefined set of size m. The method presented in Algorithm 5 computes each digit k_i first by computing the quotient q and the remainder r of the Euclidean division of t (the current scalar to decompose) by the corresponding radix b_i (lines 6 to 7).

Since all radices of $\mathcal{B}$ are known in advance, we can precompute the inverse b_i^{-1} of each radix b_i so that the quotient on line 6 can be computed using a single multiplication, as proposed by Granlund and Montgomery in [6]. Note that the inverses have to be precomputed with enough precision in order to obtain the exact quotient: according to [6, Theorem 4.2], if the scalar k fits into N bits, then the inverses require $N+1$ bits of precision. Therefore, the product on line 6 is an $N \times (N+1)$-bit multiplication. On the other hand, assuming the radices of $\mathcal{B}$ fit on a single w-bit machine word, then the remainder r can be computed using only w-bit arithmetic on line 7.

Finally, in order to avoid secret-dependent memory accesses, the value of the current radix b_i and of its precomputed inverse $(b_i)^{-1}$ are loaded into variables b and b_{inv}, respectively, by the **for** loop on lines 3 to 5: this loop goes through all the radices b_j of $\mathcal{B}$, and conditionally moves the one for which $j = \sigma(i)$ into b (and similarly for b_{inv}), where σ is a selection function from $\{1, \ldots, n\}$ to $\{1, \ldots, m\}$. These conditional moves are performed by the **cmove** instruction: **cmove**(X, Y, c) always loads the value of Y from memory (ensuring a secret-independent memory access pattern), but only sets X to this value if the bit c is 1. Quite similarly to **cswap**, **cmove** also avoids any kind of conditional branch so as to resist branch-prediction attacks as well.

Algorithm 5. Secure mixed-radix decomposition.

Input: An MRS bases $\mathcal{B} = (b_1, \ldots, b_n)$, a scalar $k \in \{X_{\mathcal{B}}^{\min}, \ldots, X_{\mathcal{B}}^{\max} - 1\}$.
Output: $(k_1, \ldots, k_n)_{\mathcal{B}}$, the MRS representation of k in base $\mathcal{B}$.
  1: $t \leftarrow k$
  2: **for** $i \leftarrow 1$ **to** n **do**
  3:     **for** $j \leftarrow 1$ **to** m **do**
  4:         **cmove**$(b, \quad b_j, \quad j = \sigma(i))$ ▷ *Load b_j into b if and only if $j = \sigma(i)$.*
  5:         **cmove**$(b_{\mathrm{inv}}, b_j^{-1}, j = \sigma(i))$ ▷ *Load the corresponding precomputed inverse.*
  6:     $q \leftarrow \lfloor t \cdot b_{\mathrm{inv}} \rfloor$ ▷ *Division by b using the precomputed inverse.*
  7:     $r \leftarrow (t - q \cdot b) \bmod 2^w$ ▷ *The remainder is computed on a single machine word.*
  8:     $k_i \leftarrow r; \ t \leftarrow q$
  9: **return** $(k_1, \ldots, k_n)$

Note that precomputing and storing in memory the inverse of each radix of $\mathcal{B}$ with $N+1$ bits of precision might prove too expensive on some embedded systems. An alternative here is to precompute the least-common multiplier of the radices of $\mathcal{B}$, $m = \mathrm{lcm}(b_1, \ldots, b_n)$, along with its inverse $m_{\mathrm{inv}} = m^{-1}$ (with $N+1$ bits of precision as well), and to always compute the quotient of t divided by m, as $\lfloor t \cdot m_{\mathrm{inv}} \rfloor$, instead of $\lfloor t \cdot b_{\mathrm{inv}} \rfloor$. Then, as long as the LCM m itself fits on a single machine word, the actual quotient and remainder of t divided by b can be retrieved using simple word-level arithmetic, requiring only word-precision precomputed inverses of the b_i's.

5.6   Randomized Yet Constant-Time Scalar Multiplication

The regular double-scalar multiplication algorithm presented in Sect. 5.3 already embeds some necessary properties for thwarting side-channel attacks. Indeed, its regular structure along with its absence of secret-dependent branching and memory access patterns should prevent the scalar multiplication from revealing information about the secret digits k_i and MRS radices b_i. However, the running time of Algorithm 3 remains proportional to the bit-length of the input scalars. Therefore, without further precaution in choosing the random base $\mathcal{B}$, an execution trace of Algorithm 4 will reveal the bit-length of the successive radices b_i used in the decomposition. This would then give an attacker a serious advantage for recovering the random base $\mathcal{B}$.

In order to prevent such kind of timing attack, we impose that all the radices of $\mathcal{B}$ have the same bit-length s. For all $1 \leq i \leq n$ we thus have $2^{s-1} \leq b_i < 2^s$. Therefore, each double-scalar multiplication computed in line 8 do generate strictly identical patterns in terms of issued instructions, branches, and memory accesses, thus reducing the number of side channels available to an attacker.

As an example of adequate family of bases $\mathcal{F}$, we define $\mathcal{F}_{s,n,m}$ as the set of all n-tuples exclusively composed of s-bit radices taken from a predefined set of size m, so that $|\mathcal{F}_{s,n,m}| = m^n$. Hence, choosing a base $\mathcal{B}$ uniformly at random in $\mathcal{F} = \mathcal{F}_{s,n,m}$ as in line 1 of Algorithm 4 provides $\rho = \lfloor \log_2(m^n) \rfloor$ bits of randomization. Observe that among all possible sets of size m, those composed of the m largest s-bit integers provide shorter MRS representations. We thus define:

$$\mathcal{F}_{s,n,m} = \{(b_1, \ldots, b_n) \ : \ 2^s - m \leq b_i \leq 2^s - 1 \text{ for } 1 \leq i \leq n\}.$$

Note that the elements of any given base $\mathcal{B} \in \mathcal{F}_{s,n,m}$ need not be distinct.

Yet, choosing s-bit radices is not sufficient to guarantee constant-time. We shall further ensure that the MRS representation of k fits on exactly $n + 1$ digits, no matter its actual value and the chosen base $\mathcal{B}$. As a consequence, the whole loop of Algorithm 4 (line 8) will repeat exactly n times. We achieve this property by adding to k a suitable multiple of the group order ℓ. More precisely, we compute $\hat{k} = k + \alpha\ell$ for a well-suited value α that guarantees that any such $X_{\mathcal{F}_{s,n,m}}^{\min} \leq \hat{k} < X_{\mathcal{F}_{s,n,m}}^{\max}$ can be written in any base $\mathcal{B} \in \mathcal{F}_{s,n,m}$ using exactly $n + 1$ digits (i.e. with $x_{n+1} > 0$).

If a base $\mathcal{B}$ is poorly chosen, it is possible that for some values of k, such an α does not exist, meaning that the base $\mathcal{B}$ cannot accommodate all possible values of the scalar. Fortunately, it is not difficult (although rather technical) to check whether a base $\mathcal{B}$ is legitimate and to adjust it accordingly if it is not the case.

At this point, we intentionally skip most of the details regarding the parameter selection, as well as the level of randomization that can be achieved and the efficiency of the algorithm for reasons that will become clear in the next section.

6   Discussions

Let us summarize what we have so far. We designed a randomized algorithm which runs in constant-time, contains no secret-dependent branching and memory access, and produces a very regular pattern of elementary operations (additions and doublings). The size and number of radices in the MRS bases can be easily determined so as to guarantee a prescribed level of randomization. It therefore presents many of the required characteristics of a robust randomized algorithm. In particular, our attack on the CSC-based approach presented at the beginning of the paper is totally ineffective.

Could it then be considered as a secure alternative to the traditional randomization strategies in a more advanced threat model? Unfortunately, the answer is probably no for reasons that we explain below.

Recall the MRS representation of the secret scalar k:

$$k = k_1 + k_2 b_1 + k_3 b_1 b_2 + \cdots + k_{n+1} \prod_{j=1}^{n} b_j = \sum_{i=1}^{n+1} k_i \Pi_{\mathcal{B}}^{(i-1)}.$$

Observe that the least significant digit k_1 depends solely on b_1 as $k_1 = k \bmod b_1$. Because b_1 is taken at random in a fixed set of size m, this represents $\log_2(m)$ bits of randomization. On the other hand, k_1 contains between $s - 1$ and s bits of information (since $b_1 \geq 2^{s-1}$). Hence, if $m < 2^{s-1}$ the least significant digit is only partially masked and we could possibly recover $s - 1 - \log_2(m)$ bits of information. Depending on the parameter choice, this may be easily taken into account, but the situation is more problematic in the advanced hardware model, where the attacker has access to the device.

Let us assume that the attacker knows the public key, i.e. the point $R = [k]P$. She can then precompute the points $R_{b,i} = [b^{-1} \bmod \ell](R - [i]P)$ for all b in $[2^s - m, 2^s - 1]$ and for all $i = 0, \ldots, b - 1$. For all b and i, the following invariant holds: $[b]R_{b,i} + [i]P = R$.

The attacker can now reprogram the hardware so that it evaluates $[b]R_{b,i} + [i]P$ for all b and i. And she stores the $m \times 2^s$ corresponding execution traces. Although the sequences of operations are identical, the bit-flips will differ depending on b and i. And it is not inconceivable at all that recent advances in deep-learning techniques for side-channel attacks could be used to differentiate these traces.

With this precomputed data at hand, the attacker may now ask the device to compute $[k]P$ many times. The last iteration of the algorithm will always go through one of the temporary points $R_{b,i}$ with $i = k \bmod b$ and will eventually evaluate $[b]R_{b,i} + [i]P$ in order to get the correct result $R = [k]P$. If the attacker runs the algorithm sufficiently many times, she should be able to distinguish m different traces which correspond to each possible b-value. By pairing these with her set of precomputed traces, she could then recover $k \bmod b$ for all $b \in [2^s - m, 2^s - 1]$. And thus, thanks to the CRT, the value $k \bmod \mathrm{lcm}(2^s - m, \ldots, 2^s - 1)$. As an example, for $s = 8$ bits, $m = 16$, this attack would require the precomputations of less than 16×2^8 traces[2]. The value of $\mathrm{lcm}(240, 241, \ldots, 255)$ is a 93-bit integer. The attacker would then recover 93 bits of information of k. She may even be able to recover the whole secret with Coppersmith-like techniques and brute force.

---

[2] $240 + 241 + \cdots + 255 = 3960$ exactly.

7   Conclusion

We presented a very powerful attack on a recently proposed randomized algorithm based on covering systems of congruences. This algorithm uses a representation of the secret scalar which resembles and shares many similarities with the mixed-radix number system. In an attempt to design a more robust algorithm that would thwart our attack, we were able to build a randomized algorithm that runs in constant-time and is free of secret-dependent branching and memory-access. However, the intrinsic nature of the mixed-radix number system, namely its positional property, combined with randomization, may allow a virtual powerful attacker to recover much more information than what was first expected. Therefore, we do not recommend the use of mixed-radix representations for randomization.

Acknowledgments. The authors would like to thank the anonymous referees for their careful reading and constructive comments, as well as Victor Lomne and Thomas Roche (https://ninjalab.io/team) for their support and invaluable suggestions.

References

1. Bernstein, D.J.: Differential addition chains (2006). https://cr.yp.to/ecdh/diffchain-20060219.pdf
2. Bernstein, D.J., Lange, T.: Topics in computational number theory inspired by Peter L. Montgomery, Chap. Montgomery Curves and the Montgomery Ladder, pp. 82–115. Cambridge University Press (2017). https://eprint.iacr.org/2017/293
3. Ciet, M., Joye, M.: (Virtually) free randomization techniques for elliptic curve cryptography. In: Qing, S., Gollmann, D., Zhou, J. (eds.) ICICS 2003. LNCS, vol. 2836, pp. 348–359. Springer, Heidelberg (2003). https://doi.org/10.1007/978-3-540-39927-8_32
4. Ebeid, N., Hasan, M.A.: On binary signed digit representations of integers. Des. Codes Crypt. **42**(1), 43–65 (2007)
5. Fouque, P.-A., Muller, F., Poupard, G., Valette, F.: Defeating countermeasures based on randomized BSD representations. In: Joye, M., Quisquater, J.-J. (eds.) CHES 2004. LNCS, vol. 3156, pp. 312–327. Springer, Heidelberg (2004). https://doi.org/10.1007/978-3-540-28632-5_23
6. Granlund, T., Montgomery, P.L.: Division by invariant integers using multiplication. In: Proceedings of the ACM SIGPLAN 1994 Conference on Programming Language Design and Implementation (PLDI 1994). ACM SIGPLAN Notices, vol. 29, pp. 61–72. ACM (1994)
7. Guerrini, E., Imbert, L., Winterhalter, T.: Randomized mixed-radix scalar multiplication. IEEE Trans. Comput. **67**(3), 418–431 (2017). https://doi.org/10.1109/TC.2017.2750677
8. Cheol Ha, J., Jae Moon, S.: Randomized signed-scalar multiplication of ECC to resist power attacks. In: Kaliski, B.S., Koç, K., Paar, C. (eds.) CHES 2002. LNCS, vol. 2523, pp. 551–563. Springer, Heidelberg (2003). https://doi.org/10.1007/3-540-36400-5_40
9. Karlof, C., Wagner, D.: Hidden Markov model cryptanalysis. In: Walter, C.D., Koç, Ç.K., Paar, C. (eds.) CHES 2003. LNCS, vol. 2779, pp. 17–34. Springer, Heidelberg (2003). https://doi.org/10.1007/978-3-540-45238-6_3

10. Méloni, N., Hasan, M.A.: Random digit representation of integers. In: Proceedings of the 23rd IEEE Symposium on Computer Arithmetic, ARITH23, pp. 118–125. IEEE Computer Society (2016)
11. Oswald, E., Aigner, M.: Randomized addition-subtraction chains as a countermeasure against power attacks. In: Koç, Ç.K., Naccache, D., Paar, C. (eds.) CHES 2001. LNCS, vol. 2162, pp. 39–50. Springer, Heidelberg (2001). https://doi.org/10.1007/3-540-44709-1_5
12. Strauss, E.G.: Addition chains of vectors (problem 5125). Am. Math. Mon. **70**, 806–808 (1964)

Cold Boot Attacks on Bliss

Ricardo Villanueva-Polanco[(✉)]

Universidad del Norte, Barranquilla, Colombia
rpolanco@uninorte.edu.co

Abstract. In this paper, we examine the feasibility of cold boot attacks against the BLISS signature scheme. We believe this to be the first time that this has been attempted. Our work is the continuation of the trend to develop cold boot attacks for different schemes as revealed by the literature. But it is also the continuation of the evaluation of post-quantum cryptographic schemes against this class of attack. Particularly, we review the BLISS implementation provided by the strongSwan project. This implementation particularly stores its private key in memory in an interesting way therefore requiring novel approaches to key recovery. We present various approaches to key recovery. We first analyse the key recovery problem in this particular case via key enumeration algorithms, and so propose different techniques for key recovery. We then turn our attention to exploit further the algebraic relation among the components of the private key, and we thus establish a connection between the key recovery problem in this particular case and an instance of Learning with Errors Problem (LWE). We then explore various key recovery techniques to tackle this instance of LWE. In particular, we show a key recovery strategy combining lattice techniques and key enumeration. Finally, we report results from experimenting with one of the key recovery algorithms for a range of parameters, showing it is able to tolerate a noise level of $\alpha = 0.001$ and $\beta = 0.09$ for a parameter set when performing a 2^{40} enumeration.

Keywords: Cold boot attacks · Enumeration algorithms ·
Noisy image · Key recovery · Learning with Errors Problem

1 Introduction

A cold boot attack is a type of data remanence attack by which sensitive data are read from a computer's main memory after supposedly having been deleted. This attack relies on the data remanence property of DRAM to retrieve memory contents that remain readable in the seconds to minutes after power has been removed. In this setting, an attacker with physical access to a computer can retrieve content from a running operating system after using a cold reboot

---

This work was supported by COLCIENCIAS and is part of my doctoral studies conducted under the supervision of Professor Kenneth G. Paterson, at Royal Holloway, University of London.

© Springer Nature Switzerland AG 2019
P. Schwabe and N. Thériault (Eds.): LATINCRYPT 2019, LNCS 11774, pp. 40–61, 2019.
https://doi.org/10.1007/978-3-030-30530-7_3

to restart the machine [10]. Unfortunately for such an adversary, the bits in memory will experience a process of degradation once the computer's power is interrupted. This implies that if the adversary can retrieve any data from the computer's main memory after the power is cut off, the extracted data will probably have bit fluctuations, i.e., the data will be noisy.

Because only a noisy version of the original key may be retrievable from main memory once the attacker discovers the location of the data in it, the adversary's main task then becomes the mathematical problem of recovering the original key from a noisy version of that key. Additionally, the adversary may have access to reference cryptographic data created using that key or have a public key available (in the asymmetric setting). So the focus of cold boot attacks after the initial work pointing out their feasibility [10] has been to develop algorithms for efficiently recovering keys from noisy versions of those keys for a range of different cryptographic schemes, whilst exploring the limits of how much noise can be tolerated. Heninger and Shacham [12] focussed on the case of RSA keys, giving an efficient algorithm based on Hensel lifting to exploit redundancy in the typical RSA private key format. This work was followed up by Henecka, May and Meurer [11] and Paterson, Polychroniadou and Sibborn [18], with both papers also focusing on the mathematically highly structured RSA setting. The latter paper in particular pointed out the asymmetric nature of the error channel intrinsic to the cold boot setting and recast the problem of key recovery for cold boot attacks in an information theoretic manner.

On the other hand, Lee et al. [15] discussed these attacks in the discrete logarithm setting, however their proposed algorithm did not take into account a bit-flipping model. Poettering and Sibborn [21] improved on the previous work by exploiting redundancies found in the in-memory private key representations from two ECC implementations found in TLS libraries. They developed cold boot key-recovery algorithms applicable to the bit-flipping model. Additional papers have considered cold boot attacks in the symmetric key setting, including Albrecht and Cid [1] who focused on the recovery of symmetric encryption keys in the cold boot setting by employing polynomial system solvers, and Kamal and Youssef [14] who applied SAT solvers to the same problem. Finally, recent research papers have explored cold boot attacks on post-quantum cryptographic schemes. [2] focused on schemes based on the ring -and module - variants of the Learning with Errors (LWE) problem, while the paper by Paterson et. al. [19] focused on cold boot attacks on NTRU.

This paper studies the feasibility of cold boot attacks against the BLISS signature scheme [8]. Our work is the continuation of the trend to develop cold boot attacks for different schemes as revealed by the literature. But it is also the continuation of the evaluation of post-quantum cryptographic schemes against this class of attack. Such an evaluation should form an important part of the overall assessment of these schemes.

When developing key recovery attacks in the cold boot setting, it is important to know the exact format used to store the private key in memory. The reason for this is that this attack depends on the physical effects in memory, which causes bit flips in the binary representation of the private key. Also, the main input to this attack is a bit-flipped version of the private key. Therefore, it is necessary to either propose natural formats in which a private key would be stored in memory or review specific implementations of this scheme. We adopt the latter, and so we study the BLISS implementation provided by the strongSwan project[1], which stores its private key in memory in an interesting way therefore requiring novel approaches to key recovery.

This paper is organised as follows. In Sect. 2, we first describe the notation, some definitions and the cold boot attack model that we will use in this paper. In Sect. 3, we then study the format the strongSwan implementation uses to store BLISS private keys. In Sect. 4, we then analyse the key recovery problem in this particular case via key enumeration, and so propose different techniques for key recovery. We then exploit further the algebraic relation among the components of the private key and establish a connection between the key recovery problem in this particular case and an instance of Learning with Errors Problem (LWE). Also, we then explore various key recovery techniques to tackle this instance of LWE. In particular, we show a key recovery strategy combining lattice techniques and key enumeration. In Sect. 5, we report results from experimenting with one of the introduced key recovery algorithms for a range of parameters, and finally we draw some conclusions in Sect. 6.

2   Preliminaries

2.1   Notation

In this paper, we write vectors and polynomials in bold lowercase letters, e.g. $\mathbf{a}$, and matrices in bold uppercase letters, e.g. $\mathbf{A}$. We frequently identify polynomials $\mathbf{a} = \sum_{i=0}^{n-1} a_i x^i$ with their coefficient vector $\mathbf{a} = (a_0, \ldots, a_{n-1})$ or $\mathbf{a}^t$. For any integer q, we identify the ring $\mathbb{Z}_q$ with the interval $[-q/2, q/2) \cap \mathbb{Z}$, and in general for a ring R, we define R_q to be the quotient ring $R/(qR)$. Whenever working in the quotient ring $R_q = \mathbb{Z}_q[x]/(x^n + 1)$ and $R_{2q} = \mathbb{Z}_{2q}[x]/(x^n + 1)$, we will assume that n is a power of 2 and q a prime number such that $q = 1 \mod 2n$. We define the rotation matrix of a polynomial $\mathbf{a} \in R_q$ as $rot(\mathbf{a}) = (\mathbf{a}, \mathbf{a} \cdot \mathbf{x}, \mathbf{a} \cdot \mathbf{x}^2, \ldots, \mathbf{a} \cdot \mathbf{x}^{n-1}) \in \mathbb{Z}_q^{n \times n}$. Then for $\mathbf{a}, \mathbf{b} \in R_q$, the matrix-vector product $rot(\mathbf{a}) \cdot \mathbf{b} \mod q$ corresponds to the product of polynomials $\mathbf{a} \cdot \mathbf{b} \in R_q$. Also, we write $\|\cdot\|$ for the Euclidean norm.

We use the following definition of lattices. Let m be a positive integer and $\mathbf{B} = \{\mathbf{b}_1, \ldots, \mathbf{b}_n\} \subset \mathbb{R}^m$ be a set of linearly independent vectors. The lattice L generated by $\mathbf{B}$, which we also denote as $\mathrm{L}(\mathbf{B})$, is the set of linear combinations of $\mathbf{b}_1, \ldots, \mathbf{b}_n$ with coefficients in $\mathbb{Z}$. Let q be a positive integer. A lattice L that contains $q\mathbb{Z}^m$ is called a q-ary lattice. For a matrix, $\mathbf{A} \in \mathbb{Z}^{m \times n}$, we define the q-ary lattice as $\mathrm{L}_q(\mathbf{A}) = \{\mathbf{v} \in \mathbb{Z}^m | \exists \mathbf{w} \in \mathbb{Z}^n : \mathbf{A} \cdot \mathbf{w} = \mathbf{v} \mod q\}$.

Let $\mathrm{L}(\mathbf{B})$ be a lattice and $\mathbf{x}$ be a point. Let $\mathbf{y} \in \mathrm{L}(\mathbf{B})$ be the lattice point for which the length $\|\mathbf{x} - \mathbf{y}\|$ is minimised. We define the distance to the lattice $\mathrm{L}(\mathbf{B})$ from the point $\mathbf{x}$ to be this length, which we denote $dist(\mathbf{x}, \mathrm{L}(\mathbf{B}))$. The length of the shortest non-zero vectors of a lattice $\mathrm{L}(\mathbf{B})$ is denoted by $\lambda_1(\mathrm{L}(\mathbf{B}))$.

---

[1] See https://www.strongswan.org/ for details of this project.

Lattice-based cryptography is based on the presumed hardness of computational problems in lattices. Two of the most important lattice problems are defined next.

Shortest Vector Problem (SVP). The task is to find a shortest non-zero vector in a lattice $L(\mathbf{B})$, i.e. find a non-zero vector $\mathbf{x} \in L(\mathbf{B})$ that minimises the Euclidean norm $\|\mathbf{x}\|$.

Bounded Distance Decoding (BDD). Given $\gamma \in \mathbb{R} \geq 0$, a lattice basis $\mathbf{B}$, and a target vector $\mathbf{t} \in \mathbb{R}^m$ with $dist(\mathbf{t}, L(\mathbf{B})) < \gamma \cdot \lambda_1(L(\mathbf{B}))$, the goal is to find a vector $\mathbf{e} \in \mathbb{R}^m$ with $\|\mathbf{e}\| < \gamma \cdot \lambda_1(L(\mathbf{B}))$ such that $\mathbf{t} - \mathbf{e} \in L(\mathbf{B})$.

Babai's Nearest Plane Algorithm. This algorithm was introduced in [3] and it has been utilised as an oracle to carry out various attacks [5,13]. The input for Babai's Nearest Plane algorithm is a lattice basis $\mathbf{B} \in \mathbb{Z}^{m \times m}$ and a target vector $\mathbf{t} \in \mathbb{R}^m$ and the corresponding output is a vector $\mathbf{e} \in R^m$ such that $\mathbf{t} - \mathbf{e} \in L(\mathbf{B})$. We denote the output by $\mathbf{NP_B}(\mathbf{t}) = \mathbf{e}$. If the lattice basis $\mathbf{B}$ consists of vectors that are pairwise orthogonal, then it is very easy to solve both SVP and BDD. In general, if the vectors in the basis are reasonably orthogonal to one another, then Babai's Nearest Plane Algorithm may solve BDD, but if the basis vectors are highly nonorthogonal, then the vector returned by the algorithm is generally far from the closest lattice vector to $\mathbf{t}$. In such a case, before applying the algorithm, we can reduce the lattice basis $\mathbf{B}$ to get a "better" basis by using some basis reduction algorithm.

2.2   Cold Boot Attack Model

Our cold boot attack model assumes that the adversary can obtain a noisy version of a secret key (using whatever format is used to store it in memory). We assume that the corresponding public parameters are known exactly (without noise). We do not consider here the important problem of how to locate the appropriate area of memory in which the secret key bits are stored, though this would be an important consideration in practical attacks. Our aim is then recover the secret key. Note that it is sufficient to recover a list of key candidates in which the true secret key is located, since we can always test a candidate by executing known algorithms linked to the scheme we are attacking.

We assume throughout that a 0 bit of the original secret key will flip to a 1 with probability $\alpha = P(0 \rightarrow 1)$ and that a 1 bit of the original private key will flip with probability $\beta = P(1 \rightarrow 0)$. We do not assume that $\alpha = \beta$; indeed, in practice, one of these values may be very small (e.g. 0.001) and relatively stable over time, while the other increases over time. Furthermore, we assume that the attacker knows the values of α and β and that they are fixed across the region of memory in which the private key is located. These assumptions are reasonable in practice: one can estimate the error probabilities by looking at a region where the memory stores known values (e.g. where the public key is located), and the regions are typically large.

3 BLISS Signature Scheme

In this section we briefly describe the BLISS key generation algorithm [8].

3.1 The BLISS Key Generation Algorithm

Given two real numbers $0 \leq \lambda_1 < 1$ and $0 \leq \lambda_2 < 1$, two random polynomials $\mathbf{f}$ and $\mathbf{g}$ are generated such that both polynomials have $d_1 = \lceil \lambda_1 n \rceil$ coefficients in $\{\pm 1\}$ and $d_2 = \lceil \lambda_2 n \rceil$ coefficients in $\{\pm 2\}$, assuring that $\mathbf{f}$ is invertible. The secret key is given by $\mathbf{S} = (\mathbf{s}_1, \mathbf{s}_2)^t = (\mathbf{f}, 2\mathbf{g} + 1)^t$. The public key is computed by setting $\mathbf{a}_q = (2\mathbf{g} + 1)/\mathbf{f} \in R_q$. If we set $\mathbf{A} = (2 \cdot \mathbf{a}_q, q - 2) \in R_{2q}^{1 \times 2}$, then one easily verifies that:

$$\mathbf{AS} = 2\mathbf{a}_q \cdot \mathbf{f} - 2(2\mathbf{g} + 1) = 0 \mod q.$$
$$\mathbf{AS} = q(2\mathbf{g} + 1) = q \cdot 1 = 1 \mod 2. \tag{1}$$

That is $\mathbf{AS} = q \mod 2q$. Finally, $(\mathbf{A}, \mathbf{S})$ is a valid key pair for the scheme.

3.2 The strongSwan Project

The strongSwan project is a multi-platform, open-source IPSec implementation. Starting with the strongSwan 5.2.2 release, BLISS is offered as an IKEv2 public key authentication method. Full BLISS key and certificate generation support is also added to the strongSwan PKI tool. With strongSwan 5.3.0, there was an upgrade to the improved BLISS-B signature algorithm described in [7].

Recent research papers [9,20] have explored other side channel attacks on this particular implementation. For example, [20] shows that cache attacks on this signature scheme are not only possible, but also practical. Its authors claim their attack recovers the secret signing key after observing roughly 6000 signature generations. However, there is no research paper, to the best of our knowledge, exploring cold boot attacks on this implementation.

3.2.1 Private Key Format

This implementation defines a C struct in the file bliss_private_key.c containing the variables used to store the polynomials $\mathbf{f}$ and $2\mathbf{g}+1$, after the subroutine bliss_private_key_gen defined in the file bliss_private_key.c has been executed. When this particular subroutine is executing, it invokes internally the subroutine create_vector_from_seed to create both $\mathbf{f}$ and $\mathbf{g}$. Each of these polynomials has d_1 coefficients with values in the set $\{-1, 1\}$, d_2 coefficients with values belonging the set $\{-2, 2\}$ and its remaining coefficients have values equal to zero. Additionally, $\mathbf{f}$ is chosen to be invertible in R_q. The algorithm also computes both the polynomial $2\mathbf{g}+1$ and the public polynomial $\mathbf{a}_q = (2\mathbf{g}+1)/\mathbf{f}$. The variable $\mathbf{s}_1$ will point to an array whose entries are the coefficient of the polynomial $\mathbf{f}$, while the variable $\mathbf{s}_2$ will point to an array whose entries are the coefficients of polynomial $2\mathbf{g} + 1$. Each entry of either of the two arrays is an 8-bit integer.

This implementation includes 4 named reference parameter sets with a range of choices for n, q, d_1 and d_2, targeting different security levels and optimisations. These parameter sets are defined in the file `bliss_param_set.c` and were proposed by the BLISS designers in [8]. For example, the parameter set `BLISS-I` targets 128 bits of security and defines $n = 512, q = 12289, d_1 = 154, d_2 = 0$, whilst the parameter set `BLISS-IV` targets 192 bits of security and defines $n = 512, q = 12289, d_1 = 231, d_2 = 31$.

4 Mounting Cold Boot Key Recovery Attacks

In this section, we will present several cold boot key recovery attacks on the `strongSwan` BLISS implementation and its corresponding private key format that was introduced in the previous section.

4.1 Initial Observations

We continue to make the assumptions outlined in Sect. 2.2. Our cold boot attack model assumes that the adversary can obtain a noisy version of the original BLISS private key (using whatever format is used to store it in memory). We assume that the corresponding BLISS public key is known exactly (without noise). We additionally assume that all relevant public parameters and private key formatting information are known to the adversary. Our aim is then recover the private key. In particular, we assume the attacker obtains $\mathbf{s}_1'$ and $\mathbf{s}_2'$, which are the noisy versions of the arrays storing $\mathbf{f}$ and $2\mathbf{g}+1$ respectively. Both the array $\mathbf{s}_1'$ and $\mathbf{s}_2'$ have n entries. We also assume the attacker knows that $\mathbf{a}_q \cdot \mathbf{f} = 2\mathbf{g}+1$ and the parameters that were used to create the private polynomials, i.e. the values of d_1 and d_2. This is a plausible assumption because the values d_1 and d_2 can be found in a public file.

According to the key generation algorithm, both the polynomial $\mathbf{f}$ and the polynomial $\mathbf{g}$ have d_1 coefficients with values in the set $\{-1, 1\}$, d_2 coefficients with values in the set $\{-2, 2\}$ and their remaining coefficients have value zero. Therefore, the polynomial $\mathbf{h} = 2\mathbf{g}+1$ has its constant coefficient value h_0 in the set $\{-1, -3, 1, 3, 5\}$ and satisfies:

1. If h_0 is 1, then $\mathbf{h}$ has d_1 coefficients with values in the set $\{-2, 2\}$, d_2 coefficients with values in the set $\{-4, 4\}$ and its remaining coefficients have value zero.
2. If $h_0 \in \{-1, 3\}$, then $\mathbf{h}$ has $d_1 - 1$ coefficients with values in the set $\{-2, 2\}$, d_2 coefficients with values in the set $\{-4, 4\}$ and its remaining coefficients have value zero.
3. If $h_0 \in \{-3, 5\}$, then $\mathbf{h}$ has d_1 coefficients with values in the set $\{-2, 2\}$ and $d_2 - 1$ coefficients with values in the set $\{-4, 4\}$ and its remaining coefficients have value zero.

We will make use of these properties of the polynomials $\mathbf{f}$ and $\mathbf{h}$ to design key recovery algorithms.

4.2 Key Recovery via Key Enumeration

In this section we will develop algorithms for tackling the problem of recovering $\mathbf{f}$ and $\mathbf{h}$ from $\mathbf{s}_1'$ and $\mathbf{s}_2'$, by running instances of key enumeration algorithms, as well as exploiting the underlying properties of the polynomials $\mathbf{f}$ and $\mathbf{h}$. We will first introduce a general key recovery strategy making use of key enumeration algorithms.

4.2.1 General Key Recovery Strategy

Suppose we have a secret key that is W bits in size, and let $\mathbf{r} = (b_0, ..., b_{W-1})$ denote the bits of the noisy key (input to the adversary in the attack). Suppose a key recovery algorithm constructs a candidate for the private key $\mathbf{c} = (c_0, \ldots, c_{W-1})$ by some means. Then, given the bit-flip probabilities α, β, we can assign a likelihood score to $\mathbf{c}$ as follows:

$$L[\mathbf{c}; \mathbf{r}] := Pr(\mathbf{r}|\mathbf{c}) = (1 - \alpha)^{n_{00}} \alpha^{n_{01}} \beta^{n_{10}} (1 - \beta)^{n_{11}}$$

where n_{00} denotes the number of positions where both $\mathbf{c}$ and $\mathbf{r}$ contain a 0 bit, n_{01} denotes the number of positions where $\mathbf{c}$ contains a 0 bit and $\mathbf{r}$ contains a 1 bit, etc. The method of maximum likelihood estimation[2] then suggests picking as $\mathbf{c}$ the value that maximises the above expression. It is more convenient to work with log-likelihoods, and equivalently to maximise these, viz:

$$\mathcal{L}[\mathbf{c}; \mathbf{r}] := \log Pr(\mathbf{r}|\mathbf{c}) = n_{00} \log(1-\alpha) + n_{01} \log \alpha + n_{10} \log \beta + n_{11} \log(1-\beta) \quad (2)$$

We will frequently refer to this log likelihood expression as a score and seek to maximise its value (or, equally well, minimise its negative). Let us suppose further that $\mathbf{r}$ can be represented as a concatenation of W/w chunks, each on w bits. Let us name the chunks $\mathbf{r}^0, \mathbf{r}^1, \ldots, \mathbf{r}^{W/w-1}$ so that $\mathbf{r}^i = b_{i \cdot w} b_{i \cdot w+1} \cdots b_{i \cdot w+(w-1)}$. Additionally, let us suppose that key candidates $\mathbf{c}$ can also be represented by concatenations of chunks $\mathbf{c}^0, \mathbf{c}^1, \ldots, \mathbf{c}^{W/w-1}$ in the same way.

Suppose further that each of the at most 2^w candidate values for chunk $\mathbf{c}^i (0 \le i < W/w)$ can be enumerated and given its own score by some procedure (formally, a sub-algorithm in an overall attack). For example, Eq. (2) for log-likelihood across all W bits can be easily modified to produce a log likelihood expression for any candidate for chunk i as follows:

$$\mathcal{L}[\mathbf{c}^i; \mathbf{r}^i] := \log Pr(\mathbf{r}^i|\mathbf{c}^i) = n_{00}^i \log(1 - \alpha) + n_{01}^i \log \alpha + n_{10}^i \log \beta + n_{11}^i \log(1 - \beta) \quad (3)$$

where the n_{ab}^i values count occurrences of bits across the i-th chunks, $\mathbf{c}^i, \mathbf{r}^i$.

We can therefore assume that we have access to W/w lists of scores, each list containing up to 2^w entries. The W/w scores, one from each of these per-chunk lists, can be added together to create a total score for a complete candidate $\mathbf{c}$. Indeed, this total score is statistically meaningful in the case where the per-chunk scores are log likelihoods because of the additive nature of the scoring

---

[2] See for example https://en.wikipedia.org/wiki/Maximum_likelihood_estimation.

function in that case. The question then becomes: can we devise efficient algorithms that traverse the lists of scores to combine chunk candidates c^i, obtaining complete key candidates c having high total scores (with total scores obtained by summation)? This is a question that has been previously addressed in the side-channel analysis literature [4,6,16,22,23], with a variety of different algorithmic approaches being possible to solve the problem.

Suppose now the attacker represents r as a concatenation of n_b blocks, where each block consists of the concatenation of n_b^j, with $n_b^j > 0$, consecutive chunks, such that $W/w = \sum_{j=0} n_b^j$. Therefore,

$$\bullet \qquad \mathbf{r} = \mathbf{b}^0||\mathbf{b}^1||\mathbf{b}^2||\cdots\mathbf{b}^{nb-1}$$

where

$$\mathbf{b}^j = \mathbf{r}^{i_j}||\mathbf{r}^{i_j+1}||\cdots||\mathbf{r}^{i_j+n_b^j-1}$$

for $0 \le j < n_b$ and some $0 \le i_j < W/w$. The attacker now proceeds with Phase I as follows.

1. For each chunk $\mathbf{r}^i$, with $0 \le i < W/w$, the attacker uses Eq. (3) to compute a log-likelihood score for each candidate c^i for the chunk $\mathbf{r}^i$.
2. For each block $\mathbf{b}^j$, the attacker presents the lists $L_{\mathbf{r}^{i_j}}, L_{\mathbf{r}^{i_j+1}}, \ldots, L_{\mathbf{r}^{i_j+n_b^j-1}}$ as inputs to an instance of an optimal key enumeration algorithm, e.g. [23], to produce a list of the M_j highest scoring candidates for the block $\mathbf{b}^j$, $L_{\mathbf{b}^j}$.

Once Phase I completes, the attacker then proceeds with Phase II as follows.

1. The lists $L_{\mathbf{b}^j}$ are given as inputs to an instance of a key enumeration algorithm, regarding each list $L_{\mathbf{b}^j}$ as a set of candidates for the block $\mathbf{b}^j$. This instance will generate high scoring candidates for the encoding of the key. For each complete candidate c output by the enumeration algorithm, it is given as input to a verification function V to verify whether the candidate is valid or not. This function is case-dependent.

In Phase II, non-optimal key enumeration algorithms would suit better [4,6, 16,22], since they are parallelisable and memory-efficient. Even though their outputs may not be given in the optimal order, the search can be customisable by either selecting a suitable interval in which the outputs' scores lie, e.g. [4,16], or selecting a suitable interval in which the outputs' ranks lie, e.g. [22].

4.2.2 Recovering f and h

The goal of the attacker is to search for key candidates of the form $(\mathbf{f}_i, \mathbf{h}_j)$ for the 2-tuple $(\mathbf{f}, \mathbf{h})$. To do so, the attacker will first need to construct both a list L_f that contains high scoring key candidates for the polynomial f and a list L_h that contains high scoring key candidates for the polynomial h. Next the attacker will take both a key candidate from the first list and a key candidate from the second list and finally verify if such pair may be the real private key. So the first task of the attacker will then be producing both the list L_f and the list L_h. Because both the list L_f and the list L_h must store high scoring key candidates for the polynomials $\mathbf{f}$ and $\mathbf{h}$ respectively, the attacker may make use of the key recovery strategy introduced in Sect. 4.2.1 to create such lists as follows.

4.2.3   Constructing L_f from $\mathbf{s}_1'$

Recall that the attacker has access to $\mathbf{s}_1'$ that is a bit string of size $W = 8n$. The attacker first sets $\mathbf{r} = \mathbf{s}_1'$ and sets a chunk to be an 8-bit string, i.e. $w = 8$, and so there are $n = W/w$ chunks. For a given chunk, its candidates are then the integers in the set $\{-2, -1, 0, 1, 2\}$. The attacker now sets a block to be a successive sequence of $l > 0$ chunks, with $l \mid n$, and so there are $n_b = n/l$ blocks. To construct the list L_f, the attacker then starts off with **Phase I** by computing log-likelihood scores for each candidate c^i for each chunk $\mathbf{r}^i, 0 \le i < n$. So the attacker obtains a list of chunk candidates with 5 entries for each chunk, since the candidates for any chunk are the integers in the set $\{-2, -1, 0, 1, 2\}$. For each block $\mathbf{b}^j, 0 \le j < n_b$, the attacker then presents the l lists corresponding to the l chunks in the block $\mathbf{b}^j$ as inputs to the optimal key enumeration algorithm (OKEA)[23] to produce a list with the M_j highest scoring chunk candidates for the block, $L_{\mathbf{b}^j}$.

At **Phase II** the attacker will have n_b lists of chunk candidates and proceed by presenting them as inputs to a key enumeration algorithm (which we will discuss in Sect. 5.2.3) in order to generate M_f high scoring key candidates $\mathbf{f}_i$ for $\mathbf{f}$, which are then stored in a list L_f. The instance of the key enumeration algorithm only outputs valid candidate polynomials $\mathbf{f}_i$ for $\mathbf{f}$, i.e. those having d_1 coefficients with values in the set $\{1, -1\}$, d_2 coefficients with values in the set $\{2, -2\}$ and the remaining coefficients with value zero. With respect to the verification of $\mathbf{f}_i$, it can be simply done by running through each entry of the array representing $\mathbf{f}_i$, while counting the array's entries with values in the set $\{-1, 1\}$, its entries with values in the set $\{-2, 2\}$ and its entries with value zero. If the three counting variables are equal to d_1, d_2 and $n - d_1 - d_2$ respectively, then $\mathbf{f}_i$ is a valid candidate for $\mathbf{f}$. It is preferable to run this check at this point because during and immediately after Phase I the algorithm can not control or know what entries will have values either in the set $\{-1, 1\}$ or in the set $\{-2, 2\}$ or value zero. Note that constructing L_h from $\mathbf{s}_2'$ can be done with a similar procedure.

4.2.4   Combining L_f and L_h

Once both the list L_f and the list L_h are created, the attacker will run another instance of a key enumeration algorithm receiving both the list L_f and the list L_h as input, which then proceeds to find high scoring candidates for $(\mathbf{f}, 2\mathbf{g} + 1)$ that are obtained by taking an $\mathbf{f}_i$ from L_f and an $\mathbf{h}_j$ from L_h, whilst ensuring that $\mathbf{a}_q \mathbf{f}_i = \mathbf{h}_j$, i.e. that there is a collision of polynomials $\mathbf{a}_q \mathbf{f}_i$ and $\mathbf{h}_j$ in the two lists. If such a collision is found, then $(\mathbf{f}_i, \mathbf{h}_j)$ is a valid candidate pair for $(\mathbf{f}, 2\mathbf{g} + 1)$; otherwise it is not.

Regarding the overall performance of the previous key recovery strategy, we note that the processes for creating the lists L_f and L_h can be run simultaneously because the dependence of the two on each other is loose. In the combining phase, it is more convenient to run a non-optimal enumeration algorithm [4,6,16,22], because the search can be parallelised and hence performed more efficiently. With regard to how successful this combining strategy might be, we note that the strategy will find a valid pair $(\mathbf{f}_i, \mathbf{h}_j)$ if and only if there is an $\mathbf{f}_i \in L_f$ and an $\mathbf{h}_i \in L_h$ with the property that $\mathbf{a}_q \cdot \mathbf{f}_i = \mathbf{h}_j$. Hence its success probability will improve by increasing the sizes of L_f and L_h. This can be problematic in terms of memory and performance when M_f and M_h grows bigger, leading us to make refinements to it as follows.

The attacker first generates M_h valid and high scoring key candidates $\mathbf{h}_i$ for $2\mathbf{g} + 1$ from $\mathbf{s}'_2$ as described previously and stores them in a hash table T_1. Specifically, for each generated $\mathbf{h}_i$, the attacker computes a hash value k_{h_i} (used as a key) from all the entries of the array representation $\mathbf{h}_i$ of $\mathbf{h}_i$, then calculates an index t_{h_i} from k_{h_i} by using a map $\mathbb{I}$ and finally adds $\mathbf{h}_i$ as the first entry of a linked list pointed to by the entry $T_1[t_{h_i}]$.

Once this is done, the attacker will generate valid and high scoring key candidates $\mathbf{f}_i$ for $\mathbf{f}$. For each $\mathbf{f}_i$, the algorithm calculates a hash value k_{af_i} (used as a key) from all the entries of the array representation $\mathbf{af}_i$ of $\mathbf{a}_q \cdot \mathbf{f}_i$, then computes the index $t_{af_i} = \mathbb{I}(k_{af_i})$ and finally checks if $\mathbf{af}_i$ can be found in the linked list pointed to by the entry $T_1[t_{af_i}]$ (if exists). If a match is found, then $\mathbf{a}_q \cdot \mathbf{f}_i = \mathbf{h}_j$, producing a valid candidate pair for $(\mathbf{f}, 2\mathbf{g} + 1)$.

Note that by using just a hash table, this variant scales better in terms of memory than the previous key recovery strategy. As far as performance is concerned, there is also less restriction on generating high scoring candidates for $2\mathbf{g} + 1$, because the order in which they are generated during an enumeration is irrelevant; what is important is that they are included in the global hash table. Note that the generation of candidates for both $2\mathbf{g} + 1$ and $\mathbf{f}$ can be done by running instances of a non-optimal enumeration algorithm, since they can be customised to perform a more efficient search.

4.2.5   Enumerating only Candidates for f

By exploiting further the relation $\mathbf{a}_q \cdot \mathbf{f} = 2\mathbf{g} + 1$ and the properties of $2\mathbf{g} + 1$ as a filter, the attacker can just enumerate candidates for $\mathbf{f}$ and not store any tables in memory. We explain how this can be done next.

By following a similar procedure as described in Sect. 4.2.3, the attacker can generate key candidates $\mathbf{f}_i$ for $\mathbf{f}$ from $\mathbf{s}'_1$. For each output $\mathbf{f}_i$, the attacker computes the polynomial $\mathbf{h}_i = \mathbf{a}_q \cdot \mathbf{f}_i$ and verifies if $\mathbf{h}_i$ satisfies the properties described in Sect. 4.1.

If the algorithm finds a pair $(\mathbf{f}_i, \mathbf{h}_i)$, then it is a candidate pair for $(\mathbf{f}, 2\mathbf{g}+1)$. In fact, it is very likely to be the correct private key. To see why, let $\mathcal{P}$ be the set of all polynomials having d_1 coefficients values in $\{-1, 1\}$, d_2 coefficient values in $\{-2, 2\}$ and the remaining coefficients values zero. We ask for the probability that some random $\mathbf{f} \in \mathcal{P}$ has the property that $\mathbf{h} = \mathbf{f} \cdot \mathbf{a}_q - 1 \in R_q$ is a polynomial having d_1 coefficients with values in the set $\{-2, 2\}$, d_2 coefficients with values in the set $\{-4, 4\}$ and its remaining coefficients have value zero. Treating the coefficients of $\mathbf{h}$ as independent random variables that are uniformly distributed modulo q, the probability that any particular coefficient is in the set either $\{-2, 2\}$ or $\{-4, 4\}$ is $2/q$, and that any particular coefficient is zero is $1/q$, then the probability we are asking for is about $\frac{n!}{d_1!d_2!(n-d_1-d_2)!}(2/q)^{d_1+d_2}(1/q)^{n-d_1-d_2}$, which is negligible for common parameters.

Regarding the verification of $\mathbf{h}_i$, it can be simply done by computing $\mathbf{h}'_i = \mathbf{h}_i - 1$ and then running through each entry of the array representing $\mathbf{h}'_i$ while counting its entries with values in the set $\{-2, 2\}$, its entries with values in the set $\{-4, 4\}$ and its entries with values zero. If the three counting variables are equal to d_1, d_2 and $n-d_1-d_2$ respectively, then $\mathbf{h}_i$ is a valid candidate for $2 \cdot \mathbf{g} + 1$. We will experimentally evaluate this key recovery algorithm in Sect. 5.2.

4.3   Casting the Problem as an LWE Instance

In this section, we establish a connection between the key recovery problem in this particular case with a non-conventional instance of Learning with Errors Problem (LWE). Let us consider the polynomials $\mathbf{s}'_1, \mathbf{s}'_2 \in R_q$ obtained from the noisy arrays $\mathbf{s}'_1$ and $\mathbf{s}'_2$ respectively. We can re-write $\mathbf{s}'_1$ as $\mathbf{s}'_1 = \mathbf{f} + \mathbf{e}_1$ and $\mathbf{s}'_2$ as $\mathbf{s}'_2 = 2\mathbf{g} + 1 + \mathbf{e}_2$, where $\mathbf{e}_1$, $\mathbf{e}_2$ are error polynomials. Hence, we have $\mathbf{a}_q \cdot \mathbf{s}'_1 = \mathbf{a}_q \cdot (\mathbf{f} + \mathbf{e}_1) = \mathbf{a}_q \cdot \mathbf{f} + \mathbf{a}_q \cdot \mathbf{e}_1 = 2\mathbf{g} + 1 + \mathbf{a}_q \cdot \mathbf{e}_1 = \mathbf{s}'_2 - \mathbf{e}_2 + \mathbf{a}_q \cdot \mathbf{e}_1$. Therefore $\mathbf{a}_q \cdot \mathbf{s}'_1 - \mathbf{s}'_2 = \mathbf{a}_q \cdot \mathbf{e}_1 - \mathbf{e}_2$. It is clear that the left-hand side of previous equation can be computed by the attacker, but the attacker does not learn any additional information on the nature of the values the coefficients of $\mathbf{e}_1$ and $\mathbf{e}_2$ may have.

Now if the attacker computes a high scoring candidate $\mathbf{c}_1$ from $\mathbf{s}'_1$ for $\mathbf{f}$ and a high candidate $\mathbf{c}_2$ from $\mathbf{s}'_2$ for $2\mathbf{g} + 1$ by using the algorithm described in Sect. 4.2.3, then there will be also polynomials $\mathbf{e}'_1$ and $\mathbf{e}'_2$ such that $\mathbf{c}_1 = \mathbf{f} + \mathbf{e}'_1$ and $\mathbf{c}_2 = 2\mathbf{g} + 1 + \mathbf{e}'_2$. Therefore, we can derive $\mathbf{a}_q \cdot \mathbf{c}_1 - \mathbf{c}_2 = \mathbf{a}_q \cdot \mathbf{e}'_1 - \mathbf{e}'_2$, where the polynomials $\mathbf{e}'_1, \mathbf{e}'_2$ probably have many coefficients with value zero and their respective non-zero coefficient values are small. Indeed, since $\mathbf{c}_1$ was chosen to be a valid candidate polynomial for $\mathbf{f}$, it follows that the coefficients of $\mathbf{e}'_1$ have values in the set $V_1 = \{-4, -3, \ldots, 3, 4\}$. Similarly, since $\mathbf{c}_2$ was chosen to be a valid candidate polynomial for $2 \cdot \mathbf{g} + 1$, then the coefficients of $\mathbf{e}'_2$ have values in the set $V_2 = \{-8, -6, \ldots, 6, 8\}$. We can now re-write $\mathbf{a}_q \cdot \mathbf{c}_1 - \mathbf{c}_2 = \mathbf{a}_q \cdot \mathbf{e}'_1 - \mathbf{e}'_2$ as

$$\mathbf{c} = \mathbf{A} \cdot \mathbf{s} + \mathbf{e} \quad \bmod q \tag{4}$$

where $\mathbf{c} \in \mathbb{Z}_q^n$ is the column vector associated with the polynomial $\mathbf{a}_q \cdot \mathbf{c}_1 - \mathbf{c}_2$, $\mathbf{s} \in \mathbb{Z}_q^n$ is the column vector associated with the polynomial $\mathbf{e}'_1$, $\mathbf{e} \in \mathbb{Z}_q^n$ is the column vector associated with the polynomial $-\mathbf{e}'_2$ and $\mathbf{A} \in \mathbb{Z}_q^{n \times n}$ is the rotation matrix of $\mathbf{a}_q$.

This shows that given a high-scoring candidate (c_1, c_2), the problem of recovering f and h can be re-cast as a Ring-LWE instance (since if s can be found, then so can f and h). However, the noise distribution in this instance, arising from e, is not the usual one in the LWE setting.

4.3.1 Meet-in-the-Middle Attacks

Here we will explore standard meet-in-the-middle attacks to solve LWE. This is a time memory trade-off approach and is therefore a faster method than a naive brute force at the cost of an increased memory requirement. The attacker starts off by splitting $s = (s^l \mid s^r)$ and $A = (A^l \mid A^r)$ into two parts and rewriting Eq. (4) as

$$c = A^l \cdot s^l + A^r \cdot s^r + e \mod q \qquad (5)$$

where $s^l \in V_1^k \subset \mathbb{Z}_q^k, s^r \in V_1^{n-k} \subset \mathbb{Z}_1^{n-k}, A^l \in \mathbb{Z}_q^{n \times (k)}, A^r \in \mathbb{Z}_q^{n \times (n-k)}$ and $e \in V_2^n \subset \mathbb{Z}_q^n$. Note that if the attacker guessed the correct vector s^l and the correct vector s^r, then the vector $A^l \cdot s^l$ would be "almost" equal to $c - A^r \cdot s^r$, because calculating $A^l \cdot s^l + e$ would likely not make $A^l \cdot s^l$ to change considerably, since e is very likely to have many zero entries and its non-zeros entries are in V_2. In other words, $c - A^r \cdot s^r$ and $A^l \cdot s^l$ differ only by a vector e such that $\max(|e_1|, |e_2|, \cdots, |e_n|) \leq 8$.

The attacker therefore may be able to choose some b such that given $u = A^l \cdot s_i^l$ and $v = c - A^r \cdot s^r$, then $MSB_b(u_p) = MSB_b(v_p)$ with overwhelming probability for all $p \in I \subseteq \{0, 1, \ldots, n-1\}$, where $MSB_b(x)$ denotes the b most significant bits of the binary representation of x. Let us define a hash function H such that $H(z)$ outputs a hash value involving all the $MSB_b(z_p)$ values for $p \in I$. Therefore, given u and v satisfying that $MSB_b(u_p) = MSB_b(v_p)$ for all $p \in I$, then $H(u) = H(v)$. Note the attacker may use H to search for collisions. Indeed, the attacker may proceed to recover s by using H and a hash table T_2, similar to the hash table T_1 described previously, as follows:

The attacker first computes guesses for s^l. For each candidate $s_i^l \in V_1^k$, the attacker first computes $u_i^l = A^l \cdot s_i^l$ and then adds the array representation of s_i^l as the first entry of a linked list pointed to by $T_2[t_i^l]$, calculating t_i^l from $H(u_i^l)$ via using a map $\mathbb{I}$ outputting indexes in the hash table T_2 from hash values.

Once the table is generated, the attacker then proceeds to compute guesses for s^r. For each candidate $s_j^r \in V^{n-k}$, the attacker computes $v_j^r = c - A^r \cdot s_j^r$, calculates $t_j^r = \mathbb{I}(H(v_j^r))$ and finally iterates through all the arrays stored at index t_j^r of T_2. For each array s_i^l found, the attacker treats $s_{i,j} = (s_i^l \mid s_j^r)$ as a candidate secret. The attacker then calculates the polynomial $f_{i,j} = c_1 - s_{i,j}$ and then verifies if $a_q \cdot f_{i,j}$ is a valid candidate for $2g + 1$ or not, as described in Sect. 4.2.5. By construction, if T_2 is queried for the guess v_j^r and returns s_i^l, then $MSB_b(v_{j,p}^r) = MSB_b(u_{i,p}^l)$ for all $p \in I$. If there is no candidate secret $s_{i,j}$ found, call for more samples and repeat.

A drawback of the above algorithm is its memory requirements, as it requires storing $|V_1|^k$ vectors in memory. In the next section, we will describe a different algorithm to search for collisions with only negligible memory requirements. This line of research started with Pollard's ρ-method, which was originally applied to factoring and discrete logarithms, but may be generalised to finding collisions in any function [17].

4.3.2   Parallel Collision Search

Parallel collision search is a method to search for colliding values x, y in the function values $F(x), F(y)$ for a given function F. This technique can be applied to meet-in-the-middle attacks [17,24]. We will follow the description of the attack in [24]. The goal in collision search is to create an appropriate function F and find two different inputs that produce the same output. F is required to have the same domain and codomain, i.e. $F : S \rightarrow S$, and to be sufficiently complex that it behaves like a random mapping. To perform a parallel collision search, each processor (thread) proceeds as follows: Select a starting point $x_0 \in S$ and produce the trail of points $x_i = F(x_{i-1})$, for $i = 1, 2, \ldots$ until a distinguished point x_d is reached based on some easily testable distinguishing property, e.g. a fixed number of leading zeros. For each trail we store the triples (x_0, x_d, d) in a single common list for all processors (threads) and start producing a new trail from a new starting point. Whenever we find two triples $(x_0, x_t, t), (x_0', x_t', t')$ with $x_t = x_t'$ and $x_0 \neq x_0'$ we have found a collision. These trails can be re-run from their starting values to find the steps $x_i \neq x_j$ for which $F(x_i) = F(x_j)$. It can then be checked if this is the collision we were looking for.

In a general meet-in-the-middle attack, we have two functions, $F_1 : W_1 \rightarrow S$ and $F_2 : W_2 \rightarrow S$, and we wish to find two particular inputs $w_1 \in W_1$ and $w_2 \in W_2$, such that $F_1(w_1) = F_2(w_2)$. To apply parallel collision search to meet-in-the-middle attacks, we construct a single function F which has identical domain and codomain to do the collision search on. This function may be constructed from the functions F_1 and F_2 as follows. Let I be the set $\{0, 1, \ldots, M-1\}$, with $M \geq \max(|W_1|, |W_2|)$, and let $D_1 : I \rightarrow W_1$ and $D_2 : I \rightarrow W_2$ be functions that map elements of the interval onto elements of W_1 and W_2 respectively. Moreover, let $G : S \rightarrow I \times \{0, 1\}$ be a mapping that maps elements from the range of F_i to elements of I and a bit selector. The mapping G should distribute the elements of S fairly uniformly across $I \times \{0, 1\}$. As a good example for G, we may take a hash function of whose output the most significant bit is split off. Therefore, we can now define the function F as $F(x, i) = G(F_{i+1}(D_{i+1}(x)))$. This is a function whose domain is equal to its codomain and on which collision search may be performed.

To apply the previous idea to search for $\mathbf{s}^l$ and $\mathbf{s}^r$, we have to define a function F with the same domain and codomain. We first define F_1 as $F_1(\mathbf{x}) = H(\mathbf{A}^l \cdot \mathbf{x})$ and F_2 as $F_2(\mathbf{x}) = H(\mathbf{c} - \mathbf{A}^r \cdot \mathbf{x})$, where H is the function defined in Sect. 4.3.1. The domain of F_1 is V_1^k, while the domain of F_2 is V_1^{n-k}, and both functions have the same codomain. We next define $|I| = \max(|V_1|^k, |V_1|^{n-k})$, the function $D_1 : I \rightarrow V_1^k$ as a function mapping an integer to a vector in V_1^k and the function $D_2 : I \rightarrow V_1^{n-k}$ as a function mapping an integer to a vector in V_1^{n-k}. The function D_1 will construct a vector $v \in V_1^k$ given a $p \in I$ as follows. Let A be the array whose entries are all the elements of V_1, i.e. $A[0] = -4, \ldots, A[7] = 4$.

It first sets $p' = p \bmod |V_1|^k$, then calculates $0 \leq c_i < |V_1|$ such that $p' = c_0 + c_1 \cdot |V_1| + \cdots + c_{k-1} \cdot |V_1|^{k-1}$, i.e. the representation of p' on base $|V_1|$. It then calculates $\mathbf{v} = [v_0, v_1, \ldots, v_{k-1}]$ by simply assigning the value $A[c_i]$ to v_i, and lastly returns the vector $\mathbf{v}$. Note the function D_2 may be defined in a similar manner.

Let H_g be a hash function. This can be any function with codomain larger than I. Hence $G(x) = (H_g(x) \bmod |I|) \times MSB(H_g(x))$ and $F(x,i) = G(F_{i+1}(D_{i+1}(x)))$. The function F can now be used for a collision attack by defining a distinguishing property D on I and creating trails starting from a point $x_0 \in I$ chosen at random. More specifically, we run trails until they reach a distinguished point $x_t \in D$ and then store the triple (x_0, x_t, t) in a hash-list. Whenever we find two triples (x_0, x_t, t), $(x'_0, x'_{t'}, t')$ with $x'_{t'} = x_t$ and $x_0 \neq x'_0$ we have found a collision. The trails then will be re-run from their starting values to find the steps $x_i \neq x_j$ for which $F(x_i, b_i) = F(x_j, b_j)$. We then compute $\mathbf{s}' = (\mathbf{s}^l | \mathbf{s}^r)$ with either $\mathbf{s}^l = D_{b_i+1}(x_i)$ and $\mathbf{s}^r = D_{b_j+1}(x_j)$ when $b_i = 0$ and $b_j = 1$ or $\mathbf{s}^l = D_{b_j+1}(x_j)$ and $\mathbf{s}^r = D_{b_i+1}(x_i)$ when $b_j = 0$ and $b_i = 1$. It is then checked if $\mathbf{f}' \cdot \mathbf{a_q}$ is a valid candidate for $2\mathbf{g} + 1$ or not, where $\mathbf{f}' = \mathbf{c}_1 - \mathbf{s}'$. If so, then return $\mathbf{f}'$ and $\mathbf{f}' \cdot \mathbf{a_q}$. If not, the triple (x_0, x_t, t) is replaced by $(x'_0, x'_{t'}, t')$ in the hash-list.

4.3.3 Hybrid Attack on LWE

Another related attack idea is to have a hybrid algorithm by combining lattice-reduction and meet-in-the-middle techniques. This attack idea has been applied against NTRU in [13], as well as on special instances of the Learning with Errors (LWE) problem in [5]. With notation as in Eq. (5), to recover $\mathbf{s}$, the attacker first tries to guess $\mathbf{s}^l$ and solve the remaining LWE instance $\mathbf{c}' = \mathbf{c} - \mathbf{A}^l \cdot \mathbf{s}^l = \mathbf{A}^r \cdot \mathbf{s}^r + \mathbf{e} \bmod q$. The newly obtained LWE instance may be solved by solving a close vector problem in the lattice $L_q(\mathbf{A}^r)$. In more detail, $\mathbf{c}' = \mathbf{A}^r \cdot \mathbf{s}^r + q\mathbf{w} + \mathbf{e}$, for some vector $\mathbf{w} \in \mathbb{Z}^n$, is close to the lattice vector $\mathbf{A}^r \cdot \mathbf{s}^r + q\mathbf{w} \in L_q(\mathbf{A}^r)$, since $\mathbf{e}$ is very likely to have many zeros and its non-zero entries are small. Hence one can hope to find $\mathbf{e}$ by running Babai's Nearest Plane algorithm in combination with a sufficient basis reduction as a pre-computation. Moreover, the attacker may speed up the guessing part of the attack by using a Meet-in-the-Middle approach, i.e. guessing vectors $\mathbf{s}_1^l \in V_1^k$ and $\mathbf{s}_2^l \in V_1^k$ such that $\mathbf{s}^l = \mathbf{s}_1^l + \mathbf{s}_2^l$.

4.3.4 Combining Lattice Techniques and Key Enumeration

We now expand on a hybrid attack similar to the previously described. First we will give a general description of the attack by following the description in [25] and then show a manner of applying it to our problem of recovering the private key in the cold boot attack setting. According to [25], the goal of this hybrid attack is to find a shortest vector in a lattice L, given a basis of L of the form

$$\mathbf{B}' = \left(\begin{array}{c|c} \mathbf{B} & \mathbf{C} \\ \hline \mathbf{O} & \mathbf{I}_k \end{array} \right)$$

where $0 < k < m$, $\mathbf{B} \in \mathbb{Z}^{(m-k) \times m-k}$, and $\mathbf{C} \in \mathbb{Z}^{(m-k) \times k}$.

Let $\mathbf{v}$ be a short vector contained in the lattice L. Let us split the short vector $\mathbf{v}$ into two parts $\mathbf{v} = (\mathbf{v}^l | \mathbf{v}^r)$ with $\mathbf{v}^l \in \mathbf{Z}^{m-k}$ and $\mathbf{v}^r \in \mathbf{Z}^k$. The left part $\mathbf{v}^l$ of $\mathbf{v}$ will be recovered with lattice techniques (solving BDD problems), while the right part $\mathbf{v}^r$ will be recovered by guessing during the attack. Because of the special form of the basis $\mathbf{B}'$, we have that

$$\begin{pmatrix} \mathbf{v}^l \\ \mathbf{v}^r \end{pmatrix} = \mathbf{B}' \begin{pmatrix} \mathbf{x} \\ \mathbf{v}^r \end{pmatrix} = \begin{pmatrix} \mathbf{B} \cdot \mathbf{x} + \mathbf{C} \cdot \mathbf{v}^r \\ \mathbf{v}^r \end{pmatrix}$$

for some vector $x \in \mathbf{Z}^{m-k}$. Thus $\mathbf{C} \cdot \mathbf{v}^r = -\mathbf{B} \cdot \mathbf{x} + \mathbf{v}^l$. Note that $\mathbf{C} \cdot \mathbf{v}^r$ is close to the lattice $\mathbf{L}(\mathbf{B})$, since it only differs from the lattice by the short vector $\mathbf{v}^l$. Therefore $\mathbf{v}^l$ may be recovered solving a BDD problem if $\mathbf{v}^r$ is known. The idea now is that if we can correctly guess the vector $\mathbf{v}^r$, then we can hope to find $\mathbf{v}^l$ by using Babai's Nearest Plane algorithm, i.e. $\mathbf{NP_B}(\mathbf{C} \cdot \mathbf{v}^r) = \mathbf{v}^l$ if the basis $\mathbf{B}$ is sufficiently reduced. The guessing of $\mathbf{v}^r$ is normally carried out by a meet-in-the-middle attack [13,25]. Note that the lattice $\mathbf{L}(\mathbf{B})$ in which we need to solve BDD has smaller dimension, i.e. $m - k$ instead of m. Thus, the newly obtained BDD problem is expected to be easier to solve than the original SVP instance.

Returning to our problem of recovering the private key, let us assume that $\mathbf{a}_q$ is invertible in R_q, which is the case with very high probability. Therefore, we may obtain the equation $\mathbf{f} = (2\mathbf{g} + 1)\mathbf{a}_q^{-1} \in R_q$. Now let us set $\mathbf{v} = (\mathbf{f} \mid 2\mathbf{g} + 1)$ and so

$$\begin{pmatrix} \mathbf{f} \\ 2\mathbf{g} + 1 \end{pmatrix} = \begin{pmatrix} (2\mathbf{g} + 1)\mathbf{a}_q^{-1} + q\mathbf{w} \\ 2\mathbf{g} + 1 \end{pmatrix} = \begin{pmatrix} q\mathbf{I}_n | \mathbf{A} \\ \mathbf{O} | \mathbf{I}_n \end{pmatrix} \begin{pmatrix} \mathbf{w} \\ 2\mathbf{g} + 1 \end{pmatrix}$$

for some $\mathbf{w} \in \mathbf{Z}^n$, where $\mathbf{A}$ is the rotation matrix of $\mathbf{a}_q^{-1}$. Hence, $\mathbf{v} \in \mathbf{L}$ with $\mathbf{L} = \mathbf{L}\left(\begin{pmatrix} q\mathbf{I}_n | \mathbf{A} \\ \mathbf{O} | \mathbf{I}_n \end{pmatrix}\right)$. Since the basis of L has the required form and $\mathbf{f}$ is a short vector[3], the attacker may perform the hybrid attack to try to recover the vector $\mathbf{f}$ by performing the guessing of the vector $2\mathbf{g} + 1$ via running an instance of a key enumeration algorithm. Specifically, the attacker now uses the algorithm described in Sect. 4.2.3 to generate valid and high scoring candidate polynomials $\mathbf{h}_i$ for $2\mathbf{g} + 1$ from $\mathbf{s}_2'$. For each $\mathbf{h}_i$, the attacker calculates $\mathbf{NP_B}(\mathbf{a}_q^{-1} \cdot \mathbf{h}_i) = \mathbf{v}^l$, where $\mathbf{B} = q\mathbf{I}_n$. If $\mathbf{f}' = \mathbf{v}^l \bmod q$ is a valid candidate for $\mathbf{f}$, then the algorithm has found the pair $(\mathbf{f}', \mathbf{h}_i)$.

Note that this technique is rather similar to the key recovery algorithm that only enumerates candidates for $\mathbf{f}$ introduced in Sect. 4.2.5. In the sense that both techniques perform an enumeration of candidates (one does for $\mathbf{f}$, while this does for $2\mathbf{g}+1$) and then each uses its corresponding oracle to find a valid pair $(\mathbf{f}_i, \mathbf{h}_i)$.

---

[3] This follows because of its form.

5   Experimental Evaluation

5.1   Simulations

To simulate the performance of our key recovery algorithms, we generate a private key (according to the format), flip its bits according to the error probabilities α, β, and then run our chosen key recovery algorithm. We refer to such a run attempting to recover a single private key as a simulation. For our experiments, we ran our simulations on a machine with Intel Xeon CPU E5-2667 v2 running at 3.30 GHz with 8 cores.

5.2   Key Recovery via Key Enumeration

In this section, we will show results obtained from running the key recovery algorithm introduced in Sect. 4.2.5.

5.2.1   Parameters

For the simulations, we used two parameter sets: BLISS-I with $n = 512, q = 12289, d_1 = 154, d_2 = 0$ and BLISS-IV with $n = 512, q = 12289, d_1 = 231, d_2 = 31$.

5.2.2   Setup

Recall that we have access to $\mathbf{s}_1'$ that is a bit string of size $W = 8(512) = 4096$. We first set a chunk to be an 8-bit string, i.e. $w = 8$, and so there are $n = 512$ chunks. When using the parameter set BLISS-I, we set the candidates for a chunk to be the integers in the set $\{-1, 0, 1\}$. On the other hand, when using the parameter set BLISS-IV, we set the candidates for a chunk to be the integers in the set $\{-2, -1, 0, 1, 2\}$. Also, we set a block to be a successive sequence of 64 chunks, resulting in 8 blocks. Besides, we set the number of candidates blsize generated for any block in Phase I to 2^r, for $r = 8, 9, 10$. Thus, eight candidate lists, each of size 2^r, will be obtained from Phase I. Regarding the key enumeration algorithm to be employed in Phase II, we will make use of a key enumeration algorithm that combines key features from the key enumeration algorithms found in the literature [4,6,16,22]. We next describe our particular choice of key enumeration algorithm.

5.2.3   Key Enumeration Algorithm for Phase II

First note that because of the nature of the log-likelihood function employed to calculate scores, many chunk candidates of any given list L_{b^i} output by any Phase I(by OKEA) will have a repeated score value. Taking advantage of this observation, we will design an algorithm to both efficiently count and enumerate all the key candidates that any Phase II will consider in any given interval $[a, b]$.

First we define a 'compact' list as a 2-tuple of the form (rscore, rlist), where rscore is a real value representing a repeated score, while rlist is a list of chunk candidates such that each chunk candidate has the repeated score as its score. From each list L_{b^i}, with $0 \le i < n_b$, we can obtain S_i 'compact' lists $C_{k_i}^i$, with $0 \le k_i < S_i$. We can then pick a 'compact' list $C_{k_i}^i$ per list L_{b^i} and simultaneously compute the sum of scores and product of counts (i.e. the sizes of $C_{k_i}^i$.rlist) to produce a 3-tuple of the form (tscore, tnumber, rtable) and insert it into the list L_{bt}. The component tnumber holds the total number of key candidates that will have the total accumulated score tscore, while rtable is a table whose size is the number of blocks and whose entry i points to the list $C_{k_i}^i$.rlist.

Since the number of 'compact' lists, S_i, obtained from each list L_{b^i} is less than 10 on average in our experiments, the total number of entries of L_{bt}, $\prod_{i=0}^{nb-1} S_i$, is not expected to be considerably large if the number of blocks, n_b, is selected suitably. Furthermore, according to our experiments, it is preferable to select the number of blocks to be less than 12 so as not to negatively affect the overall performance because of the number of entries of L_{bt}. Also, note that all the entries of the list L_{bt} may be ordered in decreasing order based on the component tscore. So we may obtain an efficient algorithm for counting and enumerating the key candidates in any given interval that our Phase II search algorithm would need to consider. Given the interval $[a, b]$, the algorithm first calculates the set of indices J such that the value $tscore_j$ from any entry with index $j \in$ J of L_{bt} lies in the given interval and then proceeds as follows.

On the one hand, as for counting, the algorithm will iterate through the indices $j \in$ J while summing the value $tnumber_j$ from the entry with index j of L_{bt}. On completion, it will return the total sum. On the other hand, as for enumeration, the algorithm will iterate through the indices $j \in$ J while generating all possible key candidates that can be formed from the table $rtable_j$ obtained from the entry with index j of L_{bt}. When enumerating, the order in which the algorithm iterates through the indices $j \in$ J helps in guaranteeing some quality in the order in which the key candidates will be generated. Indeed, assuming L_{bt} is ordered in decreasing order based on the component tscore, the set J once calculated may be seen as an array of the form $[j_{start}, j_{start} + 1, \ldots, j_{stop}]$. Therefore, the algorithm will first generate all key candidates whose accumulated score is equal to the value $tscore_{j_{start}}$ from the entry with index j_{start} of L_{bt}, followed by all key candidates whose accumulated score is equal to the value $tscore_{j_{start}+1}$ from the entry with index $j_{start} + 1$ of L_{bt} and so on.

Moreover, suppose we would like to have t independent tasks $T_1, T_2, T_3, \ldots, T_t$ executing in parallel to enumerate all key candidates whose total accumulated scores are in a given interval $[B_1, B_2]$. After creating the array J $= [j_{start}, j_{start} + 1, \ldots, j_{stop}]$, we can partition the array J into t disjoint sub-arrays J_i, and set each task T_i to iterate through the indices $j_i \in J_i$ while generating all possible key candidates that can be formed from the table rtable obtained from the entry with index j_i of L_{bt}. A consequence of the independence of the tasks is that the key candidates will be generated in no particular order, i.e. this algorithm will lose its near-optimality property when running in parallel. An example of a partition algorithm that could almost evenly distribute the workload among the tasks is removing an index $j \in$ J such that $tnumber_j$ is the maximum and add it to the corresponding J_i at each iteration, until J is empty.

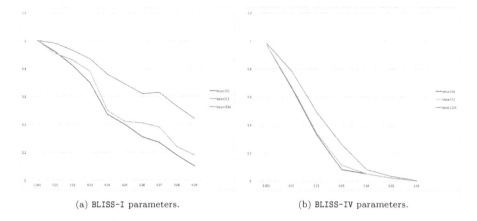

(a) BLISS-I parameters.   (b) BLISS-IV parameters.

Fig. 1. Expected success rate for a full enumeration for $\alpha = 0.001$. The y-axis represents the success rate, while the x-axis represents β.

5.2.4 Results

Complete Enumeration. Here we perform simulations to estimate the expected success rate of our overall algorithm without actually executing the expensive **Phase II**. Let p_i denote the probability that the correct chunk candidate is actually found in the list L_{b^i}; p_i will be a function of r. It follows that the probability that our **Phase II** algorithm outputs the correct candidate for **f** when performing a complete enumeration over all 2^{8r} candidate keys is given by $p = \prod_{i=1}^{8} p_i$. This simple calculation gives us a way to perform simulations to estimate the expected success rate of our overall algorithm without actually executing the expensive **Phase II**. We simply run many simulations of **Phase I** for the given value of `blsize` (each simulation generating a fresh private key and perturbing it according to α, β), and, after each simulation, test whether the correct chunks of **f** are to be found in the lists L_{b^i}.

Figure 1 shows the success rates for complete enumeration for values of `blsize` $= 2^r$ for $r \in \{8, 9, 10\}$. As expected, the greater the value of `blsize`, the higher the success rate for a fixed α and β. Also, note that when β increases, the success rate drops to zero. This is expected since it is likely that at least one chunk of **f** will not be included in the corresponding lists coming out of **Phase I** when the noise levels are high, at which point **Phase II** inevitably fails. Additionally, note that for **BLISS-IV** parameters the success rate will drop quickly (for $\beta = 0.06$), while for **BLISS-I** parameters the success rate will drop for $\beta \geq 0.09$. This is expected because $d_2 = 0$ for the latter case and so the set of candidates for a chunk was set to $\{-1, 0, 1\}$. This case is similar to the case of NTRU studied in [19].

Note that each data point in this figure (and all figures in this section) were obtained using 100 simulations. Note that the running times for **Phase I** are very low on average (≤ 50 ms), since that phase consists of calling the OKEA for each of the eight lists with `blsize` in the set $\{256, 512, 1024\}$.

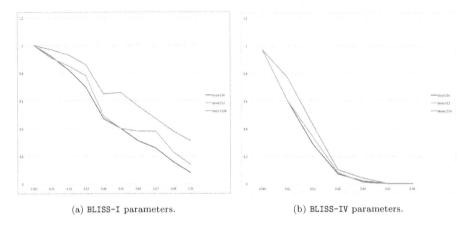

(a) BLISS-I parameters.   (b) BLISS-IV parameters.

Fig. 2. Expected success rate for a 2^{40} enumeration for $\alpha = 0.001$. The y-axis represents the success rate, while the x-axis represents β.

Partial Enumerations. We considered intervals of the form $[max - W, max]$. To calculate a suitable value for W, we exploit the key enumeration algorithm used in **Phase II** to estimate it as a function of the total number of keys considered, K. Specifically, given a value K, we run the counting method to find a suitable index i_K of L_{bt}. Therefore, the key enumeration will run through the indices $0, 1, \ldots, i_K$. Since we can easily estimate the speed at which individual keys can be assessed, we can also use this approach to control the total running time of our algorithms. Figure 2 shows how the success rate of our algorithm varies for different values of **blsize**. We observe the same trends as for full enumeration, i.e. the greater is **blsize**, the higher is the success rate for a fixed α and β. Also, for larger values of (α, β), the success rate drops rapidly to zero. Besides, Fig. 3 shows the success rates for a complete enumeration and partial enumerations with 2^{35} keys and 2^{40} keys. As expected, the success rate for a full enumeration is greater than for the partial enumerations (but note that a full enumeration here would require the testing of up to 2^{80} keys, which may be a prohibitive cost). Additionally, note that for **BLISS-IV** parameters the success rate will drop quickly (for $\beta = 0.06$), while for **BLISS-I** parameters the success rate will drop for $\beta \geq 0.09$. As noted, this is expected because $d_2 = 0$ for **BLISS-I** parameters and so the set of candidates for a chunk was set to $\{-1, 0, 1\}$. Concerning running times, we find that our code is able to test between 600 and 1000 candidates per millisecond per core during **Phase II** in our experiments.

Furthermore, our results are clearly inferior to the impressive bit-flip rates that can be handled in the RSA setting [18]. This should not come as a surprise, since analyses in the RSA setting had several benefits, such as RSA's mathematically high structure and redundant in-memory private key formats. However, our results are comparable with the results obtained for the **PolarSSL** implementation in the discrete logarithm setting [21]. They are also comparable with the results obtained for NTRU in [19], specially when using the **BLISS-I** parameters.

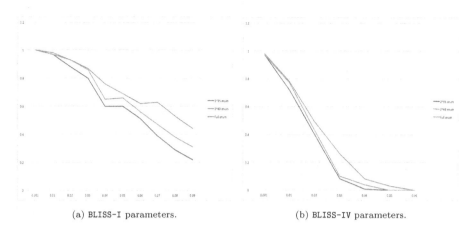

(a) BLISS-I parameters.   (b) BLISS-IV parameters.

Fig. 3. Expected success rate for various enumerations for $\alpha = 0.001$ and `blsize =` 1024. The y-axis represents the success rate, while the x-axis represents β

6   Conclusions

In this paper, we studied the cold boot attack on BLISS. Our evaluation focused on an existing BLISS implementation. We proposed a key recovery algorithm via combining key enumeration algorithms and then established a connection between the key recovery problem in this particular case and an instance of LWE. Also, we explored other techniques based on the meet-in-the-middle generic attack to tackle this instance of LWE and showed a key recovery strategy combining key enumeration and lattice techniques. We then experimented with one of the introduced key recovery algorithms to explore its performance for a range of parameters and found that our key recovery algorithm was able to tolerate a noise level of $\alpha = 0.001$ and $\beta = 0.09$ for a parameter set when performing a 2^{40} enumeration.

References

1. Albrecht, M., Cid, C.: Cold boot key recovery by solving polynomial systems with noise. In: Lopez, J., Tsudik, G. (eds.) ACNS 2011. LNCS, vol. 6715, pp. 57–72. Springer, Heidelberg (2011). https://doi.org/10.1007/978-3-642-21554-4_4
2. Albrecht, M.R., Deo, A., Paterson, K.G.: Cold boot attacks on ring and module lwe keys under the ntt. IACR Trans. Cryptogr. Hardw. Embed. Syst. (3), 173–213 (2018). https://doi.org/10.13154/tches.v2018.i3.173-213. https://tches.iacr.org/index.php/TCHES/article/view/7273
3. Babai, L.: On lováz' lattice reduction and the nearest lattice point problem. Combinatorica **6**(1), 1–13 (1986). https://doi.org/10.1007/BF02579403
4. Bogdanov, A., Kizhvatov, I., Manzoor, K., Tischhauser, E., Witteman, M.: Fast and memory-efficient key recovery in side-channel attacks. In: Dunkelman, O., Keliher, L. (eds.) SAC 2015. LNCS, vol. 9566, pp. 310–327. Springer, Cham (2016). https://doi.org/10.1007/978-3-319-31301-6_19

5. Buchmann, J., Göpfert, F., Player, R., Wunderer, T.: On the hardness of LWE with binary error: revisiting the hybrid lattice-reduction and meet-in-the-middle attack. In: Pointcheval, D., Nitaj, A., Rachidi, T. (eds.) AFRICACRYPT 2016. LNCS, vol. 9646, pp. 24–43. Springer, Cham (2016). https://doi.org/10.1007/978-3-319-31517-1_2

6. David, L., Wool, A.: A bounded-space near-optimal key enumeration algorithm for multi-subkey side-channel attacks. In: Handschuh, H. (ed.) CT-RSA 2017. LNCS, vol. 10159, pp. 311–327. Springer, Cham (2017). https://doi.org/10.1007/978-3-319-52153-4_18

7. Ducas, L.: Accelerating bliss: the geometry of ternary polynomials. Cryptology ePrint Archive, Report 2014/874 (2014). http://eprint.iacr.org/2014/874

8. Ducas, L., Durmus, A., Lepoint, T., Lyubashevsky, V.: Lattice signatures and bimodal gaussians. In: Canetti, R., Garay, J.A. (eds.) CRYPTO 2013. LNCS, vol. 8042, pp. 40–56. Springer, Heidelberg (2013). https://doi.org/10.1007/978-3-642-40041-4_3

9. Espitau, T., Fouque, P.A., Gérard, B., Tibouchi, M.: Side-channel attacks on BLISS lattice-based signatures: Exploiting branch tracing against strongSwan and electromagnetic emanations in microcontrollers. In: Thuraisingham, B.M., Evans, D., Malkin, T., Xu, D. (eds.) ACM CCS 2017: 24th Conference on Computer and Communications Security, 31 October–2 November 2017, pp. 1857–1874. ACM Press, Dallas (2017). https://doi.org/10.1145/3133956.3134028

10. Halderman, J.A., et al.: Lest we remember: cold boot attacks on encryption keys. In: van Oorschot, P.C. (ed.) USENIX Security 2008: 17th USENIX Security Symposium, USENIX Association, San Jose, CA, USA, 28 July–1 August 2008, pp. 45–60 (2008)

11. Henecka, W., May, A., Meurer, A.: Correcting errors in rsa private keys. In: Rabin, T. (ed.) CRYPTO 2010. LNCS, vol. 6223, pp. 351–369. Springer, Heidelberg (2010). https://doi.org/10.1007/978-3-642-14623-7_19

12. Heninger, N., Shacham, H.: Reconstructing RSA private keys from random key bits. In: Halevi, S. (ed.) CRYPTO 2009. LNCS, vol. 5677, pp. 1–17. Springer, Heidelberg (2009). https://doi.org/10.1007/978-3-642-03356-8_1

13. Howgrave-Graham, N.: A hybrid lattice-reduction and meet-in-the-middle attack against NTRU. In: Menezes, A. (ed.) CRYPTO 2007. LNCS, vol. 4622, pp. 150–169. Springer, Heidelberg (2007). https://doi.org/10.1007/978-3-540-74143-5_9

14. Kamal, A.A., Youssef, A.M.: Applications of sat solvers to aes key recovery from decayed key schedule images. In: Proceedings of the 2010 Fourth International Conference on Emerging Security Information, Systems and Technologies, SECURWARE 2010, IEEE Computer Society, Washington, DC, USA, pp. 216–220 (2010). https://doi.org/10.1109/SECURWARE.2010.42. http://dx.doi.org/10.1109/SECURWARE.2010.42

15. Lee, H.T., Kim, H.T., Baek, Y.-J., Cheon, J.H.: Correcting errors in private keys obtained from cold boot attacks. In: Kim, H. (ed.) ICISC 2011. LNCS, vol. 7259, pp. 74–87. Springer, Heidelberg (2012). https://doi.org/10.1007/978-3-642-31912-9_6

16. Martin, D.P., O'Connell, J.F., Oswald, E., Stam, M.: Counting keys in parallel after a side channel attack. In: Iwata, T., Cheon, J.H. (eds.) ASIACRYPT 2015. LNCS, vol. 9453, pp. 313–337. Springer, Heidelberg (2015). https://doi.org/10.1007/978-3-662-48800-3_13

17. Oorschot, P.C., Wiener, M.J.: Parallel collision search with cryptanalytic applications. J. Cryptol. 12(1), 1–28 (1999). https://doi.org/10.1007/PL00003816

18. Paterson, K.G., Polychroniadou, A., Sibborn, D.L.: A coding-theoretic approach to recovering noisy RSA keys. In: Wang, X., Sako, K. (eds.) ASIACRYPT 2012. LNCS, vol. 7658, pp. 386–403. Springer, Heidelberg (2012). https://doi.org/10.1007/978-3-642-34961-4_24

19. Paterson, K.G., Villanueva-Polanco, R.: Cold Boot attacks on NTRU. In: Patra, A., Smart, N.P. (eds.) INDOCRYPT 2017. LNCS, vol. 10698, pp. 107–125. Springer, Cham (2017). https://doi.org/10.1007/978-3-319-71667-1_6

20. Pessl, P., Bruinderink, L.G., Yarom, Y.: To BLISS-B or not to be: attacking strongSwan's implementation of post-quantum signatures. In: Thuraisingham, B.M., Evans, D., Malkin, T., Xu, D. (eds.) ACM CCS 2017: 24th Conference on Computer and Communications Security, 31 October–2 November 2017, pp. 1843–1855. ACM Press, Dallas (2017). https://doi.org/10.1145/3133956.3134023

21. Poettering, B., Sibborn, D.L.: Cold boot attacks in the discrete logarithm setting. In: Nyberg, K. (ed.) CT-RSA 2015. LNCS, vol. 9048, pp. 449–465. Springer, Cham (2015). https://doi.org/10.1007/978-3-319-16715-2_24

22. Poussier, R., Standaert, F.-X., Grosso, V.: Simple key enumeration (and rank estimation) using histograms: an integrated approach. In: Gierlichs, B., Poschmann, A.Y. (eds.) CHES 2016. LNCS, vol. 9813, pp. 61–81. Springer, Heidelberg (2016). https://doi.org/10.1007/978-3-662-53140-2_4

23. Veyrat-Charvillon, N., Gérard, B., Renauld, M., Standaert, F.-X.: An optimal key enumeration algorithm and its application to side-channel attacks. In: Knudsen, L.R., Wu, H. (eds.) SAC 2012. LNCS, vol. 7707, pp. 390–406. Springer, Heidelberg (2013). https://doi.org/10.1007/978-3-642-35999-6_25

24. van Vredendaal, C.: Reduced memory meet-in-the-middle attack against the NTRU private key. LMS J. Comput. Math. **19**(A), 43–57 (2016). https://doi.org/10.1112/S1461157016000206

25. Wunderer, T.: Revisiting the hybrid attack: improved analysis and refined security estimates. Cryptology ePrint Archive, Report 2016/733 (2016). http://eprint.iacr.org/2016/733

Symmetric Cryptography

Optimally Indifferentiable Double-Block-Length Hashing Without Post-processing and with Support for Longer Key Than Single Block

Yusuke Naito[✉]

Mitsubishi Electric Corporation, Kamakura, Kanagawa, Japan
Naito.Yusuke@ce.MitsubishiElectric.co.jp

Abstract. Existing double-block-length (DBL) hash functions, in order to achieve optimal indifferentiable security (security up to $O(2^n)$ query complexity), require a block cipher with n-bit blocks and k-bit keys such that $2n \leq k$, and a post-processing function with two block cipher calls. In this paper, we consider the indifferentiability of MDPH, a combination of the MDP domain extender and Hirose's compression function. MDPH does not require the post-processing function (thus has better efficiency), and supports block ciphers with $n < k$. We show that MDPH achieves (nearly) optimal indifferentiable security. To the best of our knowledge, this is the first result for DBL hashing with optimal indifferentiable security, with support for block ciphers with $n < k$, and without the post-processing function.

Keywords: Double-block-length hashing · Block cipher ·
Optimal indifferentiable security · Longer key than single block ·
MDP · Hirose's compression function

1 Introduction

Block-cipher-based hashing is an important design methodology for constructing a cryptographic hash function. An advantage of block-cipher-based hashing is that implementing both a hash function and a (block-cipher-based) cryptographic algorithm, one can save its memory size by sharing the block cipher algorithm. However, for single-block-length schemes such as the PGV class of functions [39], and more generally Stam's class of functions [42], the output lengths are too short against birthday attacks, using important block ciphers such as AES (FIPS 197), Camellia, SEED (ISO/IEC 18033-3), CLEFIA, PRESENT (ISO/IEC 29192-2) and other lightweight block ciphers e.g., [4,5,11,12,19,40,41,44] (these block lengths are 128 bits or less). For the birthday problem, double-block-length (DBL) design, which translates a block cipher with n-bit blocks into a hash function with $2n$-bit outputs, is an effective solution.

ⓒ Springer Nature Switzerland AG 2019
P. Schwabe and N. Thériault (Eds.): LATINCRYPT 2019, LNCS 11774, pp. 65–85, 2019.
https://doi.org/10.1007/978-3-030-30530-7_4

The idea of DBL hashing was given by Meyer and Schilling [34] in design of MDC-2 and MDC-4. After that, many DBL schemes, especially, collision resistant DBL compression functions have mainly been studied, e.g., [16,17,20,21,25–28,31,37,38,43]. Many of them achieve optimal collision security in the ideal cipher model (security up to $O(2^n)$ query complexity), and combining with domain extenders preserving collision security, e.g., the Merkle-Damgård (MD) construction [15,33], offers optimally collision secure DBL hash functions.

Since the introduction of indifferentiability of Maurer et al. [30], designing an indifferentiable (from a random oracle) secure hash function has been one of the main research topics in hash design. Indifferentiability is a stronger security notion than collision security and ensures that a hash function has no structural flaw up to the proven bound. Indeed, any MD hash function is not indifferentiable from a random oracle even with the use of an ideal compression function, whereas any indifferentiable secure hash function is collision resistance (up to the proven bound). So far, several indifferentiable secure hash functions have been proposed. Prefix-Free MD (PFMD), NMAC, HMAC [14], Enveloped MD [6] and MD with Permutation (MDP) [23] are indifferentiable secure hash functions when the underlying compression functions are random oracles or the Davies-Meyer scheme in the ideal cipher model. The Sponge function [7,8] is an indifferentiable secure permutation-based hash function when the underlying permutation is ideal, which is used in many important hash functions such as Keccak family [9] including SHA-3 functions [36], and lightweight hash functions e.g., [3,9,10].

In the research of DBL hash design, Chang et al. [13] gave indifferentiable attacks on the PBGV schemes [38] with $O(1)$ query complexity, and Mennink [32] gave indifferentiable attacks on several block-cipher-based compression functions such as MDC-2 and Hirose's schemes [20,21] with $O(1)$ query complexity. On the other hand, Gong et al. [18] proved that DBL hash functions that are combinations of PFMD/NMAC/HMAC and the PBGV schemes are indifferentiable from random oracles up to $O(2^{n/2})$ query complexity. Mennink [32] proved that Mennink's compression function [31] and MDC-4 are indifferentiable from random oracles up to $O(2^{n/2})$ and $O(2^{n/4})$ query complexities, respectively. These compression functions support block ciphers with n-bit blocks and k-bit keys such that $n \le k$. Naito [35] proposed a DBL hash function that iterates Hirose's compression function [21], then performs a post-processing function with two block cipher calls (after taking all input blocks). He proved that it achieves optimal indifferentiable security (security up to $O(2^n)$ query complexity). The DBL hash function requires a block cipher with $2n \le k$. Hirose and Kuwakado [22,24] proposed DBL hash functions that support block ciphers with $n < k$. Similar to Naito's DBL hash function, it uses a post-processing function with two block cipher calls. They proved that the DBL hash functions are indifferentiable from random oracles up to $O(2^{\min\{n,k/2\}})$ query complexity, thereby achieving optimal indifferentiable security only when $2n \le k$.

1.1 Open Problem

The existing optimally indifferentiable secure DBL hash functions

- use post-processing functions with two block cipher calls that impact on the speed especially for short inputs, and
- require a block cipher with $2n \leq k$, or compromise the security level in order to use a block cipher with $k < 2n$, e.g, using 128-bit block and 192-bit key versions of AES, Camellia, SEED and CLEFIA, Hirose-Kuwakado schemes are indifferentiable from random oracles up to 2^{96} query complexity.

Hence, an open problem from the previous works is to design an optimally indifferentiable secure DBL hash function without the post-processing functions and with support for block ciphers with $k < 2n$.

1.2 Our Contribution

In this paper, we show that a combination of the MDP domain extender [23] and Hirose's compression function [21] achieves (nearly) optimal indifferentiable security. The DBL hash function is called MDPH in this paper. The reason why the MDP domain extender and Hirose's compression function are chosen is that

- MDP has a simple structure (just iterates a compression function) and does not require costly operations (requires only a constant XOR just before the last compression function call), and
- Hirose's compression function calls a block cipher twice, the key elements are the same (i.e., the key scheduling can be shared), and the input and output lengths of Hirose's compression function are $n + k$ bits and $2n$ bits, respectively.

Hence, MDPH does not require a post-processing function, and the length of input blocks of MDPH is $k - n$ bits, thereby supporting block ciphers with $n < k$. Our indifferentiable bound is $O\big(\mu Q/2^n + 2^n \cdot (Q/(\mu 2^n))^\mu\big)$ for any positive integer μ and the number of block cipher calls Q, and gives the following results.

- Putting $\mu = n$, MDPH is indifferentiable from a random oracle up to $O(2^n/n)$ query complexity.
- When using a 128-bit block cipher ($n = 128$), putting $\mu = 15$, MDPH is indifferentiable from a random oracle up to 2^{119} query complexity.

Our result for MDPH and the existing works for the PBGV-based DBL hash functions, Mennink's compression function, MDC-4, Naito's DBL hash function, and Hirose-Kuwakado's DBL hash functions are compared in Table 1 with respect to security, message block length, block cipher lengths, the number of block cipher calls per message block, and the number of additional block cipher calls. The PBGV-based DBL hash functions support block ciphers with $n < k$ but do not achieve optimal indifferentiable security. Mennink's compression function and MDC-4 support block ciphers with $n \leq k$ (hence, single-key block

Table 1. Comparison of indifferentiable secure DBL hash functions. MB is an abbreviation for Message Block. CF is an abbreviation for Compression Function. MB Len is an abbreviation for Message Block Length. #BC/MB shows the number of block cipher calls for each message block. #BC in PP shows the number of (additional) block cipher calls by a post-processing function.

Scheme	Indifferentiable security	MB Len	Key Len	#BC/MB	#BC in PP
PBGV-based	$O(2^{n/2})$ [18]	$k-n$	$n < k$	2	0
Mennink	$O(2^{n/2})$ [32]	n	$n \leq k$	3	0
MDC-4	$O(2^{n/4})$ [32]	n	$n \leq k$	4	0
Naito	$O(2^n)$ [35]	$k-n$	$2n \leq k$	2	2
Hirose-Kuwakado	$O(2^{\min\{n,k/2\}})$ [22,24]	n	$n < k$	2	2
MDPH	$O(2^n/n)$ [Ours]	$k-n$	$n < k$	2	0

ciphers are supported) but does not achieve optimal indifferentiable security. Naito's DBL hash function achieves optimal indifferentiable security but requires two additional block cipher calls by the post-processing function and does not support block ciphers with $k < 2n$. Hirose-Kuwakado's DBL hash functions achieve optimal indifferentiable security when $k \geq 2n$, but requires two additional block cipher calls by the post-processing function, and does not achieve optimal indifferentiable security when $k < 2n$. MDPH achieves (nearly) optimal indifferentiable security when $n < k$, and does not require the post-processing functions, thus has better efficiency.

Finally, open problems from this paper are given below.

- MDPH does not support block ciphers with $k = n$, and thus designing an optimally indifferentiable secure DBL hash function with $k = n$ is an open problem.
- As the key length becomes shorter, the message block length of MDPH becomes shorter, and thus the number of block cipher calls is increased. Hence, designing an optimal indifferentiable secure DBL hash function without such efficiency degradation is an open problem.

1.3   More Related Works

Lucks [29] introduced a DBL compression function that achieves (nearly) optimal collision security in the iteration, where the message block length is $2n$ bits when using a block cipher with $k = 2n$ and for each message block, a block cipher is called once. Armknecht et al. [2] proved that Abreast-DM, Tandem-DM and Hirose's compression function achieve optimal preimage security (security up to $O(2^{2n})$ query complexity). Abed et al. [1] proposed multi-block-length compression functions with optimal collision and preimage security. Note that these results do not consider indifferentiability.

1.4 Organization

The rest of the paper is organized as follows. After introducing notations and indifferentiability in Sect. 2, we give a specification of MDPH and the indifferentiable security bound in Sect. 3, and the security proof in Sect. 4.

2 Preliminaries

2.1 Notations

Let $\{0,1\}^*$ be the set of all bit strings. Let ε be an empty string. For an integer $n \geq 0$, $\{0,1\}^n$ be the set of all n-bit strings, and $(\{0,1\}^n)^*$ be the set of all strings whose bit lengths are multiples of m. For a non-negative integer i, let $[i]$ be the set of non-negative integers equal to or less than i. For an ℓm-bit string M, we write its partition into m-bit strings as $M_1, M_2, \ldots, M_\ell \xleftarrow{m} M$. For positive integers r, s with $s \leq r$ and a r-bit string X, the most (resp. least) significant s bits of X is denoted by $[X]^s$ (resp. $[X]_s$). For a bit string Y, $X \leftarrow Y$ means that Y is assigned to X. $X \xleftarrow{\$} \mathcal{X}$ means that an element is sampled uniformly at random from a finite set $\mathcal{X}$ and is assigned to X. $\mathcal{Y} \leftarrow \mathcal{X}$ means that a finite set $\mathcal{X}$ is assigned to $\mathcal{Y}$, and $\mathcal{Y} \xleftarrow{\cup} \mathcal{X}$ means that $\mathcal{Y} \leftarrow \mathcal{X} \cup \mathcal{Y}$. For a positive integer a, $\mathsf{Func}(*, a)$ denotes the set of all functions from $\{0,1\}^*$ to $\{0,1\}^a$. For positive integers k and n, $\mathsf{BC}(k,n)$ denotes the set of all block ciphers with k-bit keys and n-bit blocks. Hence, for each $E \in \mathsf{BC}(k,n)$, $E : \{0,1\}^k \times \{0,1\}^n \to \{0,1\}^n$ is a set of permutations over $\{0,1\}^n$ indexed by a key in $\{0,1\}^k$. The decryption function of E is denoted by $D : \{0,1\}^k \times \{0,1\}^n \to \{0,1\}^n$. Though this paper, a block cipher with $n < k$ is used. For a positive integer i, let $\mathbf{i}_n$ be the n-bit representation of i, e.g., $\mathbf{1}_n = 0^{n-1}1$ and $\mathbf{2}_n = 0^{n-2}10$.

2.2 Indifferentiability from a Random Oracle

Let $\mathsf{H}^E : \{0,1\}^* \to \{0,1\}^{2n}$ be a (DBL) hash function using a block cipher $E \in \mathsf{BC}(k,n)$.

The indifferentiability of H^E from a random oracle is defined as follows. In this case, the underlying block cipher is assumed to be an ideal cipher. Here, a random oracle is defined as $\mathcal{RO} \xleftarrow{\$} \mathsf{Func}(*, 2n)$, and an ideal cipher is defined as $E \xleftarrow{\$} \mathsf{BC}(k,n)$. The security game considers indistinguishability between real and ideal worlds. In the real world, an adversary $\mathbf{A}$ interacts with the target hash function H^E and an ideal cipher (E, D). In the ideal world, for a simulator S with access to a random oracle $\mathcal{RO}$, an adversary $\mathbf{A}$ interacts with $\mathcal{RO}$ and S. After the interaction, $\mathbf{A}$ outputs a decision bit. An output of an adversary $\mathbf{A}$ with access to oracles $\mathcal{O}$ is denoted by $\mathbf{A}^{\mathcal{O}}$. For a simulator S, the advantage function of an adversary $\mathbf{A}$ is defined as

$$\mathsf{Adv}^{\mathsf{indiff}}_{\mathsf{H}, \mathcal{RO}, \mathsf{S}}(\mathbf{A}) = \Pr\left[E \xleftarrow{\$} \mathsf{BC}(k,n); \mathbf{A}^{\mathsf{H}^E, E, D} = 1\right]$$
$$- \Pr\left[\mathcal{RO} \xleftarrow{\$} \mathsf{Func}(*, 2n); \mathbf{A}^{\mathcal{RO}, \mathsf{S}^{\mathcal{RO}}} = 1\right].$$

Here, the probabilities are taken by taken over **A**, E, $\mathcal{RO}$, and S. Hence, the security goal of our target hash function is to prove that for any adversary **A**, there exists a simulator S such that the advantage function is upper-bounded by a negligible probability. Hereafter, H^E and $\mathcal{RO}$ are called hash oracles, queries to a hash oracle are called hash queries, (E, D) and S are called primitive oracles, and queries to $(E, D)/\mathsf{S}$ are called primitive queries. Queries to E resp. D are called encryption resp. decryption queries.

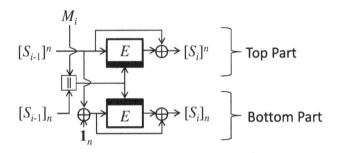

Fig. 1. Hirose compression function where $S_{i-1} \xrightarrow{M_i} S_i$.

3   MDPH: Specification and Indifferentiable Security Bound

In this section, MDPH, a combination of the MDP domain extender and Hirose's compression function, is defined, and the indifferentiable security bound of MDPH is given.

3.1   Specification

Let $m = k - n$. Let $E \in \mathsf{BC}(k, n)$ be a block cipher. The compression function $\mathsf{Hirose}^E : \{0, 1\}^{2n} \times \{0, 1\}^m \to \{0, 1\}^{2n}$ is defined as follows, and is illustrated in Fig. 1.

$\mathsf{Hirose}^E(S_{i-1}, M_i) = S_i$, where
$$[S_i]^n = E(M_i \| [S_{i-1}]_n, [S_{i-1}]^n) \oplus [S_{i-1}]^n \qquad \text{(Top Part)}$$
$$[S_i]_n = E(M_i \| [S_{i-1}]_n, [S_{i-1}]^n \oplus \mathbf{1}_n) \oplus [S_{i-1}]^n \oplus \mathbf{1}_n \qquad \text{(Bottom Part)}.$$

Next, $\mathsf{MDPH} : \{0, 1\}^* \to \{0, 1\}^{2n}$ is defined. Let $\mathsf{pad} : \{0, 1\}^* \to (\{0, 1\}^m)^*$ be an injective padding function, e.g., one-zero padding $\mathsf{pad}(M) = M \| 10^p$ where $p = m - 1 - |M| \mod m$. Then, $\mathsf{MDPH}^E(M) = H$ is defined as follows, and is illustrated in Fig. 2.

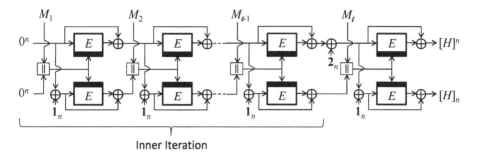

Fig. 2. MDPH^E.

1. $S_0 \leftarrow 0^{2n}$
2. $M_1, M_2, \cdots, M_\ell \overset{m}{\leftarrow} \mathrm{pad}(M)$
3. for $i = 1, \ldots, \ell - 1$ do $S_i \leftarrow \mathsf{Hirose}^E(S_{i-1}, M_i)$ $// \text{ Inner Iteration}$
4. $[S_{\ell-1}]^n \leftarrow [S_{\ell-1}]^n \oplus \mathbf{2}_n$
5. $H \leftarrow \mathsf{Hirose}^E(S_{\ell-1}, M_\ell)$

3.2   Indifferentiable Security Bound

The indifferentiable security bound of MDPH is given below, and the security proof is given in the next section (the overview of the security proof is given in the next subsection).

Theorem 1. *Let* **A** *be an adversary that makes q hash queries of σ message blocks in total and p primitive queries, and runs in time t. Let $Q = \sigma + p$ (the number of ideal cipher calls by all queries in the real world). Let μ be any positive integer. Then, there exists a simulator* S *such that*

$$\mathsf{Adv}^{\mathsf{indiff}}_{\mathsf{MDPH}, \mathcal{RO}, \mathsf{S}}(\mathbf{A}) \leq \frac{8\mu Q}{2^n - 2Q} + 3 \cdot 2^n \cdot \left(\frac{2eQ}{\mu(2^n - 2Q)} \right)^\mu,$$

where $e = 2.71828182846\ldots$ is Napier's constant. Here, S *makes at most p queries to $\mathcal{RO}$ and runs in time at most $t + O(p^2)$.*

Hereafter, the above upper-bound is studied.

– Putting $\mu = n$,

$$\mathsf{Adv}^{\mathsf{indiff}}_{\mathsf{MDPH}, \mathcal{RO}, \mathsf{S}}(\mathbf{A}) \leq \frac{8nQ}{2^n - 2Q} + 3 \cdot \left(\frac{4eQ}{n(2^n - 2Q)} \right)^n.$$

  The upper-bound ensures that MDPH is indifferentiable from a random oracle up to $O(2^n/n)$ query complexity.
– The case with $n = 128$, i.e., a 128-bit block cipher is considered. In this case, putting $\mu = 15$,

$$\mathsf{Adv}^{\mathsf{indiff}}_{\mathsf{MDPH}, \mathcal{RO}, \mathsf{S}}(\mathbf{A}) \leq \frac{120Q}{2^{128} - 2Q} + \left(\frac{148Q}{2^{128} - 2Q} \right)^{15}.$$

  The upper-bound is less than $1/2$ as long as $Q \leq 2^{119}$.

3.3 Overview of the Security Proof

In the security proof, we consider the indistinguishability between MDPH and a random oracle $\mathcal{RO}$, where the underlying block cipher is assumed to be an ideal cipher (i.e., an adversary has access to an ideal cipher). Hence, the difference between outputs of MDPH and of $\mathcal{RO}$ should carefully be handled, where an output of MDPH is defined by two ideal cipher calls and an output of $\mathcal{RO}$ is randomly chosen. In order to achieve optimal indifferentiable security, we need to prove the security so that the PRP-PRF switch term $Q^2/2^n$ that comes from the difference is not introduced.

The previous DBL hash functions, Naito's DBL hash function and Hirose-Kuwakado DBL hash function, in order to avoid introducing the PRP-PRF switch term, use a post-processing function that calls an ideal cipher twice where for each ideal cipher call, the input block is fixed to a constant value. Since an ideal cipher with a constant input block behave likes a random oracle, the PRP-PRF switch term can be avoided.

On the other hand, MDPH does not use the post-processing function. In order to avoid introducing the PRP-PRF switching term, we use the multi-collision technique that has been used in security proofs of many cryptographic algorithms including DBL hash functions such as [28,31,43]. In MDPH, the key elements at the last block are defined by the ideal cipher output on the bottom part at the second last block. This construction ensures that the number of ideal cipher outputs with the same key is upper-bounded by the number of the same ideal cipher outputs (more precisely, outputs of the Davies-Meyer mode), μ. Hence, the number of ideal cipher outputs with the same key at the last block is upper-bounded by μ (not Q), and by using the multi-collision technique, the first and second terms in Theorem 1 are introduced, instead of the PRP-PRF switch term $Q^2/2^n$. Note that by putting $\mu = Q$, the first term in Theorem 1 becomes the PRP-PRF switch term, but as shown the previous subsection, one can define the parameter as $\mu \ll Q$ and thus the PRP-PRF switch term can be avoided. Also note that the indifferentiability of MDPH is broken when a collision occurs for Hirose's compression function. By the birthday analysis, the collision probability is roughly $Q^2/2^{2n}$. The collision probability is incorporated into the first term in Theorem 1, as $Q^2/2^{2n} \leq Q/2^n$.

3.4 Remark

MDPH is a combination of existing schemes, the MDP domain extender and Hirose's compression function, and our proof is based on the existing technique (the multi-collision technique). Our contribution is to find a construction such that the multi-collision technique is used in order to avoid the PRP-PRF switching term. The construction is that the block cipher output on the bottom part at the second last block is input to the key elements at the last block.

4   Proof of Theorem 1

In this proof, for the sake of simplicity, an adversary $\mathbf{A}$ makes no repeated query, and a padding function pad in MDPH is omitted. Hence, an adversary $\mathbf{A}$ makes hash queries whose lengths are multiples of m. In this setting, $\mathbf{A}$ can select any padding rule, and thus the modification does not reduce the advantage of $\mathbf{A}$.

This proof consists of three games. Game 0 is the real world, Game 1 is defined later, and Game 2 is the ideal world. In each game, an adversary $\mathbf{A}$ interacts with three oracles (L, R_E, R_D). L is a hash oracle, and (R_E, R_D) are primitive oracles. In Game 0, $(L, R_E, R_D) = (\mathsf{H}^E, E, D)$ and in Game 1, $(L, R_E, R_D) = (\mathcal{RO}, \mathsf{S}_E^{\mathcal{RO}}, \mathsf{S}_D^{\mathcal{RO}})$, where $\mathsf{S}^{\mathcal{RO}} = (\mathsf{S}_E^{\mathcal{RO}}, \mathsf{S}_D^{\mathcal{RO}})$ is a simulator defined in Subsect. 4.2, and S_E resp. S_D simulates E resp. D.

4.1   Definitions

We denote an encryption query by $(K, X) \in \{0,1\}^k \times \{0,1\}^n$ and the response by $Y \in \{0,1\}^n$, and a decryption query by $(K, Y) \in \{0,1\}^k \times \{0,1\}^n$ and the response by $X \in \{0,1\}^n$. Hence, $Y = R_E(K, X)$ and $X = R_D(K, Y)$. Let $\mathcal{L}_{\mathsf{qr}}$ be a set of query-response triples (K, X, Y) of R_E or R_D.

Definition 1 (Block). *A block is a triple* (S_{i-1}, M_i, S_i) *which is obtained from* $\mathcal{L}_{\mathsf{qr}}$ *and satisfies the relation* $S_i = \mathsf{Hirose}^{R_E}(S_{i-1}, M_i)$. *The block is denoted by* $S_{i-1} \xrightarrow{M_i} S_i$ *(see Fig. 1).* $\mathcal{L}_{\mathsf{block}}$ *is a set of all blocks obtained from* $\mathcal{L}_{\mathsf{qr}}$.

Definition 2 (Path). *A path is a block or a concatenation of blocks which starts from the initial value* 0^{2n}. *For a sequence of blocks* $0^{2n} \xrightarrow{M_1} S_1, S_1 \xrightarrow{M_2} S_2, \ldots, S_{\ell-2} \xrightarrow{M_{\ell-1}} S_{\ell-1}$, *we denote the concatenation by* $0^{2n} \xrightarrow{M_1\|M_2\|\cdots\|M_{\ell-1}} S_{\ell-1}$. *Hence, the path represents the inner iteration of* MDPH^{R_E} *(See Fig. 2).* $\mathcal{L}_{\mathsf{path}}$ *is a set of all paths obtained from* $\mathcal{L}_{\mathsf{block}}$.

Definition 3. *For a path* $0^{2n} \xrightarrow{M'} S'$ *and a block* $S^* \xrightarrow{M^*} H$, *if there is a relation between the path and the block according to the* MDPH *structure, i.e.,* $[S']^n = [S^*]^n \oplus \mathbf{2}_n$ *and* $[S']_n = [S^*]_n$, *then the relation is denoted by* $S' \stackrel{2}{=} S^*$. *In this case,* $H = \mathsf{MDPH}^{R_E}(M'\|M^*)$.

4.2   Simulator

Next, simulator $\mathsf{S}^{\mathcal{RO}} = (\mathsf{S}_E^{\mathcal{RO}}, \mathsf{S}_D^{\mathcal{RO}})$ is defined, where $\mathsf{S}_E : \{0,1\}^k \times \{0,1\}^n \to \{0,1\}^n$ simulates an encryption oracle E, and $\mathsf{S}_D : \{0,1\}^k \times \{0,1\}^n \to \{0,1\}^n$ simulates a decryption oracle D. In the real world, for a hash query, the response is defined by using E via the MDPH structure, and thus the following is satisfied.

$$\forall \left(0^{2n} \xrightarrow{M'} S' \right) \in \mathcal{L}_{\mathsf{path}}, \left(S^* \xrightarrow{M^*} H \right) \in \mathcal{L}_{\mathsf{block}} \text{ s.t. } S' \stackrel{2}{=} S^* : L(M'\|M^*) = H. \tag{1}$$

Algorithm 1. Simulator $\mathsf{S}^{\mathcal{RO}} = (\mathsf{S}_E^{\mathcal{RO}}, \mathsf{S}_D^{\mathcal{RO}})$

Initialization

1: $\mathcal{T}_{path} \leftarrow \left\{ 0^{2n} \xrightarrow{\varepsilon} 0^{2n} \right\}$

Simulator $\mathsf{S}_E^{\mathcal{RO}}(K, X)$

1: **if** $\mathsf{E}(K, X) \neq \varepsilon$ **then return** $\mathsf{E}(K, X)$

2: **if** $\exists \left(0^{2n} \xrightarrow{M'} S' \right) \in \mathcal{T}_{path}$ s.t. $S' \stackrel{2}{=} (K, X)$ **then**

3:     $H \leftarrow \mathcal{RO}(M' \| [K]^m)$

4:     $Y_1 \leftarrow [H]^n \oplus X; Y_2 \leftarrow [H]_n \oplus X \oplus \mathbf{1}_n$

5:     **if** $Y_1 \in \mathsf{E}(K, *)$ or $Y_2 \in \mathsf{E}(K, *)$ or $Y_1 = Y_2$ **then** $\mathsf{Ecoll} \leftarrow \mathsf{true}$

6:     $\mathsf{E}(K, X) \leftarrow Y_1; \mathsf{E}(K, X \oplus \mathbf{1}_n) \leftarrow Y_2; \mathsf{D}(K, Y_1) \leftarrow X; \mathsf{D}(K, Y_2) \leftarrow X \oplus \mathbf{1}_n$

7: **end if**

8: **if** $\exists \left(0^{2n} \xrightarrow{M'} S' \right) \in \mathcal{T}_{path}$ s.t. $S' \stackrel{2}{=} (K, X \oplus \mathbf{1}_n)$ **then**

9:     $H \leftarrow \mathcal{RO}(M' \| [K]^m)$

10:    $Y_1 \leftarrow [H]^n \oplus X \oplus \mathbf{1}_n; Y_2 \leftarrow [H]_n \oplus X$

11:    **if** $Y_1 \in \mathsf{E}(K, *)$ or $Y_2 \in \mathsf{E}(K, *)$ or $Y_1 = Y_2$ **then** $\mathsf{Ecoll} \leftarrow \mathsf{true}$

12:    $\mathsf{E}(K, X \oplus \mathbf{1}_n) \leftarrow Y_1; \mathsf{E}(K, X) \leftarrow Y_2; \mathsf{D}(K, Y_1) \leftarrow X \oplus \mathbf{1}_n; \mathsf{D}(K, Y_2) \leftarrow X$

13: **end if**

14: **if** the above two conditions are not satisfied **then**

15:    $Y_1 \stackrel{\$}{\leftarrow} \{0,1\}^n \backslash \mathsf{E}(K, *); \mathsf{E}(K, X) \leftarrow Y_1; \mathsf{D}(K, Y_1) \leftarrow X$

16:    $Y_2 \stackrel{\$}{\leftarrow} \{0,1\}^n \backslash \mathsf{E}(K, *); \mathsf{E}(K, X \oplus \mathbf{1}_n) \leftarrow Y_2; \mathsf{D}(K, Y_2) \leftarrow X \oplus \mathbf{1}_n$

17: **end if**

18: run the subroutine $\mathsf{Update}(\mathcal{T}_{path}, (K, X, \mathsf{E}(K, X)), (K, X \oplus \mathbf{1}_n, \mathsf{E}(K, X \oplus \mathbf{1}_n)))$

19: **return** $\mathsf{E}(K, X)$

Simulator $\mathsf{S}_D^{\mathcal{RO}}(K, Y)$

1: **if** $\mathsf{D}(K, Y) \neq \varepsilon$ **then return** $\mathsf{D}(K, Y)$

2: $X \stackrel{\$}{\leftarrow} \{0,1\}^n \backslash \mathsf{D}(K, *); \mathsf{E}(K, X) \leftarrow Y$

3: $Y' \stackrel{\$}{\leftarrow} \{0,1\}^n \backslash \mathsf{E}(K, *); \mathsf{E}(K, X \oplus \mathbf{1}_n) \leftarrow Y'$

4: run the subroutine $\mathsf{Update}(\mathcal{T}_{path}, (K, X, \mathsf{E}(K, X)), (K, X \oplus \mathbf{1}_n, \mathsf{E}(K, X \oplus \mathbf{1}_n)))$

5: **return** $\mathsf{D}(K, Y)$

Subroutine $\mathsf{Update}(\mathcal{T}_{path}, (K, X, Y_1), (K, X \oplus \mathbf{1}_n, Y_2))$

1: Let $S^{(1)} \xrightarrow{M^*} S^{(2)}$ and $S^{(3)} \xrightarrow{M^*} S^{(4)}$ be the blocks defined from the triples (K, X, Y_1) and $(K, X \oplus \mathbf{1}_n, Y_2)$, i.e., $S^{(1)} = X \| [K]_n$, $S^{(2)} = (Y_1 \oplus X) \| (Y_2 \oplus X \oplus \mathbf{1}_n)$, $S^{(3)} = (X \oplus \mathbf{1}_n) \| [K]_n$, $S^{(4)} = (Y_2 \oplus X \oplus \mathbf{1}_n) \| (Y_1 \oplus X)$ and $M^* = [K]^m$

2: **for** $\forall \left(0^{2n} \xrightarrow{M'} S^{(1)} \right) \in \mathcal{T}_{path}$ **do** $\mathcal{T}_{path} \xleftarrow{\cup} \left(0^{2n} \xrightarrow{M' \| M^*} S^{(2)} \right)$

3: **for** $\forall \left(0^{2n} \xrightarrow{M'} S^{(3)} \right) \in \mathcal{T}_{path}$ **do** $\mathcal{T}_{path} \xleftarrow{\cup} \left(0^{2n} \xrightarrow{M' \| M^*} S^{(4)} \right)$

On the other hand, in the ideal world, for a hash query, the hash value is defined by a monolithic function $\mathcal{RO}$. Hence, the goal of simulator is to simulate an ideal cipher so that the query-responses of $\mathcal{RO}$ and of S satisfy the relation given in Eq. (1).

S is defined in Algorithm 1. S keeps query-response tripes in lists E and D whose entries are initially empty strings. If a query-response triple (K, X, Y) where $S_E(K, X) = Y$ or $S_D(K, Y) = X$ is defined, then Y is stored in $E(K, X)$ and X is stored in $D(K, Y)$, i.e., $E(K, X) = Y$ and $D(K, Y) = X$. S also keeps paths in $\mathcal{T}_{path}$ that are constructed from E and D. For $K \in \{0, 1\}^k$, let $E(K, *) = \{E(K, X) | X \in \{0, 1\}^n \wedge E(K, X) \neq \varepsilon\}$ resp. $D(K, *) = \{D(K, Y) | Y \in \{0, 1\}^n \wedge D(K, Y) \neq \varepsilon\}$ be a set of all entries associated with K in E resp. D. In order to ensure the relation in Eq. (1) in the ideal world, for an encryption query (K, X), if there exists a path $0^{2n} \xrightarrow{M'} S'$ in $\mathcal{T}_{path}$ to which the query connects, i.e., $S' = (X \oplus 2_n) \| [K]_n$ or $S' = (X \oplus 1_n \oplus 2_n) \| [K]_n$, then the response is defined by using $\mathcal{RO}$ (otherwise the response is defined by lazy sampling). Regarding the relation, we abuse the symbol "$\overset{2}{=}$" (although it appears in Definition 3): if $S' = (X \oplus 2_n) \| [K]_n$, then the relation is denoted by $S' \overset{2}{=} (K, X)$. For Hirose's compression function, when a top (resp., bottom) part is defined, the bottom (resp., top) part can immediately be defined. In addition, switching top and bottom parts, the result also has Hirose's structure. Hence, for each (encryption or decryption) query, two outputs corresponding with the top and bottom parts are defined, and two blocks are defined. The initialization procedure is performed before the first query by $\mathbf{A}$. In S, a flag Ecoll (initially false) is introduced, and is used in the following proof. Note that Ecoll = true means that a collision occurs in outputs of S with the same key, i.e., S fails to simulate an ideal cipher. $0^{2n} \overset{\varepsilon}{\rightarrow} 0^{2n}$ is an initial block such that for a block $0^{2n} \xrightarrow{M'} S'$, $0^{2n} \overset{\varepsilon}{\rightarrow} 0^{2n} \xrightarrow{M'} S'$ is regarded as $0^{2n} \xrightarrow{M'} S'$.

Regarding the number of queries from S to $\mathcal{RO}$, S makes a query to $\mathcal{RO}$ at most once for each primitive query. Hence, the number of queries to $\mathcal{RO}$ is at most p. Regarding the running time of S, for each query, Update is performed at most once and the number of other steps is a constant. Since $|\mathcal{T}_{path}| \leq 2p$ (two blocks are defined for each query), the running time is $t + O(p^2)$.

4.3 Outline of the Proof

We give an outline of the remaining proof. As mentioned above, this proof consists of three games, Game 0, Game 1 and Game 2. Let Gi be oracles in Game i. These oracles are defined as follows.

- Game 0: $G0 := (L, R_E, R_D) = (\text{MDPH}^E, E, D)$
- Game 1: $G1 := (L, R_E, R_D) = (\text{MDPH}^{S_E}, S_E^{\mathcal{RO}}, S_D^{\mathcal{RO}})$
- Game 2: $G2 := (L, R_E, R_D) = (\mathcal{RO}, S_E^{\mathcal{RO}}, S_D^{\mathcal{RO}})$

In Game 1, for each hash query, the response is defined by using S_E via the MDPH's structure. Then, we have

$$\text{Adv}_{\text{H},\mathcal{RO},\text{S}}^{\text{indiff}}(\mathbf{A}) = \left(\Pr[\mathbf{A}^{G0} = 1] - \Pr[\mathbf{A}^{G1} = 1] \right) + \left(\Pr[\mathbf{A}^{G1} = 1] - \Pr[\mathbf{A}^{G2} = 1] \right).$$

4.4   Upper-Bound of $\Pr[\mathbf{A}^{G0} = 1] - \Pr[\mathbf{A}^{G1} = 1]$

Let Ecoll_i be the event that Ecoll becomes true in Game i. Since outputs of $\mathcal{RO}$ are randomly drawn, a collision occurs in entries with the same keys of E. In other words, S behaves as an ideal cipher if and only if such collision does not occur, i.e., $\mathsf{Ecoll}_1 = \mathsf{false}$. Thus, we have

$$\Pr[\mathbf{A}^{G0} = 1] = \Pr[\mathbf{A}^{G1} = 1 | \neg\mathsf{Ecoll}_1].$$

This result gives

$$\Pr[\mathbf{A}^{G0} = 1] - \Pr[\mathbf{A}^{G1} = 1]$$
$$\leq \Pr[\mathbf{A}^{G0} = 1] - \left(\Pr[\mathbf{A}^{G1} = 1 \wedge \mathsf{Ecoll}_1] + \Pr[\mathbf{A}^{G1} = 1 | \neg\mathsf{Ecoll}_1] \cdot \Pr[\neg\mathsf{Ecoll}_1] \right)$$
$$\leq \Pr[\mathbf{A}^{G0} = 1] \cdot \left(1 - \Pr[\neg\mathsf{Ecoll}_1] \right)$$
$$\leq \Pr[\mathsf{Ecoll}_1],$$

and we have

$$\mathsf{Adv}^{\mathsf{indiff}}_{\mathsf{H},\mathcal{RO},\mathsf{S}}(\mathbf{A}) \leq \Pr[\mathsf{Ecoll}_1] + \left(\Pr[\mathbf{A}^{G1} = 1] - \Pr[\mathbf{A}^{G2} = 1] \right).$$

4.5   Upper-Bound of $\Pr[\mathbf{A}^{G1} = 1] - \Pr[\mathbf{A}^{G2} = 1]$

In this analysis, $\mathbf{A}$ is permitted to make additional encryption queries after finishing "normal" queries (q hash and p primitive queries) but before outputting a decision bit. There are two types of additional queries.

- The first type is that $\mathbf{A}$ can make queries to $R_E(= \mathsf{S}_E)$ according to the procedure of $\mathsf{MDPH}^{\mathsf{S}_E}(M)$ for all hash queries M, i.e., $\mathbf{A}$ can obtain all input-output triples of S_E to calculate $\mathsf{MDPH}^{\mathsf{S}_E}(M)$. Note that for some input-output triples that $\mathbf{A}$ has been obtained by normal queries, $\mathbf{A}$ does not make the additional queries corresponding with the input-output triples.
- The second type is that $\mathbf{A}$ can make queries to $R_E(= \mathsf{S}_E)$ whose partner according to Hirose's structure has been defined by a primitive query. More precisely, if $\mathbf{A}$ obtains a triple (K, X, Y) by a primitive query but does not obtain the partner $(K, X \oplus 1_n, Y')$, then $\mathbf{A}$ can make the additional encryption query $(K, X \oplus 1_n)$ and obtain the response Y'.

In this setting, $\mathbf{A}$ makes at most $2Q$ primitive queries. Note that the additional queries do not reduce the advantage of $\mathbf{A}$.

Let $\mathcal{T}_{block}$ be the set of the initial block $\left(0^{2n} \xrightarrow{\varepsilon} 0^{2n} \right)$ and all blocks obtained from the table E such that initially $\mathcal{T}_{block} = \left\{ 0^{2n} \xrightarrow{\varepsilon} 0^{2n} \right\}$. The following events are defined with respect to $\mathcal{T}_{block}$.

$$\text{hit} \Leftrightarrow \exists \left(S^{(1)} \xrightarrow{M'} S^{(2)}\right), \left(S^{(3)} \xrightarrow{M^*} S^{(4)}\right) \in \mathcal{T}_{block} \text{ s.t.}$$

$$\left(S^{(2)} = S^{(3)} \vee S^{(2)} \stackrel{\mathbf{2}}{=} S^{(3)}\right) \wedge$$

$$\left(S^{(3)} \xrightarrow{M^*} S^{(4)} \text{ is defined before } S^{(1)} \xrightarrow{M'} S^{(2)} \text{ is defined}\right.$$

$$\left. \vee S^{(1)} \xrightarrow{M'} S^{(2)} \text{ and } S^{(3)} \xrightarrow{M^*} S^{(4)} \text{ are defined by the same query}\right)$$

$$\text{Dhit} \Leftrightarrow \exists \left(S^{(1)} \xrightarrow{M'} S^{(2)}\right), \left(S^{(3)} \xrightarrow{M^*} S^{(4)}\right) \in \mathcal{T}_{block} \text{ s.t.}$$

$$\left(S^{(2)} \stackrel{\mathbf{2}}{=} S^{(3)}\right) \wedge \left(S^{(3)} \xrightarrow{M^*} S^{(4)} \text{ is defined by a decryption query}\right) \wedge$$

$$\left(S^{(1)} \xrightarrow{M'} S^{(2)} \text{ is defined before } S^{(3)} \xrightarrow{M^*} S^{(4)} \text{ is defined}\right)$$

$$\text{Bcoll} \Leftrightarrow \exists \left(S^{(1)} \xrightarrow{M'} S^{(2)}\right), \left(S^{(3)} \xrightarrow{M^*} S^{(4)}\right) \in \mathcal{T}_{block} \text{ s.t.}$$

$$\left(S^{(2)} = S^{(4)} \vee S^{(2)} \stackrel{\mathbf{2}}{=} S^{(4)}\right) \wedge \left((S^{(1)}, M') \neq (S^{(3)}, M^*)\right).$$

Note that if $S^{(2)} \xrightarrow{M^*} S^{(3)}$ and $S^{(1)} \xrightarrow{M'} S^{(2)}$ are defined by the same query, the top and bottom parts of the former block are switched in the latter block. Let hit_i be the event that hit occurs in Game i, Dhit_i the event that Dhit occurs in Game i, and Bcoll_i the event that Bcoll occurs in Game i. Let $\text{bad}_i := \text{hit}_i \vee \text{Dhit}_i \vee \text{Bcoll}_i$.

We next show that $\Pr[\mathbf{A}^{G1} = 1|\neg\text{bad}_1] = \Pr[\mathbf{A}^{G2} = 1|\neg\text{bad}_2]$ (Game 1 and Game 2 are indistinguishable as long as bad does not occur), i.e., the structural difference of L gives no advantage to $\mathbf{A}$. The difference is that $L = \text{MDPH}^{R_E}$ (Game 1) and $L = \mathcal{RO}$ (Game 2). Hence, we need to ensure the following two points.

1. In Game 1, for any hash query M, the response is equal to $\mathcal{RO}(M)$.
2. The additional queries to R_E in Game 1 and Game 2 do not reveal the structural difference of L. In Game 1, the additional queries are made by L for each hash query, whereas in Game 2, those are made according to $\text{MDPH}^{S_E}(M)$ for each hash query M after finishing normal queries.

To ensure these points, we show the following lemma. The lemma ensures that in Game 1, for any hash query M, $L(M) = \mathcal{RO}(M)$ (the first point is ensured), and the additional queries do not reveal the difference between Game 1 and Game 2 (the second point is ensured). Hence, we have

$$\Pr[\mathbf{A}^{G1} = 1|\neg\text{bad}_1] = \Pr[\mathbf{A}^{G2} = 1|\neg\text{bad}_2].$$

Lemma 1. *Assume that in Game i ($=1, 2$), bad_i does not occur. Then, in Game i,*

$$- \forall \left(0^{2n} \xrightarrow{M'} S'\right) \in \mathcal{L}_{\text{path}}, \left(S^* \xrightarrow{M'} H\right) \in \mathcal{L}_{\text{block}} \text{ s.t. } S' \stackrel{\mathbf{2}}{=} S^* :$$

1. *the query-response triples corresponding with* $\left(0^{2n} \xrightarrow{M'} S'\right)$ *are defined by lazy sampling, and*
2. $H = \mathcal{RO}(M' \| M^*)$.

Proof (Lemma 1). Let $0^{2n} \xrightarrow{\varepsilon} 0^{2n}$, $0^{2n} \xrightarrow{M'_1} S'_1$, $S'_1 \xrightarrow{M'_2} S'_2$, ..., $S'_{j-1} \xrightarrow{M'_j} S'_j$ be the blocks corresponding with the path $\left(0^{2n} \xrightarrow{M'} S'\right)$, i.e., the concatenation of the blocks is equal to the path and $S'_j = S'$. Let $S_0 = 0^{2n}$. Note that the block $0^{2n} \xrightarrow{\varepsilon} 0^{2n}$ is defined at first.

In Game i ($i = 1, 2$), by $\neg\mathsf{hit}_i$, firstly $0^{2n} \xrightarrow{\varepsilon} 0^{2n}$ is defined, secondly $0^{2n} \xrightarrow{M'_1} S'_1$ is defined, then for $i = 2, \ldots, j$ $S'_{i-1} \xrightarrow{M'_i} S'_i$ is defined, and finally $S^* \xrightarrow{M'} H$ is defined.

By $\neg\mathsf{Bcoll}_i$, for any path $0^{2n} \xrightarrow{M_1 \| \cdots \| M_i} S'_i$ from the initial block to the i-th block, there does not exist a distinct path $0^{2n} \xrightarrow{M^\dagger} S^\dagger$ such that $S^\dagger = S'_a$ or $S^\dagger \overset{2}{=} S'_a$.

The above two analysis ensure the followings.

1. For $\forall i \in [j-1]$, there does not exist a path $0^{2n} \xrightarrow{M^\dagger} S^\dagger$ such that $S^\dagger = S'_i$. Hence, the i-th block $S'_i \xrightarrow{M'_{i+1}} S'_{i+1}$ is defined by lazy sampling, and the first condition is satisfied.
2. Only the path $0^{2n} \xrightarrow{M'} S'$ is connected with the block $S^* \xrightarrow{M'} H$, i.e., $S' \overset{2}{=} S^*$, and the path is defined before the block is defined. In addition, by $\neg\mathsf{Dhit}_i$, the block $S^* \xrightarrow{M'} H$ is defined by an encryption query. Hence, H is defined by S_E so that $H = \mathcal{RO}(M' \| M^*)$, and the second condition is satisfied. $\square$

By $\Pr[\mathbf{A}^{G1} = 1 | \neg\mathsf{bad}_1] = \Pr[\mathbf{A}^{G2} = 1 | \neg\mathsf{bad}_2]$, we have

$$
\begin{aligned}
&\Pr[\mathbf{A}^{G1} = 1] - \Pr[\mathbf{A}^{G2} = 1] \\
&= \left(\Pr[\mathbf{A}^{G1} = 1 \wedge \mathsf{bad}_1] + \Pr[\mathbf{A}^{G1} = 1 \wedge \neg\mathsf{bad}_1] \right) \\
&\quad - \left(\Pr[\mathbf{A}^{G2} = 1 \wedge \mathsf{bad}_2] + \Pr[\mathbf{A}^{G2} = 1 \wedge \neg\mathsf{bad}_2] \right) \\
&= \left(\Pr[\mathbf{A}^{G1} = 1 | \mathsf{bad}_1] \cdot \Pr[\mathsf{bad}_1] + \Pr[\mathbf{A}^{G1} = 1 | \neg\mathsf{bad}_1] \cdot \Pr[\neg\mathsf{bad}_1] \right) \\
&\quad - \left(\Pr[\mathbf{A}^{G2} = 1 | \mathsf{bad}_2] \cdot \Pr[\mathsf{bad}_2] + \Pr[\mathbf{A}^{G2} = 1 | \neg\mathsf{bad}_2] \cdot \Pr[\neg\mathsf{bad}_2] \right) \\
&= \left(\Pr[\mathbf{A}^{G1} = 1 | \mathsf{bad}_1] - \Pr[\mathbf{A}^{G1} = 1 | \neg\mathsf{bad}_1] \right) \cdot \Pr[\mathsf{bad}_1] \\
&\quad + \left(\Pr[\mathbf{A}^{G2} = 1 | \neg\mathsf{bad}_2] - \Pr[\mathbf{A}^{G2} = 1 | \mathsf{bad}_2] \right) \cdot \Pr[\mathsf{bad}_2] \\
&\leq \Pr[\mathsf{bad}_1] + \Pr[\mathsf{bad}_2],
\end{aligned}
$$

and thus

$$\mathsf{Adv}^{\mathsf{indiff}}_{\mathsf{H},\mathcal{RO},\mathsf{S}}(\mathbf{A}) \leq \Pr[\mathsf{Ecoll}_1] + \Pr[\mathsf{bad}_1] + \Pr[\mathsf{bad}_2].$$

4.6   Upper-Bound of $\mathsf{Adv}^{\mathsf{indiff}}_{\mathsf{H},\mathcal{RO},\mathsf{S}}(\mathbf{A})$

First, the following multi-collision event is defined. Let μ be a positive integer and a free parameter.

$$\mathsf{mcoll}(\mu) \Leftrightarrow \exists\text{distinct pairs } (K_1, X_1), \dots, (K_\mu, X_\mu)$$
$$\text{s.t. } \mathsf{E}(K_1, X_1) \neq \varepsilon, \dots, \mathsf{E}(K_\mu, X_\mu) \neq \varepsilon$$
$$\wedge\, \mathsf{E}(K_1, X_1) \oplus X_1 = \dots = \mathsf{E}(K_\mu, X_\mu) \oplus X_\mu.$$

Let $\mathsf{mcoll}_i(\mu)$ be the event that $\mathsf{mcoll}(\mu)$ occurs in Game i. Then we have

$\mathsf{Adv}^{\mathsf{indiff}}_{\mathsf{H},\mathcal{RO},\mathsf{S}}(\mathbf{A})$
$\leq \Pr[\mathsf{Ecoll}_1] + \Pr[\mathsf{bad}_1] + \Pr[\mathsf{bad}_2]$
$\leq \Pr[\mathsf{Ecoll}_1|\neg\mathsf{mcoll}_1(\mu)] + \Pr[\mathsf{mcoll}_1(\mu)]$
$\quad + \Pr[\mathsf{hit}_1 \vee \mathsf{Dhit}_1 \vee \mathsf{Bcoll}_1] + \Pr[\mathsf{hit}_2 \vee \mathsf{Dhit}_2 \vee \mathsf{Bcoll}_2]$
$\leq \Pr[\mathsf{Ecoll}_1|\neg\mathsf{mcoll}_1(\mu)] + \Pr[\mathsf{mcoll}_1(\mu)] + \Pr[\mathsf{mcoll}_1(\mu)] + \Pr[\mathsf{mcoll}_2(\mu)]$
$\quad + \Pr[\mathsf{hit}_1] + \Pr[\mathsf{hit}_2] + \Pr[\mathsf{Dhit}_1|\neg\mathsf{mcoll}_1(\mu)] + \Pr[\mathsf{Dhit}_2|\neg\mathsf{mcoll}_2(\mu)]$
$\quad + \Pr[\mathsf{Bcoll}_1] + \Pr[\mathsf{Bcoll}_2].$

Hereafter, these probabilities are upper-bounded.

Upper-Bound of $\Pr[\mathsf{Ecoll}_1|\neg\mathsf{mcoll}_1(\mu)]$. The first two conditions in Ecoll_1: $Y_1 \in \mathsf{E}(K, *)$ and $Y_2 \in \mathsf{E}(K, *)$ are considered. Fixing an encryption query (K, X) such that the condition on Step 2 or Step 8 in S_E is satisfied, there exists a pair (K', X') such that $[K]_n = \mathsf{E}(K', X') \oplus X'$. By $\neg\mathsf{mcoll}_1(\mu)$, for each $K \in \{0,1\}^k$, the number of encryption queries with K such that the condition is satisfied is at most $\mu - 1$. That is, for each K, the number of chances that $Y_1 \in \mathsf{E}(K, *)$ or $Y_2 \in \mathsf{E}(K, *)$ is satisfied is at most $\mu - 1$, and for each chance, the probability that $Y_1 \in \mathsf{E}(K, *)$ or $Y_2 \in \mathsf{E}(K, *)$ is satisfied is at most $2|\mathsf{E}(K, *)|/2^n$. Since $\sum_{K \in \{0,1\}^k} |\mathsf{E}(K, *)| \leq 2Q$, the probability that for some encryption query, $Y_1 \in \mathsf{E}(K, *)$ or $Y_2 \in \mathsf{E}(K, *)$ is satisfied is at most

$$\sum_{K \in \{0,1\}^n} \frac{2(\mu - 1)|\mathsf{E}(K, *)|}{2^n} \leq \frac{4(\mu - 1)Q}{2^n}.$$

The third condition in Ecoll_1: $Y_1 = Y_2$ is considered. As Y_1 and Y_2 are randomly and independently drawn and the number of pairs (Y_1, Y_2) is at most Q, the probability that for some encryption query $Y_1 = Y_2$ is satisfied is at most $Q/2^n$.

Finally, we have

$$\Pr[\mathsf{Ecoll}_1 | \neg \mathsf{mcoll}_1(\mu)] \leq \frac{(4\mu - 3)Q}{2^n}.$$

Upper-Bounds of $\Pr[\mathsf{mcoll}_1(\mu)]$ and $\Pr[\mathsf{mcoll}_2(\mu)]$. First $\Pr[\mathsf{mcoll}_1(\mu)]$ is upper-bounded. Fix μ distinct pairs $(K_1, X_1), \ldots, (K_\mu, X_\mu)$ and an n-bit value W. Since for each i, either X_1 or $\mathsf{E}(K_1, X_1)$ is randomly drawn from at least $2^n - 2Q$ values, the probability that $\mathsf{E}(K_1, X_1) \oplus X_1 = \cdots = \mathsf{E}(K_\mu, X_\mu) \oplus X_\mu = W$ is at most $1/(2^n - 2Q)^\mu$. Hence, we have

$$\Pr[\mathsf{mcoll}_1(\mu)] \leq 2^n \cdot \binom{2Q}{\mu} \cdot \left(\frac{1}{2^n - 2Q}\right)^\mu \leq 2^n \cdot \left(\frac{2eQ}{\mu(2^n - 2Q)}\right)^\mu,$$

using Stirling's approximation $(x! \geq (x/e)^x$ for any $x)$.

$\Pr[\mathsf{mcoll}_2(\mu)]$ can be upper-bounded by the same analysis as the above one. Hence, we have

$$\Pr[\mathsf{mcoll}_2(\mu)] \leq 2^n \cdot \left(\frac{2eQ}{\mu(2^n - 2Q)}\right)^\mu.$$

Upper-Bounds of $\Pr[\mathsf{hit}_1]$ and $\Pr[\mathsf{hit}_2]$. First $\Pr[\mathsf{hit}_1]$ is upper-bounded. Fix two blocks $S^{(1)} \xrightarrow{M'} S^{(2)}$ and $S^{(3)} \xrightarrow{M^*} S^{(4)}$ where these blocks are defined by the same query or the former block is defined after the latter block is defined. $S^{(2)}$ is defined as follows.

$$[S^{(2)}]^n = \mathsf{E}(M' \| [S^{(1)}]_n, [S^{(1)}]^n) \oplus [S^{(1)}]^n \qquad \text{(top part)}$$

$$[S^{(2)}]_n = \mathsf{E}(M' \| [S^{(1)}]_n, [S^{(1)}]^n \oplus 1_n) \oplus [S^{(1)}]^n \oplus 1_n \qquad \text{(bottom part)}$$

Regarding the top part, either $\mathsf{E}(M' \| [S^{(1)}]_n, [S^{(1)}]^n)$ or $[S^{(1)}]^n$ is randomly drawn from at least $2^n - 2Q$ values. Regarding the bottom part, either $\mathsf{E}(M' \| [S^{(1)}]_n, [S^{(1)}]^n \oplus 1_n)$ or $([S^{(1)}]^n \oplus 1_n)$ is randomly drawn from at least $2^n - 2Q$ values. Hence, the probability that $S^{(2)} = S^{(3)} \vee S^{(2)} \overset{2}{=} S^{(3)}$ is at most $2/(2^n - 2Q)^2$. Since the number of blocks is at most $2Q$, we have

$$\Pr[\mathsf{hit}_1] \leq (2Q)^2 \cdot \frac{2}{(2^n - 2Q)^2} \leq \frac{8Q^2}{(2^n - 2Q)^2}.$$

$\Pr[\mathsf{hit}_2]$ can be upper-bounded by the same analysis as the above one. Hence, we have

$$\Pr[\mathsf{hit}_2] \leq \frac{8Q^2}{(2^n - 2Q)^2}.$$

Upper-Bounds of $\Pr[\mathsf{Dhit}_1|\neg\mathsf{mcoll}_1(\mu)]$ and $\Pr[\mathsf{Dhit}_2|\neg\mathsf{mcoll}_2(\mu)]$. First, $\Pr[\mathsf{Dhit}_1|\neg\mathsf{mcoll}_1(\mu)]$ is upper-bounded. Fix a block $S^{(3)} \xrightarrow{M^*} S^{(4)}$ that is defined by a decryption query. By $\neg\mathsf{mcoll}_1(\mu)$, the number of blocks $S^{(1)} \xrightarrow{M'} S^{(2)}$ that have been defined such that $[S^{(2)}]_n = [S^{(3)}]_n$ is at most $\mu - 1$. Since $[S^{(3)}]^n = D(M^* \| [S^{(3)}]_n, [S^{(3)}]^n \oplus [S^{(4)}]^n)$ is randomly drawn from at least $2^n - 2Q$ values, the probability that Dhit_1 occurs due to the block $S^{(3)} \xrightarrow{M^*} S^{(4)}$ is at most $(\mu - 1)/(2^n - 2Q)$. Since there are at most $2Q$ blocks, we have

$$\Pr[\mathsf{Dhit}_1|\neg\mathsf{mcoll}_1(\mu)] \leq \frac{2(\mu - 1)Q}{2^n - 2Q}.$$

$\Pr[\mathsf{Dhit}_2|\neg\mathsf{mcoll}_2(\mu)]$ can be upper-bounded by the same analysis as the above one. Hence, we have

$$\Pr[\mathsf{Dhit}_2|\neg\mathsf{mcoll}_2(\mu)] \leq \frac{2(\mu - 1)Q}{2^n - 2Q}.$$

Upper-Bounds of $\Pr[\mathsf{Bcoll}_1]$ and $\Pr[\mathsf{Bcoll}_2]$. First $\Pr[\mathsf{Bcoll}_1]$ is upper-bounded. Fix two distinct blocks $S^{(1)} \xrightarrow{M'} S^{(2)}$ and $S^{(3)} \xrightarrow{M^*} S^{(4)}$, and upper-bound the probability that $S^{(2)} = S^{(4)}$ or $S^{(2)} \overset{2}{=} S^{(4)}$. The following cases are considered.

- The first case is that $\left([S^{(1)}]^n = [S^{(3)}]^n \oplus \mathbf{1}_n\right) \wedge \left([S^{(1)}]_n = [S^{(3)}]_n\right) \wedge \left(M' = M^*\right)$ ($S^{(1)} \xrightarrow{M'} S^{(2)}$ and $S^{(3)} \xrightarrow{M^*} S^{(4)}$ are defined by the same query and the top and bottom parts of the former block are switched in the latter blocks). In this case, $S^{(2)} \overset{2}{=} S^{(4)}$ is not satisfied, and thus the probability that $S^{(2)} = S^{(4)}$ is satisfied is considered. $S^{(2)} = S^{(4)}$ implies $[S^{(2)}]^n = [S^{(2)}]_n$, i.e.,

$$E(M'\|[S^{(1)}]_n, [S^{(1)}]^n) \oplus [S^{(1)}]^n = E(M'\|[S^{(1)}]_n, [S^{(1)}]^n \oplus \mathbf{1}_n) \oplus [S^{(1)}]^n \oplus \mathbf{1}_n.$$

Since $E(M'\|[S^{(1)}]_n, [S^{(1)}]^n)$ or $E(M'\|[S^{(1)}]_n, [S^{(1)}]^n \oplus \mathbf{1}_n)$ is randomly drawn from at least $2^n - 2Q$ values, the probability that $S^{(2)} = S^{(4)}$ is satisfied is at most $1/(2^n - 2Q)$.

- The second case is that $\left([S^{(1)}]^n \neq [S^{(3)}]^n \oplus \mathbf{1}_n\right) \vee \left([S^{(1)}]_n \neq [S^{(3)}]_n\right) \vee \left(M' \neq M^*\right)$ ($S^{(1)} \xrightarrow{M'} S^{(2)}$ and $S^{(3)} \xrightarrow{M^*} S^{(4)}$ are defined by distinct queries). In this case, $S^{(2)} = S^{(4)}$ implies

$$E(M'\|[S^{(1)}]_n, [S^{(1)}]^n) \oplus [S^{(1)}]^n = E(M^*\|[S^{(3)}]_n, [S^{(3)}]^n) \oplus [S^{(3)}]^n$$
$$E(M'\|[S^{(1)}]_n, [S^{(1)}]^n \oplus \mathbf{1}_n) \oplus [S^{(1)}]^n \oplus \mathbf{1}_n,$$
$$= E(M^*\|[S^{(3)}]_n, [S^{(3)}]^n \oplus \mathbf{1}_n) \oplus [S^{(3)}]^n \oplus \mathbf{1}_n,$$

where for $i = 1, 3$, either $\mathsf{E}(M' \| [S^{(i)}]_n, [S^{(i)}]^n)$ or $[S^{(i)}]^n$ is randomly drawn from at least $2^n - 2Q$ values, and either $\mathsf{E}(M' \| [S^{(i)}]_n, [S^{(i)}]^n \oplus \mathbf{1}_n)$ or $([S^{(i)}]^n \oplus \mathbf{1}_n)$ is randomly drawn from at least $2^n - 2Q$ values. In this case, these values are independently drawn, since the blocks are defined by distinct queries. Hence, the probability that $S^{(2)} = S^{(4)}$ is at most $1/(2^n - 2Q)^2$. Similarly, the probability that $S^{(2)} \overset{2}{=} S^{(4)}$ is at most $1/(2^n - 2Q)^2$.

The numbers of chances are at most Q for the first case, and at most $\binom{2Q}{2}$ for the second case. Hence, we have

$$\Pr[\mathsf{Bcoll}_1] \leq \frac{Q}{2^n - 2Q} + \binom{2Q}{2} \cdot \frac{2}{(2^n - 2Q)^2} \leq \frac{Q}{2^n - 2Q} + \frac{4Q^2}{(2^n - 2Q)^2}.$$

$\Pr[\mathsf{Bcoll}_2]$ can be upper-bounded by the same analysis as the above one. Hence, we have

$$\Pr[\mathsf{Bcoll}_2] \leq \frac{Q}{2^n - 2Q} + \frac{4Q^2}{(2^n - 2Q)^2}.$$

Summing the Upper-Bounds. Finally, the above upper-bounds give

$$\begin{aligned}
\mathsf{Adv}_{\mathsf{H}, \mathcal{RO}, \mathsf{S}}^{\mathrm{indiff}}(\mathbf{A}) &\leq \frac{(4\mu - 3)Q}{2^n - 2Q} + 3 \cdot 2^n \cdot \left(\frac{2eQ}{\mu(2^n - 2Q)}\right)^\mu \\
&\quad + \frac{16Q^2}{(2^n - 2Q)^2} + \frac{4(\mu - 1)Q}{2^n} + \frac{2Q}{2^n - 2Q} + \frac{8Q^2}{(2^n - 2Q)^2} \\
&\leq \frac{24Q^2}{(2^n - 2Q)^2} + \frac{8\mu Q}{2^n - 2Q} - \frac{5Q}{2^n - 2Q} + 3 \cdot 2^n \cdot \left(\frac{2eQ}{\mu(2^n - 2Q)}\right)^\mu \\
&\leq \frac{24Q^2}{(2^n - 2Q)^2} + \frac{8\mu Q}{2^n - 2Q} - \frac{25Q^2}{(2^n - 2Q)^2} + 3 \cdot 2^n \cdot \left(\frac{2eQ}{\mu(2^n - 2Q)}\right)^\mu \\
&\leq \frac{8\mu Q}{2^n - 2Q} + 3 \cdot 2^n \cdot \left(\frac{2eQ}{\mu(2^n - 2Q)}\right)^\mu.
\end{aligned}$$

References

1. Abed, F., Forler, C., List, E., Lucks, S., Wenzel, J.: Counter-bDM: a provably secure family of multi-block-length compression functions. In: Pointcheval, D., Vergnaud, D. (eds.) AFRICACRYPT 2014. LNCS, vol. 8469, pp. 440–458. Springer, Cham (2014). https://doi.org/10.1007/978-3-319-06734-6_26
2. Armknecht, F., Fleischmann, E., Krause, M., Lee, J., Stam, M., Steinberger, J.: The preimage security of double-block-length compression functions. In: Lee, D.H., Wang, X. (eds.) ASIACRYPT 2011. LNCS, vol. 7073, pp. 233–251. Springer, Heidelberg (2011). https://doi.org/10.1007/978-3-642-25385-0_13
3. Aumasson, J.-P., Henzen, L., Meier, W., Naya-Plasencia, M.: QUARK: a lightweight hash. In: Mangard, S., Standaert, F.-X. (eds.) CHES 2010. LNCS, vol. 6225, pp. 1–15. Springer, Heidelberg (2010). https://doi.org/10.1007/978-3-642-15031-9_1

4. Banik, S., Pandey, S.K., Peyrin, T., Sasaki, Y., Sim, S.M., Todo, Y.: GIFT: a small present - towards reaching the limit of lightweight encryption. In: CHES 2017. LNCS, vol. 10529, pp. 321–345. Springer (2017). https://doi.org/10.1007/978-3-319-66787-4_16

5. Beierle, C., et al.: The SKINNY family of block ciphers and its low-latency variant MANTIS. In: Robshaw, M., Katz, J. (eds.) CRYPTO 2016. LNCS, vol. 9815, pp. 123–153. Springer, Heidelberg (2016). https://doi.org/10.1007/978-3-662-53008-5_5

6. Bellare, M., Ristenpart, T.: Multi-property-preserving hash domain extension and the EMD transform. In: Lai, X., Chen, K. (eds.) ASIACRYPT 2006. LNCS, vol. 4284, pp. 299–314. Springer, Heidelberg (2006). https://doi.org/10.1007/11935230_20

7. Bertoni, G., Daemen, J., Peeters, M., Assche, G.V.: Sponge Functions. In: Ecrypt Hash Workshop 2007 (2007)

8. Bertoni, G., Daemen, J., Peeters, M., Van Assche, G.: On the indifferentiability of the sponge construction. In: Smart, N. (ed.) EUROCRYPT 2008. LNCS, vol. 4965, pp. 181–197. Springer, Heidelberg (2008). https://doi.org/10.1007/978-3-540-78967-3_11

9. Bertoni, G., Daemen, J., Peeters, M., Van Assche, G.: Keccak. In: Johansson, T., Nguyen, P.Q. (eds.) EUROCRYPT 2013. LNCS, vol. 7881, pp. 313–314. Springer, Heidelberg (2013). https://doi.org/10.1007/978-3-642-38348-9_19

10. Bogdanov, A., Knežević, M., Leander, G., Toz, D., Varıcı, K., Verbauwhede, I.: SPONGENT: a lightweight hash function. In: Preneel, B., Takagi, T. (eds.) CHES 2011. LNCS, vol. 6917, pp. 312–325. Springer, Heidelberg (2011). https://doi.org/10.1007/978-3-642-23951-9_21

11. Bogdanov, A., et al.: PRESENT: an ultra-lightweight block cipher. In: Paillier, P., Verbauwhede, I. (eds.) CHES 2007. LNCS, vol. 4727, pp. 450–466. Springer, Heidelberg (2007). https://doi.org/10.1007/978-3-540-74735-2_31

12. Borghoff, J., et al.: PRINCE – a low-latency block cipher for pervasive computing applications. In: Wang, X., Sako, K. (eds.) ASIACRYPT 2012. LNCS, vol. 7658, pp. 208–225. Springer, Heidelberg (2012). https://doi.org/10.1007/978-3-642-34961-4_14

13. Chang, D., Lee, S., Nandi, M., Yung, M.: Indifferentiable security analysis of popular hash functions with prefix-free padding. In: Lai, X., Chen, K. (eds.) ASIACRYPT 2006. LNCS, vol. 4284, pp. 283–298. Springer, Heidelberg (2006). https://doi.org/10.1007/11935230_19

14. Coron, J.-S., Dodis, Y., Malinaud, C., Puniya, P.: Merkle-Damgård revisited: how to construct a hash function. In: Shoup, V. (ed.) CRYPTO 2005. LNCS, vol. 3621, pp. 430–448. Springer, Heidelberg (2005). https://doi.org/10.1007/11535218_26

15. Damgård, I.B.: A design principle for hash functions. In: Brassard, G. (ed.) CRYPTO 1989. LNCS, vol. 435, pp. 416–427. Springer, New York (1990). https://doi.org/10.1007/0-387-34805-0_39

16. Fleischmann, E., Forler, C., Gorski, M., Lucks, S.: Collision resistant double-length hashing. In: Heng, S.-H., Kurosawa, K. (eds.) ProvSec 2010. LNCS, vol. 6402, pp. 102–118. Springer, Heidelberg (2010). https://doi.org/10.1007/978-3-642-16280-0_7

17. Fleischmann, E., Forler, C., Lucks, S., Wenzel, J.: Weimar-DM: a highly secure double-length compression function. In: Susilo, W., Mu, Y., Seberry, J. (eds.) ACISP 2012. LNCS, vol. 7372, pp. 152–165. Springer, Heidelberg (2012). https://doi.org/10.1007/978-3-642-31448-3_12

18. Gong, Z., Lai, X., Chen, K.: A synthetic indifferentiability analysis of some block-cipher-based hash functions. Des. Codes Cryptogr. **48**(3), 293–305 (2008)

19. Guo, J., Peyrin, T., Poschmann, A., Robshaw, M.: The LED block cipher. In: Preneel, B., Takagi, T. (eds.) CHES 2011. LNCS, vol. 6917, pp. 326–341. Springer, Heidelberg (2011). https://doi.org/10.1007/978-3-642-23951-9_22

20. Hirose, S.: Provably secure double-block-length hash functions in a black-box model. In: Park, C., Chee, S. (eds.) ICISC 2004. LNCS, vol. 3506, pp. 330–342. Springer, Heidelberg (2005). https://doi.org/10.1007/11496618_24

21. Hirose, S.: Some plausible constructions of double-block-length hash functions. In: Robshaw, M. (ed.) FSE 2006. LNCS, vol. 4047, pp. 210–225. Springer, Heidelberg (2006). https://doi.org/10.1007/11799313_14

22. Hirose, S., Kuwakado, H.: A block-cipher-based hash function using an MMO-type double-block compression function. In: Chow, S.S.M., Liu, J.K., Hui, L.C.K., Yiu, S.M. (eds.) ProvSec 2014. LNCS, vol. 8782, pp. 71–86. Springer, Cham (2014). https://doi.org/10.1007/978-3-319-12475-9_6

23. Hirose, S., Park, J.H., Yun, A.: A simple variant of the Merkle-Damgård scheme with a permutation. In: Kurosawa, K. (ed.) ASIACRYPT 2007. LNCS, vol. 4833, pp. 113–129. Springer, Heidelberg (2007). https://doi.org/10.1007/978-3-540-76900-2_7

24. Kuwakado, H., Hirose, S.: Hashing mode using a lightweight blockcipher. In: Stam, M. (ed.) IMACC 2013. LNCS, vol. 8308, pp. 213–231. Springer, Heidelberg (2013). https://doi.org/10.1007/978-3-642-45239-0_13

25. Lai, X., Massey, J.L.: Hash functions based on block ciphers. In: Rueppel, R.A. (ed.) EUROCRYPT 1992. LNCS, vol. 658, pp. 55–70. Springer, Heidelberg (1993). https://doi.org/10.1007/3-540-47555-9_5

26. Lee, J., Kwon, D.: The security of Abreast-DM in the ideal cipher model. IEICE Trans. **94-A**(1), 104–109 (2011)

27. Lee, J., Stam, M.: MJH: a faster alternative to MDC-2. In: Kiayias, A. (ed.) CT-RSA 2011. LNCS, vol. 6558, pp. 213–236. Springer, Heidelberg (2011). https://doi.org/10.1007/978-3-642-19074-2_15

28. Lee, J., Stam, M., Steinberger, J.: The collision security of Tandem-DM in the ideal cipher model. In: Rogaway, P. (ed.) CRYPTO 2011. LNCS, vol. 6841, pp. 561–577. Springer, Heidelberg (2011). https://doi.org/10.1007/978-3-642-22792-9_32

29. Lucks, S.: A collision-resistant rate-1 double-block-length hash function. In: Symmetric Cryptography, Dagstuhl Seminar Proceedings, vol. 07021 (2007)

30. Maurer, U., Renner, R., Holenstein, C.: Indifferentiability, impossibility results on reductions, and applications to the random oracle methodology. In: Naor, M. (ed.) TCC 2004. LNCS, vol. 2951, pp. 21–39. Springer, Heidelberg (2004). https://doi.org/10.1007/978-3-540-24638-1_2

31. Mennink, B.: Optimal collision security in double block length hashing with single length key. In: Wang, X., Sako, K. (eds.) ASIACRYPT 2012. LNCS, vol. 7658, pp. 526–543. Springer, Heidelberg (2012). https://doi.org/10.1007/978-3-642-34961-4_32

32. Mennink, B.: Indifferentiability of double length compression functions. In: Stam, M. (ed.) IMACC 2013. LNCS, vol. 8308, pp. 232–251. Springer, Heidelberg (2013). https://doi.org/10.1007/978-3-642-45239-0_14

33. Merkle, R.C.: One way hash functions and DES. In: Brassard, G. (ed.) CRYPTO 1989. LNCS, vol. 435, pp. 428–446. Springer, New York (1990). https://doi.org/10.1007/0-387-34805-0_40

34. Meyer, C., Matyas, S.: Secure program load with manipulation detection code. In: SECURICOM, pp. 111–130 (1988)

35. Naito, Y.: Blockcipher-based double-length hash functions for pseudorandom oracles. In: Miri, A., Vaudenay, S. (eds.) SAC 2011. LNCS, vol. 7118, pp. 338–355. Springer, Heidelberg (2012). https://doi.org/10.1007/978-3-642-28496-0_20

36. NIST: SHA-3 Standard: Permutation-Based Hash and Extendable-Output Functions. FIPS PUB 202 (2015)

37. Özen, O., Stam, M.: Another glance at double-length hashing. In: Parker, M.G. (ed.) IMACC 2009. LNCS, vol. 5921, pp. 176–201. Springer, Heidelberg (2009). https://doi.org/10.1007/978-3-642-10868-6_11

38. Preneel, B., Bosselaers, A., Govaerts, R., Vandewalle, J.: Collision-free hash-functions based on blockcipher algorithms. In: Proceedings of 1989 International Carnahan Conference on Security Technology, pp. 203–210 (1989)

39. Preneel, B., Govaerts, R., Vandewalle, J.: Hash functions based on block ciphers: a synthetic approach. In: Stinson, D.R. (ed.) CRYPTO 1993. LNCS, vol. 773, pp. 368–378. Springer, Heidelberg (1994). https://doi.org/10.1007/3-540-48329-2_31

40. Shibutani, K., Isobe, T., Hiwatari, H., Mitsuda, A., Akishita, T., Shirai, T.: *Piccolo*: an ultra-lightweight blockcipher. In: Preneel, B., Takagi, T. (eds.) CHES 2011. LNCS, vol. 6917, pp. 342–357. Springer, Heidelberg (2011). https://doi.org/10.1007/978-3-642-23951-9_23

41. Shirai, T., Shibutani, K., Akishita, T., Moriai, S., Iwata, T.: The 128-bit blockcipher CLEFIA (extended abstract). In: Biryukov, A. (ed.) FSE 2007. LNCS, vol. 4593, pp. 181–195. Springer, Heidelberg (2007). https://doi.org/10.1007/978-3-540-74619-5_12

42. Stam, M.: Blockcipher-based hashing revisited. In: Dunkelman, O. (ed.) FSE 2009. LNCS, vol. 5665, pp. 67–83. Springer, Heidelberg (2009). https://doi.org/10.1007/978-3-642-03317-9_5

43. Steinberger, J.P.: The collision intractability of MDC-2 in the ideal-cipher model. In: Naor, M. (ed.) EUROCRYPT 2007. LNCS, vol. 4515, pp. 34–51. Springer, Heidelberg (2007). https://doi.org/10.1007/978-3-540-72540-4_3

44. Suzaki, T., Minematsu, K., Morioka, S., Kobayashi, E.: *TWINE*: a lightweight block cipher for multiple platforms. In: Knudsen, L.R., Wu, H. (eds.) SAC 2012. LNCS, vol. 7707, pp. 339–354. Springer, Heidelberg (2013). https://doi.org/10.1007/978-3-642-35999-6_22

On the Fast Algebraic Immunity
of Majority Functions

Pierrick Méaux[✉]

ICTEAM/ELEN/Crypto Group, Université catholique de Louvain,
Ottignies-Louvain-la-Neuve, Belgium
pierrick.meaux@uclouvain.be

Abstract. In different contexts such as filtered LFSR, Goldreich's PRG, and FLIP stream ciphers, the security of a cryptographic primitive mostly depends on the algebraic properties of one Boolean function. Since the Seventies, more and more efficient attacks have been exhibited in this context, related to more and more general algebraic properties, such as the degree, the algebraic immunity, and finally, the fast algebraic immunity. Once the properties to estimate the attack complexities are identified, it remains to determine the exact parameters of interesting family of functions with these properties. Then, these functions can be combined in secondary constructions to guarantee the good algebraic properties of a main function. In particular, the family of symmetric functions, and more precisely the subclass of majority functions, has been intensively studied in the area of cryptography, because of their practical advantages and good properties.

The degree of all these functions is known, and they have been proven to reach the optimal algebraic immunity, but still very few is known relatively to its fast algebraic immunity. For a function in $n = 2^m + j$ variables, an upper bound is known for all m and j, proving that these functions do not reach the optimal fast algebraic immunity. However, the exact fast algebraic immunity is known only for very few families indexed by j, where the parameter is exhibited for all members of the family since m is big enough. Recent works gave exact values for $j = 0$ and $j = 1$ (in the first case), and for $j = 2$ and $j = 3$ with $m \geq 2$ (in the second case). In this work, we determine the exact fast algebraic immunity for all possible values of j, for all member of the family assuming $m \geq 1 + \log_2(j + 1)$.

Keywords: Boolean functions · Fast algebraic attacks ·
Symmetric functions · Majority functions

1 Introduction

1.1 Cryptographic Primitives with Security Determined
by the Algebraic Properties of One Boolean Function

For some constructions, the security of a cryptographic primitive mostly depends on the algebraic properties of one Boolean function. This strong connection

© Springer Nature Switzerland AG 2019
P. Schwabe and N. Thériault (Eds.): LATINCRYPT 2019, LNCS 11774, pp. 86–105, 2019.
https://doi.org/10.1007/978-3-030-30530-7_5

between security and algebraic properties happens when two conditions hold. First, the primitive has a simple structure where the non-linear part is provided by an unique Boolean function. Second, an adversary is only able to obtain a system of equations as the output of this function (non iterated). The typical example of such context relates to stream-cipher encryption schemes, more particularly to the family of designs called (combined) filtered Linear Feedback Shift Register (LFSR) (*e.g.* [32]). This design is characterized by the combination of linear components applying on the secret key, which output is filtered by a Boolean function of degree at least two, generating the key-stream. An adversary can have access to the key-stream (this corresponds to the known plaintext-ciphertext pairs model) and build the corresponding algebraic system. Solving this system gives the secret variables, *i.e.* the secret key, directly breaking the security (as it enables to decrypt any message encrypted with this key).

Other examples of constructions for which the security mostly depends on the algebraic properties of a Boolean functions are given by the family of stream-ciphers FLIP [29], and the local PseudoRandom Generators (PRG) following the blueprint of Goldreich's PRG [21]. The first example is a recent design of symmetric encryption scheme which goal is to facilitate the use of Fully Homomorphic Encryption [20] for outsourcing computation. In this construction, for each produced key-stream bit, a public reordering of the key-bits is performed, and a fixed Boolean function is applied. The second example relates to cryptographic primitives that can exist in low-complexity classes such as NC0, and these PRG have been the focus of many attentions lastly. These are considered as potential building blocks for indistinguishability obfuscation [1,24,25]. For these PRG, each output is the result of a fixed Boolean function applied on a subpart of the seed, the subpart being publicly determined. In these two cases (as for filtered LFSR), an adversary can build an algebraic system of equation in the secret variables, from the main function only, and attacks solving these algebraic systems are amongst the most efficient against those primitives.

Many algorithms are known to solve algebraic systems of equations, one of the most efficient being based on Grobner bases such as F5 [19]. The algorithms based on linearization techniques are generally less efficient but with easier to determine time and data complexities. For these algorithms and corresponding attacks, the complexities can be determined only based on algebraic criteria on the Boolean function. The first attack known to apply on the constructions we listed is an attack based on the algebraic degree of the function, that we note d. Indeed, as all the equations of algebraic system have this degree, it is possible for the attacker to rewrite any monomial of degree at most d in a new variable. Then, it corresponds to a linear system in at most $D = \sum_{i=0}^{d} \binom{n}{d}$ variables, where we note n the number of secret variables. Finally, solving such linear system can be performed in time complexity $O(D^{\omega})$ (where ω is the exponent in linear system inversion, such as $\omega = 2.807$ for Strassen's algorithm, and 2.373 for the latest results), giving the cost of these attacks.

A simpler system may be obtained by considering algebraic properties of the function other than its degree. Calling f the Boolean function giving the equations, the Algebraic Immunity (AI) of f is defined as the smallest integer d such that there exists a function g (nonzero) of degree d for which $fg = 0$ on all inputs (or $g(f + 1) = 0$ on all inputs). In 2003, Courtois and Meier [14] showed that an attack can be mounted on filtered LFSR using algebraic systems of degree at most the algebraic immunity of the function f. As the algebraic immunity is at most equal to the degree of a function, the so-called algebraic attack has a better complexity than the one targeting the degree. Recently, the algebraic attacks have been rediscovered in the context of Goldreich's PRG [2], also giving better attacks than the one based on the degree. A more general algebraic property of f is its Fast Algebraic Immunity (FAI). This property takes in account the degrees of both the function g and of the product fg, where g is a nonzero function of degree smaller than $\mathsf{AI}(f)$. The principle of the corresponding attack is to perform linear combinations of the system's equations to cancel the monomials of degree between $\deg(g)$ and $\deg(fg)$. Hence, it gives an algebraic system of even smaller degree than those obtained from other algebraic properties of f, and which can be more easily linearized. It corresponds to a more efficient class of attack called fast algebraic attack [13].

1.2   Determining Algebraic Properties, and Good Functions

Once the properties required for security are exhibited, two natural questions have to been answered. The first concern is how to (efficiently) determine the parameter of each function relatively to one property. The second one consists in determining which functions have good parameters for these properties.

For the first question, the situation is very different depending on which algebraic property is targeted. The algebraic degree of a Boolean function is directly given by its Algebraic Normal Form (ANF), one of the most common representation. Various works focus on efficient algorithms to determine the degree directly from the truth table of a Boolean function such as [12]. The algebraic immunity is more complex to determine from the ANF, or any other common representation. This parameter for a particular function f can be determined by considering the rank of Reed-Muller codes punctured at the support of f, and at the support of $f + 1$. In [4] a more efficient algorithm using multivariate interpolation is given, and further works are dedicated to assess the complexity of such algorithms [16,22]. Determining the fast algebraic immunity is a more intricate task, since all known algorithms to do this become less efficient in this case. An algorithm to determine this parameter is also given in [4], with a running time complexity in $\mathcal{O}(DE^2)$ where $D = \binom{n}{d}$ and $E = \binom{n}{e}$, n being the number of variables of the function f, e the degree of g and d the degree of fg. Note that in the worst case this complexity is exponential as d can be as high as $\lceil (n+1)/2 \rceil$, giving $D \approx 2^{n/2}$ (using Stirling approximation). As a result, this kind of algorithms cannot be used to determine the fast algebraic immunity of arbitrary functions of hundreds of variables that are used in some cryptographic constructions.

For the second question, the difficulty of finding functions with good parameters is scaling up with the generality of the property. Any n-variable function with monomials of degree n in its ANF has maximum algebraic degree (or equivalently, odd weight truth table), which allows to easily define families of functions (indexed by n) with good algebraic degree. Finding functions with optimal algebraic immunity is the central topic of different works such as [17,18]. This line of works shows that exhibiting families of functions with good algebraic immunity is much more complex than exhibiting functions with good algebraic degree. Typical examples of such families are the majority functions and modifications, or Carlet-Feng [9] functions. In comparison, only partial results have been obtained about families of functions with optimal, or good, fast algebraic immunity. In various works, this concern is tackled by showing a lower bound on this parameter for functions already known to have good characteristics relatively to other properties. For example, Carlet-Feng functions have optimal fast algebraic immunity when they are defined in $2^s + 1$ variables [27]. T-C-T functions [35] have optimal AI and almost optimal FAI [26], and the functions introduced in [34] have optimal AI and FAI of at least $n - 6$.

Another approach to build sufficiently good functions for the algebraic criteria is to combine good functions with others such that the properties of the combination can only increase. This principle is used for Goldreich's PRG [21], and for FLIP [29], where a function with good (F)AI is one of the constituent of a direct sum giving the main function. In these cases, the algebraic degree, AI, and FAI of the main functions are at least equal to the one of the function with good algebraic properties. Then, determining the exact algebraic parameters of a good function directly leads to a lower bound on the parameters of the more complex function, which is the main component of the cryptographic primitive.

1.3   Majority Functions, and Their Fast Algebraic Immunity

The family of majority functions has been the center of various studies in the context of cryptographic constructions. It is one of the first examples of functions proven to reach the optimal algebraic immunity [18]. As it is the most particular case of symmetric functions, this family is known and studied in diverse contexts, for example as easy-to-compute functions with branching programs. Despite their optimal algebraic immunity, majority functions are not good for all cryptographic properties (for non-linearity or resilience for example [15,18]), hence they are not directly used as filtering functions. Nevertheless, they are used in diverse constructions combined with other functions, for example in the XOR-MAJ functions [2,3], or in the Caesar competitor ACORN [23]. In the context of Goldreich's PRG [2,3], or Improved Filter Permutator [28] (a paradigm of stream-cipher), the main function is the result of a secondary construction (a direct sum) where one of the two components is a majority function. The degree, AI and FAI of the majority function used are then giving lower bounds of the same parameters for the main function.

The cryptographic properties of majority functions and more generally of symmetric functions are investigated in many works such as [5–7,18,30,31,33]. From these series of works some properties of symmetric functions are better known that others. The balancedness, and more generally resilience of (non affine) symmetric function is still the object of conjectures. On the opposite extreme the algebraic degree is the property which is better known for this class of functions. As majority functions are known to have optimal algebraic immunity since a decade, and balanced for n odd, there are more results on the parameters of this subclass. The resilience, nonlinearity and algebraic immunity are exhibited for all elements of this family, but it is still not the case for the fast algebraic immunity.

A fundamental result regarding the algebraic properties of majority function is given in [4]. Despite having optimal algebraic immunity, majority functions do not reach the optimal fast algebraic immunity. More specifically, in this paper the authors show an upper bound smaller than n for majority functions, considering as function g a particular symmetric function. However, this result does not allow us to obtain the exact fast algebraic immunity of majority function, which affects their use as building blocks in secondary constructions. Up to now, very little has been shown for these exact parameters. Two papers focus on this specific question, proving the exact parameter for particular subclasses. [36] gave the first relative result, where the exact FAI is exhibited for the subclasses of majority function in 2^m and $2^m + 1$ variables. More recently, the parameter of two other subclasses have been determined in [11], where the cases $2^m + 2$ and $2^m + 3$ are tackled for $m \geq 2$.

1.4   Our Contributions

In this article we exhibit the fast algebraic immunity of all majority function in $2^m + j$ variables with $m \geq 2$ and $0 \leq j < 2^{m-1}$. These results are obtained using different properties relatively to the annihilators of threshold functions (a subclass of symmetric functions containing majority functions), to their algebraic immunity, and to the structure of their algebraic normal form. These results give lower bounds on the complexity of fast algebraic attack on Goldreich's PRG or FILIP stream-cipher instantiated with XOR-MAJ functions [2,3,28].

To obtain these results, we first focus on the minimal degree of the nonzero annihilators of majority functions and their complementary. Combining it with the upper bound of [4], we can derive an interval for the FAI of any majority function in $n \geq 2$ variables. We show how this interval directly implies the result of [36]. Then, we use and combine different results on the representation of symmetric functions. These results allow us to exhibit an expression of the algebraic normal form of any threshold function. Finally, we show that for many values of n the functions reach the upper bound of [4]. To get this result, we show that multiplying the majority function by a low degree function cannot degrade too much the degree of the product, which corresponds to the case of low FAI. This is done by partitioning the majority function in two parts, one with the monomials of degree less that t, the other one with the monomials of degree equal or greater than t. We show that there is a quantified gap between the highest degree appearing in the low degree part, and the lowest degree appearing in the high degree part. We prove that the upper part corresponds to a threshold function. Moreover, using results on the degree of the annihilators of threshold functions we can derive results on the initial (partitioned) majority function, allowing us to state the final result.

1.5   Paper Organization

The article is organized in the following way: In Sect. 2 we define the notations and preliminary notions necessary to follow the main results. Section 3 is dedicated to the lower and upper bound of the FAI of majority functions. Section 4 shows results relative to the ANF of threshold functions. In Sect. 5 we present the main theorem, giving the exact FAI of several families of majority functions. Finally, Sect. 6 concludes on the results and open problems relative to this work.

2   Preliminaries

In addition to classic notations we use $[n]$ to denote the subset of all integers between 1 and n: $\{1, \ldots, n\}$. For readability we use the notation $+$ instead of $\oplus$ to denote the addition in $\mathbb{F}_2$ and $\sum$ instead of $\bigoplus$. Let $v \in \mathbb{F}_2^n$, we refer to the element v as a word, or a Boolean vector of length n, we denote its coefficient v_i (for $i \in [n]$). When we consider $v \in \mathbb{F}_2^n$ as an integer we refers to the integer $\sum_{i=1}^n 2 v_i^{i-1}$. The Hamming weight (or weight) of v is $\mathsf{w}_\mathsf{H}(v) = \#\{v_i \neq 0 \mid i \in [n]\}$. We denote $\overline{v} \in \mathbb{F}_2^n$ the complementary of v: $\forall i \in [n]$, $\overline{v_i} = 1 - v_i$. We call support of v and denote $\mathsf{supp}(v)$ the set of elements i in $[n]$ such that $v_i \neq 0$.

2.1   Boolean Functions, and Order on $\mathbb{F}_2^n$

Definition 1 (Boolean Function). *A Boolean function f with n variables is a function from $\mathbb{F}_2^n$ to $\mathbb{F}_2$.*

Definition 2 (Algebraic Normal Form (ANF)). *We call Algebraic Normal Form of a Boolean function f its n-variable polynomial representation over $\mathbb{F}_2$ (i.e. belonging to $\mathbb{F}_2[x_1, \ldots, x_n]/(x_1^2 + x_1, \ldots, x_n^2 + x_n))$:*

$$f(x) = \sum_{I \subseteq [n]} a_I \left(\prod_{i \in I} x_i \right) = \sum_{I \subseteq [n]} a_I x^I,$$

where $a_I \in \mathbb{F}_2$.

Definition 3 (Order $\preceq$). *We denote $\preceq$ the partial order on $\mathbb{F}_2^n$ defined as:*

$$a \preceq b \Leftrightarrow \forall i \in [n], a_i \leq b_i,$$

where $\leq$ denotes the usual order on $\mathbb{Z}$ and the elements a_i and b_i of $\mathbb{F}_2$ are identified to 0 or 1 in $\mathbb{Z}$.

Property 1 (Corollary of Lucas's Theorem (*e.g.* [8])). *Let $u, v \in \mathbb{F}_2^n$:*

$$u \preceq v \Leftrightarrow \binom{v}{u} \equiv 1 \mod 2,$$

where the inputs of the binomial coefficient are the integers whose binary decomposition corresponds to u and v.

2.2   Algebraic Immunity and Fast Algebraic Immunity

Definition 4 (Algebraic Immunity and Annihilators). *The algebraic imm-unity of a Boolean function $f \in \mathcal{B}_n$, denoted as $\mathsf{AI}(f)$, is defined as:*

$$\mathsf{AI}(f) = \min_{g \neq 0}\{\deg(g) \mid fg = 0 \text{ or } (f+1)g = 0\},$$

where $\deg(g)$ is the algebraic degree of g. The function g is called an annihilator of f (or $f + 1$).

We also use the notation $\mathsf{AN}(f)$ for the minimum algebraic degree of nonzero annihilator of f:

$$\mathsf{AN}(f) = \min_{g \neq 0}\{\deg(g) \mid fg = 0\}.$$

Property 2 (Algebraic Immunity Properties (*e.g.* [8])). *Let f be a Boolean function:*

- *The null and the all-one functions are the only functions such that $\mathsf{AI}(f) = 0$,*
- *All monomial (non constant) functions f are such that $\mathsf{AI}(f) = 1$,*
- *For all non constant f it holds that: $\mathsf{AI}(f) \leq \mathsf{AN}(f) \leq \deg(f)$,*
- *$\mathsf{AI}(f) \leq \lfloor \frac{n+1}{2} \rfloor$.*

Definition 5 (Fast Algebraic Immunity [4]). *The fast algebraic immunity of a Boolean function $f \in \mathcal{B}_n$, denoted as $\mathsf{FAI}(f)$, is defined as:*

$$\mathsf{FAI}(f) = \min\left\{2\mathsf{AI}(f), \min_{1 \leq \deg(g) < \mathsf{AI}(f)}[\deg(g) + \deg(fg)]\right\}.$$

Property 3 (Fast Algebraic Immunity Properties (*e.g.* [8])). *Let f be a Boolean function:*

- *$\mathsf{FAI}(f) = \mathsf{FAI}(f + 1)$,*
- *$\mathsf{FAI}(f) \leq n$,*
- *$\mathsf{FAI}(f) \geq \mathsf{AN}(f + 1) + 1$.*

Remark 1. The last item comes from the fact that $\deg(fg)$ is at least the degree of $\mathsf{AN}(f + 1)$ as by construction fg is a nonzero annihilator of $f + 1$.

2.3   Symmetric Functions

Symmetric functions are functions such that changing the order of the inputs does not change the output. They have been the focus of many studies *e.g.* [6,7,18,30,31,33]. These functions can be described more succinctly through the simplified value vector.

Definition 6 (Simplified Value Vector). *Let f be a symmetric function in n variables, we define its simplified value vector:*

$$\mathbf{s}_f = [w_0, w_1, \ldots, w_n]$$

of length n, where for each $k \in \{0, \ldots, n\}$, $w_k = f(x)$ for x such that $\mathsf{w_H}(x) = k$, i.e. w_k is the value of f on all inputs of Hamming weight k.

Definition 7 (Elementary Symmetric Functions). *Let $n \in \mathbb{N}^*$, let $i \in \{0, \cdots, n\}$, the elementary symmetric function of degree i in n variables, denoted σ_i, is the function which ANF contains all monomials of degree i and no monomials of other degrees. The $n + 1$ elementary symmetric functions in n variables form a basis of the symmetric functions in n variables.*

We define the sub-family of threshold functions, and then a sub-family of threshold functions of particular interest: the family of majority functions.

Definition 8 (Threshold Function). *For any positive integers $d \le n + 1$ we define the Boolean function $\mathsf{T}_{d,n}$ as:*

$$\forall x \in \mathbb{F}_2^n, \quad \mathsf{T}_{d,n}(x) = \begin{cases} 0 & \text{if } \mathsf{w_H}(x) < d, \\ 1 & \text{otherwise.} \end{cases}$$

Definition 9 (Majority Function). *For any positive integer n we define the Boolean function MAJ_n as:*

$$\forall x \in \mathbb{F}_2^n, \quad \mathsf{MAJ}_n(x) = \begin{cases} 0 & \text{if } \mathsf{w_H}(x) \le \lfloor \frac{n}{2} \rfloor, \\ 1 & \text{otherwise.} \end{cases}$$

Note that for a threshold function, we have $w_k = 0$ for $k < d$ and 1 otherwise, so the simplified value vector of a threshold function $\mathsf{T}_{d,n}$ is the $n + 1$-length vector of d consecutive 0's and $n + 1 - d$ consecutive 1's.

Remark 2 (Convention on Majority). Note that for n even it gives $\mathsf{MAJ}_n = \mathsf{T}_{\frac{n}{2}+1,n}$ and for n odd $\mathsf{MAJ}_n = \mathsf{T}_{\frac{n+1}{2},n}$. In the case of n even, the choice of $\mathsf{T}_{\frac{n}{2},n}$ or $\mathsf{T}_{\frac{n}{2}+1,n}$ as the majority function is arbitrary, some papers considers the second choice. As shown by the following proposition, it does not matter in this work as both functions have the same behavior relatively to fast algebraic immunity. We include the proof of [10] for the ease of the reader.

Proposition 1 ([10]). *Let $n \in \mathbb{N}^*$ and $d \in [0, n + 1]$, for all $x \in \mathbb{F}_2^n$ let $1_n + x$ denote the element $(1 + x_1, \ldots, 1 + x_n) \in \mathbb{F}_2^n$, then the following relation holds for $\mathsf{T}_{d,n}$ and $\mathsf{T}_{n-d+1,n}$:*

$$\forall x \in \mathbb{F}_2^n, \quad 1 + \mathsf{T}_{d,n}(1_n + x) = \mathsf{T}_{n-d+1,n}(x).$$

Proof. We use the simplified value vector formalization (see Definition 6) to show this result. For all elements $x \in \mathbb{F}_2^n$, we have $\mathsf{w_H}(x + 1_n) = \mathsf{w_H}(1_n) - \mathsf{w_H}(x) = n - \mathsf{w_H}(x)$. So denoting w_k' the coefficients of the simplified value vector of $\mathsf{T}_{d,n}(1_n + x)$ we get: $w_k' = w_{n-k}$ for all $k \in [0, n]$. It gives a vector symmetric to the first simplified value vector, *i.e.* with the elements from 0 to $n - d$ being 1 and from $n - d + 1$ to n being 0.

For all $x \in \mathbb{F}_2^n$, $1 + \mathsf{T}_{d,n}(1_n + x) = \overline{\mathsf{T}_{d,n}(1_n + x)}$, its complement to 1. Then, denoting $w"_k$ the coefficients of the simplified value vector of $1 + \mathsf{T}_{d,n}(1_n + x)$ we get: $w"_k = \overline{w_{n-k}}$ for all $k \in [0, n]$. It gives a vector which is the complement of the precedent simplified value vector to the $(n + 1)$-length all-1 vector, *i.e.* with the elements from 0 to $n - d$ being 0 and from $n - d + 1$ to n being 1. This simplified value vector is the one of $\mathsf{T}_{n-d+1,n}$, finishing the proof.   □

More precisely, for the case $d = n/2$ it gives that $\mathsf{T}_{\frac{n}{2},n}$ and $\mathsf{T}_{\frac{n}{2}+1,n}$ are extended affine equivalent, then having the same degree, algebraic immunity, and fast algebraic immunity.

3   Lower and Upper Bound on the Fast Algebraic Immunity of Majority Functions

In the following we will express n as $2^m + 2k + \varepsilon$ where $0 \le k < 2^{m-1}$, and $\varepsilon = 0$ or 1, as this writing will be convenient to highlight the properties of the functions used. First we recall the result of [4] giving the upper bound on MAJ_n, using the formulation developed in [36] and [11]:

Lemma 1 (Upper Bound on $\mathsf{FAI}(\mathsf{MAJ}_n)$, [4] Theorem 2). *Let $n \ge 2$ such that $n = 2^m + 2k + \varepsilon$, $m \ge 1$, $0 \le k < 2^{m-1}$, and $\varepsilon \in \{0,1\}$, Then:*

$$\mathsf{FAI}(\mathsf{MAJ}_n) \le 2^{m-1} + 2k + 2.$$

For the lower bound we recall the result of [10] on the nonzero annihilator of minimal degree of threshold functions and then we combine it with Property 3. We include the proof of [10] for the ease of the reader.

Lemma 2 (AN of Threshold Functions, [10]). *Let n be a nonzero positive integer, $1 \le d \le n$, the threshold function $\mathsf{T}_{d,n}$ has the following property:*

$$\mathsf{AN}(\mathsf{T}_{d,n}) = n - d + 1, \ \text{and} \ \mathsf{AN}(1 + \mathsf{T}_{d,n}) = d.$$

Proof. Applying the transformation $x \mapsto x + 1_n$, where 1_n is the all-1 vector of length n, changes $\mathsf{T}_{d,n}$ into the indicator of the set of vectors of Hamming weight at most $n-d$. The relations between the expressions of the coefficients of the ANF $\sum_{I \subseteq [n]} a_I x^I$ by means of the values of the function, namely, $a_I = \sum_{\mathsf{supp}(x) \subseteq I} f(x)$ and $f(x) = \sum_{I \subseteq \mathsf{supp}(x)} a_I$, show that the annihilators of this indicator are all the linear combinations over $\mathbb{F}_2$ of the monomials of degrees at least $n-d+1$. Hence, the annihilators of $\mathsf{T}_{d,n}$ are obtained from these latter linear combinations by the transformation $x \mapsto x+1_n$. They can have every algebraic degree at least $n-d+1$. And the annihilators of $1 + \mathsf{T}_{d,n}$ are similarly the linear combinations over $\mathbb{F}_2$ of the monomials of degrees at least d. They can have every algebraic degree at least d. Hence $\mathsf{AN}(\mathsf{T}_{d,n}) = n-d+1$, $\mathsf{AN}(1+\mathsf{T}_{d,n}) = d$, and $\mathsf{AI}(\mathsf{T}_{d,n}) = \min(d, n-d+1)$. $\qquad\square$

Lemma 3 (Lower Bound on $\mathsf{FAI}(\mathsf{MAJ}_n)$). *Let $n > 2$ such that $n = 2^m + 2k + \varepsilon$, $m \ge 1$, $0 \le k < 2^{m-1}$, and $\varepsilon \in \{0,1\}$, Then:*

$$\mathsf{FAI}(\mathsf{MAJ}_n) \ge 2^{m-1} + k + 2.$$

Proof. First, for such values of n note that MAJ_n is the threshold function $\mathsf{T}_{d,n}$ with $d = 2^{m-1} + k + 1$. Using Lemma 2 gives $\mathsf{AN}(\mathsf{T}_{d,n}) = 2^{m-1} + k + \varepsilon$ and $\mathsf{AN}(1+\mathsf{T}_{d,n}) = 2^{m-1}+k+1$. As for any function f $\mathsf{AI}(f) = \min(\mathsf{AN}(f), \mathsf{AN}(f+1))$, it leads to $\mathsf{AI}(\mathsf{MAJ}_n) = 2^{m-1} + k + \varepsilon$. The third item of Property 3 enables to obtain:

$$\mathsf{FAI}(\mathsf{MAJ}_n) \geq \min(2^m + 2k + 2\varepsilon, 2^{m-1} + k + 2).$$

When $m \geq 2$ or $\varepsilon = 1$ this minimum is reached by $2^{m-1} + k + 2$, then gives the final result for $n > 2$. $\qquad\qquad\qquad\qquad\qquad\qquad\qquad\qquad\qquad\qquad\qquad$ $\square$

Note that the difference between the upper and lower bound is only of k, then they coincide when $k = 0$, giving the result previously obtained in [36]:

Corollary 1 (Fast Algebraic Immunity of MAJ_n for $n = 2^m + \varepsilon$). *Let $n = 2^m + \varepsilon$, $n > 2$, $m \geq 1$, $\varepsilon \in \{0,1\}$, then $\mathsf{FAI}(\mathsf{MAJ}_n) = 2^{m-1} + 2$.*

The intuition behind our main result is that many functions are reaching the upper bound. A way of proving this consists in showing that for all functions of degree at most k, the product with the majority function is higher that the lower bound given by $\mathsf{AN}(\mathsf{MAJ}_n)$. A difference of k with this bound is sufficient to show that $\mathsf{FAI}(\mathsf{MAJ}_n)$ reaches the upper bound. In order to determine when this difference happens, we will use the properties of algebraic immunity of various threshold functions. Such strategy is possible since considering the ANF of a majority function restricted to its monomials of degree superior to a fixed level corresponds to the ANF of another threshold function.

4   Exhibiting the Algebraic Normal Form of Threshold Functions

In order to prove our main result we need to exhibit the ANF of threshold function as a sum of elementary symmetric functions, a form which is easier to use to reach our objective. First we show some properties on the ANF of these functions, and then we give a general expression. In this part we use the fact that some properties of symmetric functions can be derived from the periodicity of their simplified value vector [6].

4.1   Some Properties on the ANF of Threshold Functions

We first recall how a symmetric function can be written as a sum of elementary symmetric function, using Lucas's theorem and the simplified value vector (*e.g.* [8]).

Lemma 4 (Symmetric Function as a Sum of Elementary Symmetric Function, [8] p144). *Let f be a symmetric n-variable Boolean function with simplified value vector $\mathbf{s}_f = [w_0, w_1, \ldots, w_n]$, then $\forall x \in \mathbb{F}_2^n$:*

$$f(x) = \sum_{i=0}^{n} \lambda_i \sigma_i(x), \qquad \text{where } \lambda_i = \sum_{j \preceq i} w_j.$$

Let us denote $D = 2^{\lceil \log d \rceil}$, we show that the indices of the elementary symmetric functions appearing in the ANF of the threshold function $\mathsf{T}_{d,n}$ follow a period of D.

Lemma 5 (ANF of Threshold Functions and Periodicity). *Let n and d be two integers such that $0 < d \leq n + 1$, let $D = 2^{\lceil \log d \rceil}$, if $\mathsf{T}_{d,n} = \sum_{i'=0}^{n} \lambda_{i'} \sigma_{i'}$ then the following relation holds on its coefficients:*

$$\forall i' \in [n], \ \lambda_{i'} = \lambda_i \,|\, i' \equiv i \mod D, \ and \ i \in [D].$$

Proof. Let us consider the integer $i' \in [n]$, it can be written as $i' = i + kD$ with $i \in [D]$ and $k \in \mathbb{N}$. Using Lemma 4 and partitioning the sum in intervals of size D (except the last one stopping at $i + kD$ since no bigger element complies the order relation) we get:

$$\lambda_{i'} = \sum_{\substack{j \preceq i+kD \\ 0 \leq j < D}} w_j + \cdots + \sum_{\substack{j \preceq i+kD \\ \ell D \leq j < (\ell+1)D}} w_j + \cdots + \sum_{\substack{j \preceq i+kD \\ kd \leq j \leq i+kD}} w_j. \tag{1}$$

We first consider the case $i \neq D$. In the set $[0, i]$ the number of elements j such that $0 \leq j \leq i$, $j \preceq i$ is even (it can be seen using Property 1 and $\sum_{j=0}^{i} \binom{i}{j} = 2^i \equiv 0 \mod 2$). Since $j > i$ implies $j \not\preceq i$, then an even number of elements of $[0, \text{D-1}]$ are such that $j \preceq i$. When $j = \ell D + r$ with $0 \leq r < D$ we have $j \preceq i + kD \Leftrightarrow r \preceq i$ and $\ell \preceq k$, allowing us to conclude that all the sums from the second to the last contain an even number of w_j. Since all these coefficients are for $j \geq D$ and we set $D \geq d$, and by the definition of threshold function $\mathsf{T}_{d,n}$, all these coefficients are equal to 1, giving:

$$\lambda_{i'} = \sum_{\substack{j \preceq i+kD \\ 0 \leq j < D}} w_j = \lambda_i.$$

For the remaining case, $i = D$, we need to show that $\lambda_{kD} = \lambda_D$ for $k \in \mathbb{N}^*$ (note that λ_0 is not considered). Since i' is a multiple of D, at most one coefficient of each sum can contribute to the total sum, and in this case Eq. 1 gives:

$$\lambda_{kD} = \sum_{\substack{j \preceq kD \\ j=0}} w_j + \cdots + \sum_{\substack{j \preceq kD \\ j=\ell D}} w_j + \cdots + \sum_{\substack{j \preceq kD \\ j=kD}} w_j.$$

The number of elements $j \preceq kD$ such that j is a multiple of D corresponds to the number of elements of $[0, k]$ preceding k, which is even as $k > 0$. All coefficients $w_{\ell D}$ with $\ell \in [k]$ are equal to 1 and w_0 is equal to 0 as $0 < d \leq D$, therefore (since $0 \preceq kD$ for all k), it implies $\lambda_{kD} = 1$ for $k \in \mathbb{N}^*$. We can then conclude that $\lambda_{kD} = \lambda_D$ for $k \in \mathbb{N}^*$. □

As a result we can link the presence of an elementary symmetric function in the ANF of a threshold function to a property on a small set.

Proposition 2. *Let n and d be two integers such that $0 < d \leq n + 1$, let $D = 2^{\lceil \log d \rceil}$, let $\mathsf{T}_{d,n} = \sum_{i'=0}^{n} \lambda_{i'} \sigma_{i'}$. For all $i' \in [n]$ let i be the integer such that $i' \equiv i \mod D$ and $i \in [D]$, then:*

$$\forall i' \in [n], \ \lambda_{i'} = \#\{j \preceq i \mid j \in [d, D]\} \mod 2.$$

Proof. From Lemma 5 we know that $\lambda_{i'} = \lambda_i$, and using Lemma 4, $\lambda_i = \sum_{j \preceq i} w_j$, since $w_j = 0$ for $j < d$ and $w_j = 1$ for $j \geq d$, and $i \leq D$ gives $\lambda_i = \sum_{d \leq j \leq D \mid j \preceq i} 1$, which is equivalent to the final result.   □

Finally, we highlight that for majority functions, only the set $[d, D]$ is important to exhibit the ANF.

Proposition 3. *Let $n > 2$ and $\mathsf{MAJ}_n = \mathsf{T}_{d,n} = \sum_{i'=0}^{n} \lambda_{i'} \sigma_{i'}$, $D = 2^{\lceil \log d \rceil}$, then: $\lambda_{i'} = 1 \Rightarrow d \leq i' \leq D$.*

Proof. Let us write n as $2^m + 2k + \varepsilon$ such as $m \geq 1$, $0 \leq k < 2^{m-1}$, and $\varepsilon \in \{0, 1\}$. This fixes $d = 2^{m-1} + k + 1$ and $D = 2^m$. We first show that none of the indices smaller than d can appear in the ANF, and that the same holds for all indexes between $D + 1$ and n.

When $d > 0$ we have $\lambda_0 = w_0 = 0$. For all $i \in [d - 1]$ we have $\{j \preceq i \mid j \in [d, D]\} = \emptyset$, so Proposition 2 gives $\lambda_i = 0$. Hence, no coefficient smaller than $2^{m-1} + k + 1$ appears in the ANF of a majority function.

Now, note that all the elements in $[D + 1, n]$ have their representative in $[D]$ (the element with same congruence modulus D) belonging to $[2k + \varepsilon]$ since $n = D + 2k + \varepsilon$. Because $k < 2^{m-1}$, we have $2k + \varepsilon < 2^{m-1} + k + 1 = d$ and combining Lemma 5 with Proposition 3 implies that $\forall i' \in [D + 1, n], \lambda_{i'} = 0$. Hence, no coefficient bigger than 2^m appears in the ANF of a majority function. In conclusion only coefficients between $2^{m-1} + k + 1$ and 2^m appear in the ANF.   □

4.2 A Simple Expression of the Algebraic Normal Form of Threshold Functions

In this section, we give a simple expression of the ANF of threshold functions using some set representation. This expression will be used to exhibit the main results of Sect. 5. We begin with a preliminary lemma relative to the order $\preceq$ which simplifies the proof of the main theorem of this section.

Lemma 6. *Let $a, b - 1 \in \mathbb{F}_2^n$ then $a \preceq \overline{b - 1} \Leftrightarrow a \preceq a + b - 1$.*

Proof. We first show $a \preceq \overline{b - 1} \Rightarrow a \preceq a + b - 1$. $a \preceq \overline{b - 1}$ implies $\mathsf{supp}(a) \cap \mathsf{supp}(b - 1) = \emptyset$, so $a \preceq a + b - 1$. We prove the other direction by contrapositive:

$$a \npreceq \overline{b - 1} \Rightarrow \exists i \in [n] \mid a_i = 1 \text{ and } \overline{b - 1}_i = 0.$$

Taking the smallest index i with this property, $a_i = 1$ and $(b - 1)_i = 1$ and it is the first carry, hence $a_i = 1$ and $(a + b - 1)_i = 0$ giving $a \npreceq a + b - 1$, finishing the proof.   □

Theorem 1 (Algebraic Normal Form of Threshold Functions). *Let n and d be two integers such that $0 < d \leq n+1$, let $D = 2^{\lceil \log d \rceil}$. Let $\mathsf{T}_{d,n} = \sum_{i'=0}^{n} \lambda_{i'} \sigma_{i'}$, and let S_d denote the set $\{v \in [0, D-1] \,|\, v \preceq D-d\}$ also equal to $\{v \in \mathbb{F}_2^{\lceil \log d \rceil} \,|\, v \preceq \overline{d-1}\}$ where $d-1$ is considered over $\log(D)-1$ bits. The following relation holds:*

$$\lambda_{i'} = 1 \Leftrightarrow i' \in S'_d,$$

where $S'_d = \{kD + d + v \,|\, k \in \mathbb{N}, v \in S_d\} \cap [n] = \{kD - v \,|\, k \in \mathbb{N}^*, v \in S_d\} \cap [n]$. Or equivalently:

$$\mathsf{T}_{d,n} = \sum_{i \in S'_d} \sigma_i.$$

Proof. We will first show that σ_0 is never in the ANF of these threshold functions, then that the two definitions of S_d are equivalent, as the two definitions of S'_d, and finally that the appearance in the ANF is equivalent to the membership in S'_d.

For $d > 0$, $w_0 = \lambda_0 = 0$ and no threshold functions with $d > 0$ can have σ_0 in the ANF. By definition, $\mathsf{T}_{0,n}$ is the constant n-variable function 1, for which the ANF is $1 = \sigma_0$.

For the set equivalences, we consider both the integer representation and the Boolean vector representation. We first focus on the set S_d, $v \in [0, D-1]$ means that v is a positive integer smaller than $D = 2^{\lceil \log d \rceil}$ which is equivalent to a Boolean vector of length $\lceil \log d \rceil$. Then, as $D = 2^{\lceil \log d \rceil}$, $D - d = D - 1 - (d-1)$ where $D-1$ and $d-1$ can both be written on $\lceil \log d \rceil - 1$ bits and $D-1$ is the all 1 vector of this length. Therefore $D - d = \overline{d-1}$ on $\log(D)-1$ bits, which proves the equivalent representations of S_d. Note that $v \preceq D-d \Leftrightarrow v = D-d-v' \,|\, v' \preceq D-d$, and $\{d + v \,|\, v \in S_d\} = \{D - v' \,|\, v' \in S_d\}$ implies the equivalence of the two definitions of S'_d.

Using Proposition 2, for all $i' \in [n]$ we have $\lambda_{i'} = 1$ if and only if the set $\{j \preceq i \,|\, j \in [d, D]\}$ has odd cardinality. Property 1 gives that the Boolean value $j \preceq i$ equals the parity of the binomial coefficient i choose j. Using Pascal's identity as $d > 0$ we get:

$$\sum_{j=d}^{D} \binom{i}{j} \equiv \sum_{j=d}^{D} \left[\binom{i-1}{j} + \binom{i-1}{j-1} \right] \equiv \binom{i-1}{d-1} + \binom{i-1}{D} \quad \mod 2,$$

$$\equiv \binom{i-1}{d-1} \equiv \binom{i-1}{i-d} \quad \mod 2.$$

The parity of the cardinality of the set is then the Boolean value $i - d \preceq i - 1$. If $i - d < 0$ then $\lambda_{i'} = 0$ from Proposition 3, and both $i - d$ and $i - 1$ are non negative integers smaller than D (the case $i' = 0$ has already been considered). Therefore, we can identify a to $i - d$ and b to i in Lemma 6, which gives that $\lambda_{i'}$ is equal to the Boolean value $i - d \preceq \overline{d-1}$. It enables us to conclude:

$$\lambda_{i'} = 1 \Leftrightarrow i' \in [n], i' = kD + i, i \in [D], k \in \mathbb{N}, i - d \in S_d,$$
$$\Leftrightarrow i' \in [n], i' = kD + d + v, d + v \in [D], k \in \mathbb{N}, v \in S_d,$$
$$\Leftrightarrow i' \in S'_d.$$

$\square$

Remark 3. Note that the threshold functions in n variables form a basis of the n-variable symmetric function, then this representation with the sets S'_d can be used to obtain the ANF of any symmetric function. For example, the ANF of the indicator function of the elements of Hamming weight d, $\varphi_{d,n} = \mathsf{T}_{d,n} + \mathsf{T}_{d+1,n}$, is given by $S'_d \Delta S'_{d+1}$, where Δ denotes the symmetric difference of sets.

5 Exact Fast Algebraic Immunity of Several Families

In this section we show that many majority functions reach the upper bound of [4]. To do so, we use the ANF formulation of Theorem 1 to show a gap between two consecutive elementary symmetric functions appearing in the ANF of a majority function, σ_a and σ_b. We use the fact that for functions of degree smaller than this gap the product with the part of degree up to a has a smaller degree than b. Then, when the function obtained by the part of degree at least b is a threshold function, we can determine a lower bound on the degree of its product with a function of degree at most the gap. By construction, this lower bound also applies to the degree of the product of the majority function with a function of degree at most the gap, giving a lower bound on the fast algebraic immunity.

We write the integer n as in Sect. 3: $n = 2^m + 2k + \varepsilon$ but with $k < 2^{m-2}$ this time, and we show that in this case the ANF of MAJ_n has no monomials of degree between $2^m - 2^{m-2} - 1$ and $2^m - 2^{m-2} + k$.

Lemma 7. *Let $n > 2$ be an integer such that $n = 2^m + 2k + \varepsilon, m \geq 2, 0 \leq k < 2^{m-2}, \varepsilon \in \{0,1\}$. Let $\mathsf{MAJ}_n = \sum_{i'=0}^{n} \lambda_{i'} \sigma_{i'}$, the following holds:*

$$\{i' \in [2^m - 2^{m-2}, 2^m - 2^{m-2} + k + 1] \mid \lambda_{i'} = 1\} = \{2^m - 2^{m-2}, 2^m - 2^{m-2} + k + 1\}.$$

Proof. Using Theorem 1 we know that $S'_d = \{\ell D - v \mid \ell \in \mathbb{N}^*, v \in S_d\} \cap [n]$, and using Proposition 3:

$$S'_d = \{2^m - v \mid v \in S_d\}.$$

Since $d = 2^{m-1} + k + 1$, we have $S_d = \{v \in \mathbb{F}_2^m \mid v \preceq \overline{2^{m-1} + k + 1 - 1}\}$. Then, $\overline{2^{m-1} + k} = 2^m - 1 - (2^{m-1} + k) = 2^{m-1} - k - 1$. In the following we show which integers are covered or not by $2^{m-1} - k - 1$ in the set we are interested in.

Writing $2^{m-1} - k - 1$ as $2^{m-2} + 2^{m-2} - k - 1$, and since $2^{m-2} - k - 1 < 2^{m-2}$ (2^{m-2} and $2^{m-2} - k - 1$ have disjoint support) we see that $2^{m-2} - k - 1 \preceq 2^{m-2} + 2^{m-2} - k - 1$ (and $2^{m-2} \preceq 2^{m-2} + 2^{m-2} - k - 1$). It means that $2^{m-2} - k - 1 \preceq 2^{m-1} - k - 1$ (and $2^{m-2} \preceq 2^{m-1} - k - 1$), hence $2^{m-2} - k - 1$ and 2^{m-2} are both in S_d.

The elements in $[2^{m-2} - k - 1, 2^{m-2}]$ are smaller than 2^{m-2} so they are covered by $2^{m-2} + 2^{m-2} - k - 1$ if and only if the are covered by $2^{m-2} - k - 1$, which is not the case as they are bigger than this number. Finally $S_d \cap [2^{m-2} - k - 1, 2^{m-2}] = \emptyset$. □

In the following we prove that the function obtained by considering only the monomials of degree at least $2^m - 2^{m-2} + k + 1$ of the MAJ_n function corresponds to the threshold function with $d = 2^m - 2^{m-2} + k + 1$.

Lemma 8. *Let $n > 2$ be an integer such that $n = 2^m + 2k + \varepsilon, m \geq 2, 0 \leq k < 2^{m-2}, \varepsilon \in \{0,1\}$. Let $\mathsf{MAJ}_n = \sum_{i'=0}^{n} \lambda_{i'} \sigma_{i'}$, then the following holds:*

$$\forall x \in \mathbb{F}_2^n, \sum_{i'=2^m-2^{m-2}+k+1}^{n} \lambda_{i'} \sigma_{i'}(x) = \mathsf{T}_{2^m-2^{m-2}+k+1,n}(x).$$

Proof. In order to prove that these functions coincide we can use the formalization of Theorem 1, it consists in showing:

$$S'_{2^{m-1}+k+1} \cap [2^m - 2^{m-2} + k + 1, n] = S'_{2^m-2^{m-2}+k+1}. \tag{2}$$

First, we show that both sets are subsets of $[2^m - 2^{m-2} + k + 1, 2^m]$. For the first one it is a direct consequence of Proposition 3 since $S'_{2^{m-1}+k+1} \subseteq [2^{m-1} + k + 1, 2^m]$. For the other set, due to the periodicity proven in Lemma 5, there are elements greater than 2^m in $S'_{2^m-2^{m-2}+k+1}$ only if there are indexes i in $[2k + \varepsilon]$ such that the ANF coefficients of $\mathsf{T}_{2^m-2^{m-2}+k+1,n}$ are equal to 1. It is not the case as $k < 2^{m-2}$, implying that $2k + \varepsilon < 2^{m-2} + k + 1 < 2^m - 2^{m-2} + k + 1$.

Then, writing $[2^m - 2^{m-2} + k + 1, 2^m]$ as $[2^m - v \mid v \in [0, 2^{m-2} - k - 1]]$, using the definitions of the sets S_d given in Theorem 1, Eq. 2 can be simplified to:

$$\{v \in [0, 2^{m-2} - k - 1] \mid v \preceq 2^{m-1} - k - 1\} = \{v \in [0, 2^m - 1] \mid v \preceq 2^{m-2} - k - 1\}.$$

We show that both sets are equal to $\{v \in [0, 2^{m-2} - k - 1] \mid v \preceq 2^{m-2} - k - 1\}$. For the first one, note that $v < 2^{m-2}$ then $v \preceq 2^{m-1} - k - 1 \Rightarrow v \preceq 2^{m-2} - k - 1$. For the other one, note that $v > 2^{m-2} - k - 1 \Rightarrow v \npreceq 2^{m-2} - k - 1$. The equivalence of these sets finishes the proof. $\square$

The next lemma shows a lower bound on the degree of a (particular case of) majority function multiplied by a low degree function. This lemma is the corner stone of the main theorem.

Lemma 9. *Let $n > 2$ be an integer such that $n = 2^m + 2k + \varepsilon$, with $m \geq 2, 0 \leq k < 2^{m-2}$, and $\varepsilon \in \{0,1\}$. For all nonzero $n-$variable function g such that $\deg(g) \leq k$, the following holds:*

$$\deg(g\mathsf{MAJ}_n) \geq 2^m - 2^{m-2} + k + 1.$$

Proof. We begin by writing MAJ_n as the sum of a function of degree less than or equal to $2^m - 2^{m-2} + k$ and the the part of MAJ_n of degree at least $2^m - 2^{m-2} + k + 1$. Note that in terms of ANF it corresponds to a partition of the ANF of MAJ_n, we use the following notation:

$$\mathsf{MAJ}_n = f_{\leq t} + f_{>t},$$

where $f_{\leq t}$ is the degree less than or equal to $2^m - 2^{m-2} + k$ part, and $f_{>t}$ is the remaining part: all the monomials of degree between $2^m - 2^{m-2} + k + 1$ and $2^m + 2k + \varepsilon$. Applying Lemma 7, $\deg f_{\leq t} = 2^m - 2^{m-2}$, and applying Lemma 8, $f_{>t} = \mathsf{T}_{2^m - 2^{m-2} + k + 1, n}$.

Then, for any nonzero function g such that $\deg(g) \leq k$, the degree of $g f_{\leq t}$ is at most $2^m - 2^{m-2} + k$. Using Lemma 2 on $\mathsf{T}_{2^m - 2^{m-2} + k + 1, n}$, and since $\mathsf{AI}(\mathsf{T}_{2^m - 2^{m-2} + k + 1, n}) = \min(2^m - 2^{m-2} + k + 1, 2^{m-2} + k + \varepsilon) > k$, we have:

$$\deg(g\mathsf{T}_{2^m - 2^{m-2} + k + 1, n}) \geq \mathsf{AN}(1 + \mathsf{T}_{2^m - 2^{m-2} + k + 1, n}) = 2^m - 2^{m-2} + k + 1.$$

The degree of $g f_{\leq t}$ being at most $2^m - 2^{m-2} + k$ and the one of $g f_{>t}$ at least $2^m - 2^{m-2} + k + 1$, it gives for all g nonzero of degree at most f:

$$\deg(g\mathsf{MAJ}_n) = \deg(g(f_{\leq t} + f_{>t})) \geq 2^m - 2^{m-2} + k + 1.$$

$\square$

This lemma enables us to state the theorem for the exact fast algebraic immunity of several families of majority functions:

Theorem 2 (Exact Fast Algebraic Immunity of Majority Functions). *Let* MAJ_n *be the* $n-$*variable majority function such that* $n = 2^m + 2k + \varepsilon$, *where* $m \geq 2$, $0 \leq k < 2^{m-2}$, *and* $\varepsilon \in \{0, 1\}$:

$$\mathsf{FAI}(\mathsf{MAJ}_n) = 2^{m-1} + 2k + 2.$$

Proof. First we recall the definition of the fast algebraic immunity, applied on MAJ_n:

$$\mathsf{FAI}(\mathsf{MAJ}_n) = \min\left\{ 2\mathsf{AI}(\mathsf{MAJ}_n), \min_{1 \leq \deg(g) < \mathsf{AI}(\mathsf{MAJ}_n)} [\deg(g) + \deg(g\mathsf{MAJ}_n)] \right\}.$$

Lemma 2 gives $2\mathsf{AI}(\mathsf{MAJ}_n) = 2^m + 2k + 2\varepsilon$ which is greater than the upper bound stated in Lemma 1. Then, we consider the degree of the right term depending on the degree of g. The degree of $g\mathsf{MAJ}_n$ for $1 \leq \deg(g) < \mathsf{AI}(\mathsf{MAJ}_n)$ is at least $2^{m-1} + k + 1$ using Property 3 and Lemma 2. Then we have two cases:

- If $\deg(g) > k$, then $\deg(g\mathsf{MAJ}_n) + \deg g \geq 2^{m-1} + k + 1 + k + 1 = 2^{m-1} + 2k + 2$, which is the upper bound of $\mathsf{FAI}(\mathsf{MAJ}_n)$ from [4].
- If $\deg(g) \leq k$, then applying Lemma 9, $\deg(g\mathsf{MAJ}_n) \geq 2^m - 2^{m-2} + k + 1 = 2^{m-1} + 2^{m-2} + k + 1$. As $k < 2^{m-2}$, it gives $\deg(g\mathsf{MAJ}_n) \geq 2^{m-1} + 2k + 2$, also reaching the upper bound.

We can therefore conclude: $\mathsf{FAI}(\mathsf{MAJ}_n) = 2^{m-1} + 2k + 2$. $\square$

6 Conclusion

In conclusion, in this article we developed different techniques to determine the exact fast algebraic immunity of majority functions over n bits:

- First, we gave an expression of the ANF of any threshold function, using a particular set representation to determine more easily its decomposition in terms of elementary symmetric functions.
- Then, we showed some gaps between two consecutive degrees appearing in the ANF of a threshold function. We used these gaps to bound the degree of the products with functions of upper bounded degree.
- Finally, we exhibited that a subpart of a threshold function can correspond to another threshold function of higher threshold. The known properties of this second function can then be used to derive properties on the first one.

We used these techniques on a sub-case of majority functions, writing any integer n as $2^m + 2k + \varepsilon$ with m the biggest power of 2 smaller than or equal to n and ε used for the parity of n, our results applies for $m \geq 2$ and $k < 2^{m-2}$. Since $m \geq 2$, Theorem 2 gives the exact fast algebraic immunity of all function with $n \in [2^m, 2^m + 2^{m-1} - 1]$, which corresponds to half of the functions. In the formulation of [11,36], the majority functions are considered in terms of family indexed by j such that $n = 2^m + j$. It corresponds to a more asymptotic oriented definition, where the result applies since m is bigger than a fixed value. In these terms, Theorem 2 applies to any j, giving that the exact FAI of the majority in $2^m + j$ variables is $2^{m-1} + j + 2$ for j even and $2^{m-1} + j + 1$ for j odd, and the result applies since $m \geq \log(j + 1) + 1$.

Concerning the remaining cases, for $m < 2$, it corresponds to $n \in \{1, 2, 3\}$, where $k = 0$, the case $n = 3$ is taken in Corollary 1. The other cases are exceptions, for $n = 2$ the minimum is given by $2\mathsf{AI}(\mathsf{MAJ}_2) = 2$ which is optimal. For $n = 1$ the definition of FAI is not accurate as the formula would give 2 (whereas the FAI is supposed to be at most n). For $m \geq 2$, note that no majority function such that $2^{m-2} < k < 2^{m-1}$ can reach the upper bound of Lemma 1. Indeed, These majority functions have degree 2^m and then for any degree 1 function g:

$$\deg(g\mathsf{MAJ}_n) + \deg(g) \leq 2^m + 2, \text{ and } 2^m + 2 < 2^{m-1} + 2k + 2,$$

where we only use that $\mathsf{AI}(\mathsf{MAJ}_n) > 1$, and $\mathsf{AN}(1 + \mathsf{MAJ}_n) = 2^{m-1} + k + 1$ (from Lemma 2). This explains why no such values of k are taken in consideration it the main theorem. Nevertheless, for the remaining values the techniques we developed could still be used, but targeting a tighter upper bound.

As noted in Remark 3, the $n-$variable threshold functions form a basis of $n-$variable symmetric functions. As such, the results we presented allow to obtain the exact fast algebraic immunity of several families of majority functions. We hope than such techniques can be used to determine more precisely the algebraic properties (such as ANF, degree, AI, and FAI) of all symmetric functions.

Acknowledgements. The author is a beneficiary of a FSR Incoming Post-doctoral Fellowship.

References

1. Ananth, P., Sahai, A.: Projective arithmetic functional encryption and indistinguishability obfuscation from degree-5 multilinear maps. In: Coron, J.-S., Nielsen, J.B. (eds.) EUROCRYPT 2017. LNCS, vol. 10210, pp. 152–181. Springer, Cham (2017). https://doi.org/10.1007/978-3-319-56620-7_6
2. Applebaum, B., Lovett, S.: Algebraic attacks against random local functions and their countermeasures. In: Wichs, D., Mansour, Y. (eds.) 48th ACM STOC. ACM Press, June 2016
3. Applebaum, B., Lovett, S.: Algebraic attacks against random local functions and their countermeasures. SIAM J. Comput. **47**(1), 52–79 (2018)
4. Armknecht, F., Carlet, C., Gaborit, P., Künzli, S., Meier, W., Ruatta, O.: Efficient computation of algebraic immunity for algebraic and fast algebraic attacks. In: Vaudenay, S. (ed.) EUROCRYPT 2006. LNCS, vol. 4004, pp. 147–164. Springer, Heidelberg (2006). https://doi.org/10.1007/11761679_10
5. Braeken, A., Preneel, B.: On the algebraic immunity of symmetric Boolean functions. In: Maitra, S., Veni Madhavan, C.E., Venkatesan, R. (eds.) INDOCRYPT 2005. LNCS, vol. 3797, pp. 35–48. Springer, Heidelberg (2005). https://doi.org/10.1007/11596219_4
6. Canteaut, A., Videau, M.: Symmetric Boolean functions. IEEE Trans. Inf. Theor. **51**(8), 2791–2811 (2005)
7. Carlet, C.: On the degree, nonlinearity, algebraic thickness, and nonnormality of Boolean functions, with developments on symmetric functions. IEEE Trans. Inf. Theor. **50**(9), 2178–2185 (2004)
8. Carlet, C.: Boolean functions for cryptography and error-correcting codes. In: Encyclopedia of Mathematics and Its Applications, pp. 257–397, Cambridge University Press (2010)
9. Carlet, C., Feng, K.: An Infinite class of balanced functions with optimal algebraic immunity, good immunity to fast algebraic attacks and good nonlinearity. In: Pieprzyk, J. (ed.) ASIACRYPT 2008. LNCS, vol. 5350, pp. 425–440. Springer, Heidelberg (2008). https://doi.org/10.1007/978-3-540-89255-7_26
10. Carlet, C., Méaux, P.: Boolean functions for homomorphic-friendly stream ciphers (2019, to appear)
11. Chen, Y., Guo, F., Zhang, L.: Fast algebraic immunity of $2^m + 2$ and $2^m + 3$ variables majority function. Cryptology ePrint Archive, Report 2019/286 (2019)
12. Climent, J.J., García, F., Requena, V.: The degree of a Boolean function and some algebraic properties of its support. **45**, 25–36 (2013). https://doi.org/10.2495/DATA130031
13. Courtois, N.T.: Fast algebraic attacks on stream ciphers with linear feedback. In: Boneh, D. (ed.) CRYPTO 2003. LNCS, vol. 2729, pp. 176–194. Springer, Heidelberg (2003). https://doi.org/10.1007/978-3-540-45146-4_11
14. Courtois, N.T., Meier, W.: Algebraic attacks on stream ciphers with linear feedback. In: Biham, E. (ed.) EUROCRYPT 2003. LNCS, vol. 2656, pp. 345–359. Springer, Heidelberg (2003). https://doi.org/10.1007/3-540-39200-9_21
15. Cusick, T.: Simpler proof for nonlinearity of majority function. arXiv:1710.02034v2 (2018)
16. Dalai, D.K.: Computing the rank of incidence matrix and the algebraic immunity of Boolean functions. Cryptology ePrint Archive, Report 2013/273 (2013). http://eprint.iacr.org/2013/273

17. Dalai, D.K., Gupta, K.C., Maitra, S.: Cryptographically significant Boolean functions: construction and analysis in terms of algebraic immunity. In: Gilbert, H., Handschuh, H. (eds.) FSE 2005. LNCS, vol. 3557, pp. 98–111. Springer, Heidelberg (2005). https://doi.org/10.1007/11502760_7

18. Dalai, D.K., Maitra, S., Sarkar, S.: Basic theory in construction of Boolean functions with maximum possible annihilator immunity. Des. Codes Crypt. **40**(1), 41–58 (2006)

19. Faugère, J.C.: A new efficient algorithm for computing Grobner bases without reduction to zero. In: Workshop on application of Groebner Bases 2002, Catania, Spain (2002). https://hal.inria.fr/inria-00100997

20. Gentry, C.: Fully homomorphic encryption using ideal lattices. In: Mitzenmacher, M. (ed.) 41st ACM STOC, pp. 169–178. ACM Press, May/June 2009

21. Goldreich, O.: Candidate one-way functions based on expander graphs. Electron. Colloq. Comput. Complex. (ECCC) **7**(90), 76–87 (2000)

22. Hawkes, P., Rose, G.G.: Rewriting variables: the complexity of fast algebraic attacks on stream ciphers. In: Franklin, M. (ed.) CRYPTO 2004. LNCS, vol. 3152, pp. 390–406. Springer, Heidelberg (2004). https://doi.org/10.1007/978-3-540-28628-8_24

23. Hongjun, W.: A lightweight authenticated cipher (2016). https://competitions.cr.yp.to/round3/acornv3.pdf

24. Lin, H., Tessaro, S.: Indistinguishability obfuscation from trilinear maps and blockwise local PRGs. In: Katz, J., Shacham, H. (eds.) CRYPTO 2017. LNCS, vol. 10401, pp. 630–660. Springer, Cham (2017). https://doi.org/10.1007/978-3-319-63688-7_21

25. Lin, H., Vaikuntanathan, V.: Indistinguishability obfuscation from DDH-like assumptions on constant-degree graded encodings. In: Dinur, I. (ed.) 57th FOCS, pp. 11–20. IEEE Computer Society Press, October 2016. https://doi.org/10.1109/FOCS.2016.11

26. Liu, M., Lin, D.: Almost perfect algebraic immune functions with good nonlinearity. In: 2014 IEEE International Symposium on Information Theory, pp. 1837–1841, June 2014. https://doi.org/10.1109/ISIT.2014.6875151

27. Liu, M., Zhang, Y., Lin, D.: Perfect algebraic immune functions. In: Wang, X., Sako, K. (eds.) ASIACRYPT 2012. LNCS, vol. 7658, pp. 172–189. Springer, Heidelberg (2012). https://doi.org/10.1007/978-3-642-34961-4_12

28. Méaux, P., Carlet, C., Journault, A., Standaert, F.X.: Improved filter permutators: combining symmetric encryption design, Boolean functions, low complexity cryptography, and homomorphic encryption, for private delegation of computations. Cryptology ePrint Archive, Report 2019/483 (2019). https://eprint.iacr.org/2019/483

29. Méaux, P., Journault, A., Standaert, F.-X., Carlet, C.: Towards stream ciphers for efficient FHE with low-noise ciphertexts. In: Fischlin, M., Coron, J.-S. (eds.) EUROCRYPT 2016. LNCS, vol. 9665, pp. 311–343. Springer, Heidelberg (2016). https://doi.org/10.1007/978-3-662-49890-3_13

30. Qu, L., Feng, K., Liu, F., Wang, L.: Constructing symmetric Boolean functions with maximum algebraic immunity. IEEE Trans. Inf. Theor. **55**(5), 2406–2412 (2009)

31. Qu, L., Li, C., Feng, K.: A note on symmetric Boolean functions with maximum algebraic immunity in odd number of variables. IEEE Trans. Inf. Theor. **53**(8), 2908–2910 (2007)

32. Geffe, P.R.: How to protect data with ciphers that are really hard to break. Electronics **46**(1), 99–101 (1973)

33. Sarkar, P., Maitra, S.: Balancedness and correlation immunity of symmetric Boolean functions. Discrete Math. **307**(19–20), 2351–2358 (2007)
34. Tang, D., Carlet, C., Tang, X., Zhou, Z.: Construction of highly nonlinear 1-resilient Boolean functions with optimal algebraic immunity and provably high fast algebraic immunity. IEEE Trans. Inf. Theor. **63**(9), 6113–6125 (2017). https://doi.org/10.1109/TIT.2017.2725918
35. Tang, D., Carlet, C., Tang, X.: Highly nonlinear Boolean functions with optimal algebraic immunity and good behavior against fast algebraic attacks. IEEE Trans. Inf. Theor. **63**(9), 653–664 (2013). https://doi.org/10.1109/TIT.2012.2217476
36. Tang, D., Luo, R., Du, X.: The exact fast algebraic immunity of two subclasses of the majority function. IEICE Trans. **99**(11), 2084–2088 (2016)

Side-Channel Analysis

Don't Forget Your Roots: Constant-Time Root Finding over $\mathbb{F}_{2^m}$

Douglas Martins[1($\boxtimes$)], Gustavo Banegas[2,3], and Ricardo Custódio[1]

[1] Departamento de Informática e Estatística, Universidade Federal
de Santa Catarina, Florianópolis, SC 88040-900, Brazil
marcelino.douglas@posgrad.ufsc.br, ricardo.custodio@ufsc.br
[2] Department of Mathematics and Computer Science, Technische Universiteit
Eindhoven, P.O. Box 513, 5600 Eindhoven, MB, The Netherlands
[3] Chalmers University of Technology, Gothenburg, Sweden
gustavo@cryptme.in

Abstract. In the last few years, post-quantum cryptography has received much attention. NIST is running a competition to select some post-quantum schemes as standard. As a consequence, implementations of post-quantum schemes have become important and with them side-channel attacks. In this paper, we show a timing attack on a code-based scheme which was submitted to the NIST competition. This timing attack recovers secret information because of a timing variance in finding roots in a polynomial. We present four algorithms to find roots that are protected against remote timing exploitation.

Keywords: Side-channel attack · Post-quantum cryptography ·
Code-based cryptography · Roots finding

1 Introduction

In recent years, the area of post-quantum cryptography has received considerable attention, mainly because of the call by the National Institute of Standards and Technology (NIST) for the standardization of post-quantum schemes. On this call, NIST did not restrict to specific hard problems. However, most schemes for the Key Encapsulation Mechanism (KEM) are lattice-based and code-based. The latter type is based on coding theory and includes one of the oldest unbroken cryptosystems, namely the McEliece cryptosystem [15].

This study was financed in part by the Coordenação de Aperfeiçoamento de Pessoal de Nível Superior - Brasil (CAPES) - Finance Code 001; through the European Union's Horizon 2020 research and innovation programme under the Marie Skłodowska-Curie grant agreement No. 643161; and by Sweden through the WASP expedition project Massive, Secure, and Low-Latency Connectivity for IoT Applications.

P. Schwabe and N. Thériault (Eds.): LATINCRYPT 2019, LNCS 11774, pp. 109–129, 2019.
https://doi.org/10.1007/978-3-030-30530-7_6

One of the requirements for those proposals is that they are resistant to all known cryptanalysis methods. However, even if a scheme is immune to such attacks, it may be subject to attacks related to its implementation. In particular, submissions need to avoid side-channel attacks.

There are different ways to apply side-channel attacks to a cryptosystem. As an example, an attacker can measure the execution time of the operations performed by an algorithm and, based on these measures, estimate some secret information of the scheme. This approach is thriving even in a data communication network environment. Bernstein, for instance, demonstrated how to recover AES keys by doing timing attacks on the cache "access speed" [5].

In code-based cryptography, timing attacks on the decryption process are mostly done during the retrieval of the Error Locator Polynomial (ELP) as shown by [20]. The attack is usually done during the polynomial evaluation process, while computing its roots. This attack was demonstrated first in [20] and later in an improved version in [10].

[21] demonstrates algorithms to find roots efficiently in code-based cryptosystems. However, the author shows only timings in different types of implementations and selects the one that has the least timing variability. In other words, the author does not present an algorithm to find the roots in constant time and eliminate a remote timing attack as remarked in Section 6 of [22]. In our work, we use strategies to make the execution time of those algorithms constant. The first and most important one is to write the algorithms iteratively, eliminating all recursions. We also use permutations and simulated operations to uncouple possible measurements of the side effects of the data being measured. The implementation for finding roots in [12] uses Fast Fourier Transform (FFT), which is efficient, but is built and optimized for $\mathbb{F}_{2^{13}}$. In this paper, we aim at developing a more generic implementation that does not require specific optimization in the finite field arithmetic.

Contributions of this Paper: In this paper, we show how to perform a timing attack on a code-based key encapsulation mechanism called BIGQUAKE, which was submitted to NIST [2]. The attack was based on timing leakage on root finding process on the decoding step. The original implementation submitted to NIST uses a variation of the Berlekamp Trace Algorithm (BTA) to find roots in the ELP. We provide other methods to find roots and implement them avoiding timing attacks. Moreover, we make a comparison between methods, showing the number of CPU cycles required for our implementation.

Structure of this Paper: In Sect. 2, we give a brief description of Goppa codes, the McEliece cryptosystem and BIGQUAKE for an understanding about how the cryptosystems work and the basic notation used in this paper. In Subsect. 2.4, we show how to use a timing attack for recovering the error vector in BIGQUAKE. In Sect. 3, the core of the paper, we present four methods for finding roots over $\mathbb{F}_{2^m}$. We also include countermeasures for avoiding timing attacks. Section 4 provides a comparison of the number of cycles of the original implementation and the implementation with countermeasures. At last, we conclude and discuss open problems.

2   Preliminaries

In this section, we briefly introduce key concepts about Goppa codes and the McEliece cryptosystem [15], relevant for this paper. For more details about algebraic codes, see [3]. After that, we introduce the BIGQUAKE submission, which is the focus of a timing attack presented in Subsect. 2.4.

Our focus is on binary Goppa codes since BIGQUAKE [2] and other McEliece schemes use them in their constructions. Moreover, Goppa codes are being used in other submissions in the Second Round of the NIST standardization process.

2.1   Goppa Codes

Let $m, n, t \in \mathbb{N}$. A binary Goppa code $\Gamma(L, g(z))$ is defined by a polynomial $g(z) = \sum_{i=0}^{t} g_i z^i$ over $\mathbb{F}_{2^m}$ with degree t and $L = (\alpha_1, \alpha_2, \ldots, \alpha_n) \in \mathbb{F}_{2^m}$ with $\alpha_i \neq \alpha_j$ for $i \neq j$, such that $g(\alpha_i) \neq 0$ for all $\alpha_i \in L$ and $g(z)$ is square free. To a vector $c = (c_1 \ldots, c_n) \in \mathbb{F}_2^n$ we associate a syndrome polynomial such as

$$S_c(z) = \sum_{i=1}^{n} \frac{c_i}{z + \alpha_i}, \tag{1}$$

where $\frac{1}{z+\alpha_i}$ is the unique polynomial with $(z + \alpha_i)\frac{1}{z+\alpha_i} \equiv 1 \mod g(z)$.

Definition 1. *The binary Goppa code $\Gamma(L, g(z))$ consists of all vectors $c \in \mathbb{F}_2^n$ such that*

$$S_c(z) \equiv 0 \mod g(z). \tag{2}$$

The parameters of a linear code are the size n, dimension k and minimum distance d. We use the notation $[n, k, d]$−Goppa code for a binary Goppa code with parameters n, k and d. If the polynomial $g(z)$, which defines a Goppa code, is irreducible over $\mathbb{F}_{2^m}$, we call the code an irreducible Goppa code.

The length of a Goppa code is given by $n = |L|$ and its dimension is $k \geq n - mt$, where $t = deg(g)$, and the minimum distance of $\Gamma(L, g(z))$ is $d \geq 2t + 1$. The syndrome polynomial $S_c(z)$ can be written as:

$$S_c(z) \equiv \frac{w(z)}{\sigma(z)} \mod g(z), \tag{3}$$

where $\sigma(z) = \prod_{i=1}^{l}(z + \alpha_i)$ is the product over those $(z + \alpha_i)$, where there is an error in position i of c. This polynomial $\sigma(z)$ is called Error-Locator Polynomial (ELP).

A binary Goppa code can correct a codeword $c \in \mathbb{F}_2^n$, which is obscured by an error vector $e \in \mathbb{F}_2^n$ with Hamming weight $w_h(e)$ up to t, i.e., the numbers of non-zero entries in e is at most t. The way to correct errors is using a decoding algorithm. For irreducible binary Goppa codes, we have three alternatives: Extended Euclidean Algorithm (EEA), Berlekamp-Massey algorithm and Patterson algorithm [17]. The first two are out of the scope of this paper since they need a parity-check matrix that has twice more rows than columns. The Patterson algorithm, which is the focus of this paper, can correct up to t errors with a smaller structure.

2.2 McEliece Cryptosystem

In this section, we describe the three important algorithms of the McEliece cryptosystem [15], i.e., key generation, message encryption, and message decryption. To give a practical explanation, we describe the McEliece scheme based on binary Goppa codes. However, it can be used with any q-ary Goppa codes or Generalized Srivastava codes with small modifications as shown by [16] and [1].

Algorithm 1. McEliece key generation.

   Data: t, k, n, m as integers.
   Result: pk as public key, sk as secret key.
 1 Select a random binary Goppa polynomial $g(z)$ of degree t over $\mathbb{F}_{2^m}$;
 2 Randomly choose n distinct elements of $\mathbb{F}_{2^m}$ that are not roots of $g(z)$ as the support L;
 3 Compute the $k \times n$ parity check matrix $\hat{H}$ according to L and $g(z)$;
 4 Bring H to systematic form: $H_{sys} = [I_{k-n}|H']$;
 5 Compute generator matrix G from H_{sys};
 6 **return** sk $= (L, g(z))$, pk $= (G)$;

Algorithm 1 is the key generation of McEliece. First, it starts by generating a binary Goppa polynomial $g(z)$ of degree t, which can be an irreducible Goppa polynomial. Second, it generates the support L as an ordered subset of $\mathbb{F}_{2^m}$ satisfying the root condition. Third, it is the computation of the systematic form of $\hat{H}$ is done using the Gauss-Jordan elimination algorithm. Steps four, five, and six compute the generator matrix from the previous systematic matrix and return secret and public key.

Algorithm 2. McEliece encryption.

   Data: Public key $pk = G$, message $m \in \mathbb{F}_2^k$.
   Result: c as ciphertext of length n.
 1 Choose randomly an error vector e of length n with $w_h(e) \leq t$;
 2 Compute $c = (m \cdot G) \oplus e$;
 3 **return** c;

Algorithm 2 shows the encryption process of McEliece. The process is simple and efficient, requiring only a random vector e with $w_h(e) \leq t$ and a multiplication of a vector by a matrix.

Algorithm 3 gives the decryption part of McEliece. This algorithm consists of the removal of the applied errors using a decoding algorithm. First, we compute the syndrome polynomial $S_c(z)$. Second, we recover the error vector e from the syndrome polynomial. Finally, we can recover the plaintext m computing $c \oplus e$, i.e., the exclusive-or of the ciphertext and the error vector. Note that in modern KEM versions of McEliece, $m \in \mathbb{F}_2^n$ is a random bit string used to compute a session key using a hash function. Hence, there is no intelligible information in seeing the first k positions of m with almost no error.

Algorithm 3. McEliece decryption.

Data: c as ciphertext of length n, secret key $sk = (L, g(z))$.
Result: Message m
1 Compute the syndrome $S_c(z) = \sum \frac{c_i}{z + \alpha_i} \mod g(z)$;
2 Compute $\tau(z) = \sqrt{S_c^{-1}(z) + z}$;
3 Compute $b(z)$ and $a(z)$, so that $b(z)\tau(z) = a(z) \mod g(z)$, such that $\deg(a) \le \lfloor \frac{t}{2} \rfloor$ and $\deg(b) \le \lfloor \frac{t-1}{2} \rfloor$;
4 Compute the error locator polynomial $\sigma(z) = a^2(z) + zb^2(z)$ and $\deg(\sigma) \le t$;
5 The position in L of the roots of $\sigma(z)$ define the error vector e;
6 Compute the plaintext $m = c \oplus e$;
7 **return** m;

In the decryption algorithm, steps 2-5 are the description of Patterson's algorithm [17]. This same strategy can be used in schemes that make use of the Niederreiter cryptosystem [11]. These schemes differ in their public-key structure, encryption, and decryption step, but both of them, in the decryption steps, decode the message from the syndrome.

The roots of the ELP can be acquired with different methods. Although these methods can be implemented with different forms, it is essential that the implementations do not leak any timing information about their execution. This leakage can lead to a side-channel attack using time differences in the decryption algorithm, as we explore in a scheme in Subsect. 2.4.

2.3   BIGQUAKE Key Encapsulation Mechanism

BIGQUAKE (BInary Goppa QUAsi-cyclic Key Encapsulation) [2] uses binary Quasi-cyclic (QC) Goppa codes in order to accomplish a KEM between two distinct parts. Instead of using binary Goppa codes, BIGQUAKE uses QC Goppa codes, which have the same properties as Goppa codes but allow smaller keys. Furthermore, BIGQUAKE aims to be IND-CCA [6], which makes the attack scenario in Sect. 2.4 meaningful.

Let us suppose that Alice and Bob (A and B respectively) want to share a session secret key K using BIGQUAKE. Then Bob needs to publishes his public key and Alice needs to follow the encapsulation mechanism. $\mathcal{F}$ is a function that maps an arbitrary binary string as input and returns a word of weight t, i.e $\mathcal{F} : \{0,1\}^* \to \{x \in \mathbb{F}_2^n | w_h(x) = t\}$. The detailed construction of the function $\mathcal{F}$

can be found at subsection 3:4:4 in [2]. $\mathcal{H} : \{0,1\}^k \rightarrow \{0,1\}^s$ is a hash function. The function $\mathcal{H}$ in the original implementation is SHA-3. The encapsulation mechanism can be described as:

1. A generates a random $m \in \mathbb{F}_2^s$;
2. Generate $e \leftarrow \mathcal{F}(m)$;
3. A sends $c \leftarrow (m \oplus \mathcal{H}(e), H \cdot e^T, \mathcal{H}(m))$ to B;
4. The session key is defined as: $K \leftarrow \mathcal{H}(m, c)$.

After Bob receives c from Alice, he initiates the decapsulation process:

1. B receives $c = (c_1, c_2, c_3)$;
2. Using the secret key, Bob decodes c_2 to e' with $w_h(e') \leq t$ such that $c_2 = H \cdot e'^T$;
3. B computes $m' \leftarrow c_1 \oplus \mathcal{H}(e')$;
4. B computes $e'' \leftarrow \mathcal{F}(m')$;
5. If $e'' \neq e'$ or $\mathcal{H}(m') \neq c_3$ then B aborts.
6. Else, B computes the session key: $K \leftarrow \mathcal{H}(m', c)$.

After Bob executes the decapsulation process successfully, both parties of the protocol agree on the same session secret key K.

2.4 Attack Description

In [20], the attack exploits the fact that flipping a bit of the error e changes the Hamming weight w and per consequence the timing for its decryption. If we flip a position that contains an error ($e_i = 1$) then the error will be removed and the time of computation will be shorter. However, if we flip a bit in a wrong position ($e_i = 0$) then it will add another error, and it will increase the decryption time. The attack described in [10] exploits the root finding in the polynomial ELP. It takes advantage of sending ciphertexts with fewer errors than expected, which generate an ELP with degree less than t, resulting in less time for finding roots. We explore both ideas applied to the implementation of BIGQUAKE.

Algorithm 4 is the direct implementation of the attack proposed in [20]. We reused the attack presented to show that the attack still works in current implementations such as BIGQUAKE when the root finding procedure is vulnerable to remote timing attacks.

After finding the position of the errors, one needs to verify if the error e' found is the correct one, and then recover the message m. In order to verify for correctness, one can check e' by computing $\mathcal{H}(e) \oplus \mathcal{H}(e') \oplus m = m'$ and if c_3 is equal to $\mathcal{H}(m')$. As mentioned in Subsect. 2.3, the ciphertext is composed by $c = (m \oplus \mathcal{H}(e), H \cdot e^T, \mathcal{H}(m))$ or $c = (c_1, c_2, c_3)$.

2.5 Constant-Time $\mathbb{F}_{2^m}$ operations

In our analysis, we noticed that the original implementation of BIGQUAKE uses log and antilog tables for computing multiplications and inversions. These lookup tables give a speedup in those operations. However, this approach is subject

---

Algorithm 4. Attack on ELP.

Data: n-bit ciphertext c, t as the number of errors and precision parameter M
Result: Attempt to obtain an error vector e hidden in c.

1 $e \leftarrow [0, \ldots, 0]$;
2 **for** $i \leftarrow 0$ **to** $n - 1$ **do**
3 $\quad$ $T \leftarrow 0$;
4 $\quad$ $c' \leftarrow c \oplus \text{setBit}(n, i)$;
5 $\quad$ $time_m \leftarrow 0$;
6 $\quad$ **for** $j \leftarrow 0$ **to** M **do**
7 $\quad\quad$ $time_s \leftarrow time()$;
8 $\quad\quad$ $\text{decrypt}(c')$;
9 $\quad\quad$ $time_e \leftarrow time()$;
10 $\quad\quad$ $time_m \leftarrow time_m + (time_e - time_s)$;
11 $\quad$ **end**
12 $\quad$ $T \leftarrow time_m/M$;
13 $\quad$ $L \leftarrow (T, i)$;
14 **end**
15 Sort L in descending order of T;
16 **for** $k \leftarrow 0$ **to** $t - 1$ **do**
17 $\quad$ $index \leftarrow L[k].i$;
18 $\quad$ $e[index] \leftarrow 1$;
19 **end**
20 **return** e;

---

to cache attacks in a variation of [9], where the attacker tries to induce cache misses and infer the data.

Since we want to avoid the use of look-up tables, we made a constant time implementation for multiplication and inversion, using a similar approach as [12]. In order to illustrate that, Listing 1.1 shows the multiplication in constant-time between two elements over $\mathbf{F}_{2^{12}}$ followed by the reduction of the result by the irreducible polynomial $f(x) = x^{12} + x^6 + x^4 + x + 1$. The inversion in finite fields can be computed by raising an element a to the power $2^m - 2$, i.e., a^{2^m-2}, as shown in Listing 1.1.

3   Root Finding Methods

As argued, the leading cause of information leakage in the decoding algorithm is the process of finding the roots of the ELP. In general, the time needed to find these roots varies, often depending on the roots themselves. Thus, an attacker who has access to the decoding time can infer these roots, and hence get the vector of errors e. Next, we propose modifications in four of these algorithms to avoid the attack presented in Subsect. 2.4.

Strenzke [21] presents an algorithm analysis for fast and secure root finding for code-based cryptosystems. He uses as a basis for his results the implementation of "Hymes" [7]. Some of that implementation uses, for instance, log and antilog tables for some operations in finite fields, which are known to be vulnerable. Given that, we rewrote those operations without tables and analyzed each line of code from the original implementations, taking care of modifying them in order to eliminate processing that could indicate root-dependent execution time. The adjustments were made in the following algorithms to find roots: exhaustive search, linearized polynomials, Berlekamp trace algorithm (BTA), and successive resultant algorithm (SRA).

In this work, we use the following notation: given a univariate polynomial f, with degree d and coefficients over $\mathbb{F}_{p^n}$, one needs to find its roots. In our case, we are concerned about binary fields, i.e., $p = 2$. Additionally, we assume that all the factors of f are linear and distinct.

3.1 Exhaustive Search

The exhaustive search is a direct method, in which the evaluation of f for all the elements in $\mathbb{F}_{2^m}$ is performed. A root is found whenever the evaluation result is zero. This method is acceptable for small fields and can be made efficient with a parallel implementation. Algorithm 5 describes this method.

As can be seen in Algorithm 5, this method leaks information. This is because whenever a root is found, i.e., $dummy = 0$, an extra operation is performed. In this way, the attacker can infer from this additional time that a root was found, thus providing ways to obtain data that should be secret.

Algorithm 5. Exhaustive search algorithm for finding roots of a univariate polynomial over $\mathbb{F}_{2^m}$.

Data: $p(x)$ as univariate polynomial over $\mathbb{F}_{2^m}$ with d roots, $A = [a_0, \ldots, a_{n-1}]$ as all elements in $\mathbb{F}_{2^m}$, n as the length of A.
Result: R as a set of roots of $p(x)$.
1 $R \leftarrow \emptyset$;
2 **for** $i \leftarrow 0$ **to** $n - 1$ **do**
3 $\quad$ $dummy \leftarrow p(A[i])$;
4 $\quad$ **if** $dummy == 0$ **then**
5 $\quad\quad$ $R.add(A[i])$;
6 $\quad$ **end**
7 **end**
8 **return** R;

One solution to avoid this leakage is to permute the elements of vector A. Using this technique, an attacker can identify the extra operation, but without learning any secret information. In our case, we use the Fisher-Yates shuffle [8] for shuffling the elements of vector A. In [25], the authors show an implementation of the shuffling algorithm safe against timing attacks. Algorithm 6 shows the permutation of the elements and the computation of the roots.

Algorithm 6. Exhaustive search algorithm with a countermeasure for finding roots of an univariate polynomial over $\mathbb{F}_{2^m}$.

Data: $p(x)$ as a univariate polynomial over $\mathbb{F}_{2^m}$ with d roots,
  $A = [a_0, \ldots, a_{n-1}]$ as all elements in $\mathbb{F}_{2^m}$, n as the length of A.
Result: R as a set of roots of $p(x)$.

```
1  permute(A);
2  R ← ∅;
3  for i ← 0 to n − 1 do
4  │   dummy ← p(A[i]);
5  │   if dummy == 0 then
6  │   │   R.add(A[i]);
7  │   end
8  end
9  return R;
```

Using this approach, we add one extra step to the algorithm. However, this permutation blurs the sensitive information of the algorithm, making the usage of Algorithm 6 slightly harder for the attacker to acquire timing leakage.

The main costs for Algorithms 5 and 6 are the polynomial evaluation and we define as C_{pol_eval}. Since we need to evaluate each element in A, it is safer to assume that the total cost is:

$$C_{exh} = n(C_{pol\_eval}). \tag{4}$$

We can go further and express the cost for one polynomial evaluation by the number of operations in finite fields. In our implementation[1] the cost is determined by the degree d of the polynomial and basic finite field operations such as addition and multiplication. As a result, the cost for one polynomial evaluation is:

$$C_{pol\_eval} = d(C_{gf\_add} + C_{gf\_mul}). \tag{5}$$

3.2 Linearized Polynomials

The second countermeasure proposed is based on linearized polynomials. The authors in [14] propose a method to compute the roots of a polynomial over $\mathbb{F}_{2^m}$, using a particular class of polynomials, called linearized polynomials. In [21], this approach is a recursive algorithm which the author calls "dcmp-rf". In our solution, however, we present an iterative algorithm. We define linearized polynomials as follows:

Definition 2. *A polynomial $\ell(y)$ over $\mathbb{F}_{2^m}$ is called a linearized polynomial if*

$$\ell(y) = \sum_i c_i y^{2^i}, \tag{6}$$

where $c_i \in \mathbb{F}_{2^m}$.

---

[1] available in https://git.dags-project.org/gustavo/roots_finding.

In addition, from [24], we have Lemma 1 that describes the main property of linearized polynomials for finding roots.

Lemma 1. *Let $y \in \mathbb{F}_{2^m}$ and let $\alpha^0, \alpha^1, \ldots, \alpha^{m-1}$ be a standard basis over $\mathbb{F}_2$. If*

$$y = \sum_{k=0}^{m-1} y_k \alpha^k, y_k \in \mathbb{F}_2 \tag{7}$$

and $\ell(y) = \sum_j c_j y^{2^j}$, then

$$\ell(y) = \sum_{k=0}^{m-1} y_k \ell(\alpha^k). \tag{8}$$

We call $A(y)$ over $\mathbb{F}_{2^m}$ as an affine polynomial if $A(y) = \ell(y) + \beta$ for $\beta \in \mathbb{F}_{2^m}$, where $\ell(y)$ is a linearized polynomial.

We can illustrate a toy example to understand the idea behind finding roots using linearized polynomials.

Example 1. Let us consider the polynomial $f(y) = y^2 + (\alpha^2 + 1)y + (\alpha^2 + \alpha + 1)y^0$ over $\mathbb{F}_{2^3}$ and α are elements in $\mathbb{F}_2[x]/x^3 + x^2 + 1$. Since we are trying to find roots, we can write $f(y)$ as

$$y^2 + (\alpha^2 + 1)y + (\alpha^2 + \alpha + 1)y^0 = 0$$

or

$$y^2 + (\alpha^2 + 1)y = (\alpha^2 + \alpha + 1)y^0 \tag{9}$$

We can point that on the left hand side of Eq. 9, $\ell(y) = y^2 + (\alpha^2 + 1)y$ is a linearized polynomial over $\mathbb{F}_{2^3}$ and Eq. 9 can be expressed just as

$$\ell(y) = \alpha^2 + \alpha + 1 \tag{10}$$

If $y = y_2 \alpha^2 + y_1 \alpha + y_0 \in \mathbb{F}_{2^3}$ then, according to Lemma 1, Eq. 10 becomes

$$y_2 \ell(\alpha^2) + y_1 \ell(\alpha) + y_0 \ell(\alpha^0) = \alpha^2 + \alpha + 1 \tag{11}$$

We can compute $\ell(\alpha^0), \ell(\alpha)$ and $\ell(\alpha^2)$ using the left hand side of Eq. 9 and we have the following values

$$\ell(\alpha^0) = (\alpha^0)^2 + (\alpha^2 + 1)(\alpha^0) = \alpha^2 + 1 + 1 = \alpha^2$$
$$\ell(\alpha) = (\alpha)^2 + (\alpha^2 + 1)(\alpha) = \alpha^2 + \alpha^2 + \alpha + 1 = \alpha + 1 \tag{12}$$
$$\ell(\alpha^2) = (\alpha^2)^2 + (\alpha^2 + 1)(\alpha^2) = \alpha^4 + \alpha^4 + \alpha^2 = \alpha^2.$$

A substitution of Eq. 12 into Eq. 11 gives us

$$(y_2 + y_0)\alpha^2 + (y_1)\alpha + (y_1)\alpha^0 = \alpha^2 + \alpha + 1 \tag{13}$$

Equation 13 can be expressed as a matrix in the form

$$
\begin{bmatrix} y_2 & y_1 & y_0 \end{bmatrix}
\begin{bmatrix} 1 & 0 & 0 \\ 0 & 1 & 1 \\ 1 & 0 & 0 \end{bmatrix}
= \begin{bmatrix} 1 & 1 & 1 \end{bmatrix}.
\tag{14}
$$

If one solves simultaneously the linear system in Eq. 14 then the results are the roots of the polynomial given in Eq. 9. From Eq. 13, one observes that the solutions are $y = 110$ and $y = 011$, which can be translated to $\alpha + 1$ and $\alpha^2 + \alpha$.

Fortunately, the authors in [14] provide a generic decomposition for finding affine polynomials. In their work, each polynomial in the form $F(y) = \sum_{j=0}^{t} f_j y^j$ for $f_j \in \mathbb{F}_{2^m}$ can be represented as

$$
F(y) = f_3 y^3 + \sum_{i=0}^{\lceil (t-4)/5 \rceil} y^{5i} \left(f_{5i} + \sum_{j=0}^{3} f_{5i+2^j} y^{2^j} \right)
\tag{15}
$$

After that, we can summarize all the steps as Algorithm 7. The function "generate(m)" refers to the generation of the elements in $\mathbb{F}_{2^m}$ using Gray codes, see [19] for more details about Gray codes.

Algorithm 7 presents a countermeasure in the last steps of the algorithm, i.e., we added a dummy operation for blinding if $X[j]$ is a root of polynomial $F(x)$.

Using Algorithm 7, the predominant cost for its implementation is:

$$
C_{lin} = m(C_{gf\_pow} + C_{pol\_eval}) + 2^m(C_{gf\_pow} + 2C_{gf\_mul})
\tag{16}
$$

3.3 Berlekamp Trace Algorithm – BTA

In [4], Berlekamp presents an efficient algorithm to factor a polynomial, which can be used to find its roots. We call this algorithm *Berlekamp trace algorithm* since it works with a trace function defined as $Tr(x) = x + x^2 + x^{2^2} + \cdots + x^{2^{m-1}}$. It is possible to change BTA for finding roots of a polynomial $p(x)$ using $\beta = \{\beta_1, \beta_2, \ldots, \beta_m\}$ as a standard basis of $\mathbb{F}_{2^m}$, and then computing the greatest common divisor between $p(x)$ and $Tr(\beta_0 \cdot x)$. After that, it starts a recursion where BTA performs two recursive calls; one with the result of gcd algorithm and the other with the remainder of the division $p(x)/\gcd(p(x), Tr(\beta_i \cdot x))$. The base case is when the degree of the input polynomial is smaller than one. In this case, BTA returns the root, by getting the independent term of the polynomial. In summary, the BTA is a divide and conquer like algorithm since it splits the task of computing the roots of a polynomial $p(x)$ into the roots of two smalls polynomials. The description of BTA algorithm is presented in Algorithm 8.

As we can see, a direct implementation of Algorithm 8 has no constant execution time. The recursive behavior may leak information about the characteristics of roots in a side-channel attack. Additionally, in our experiments, we noted that the behavior of the gcd with the trace function may result in a polynomial with

---

Algorithm 7. Linearized polynomials for finding roots over $\mathbb{F}_{2^m}$.

Data: $F(x)$ as a univariate polynomial over $\mathbb{F}_{2^m}$ with degree t and m as the
extension field degree.

Result: R as a set of roots of $p(x)$.

```
1  ℓᵢᵏ ← ∅; ℓᵢₛ ← ∅; Aₖʲ ← ∅; R ← ∅; dummy ← ∅;
2  if f₀ == 0 then
3  |   R.append(0);
4  end
5  for i ← 0 to ⌈(t − 4)/5⌉ do
6  |   ℓᵢ(x) ← 0;
7  |   for j ← 0 to 3 do
8  |   |   ℓᵢ(x) ← ℓᵢ(x) + f₅ᵢ₊₂ⱼ x^{2ʲ};
9  |   end
10 |   ℓᵢₛ[i] ← ℓᵢ(x);
11 end
12 for k ← 0 to m − 1 do
13 |   for i ← 0 to ⌈(t − 4)/5⌉ do
14 |   |   ℓᵢᵏ ← ℓᵢₛ(αᵏ);
15 |   end
16 end
17 Aᵢ⁰ ← ∅;
18 for i ← 0 to ⌈(t − 4)/5⌉ do
19 |   Aᵢ⁰ ← f₅ᵢ;
20 end
21 X ← generate(m);
22 for j ← 1 to 2ᵐ − 1 do
23 |   for i ← 0 to ⌈(t − 4)/5⌉ do
24 |   |   A ← Aᵢʲ⁻¹;
25 |   |   A ← A + ℓᵢ^{δ(X[j],X[j−1])};
26 |   |   Aᵢʲ ← A;
27 |   end
28 end
29 for j ← 1 to 2ᵐ − 1 do
30 |   result ← 0;
31 |   for i ← 0 to ⌈(t − 4)/5⌉ do
32 |   |   result = result + (X[j])^{5i} Aᵢʲ;
33 |   end
34 |   eval = result + f₃(X[j])³;
35 |   if eval == 0 then
36 |   |   R.append(X[j]);
37 |   else
38 |   |   dummy.append(X[j]);
39 |   end
40 end
41 return R;
```

Algorithm 8. Berlekamp Trace Algorithm [21] – $BTA(p(x), i) - rf$.

Data: $p(x)$ as a univariate polynomial over $\mathbb{F}_{2^m}$ and i.
Result: The set of roots of $p(x)$.

1 **if** $deg(p(x)) \leq 1$ **then**
2   **return** root of $p(x)$;
3 **end**
4 $p_0(x) \leftarrow gcd(p(x), Tr(\beta_i \cdot x))$;
5 $p_1(x) \leftarrow p(x)/p_0(x)$;
6 **return** $BTA(p_0(x), i+1) \cup BTA(p_1(x), i+1)$;

---

the same degree. Therefore, BTA will divide this input polynomial in a future call with a different basis. Consequently, there is no guarantee of a constant number of executions.

In order to avoid the nonconstant number of executions, here referred as $BTA - it$, we propose an iterative implementation of Algorithm 8. In this way, our proposal iterates in a fixed number of iterations instead of calling itself until the base case. The main idea is not changed; we still divide the task of computing the roots of a polynomial $p(x)$ into two smaller instances. However, we change the approach of the division of the polynomial. Since we want to compute the same number of operations independent of the degree of the polynomial, we perform the gcd with a trace function for all basis in β, and choose a division that results in two new polynomials with approximate degree.

This new approach allows us to define a fixed number of iterations for our version of BTA. Since we always divide into two small instances, we need $t - 1$ iterations to split a polynomial of degree t in t polynomials of degree 1. Algorithm 9 presents this approach.

Algorithm 9 extracts a root of the polynomial when the variable *current* has a polynomial with degree equal to one. If this degree is greater than one, then the algorithm needs to continue dividing the polynomial until it finds a root. The algorithm does that by adding the polynomial in a stack and reusing this polynomial in a division.

As presented in the previous methods, the overall cost of Algorithm 9 is:

$$C_{BTA-it} = t(mC_{gcd} + C_{QuoRem}). \tag{17}$$

where C_{gcd} is the cost of computing the gcd of two polynomials, with d the higher degree of those polynomials. In our implementation, the cost of C_{gcd} is:

$$C_{gcd} = d(C_{gf\_inv} + 3C_{gf\_mul}), \tag{18}$$

and C_{QuoRem} is the cost for computing the quotient and remainder between two polynomials. The cost for this computation is:

$$C_{QuoRem} = d(C_{gf\_inv} + (d+1)C_{gf\_mul} + C_{gf\_add}). \tag{19}$$

Algorithm 9. Iterative Berlekamp Trace Algorithm – $BTA(p(x)) - it$.

Data: $p(x)$ as an univariate polynomial over $\mathbb{F}_{2^m}$, t as number of expected
     roots.

Result: The set of roots of $p(x)$.

1 $g \leftarrow \{p(x)\}$; // The set of polynomials to be computed
2 **for** $k \leftarrow 0$ **to** t **do**
3 | $current = g.pop()$;
4 | Compute $candidates = gcd(current, Tr(\beta_i \cdot x))\ \forall\ \beta_i \in \beta$;
5 | Select $p_0 \in candidates$ such as $p_0.degree \simeq \frac{current}{2}$;
6 | $p_1(x) \leftarrow current/p_0(x)$;
7 | **if** $p_0.degree == 1$ **then**
8 | | $R.add(\text{root of } p_0)$
9 | **end**
10 | **else**
11 | | $g.add(p_0)$;
12 | **end**
13 | **if** $p_1.degree == 1$ **then**
14 | | $R.add(\text{root of } p_1)$
15 | **end**
16 | **else**
17 | | $g.add(p_1)$;
18 | **end**
19 **end**
20 **return** R

3.4   Successive Resultant Algorithm

In [18], the authors present an alternative method for finding roots in $\mathbb{F}_{p^m}$. Later on, the authors better explain the method in [13]. The Successive Resultant Algorithm (SRA) relies on the fact that it is possible to find roots exploiting properties of an ordered set of rational mappings.

Given a polynomial f of degree d and a sequence of rational maps $K_1, \ldots, K_t$, the algorithm computes finite sequences of length $j \leq t + 1$ obtained by successively transforming the roots of f by applying the rational maps. The algorithm is as follows: Let $\{v_1, \ldots, v_m\}$ be an arbitrary basis of $\mathbb{F}_{p^m}$ over $\mathbb{F}_p$, then it is possible to define $m + 1$ functions $\ell_0, \ell_1, \ldots, \ell_m$ from $\mathbb{F}_{p^m}$ to $\mathbb{F}_{p^m}$ such that

$$
\begin{cases}
\ell_0(z) = z \\
\ell_1(z) = \prod_{i \in \mathbb{F}_p} \ell_0(z - iv_1) \\
\ell_2(z) = \prod_{i \in \mathbb{F}_p} \ell_1(z - iv_2) \\
\ldots \\
\ell_m(z) = \prod_{i \in \mathbb{F}_p} \ell_{m-1}(z - iv_m)
\end{cases}
$$

The functions ℓ_j are examples of linearized polynomials, as previously defined in Subsect. 3.2. Our next step is to present the theorems from [18]. Check original work for the proofs.

Theorem 1. *(a) Each polynomial ℓ_i is split and its roots are all elements of the vector space generated by $\{v_1, \ldots, v_i\}$. In particular, we have $\ell_n(z) = z^{p^m} - z$.*
(b) We have $\ell_i(z) = \ell_{i-1}(z)^p - a_i\ell_{i-1}(z)$ where $a := (\ell_{i-1}(v_i))^{p-1}$.
(c) If we identify $\mathbb{F}_{p^m}$ with the vector space $(\mathbb{F}_p)^m$, then each ℓ_i is a p-to-1 linear map of $\ell_{i-1}(z)$ and a p^i to 1 linear map of z.

From Theorem 1 and its properties, we can reach the following polynomial system:

$$\begin{cases} f(x_1) = 0 \\ x_j^p = a_j x_j = x_{j+1} \quad j = 1, \ldots, m-1 \\ x_n^p - a_n x_n = 0 \end{cases} \tag{20}$$

where the $a_i \in \mathbb{F}_{p^n}$ are defined as in Theorem 1. Any solution of this system provides us with a root of f by the first equation, and the n last equations together imply this root belongs to $\mathbb{F}_{p^n}$. From this system of equations, [18] derives Theorem 2.

Theorem 2. *Let $(x_1, x_2, \ldots, x_m)$ be a solution of the equations in Eq. 20. Then $x_1 \in \mathbb{F}_{p^m}$ is a solution of f. Conversely, given a solution $x_1 \in \mathbb{F}_{p^m}$ of f, we can reconstruct a solution of all equations in Eq. 20 by setting $x_2 = x_1^p - a_1 x_1$, etc.*

In [18], the authors present an algorithm for solving the system in Eq. 20 using resultants. The solutions of the system are the roots of polynomial $f(x)$. We implemented the method presented in [18] using SAGE Math [23] due to the lack of libraries in C that work with multivariate polynomials over finite fields. It is worth remarking that this algorithm is almost constant-time and hence we just need to protect the branches presented on it. The countermeasure adopted was to add dummy operations, as presented in Subsect. 3.2.

4 Comparison

In this section, we present the results of the execution of each of the methods presented in Sect. 3. We used an Intel® Core(TM) i5-5300U CPU @ 2.30GHz. The code was compiled with GCC version 8.3.0 and the following compilation flags "-O3 -g3 -Wall -march=native -mtune=native -fomit-frame-pointer -ffast-math". We ran 100 times the code and got the average number of cycles. Table 1 shows the number of cycles of root finding methods without countermeasures, while Table 2 shows the number of cycles when there is a countermeasure. In both cases, we used $d = \{55, 65, 100\}$ where d is the number of roots. We remark that the operations in the tables are over $\mathbb{F}_{2^{12}}$ and $\mathbb{F}_{2^{16}}$. We used two different finite fields for showing the generality of our implementations and the costs for a small field and a larger field.

Figure 1 shows the number of cycles for random polynomials with degree 55, 65 and 100 and all the operations are over $\mathbb{F}_{2^{16}}$. Figure 1a shows a time variation in the execution time of the exhaustive method, as expected, the average time was increased. In Fig. 1b, note a variation of time when we did not add the countermeasures, but when we add them, we see a constant behavior. In Fig. 1c, it is possible to see a nonconstant behavior of $BTA-rf$. However, this is different for $BTA-it$, which shows a constant behavior.

Table 1. Number of cycles divided by 10^6 for each method of finding roots without countermeasures.

Nr. Roots	Field	Exhaustive search	Linearized polynomials	BTA-rf	SRA
55	$\mathbb{F}_{2^{12}}$	10.152	45.697	9.801	2,301.663
	$\mathbb{F}_{2^{16}}$	117.307	425.494	72.766	2,333.519
65	$\mathbb{F}_{2^{12}}$	12.103	56.270	11.933	2,711.318
	$\mathbb{F}_{2^{16}}$	139.506	522.208	80.687	2,782.838
100	$\mathbb{F}_{2^{12}}$	18.994	84.076	17.322	3,555.221
	$\mathbb{F}_{2^{16}}$	213.503	863.063	133.487	3,735.954

Table 2. Number of cycles divided by 10^6 for each method of finding roots with countermeasures.

Nr. Roots	Field	Exhaustive search	Linearized polynomials	BTA-it	SRA
55	$\mathbb{F}_{2^{12}}$	11.741	45.467	11.489	2,410.410
	$\mathbb{F}_{2^{16}}$	142.774	433.645	75.467	2,660.052
65	$\mathbb{F}_{2^{12}}$	13.497	55.908	14.864	2,855.899
	$\mathbb{F}_{2^{16}}$	164.951	533.946	86.869	2,929.608
100	$\mathbb{F}_{2^{12}}$	20.287	89.118	20.215	4,211.459
	$\mathbb{F}_{2^{16}}$	238.950	882.101	138.956	4,212.493

The main focus of our proposal was to find alternatives to compute roots of ELP that has constant execution time. Figure 2 presents an overview between the original implementations and the implementations with countermeasures. It is possible that when a countermeasure is present on Linearized and on BTA approach, the number of cycles increases. However, the variance of time decreases. Additionally, Fig. 2 shows an improvement in time variance for SCA method, without a huge increase on the average time. We remark that the "points" out

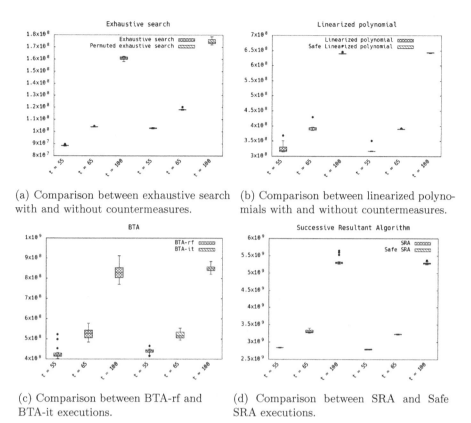

(a) Comparison between exhaustive search with and without countermeasures.

(b) Comparison between linearized polynomials with and without countermeasures.

(c) Comparison between BTA-rf and BTA-it executions.

(d) Comparison between SRA and Safe SRA executions.

Fig. 1. Plots of measurements cycles for methods presented in Sect. 3. Our evaluation of SRA was made using a Python implementation and cycles measurement with C. In our tests, the drawback of calling a Python module from C has behavior bordering to constant.

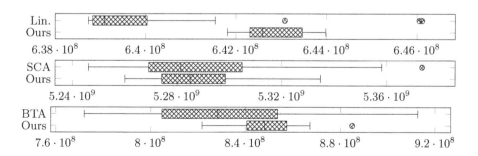

Fig. 2. Comparison of original implementation and our proposal for Linearized, Successive resultant algorithm and Berlekamp trace algorithm with $t = 100$.

of range can be ignored since we did not run the code under a separated environment, and as such it could be that some process in our environment influenced the result.

5 Conclusion

In our study, we demonstrated countermeasures that can be used to avoid remote timing attacks. In our empirical analysis, i.e, the results in Table 2, BTA-it shows an advantage in the number of cycles which makes it a more efficient and safer choice. However, the exhaustive search with shuffling shows the smallest variation of time, which can be an alternative for usage. Still, the problem for this method is that if the field is large, then it becomes costly to shuffle and iterate all elements.

5.1 Open Problems

We bring to the attention of the reader that we did not use any optimization in our implementations, i.e., we did not use vectorization or bit slicing techniques or any specific instructions such as Intel® IPP Cryptography for finite field arithmetic in our code. Therefore, these techniques and instructions can improve the finite fields operations and speed up our algorithms.

We remark that for achieving a safer implementation, one needs to improve the security analysis, by removing conditional memory access and protecting memory access of instructions. Moreover, one can analyze the security of the implementations, by considering different attack scenarios and performing an in-depth analysis of hardware side-channel attacks.

Acknowledgments. We want to thank the reviewers for the thoughtful comments on this work. We would also like to thank Tanja Lange for her valuable feedback. We want to extend the acknowledgments to Sonia Belaïd from Cryptoexperts for the discussions about timing attacks.

A   Implementation Code

```
#include <stdint.h>
typedef uint16_t gf;
gf gf_q_m_mult(gf in0, gf in1) {
    uint64_t i, tmp, t0 = in0, t1 = in1;
    //Multiplication
    tmp = t0 * (t1 & 1);
    for (i = 1; i < 12; i++)
        tmp ^= (t0 * (t1 & (1 << i)));
    //reduction
    tmp = tmp & 0x7FFFFF;
    //first step of reduction
    gf reduction = (tmp >> 12);
    tmp = tmp & 0xFFF;
    tmp = tmp ^ (reduction << 6);
    tmp = tmp ^ (reduction << 4);
    tmp = tmp ^ reduction << 1;
    tmp = tmp ^ reduction;
    //second step of reduction
    reduction = (tmp >> 12);
    tmp = tmp ^ (reduction << 6);
    tmp = tmp ^ (reduction << 4);
    tmp = tmp ^ reduction << 1;
    tmp = tmp ^ reduction;
    tmp = tmp & 0xFFF;
    return tmp;
} gf gf_inv(gf in) {
    gf tmp_11 = 0;
    gf tmp_1111 = 0;
    gf out = in;
    out = gf_sq(out); //a^2
    tmp_11 = gf_mult(out, in); //a^2*a = a^3
    out = gf_sq(tmp_11); //(a^3)^2 = a^6
    out = gf_sq(out); // (a^6)^2 = a^12
    tmp_1111 = gf_mult(out, tmp_11); //a^12*a^3 = a^15
    out = gf_sq(tmp_1111); //(a^15)^2 = a^30
    out = gf_sq(out); //(a^30)^2 = a^60
    out = gf_sq(out); //(a^60)^2 = a^120
    out = gf_sq(out); //(a^120)^2 = a^240
    out = gf_mult(out, tmp_1111); //a^240*a^15 = a^255
    out = gf_sq(out); // (a^255)^2 = 510
    out = gf_sq(out); //(a^510)^2 = 1020
    out = gf_mult(out, tmp_11); //a^1020*a^3 = 1023
    out = gf_sq(out); //(a^1023)^2 = 2046
    out = gf_mult(out, in); //a^2046*a = 2047
    out = gf_sq(out); //(a^2047)^2 = 4094
    return out;
}
```

Listing 1.1. Multiplication of two elements in $\mathbb{F}_{2^{12}}$ and inversion of an element in $\mathbb{F}_{2^{12}}$

References

1. Banegas, G., et al.: DAGS: key encapsulation using dyadic GS codes. J. Math. Cryptol. **12**(4), 221–239 (2018)
2. Bardet, M., et al.: BIG QUAKE BInary Goppa QUAsi-cyclic Key Encapsulation, Technical report, National Institute of Standards and Technology (NIST) (2017)
3. Berlekamp, E.: Algebraic Coding Theory. World Scientific (2015)

128   D. Martins et al.

4. Berlekamp, E.R.: Factoring polynomials over large finite fields. Math. Comput. **24**(111), 713–735 (1970)
5. Bernstein, D.J.: Cache-timing attacks on AES (2005). https://cr.yp.to/antiforgery/cachetiming-20050414.pdf
6. Bernstein, D.J., Persichetti, E.: Towards KEM unification. Cryptology ePrint Archive, Report 2018/526 (2018). https://eprint.iacr.org/2018/526
7. Biswas, B., Sendrier, N.: HyMES - an open source implementation of the McEliece cryptosystem (2008). http://www-rocq.inria.fr/secret/CBCrypto/index.php?pg=hyme
8. Black, P.E.: Fisher-Yates shuffle. In: Dictionary Algorithms Data Structures. https://xlinux.nist.gov/dads/HTML/fisherYatesShuffle.html. Accessed 23 Aug 2019
9. Bruinderink, L.G., Hülsing, A., Lange, T., Yarom, Y.: Flush, gauss, and reload - a cache attack on the BLISS lattice-based signature scheme. In: Proceedings of the 18th International Conference Cryptographic Hardware and Embedded Systems - CHES 2016, Santa Barbara, CA, USA, 17–19 August 2016, pp. 323–345 (2016). https://doi.org/10.1007/978-3-662-53140-2_16
10. Bucerzan, D., Cayrel, P.L., Dragoi, V., Richmond, T.: Improved timing attacks against the secret permutation in the McEliece PKC. Int. J. Comput. Commun. Control **12**(1), 7–25 (2017)
11. Chor, B., Rivest, R.L.: A knapsack-type public key cryptosystem based on arithmetic in finite fields. IEEE Trans. Inf. Theor. **34**(5), 901–909 (1988)
12. Chou, T.: McBits revisited. In: Proceedings of the 19th International Conference on Cryptographic Hardware and Embedded Systems - CHES 2017, Taipei, Taiwan, 25–28 September 2017, pp. 213–231 (2017). https://doi.org/10.1007/978-3-319-66787-4_11
13. Davenport, J.H., Petit, C., Pring, B.: A generalised successive resultants algorithm. In: Duquesne, S., Petkova-Nikova, S. (eds.) WAIFI 2016. LNCS, vol. 10064, pp. 105–124. Springer, Cham (2016). https://doi.org/10.1007/978-3-319-55227-9_9
14. Fedorenko, S.V., Trifonov, P.V.: Finding roots of polynomials over finite fields. IEEE Trans. Commun. **50**(11), 1709–1711 (2002)
15. McEliece, R.J.: A public-key cryptosystem based on algebraic coding theory. Deep Space Netw. Prog. Rep. **44**, 114–116 (1978)
16. Misoczki, R., Barreto, P.S.L.M.: Compact McEliece keys from Goppa codes. In: 16th Annual International Workshop on Selected Areas in Cryptography, SAC 2009, Calgary, Alberta, Canada, August 13–14, 2009, Revised Selected Papers, pp. 376–392 (2009). https://doi.org/10.1007/978-3-642-05445-7_24
17. Patterson, N.: The algebraic decoding of Goppa codes. IEEE Trans. Inf. Theor. **21**(2), 203–207 (1975)
18. Petit, C.: Finding roots in $GF(p^n)$ with the successive resultant algorithm. IACR Cryptology ePrint Archive 2014, 506 (2014)
19. Savage, C.: A survey of combinatorial Gray codes. SIAM Rev. **39**(4), 605–629 (1997)
20. Shoufan, A., Strenzke, F., Molter, H.G., Stöttinger, M.: A timing attack against Patterson algorithm in the McEliece PKC. In: 12th International Conference on Information, Security and Cryptology - ICISC 2009, Seoul, Korea, 2–4 December 2009, Revised Selected Papers, pp. 161–175 (2009). https://doi.org/10.1007/978-3-642-14423-3_12

21. Strenzke, F.: Fast and secure root finding for code-based cryptosystems. In: Proceedings of the 11th International Conference on Cryptology and Network Security, CANS 2012, Darmstadt, Germany, 12–14 December 2012, pp. 232–246 (2012). https://doi.org/10.1007/978-3-642-35404-5_18
22. Strenzke, F.: Efficiency and implementation security of code-based cryptosystems. Ph.D. thesis, Technische Universität (2013)
23. The Sage Developers: SageMath, the Sage Mathematics Software System (Version 8.7) (2019). https://www.sagemath.org
24. Truong, T.K., Jeng, J.H., Reed, I.S.: Fast algorithm for computing the roots of error locator polynomials up to degree 11 in Reed-Solomon decoders. IEEE Trans. Commun. **49**(5), 779–783 (2001)
25. Wang, W., Szefer, J., Niederhagen, R.: FPGA-based Niederreiter cryptosystem using binary Goppa codes. In: Proceedings of the 9th International Conference Post-Quantum Cryptography, PQCrypto 2018, Fort Lauderdale, FL, USA, 9–11 April 2018, pp. 77–98 (2018). https://doi.org/10.1007/978-3-319-79063-3_4

More Practical Single-Trace Attacks on the Number Theoretic Transform

Peter Pessl$^{(\boxtimes)}$ and Robert Primas

Graz University of Technology, Graz, Austria
`peter.pessl@iaik.tugraz.at, rprimas@gmail.com`

Abstract. Single-trace side-channel attacks are a considerable threat to implementations of classic public-key schemes. For lattice-based cryptography, however, this class of attacks is much less understood, and only a small number of previous works show attacks. Primas et al., for instance, present a single-trace attack on the Number Theoretic Transform (NTT), which is at the heart of many efficient lattice-based schemes.

They, however, attack a variable-time implementation and also require a rather powerful side-channel adversary capable of creating close to a million multivariate templates. Thus, it was an open question if such an attack can be made practical while also targeting state-of-the-art constant-time implementations.

In this paper, we answer this question positively. First, we introduce several improvements to the usage of belief propagation, which underlies the attack. And second, we change the target to encryption instead of decryption; this limits attacks to the recovery of the transmitted symmetric key, but in turn, increases attack performance. All this then allows successful attacks even when switching to univariate Hamming-weight templates. We evaluate the performance and noise resistance of our attack using simulations, but also target a real device. Concretely, we successfully attack an assembly-optimized constant-time Kyber implementation running on an ARM Cortex M4 microcontroller while requiring the construction of only 213 templates.

Keywords: Side-channel attacks · Post-quantum cryptography · Lattice-based cryptography · Belief propagation

1 Introduction

For implementations of classic public-key schemes, such as RSA, DH, and ECC, there exist many side-channel attacks capable of retrieving the secret key using just a single execution trace. Ranging from the textbook example of distinguishing squarings and multiplications with the naked eye to more sophisticated methods, such as horizontal collision correlation [9] capable of attacking even constant-time implementations, such single-trace attacks can be considered to be a prime threat and are able to bypass many randomization countermeasures.

© Springer Nature Switzerland AG 2019
P. Schwabe and N. Thériault (Eds.): LATINCRYPT 2019, LNCS 11774, pp. 130–149, 2019.
https://doi.org/10.1007/978-3-030-30530-7_7

For lattice-based cryptography, the largest family of schemes currently running in the second round of the NIST post-quantum standardization process [21], the sincerity of this threat is much less clear. Compared to most classic constructions, it is relatively straightforward to make implementations of lattice-based cryptography both constant time[1] and free of secret-dependent memory accesses, thereby eliminating the most glaring side-channel leaks. Possibly due to this reason, many previous works on secure implementations of lattice-based cryptography primarily focused on masking and thus differential side-channel attacks [8,22,24,25].

Still, single-trace attacks have received some prior attention and were shown to be possible. In particular, Primas et al. [23] proposed an attack on the Number Theoretic Transform (NTT), which is an integral part of efficient implementations of many lattice-based schemes, e.g., NewHope [2] and Kyber [6]. Simply speaking, the NTT resembles a Fast Fourier Transform (FFT), but works over $\mathbb{Z}_q$ instead of over the complex plane. It enables fast multiplication of polynomials in the ring $\mathcal{R}_q = \mathbb{Z}_q[x]/\langle x^n + 1\rangle$, which are a common sight in schemes based on structured lattices. The attacks of Primas et al. follow the path of soft-analytical side-channel attacks [28]. That is, they first perform a side-channel template matching [12] on certain intermediates, construct a graph describing the NTT and all of its intermediate computations, include the observed leakage information in this graph, and finally run a message-passing algorithm known as belief propagation. The recovered secret input is either the key itself or can be used to recover said key.

However, while this attack can even bypass certain countermeasures, it does leave open the question of practicality. For their evaluations on a real device, they build close to one million templates. Besides, they attack a variable-time implementation. While the attack, as such, does not require timing differences, it does benefit from them. And finally, they mainly focus on attacking the decryption process. While the most apparent target, the involvement of long-term secrets makes the need for side-channel protections obvious. Encryption, however, only deals with ephemeral secrets and might thus see less care in side-channel protections. Still, a successful attack on encryption can lead to a compromise of the entire system.

Our Contribution. In this paper, we address the above limitations and show that single-trace attacks on the NTT can be made truly practical. Several improvements to the attack, alongside the choice of a different target, allow us to attack a constant-time microcontroller implementation of the Kyber lattice-based key exchange [6], all while requiring only 213 univariate Hamming-weight templates.

More concretely, we include three improvements to belief propagation in the context of side-channel attacks on the NTT. We merge certain nodes in the graph representation of the NTT, make use of message damping, and introduce a new message schedule. These changes lead to higher accuracy of computed

---

[1] At least when using a simple error distribution, such as centered binomials.

marginal probabilities and thus to better attack performance. The runtime of belief propagation, while increased, still stays very reasonable.

As already hinted above, we change the concrete target of our attack. Primas et al. attacked the inverse NTT transformation during decryption. Decryption involves the private key, which makes not only attacks worthwhile, but also the need for careful side-channel protection obvious. We target encryption instead. While this limits attacks to recovering the exchanged symmetric keys, it focuses on a part seemingly requiring less side-channel protection. Also, in encryption, the inputs of the NTT are confined to a narrow interval, which further aids attack performance.

These changes and performance improvements allow a simplification of the physical part of the attack. That is, by switching to Hamming-weight templates and targeting load/store operations instead of multiplications, the number of required templates and thus also traces for template building is cut down drastically.

We evaluate our attack for different noise levels using simulations. Furthermore, we study the effects of masking and recent implementation techniques, such as lazy reduction, on the attack performance. Finally, we demonstrate the attack using real power measurements of an STM32F4 microcontroller running a constant-time ASM-optimized Kyber implementation. Using just 213 univariate Hamming-weight templates, the entire secret NTT input can be recovered with a probability of up to 95%. Finally, we note that our attacks can be easily ported to many other implementations that make use of the NTT.

Outline. In Sect. 2, we briefly describe the concrete target of our attacks, namely the Kyber key exchange, and discuss its implementation aspects. In Sect. 3, we present details of the attack by Primas et al. [23] and also discuss its shortcomings. After having covered the necessary background, we show all our improvements and adaptations in Sect. 4. We then evaluate the attack using simulations in Sect. 5 and target a real device in Sect. 6. In Sect. 7, we discuss the applicability and effectiveness of previously proposed countermeasures.

2   Lattice-Based Cryptography

In this section, we briefly recall the lattice-based key-exchange Kyber. We also describe efficient implementation techniques, both for Kyber and lattice-based cryptography in general.

2.1   Kyber

The Kyber key exchange [6] is currently running in the second round of the NIST standardization process [21]. In its core, Kyber resembles the Ring-LWE encryption scheme proposed by Lyubashevsky, Peikert, and Regev [18], but it bases its security on the Module Learning-With-Errors assumption (MLWE) [16] instead of Ring-LWE. This means that it operates with matrices/vectors containing polynomials defined over the ring $\mathcal{R}_q = \mathbb{Z}_q[x]/\langle x^n + 1 \rangle$. We use boldface letters to differentiate matrices/vectors of polynomials from single polynomials.

Already in its specification, Kyber prescribes usage of the NTT for efficient polynomial multiplication. Via point-wise multiplication of transformed polynomials, i.e., $ab = \mathsf{NTT}^{-1}(\mathsf{NTT}(a) \circ \mathsf{NTT}(b))$, multiplication can be performed in time $\mathcal{O}(n \log n)$. We use $\hat{a}$ as shorthand for the NTT-transformed of a, with $\hat{\mathbf{a}}$ we denote vectors where all component polynomials are transformed.

The core public-key encryption scheme (PKE) only offers IND-CPA security. For this reason, the Kyber authors apply a variant of the Fujisaki-Okamoto transform [14] to build an IND-CCA2 secure key-encapsulation mechanism (KEM). In essence, the transform requires a re-encryption of the decrypted message using the randomness seed used for the original encryption, which is embedded in the ciphertext. Only if the recomputed and the received ciphertexts match, the decrypted message is released. Since recovering the key/message used in the underlying PKE directly leads to key/message recovery of the KEM, we omit details of the transform and only focus on the PKE. We further omit aspects regarding, e.g., efficient packing, and give a simplified but conceptually identical description. For further details, we refer to the Kyber specification [6].

Algorithm 1 gives the key-generation procedure. The function Sample_U samples the $(k \times k)$-matrix $\hat{\mathbf{A}}$ from uniform using the seed ρ, which is also part of the public key. The sampling is performed directly in the NTT domain. Then, the coefficients of $\mathbf{s}$ and $\mathbf{e}$ are sampled following a centered binomial distribution with support $[-\eta, \eta]$ using Sample_B with seed σ. Afterward, the NTT is applied to all component polynomials of $\mathbf{s}$ independently to receive the secret key $\hat{\mathbf{s}}$. The result $\mathbf{t} := \mathbf{As} + \mathbf{e}$ is the public key.

Algorithm 1. Kyber-PKE Key Generation (simplified)

Output: Public key pk, private key sk

1: Choose uniform seeds ρ, σ
2: $\hat{\mathbf{A}} \in R_q^{k \times k} := \mathsf{Sample}_U(\rho)$ ▷ Generate uniform $\hat{\mathbf{A}}$ in NTT domain
3: $\mathbf{s} \in R_q^k := \mathsf{Sample}_B(\sigma \| 0)$ ▷ Sample private key $\mathbf{s}$ (binomial distribution)
4: $\mathbf{e} \in R_q^k := \mathsf{Sample}_B(\sigma \| 1)$ ▷ Sample error $\mathbf{e}$ (binomial distribution)
5: $\hat{\mathbf{s}} := \mathsf{NTT}(\mathbf{s})$ ▷ NTT for efficient multiplication
6: $\mathbf{t} := \mathsf{NTT}^{-1}(\hat{\mathbf{A}} \circ \hat{\mathbf{s}}) + \mathbf{e}$ ▷ $\mathbf{t} := \mathbf{As} + \mathbf{e}$
7: **return** $(pk := (\mathbf{t}, \rho), sk := \hat{\mathbf{s}})$

Encryption is shown in Algorithm 2. After recomputation of $\hat{\mathbf{A}}$ from the seed ρ, the variables $\mathbf{r}, \mathbf{e}_1, e_2$ are sampled. The seed τ used for this sampling is made explicit to allow the re-encryption required for the CCA2 transform. The ciphertext c consists of two parts, where the second component c_2 contains m encoded as an element in $\mathcal{R}_q$. The decryption process (Algorithm 3) requires to recover this m from a noisy version.

The Kyber authors originally specified three parameter sets. In this paper, we primarily focus on the original Kyber768 set given by ($n = 256, k = 3, q = 7681, \eta = 4$). Kyber512 and Kyber1024 mainly differ in the used k. Since we

Algorithm 2. Kyber-PKE Encryption (simplified)

Input: Public key $pk = (\mathbf{t}, \rho)$, message m, seed τ
Output: Ciphertext c

1: $\hat{\mathbf{A}} \in R_q^{k \times k} := \mathsf{Sample}_\mathsf{U}(\rho)$ $\triangleright$ Regenerate uniform $\hat{\mathbf{A}}$
2: $\mathbf{r} \in R_q^k := \mathsf{Sample}_\mathsf{B}(\tau||0)$
3: $\mathbf{e}_1 \in R_q^k := \mathsf{Sample}_\mathsf{B}(\tau||1)$ $\triangleright$ Sample noise $\mathbf{r}, \mathbf{e}_1, e_2$
4: $e_2 \in R_q := \mathsf{Sample}_\mathsf{B}(\tau||2)$
5: $\hat{\mathbf{r}} := \mathsf{NTT}(\mathbf{r})$ $\triangleright$ NTT for efficient multiplication
6: $\mathbf{c}_1 := \mathsf{NTT}^{-1}(\hat{\mathbf{A}}^T \circ \hat{\mathbf{r}}) + \mathbf{e}_1$ $\triangleright$ $\mathbf{c}_1 := \mathbf{A}^T \mathbf{r} + \mathbf{e}_1$
7: $c_2 := \mathsf{NTT}^{-1}(\mathsf{NTT}(\mathbf{t})^T \circ \hat{\mathbf{r}}) + e_2 + \mathsf{Encode}(m)$ $\triangleright$ $c_2 := \mathbf{t}^T \mathbf{r} + e_2 + \mathsf{Encode}(m)$
8: **return** $c := (\mathbf{c}_1, c_2)$

Algorithm 3. Kyber-PKE Decryption (simplified)

Input: Public key $pk = (\mathbf{t}, \rho)$, secret key $sk = \hat{\mathbf{s}}$, ciphertext $c = (\mathbf{c}_1, c_2)$
Output: Message m

1: $m := \mathsf{Decode}(c_2 - \mathsf{NTT}^{-1}(\hat{\mathbf{s}}^T \circ \mathsf{NTT}(\mathbf{c}_1)))$ $\triangleright$ $m := \mathsf{Decode}(c_2 - \mathbf{s}^T \mathbf{c}_1)$
2: **return** m

will target individual NTT executions, k does not impact attack performance, at least as long the success probability on single NTTs is close to 1. We note that very recently, the Kyber parameters were tweaked for round 2 of the NIST standardization process. All parameter sets now feature $(q = 3329, \eta = 2)$.[2] We will later show that this change is beneficial to our attack. Note that we will always use the original parameter set unless stated otherwise.

2.2 Efficient and Secure Implementation

The rising popularity of lattice-based cryptography in the last decade has also led to many efficient constant-time implementation techniques. We now give details to the two most relevant for this work.

Number Theoretic Transform (NTT). As already stated above, the NTT allows efficient multiplication in $\mathcal{R}_q$ by pointwise multiplying two forward transformed polynomials and transforming the result back[3]. In essence, the NTT is a Discrete Fourier Transform (DFT) over a prime field $\mathbb{Z}_q$ and can thus be implemented using the same techniques as found in the Fast Fourier Transform (FFT). As shown in Fig. 1 with the example of a 4-coefficient NTT, the transformation consists of chaining $\log_2 n$ layers of so-called butterflies. A butterfly takes two inputs, one of them is multiplied with a certain power of ω_n, where ω_n is a primitive n-th root of unity in $\mathbb{Z}_q$. The product is then both added to (upper branch) and subtracted from (lower branch) the second input.

---

[2] The new parameter set also requires some minor modifications to the NTT, such as different constants and omission of the last butterfly layer.

[3] Here, the NTT is defined to include the scaling required to compute products in $\mathbb{Z}_q[x]/\langle x^n + 1 \rangle$ instead of $\mathbb{Z}_q[x]/\langle x^n - 1 \rangle$. We point to [6] for further details.

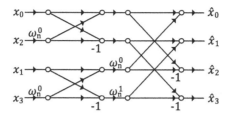

Fig. 1. 4-coefficient NTT

Constant-Time and Efficient Reductions. Early implementations of the NTT often used straight-forward and variable-time modular reduction techniques. For instance, de Clercq et al. [13] use ARMs conditional operations for reductions after additions and subtractions, as well as integer divisions for reductions after multiplications. On most embedded devices, such divisions do not run in constant time.

More recent implementations, e.g., the Cortex-M optimized NewHope implementation by Alkim, Jakubeit, and Schwabe [4], frequently make use of constant-time variants of the established Montgomery and Barret reduction techniques. Constant-time is reached by omitting the final conditional subtractions. In other words, the result is not always reduced back to $[0, q-1]$, but can be larger. This can also be used for efficiency gains by, e.g., skipping reductions after additions (*lazy reduction*).

2.3   Protected Implementations

Constant-time operations mitigate timing attacks, both on small devices such as microcontrollers and large ones like PCs. Protecting against other types of side-channel attacks, e.g., Differential Power Analysis (DPA), requires more effort. There do already exist works addressing this issue and proposing DPA-secured implementations of lattice-based cryptography; they use masking as their main protection mechanism [8, 22, 25].

Since the NTT is a linear transformation, it is trivial to mask. When s is the sensitive input, then one can sample a uniformly random masking polynomial $m \in \mathcal{R}_q$, compute the NTT on m and $(s-m)$ independently, and finally add the shares back again if needed. Masking the sampling of error polynomials and the decoding of the noisy message in decryption is much more intricate. Since we do not attack these operations, we refer to Oder et al. [22] for details.

Oder et al. [22] further employ hiding techniques. They shuffle the ordering of linear operations, such as the pointwise multiplication, and blind polynomials with a random scalar. The latter method was first introduced by Saarinen [26].

3   Single-Trace Attacks on Lattice-Based Cryptography

Masking is very efficient in protecting against DPA-like attacks. Still, single-trace attacks are potentially able to bypass masking as well as other defenses. There do already exist earlier works showing the feasibility of such attacks in the context of lattice-based cryptography. Recently, horizontal side-channel attacks on matrix-vector multiplications found in schemes over unstructured lattices, such as Frodo [3], were demonstrated [7,11]. These attacks, however, do not carry over to schemes using structured lattices, as they typically use faster multiplication methods such as the NTT or Karatsuba's method.[4]

Primas et al. [23] propose a single-trace attack on the NTT. Since this attack is the basis of our work, we now introduce the required background. First, we recall soft-analytical side-channel attacks and the belief propagation algorithm, which form the basis of the attack. Then, we will present the attack details and discuss some of its shortcomings.

3.1 Soft-Analytical Side-Channel Attacks

The attack of Primas et al. is an instance of a soft-analytical side-channel attack (SASCA), which were first proposed by Veyrat-Charvillon et al. [28]. In SASCA, one first performs a side-channel template attack [12] on certain intermediates and retrieves probabilities conditioned on the leakage. In other words, one gets $\Pr(T = t|\ell)$, where T is an attacked intermediate, t runs through all of the possible values of T, and ℓ is the observed side-channel leakage. Then, one constructs a factor graph modeling the attacked algorithm and its specific implementation. After including the conditioned probabilities into this graph, the belief-propagation algorithm is run, which returns marginal probabilities for all inputs (including the involved key components), outputs, and intermediates processed by the algorithm. We now give a more thorough explanation.

Belief Propagation. We base our descriptions of belief propagation (BP) on MacKay [19, Chapter 26], as also done by previous works using SASCA [23,28].

BP allows efficient marginalization in certain probabilistic models. Given is a function $P^*(\mathbf{x}) = \prod_{m=1}^{M} f_m(\mathbf{x}_m)$, which is defined over a set of N variables $\mathbf{x} \equiv \{x_n\}_{n=1}^{N}$ and the product of M factors. Each of the factors $f_m(\mathbf{x}_m)$ is a function of a subset $\mathbf{x}_m$ of $\mathbf{x}$. The problem of marginalization is then defined as computing the marginal function $Z_n(x_n) = \sum_{\{x_{n'}\}, n' \neq n} P^*(\mathbf{x})$, or the normalized version $P_n(x_n) = Z_n(x_n)/Z$, with $Z = \sum_{\mathbf{x}} \prod_{m=1}^{M} f_m(\mathbf{x})$.

BP solves this task efficiently by exploiting the known factorization of P^*. First, it represents the factorization in a probabilistic graphical model called factor graph (FG). Factor graphs are comprised of variable nodes, each representing one variable $x_n \in \mathbf{x}$, and factor nodes, each representing one f_m. Factor f_m and variable x_n are connected in the graph if f_m depends on x_n. Second, it performs message-passing on the factor graph. Concretely, it iteratively runs the following two steps until convergence is reached:

---

[4] Aysu et al. [7] do also run their attack for the RLWE-based scheme NewHope [2]. However, their attacked implementation uses schoolbook multiplication instead of the NTT, resulting in a drastically increased runtime.

(1) from variable to factor:

$$u_{n \to m}(x_n) = \prod_{m' \in \mathcal{M}(n) \backslash \{m\}} v_{m' \to n}(x_n), \tag{1}$$

where $\mathcal{M}(n)$ denotes the set of factors in which n participates.
(2) from factor to variable:

$$v_{m \to n}(x_n) = \sum_{x_m \backslash n} \left(f_m(\mathbf{x}_m) \prod_{n' \in \mathcal{N}(m) \backslash m} u_{n' \to m}(x'_n) \right), \tag{2}$$

where $\mathcal{N}(m)$ denotes the indices of the variables that the m-th factor depends on and $\mathbf{x}_{m \backslash n}$ denotes the set of variables in $\mathbf{x}_m$ without x_n.

After convergence, the marginal function $Z_n(x_n)$ can be computed by multiplying all incoming messages at each node: $Z_n(x_n) = \prod_{m \in \mathcal{M}(n)} v_{m \to n}(x_n)$. The normalized marginals are given by $P_n(x_n) = Z_n(x_n)/Z$, where $Z = \sum_{x_n} Z_n(x_n)$.

BP is guaranteed to return the correct marginals only if the factor graph is acyclic. If this is not the case, then the same update rules can still be used in what is then called loopy BP. This variant might not even converge, but when it does, it often gives sufficiently precise approximations to the true marginals. The performance of loopy BP, i.e., the quality of the approximations and converge properties, is inversely proportional to the length of the loops. Put simply, loops in the factor graph introduce positive feedback, which can cause overconfidence in certain beliefs and subsequently even oscillations, especially when deterministic factors are involved. Longer loops are less susceptible to this effect. Note that there do exist approaches, such as generalized belief propagation [30], aiming at significantly improving the quality of the marginal probabilities in loopy graphs. They, however, can come with significantly increased computational runtime.

3.2 Single-Trace Attacks on the NTT

By running a soft-analytical side-channel attack, Primas et al. [23] can recover the secret NTT inputs after observing just a single trace. Concretely, they recover the inputs of the inverse NTT in decryption (Algorithm 3), and can then derive the key $\mathbf{s}$.[5] The NTT appears to be a fitting target for SASCA since each stored intermediate is computed using relatively simple combinations (additions and subtractions) of just two intermediates of the previous NTT layer.

Figure 2 demonstrates how one can construct a factor graph for the NTT. Figure 2a shows a single butterfly for reference. Note that since such a butterfly is equivalent to a length-2 NTT, we denote the outputs as $\hat{x}_0$ and $\hat{x}_1$. Figure 2b then depicts the corresponding factor graph as constructed by Primas et al. In this graph, variable nodes and factor nodes are represented by circles and

---

[5] They target the original LPR scheme, which has very similar encryption and decryption routines.

squares, respectively. The factor nodes can be further split into two groups. Factor f_ℓ models the observed side-channel information, i.e., the outcome of the template matching. More concretely, we have $f_\ell(i) = \Pr(x = i|\ell)$, where x is the matched intermediate. Primas et al. perform template matching on the modular multiplication with ω, which is why they receive information on x_1.

The second group of factors, consisting of f_{add} and f_{sub}, then model the deterministic relationships between the variable nodes as specified by the NTT. For, e.g., the addition in the upper branch, we get:

$$f_{\mathrm{add}}(x_0, x_1, \hat{x}_0) = \begin{cases} 1 & \text{if } x_0 + x_1\omega = \hat{x}_0 \bmod q \\ 0 & \text{otherwise} \end{cases}$$

Due to the deterministic nature of f_{add} and f_{sub}, the factor-to-variable update rule stated in Eq. 2 can be computed in time $\mathcal{O}(q^2)$ by simply enumerating all q^2 possible input combinations. Primas et al. can decrease the runtime to $\mathcal{O}(q \log q)$ by using cyclic properties of modular addition and FFTs of length q.

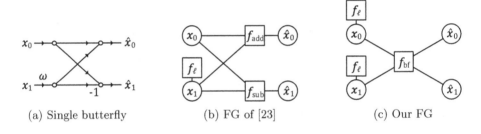

(a) Single butterfly   (b) FG of [23]   (c) Our FG

Fig. 2. Comparison of a single butterfly with possible factor-graph representations

Shortcomings. While Primas et al. demonstrate the possibility of side-channel attacks on the NTT, their attack falls somewhat short of being fully practical.

They perform template matching on modular multiplications. This requires constructing templates for all possible combinations of x_1 and ω taking q and $n/2$ possible values, respectively. For their evaluated parameter set, also featuring $(n = 256, q = 7681)$, close to a million templates are required. Each template is constructed using 100 traces, thus summing up to 100 million traces used for evaluation. They also assume time-invariance of leakage, which allows them to condense analysis to just that of butterflies without regarding its position in the trace. We found that this assumption might not always hold (cf. Sect. 6.2).

In addition, they attack the variable-time NTT implementation by de Clercq et al. [13], which makes use of ARMs conditional instructions and variable-time integer division. Note that the attack as such does not require timing leakage, it can easily be adapted to constant-time implementations. However, the inclusion of timing information is beneficial to attack performance. Thus, the applicability to constant-time implementations is unknown.

Finally, we note that the butterfly factor graph shown in Fig. 2b contains short loops, which is detrimental to the performance of BP. In fact, due to the bipartite and singly-connected nature of factor graphs, no shorter loops are possible in any such graph.

4   Reaching Practical Single-Trace Attacks

We now address these problems and show how single-trace attacks on the NTT can be made truly practical, even on constant-time implementations. First, in Sect. 4.1, we decrease the number of required templates. In combination with the lack of timing information, the attack now fails. For this reason, we adopt several improvements to the belief-propagation algorithm for our scenario, as explained in Sect. 4.2. Then, in Sect. 4.3, we explain why attacking encryption instead of decryption can boost performance even further.

4.1   Decreasing the Number of Templates

Our method to decrease the number of required templates and thus also traces for template building to a more considerate amount is relatively simple. Instead of performing a template matching on modular multiplication and constructing templates for each possible input combination, we target loading/storing of butterfly inputs/outputs to and from RAM (cf. Fig. 2c using leakage of just loading inputs). In addition, we do not construct templates for every single possible value, but only for Hamming weights. Under ideal circumstances, this limits the number of templates to just $\lceil \log_2 q \rceil + 1 = 14$, which, compared to the previous attack, is a reduction by a factor of over $70\,000$. Apart from this reduction, (univariate) Hamming-weight templates are also significantly easier to port from one device to another (compared to multivariate value-based templates).

As it turns out, however, the information loss due to switching to such simpler templates and additionally losing all timing leakage–we only target constant-time implementations–is too high. The attack fails, even for the noise-free case. For this reason, we will now propose improvements to the attack, which allow successful message recovery for such a more constrained attacker.

4.2   Improving Belief Propagation for the NTT

There already exists a large body of work studying ways to improve the performance of belief propagation in cyclic factor graphs. We adopted three concrete methods for use with the NTT and will now describe them in depth.

Butterfly Factors. The factor graph shown in Fig. 2b contains very short loops, which, especially in conjunction with deterministic factors, can lead to convergence problems and overall bad performance of loopy BP [27]. Such network configurations and the resulting problems are however not exclusive to the NTT. As shown by Storkey [27] and Yedidia [29], similar problems also appear when applying BP to other FFT-like networks. Storkey analyzes BP in context of ordinary real-valued FFTs, whereas Yedidia focuses on Reed-Solomon codes, which can be represented by NTTs/FFTs over $GF(q)$.

To increase BP performance, both Stork and Yedidia propose to cluster the factors belonging to the same butterfly and thereby enforce all of its input/output relations at once. We follow their approach and replace factors f_{add}, f_{sub} with a single *butterfly factor* f_{bf}. As seen in Fig. 2c, this eliminates the loop inside each butterfly. The full factor graph of the NTT, built by connecting multiple instances of the butterfly FG (cf. Fig. 1), will still contain loops. These loops, however, are longer, which will lead to increased performance. Yedidia notes that this clustering constitutes a simple form of generalized belief propagation [29, 30].

Butterfly factors are specified as:

$$f_{bf}(x_0, x_1, \hat{x}_0, \hat{x}_1) = \begin{cases} 1 & \text{if } x_0 + x_1\omega = \hat{x}_1 \bmod q \text{ and } x_0 - x_1\omega = \hat{x}_1 \bmod q \\ 0 & \text{otherwise} \end{cases}$$

With the increased accuracy, however, comes also an increase in computational runtime. By making use of an FFT of length q, the update rules for f_{add} and f_{sub} can be evaluated in time $\mathcal{O}(q \log q)$. This does not carry over to f_{bf}. Instead, all input combinations need to be enumerated, thereby increasing the runtime to $\mathcal{O}(q^2)$.

For typical parameters of lattice-based encryption, with $q \approx 2^{13} - 2^{14}$ [2, 6], this is still very much practical, as will later be demonstrated. For the moduli used by lattice-based signatures, e.g., the schemes Dilithium [17] and qTesla [10] both use $q \approx 2^{23}$, practicality cannot be claimed anymore. When also considering that the NTT in, e.g., Dilitihium, consists of 2^{10} butterfly invocations, then it becomes clear that the previous method with split factors needs to be used there.

Optimized Message Schedule. Another property that can influence convergence and accuracy in loopy BP is the chosen message schedule, i.e., the order in which messages are computed and passed between nodes. The most straightforward schedule is to update all variable or factor nodes simultaneously. This approach is followed by Primas et al. [23]. When using the original representation of Fig. 2b, then completing a loop requires just 2 iterations of evaluating Eqs. (1) and (2) (for our proposed representation, this number increases to 4). It, however, can take up to $2 \log_2 n$ iterations for any two nodes in the full NTT graph to communicate.

This is clearly not ideal, which is why we adopt the schedule also used by Storkey [27]. That is, we first pass messages from the NTT input to the output (layer by layer), and then back again. This does not affect the number of iterations required for completing a loop but allows any two nodes in the factor graph to communicate in just a single iteration. This becomes especially advantageous when changing the target to encryption, which features inputs with small support.

Message Damping. While the above two methods greatly increase accuracy, convergence is still not guaranteed. For this reason, we finally also adopt message damping. It aims to dampen oscillations by computing a weighted average of the new and the previous message. When denoting α as the damping factor and $u_{n\to m}^{\mathrm{prev}}$ as the message sent from node to factor in the previous iteration, then the dampened version of (1) is:

$$u_{n\to m}(x_n) = \alpha \left(\prod_{m'\in\mathcal{M}(n)\setminus\{m\}} v_{m'\to n}(x_n) \right) + (1-\alpha)u_{n\to m}^{\mathrm{prev}}(x_n) \qquad (3)$$

For all of our later experiments, we set the damping factor α to 0.9.

4.3 Changing Targets

The decryption process described in Algorithm 3 involves the secret key $\mathbf{s}$ and is thus the obvious first target of a side-channel attack. We now argue that encryption, while not involving $\mathbf{s}$, can also be a very interesting target and is significantly easier to attack.

First, encryption only deals with ephemeral secrets. While this means that the side-channel attack has to be performed for each individual message, the lack of long-term secrets makes it very tempting to use implementations devoting fewer resources for side-channel protections, or maybe even an unprotected implementation. We want to prove this intuition wrong.

Second, the Fujisaki-Okamoto CCA2-transform employed by Kyber and many other lattice-based KEMs requires a re-encryption of the message. The message is then only released if the recomputed ciphertext matches the received one. This means that attacks are not restricted to sending devices, but can also be mounted on the receiving end, i.e., on devices having access to the secret key.

Third, encryption involves an NTT with inputs over a very narrow support: error polynomials follow a centered binomial distribution over $[-\eta, \eta]$, with $\eta = 4$ in our analyzed parameter set. The inputs to the inverse NTT in decryption, however, can be considered uniform in $\mathbb{Z}_q$. Information on the narrow support can easily be integrated into the factor graph; it suffices to apply Bayes' theorem to the leakage-likelihood obtained in the input layer and use the result in the factor nodes f_ℓ. The first iteration of our forward-backward message passing then immediately spreads the information to all later layers and ensures, e.g., that in the second layer, only $(2\eta + 1)^2$ values have a non-zero probability. The narrow support allows BP to pick the correct value under much more noise, as we will later demonstrate.

Fourth and finally, we note that key generation (Algorithm 1) also features an NTT with small inputs, namely that of the private key $\mathbf{s}$. Thus, our attack also applies here. This becomes interesting on devices which either use the plain IND-CPA secure scheme described in Sect. 2.1 and thus only use ephemeral keys, or only store the seed σ and regenerate $\mathbf{s}$ each time to save space in secure non-volatile storage.

Attacking Encryption. For the actual attack on encryption, we target the forward NTT of $\mathbf{r}$, found in line 5 of Algorithm 2. We picked this invocation of the NTT, since all others in Algorithm 2 work on polynomials which are uniform over $\mathbb{Z}_q$. Since $\mathbf{r} \in \mathcal{R}_q^k$ is comprised of k polynomials, we have to attack all k independent invocations of the NTT. Then, we can compute the message m by using line 7. That is, $m = \mathsf{Decode}(c_2 - \mathbf{t}^T \mathbf{r}) = \mathsf{Decode}(e_2 + \mathsf{Encode}(m))$.

5 Evaluation and Additional Scenarios

After having described our attack in depth, we now evaluate it using leakage simulations and additionally explore more attack scenarios. First, in Sect. 5.1, we analyze the improvements proposed for BP in the context of the NTT. Then, we focus on implementations employing the masking countermeasure in Sect. 5.2. In Sect. 5.3, we finally study the effects of state-of-the-art implementation techniques.

Leakage Simulation. For all our simulations, we make use of the established *Hamming weight with additive Gaussian noise* model. Thus, when processing a value x, we receive simulated leakage $\ell = \mathsf{HW}(x) + \mathcal{N}(0, \sigma_{\mathsf{HW}})$. Here, HW denotes the Hamming-weight function, and $\mathcal{N}(0, \sigma_{\mathsf{HW}})$ describes a random sample from the normal distribution with zero mean and standard deviation σ_{HW}.

For each simulation run, we generate one such sample for each intermediate state variable. Thus, we have n samples in each layer (including inputs and outputs), this sums up to $n(\log_2(n) + 1) = 2\,304$ samples. Note that in practice, intermediates in inner layers of the NTT would leak twice: once during storing, once during loading. For the sake of simplicity, we only generate a single sample here. Finally, we perform a template matching on all generated samples and retrieve the corresponding conditioned probabilities $\Pr(X = x | \ell)$.

Attack Implementation. We implemented our evaluations and attacks, including the belief-propagation algorithm, in Matlab. The most time-critical component, namely the factor-to-variable update of butterfly factors f_{bf}, was outsourced to multi-threaded C++ code. We performed up to 50 full message-passing iterations but abort as soon as convergence is reached for all variable nodes in the network. All experiments were run on an Intel Xeon E5-4669 v4 (2.2 GHz).

Evaluation of attack performance is done for varying values of σ_{HW}. For each scenario and analyzed noise level, we performed at least 100 experiments. We computed the success rate by counting the experiments where belief propagation correctly classifies all n NTT inputs, i.e., assigns the highest probability to the correct values.

5.1 Evaluating Improvements to BP

For our first evaluations, we analyze the effects of the improvements proposed in Sect. 4.2: the introduction of butterfly factor nodes, a changed message schedule, and the use of damping. This evaluation also doubles as a general analysis of the noise resistance of our attack.

We target a generic constant-time but otherwise unprotected implementation of the Kyber-NTT. The exact internal operations of this implementation are not important, at least as long the factor graph model and the actual implementation are consistent regarding the attacked intermediates. As we target the loads and stores at the inputs and outputs of butterflies, the exact methods used for, e.g., modular multiplication, are mostly irrelevant.

Figure 3 shows the outcome, for both the original ($q = 7681, \eta = 4$) and the tweaked ($q = 3329, \eta = 2$) Kyber parameter sets. Without the improvements, but still using the same load/store leakage, a success rate of more than 0.9 can be maintained up to and including $\sigma_{HW} = 0.9$. With our changes, this threshold is increased to $\sigma_{HW} = 1.5$. When computing an SNR and thus looking at the variance σ_{HW}^2, then this difference corresponds to almost a tripling of the acceptable noise level. The smaller values used by the new parameter set lead to a slight improvement in the success rate.

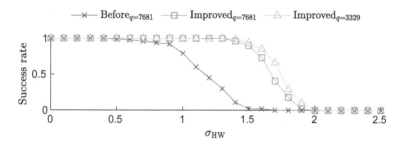

Fig. 3. Comparison of the attack success rate, with and without the optimizations proposed in Sect. 4.2. The improved version was evaluated for both the original ($q = 7681$) and tweaked ($q = 3329$) parameter sets.

On a single core of our system, the runtime of a full forward-backward iteration of belief propagation using $q = 7681$ is roughly 2 min. In low-noise cases, 2 such iterations are already sufficient. For $\sigma_{HW} = 1.5$, the average number of iterations (for convergent experiments) rises to 9. For this noise level, all failed experiments correspond to non-convergence of BP.

5.2   The Case of Masking

As noted in Sect. 2.3, masking the NTT is straightforward. So is, at least in theory, the adaptation of a single-trace attack to the masked case. One can simply recover each share individually and add them up to receive the unmasked input. This approach is used by Primas et al. [23]. In their evaluations, masking alone does not significantly decrease the attack success rate. In our scenario, this is no longer the case. We specifically target the NTT of **r** due to the small input coefficients. When using masking, this advantage is lost, as all input coefficients become uniformly distributed over $\mathbb{Z}_q$.

We reintroduce the information on the narrow support as follows. Instead of running belief propagation on two factor graphs corresponding to the two shares individually, we adjoin graphs at the input layer using factor nodes f_{bino}. These nodes ensure that the sum of the two inputs is consistent with the centered binomial distribution over $[-\eta, \eta]$. When using $\mathcal{B}_\eta$ to denote the density of said distribution, and x', x'' as the two shares of the input, then we can write $f_{\text{bino}}(x', x'') = \mathcal{B}_\eta(x' + x'' \bmod q)$.

Figure 4 shows the simulation results. Running BP on the shares independently does not yield satisfactory results, even for perfect Hamming-weight leakage. The introduction of f_{bino} brings the success rate close to 1, at least when $\sigma_{\text{HW}} \leq 0.3$. While this is a drastic reduction compared to the unprotected case, it at least allows attacks in low noise scenarios. Here, also note that our attacker only uses Hamming-weight templates. A more powerful adversary might attack masked implementations even in high-noise settings.

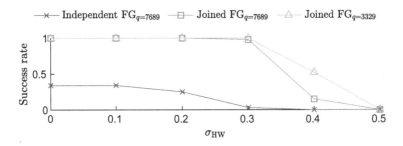

Fig. 4. Success rate of our attack on a masked implementation, both using independent factor graphs and joined graphs

5.3   The Case of Lazy Reductions

Up until now, we analyzed a relatively generic implementation of the NTT. There, operands are always in the range $[0, q - 1]$. As mentioned in Sect. 2.2, this is not true for many recent implementations. They make use of constant-time variants of the Montgomery and Barret reduction, both of which do not necessarily reduce operands down to the base range. Instead, they reduce to a representative (of the equivalence class) only guaranteed to be smaller than, e.g., 2^{16}. Also, reductions after, e.g., additions, can be skipped for performance improvements (lazy reduction).

Such an implementation could, at least theoretically, be attacked using the same factor-graph representation. After performing the template matching on the now larger range of possible values, one could compute the probability of each equivalence class by summing up the probability of each possible representative. Due to just using Hamming-weight leakages, we do not think that such an approach is fruitful.

Instead, we modify the graph to directly model the changed operations. Concretely, we target the assembly-optimized ARM Cortex M4 implementation of Kyber provided by the PQM4 library [15].[6] It uses Montgomery reductions after modular multiplications and Barret reductions after additions and subtractions. Reductions after additions are skipped in each other layer. We integrate all that in the butterfly factors. When denoting MRed and BRed as the used reduction routines, and looking at a layer where no reduction is skipped, then we have

$$
f_{bf}(x_0, x_1, \hat{x}_0, \hat{x}_1) = \begin{cases} 1 & \text{if } \mathsf{BRed}(x_0 + \mathsf{MRed}(x_1\omega)) = \hat{x}_0 \text{ and} \\ & \quad \mathsf{BRed}(x_0 + 4q - \mathsf{MRed}(x_1\omega)) = \hat{x}_1 \\ 0 & \text{otherwise} \end{cases} .
$$

The results of the simulations using this model are shown in Fig. 5. The analyzed implementation only supports the original parameter set with $q = 7681$, which is why we limit analysis to this scenario. Note, however, that our earlier results indicate better attack performance for the tweaked parameter set. Compared to our earlier results, the 90% success-rate threshold is now decreased to $\sigma_{HW} = 1.3$. As an effect of the larger input ranges, the single-core runtime of a full iteration increases to approximately 8 min.

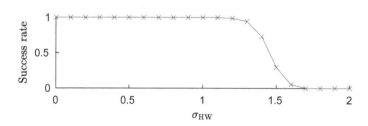

Fig. 5. Success rate of our attack when modeling constant-time and lazy reductions

6   Attacking a Real Device

The previous section already analyzed an optimized microcontroller implementation, but still resorts to leakage simulations. We now show that our attack carries over to an actual device.

6.1   Measurement Setup

The ARM Cortex M4 appears to be the standard target for embedded software implementations of post-quantum cryptography [5]. For this reason, we also performed our side-channel analysis on such a device. More concretely, we performed

---

[6] Shortly after the initial publication of this paper, the Kyber implementation in PQM4 was updated. For reference, we used the version found at https://github.com/mupq/pqm4/releases/tag/Round1.

power measurements of an STM32F405 microcontroller atop the STM32F4 target for the ChipWhisperer UFO board [20]. The power consumption was measured using an AD8129A differential amplifier across an onboard shunt resistor. The 8 MHz device clock was externally generated using a function generator. This was done to simplify synchronization across traces.

This device then ran the optimized Kyber implementation of the PQM4 library [15], which we already targeted in the previous section. More correctly, we only run the forward NTT of error polynomials. Each trace captures an entire NTT execution; we used a dedicated trigger pin to signal the start and end of this operation. We recorded 2 000 traces and then split this set into 1 900 templating traces and 100 attack traces. Note that, while both sets of traces were recorded on the same device, the use of simple univariate Hamming-weight templates makes porting of templates to similar but different devices much more realistic compared to the previous attack.

6.2   Trace Analysis and Attack

As we want to demonstrate practicality, we keep the trace analysis relatively simple by using univariate Hamming-weight templates. For determining the position of leaking operations, we run a correlation analysis along the entire length of the traces, for each of the 2 304 attacked intermediates. The single position of the highest peak (in absolute value) was then selected as point of interest.

The switch to Hamming-weight templates would ideally allow a reduction to just 14 templates. However, we found that the power leakage does show a certain degree of time dependence. Even after basic trace normalization, such as point-wise subtraction of the mean and normalization to a standard deviation of 1, the same operation showed slightly different behavior when executed at a different point in time. We suspect the different flow of instructions preceding our attacked operations, alongside the low-pass behavior of the power network, to be the cause.

Construction of templates for each position is still not required, as we follow an intermediate approach. We build two sets of templates for each NTT layer. The first set targets the upper branch in all butterflies of the respective layer, the second set targets the lower branch (cf. Fig. 2a). Each template is thus used $n/2 = 128$ times. As not all Hamming weights are possible in all layers, one has to build a total of 213 templates.

After matching these templates on an attacked trace, we use the factor-graph representation already established in Sect. 5.3. Out of our 100 performed experiments, 83 yield the correct NTT input. Since we need to attack $k = 3$ independent NTTs, the total success rate can be estimated to be $0.83^3 \approx 0.57$.

6.3   Increasing the Success Rate

The stated success rate can be improved by making use of lattice-reduction techniques. Previously, we defined an attack to be successful if all n NTT inputs are correctly recovered. For the full Kyber scheme, one needs to accomplish this k times to recover all nk coefficients of $\mathbf{r}$.

One can, however, also recover the message when only using the $nk - l$ most probable coefficients, for some small l. That is, one only picks the $nk - l$ coefficients where the final probability of the most likely value is closest to 1. These values are then plugged into the equation $\mathbf{c}_1 := \mathbf{A}^T\mathbf{r} + \mathbf{e}_1$, the remaining l coefficients can then be recovered using lattice-reduction techniques. Such an approach was also used by Primas et al. [23], which is why we do not give further details here.

When using $l = 120$, a conversion to unique-SVP [1], and the BKZ lattice-reduction algorithm with block size 25, then the unknown coefficients can be recovered in approximately 5–10 min. When picking $k = 3$ out of the 100 real experiments at random, then the success rate is increased to 0.95 when using this approach with the stated parameters.

7 Countermeasures

In the previous sections, we established that single-trace attacks on the NTT can be made truly practical. Several improvements to the underlying use of belief propagation in conjunction with the exploitation of small coefficients allow attacks even with simple Hamming-weight templates. This clearly shows that countermeasures are needed even for encryption where no long-term secrets are involved. We now discuss some possible options.

Masking. Masking is firstly a DPA countermeasure, but in our scenario also somewhat counteracts single-trace attacks. They are still possible, as shown in Sect. 5.2, but the acceptable noise level is drastically decreased. Nonetheless, further countermeasures are likely needed to protect against more sophisticated attackers.

Blinding. Saarinen [26] and Oder et al. [22] make use of a blinding technique, which can be seen as a simple form of masking. They blind the two to-be-multiplied polynomials by first multiplying them with two random scalars $(a, b) \in \mathbb{Z}_q$. The product is then unblinded via a multiplication with $(ab)^{-1} \bmod q$. Note that this scalar blinding does keep the narrow support of, e.g., $\mathbf{r}$, intact. The concrete values of the support are however changed. Such a countermeasure might not be able to prevent attacks. First, one can mount a horizontal side-channel template attack, e.g., on all n multiplications with a, to recover the fixed blinding value. Second, one can model the blinding value as an additional variable node in the factor graph and let belief propagation recover its value. We do not further study these scenarios here.

Shuffling. Similar to other algebraic side-channel attacks, shuffling is probably a very effective countermeasure. By randomizing the order of executed operations within each NTT layer, the leakage points cannot be trivially assigned to the correct variable nodes anymore. Note that shuffling linear operations, such as pointwise multiplications, was proposed by Oder et al. [22], but does not affect an attack on the NTT. We leave an analysis of the required granularity of shuffling and the overall cost of this countermeasure for future work.

Acknowledgements. This work has been supported by the Austrian Research Promotion Agency (FFG) via the K-project DeSSnet, which is funded in the context of COMET – Competence Centers for Excellent Technologies by BMVIT, BMWFW, Styria and Carinthia, and via the project ESPRESSO, which is funded by the province of Styria and the Business Promotion Agencies of Styria and Carinthia.

References

1. Albrecht, M.R., Göpfert, F., Virdia, F., Wunderer, T.: Revisiting the expected cost of solving uSVP and applications to LWE. In: Takagi, T., Peyrin, T. (eds.) ASIACRYPT 2017. LNCS, vol. 10624, pp. 297–322. Springer, Cham (2017). https://doi.org/10.1007/978-3-319-70694-8_11
2. Alkim, E., et al.: NewHope (2017). https://newhopecrypto.org/. Submission to [21]
3. Alkim, E., et al.: FrodoKEM (2017). https://frodokem.org/. Submission to [21]
4. Alkim, E., Jakubeit, P., Schwabe, P.: NewHope on ARM Cortex-M. In: Carlet, C., Hasan, M.A., Saraswat, V. (eds.) SPACE 2016. LNCS, vol. 10076, pp. 332–349. Springer, Cham (2016). https://doi.org/10.1007/978-3-319-49445-6_19
5. Alperin-Sheriff, J.: Programmable hardware, microcontrollers and vector instructions. Post on the NIST PQC-forum (2018). https://groups.google.com/a/list.nist.gov/d/msg/pqc-forum/_0mDoyry1Ao/Tt7yHpjSDgAJ
6. Avanzi, R., et al.: CRYSTALS-Kyber (2017). https://pq-crystals.org/kyber. Submission to [21]
7. Aysu, A., Tobah, Y., Tiwari, M., Gerstlauer, A., Orshansky, M.: Horizontal side-channel vulnerabilities of post-quantum key exchange protocols. In: HOST, pp. 81–88. IEEE Computer Society (2018)
8. Barthe, G., et al.: Masking the GLP lattice-based signature scheme at any order. In: Nielsen, J.B., Rijmen, V. (eds.) EUROCRYPT 2018. LNCS, vol. 10821, pp. 354–384. Springer, Cham (2018). https://doi.org/10.1007/978-3-319-78375-8_12
9. Bauer, A., Jaulmes, E., Prouff, E., Wild, J.: Horizontal collision correlation attack on elliptic curves. In: Lange, T., Lauter, K., Lisoněk, P. (eds.) SAC 2013. LNCS, vol. 8282, pp. 553–570. Springer, Heidelberg (2014). https://doi.org/10.1007/978-3-662-43414-7_28
10. Bindel, N., et al.: qTESLA (2017). https://qtesla.org. Submission to [21]
11. Bos, J.W., Friedberger, S., Martinoli, M., Oswald, E., Stam, M.: Assessing the feasibility of single trace power analysis of frodo. In: Cid, C., Jacobson Jr., M. (eds.) SAC 2018. LNCS, vol. 11349, pp. 216–234. Springer, Cham (2019). https://doi.org/10.1007/978-3-030-10970-7_10
12. Chari, S., Rao, J.R., Rohatgi, P.: Template attacks. In: Kaliski, B.S., Koç, K., Paar, C. (eds.) CHES 2002. LNCS, vol. 2523, pp. 13–28. Springer, Heidelberg (2003). https://doi.org/10.1007/3-540-36400-5_3
13. de Clercq, R., Roy, S.S., Vercauteren, F., Verbauwhede, I.: Efficient software implementation of ring-LWE encryption. In: DATE, pp. 339–344. ACM (2015)
14. Fujisaki, E., Okamoto, T.: Secure integration of asymmetric and symmetric encryption schemes. In: Wiener, M. (ed.) CRYPTO 1999. LNCS, vol. 1666, pp. 537–554. Springer, Heidelberg (1999). https://doi.org/10.1007/3-540-48405-1_34

15. Kannwischer, M.J., Rijneveld, J., Schwabe, P., Stoffelen, K.: PQM4: post-quantum crypto library for the ARM Cortex-M4. https://github.com/mupq/pqm4
16. Langlois, A., Stehlé, D.: Worst-case to average-case reductions for module lattices. Des. Codes Crypt. **75**(3), 565–599 (2015)
17. Lyubashevsky, V., et al.: CRYSTALS-Dilithium (2017). https://pq-crystals.org/dilithium. Submission to [21]
18. Lyubashevsky, V., Peikert, C., Regev, O.: On ideal lattices and learning with errors over rings. In: Gilbert, H. (ed.) EUROCRYPT 2010. LNCS, vol. 6110, pp. 1–23. Springer, Heidelberg (2010). https://doi.org/10.1007/978-3-642-13190-5_1
19. MacKay, D.J.C.: Information Theory, Inference, and Learning Algorithms. Cambridge University Press, Cambridge (2003)
20. NewAE: CW308T-STM32F. https://wiki.newae.com/CW308T-STM32F
21. NIST: Post-quantum cryptography standardization. https://csrc.nist.gov/projects/post-quantum-cryptography/post-quantum-cryptography-standardization
22. Oder, T., Schneider, T., Pöppelmann, T., Güneysu, T.: Practical CCA2-secure and masked ring-LWE implementation. IACR Trans. Cryptogr. Hardw. Embed. Syst. **2018**(1), 142–174 (2018)
23. Primas, R., Pessl, P., Mangard, S.: Single-trace side-channel attacks on masked lattice-based encryption. In: Fischer, W., Homma, N. (eds.) CHES 2017. LNCS, vol. 10529, pp. 513–533. Springer, Cham (2017). https://doi.org/10.1007/978-3-319-66787-4_25
24. Reparaz, O., de Clercq, R., Roy, S.S., Vercauteren, F., Verbauwhede, I.: Additively homomorphic ring-LWE masking. In: Takagi, T. (ed.) PQCrypto 2016. LNCS, vol. 9606, pp. 233–244. Springer, Cham (2016). https://doi.org/10.1007/978-3-319-29360-8_15
25. Reparaz, O., Sinha Roy, S., Vercauteren, F., Verbauwhede, I.: A masked ring-LWE implementation. In: Güneysu, T., Handschuh, H. (eds.) CHES 2015. LNCS, vol. 9293, pp. 683–702. Springer, Heidelberg (2015). https://doi.org/10.1007/978-3-662-48324-4_34
26. Saarinen, M.O.: Arithmetic coding and blinding countermeasures for lattice signatures - engineering a side-channel resistant post-quantum signature scheme with compact signatures. J. Cryptographic Eng. **8**(1), 71–84 (2018)
27. Storkey, A.J.: Generalised propagation for fast fourier transforms with partial or missing data. In: NIPS, pp. 433–440. MIT Press (2003)
28. Veyrat-Charvillon, N., Gérard, B., Standaert, F.-X.: Soft analytical side-channel attacks. In: Sarkar, P., Iwata, T. (eds.) ASIACRYPT 2014. LNCS, vol. 8873, pp. 282–296. Springer, Heidelberg (2014). https://doi.org/10.1007/978-3-662-45611-8_15
29. Yedidia, J.S.: Sparse factor graph representations of Reed-Solomon and related codes. In: Algebraic Coding Theory and Information Theory. DIMACS Series in Discrete Mathematics and Theoretical Computer Science, vol. 68, pp. 91–98. DIMACS/AMS (2003). http://www.merl.com/publications/docs/TR2003-135.pdf
30. Yedidia, J.S., Freeman, W.T., Weiss, Y.: Generalized belief propagation. In: NIPS, pp. 689–695. MIT Press (2000)

Authenticated Encryption with Nonce Misuse and Physical Leakage: Definitions, Separation Results and First Construction
(Extended Abstract)

Chun Guo[✉], Olivier Pereira, Thomas Peters, and François-Xavier Standaert

ICTEAM/ELEN/Crypto Group, UCLouvain, Louvain-la-Neuve, Belgium
chun.guo.sc@gmail.com,
{olivier.pereira,thomas.peters,francois-xavier.standaert}@uclouvain.be

Abstract. We propose definitions of authenticated encryption (AE) schemes that offer security guarantees even in the presence of nonce misuse and side-channel information leakage. This is part of an important ongoing effort to make AE more robust, while preserving appealing efficiency properties. Our definitions consider an adversary enhanced with the leakage of all the computations of an AE scheme, together with the possibility to misuse nonces, be it during all queries (in the spirit of misuse-resistance), or only during training queries (in the spirit of misuse-resilience recently introduced by Ashur et al.). These new definitions offer various insights on the effect of leakage in the security landscape. In particular, we show that, in contrast with the black-box setting, leaking variants of INT-CTXT and IND-CPA security do not imply a leaking variant IND-CCA security, and that leaking variants of INT-PTXT and IND-CCA do not imply a leaking variant of INT-CTXT. They also bring a useful scale to reason about and analyze the implementation properties of emerging modes of operation with different levels of leakage-resistance, such as proposed in the ongoing NIST lightweight cryptography competition. We finally propose the first instance of mode of operation that satisfies our most demanding definitions.

1 Introduction

Authenticated encryption (AE) has become the de facto standard primitive for the protection of secure communications, by offering a robust and efficient alternative to the combination of encryption and MACs, a combination that is challenging enough to have been the source of security issues in numerous high-profile systems [2,18,29]. This effort towards robustness has been intensely pursued and, as a result, a number of strengthened requirements for AE schemes have been proposed in the literature.

A first focus has been on reducing functional requirements, in order to protect users from their failure to provide appropriate inputs to the system. The

© Springer Nature Switzerland AG 2019
P. Schwabe and N. Thériault (Eds.): LATINCRYPT 2019, LNCS 11774, pp. 150–172, 2019.
https://doi.org/10.1007/978-3-030-30530-7_8

typical requirement of using random IVs has been lowered to the requirement of providing unique nonces. Further efforts have then been made to reduce the impact of a repeated nonce, by requiring that such a repetition only makes it possible to recognize the repetition of a message, which is the strict minimal consequence. These considerations led Rogaway and Shrimpton to define the central notion of misuse-resistant nonce-based AE [32], which goes even one step further, by requiring ciphertexts to be indistinguishable from random strings. Satisfying this notion of misuse-resistance is extremely appealing, as it goes as far as possible in protecting users from their own mistakes or from devices offering poor sources of randomness. However, it comes with a significant memory penalty (two successive passes are needed to perform encryption) and, as we will argue, may also be infeasible to achieve in the presence of many natural types of leakage (e.g., based on the power consumption or electromagnetic radiation of an implementation). More recently, Ashur et al. [4] proposed the relaxed security notion of misuse-resilience, which requires that nonce misuse does not have an impact on the security of messages encrypted with a fresh nonce. This notion can be satisfied by much more efficient schemes, and we will show that it is also compatible with the side-channel attack scenarios mentioned above.

A second line of efforts aims at protecting from weaknesses that implementers could introduce in an AE scheme, by creating observable behaviors that are not part of its specifications. One type of implementation weakness comes from the decryption of invalid ciphertexts [3,4,13,24,27]. While security models usually assume that the decryption of an invalid ciphertext returns an error signal, the reality is often different, and some implementations return different messages depending on the step at which decryption fails, or would even go as far as releasing the partially decrypted message to the adversary, either explicitly, or by treating it as public garbage. Another source of weakness coming from implementation is the possibility of side-channel attacks [5,10,11]. Here, the attacker does not (only) exploit explicit software messages, but extracts information from side-effects such as the computation time, the power consumption, or the electromagnetic radiation of the device performing cryptographic operations. In this context, the previous focus on decryption failures must be broadened, as side-channel leakage happens at encryption and decryption times, and happen at decryption time whether a ciphertext is valid or not.

What can be achieved in the presence of leakage of course depends on the type, the permanence and the amount of leakage granted to the adversary. As far as the type is concerned, we separate scalar leakage (like timing) that allows so-called univariate attacks and vector leakage (like the aforementioned power consumption or electromagnetic radiation) that allows so-called multivariate attacks. As far as the permanence is concerned, we separate between full leakage (that allows leakage during all interactions with the device) and partial leakage that excludes the leakage of some interactions. This leads us to define a first taxonomy of leakage as Vector & Full (VF), Scalar & Full (SF), Vector and Partial (VP), Scalar & Partial (SP). In the rest of this paper, we are concerned with the strongest category of VF leakage.

As for the amount of information leaked, it is in general hard to quantify and highly depends on the implementation and measurement devices that are at hand. In this respect, our starting observation is that the leakage of all secrets makes confidentiality-preserving cryptography impossible, but the full protection against leakage at the implementation level brings us back to a situation in which we put a lot of pressure on implementers, who we must completely trust to limit the leakage. Furthermore, even in that case, this will come at high cost in terms of extra computation time, energy, or circuit area, since strong protections against side-channel attacks (especially in the case of VF leakage) typically increase the "code size × cycle count" metric by 2 or 3 orders of magnitude compared to a non-protected implementation [7, 19].

This state-of-the-art motivated the design of authentication, encryption and AE schemes allowing "leveled implementation" (or implementation in the leveled leakage setting). By leveled implementation, we mean that different levels of security are required for different parts of the computations: some computations must be well protected, while a weaker protection would be sufficient for others. As put forward in [10, 11, 30], this setting usually allows lower cost or more efficient implementation with symmetric building blocks.

The design of such schemes being guided by the security definitions to target, it can be viewed as a tradeoff between the pressure on implementers to limit the leakage and the pressure on the modes to deal with the remaining leakage. Our contributions therefore aim at defining security targets and modes of operation with an effective balance between leakage reduction at the implementation level and leakage-resistance at the cryptographic mode level, in order to reach AE with high physical security and a minimum implementation cost.

Contributions. Our main contributions target deterministic (nonce-based) authenticated encryption with associated data (AEAD) [31]. We:

(i) Define confidentiality and integrity notions in the presence of nonce misuse and leakage. Our security notions capture leakage in encryption and decryption and allow the computation of the "challenge ciphertexts" to leak. Several variants are explored and compared.

(ii) Identify the strongest form of security that an AEAD can offer to protect messages in the presence of nonce misuse and VF leakage, which we call AEML-VF security, as a combination of black-box misuse-resistance, ciphertext integrity with VF leakage and misuse-resistance and CCA security with VF leakage, and misuse-resilience. We also argue why CCA security with VF leakage and misuse-resistance cannot be achieved.

Inspired by the misuse-resistance vs. misuse-resilience terminology, we denote as leakage-resistant the modes that aim to cope with full leakage, and as leakage-resilient the modes that aim to cope with partial leakage. The resulting set of definitions is relatively large, but we believe that it offers a valuable resource.

– An increased number of AE schemes claim to offer some form of leakage-resistance: among the candidates to the NIST lightweight cryptographic algorithm competition, we may mention Ascon, ISAP, Spook and others.[1] Our structured set of definitions should help comparing the claimed guarantees, which we would view as an interesting future work.

- Applications may raise different risks in terms of side-channel attacks, resulting in the adoption of different security requirements. For instance, we may have an encrypting device exposed to side-channel attacks, while decryption would only happen in a very well protected environment, which may suggest the adoption of a security definition that excludes decryption leakages. And aiming at weaker requirement could very well lead to the adoption of more efficient schemes.

- Exploring relations between definitions may sometimes offer implications that would support simpler security proofs. We compare all our definition variants, and demonstrate that none of our security notions are equivalent.

SECURITY DEFINITION. Our definition of AEML-VF security (cAEML security when VF is understood) is a combination of three requirements: (i) The AE scheme must be misuse-resistant (MR) in the black-box setting (without leakage), in the usual sense of Rogaway and Shrimpton [32]. (ii) The AE scheme must offer CIML2 security, which is a natural extension of ciphertext integrity and nonce misuse resistance in the presence of (full) leakages, as introduced by Berti et al. [10,11]. (iii) The AE scheme must offer CCAmL2 security, which is an extension of CCA security with misuse-resilience in the presence of (full) leakage that we propose here. Misuse-resilience and full leakage are reflected by the small m and large L in these notations.

The first requirement is there to ensure that, for someone who does not have access to leakage, an AEML scheme is also a traditional MR AE scheme.

In the presence of leakage, we unfortunately cannot just easily extend the Rogaway-Shrimpton definition of MR AE in any natural way that would uniformly combine confidentiality and integrity. Indeed, their definition requires that ciphertexts look random as soon as they are produced from a fresh (nonce, message) pair. But defining the leakage function corresponding to the generation of such random-looking ciphertexts is difficult, since the very definition of this function is implementation-dependent. In order to avoid this caveat, we therefore turn back to the original definitional approach for AE security, as a combination of confidentiality and ciphertext integrity, which we gradually extend to the leakage world in the presence of nonce misuse. Such a combination turns out to be especially relevant in the leakage setting where ensuring confidentiality and integrity may benefit from different types of physical assumptions.

The extension of INT-CTXT (the hardness to forge a fresh ciphertext that would pass decryption) to the setting of misuse and leakage has been recently proposed as the CIML2 notion [11]. (The same notion excluding decryption leakage is denoted as CIML1 [10]). This extension can be viewed as natural as it provides the adversary with full nonce misuse capabilities (as in the black box setting) and leakage from all the computations performed in encryption and

---

[1] https://csrc.nist.gov/projects/lightweight-cryptography/.

decryption. Furthermore and as will be detailed next, it can be obtained under quite mild leakage assumptions, making it a particularly desirable property to reach in practice.

It would be tempting to complete this picture with an extension of CPA security to the misuse and leakage setting, e.g., based on the notions defined/used in [10,33]. However, this leads to guarantees that are weaker than what we can hope to achieve. While INT-CTXT + IND-CPA implies (the desired) IND-CCA security in the black box setting [8], we show that this is not true anymore when leakage enters the picture: the implication towards an extension of CCA security with leakage does not hold, mainly because it does not capture the risks associated to decryption leakage.

With this difficulty in mind, we introduce the notion of CCAmL2 security as an extension of CCA security that also offers nonce misuse-resilience [4] in the presence of full leakage: as long as the nonce used in the test query is fresh, confidentiality must hold. Besides the aforementioned separation, we also show that leaking variants of INT-PTXT (the hardness to forge a ciphertext that would decrypt to a fresh message) and CCAmL2 do not imply CIML2 security: the alternate definition of AE as INT-PTXT and IND-CCA security [25] does not suffice in the leaking setting either. By the above, we propose to use CCAmL2 in combination with CIML2 (and MR) to define AEML-VF security.

Finally, the reason of our focus on nonce misuse-resilience for CCAmL2 security, rather than on the stronger requirement of nonce misuse-resistance, is due to the nature of VF leakage. Concretely, if an implementation of an AE scheme processes a message block-by-block, as it is standard, the leakage happening during the processing of the first blocks will only depend on these blocks, and not on all blocks. So, if an adversary asks for an encryption of two messages that have identical first blocks (but differ otherwise), using a single nonce, the leakage of the computation associated to these first blocks will be highly similar, something that can be easily observed and trivially contradicts misuse-resistance. Nonce misuse-resilience is then the natural form of protection against misuse that can be aimed for in the VF setting. Note that this argument may not hold for scalar leakage (i.e., in the SF or SP settings): if there is a single scalar leaked for a full message encryption process, then that scalar may depend on the full message, not just on its first blocks. It also does not hold in the VP setting since, in that case, the security game does not provide the adversary with the challenge leakage that can help her to distinguish.

NEW MODE OF OPERATION. Based on the above definitions, we propose a new mode of operation for which the driving motivation, and our choice of leakage models, is to push towards the most effective balance between the pressure on implementers and the pressure on designers of modes (i.e., trading more complicated leakage-resistant modes for simpler implementations).

Traditional (non leakage-resistant) encryption modes, when intended to be used in a VF leakage setting, require implementers to offer an implementation that can at least withstand so-called Differential Power Analysis attacks (DPAs). Informally, DPAs are the most commonly exploited side-channel attacks and take advantage of the leakage about a secret (e.g., key) obtained from computations based on different inputs (e.g., [14,15,26] and follow ups). A DPA reduces the computational secrecy of the state manipulated by a device at a rate that is exponential in the number of leakage traces, by combining the information of these different inputs (e.g., plaintexts).

Leakage-resistant modes have the potential to considerably lower the costs of physical protection (in terms of time/energy/code size needed to perform an encryption) by removing, to a large extent, DPAs from the attack surface (mostly via consistently refreshing internal secrets, so that it's impossible to collect multiple traces), leaving the adversary with the more challenging task of exploiting leakage with Simple Power Analysis attacks (SPAs). SPAs are side-channel attacks taking advantage of the leakage of a single input, possibly measured multiple times to reduce the measurement noise, and therefore correspond to a minimum threat that targets the unavoidable manipulation of the messages to encrypt/decrypt. SPA protection is considerably cheaper than DPA protection (see [16]), and it is expected that the overhead coming from the use of a more demanding encryption mode (e.g., requiring more block cipher calls per message block) can be compensated by the cheaper physical protections against SPA.

With the above spirit, we define a mode of operation FEMALE (for Feedback-based Encryption with Misuse, Authentication and LEakage) that is based on a block cipher and a hash function and offers AEML-VF security. As encouraged by our composite definitions, the security proofs of FEMALE are obtained under physical assumptions that differ depending on whether we target confidentiality or integrity guarantees. In this respect, it is important to note that our definition of AEML security allows expressing gradual security degradations in the sense (present in our modes) that a weakly protected component that would leak too much to satisfy the assumptions that we need for CCAmL2 security may still offer CIML2 security. In other words, CIML2 and CCAmL2 should be seen as gradual improvements that modes of operation can bring to better cope with leakage, with a risk of non-negligible adversarial advantages (especially for CCAmL2) that are at the same time inherent to physical security issues, but also significantly reduced compared to modes of operations ignoring physical leakage in their design.

In the extended version of this work, we additionally propose a more efficient (one-pass) mode of operation, that ensures CIML2 and CCAmL2 without black box MR, a combination that we denoted as AEmL [20].

Related Works. Recently, Barwell et al. [5] introduced notions of misuse-resistant and leakage-resilient AE, and proposed modes of operation satisfying their definitions. We will refer to this work as BMOS, by the initial of its authors. The BMOS definition captures leakage-resilient AE security as follows (we just focus on encryption queries for simplicity): they first follow the Rogaway-Shrimpton strategy by challenging the adversary to distinguish between non-leaking real or random encryption oracles, then augment the power of the adversary by giving him access to a leaking encryption oracle that cannot be queried with inputs identical to those of the non-leaking oracles. As a result, it is impossible to win their game by exploiting a leakage that would reveal information about the messages that the AE scheme is supposed to hide: leakage is excluded from the "challenge" queries. In our terminology, BMOS focuses on the VP (Vector & Partial) leakage model, which we reflect with a small l in our notations.

As a result of the weaker VP leakage model, BMOS can realistically require misuse-resistance to hold for confidentiality, and not only misuse-resilience (i.e., CCAMl1, CCAMl2), which is in line with our previous discussions. As such, the BMOS work can be viewed as dual to ours: we consider full leakage (i.e., leakage-resistance), and as a consequence have to exclude full misuse-resistance; they consider partial leakage (i.e., leakage-resilience), which makes misuse-resistance possible. On the positive side, the BMOS authors show that their definition is compatible with strong composition results. Yet, the VP model may be insufficient in many practical cases: an implementation that leaks plaintexts in full during encryption may still satisfy the BMOS security definition. By contrast, such an implementation would be considered insecure in the VF model.

Our CCAmL2 definition builds on the notion of misuse-resilience introduced by Ashur, Dunkelman and Luykx [4]. The actual definitions and their motivations are quite different, though. Ashur et al. introduce misuse-resilience to offer a finer grained evaluation of several standard AE schemes that are not misuse-resistant. They do not consider side-channel leakage. In contrast, this type of leakage is the central concern of our definitions, and is our motivation for departing from traditional misuse-resistance in the VF leakage model.

Eventually, we mention the line of works about "after-the-fact" leakage which is complementary to ours [23] and allows the adversary to obtain leakage information after the challenge ciphertext. While the latter is meaningful in certain scenarios (e.g., in the context of a cold boot attack [22], the adversary could first see the encrypted disk – hence getting access to the ciphertext – and then try to design a method of measuring the memory for the purpose of decrypting this ciphertext), it still excludes information leakage during the challenge phase, as will be available in the context of a side-channel attack based on power consumption leakage, which is our main concern here.

2   Preliminaries

Throughout the paper n denotes the security parameter.

2.1   Notations

Adversary. We denote by a $(q_1, \ldots, q_\omega, t)$-bounded adversary a probabilistic algorithm that has access to ω oracles, can make at most q_i queries to its i-th oracle, and can perform computations bounded by running time t. For algorithms that have no oracle to access, we simply call them t-bounded. In this paper, we use subscripts to make a clear distinction between the number of queries to different oracles: the number of queries to the (authenticated) encryption oracle, decryption oracle, and leakage oracle L are denoted by q_e, q_d, and q_l respectively. For example, a (q_e, q_d, q_l, t)-bounded adversary runs in time t, makes q_e and q_d queries to the encryption and decryption oracles of the Authenticated Encryption with Associated Data (AEAD) scheme respectively, and makes q_l additional queries to the leakage oracle L. In all cases, the access to leakage happens through oracle queries. This captures the fact that the leakage function is typically unknown, and that it is only queried by running a physical computation process (rather than being emulated).

Leaking Algorithm. For an algorithm Algo, a leaking version is denoted LAlgo. It runs both Algo and a *leakage function* L_{algo} which captures the additional information given by an implementation of Algo during its execution. LAlgo returns the outputs of both Algo and L_{algo} which all take the same input.

2.2 Definitions of Primitives

We will focus on authenticated encryption with the following formalism.

Definition 1 (Nonce-Based AEAD [31]). *A nonce-based authenticated encryption scheme with associated data is a tuple* AEAD = (Gen, Enc, Dec) *such that, for any security parameter n, and keys in $\mathcal{K}$ generated from* Gen(1^n):

- Enc : $\mathcal{K} \times \mathcal{N} \times \mathcal{AD} \times \mathcal{M} \to \mathcal{C}$ *deterministically maps a key selected from $\mathcal{K}$, a nonce value from $\mathcal{N}$, some associated data selected from $\mathcal{AD}$, and a message from $\mathcal{M}$ to a ciphertext in $\mathcal{C}$.*
- Dec : $\mathcal{K} \times \mathcal{N} \times \mathcal{AD} \times \mathcal{C} \to \mathcal{M} \cup \{\perp\}$ *deterministically maps a key from $\mathcal{K}$, a nonce from $\mathcal{N}$, associated data from $\mathcal{AD}$, and a ciphertext from $\mathcal{C}$, to a message in $\mathcal{M}$ or to a special symbol $\perp$ if integrity verification fails.*

The sets $\mathcal{K}, \mathcal{N}, \mathcal{AD}, \mathcal{M}, \mathcal{C}$ are completely specified by n. Given a key $k \leftarrow$ Gen(1^n), Enc$_k(N, A, M) :=$ Enc(k, N, A, M) and Dec$_k(N, A, M) :=$ Dec(k, N, A, M) are deterministic functions whose implementations may be probabilistic. Furthermore, the input length of Enc publicly determines its output length.

The correctness is defined in the natural way (see [31]). Since we only focus on (correct) nonce-based authenticated encryption with associated data in this paper, we will simply refer to it as *authenticated encryption*.

We recall the definition of Misuse-Resistance (MR) formalized in [32].

Definition 2 (MR). *A nonce-based authenticated encryption scheme with associated data* AEAD = (Gen, Enc, Dec) *is $(q_e, q_d, t, \varepsilon)$ misuse resistant for a security parameter n if, for all (q_e, q_d, t)-bounded adversaries $\mathcal{A}$,*

$$\left| \Pr\left[k \xleftarrow{\$} \text{Gen}(1^n) : \mathcal{A}^{\text{Enc}_k, \text{Dec}_k}(1^n) \Rightarrow 1\right] - \Pr\left[\mathcal{A}^{\$, \perp}(1^n) \Rightarrow 1\right] \right| \leq \varepsilon,$$

where $\$(N, A, M)$ outputs and associates a fresh random ciphertext $C \leftarrow \mathcal{C}$ of appropriate length to fresh inputs, and the associated C otherwise, and $\perp(N, A, C)$ outputs $\perp$ except if C was associated to (N, A, M) for some message M, in which case it returns M.

3   AE with Full Vectorial Leakage

In order to define AEML security, our proposed security notion for authenticated encryption in the full vectorial leakage setting in the presence of nonce misuse, we start by extending the existing black-box security notions to the leakage setting. Surprisingly, the combination of our strongest extensions of confidentiality and integrity is separated from *any other* combinations unlike the situation without misuse and leakages. This motivates our definition to be at least as secure as this strongest combination.

3.1   Variants of Black-Box Notions with Misuse and Leakages

We first adapt the IND-CPA and the IND-CCA confidentiality notions of nonce-based authenticated encryption in the setting of nonce misuse and leakages. We focus then on the extension of the INT-PTXT and INT-CTXT integrity notions.

Confidentiality. Contrary to existing confidentiality notions in a leaking setting (e.g., [5]), our definition includes leakages during encryption and decryption even on the challenge ciphertext(s). We first focus on security against chosen-ciphertext attacks with misuse-resilience and leakages, denoted CCAmL2. Then, we derive the weaker notion of security against chosen-plaintext attacks with misuse-resilience and leakages, denoted CPAmL2.

Chosen-Ciphertext Security with Misuse and Leakages. To capture CCAmL2 security, as motivated in the introduction, we define the game $\mathsf{PrivK}_{\mathcal{A},\mathsf{AEAD},\mathsf{L}}^{\mathsf{CCAmL2},b}$ detailed in Fig. 1. This game takes as parameters an adversary $\mathcal{A}$, a nonce-based authenticated encryption AEAD and a (possibly probabilistic) leakage function pair $\mathsf{L} = (\mathsf{L}_{\mathsf{enc}}, \mathsf{L}_{\mathsf{dec}})$ resulting from the implementation of the scheme. During $\mathsf{PrivK}_{\mathcal{A},\mathsf{AEAD},\mathsf{L}}^{\mathsf{CCAmL2},b}$, the adversary $\mathcal{A}$ selects and submits a tuple $(N_{ch}, A_{ch}, M^0, M^1)$, where the nonce N_{ch} must be fresh and the messages M^0, M^1 must have identical block length. It then receives an encryption of (N_{ch}, A_{ch}, M^b) and the associated leakage, and must guess the bit b. All along this game $\mathcal{A}$ is also granted unbounded and adaptive access to three types of oracles: LEnc, a leaking encryption oracle; LDec, a leaking decryption oracle; and $\mathsf{L}_{\mathsf{decch}}$, a challenge decryption leakage oracle that provides the leakage of the decryption process, but not the resulting plaintext.

Overall, this definition follows the general pattern of CCA security. In terms of misuse-resilience, it only forbids the adversary to reuse a nonce N_{ch} in its challenge query. This captures real situations where, for instance, a counter providing the nonce has been unintentionally reset or shifted. As long as the counter recovers increments and provides fresh nonce values, the security of the challenges should remain unaltered even if the previous encryptions leaked. In terms of leakage, both the encryption and the decryption oracles leak (hence the "2" of CCAmL2 for the two leaking oracles), including during the challenge query. We go one step further with the $\mathsf{L}_{\mathsf{decch}}$ oracle, which offers the leakages

---

$\mathsf{PrivK}_{\mathcal{A},\mathsf{AEAD},\mathsf{L}}^{\mathsf{CCAmL2},b}(1^n)$ is the output of the following experiment:

Initialization: generates a secret key $k \leftarrow \mathsf{Gen}(1^n)$ and sets $\mathcal{E} \leftarrow \emptyset$

Pre-challenge queries: $\mathcal{A}^\mathsf{L}$ gets adaptive access to $\mathsf{LEnc}(\cdot,\cdot,\cdot)$ and $\mathsf{LDec}(\cdot,\cdot,\cdot)$
    (1) $\mathsf{LEnc}(N,A,M)$ computes $C \leftarrow \mathsf{Enc}_k(N,A,M)$ and $\mathsf{leak}_e \leftarrow \mathsf{L}_{\mathsf{enc}}(k,N,A,M)$
        updates $\mathcal{E} \leftarrow \mathcal{E} \cup \{N\}$ and finally returns (C,leak_e)
    (2) $\mathsf{LDec}(N,A,C)$ computes $M \leftarrow \mathsf{Dec}_k(N,A,C)$ and $\mathsf{leak}_d \leftarrow \mathsf{L}_{\mathsf{dec}}(k,N,A,C)$
        and returns (M,leak_d) — we stress that $M = \bot$ may occur

Challenge query: on a single occasion $\mathcal{A}^\mathsf{L}$ submits a tuple $(N_{\mathsf{ch}},A_{\mathsf{ch}},M^0,M^1)$
    If M^0 and M^1 have different (block) length or $N_{\mathsf{ch}} \in \mathcal{E}$ return $\bot$
    Else compute $C^b \leftarrow \mathsf{Enc}_k(N_{\mathsf{ch}},A_{\mathsf{ch}},M^b)$ and $\mathsf{leak}_e^b \leftarrow \mathsf{L}_{\mathsf{enc}}(k,N_{\mathsf{ch}},A_{\mathsf{ch}},M^b)$
    and return (C^b,leak_e^b)

Post-challenge queries: $\mathcal{A}^\mathsf{L}$ can keep accessing LEnc and LDec with some restrictions
    but it can also get an unlimited access to $\mathsf{L}_{\mathsf{decch}}$
    (3) $\mathsf{LEnc}(N,A,M)$ returns $\bot$ if $N = N_{\mathsf{ch}}$ otherwise computes $C \leftarrow \mathsf{Enc}_k(N,A,M)$
        and $\mathsf{leak}_e \leftarrow \mathsf{L}_{\mathsf{enc}}(k,N,A,M)$ and finally returns (C,leak_e)
    (4) $\mathsf{LDec}(N,A,C)$ returns $\bot$ if $(N,A,C) = (N_{\mathsf{ch}},A_{\mathsf{ch}},C^b)$ otherwise computes
        $M \leftarrow \mathsf{Dec}_k(N,A,C)$ and $\mathsf{leak}_d \leftarrow \mathsf{L}_{\mathsf{dec}}(k,N,A,C)$ and returns (M,leak_d)
    (5) $\mathsf{L}_{\mathsf{decch}}$ outputs the leakage trace $\mathsf{leak}_d^b \leftarrow \mathsf{L}_{\mathsf{dec}}(k,N_{\mathsf{ch}},A_{\mathsf{ch}},C^b)$ of the challenge

Finalization: $\mathcal{A}^\mathsf{L}$ outputs a guess bit b' which is defined as the output of the game

---

Fig. 1. The $\mathsf{PrivK}_{\mathcal{A},\mathsf{AEAD},\mathsf{L}}^{\mathsf{CCAmL2},b}(1^n)$ game.

corresponding to the decryption of the challenge ciphertext (but not the corresponding plaintext, as it would offer a trivial win). This addition captures the fact that the adversary may be allowed to observe the decryption of this challenge ciphertext through side-channels, which might be valuable in applications such as secure bootloading or firmware update with a device controlled by $\mathcal{A}$ [28] (see [11] for more discussion). We let the adversary query the $\mathsf{L}_{\mathsf{decch}}$ oracle multiple times, as leakages can be non-deterministic (e.g., contain noise), and $\mathcal{A}$ may benefit from observing the leakages from multiple decryptions of the same plaintext. However, a single leakage is provided for the encryption of the challenge message, as we require the encrypting party to be nonce-respecting for that query: as a result, the challenge encryption process can happen only once.

We focus on a single challenge definition but the multi-challenge setting is treated in the extended version of our work, where we establish their equivalence.

Definition 3 (CCAmL2). *A nonce-based authenticated encryption with associated data* $\mathsf{AEAD} = (\mathsf{Gen},\mathsf{Enc},\mathsf{Dec})$ *with leakage function pair* $\mathsf{L} = (\mathsf{L}_{\mathsf{enc}},\mathsf{L}_{\mathsf{dec}})$ *is* $(q_e,q_d,q_c,q_l,t,\varepsilon)$*-CCAmL2 secure for a security parameter* n *if, for every* (q_e,q_d,q_c,q_l,t)*-bounded adversary* $\mathcal{A}^\mathsf{L}$,[2] *we have:*

$$\left| \Pr\left[\mathsf{PrivK}_{\mathcal{A},\mathsf{AEAD},\mathsf{L}}^{\mathsf{CCAmL2},0}(1^n) \Rightarrow 1\right] - \Pr\left[\mathsf{PrivK}_{\mathcal{A},\mathsf{AEAD},\mathsf{L}}^{\mathsf{CCAmL2},1}(1^n) \Rightarrow 1\right] \right| \leq \varepsilon,$$

---

[2] The notation of $\mathcal{A}^\mathsf{L}$ indicates that the adversary may query L on chosen inputs including *chosen keys* selected and known by $\mathcal{A}$.

where the adversary $\mathcal{A}^{L}$ *makes at most* q_{e} *leaking encryption queries,* q_{d} *leaking decryption queries,* q_{c} *challenge decryption leakage queries and* q_{l} *leakage evaluation queries on arbitrarily chosen keys.*

We will sometimes refer to CCAmL2* as a weakened version of CCAmL2 where we drop the challenge decryption leakage oracle L_{decch} from the game of Fig. 1.

Chosen-Plaintext Security with Misuse and Leakages. Derived from CCAmL2, CPAmL2 is defined by a game $\text{PrivK}_{\mathcal{A},\text{AEAD},L}^{\text{CPAmL2},b}$ which is exactly as $\text{PrivK}_{\mathcal{A}^{L},\text{AEAD}}^{\text{CCAmL2},b}$ except that we remove $\mathcal{A}$'s access to the leaking decryption oracle LDec in Fig. 1 (Items 2, 4). Yet, $\mathcal{A}$ is still able to get challenge decryption leakages leak_{d}^{b}—this corresponds to settings in which a passive adversary tries to break confidentiality while being able to observe leakages of encryption and decryption operations. In Sect. 4.1, we will also introduce the CPAmL1 security notion, which can be seen as the CPAmL2 variant without L_{decch}, corresponding to situations in which an adversary cannot observe any decryption operation, which could happen in settings where keys are dependent of the communication direction, and the adversary only has physical access to one end of the communication.

Definition 4 (CPAmL2). *A nonce-based authenticated encryption with associated data* $\text{AEAD} = (\text{Gen}, \text{Enc}, \text{Dec})$ *with leakage function pair* $L = (L_{\text{enc}}, L_{\text{dec}})$ *is* $(q_{e}, q_{c}, q_{l}, t, \varepsilon)$-CPAmL2 *secure for a security parameter* n *if, for every* (q_{e}, q_{c}, q_{l}, t)-*bounded adversary* $\mathcal{A}$, *we have:*

$$\left| \Pr\left[\text{PrivK}_{\mathcal{A},\text{AEAD},L}^{\text{CPAmL2},0}(1^{n}) \Rightarrow 1\right] - \Pr\left[\text{PrivK}_{\mathcal{A},\text{AEAD},L}^{\text{CPAmL2},1}(1^{n}) \Rightarrow 1\right] \right| \leq \varepsilon,$$

where the adversary $\mathcal{A}^{L}$ *makes at most* q_{e} *leaking encryption queries,* q_{c} *challenge decryption leakage queries and* q_{l} *leakage evaluation queries on chosen keys.*

Integrity. We next adopt the natural and strong extensions of INT-CTXT and INT-PTXT to nonce-misuse resistance and (full) leakages in encryption and decryption. The INT-CTXT extension, called Ciphertext Integrity with Misuse and Leakages, noted CIML2, comes from [11] and is an earlier proposal CIML1 [10] extended with with decryption leakage. Based on this definition, we propose here the corresponding extension of INT-PTXT security, which we call PIML2.

Definition 5 (CIML2, PIML2). *An authenticated encryption* $\text{AEAD} = (\text{Gen}, \text{Enc}, \text{Dec})$ *with leakage function pair* $L = (L_{\text{enc}}, L_{\text{dec}})$ *provides* $(q_{e}, q_{d}, q_{l}, t, \varepsilon)$-*ciphertext (resp. plaintext) integrity with nonce misuse and leakages for security parameter* n *if, for all* (q_{e}, q_{d}, q_{l}, t)-*bounded adversaries* $\mathcal{A}^{L}$, *we have:*

$$\Pr\left[\text{PrivK}_{\mathcal{A},\text{AEAD},L}^{\text{CIML2}}(1^{n}) \Rightarrow 1\right] \leq \varepsilon,$$

$$\textit{(resp. } \Pr\left[\text{PrivK}_{\mathcal{A},\text{AEAD},L}^{\text{PIML2}}(1^{n}) \Rightarrow 1\right] \leq \varepsilon),$$

where the security game $\text{PrivK}_{\mathcal{A},\text{AEAD},L}^{\text{CIML2}}$ *(resp.* $\text{PrivK}_{\mathcal{A},\text{AEAD},L}^{\text{PIML2}}$*) is defined in the left part of Table 1 (resp. right part) when* $\mathcal{A}^{L}$ *makes at most* q_{e} *leaking encryption queries,* q_{d} *leaking decryption queries and* q_{l} *leakage evaluation queries.*

Table 1. The CIML2 and PIML2 security games. Both games ask the adversary to forge a fresh (N, A, C) triple, based on inputs received from leaking encryption and decryption oracles. The CIML2 is won as soon as (N, A, C) is valid, while PIML2 also requires that its decryption leads to a fresh pair of message and associated data.

$\mathsf{PrivK}^{\mathsf{CIML2}}_{\mathcal{A},\mathsf{AEAD},\mathsf{L}}(1^n)$ experiment	$\mathsf{PrivK}^{\mathsf{PIML2}}_{\mathcal{A},\mathsf{AEAD},\mathsf{L}}(1^n)$ experiment
Initialization:	*Initialization:*
1. $k \leftarrow \mathsf{Gen}(1^n)$, $\mathcal{S} \leftarrow \emptyset$	1. $k \xleftarrow{\$} \mathsf{Gen}(1^n)$, $\mathcal{S} \leftarrow \emptyset$
Finalization:	*Finalization:*
1. $(N, A, C) \leftarrow \mathcal{A}^{\mathsf{LEnc}_k,\mathsf{LDec}_k,\mathsf{L}}(1^n)$	1. $(N, A, C) \leftarrow \mathcal{A}^{\mathsf{LEnc}_k,\mathsf{LDec}_k,\mathsf{L}}(1^n)$
2. If $(N, A, C) \in \mathcal{S}$, return 0	2. $M \leftarrow \mathsf{Dec}_k(N, A, C)$
3. If $\mathsf{Dec}_k(N, A, C) = \bot$, return 0	3. If $M = \bot$ or $(A, M) \in \mathcal{S}$, return 0
4. Return 1	4. Return 1
Leaking encryption: $\mathsf{LEnc}_k(N, A, M)$	*Leaking encryption:* $\mathsf{LEnc}_k(N, A, M)$
1. $C \leftarrow \mathsf{Enc}_k(N, A, M)$	1. $C \leftarrow \mathsf{Enc}_k(N, A, M)$
2. $\mathcal{S} \leftarrow \mathcal{S} \cup \{(N, A, C)\}$	2. $\mathcal{S} \leftarrow \mathcal{S} \cup \{(A, M)\}$
3. Return $(C, \mathsf{L}_{\mathsf{enc}}(k, N, A, M))$	3. Return $(C, \mathsf{L}_{\mathsf{enc}}(k, N, A, M))$
Leaking decryption: $\mathsf{LDec}_k(N, A, C)$	*Leaking decryption:* $\mathsf{LDec}_k(N, A, C)$
1. Return $(\mathsf{Dec}_k(N, A, C), \mathsf{L}_{\mathsf{dec}}(k, N, A, C))$	1. Return $(\mathsf{Dec}_k(N, A, C), \mathsf{L}_{\mathsf{dec}}(k, N, A, C))$

3.2 Overall Requirement on AE

We eventually require that a secure AE intended to support nonce misuse and full leakage satisfies the strongest achievable guarantee presented in the paper: an AEML scheme is expected to offer CCAmL2 and CIML2 security, together with being a MR AEAD scheme without leakages. This definition departs from the traditional ones in the black-box setting, which is based on the combination of CPA and INT-CTXT security [8] or CCA and INT-PTXT security [25]. We will actually show that there are important separations between these notions: CCAmL2 + PIML2 + MR $\not\Rightarrow$ CIML2, and CPAmL2 + CIML2 + MR $\not\Rightarrow$ CCAmL2. Furthermore, even if CCAmL2 (resp., CIML2) implies both IND-CCA and CPAmL2 (resp., INT-CTXT and PIML2), the combination of CCAmL2 and CIML2 security does not imply MR, which is therefore a separate requirement.

Definition 6 (AEML-VF). *An AE scheme with security against nonce misuse and full vectorial leakages (denoted as AEML-VF) is an AE scheme AEAD = (Gen, Enc, Dec) with a leakage function pair $\mathsf{L} = (\mathsf{L}_{\mathsf{enc}}, \mathsf{L}_{\mathsf{dec}})$ satisfying the following assertions: (i) AEAD is misuse resistant; (ii) AEAD is CIML2 secure with leakage function L; (iii) AEAD is CCAmL2 secure with leakage function L.*

As indicated above, AEML-VF security will typically be abbreviated as AEML in our paper, since the VF attack setting is understood.

3.3 Separation Results

We now explain why the strong security notions of MR, CCAmL2 and CIML2 are needed to define AEML, while one could be tempted to make a definition as

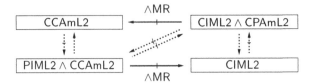

Fig. 2. Relations among notions. Arrows (resp., barred arrows) denote implications (resp., separations). Dotted arrows are trivially implied by other relations.

a combination of weaker notions, which may be easier to prove. Unfortunately, there is no such equivalence and we show that AEML is strictly stronger than any other combinations, assuming that AEML-secure AEAD exists.

We summarize even more relations in Fig. 2. In contrast to the black-box setting, these relations show that one cannot choose between different ways to achieve AEML since, for instance, CCAmL2 ∧ PIML2 ≢ CPAmL2 ∧ CIML2.

MR∧CPAmL2∧CIML2⇏CCAML2*. It is not surprising that MR does not imply CCAmL2 since the leakage function L is absent from the black-box notion. Contrarily, L appears both in CPAmL2 and CIML2. This claim thus says that leakages in decryption may not alter integrity but may alter confidentiality. To reflect this intrinsic separation of the leakage setting, we show that the implication does not even hold for CCAmL2* where the challenge decryption leakage oracle $\mathsf{L}_{\mathsf{decch}}$ is unavailable. While the latter leakages are motivated in the context of side-channel attacks [11], is is also quite specific to such attacks. So ignoring it in the separation makes our result stronger and more general.

Theorem 1. *Assuming that there exists an AE scheme which satisfies* MR, CPAmL2, *and* CIML2 *in the unbounded leakage setting, then there exists an AE with the same security properties but which fails to achieve* CCAmL2, *even without challenge decryption leakages (i.e.,* CCAmL2**).*

The proof utilizes information leaked by invalid decryption queries, which was also exploited in the "protocol leakage" setting [6]. The implication does not hold either when starting from the multiple challenge variant of CPAmL2.

Proof. Let AEAD = (Gen, Enc, Dec) with leakage function $\mathsf{L} = (\mathsf{L}_{\mathsf{enc}}, \mathsf{L}_{\mathsf{dec}})$ be MR, CPAmL2 with respect to L and CIML2 with respect to L^* as such authenticated encryption exists by assumption. Then we build AEAD′ = (Gen′, Enc, Dec) with leakage $\mathsf{L}' = (\mathsf{L}'_{\mathsf{enc}}, \mathsf{L}'_{\mathsf{dec}})$ such that, for a fixed message $M^\dagger \in \mathcal{M}$:

Gen′(1^n): returns $k \leftarrow$ Gen(1^n) and $k' \leftarrow$ Gen(1^n);

$\mathsf{L}'_{\mathsf{enc}}((k, k'), N, A, M)$: outputs $(\mathsf{leak}_{\mathsf{e}}, C', \mathsf{leak}_{\mathsf{e'}})$ where $\mathsf{leak}_{\mathsf{e}} = \mathsf{L}_{\mathsf{enc}}(k, N, A, M)$ (comes from the computation of $C \leftarrow \mathsf{Enc}_k(N, A, M)$), the ciphertext $C' = \mathsf{Enc}_{k'}(N, A, M)$ and consequently $\mathsf{leak}_{\mathsf{e'}} = \mathsf{L}_{\mathsf{enc}}(k', N, A, M)$;

$\mathsf{L}'_{\mathsf{dec}}((k, k'), N, A, C)$: outputs $\mathsf{leak}_{\mathsf{d}} = \mathsf{L}_{\mathsf{dec}}(k, N, A, C)$ if $M \neq \bot$ (which comes from the computation of $M \leftarrow \mathsf{Dec}_k(N, A, C)$) and outputs

$(\mathsf{leak_d}, C^\dagger, \mathsf{leak}_{e'}^\dagger)$ otherwise, where $\mathsf{leak_d} = \mathsf{L_{dec}}(k, N, A, C)$, $C^\dagger \leftarrow \mathsf{Enc}_{k'}(N, A, M^\dagger)$ and consequently also $\mathsf{leak}_{e'}^\dagger = \mathsf{L_{enc}}(k', N, A, M^\dagger)$.

From a black-box standpoint, k' does not even exist so AEAD' is still MR. Therefore, let us focus on the security notions involving leakages.

CPAmL2. In the $\mathsf{PrivK}_{\mathcal{A}', \mathsf{AEAD}', \mathsf{L}'}^{\mathsf{CPAmL2}, b}(1^n)$ game, the adversary $\mathcal{A}'$ does not have access to $\mathsf{L}'_{\mathsf{dec}}$ except from the challenge decryption leakage through $\mathsf{L}'_{\mathsf{decch}}$. But since the challenge ciphertext is valid, $\mathsf{L}'_{\mathsf{decch}} = \mathsf{L_{decch}}$ which returns $\mathsf{L_{dec}}(k, N_{\mathsf{ch}}, A_{\mathsf{ch}}, C^b)$. Consequently, an adversary $\mathcal{A}$ in $\mathsf{PrivK}_{\mathcal{A}, \mathsf{AEAD}, \mathsf{L}}^{\mathsf{CPAmL2}, b}$ can easily simulate the view of $\mathcal{A}'$, simply by picking $k' \leftarrow \mathsf{Gen}(1^n)$, transmitting all the queries to its own oracles, and adding the encryption leakage $(C', \mathsf{leak}_{e'})$ if necessary.

CIML2. In the $\mathsf{PrivK}_{\mathcal{A}', \mathsf{AEAD}', (\mathsf{L}')^*}^{\mathsf{CIML2}}(1^n)$ game, the adversary $\mathcal{A}'$ still needs to forge a fresh ciphertext of AEAD with key k while the additional unbounded leakage given by $(\mathsf{L}')^*$ only depends k'. Then, building a reduction to $\mathsf{PrivK}_{\mathcal{A}, \mathsf{AEAD}, \mathsf{L}^*}^{\mathsf{CIML2}}(1^n)$ is straightforward.

¬CCAmL2*. We build a distinguisher $\mathcal{A}'$ against AEAD'. In the security game $\mathsf{PrivK}_{\mathcal{A}', \mathsf{AEAD}', \mathsf{L}'}^{\mathsf{CCAmL2}, b}(1^n)$, the adversary queries leaking decryption of $(N_{\mathsf{ch}}, A_{\mathsf{ch}}, C)$ for any chosen $N_{\mathsf{ch}}, A_{\mathsf{ch}}$ and C. If the ciphertext is valid, it receives some $M \neq \perp$ and it sets $(M^0, C^0) = (M, C)$. If not, it receives $(\perp, (\mathsf{leak_e}, C^\dagger, \mathsf{leak}_{e'}^\dagger))$ from $\mathsf{LDec}_{k, k'}(N_{\mathsf{ch}}, A_{\mathsf{ch}}, C)$ and sets $(M^0, C^0) = (M^\dagger, C^\dagger)$. In the challenge phase, $\mathcal{A}'$ sends $(N_{\mathsf{ch}}, A_{\mathsf{ch}}, M^0, M^1)$ for any distinct M^1 than M^0. Since the pair $(N_{\mathsf{ch}}, A_{\mathsf{ch}})$ has never been queried for (leaking) encryption, $\mathcal{A}'$ does not receive $\perp$. In the answer $\mathsf{LEnc}_k(N_{\mathsf{ch}}, A_{\mathsf{ch}}, M^b)$, $\mathcal{A}'$ gets C^b. If C^b equals the known C^0, $\mathcal{A}'$ outputs 0, otherwise it outputs 1. Obviously the distinction holds with probability 1.

Now, it is easy to see that AEAD' with leakage L' fulfills all the desired requirements of the theorem based on the existence of AEAD. □

MR ∧ CCAmL2 ∧ PIML2 ⇏ CIML2. As for the previous assertion, being MR does not say anything about leakages, so not being CIML2 is obviously compatible. The most interesting part comes from CCAmL2 and PIML2 which include leakages. This claim exploits the fact that leakages on repeated queries may degrade ciphertext integrity but neither confidentiality nor plaintext integrity.

Theorem 2. *Assuming that there exists an AE scheme which satisfies* MR, CCAmL2, *and* PIML2 *in the unbounded leakage model, then there exists an AE which satisfies the same security properties but which fails to achieve* CIML2 *(even if not in the unbounded leakage model).*

The proof is available in the full version. It proceeds by building a ¬CIML2 scheme AEAD' from an MR ∧ CCAmL2 ∧ PIML2 scheme AEAD. An interesting feature is that this counterexample AEAD' preserves the tidiness of AEAD, that is, the property that $\mathsf{Enc}_k(N, A, \mathsf{Dec}_k(N, A, C)) = C$ when $\mathsf{Dec}_k(N, A, C) \neq \perp$. This deviates from Bellare and Namprempre's well-known approach for establishing INT-PTXT ⇏ INT-CTXT, which did utilize non-tidy counterexamples [8]. It is possible in our case due to the presence of leakages.

4   Completing the Definitions' Zoo

To give a complete picture of the different security flavors of AE with misuse-resistance or resilience and full vectorial leakages, we list all the security definitions that can be derived from our confidentiality and integrity notions. We then study their relations which may be useful in order to guide future designs with relaxed requirements (e.g., in order to reach better performances). It shows that, apart from the obvious implications between the different flavors of confidentiality (resp., integrity), all the notions are separated from each other. In this section we concentrate on the single challenge notions. The extension to the multi-challenge setting is discussed in the extended version of our work.

4.1   Security Definition List (Single Challenge Setting)

The CCAmL2 security game $\mathsf{PrivK}^{\mathsf{CCAmL2},b}_{\mathcal{A},\mathsf{AEAD},\mathsf{L}}$ is defined in Sect. 3.1, Fig. 1. By dropping some accesses to the distinct oracles of this game, we naturally derive other confidentiality notions. For instance CPAmL2 is defined by removing items (2) and (4) from the security game. By doing similar modifications, we can define different integrity notions from the CIML2 security game $\mathsf{PrivK}^{\mathsf{CIML2}}_{\mathcal{A},\mathsf{AEAD},\mathsf{L}}$ defined in Sect. 2.2, Table 1. We next formalize these variants.

Prefix-Suffix Definitions. In all the notions derived from CCAmL2 and CIML2 we only focus on those capturing full leakages (partial leakage is covered by BMOS). Therefore all the definitions below keep the large L in their notation. This leads us to consider 16 different notions denoted as "pre-suf" with prefix pre $\in$ {CCA, CPA, CI, PI} and suffix suf $\in$ {ML2, ML1, mL2, mL1, L2, L1}: a large "M" corresponds to misuse resistance, a small "m" corresponds to misuse-resilience and no "M/m" means that the security game is nonce-respecting (which only restricts leaking encryption queries).

Zoo of Confidentiality Notions. For pre $\in$ {CCA, CPA} we obtain the following 8 notions, by starting from CCAmL2 and by removing one security layer at a time:

CCAmL2 → CCAmL1, CCAL2, CPAmL2 → CPAmL1, CPAL2, CCAL1 → CPAL1.

Definition 7. *A nonce-based authenticated encryption with associated data* AEAD = (Gen, Enc, Dec) *with leakages* L = (L_enc, L_dec) *is* $(q_{\mathsf{pre-suf}}, q_l, t, \varepsilon)$*-pre-suf secure for a security parameter n if, for every* $(q_{\mathsf{pre-suf}}, q_l, t)$*-bounded adversary* $\mathcal{A}^{\mathsf{L}}$, *we have* pre $\in$ {CCA, CPA} *and:*

$$\left| \Pr\left[\mathsf{PrivK}^{\mathsf{pre-suf},0}_{\mathcal{A},\mathsf{AEAD},\mathsf{L}}(1^n) \Rightarrow 1\right] - \Pr\left[\mathsf{PrivK}^{\mathsf{pre-suf},1}_{\mathcal{A},\mathsf{AEAD},\mathsf{L}}(1^n) \Rightarrow 1\right] \right| \leq \varepsilon,$$

where the adversary $\mathcal{A}^{\mathsf{L}}$ *makes at most* $q_{\mathsf{pre-suf}}$ *queries defined in* $\mathsf{PrivK}^{\mathsf{pre-suf},b}_{\mathcal{A},\mathsf{AEAD},\mathsf{L}}$ *below, and* q_l *leakage evaluation queries on arbitrarily chosen keys.*

(i) $\mathsf{PrivK}^{\mathsf{CCAmL2},b}_{\mathcal{A},\mathsf{AEAD},\mathsf{L}}$: $q_{\mathsf{CCAmL2}} = (q_e, q_d, q_c)$ *with the* CCAmL2 *game in Fig. 1.*

(ii) $\mathsf{PrivK}^{\mathsf{CCAmL1},b}_{\mathcal{A},\mathsf{AEAD},\mathsf{L}}$: $q_{\mathsf{CCAmL1}} = (q_e, q_d)$ and the CCAmL1 security game "removes 2" from the CCAmL2 game, meaning that $\mathsf{L}_{\mathsf{dec}}$ is removed from all the oracles. In other words items (2), (4) become black-box and (5) disappears.

(iii) $\mathsf{PrivK}^{\mathsf{CCAL2},b}_{\mathcal{A},\mathsf{AEAD},\mathsf{L}}$: $q_{\mathsf{CCAL2}} = (q_e, q_d, q_c)$ and the CCAL2 security game "removes M" from the CCAmL2 game which becomes nonce-respecting.

(iv) $\mathsf{PrivK}^{\mathsf{CPAmL2},b}_{\mathcal{A},\mathsf{AEAD},\mathsf{L}}$: $q_{\mathsf{CPAmL2}} = (q_e, q_c)$ and no decryption oracle access is given in Fig. 1: items (2) and (4) are removed but not item (5), hence the 2.

(v) $\mathsf{PrivK}^{\mathsf{CPAmL1},b}_{\mathcal{A},\mathsf{AEAD},\mathsf{L}}$: $q_{\mathsf{CPAmL1}} = (q_e)$ and the CPAmL1 game only keeps items (1) and (3) from the CCAmL2 game, (like the CPAmL2 game without $\mathsf{L}_{\mathsf{decch}}$).

(vi) $\mathsf{PrivK}^{\mathsf{CPAL2},b}_{\mathcal{A},\mathsf{AEAD},\mathsf{L}}$: $q_{\mathsf{CPAL2}} = (q_e, q_c)$, the CPAL2 game is a nonce-respecting version of the CPAmL2 and $\mathsf{L}_{\mathsf{decch}}$ is still available in item (5).

(vii) $\mathsf{PrivK}^{\mathsf{CCAL1},b}_{\mathcal{A},\mathsf{AEAD},\mathsf{L}}$: $q_{\mathsf{CCAL1}} = (q_e, q_d)$ and the CCAL1 is a nonce-respecting version of CCAmL1 (with black-box dec. and nonce-respecting leaking enc.).

(viii) $\mathsf{PrivK}^{\mathsf{CPAL1},b}_{\mathcal{A},\mathsf{AEAD},\mathsf{L}}$: $q_{\mathsf{CPAL1}} = (q_e)$ with only nonce-respecting leaking encryption.

Zoo of Integrity Notions. For $\mathsf{pre} \in \{\mathsf{CI}, \mathsf{PI}\}$ we obtain the following 8 notions, by starting from CIML2 and by removing one security layer at a time:

$$\mathsf{CIML2} \rightarrow \mathsf{CIML1}, \mathsf{CIL2}, \mathsf{PIML2} \rightarrow \mathsf{PIML1}, \mathsf{PIL2}, \mathsf{CIL1} \rightarrow \mathsf{PIL1}.$$

Definition 8. *A nonce-based authenticated encryption with associated data* $\mathsf{AEAD} = (\mathsf{Gen}, \mathsf{Enc}, \mathsf{Dec})$ *with leakages* $\mathsf{L} = (\mathsf{L}_{\mathsf{enc}}, \mathsf{L}_{\mathsf{dec}})$ *is* $(q_e, d_d, q_l, t, \varepsilon)$-*pre-suf secure for a security parameter* n *if, for every* (q_e, q_d, q_l, t)-*bounded adversary* $\mathcal{A}^\mathsf{L}$, *we have* $\mathsf{pre} \in \{\mathsf{CI}, \mathsf{PI}\}$ *and:*

$$\Pr\left[\mathsf{PrivK}^{\mathsf{pre\text{-}suf}}_{\mathcal{A},\mathsf{AEAD},\mathsf{L}}(1^n) \Rightarrow 1\right] \leq \varepsilon,$$

where the adversary $\mathcal{A}^\mathsf{L}$ *makes at most* q_e *encryption queries and* q_d *decryption queries defined in* $\mathsf{PrivK}^{\mathsf{pre\text{-}suf}}_{\mathcal{A},\mathsf{AEAD},\mathsf{L}}$ *below, and* q_l *leakage evaluation queries on arbitrarily chosen keys.*

(i) $\mathsf{PrivK}^{\mathsf{CIML2}}_{\mathcal{A},\mathsf{AEAD},\mathsf{L}}$: the CIML2 game, see Table 1.

(ii) $\mathsf{PrivK}^{\mathsf{CIML1}}_{\mathcal{A},\mathsf{AEAD},\mathsf{L}}$: the CIML1 game removes $\mathsf{L}_{\mathsf{dec}}$ (i.e., decryption is black-box).

(iii) $\mathsf{PrivK}^{\mathsf{CIL2}}_{\mathcal{A},\mathsf{AEAD},\mathsf{L}}$: the CIL2 game is a nonce-respecting version of CIML2.

(iv) $\mathsf{PrivK}^{\mathsf{PIML2}}_{\mathcal{A},\mathsf{AEAD},\mathsf{L}}$: in the PIML2 game the winning condition changed (Table 1).

(v) $\mathsf{PrivK}^{\mathsf{PIML1}}_{\mathcal{A},\mathsf{AEAD},\mathsf{L}}$: the PIML1 game removes $\mathsf{L}_{\mathsf{dec}}$ from PIML2.

(vi) $\mathsf{PrivK}^{\mathsf{PIL2}}_{\mathcal{A},\mathsf{AEAD},\mathsf{L}}$: the PIL2 game is a nonce respecting version of PIML2.

(vii) $\mathsf{PrivK}^{\mathsf{CIL1}}_{\mathcal{A},\mathsf{AEAD},\mathsf{L}}$: the CIL1 game is a nonce-respecting version of CIML2 free of $\mathsf{L}_{\mathsf{dec}}$.

(viii) $\mathsf{PrivK}^{\mathsf{PIL1}}_{\mathcal{A},\mathsf{AEAD},\mathsf{L}}$: the PIL1 game is a nonce-respecting version of PIML2 free of $\mathsf{L}_{\mathsf{dec}}$.

Connection with Previous Works. Among the above sixteen notions, three of them are equivalent to already defined ones: CPAL1 appeared in [30] under the name of LMCPA, CIML1 was introduced in [10] (under the name CIML) and CIML2 was introduced in [11].

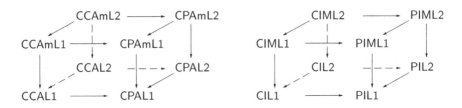

Fig. 3. Single-challenge security notions with various combinations of C/P (Ciphertext/Plaintext), m/M (misuse), 1/2 (# of leaking oracles). Left: confidentiality notions, right: integrity notions. Arrows indicate implications.

4.2 Relations Within the Zoo (Single Challenge Setting)

We picture all the 16 notions with their natural implications in Fig. 3.

Theorem 3 (Long diagonals). *There exist authenticated encryptions schemes showing that:*

$$\text{CCAmL1} \not\Rightarrow \text{CPAL2} \quad \text{CCAL2} \not\Rightarrow \text{CPAmL1} \quad \text{CPAmL2} \not\Rightarrow \text{CCAL1}$$
$$\text{CIML1} \not\Rightarrow \text{PIL2} \quad \text{CIL2} \not\Rightarrow \text{PIML1} \quad \text{PIML2} \not\Rightarrow \text{CIL1}$$

As a corollary, all the arrows of Fig. 3 are strict. The proof only requires to show 4 of the 6 assertions.

Proof We are to prove 12 non-implications:

(i) CCAmL1 $\not\Rightarrow$ CPAL2,   (vii) CIML1 $\not\Rightarrow$ PIL2,

(ii) CPAL2 $\not\Rightarrow$ CCAmL1,   (viii) PIL2 $\not\Rightarrow$ CIML1,

(iii) CCAL2 $\not\Rightarrow$ CPAmL1,   (ix) CIL2 $\not\Rightarrow$ PIML1,

(iv) CPAmL1 $\not\Rightarrow$ CCAL2,   (xi) PIML1 $\not\Rightarrow$ CIL2,

(v) CPAmL2 $\not\Rightarrow$ CCAL1,   (xi) PIML2 $\not\Rightarrow$ CIL1,

(vi) CCAL1 $\not\Rightarrow$ CPAmL2,   (xii) CIL1 $\not\Rightarrow$ PIML2.

We first show that a security notion X1 *without* decryption leakages cannot imply the corresponding notion X2 *with* decryption leakages. This would establish six separations (i), (iv), (vi), (vii), (x), and (xii). For this, assume that AEAD is a X1 secure scheme with master-key K. We define a new scheme AEAD*, which is the same as AEAD except that its leakages for decryption queries explicitly include the master-key K. In this way, AEAD* is clearly not X2 secure (as the key is leaked). But it remains X1 secure, since this enhancement of decryption leakage *cannot* be observed in the X1 security game.

We then show that a security notion X *without* supporting nonce-misuse resistance/resilience cannot imply the corresponding notion XM *with* misuse-resilience. This would establish four separations (ii), (iii), (viii), and (ix). For this, assume that AEAD = (Gen, Enc, Dec) with leakage L = (L_{enc}, L_{dec}) is a X secure scheme. We define a new scheme AEAD* = (Gen', Enc, Dec) with leakage L = (L'_{enc}, L'_{dec}) as follows:

$\mathsf{Gen}'(1^n)$: generates two keys $k \leftarrow \mathsf{Gen}(1^n)$ and $k' \leftarrow \mathsf{Gen}(1^n)$, and selects a public pair $(N^\dagger, A^\dagger)$.

$\mathsf{L}'_{\mathsf{enc}}((k, k'), N, A, M)$: outputs $\mathsf{leak}_e = \mathsf{L}_{\mathsf{enc}}(k, N, A, M)$ as well as the additional value B but in only two cases:

– if $N = N^\dagger$ and $A = A^\dagger$, $B = k \oplus k'$;
– if $N = N^\dagger$ and $A \neq A^\dagger$, $B = k'$;

Clearly, when multiple encryption queries with the same nonce $N^\dagger$ is made, then both $k \oplus k'$ and k' could be leaked, and the key of the underlying scheme AEAD could be recovered. Therefore, AEAD* is not misuse-resistant in *any* security setting. This is not the case in the nonce-respecting setting, and it thus remains X secure.

It remains to prove CPAmL2 $\not\Rightarrow$ CCAL1 and PIML2 $\not\Rightarrow$ CIL1. For this we follow the standard idea of showing CPA$\not\Rightarrow$CCA and INT-PTXT $\not\Rightarrow$ INT-CTXT. In detail, consider CPAmL2 $\not\Rightarrow$ CCAL1 first, and assume that AEAD = (Gen, Enc, Dec) is CPAmL2 secure. We define a new scheme AEAD* = (Gen, Enc, Dec') as follows:

$\mathsf{Dec}'_k(N, A, C)$: outputs $\mathsf{Dec}_k(N, A, C) \| k$, i.e. the main key k is appended to the decrypted plaintext.

This very artificial scheme "gives up" by appending its key to the decrypted message upon any decryption query. Therefore, it cannot be CCA secure under any reasonable definition. Thus CPAmL2 $\not\Rightarrow$ CCAL1.

For PIML2 $\not\Rightarrow$ CIL1, assume that AEAD = (Gen, Enc, Dec) is PIML2 secure. We define a new scheme AEAD* = (Gen, Enc', Dec') as follows:

$\mathsf{Enc}'_k(N, A, M)$: outputs $\mathsf{Enc}_k(N, A, M) \| 0 \| 0$, i.e., two bits are appended to the ciphertext.
$\mathsf{Dec}'_k(N, A, C)$: parses $C = C' \| b \| b'$, and outputs $\mathsf{Dec}_k(N, A, C')$ if and only if $b = b'$.

Then it's clear that AEAD* is not CIL1 since from any valid ciphertext $(N, A, C \| 0 \| 0)$ obtained before the adversary could use $(N, A, C \| 1 \| 1)$ as a forgery. Yet, it remains PIML2 secure.

Remark. By revisiting the proof for MR $\wedge$ CCAmL2 $\wedge$ PIML2 $\not\Rightarrow$ CIML2 in Subsect. 3.3, it can be seen that the exhibited CIML2 adversary *only* relies on the leaking encryption. This means that it also breaks the CIML1 security. Therefore, we already know that MR $\wedge$ CCAmL2 $\wedge$ PIML2 $\not\Rightarrow$ CIML1.

5 First AEML Instantiation: FEMALE

We finally present the AEML mode FEMALE that makes only two calls to a strongly protected block cipher per message to be encrypted and enables leveled

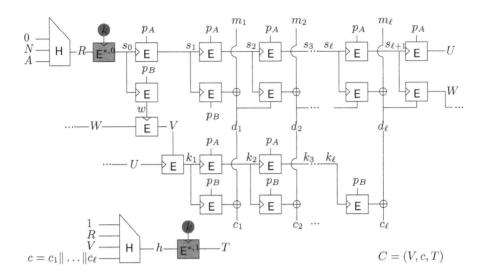

Fig. 4. FEMALE encryption algorithm. "Leak free" block ciphers are in gray with "*". $\mathsf{E}^{*,b} : \mathcal{B} \mapsto \mathcal{M}$ is such that $\mathsf{E}^{*,b}(B) := \mathsf{E}^{*}(b, B)$. Triangles in block ciphers indicate key inputs. If $M \in \mathcal{M}^{*}$ is such that $M = (m_1, \ldots, m_{\ell})$, the output ciphertext is $C = (V, c, T) \in \mathcal{M}^{\ell+2}$. (Top) Generates (U, V) and $d = (d_1, \ldots, d_{\ell})$, a pre-encryption of $M = (m_1, \ldots, m_{\ell})$. (Middle) One-time encryption of d into $c = (c_1, \ldots, c_{\ell})$ with one-time key U and pseudorandom IV V. (Bottom) Authentication from tag T.

implementations. FEMALE is named after *Feedback-based Encryption with Misuse, Authentication and LEakage* as it starts processing the message blocks using a (re-keying) ciphertext feedback mode (see the top of Fig. 4). The encryption processes the key only twice and the message blocks only once.

Given a hash function $\mathsf{H} : \{0,1\}^* \mapsto \mathcal{B}$ and a block cipher E on $\mathcal{M} = \{0,1\} \times \mathcal{B}$ as well as two distinct public constants p_A and p_B of $\mathcal{M}$, the FEMALE encryption algorithm has 3 stages:

(i) *Ephemeral key-IV generation:* on input (N, A, M) with $M \in \mathcal{M}^*$, derives a pseudorandom ephemeral key U depending only on (N, A) as well as a pseudorandom IV V depending on the whole triple. During this process all the blocks m_i of $M = (m_1, \ldots, m_{\ell})$ are "pre-encrypted" as d_i, resulting in $d = (d_1, \ldots, d_{\ell})$, where d_i depends on $(N, A, m_1, \ldots, m_i)$;

(ii) *One-time encryption:* on input (V, d) and the ephemeral key U, produces a one-time encryption c of d with initialized vector V;

(iii) *Authentication:* on input (R, V, c), where $R = \mathsf{H}(0\|N\|A)$, computes a pseudorandom tag T.

The ciphertext is given by $C = (V, c, T)$ and it does not include d. To decrypt the ciphertext (N, A, C), FEMALE first checks (iii) before deriving the one-time key U from (N, A) as in step (i) in order to decrypt c into d as the reverse

---

Description of FEMALE:

Gen(1^n) picks a random key $k \xleftarrow{\$} \{0,1\}^n = \mathcal{K}$.

Enc$_k(N, A, M)$ parses $M \in \mathcal{M}^*$ into as many blocks as needed as $M = (m_1, \ldots, m_\ell)$ for some ℓ. Computes $R \leftarrow \mathsf{H}(0\|N\|A)$. Then:

1. *Ephemeral key-IV generation:* (skip step (b) if $\ell = 0$)
   - (a) Computes $s_0 \leftarrow \mathsf{E}_k^*(0\|R)$, $w \leftarrow \mathsf{E}_{s_0}(p_B)$, $s_1 \leftarrow \mathsf{E}_{s_0}(p_A)$, and sets $d_0 \leftarrow p_B$;
   - (b) Computes $s_{i+1} \leftarrow \mathsf{E}_{s_i}(p_A)$, $y_i \leftarrow \mathsf{E}_{s_i}(d_{i-1})$, $d_i \leftarrow y_i \oplus m_i$, for $i = 1$ to ℓ;
   - (c) Computes $U \leftarrow \mathsf{E}_{s_{\ell+1}}(p_A)$, $W \leftarrow \mathsf{E}_{s_{\ell+1}}(d_\ell)$, $V \leftarrow \mathsf{E}_w(W)$.
2. *One-time encryption:* first computes $k_1 \leftarrow \mathsf{E}_U(V)$ and then, for $i = 1$ to $\ell - 1$, computes $k_{i+1} \leftarrow \mathsf{E}_{k_i}(p_A)$, $z_i \leftarrow \mathsf{E}_{k_i}(p_B)$, and $c_i \leftarrow z_i \oplus d_i$.
3. *Authentication:* sets $c = c_1\| \ldots \|c_\ell$, computes $h \leftarrow \mathsf{H}(1\|R\|V\|c)$, and computes $T \leftarrow \mathsf{E}_k^*(1\|h)$.

Eventually, returns the ciphertext $C = (V, c, T)$.

Dec$_k(N, A, C)$ parses $C = (V, c, T)$, $c = c_1\| \ldots \|c_\ell$, then proceeds in four phases:

1. *Integrity Checking:* computes $R \leftarrow \mathsf{H}(0\|N\|A)$, $h \leftarrow \mathsf{H}(1\|R\|V\|c)$, and $h^* \leftarrow \mathsf{trunc}((\mathsf{E}_k^*)^{-1}(T))$, where trunc drops the first bit of its input. Then, if $h^* = h$, it enters the next phase, and returns $\perp$ otherwise.
2. *Ephemeral key extraction:* first computes $s_0 \leftarrow \mathsf{E}_k^*(0\|R)$ and $s_{i+1} \leftarrow \mathsf{E}_{s_i}(p_A)$, for $i = 0$ to ℓ, and finally $U \leftarrow \mathsf{E}_{s_{\ell+1}}(p_A)$.
3. *One-time decryption:* first computes $k_1 \leftarrow \mathsf{E}_U(V)$ and then, for $i = 1$ to $\ell - 1$, computes $k_{i+1} \leftarrow \mathsf{E}_{k_i}(p_A)$, $z_i \leftarrow \mathsf{E}_{k_i}(p_B)$, and $d_i \leftarrow z_i \oplus c_i$; Set $d_0 \leftarrow p_B$.
4. *Message recovery:* for $i = 1$ to ℓ, computes $y_i \leftarrow \mathsf{E}_{s_i}(d_{i-1})$ and $m_i \leftarrow y_i \oplus d_i$.

Eventually, returns the message $M = (m_1, \ldots, m_\ell)$.

Fig. 5. The FEMALE AEAD scheme.

process of step (ii). Eventually, (N, A, d) allows retrieving M at step (i). The full specification of FEMALE is available in Fig. 5.

For the sake of space, the security analysis of FEMALE is deferred to the full version of this paper [20]. Informally, built upon secure cryptographic functions and assuming that the circuits of E^* is "leak-free", FEMALE offers a (somewhat standard) birthday security, i.e., it can preserve MR, CIML2, and CCAmL2 up to $2^{n/2}$ computations and processing $2^{n/2}$ message and associated data blocks.

5.1 Other Possible Instances

To demonstrate the usefulness of the various definitions, we also list some other possible instances of modes that satisfy some form of resistance against leakage. First, it has been known that the state of a duplex construction [12] can be easily recovered when the initial state can be fixed [1], which may enable universal forgery. A standard 1-pass duplex AE starts processing the inputs by deriving a secret duplex state from the nonce N and the AE key, and thus runs a duplex construction on A and M. For such an AE, the initial state indeed can be fixed if N can be reused for encryption, or if decryption leakages are available. This means such a standard 1-pass duplex AE cannot be CIML1 not CIL2. The inability to offer CIL2 enables a simple forging-and-testing attack against the

CCAL2 security. However, given a side-channel secure state-derivation function (like our leak-free block cipher), such a 1-pass duplex AE seems to offer CIL1 and CCAL1, since in these settings N cannot be reused and the above attacks turn impossible. We leave the proof of this conjecture as an open problem.

On the other hand, if a (side-channel secure) keyed finalization function is added to the 1-pass duplex AE, which is adopted by a CAESAR final winner Ascon [17], then the above universal forgery disappears. Indeed, Ascon is CIML2 and CCAmL1 under certain assumptions: see our recent work [21]. Furthermore, if we can use 2 passes, then we can achieve CIML2 and CCAmL2: this is achieved by the AEDT design [20], or the recent TEDT [9]. Sponge-based 2-pass AEs like ISAP [16] or S1P [21] are also expected to offer similar guarantees.

Acknowledgments. Thomas Peters and François-Xavier Standaert are post-doctoral researcher and senior associate researcher of the Belgian Fund for Scientific Research (FNRS-F.R.S). This work has been funded in part by the ERC consolidator grant SWORD (724725), and also by the EU and Walloon Region through the FEDER project USERMedia (501907-379156).

References

1. Adomnicai, A., Fournier, J.J., Masson, L.: Masking the lightweight authenticated ciphers ACORN and ascon in software. Cryptology ePrint Archive, Report 2018/708 (2019). Appeared at BalkanCryptSec 2018
2. Albrecht, M.R., Paterson, K.G., Watson, G.J.: Plaintext recovery attacks against SSH. In: IEEE Symposium on Security and Privacy, pp. 16–26. IEEE Computer Society (2009)
3. Andreeva, E., Bogdanov, A., Luykx, A., Mennink, B., Mouha, N., Yasuda, K.: How to securely release unverified plaintext in authenticated encryption. In: Sarkar, P., Iwata, T. (eds.) ASIACRYPT 2014. LNCS, vol. 8873, pp. 105–125. Springer, Heidelberg (2014). https://doi.org/10.1007/978-3-662-45611-8_6
4. Ashur, T., Dunkelman, O., Luykx, A.: Boosting authenticated encryption robustness with minimal modifications. In: Katz, J., Shacham, H. (eds.) CRYPTO 2017. LNCS, vol. 10403, pp. 3–33. Springer, Cham (2017). https://doi.org/10.1007/978-3-319-63697-9_1
5. Barwell, G., Martin, D.P., Oswald, E., Stam, M.: Authenticated encryption in the face of protocol and side channel leakage. In: Takagi, T., Peyrin, T. (eds.) ASIACRYPT 2017. LNCS, vol. 10624, pp. 693–723. Springer, Cham (2017). https://doi.org/10.1007/978-3-319-70694-8_24
6. Barwell, G., Page, D., Stam, M.: Rogue decryption failures: reconciling AE robustness notions. In: Groth, J. (ed.) IMACC 2015. LNCS, vol. 9496, pp. 94–111. Springer, Cham (2015). https://doi.org/10.1007/978-3-319-27239-9_6
7. Belaïd, S., Grosso, V., Standaert, F.: Masking and leakage-resilient primitives: one, the other(s) or both? Crypt. Commun. **7**(1), 163–184 (2015)
8. Bellare, M., Namprempre, C.: Authenticated encryption: relations among notions and analysis of the generic composition paradigm. J. Cryptology **21**(4), 469–491 (2008)
9. Berti, F., Guo, C., Pereira, O., Peters, T., Standaert, F.: TEDT, a leakage-resilient AEAD mode for high (physical) security applications. IACR Cryptology ePrint Archive 2019/137 (2019). https://eprint.iacr.org/2019/137

10. Berti, F., Koeune, F., Pereira, O., Peters, T., Standaert, F.: Ciphertext integrity with misuse and leakage: definition and efficient constructions with symmetric primitives. In: AsiaCCS, pp. 37–50. ACM (2018)
11. Berti, F., Pereira, O., Peters, T., Standaert, F.: On leakage-resilient authenticated encryption with decryption leakages. IACR Trans. Symmetric Cryptology **2017**(3), 271–293 (2017)
12. Bertoni, G., Daemen, J., Peeters, M., Van Assche, G.: Duplexing the sponge: single-pass authenticated encryption and other applications. In: Miri, A., Vaudenay, S. (eds.) SAC 2011. LNCS, vol. 7118, pp. 320–337. Springer, Heidelberg (2012). https://doi.org/10.1007/978-3-642-28496-0_19
13. Boldyreva, A., Degabriele, J.P., Paterson, K.G., Stam, M.: On symmetric encryption with distinguishable decryption failures. In: Moriai, S. (ed.) FSE 2013. LNCS, vol. 8424, pp. 367–390. Springer, Heidelberg (2014). https://doi.org/10.1007/978-3-662-43933-3_19
14. Brier, E., Clavier, C., Olivier, F.: Correlation power analysis with a leakage model. In: Joye, M., Quisquater, J.-J. (eds.) CHES 2004. LNCS, vol. 3156, pp. 16–29. Springer, Heidelberg (2004). https://doi.org/10.1007/978-3-540-28632-5_2
15. Chari, S., Rao, J.R., Rohatgi, P.: Template attacks. In: Kaliski, B.S., Koç, K., Paar, C. (eds.) CHES 2002. LNCS, vol. 2523, pp. 13–28. Springer, Heidelberg (2003). https://doi.org/10.1007/3-540-36400-5_3
16. Dobraunig, C., Eichlseder, M., Mangard, S., Mendel, F., Unterluggauer, T.: ISAP - towards side-channel secure authenticated encryption. IACR Trans. Symmetric Cryptology **2017**(1), 80–105 (2017)
17. Dobraunig, C., Eichlseder, M., Mendel, F., Schlaffer, M.: Ascon v1.2. Submission to the CAESAR Competition (2016). https://competitions.cr.yp.to/round3/asconv12.pdf
18. Duong, T., Rizzo, J.: Cryptography in the web: the case of cryptographic design flaws in ASP.NET. In: IEEE Symposium on Security and Privacy, pp. 481–489. IEEE Computer Society (2011)
19. Goudarzi, D., Rivain, M.: How fast can higher-order masking be in software? In: Coron, J.-S., Nielsen, J.B. (eds.) EUROCRYPT 2017. LNCS, vol. 10210, pp. 567–597. Springer, Cham (2017). https://doi.org/10.1007/978-3-319-56620-7_20
20. Guo, C., Pereira, O., Peters, T., Standaert, F.: Authenticated encryption with nonce misuse and physical leakages: definitions, separation results and leveled constructions. IACR Cryptology ePrint Archive 2018/484 (2018). https://eprint.iacr.org/2018/484
21. Guo, C., Pereira, O., Peters, T., Standaert, F.: Towards lighter leakage-resilient authenticated encryption from the duplex construction. IACR Cryptology ePrint Archive 2019/193 (2019). https://eprint.iacr.org/2019/193
22. Halderman, J.A., et al.: Lest we remember: cold-boot attacks on encryption keys. Commun. ACM **52**(5), 91–98 (2009)
23. Halevi, S., Lin, H.: After-the-fact leakage in public-key encryption. In: Ishai, Y. (ed.) TCC 2011. LNCS, vol. 6597, pp. 107–124. Springer, Heidelberg (2011). https://doi.org/10.1007/978-3-642-19571-6_8
24. Hoang, V.T., Krovetz, T., Rogaway, P.: Robust authenticated-encryption AEZ and the problem that it solves. In: Oswald, E., Fischlin, M. (eds.) EUROCRYPT 2015. LNCS, vol. 9056, pp. 15–44. Springer, Heidelberg (2015). https://doi.org/10.1007/978-3-662-46800-5_2

25. Katz, J., Yung, M.: Unforgeable encryption and chosen ciphertext secure modes of operation. In: Goos, G., Hartmanis, J., van Leeuwen, J., Schneier, B. (eds.) FSE 2000. LNCS, vol. 1978, pp. 284–299. Springer, Heidelberg (2001). https://doi.org/10.1007/3-540-44706-7_20
26. Kocher, P., Jaffe, J., Jun, B.: Differential power analysis. In: Wiener, M. (ed.) CRYPTO 1999. LNCS, vol. 1666, pp. 388–397. Springer, Heidelberg (1999). https://doi.org/10.1007/3-540-48405-1_25
27. Martin, D.P., Oswald, E., Stam, M., Wójcik, M.: A leakage resilient MAC. In: Groth, J. (ed.) IMACC 2015. LNCS, vol. 9496, pp. 295–310. Springer, Cham (2015). https://doi.org/10.1007/978-3-319-27239-9_18
28. O'Flynn, C., Chen, Z.D.: Side channel power analysis of an AES-256 bootloader. In: CCECE, pp. 750–755. IEEE (2015)
29. Paterson, K.G., AlFardan, N.J.: Plaintext-recovery attacks against datagram TLS. In: NDSS. The Internet Society (2012)
30. Pereira, O., Standaert, F., Vivek, S.: Leakage-resilient authentication and encryption from symmetric cryptographic primitives. In: ACM Conference on Computer and Communications Security, pp. 96–108. ACM (2015)
31. Rogaway, P.: Authenticated-encryption with associated-data. In: ACM Conference on Computer and Communications Security, pp. 98–107. ACM (2002)
32. Rogaway, P., Shrimpton, T.: A provable-security treatment of the key-wrap problem. In: Vaudenay, S. (ed.) EUROCRYPT 2006. LNCS, vol. 4004, pp. 373–390. Springer, Heidelberg (2006). https://doi.org/10.1007/11761679_23
33. Standaert, F.-X., Pereira, O., Yu, Y.: Leakage-resilient symmetric cryptography under empirically verifiable assumptions. In: Canetti, R., Garay, J.A. (eds.) CRYPTO 2013. LNCS, vol. 8042, pp. 335–352. Springer, Heidelberg (2013). https://doi.org/10.1007/978-3-642-40041-4_19

Stronger and Faster Side-Channel Protections for CSIDH

Daniel Cervantes-Vázquez[1]($\boxtimes$), Mathilde Chenu[2,3],
Jesús-Javier Chi-Domínguez[1], Luca De Feo[4], Francisco Rodríguez-Henríquez[1],
and Benjamin Smith[2,3]

[1] CINVESTAV - Centro de Investigaciòn y de Estudios Avanzados del Instituto Politécnico Nacional, Mexico City, Mexico
dcervantes@computacion.cs.cinvestav.mx
[2] École polytechnique, Institut Polytechnique de Paris, Palaiseau, France
[3] Inria, équipe-projet GRACE, Université Paris–Saclay, Paris, France
[4] Université Paris Saclay – UVSQ, Versailles, France

Abstract. CSIDH is a recent quantum-resistant primitive based on the difficulty of finding isogeny paths between supersingular curves. Recently, two constant-time versions of CSIDH have been proposed: first by Meyer, Campos and Reith, and then by Onuki, Aikawa, Yamazaki and Takagi. While both offer protection against timing attacks and simple power consumption analysis, they are vulnerable to more powerful attacks such as fault injections. In this work, we identify and repair two oversights in these algorithms that compromised their constant-time character. By exploiting Edwards arithmetic and optimal addition chains, we produce the fastest constant-time version of CSIDH to date. We then consider the stronger attack scenario of fault injection, which is relevant for the security of CSIDH static keys in embedded hardware. We propose and evaluate a dummy-free CSIDH algorithm. While these CSIDH variants are slower, their performance is still within a small constant factor of less-protected variants. Finally, we discuss derandomized CSIDH algorithms.

1 Introduction

Isogeny-based cryptography was introduced by Couveignes [10], who defined a key exchange protocol similar to Diffie–Hellman based on the action of an ideal class group on a set of ordinary elliptic curves. Couveignes' protocol was independently rediscovered by Rostovtsev and Stolbunov [27,28], who were the first to recognize its potential as a post-quantum candidate. Recent efforts to make this system practical have put it back at the forefront of research in post-quantum cryptography [13]. A major breakthrough was achieved by Castryck, Lange, Martindale, Panny, and Renes with CSIDH [6], a reinterpretation of Couveignes' system using supersingular curves defined over a prime field.

The first implementation of CSIDH completed a key exchange in less than 0.1 seconds, and its performance has been further improved by Meyer and Reith [22]. However, both [6] and [22] recognized the difficulty of implementing CSIDH with

© Springer Nature Switzerland AG 2019
P. Schwabe and N. Thériault (Eds.): LATINCRYPT 2019, LNCS 11774, pp. 173–193, 2019.
https://doi.org/10.1007/978-3-030-30530-7_9

constant-time algorithms, that is, algorithms whose running time, sequence of operations, and memory access patterns do not depend on secret data. The implementations of [6] and [22] are thus vulnerable to simple timing attacks.

The first attempt at implementing CSIDH in constant-time was realized by Bernstein, Lange, Martindale, and Panny [3], but their goal was to obtain a fully deterministic reversible circuit implementing the class group action, to be used in quantum cryptanalyses. The distinct problem of efficient CSIDH implementation with side-channel protection was first tackled by Jalali, Azarderakhsh, Mozaffari Kermani, and Jao [16], and independently by Meyer, Campos, and Reith [21], whose work was improved by Onuki, Aikawa, Yamazaki, and Takagi [26].

The approach of Jalali *et al.* is similar to that of [3], in that they achieve a stronger notion of constant time (running time independent from *all* inputs), at the cost of allowing the algorithm to fail with a small probability. In order to make the failure probability sufficiently low, they introduce a large number of useless operations, which make the performance significantly worse than the original CSIDH algorithm. This poor performance and possibility of failure reduces the interest of this implementation; we will not analyze it further here.

Meyer *et al.* take a different path: the running time of their algorithm is independent of the secret key, but not of the output of an internal random number generator. They claim a speed only 3.10 times slower than the unprotected algorithm in [22]. Onuki *et al.* introduced new improvements, claiming a speed-up of 27.35% over Meyer *et al.*, i.e., a net slow-down factor of 2.25 compared to [22].

Our Contribution. In this work we take a new look at side-channel protected implementations of CSIDH. We start by reviewing the implementations in [21] and [26]. We highlight some flaws that make their constant-time claims disputable, and propose fixes for them. Since these fixes introduce some minor slow-downs, we report on the performance of the revised algorithms.

Then, we introduce new optimizations to make both [21] and [26] faster: we improve isogeny formulas for the model, and we introduce the use of optimal addition chains in the scalar multiplications. With these improvements, we obtain a version of CSIDH protected against timing and some simple power analysis (SPA) attacks that is 25% more efficient than [21] and 15% more efficient than a repaired version of [26].

Then, we shift our focus to stronger security models. All constant-time versions of CSIDH presented so far use so-called "dummy operations", i.e., computations whose result is not used, but whose role is to hide the conditional structure of the algorithm from timing and SPA attacks that read the sequence of operations performed from a single power trace. However, this countermeasure is easily defeated by fault-injection attacks, where the adversary may modify values during the computation. We propose a new constant-time variant of CSIDH without dummy operations as a first-line defence. The new version is only twice as slow as the simple constant-time version.

We conclude with a discussion of derandomized variants of CSIDH. The versions discussed previously are "constant-time" in the sense that their running time is uncorrelated to the secret key, however it depends on some (necessarily secret) seed to a PRNG. While this notion of "constant-time" is usually considered good enough for side-channel protection, one may object that a compromise of the PRNG or the seed generation would put the security of the implementation at risk, even if the secret was securely generated beforehand (with an uncomprised PRNG) as part of a long-term or static keypair. We observe that this dependence on additional randomness is not necessary: a simple modification of CSIDH, already considered in isogeny-based signature schemes [11,14], can easily be made constant-time and free of randomness. Unfortunately this modification requires increasing substantially the size of the base field, and is thus considerably slower and not compatible with the original version. On the positive side, the increased field size makes it much more resistant to quantum attacks, a non-negligible asset in a context where the quantum security of CSIDH is still unclear; it can thus be seen as CSIDH variant for the paranoid.

Organization. In Sect. 2 we briefly recall ideas, algorithms and parameters from CSIDH [6]. In Sect. 3 we highlight shortcomings in [21] and [26] and propose ways to fix them. In Sect. 4 we introduce new optimizations compatible with all previous versions of CSIDH. In Sect. 5 we introduce a new algorithm for evaluating the CSIDH group action that is resistant against timing and some simple power analysis attacks, while providing protection against some fault injections. Finally, in Sect. 6 we discuss a more costly variant of CSIDH with stronger security guarantees.

Notation. $\mathbf{M}$, $\mathbf{S}$, and $\mathbf{A}$ denote the cost of computing a single multiplication, squaring, and addition (or subtraction) in $\mathbb{F}_p$, respectively. We assume that a constant-time equality test $\mathtt{isequal}(X, Y)$ is defined, returning 1 if $X = Y$ and 0 otherwise. We also assume that a constant-time conditional swap $\mathtt{cswap}(X, Y, b)$ is defined, exchanging (X, Y) if $b = 1$ (and not if $b = 0$).

2   CSIDH

CSIDH is an isogeny based primitive, similar to Diffie–Hellman, that can be used for key exchange and encapsulation [6], signatures [4,11,14], and other more advanced protocols. Compared to the other main isogeny-based primitive SIDH [12,17], CSIDH is slower. On the positive side, CSIDH has smaller public keys, is based on a better understood security assumption, and supports an easy key validation procedure, making it better suited than SIDH for CCA-secure encryption, static-dynamic and static-static key exchange. In this work we will use the jargon of key exchange when we refer to cryptographic concepts.

CSIDH works over a finite field $\mathbb{F}_p$, where p is a prime of the special form

$$p := 4 \prod_{i=1}^{n} \ell_i - 1$$

with $\ell_1, \ldots, \ell_n$ a set of small odd primes. Concretely, the original CSIDH article [6] defined a 511-bit p with $\ell_1, \ldots, \ell_{n-1}$ the first 73 odd primes, and $\ell_n = 587$.

The set of public keys in CSIDH is a subset of all supersingular elliptic curves defined over $\mathbb{F}_p$, in *Montgomery form* $y^2 = x^3 + Ax^2 + x$, where $A \in \mathbb{F}_p$ is called the *A-coefficient* of the curve.[1] The endomorphism rings of these curves are isomorphic to orders in the imaginary quadratic field $\mathbb{Q}(\sqrt{-4p})$. Castryck *et al.* [6] choose to restrict the public keys to the *horizontal isogeny class* of the curve with $A = 0$, so that all endomorphism rings are isomorphic to $\mathbb{Z}[\sqrt{-p}]$.

2.1 The Class Group Action

Let $E/\mathbb{F}_p$ be an elliptic curve with $\text{End}(E) \cong \mathbb{Z}[\sqrt{-p}]$. If $\mathfrak{a}$ is a nonzero ideal in $\mathbb{Z}[\sqrt{-p}]$, then it defines a finite subgroup $E[\mathfrak{a}] = \bigcap_{\alpha \in \mathfrak{a}} \ker(\alpha)$, where we identify each α with its image in $\text{End}(E)$. We then have a quotient isogeny $\phi : E \rightarrow E' = E/E[\mathfrak{a}]$ with kernel $\mathfrak{a}$; this isogeny and its codomain is well-defined up to isomorphism. If $\mathfrak{a} = (\alpha)$ is principal, then $\phi \cong \alpha$ and $E/E[\mathfrak{a}] \cong E$. Hence, we get an action of the ideal class group $\text{Cl}(\mathbb{Z}[\sqrt{-p}])$ on the set of isomorphism classes of elliptic curves E over $\mathbb{F}_p$ with $\text{End}(E) \cong \mathbb{Z}[\sqrt{-p}]$; this action is faithful and transitive. We write $\mathfrak{a} * E$ for the image of (the class of) E under the action of $\mathfrak{a}$, which is (the class of) $E/E[\mathfrak{a}]$ above.

For CSIDH, we are interested in computing the action of small prime ideals. Consider one of the primes ℓ_i dividing $p + 1$; the principal ideal $(\ell_i) \subset \mathbb{Z}[\sqrt{-p}]$ splits into two primes, namely $\mathfrak{l}_i = (\ell_i, \pi - 1)$ and $\bar{\mathfrak{l}}_i = (\ell_i, \pi + 1)$, where π is the element of $\mathbb{Z}[\sqrt{-p}]$ mapping to the Frobenius endomorphism of the curves. Since $\bar{\mathfrak{l}}_i \mathfrak{l}_i = (\ell_i)$ is principal, we have $\bar{\mathfrak{l}}_i = \mathfrak{l}_i^{-1}$ in $\text{Cl}(\mathbb{Z}[\sqrt{-p}])$, and hence

$$\bar{\mathfrak{l}}_i * (\mathfrak{l}_i * E) = \mathfrak{l}_i * (\bar{\mathfrak{l}}_i * E) = E$$

for all $E/\mathbb{F}_p$ with $\text{End}(E) \cong \mathbb{Z}[\sqrt{-p}]$.

2.2 The CSIDH Algorithm

At the heart of CSIDH is an algorithm that evaluates the class group action described above on any supersingular curve over $\mathbb{F}_p$. Cryptographically, this plays the same role as modular exponentiation in classic Diffie–Hellman.

The input to the algorithm is an elliptic curve $E : y^2 = x^3 + Ax^2 + x$, represented by its A-coefficient, and an ideal class $\mathfrak{a} = \prod_{i=1}^n \mathfrak{l}_i^{e_i}$, represented by its list of exponents $(e_1, \ldots, e_n) \in \mathbb{Z}^n$. The output is the ($A$-coefficient of the) elliptic curve $\mathfrak{a} * E = \mathfrak{l}_1^{e_1} * \cdots * \mathfrak{l}_n^{e_n} * E$.

The isogenies corresponding to $\mathfrak{l}_i = (\ell_i, \pi - 1)$ can be efficiently computed using Vélu's formulæ and their generalizations: exploiting the fact that $\#E(\mathbb{F}_p) = p + 1 = 4 \prod \ell_i$, one looks for a point R of order ℓ_i in $E(\mathbb{F}_p)$ (i.e., a point that is in the kernels of both the multiplication-by-ℓ_i map and $\pi - 1$), computes the isogeny $\phi : E \rightarrow E/\langle R \rangle$ with kernel $\langle R \rangle$, and sets $\mathfrak{l}_i * E = E/\langle R \rangle$. Iterating this procedure lets us compute $\mathfrak{l}_i^e * E$ for any exponent $e \geq 0$.

The isogenies corresponding to $\mathfrak{l}_i^{-1}$ are computed in a similar fashion: this time one looks for a point R of order ℓ_i in the kernel of $\pi + 1$, i.e., a point in $E(\mathbb{F}_{p^2})$

---

[1] Following [8], we represent $A = A'/C'$ as a projective point $(A' : C')$; see Sect. 4.1.1.

of the form (x, iy) where both x and y are in $\mathbb{F}_p$ (since $i = \sqrt{-1}$ is in $\mathbb{F}_{p^2} \setminus \mathbb{F}_p$ and satisfies $i^p = -i$). Then one proceeds as before, setting $\mathfrak{l}_i^{-1} * E = E/\langle R \rangle$.

In the sequel we assume that we are given an algorithm `QuotientIsogeny` which, given a curve $E/\mathbb{F}_p$ $\phi: E \to E' \cong E/\langle R \rangle$, and returns the pair (ϕ, E'). We refer to this operation as *isogeny computation*. Algorithm 1, taken from the original CSIDH article [6], computes the class group action.

Algorithm 1. The original CSIDH class group action algorithm for supersingular curves over $\mathbb{F}_p$ where $p = 4\prod_{i=1}^{n} \ell_i - 1$. The choice of ideals $\mathfrak{l}_i = (\ell_i, \pi - 1)$, where π is the element of $\mathbb{Q}(\sqrt{-p})$ is mapped to the p-th power Frobenius endomorphism on each curve in the isogeny class, is a system parameter. This algorithm constructs exactly $|e_i|$ isogenies for each ideal $\mathfrak{l}_i$.

Input: $A \in \mathbb{F}_p$ such that $E_A: y^2 = x^3 + Ax^2 + x$ is supersingular, and an integer exponent vector $(e_1, \ldots, e_n)$
Output: B such that $E_B: y^2 = x^3 + Bx^2 + x$ is $\mathfrak{l}_1^{e_1} * \cdots * \mathfrak{l}_n^{e_n} * E_A$,

1 $B \leftarrow A$;
2 **while** *some* $e_i \neq 0$ **do**
3   Sample a random $x \in \mathbb{F}_p$;
4     $s \leftarrow +1$ if $x^3 + Bx^2 + x$ is square in $\mathbb{F}_p$, else $s \leftarrow -1$;
5     $S \leftarrow \{i \mid e_i \neq 0, \text{sign}(e_i) = s\}$
6   ;
7   **if** $S \neq \emptyset$ **then**
8         $k \leftarrow \prod_{i \in S} \ell_i$;
9         $Q \leftarrow [(p+1)/k]P$, where P is the projective point with x-coordinate x. ;
10   **for** $i \in S$ **do**
11            $R \leftarrow [k/\ell_i]Q$;   // Point to be used as kernel generator
12   **if** $R \neq \infty$ **then**
13                $(E_B, \phi) \leftarrow \text{QuotientIsogeny}(E_B, R)$;
14                $Q \leftarrow \phi(Q)$;
15                $(k, e_i) \leftarrow (k/\ell_i, e_i - s)$

16 **return** B

For cryptographic purposes, the exponent vectors $(e_1, \ldots, e_n)$ must be taken from a space of size at least $2^{2\lambda}$, where λ is the (classical) security parameter. The CSIDH-512 parameters in [6] take $n = 74$, and all e_i in the interval $[-5, 5]$, so that $74\log_2(2 \cdot 5 + 1) \simeq 255.99$, consistent with the NIST-1 security level. With this choice, the implementation of [6] computes one class group action in 40 ms on average. Meyer and Reith [22] further improved this to 36 ms on average. Neither implementation is constant-time.

2.3   The Meyer–Campos–Reith Constant-Time Algorithm

As Meyer, Campos and Reith observe in [21], Algorithm 1 performs fewer scalar multiplications when the key has the same number of positive and negative exponents than it does in the unbalanced case where these numbers differ. Algorithm 1 thus leaks information about the distribution of positive and negative exponents under timing attacks. Besides this, analysis of power traces would reveal the cost of each isogeny computation, and the number of such isogenies computed, which would leak the exact exponents of the private key.

In view of this vulnerability, Meyer, Campos and Reith proposed in [21] a constant-time CSIDH algorithm whose running time does not depend on the private key (though, unlike [16], it still varies due to randomness). The essential differences between the algorithm of [21] and classic CSIDH are as follows. First, to address the vulnerability to timing attacks, they choose to use only positive exponents in $[0, 10]$ for each ℓ_i, instead of $[-5, 5]$ in the original version, while keeping the same prime $p = \prod_{i=1}^{74} \ell_i - 1$. To mitigate power consumption analysis attacks, their algorithm always computes the maximal amount of isogenies allowed by the exponent, using dummy isogeny computations if needed.

Since these modifications generally produce more costly group action computations, the authors also provide several optimizations that limit the slow-down in their algorithm to a factor of 3.10 compared to [22]. These include the Elligator 2 map of [2] and [3], multiple batches for isogeny computation (SIMBA), and sample the exponents e_i from intervals of different sizes depending on ℓ_i.

2.4   The Onuki–Aikawa–Yamazaki–Takagi Constant-Time Algorithm

Still assuming that the attacker can perform only power consumption analysis and timing attacks, Onuki, Aikawa, Yamazaki and Takagi proposed a faster constant-time version of CSIDH in [26].

The key idea is to use two points to evaluate the action of an ideal, one in $\ker(\pi - 1)$ (i.e., in $E(\mathbb{F}_p)$) and one in $\ker(\pi + 1)$ (i.e., in $E(\mathbb{F}_{p^2})$ with x-coordinate in $\mathbb{F}_p$). This allows them to avoid timing attacks, while keeping the same primes and exponent range $[-5, 5]$ as in the original CSIDH algorithm. Their algorithm also employs dummy isogenies to mitigate some power analysis attacks, as in [21]. With these improvements, they achieve a speed-up of 27.35% compared to [21].

We include pseudo-code for the algorithm of [26] in Algorithm 2, to serve both as a reference for a discussion of some subtle leaks in Sect. 3 and also as a departure point for our dummy-free algorithm in Sect. 5.

3   Repairing Constant-Time Versions

3.1   Projective Elligator

Both [21] and [26] use the Elligator 2 map to sample a random point on the current curve E_A in step 6 of Algorithm 2. Elligator takes as input a random field

Algorithm 2. The Onuki–Aikawa–Yamazaki–Takagi CSIDH algorithm for supersingular curves over $\mathbb{F}_p$, where $p = 4 \prod_{i=1}^{n} \ell_i - 1$. The ideals $\mathfrak{l}_i = (\ell_i, \pi - 1)$, where π maps to the p-th power Frobenius endomorphism on each curve, and the exponent bound vector $(m_1, \ldots, m_n)$, are system parameters. This algorithm computes exactly m_i isogenies for each ℓ_i.

Input: A supersingular curve $E_A: y^2 = x^3 + Ax^2 + x$ over $\mathbb{F}_p$, and an integer exponent vector $(e_1, \ldots, e_n)$ with each $e_i \in [-m_i, m_i]$.
Output: $E_B: y^2 = x^3 + Bx^2 + x$ such that $E_B = \mathfrak{l}_1^{e_1} * \cdots * \mathfrak{l}_n^{e_n} * E_A$.

```
1  (e′₁,…,e′ₙ) ← (m₁ − |e₁|,…,mₙ − |eₙ|) ;    // Number of dummy computations
2  E_B ← E_A ;
3  while some eᵢ ≠ 0 or e′ᵢ ≠ 0 do
4  |   S ← {i | eᵢ ≠ 0 or e′ᵢ ≠ 0}
5  |   ;
6  |   k ← ∏_{i∈S} ℓᵢ ;
7  |   (T₋,T₊) ← Elligator(E_B,u) ;    // T₋ ∈ E_B[π − 1] and T₊ ∈ E_B[π + 1]
8  |   (P₀,P₁) ← ([(p + 1)/k]T₊,[(p + 1)/k]T₋) ;
9  |   for i ∈ S do
10 |   |   s ← sign(eᵢ) ;                          // Ideal 𝔩ᵢˢ to be used
11 |   |   Q ← [k/ℓᵢ]P_{(1−s)/2} ;         // Secret kernel point generator
12 |   |   P_{(1+s)/2} ← [ℓᵢ]P_{(1+s)/2} ;    // Secret point to be multiplied
13 |   |   if Q ≠ ∞ then
14 |   |   |   if eᵢ ≠ 0 then
15 |   |   |   |   (E_B,φ) ← QuotientIsogeny(E_B,Q) ;
16 |   |   |   |   (P₀,P₁) ← (φ(P₀),φ(P₁)) ;
17 |   |   |   |   eᵢ ← eᵢ − s.
18 |   |   |   else
19 |   |   |   |   E_B ← E_B; P_{(1−s)/2} ← [ℓᵢ]P_{(1−s)/2}; e′ᵢ ← e′ᵢ − 1 ;    // Dummies
20 |   |   k ← k/ℓᵢ
21 return B
```

---

element $u \in \{2, \ldots, \frac{p-1}{2}\}$ and the Montgomery A-coefficient from the current curve and returns a pair of points in $E_A[\pi - 1]$ and $E_A[\pi + 1]$ respectively.

To avoid a costly inversion of $u^2 - 1$, instead of sampling u randomly, Meyer, Campos and Reith[2] follow [3] and precompute a set of ten pairs $(u, (u^2 - 1)^{-1})$; they try them in order until one that produces a point Q passing the test in Step 12 is found. When this happens, the algorithm moves to the next curve, and Elligator can keep on using the next precomputed value of u, going back to the first value when the tenth has been reached. This is a major departure from [3], where *all* precomputed values of u are tried *for each isogeny computation*, and the algorithm succeeds if at least one passes the test. And indeed the implementation

---

[2] Presumably, Onuki *et al.* do the same, however their exposition is not clear on this point, and we do not have access to their code.

of [21] leaks information on the secret via the timing channel:[3] since Elligator uses no randomness for u, its output only depends on the A-coefficient of the current curve, which itself depends on the secret key; but the running time of the algorithm varies and, not being correlated to u, it is necessarily correlated to A and thus to the secret.

Fortunately this can be easily fixed by (re)introducing randomness in the input to Elligator. To avoid field inversions, we use a projective variant: given $u \neq 0, 1$ and assuming $A \neq 0$, we write $V = (A : u^2 - 1)$, and we want to determine whether V is the abscissa of a projective point on E_A. Plugging V into the homogeneous equation

$$E_A : Y^2 Z^2 = X^3 Z + A X^2 Z^2 + X Z^3$$

gives

$$Y^2 (u^2 - 1)^2 = ((A^2 u^2 + (u^2 - 1)^2) A (u^2 - 1).$$

We can test the existence of a solution for Y by computing the Legendre symbol of the right hand side: if it is a square, the points with projective XZ-coordinates

$$T_+ = (A : u^2 - 1), \qquad\qquad T_- = (-Au^2 : u^2 - 1)$$

are in $E_A[\pi - 1]$ and $E_A[\pi + 1]$ respectively, otherwise their roles are swapped.

We are left with the case $A = 0$. Following [3], Meyer, Campos and Reith precompute once and for all a pair of generators T_+, T_- of $E_0[\pi - 1]$ and $E_0[\pi + 1]$, and output those instead of random points. This choice suffers from a similar issue to the previous one: because the points are output in a deterministic way, the running time of the whole algorithm will be correlated to the number of times the curve E_0 is encountered during the isogeny walk.

In practice, E_0 is unlikely to ever be encountered in a random isogeny walk, except as the starting curve in the first phase of a key exchange, thus this flaw seems hard to exploit. Nevertheless, we find it not significantly more expensive to use a different approach, also suggested in [3]: with $u \neq 0$, only on E_0, we define the output of Elligator as $T_+ = (u : 1), T_- = (-u : 1)$ when $u^3 + u$ is a square, and we swap the points when $u^3 + u$ is not a square.

With these choices, under reasonable heuristics experimentally verified in [3], the running time of the whole algorithm is uncorrelated to the secret key as long as the values of u are unknown to an adversary. We summarize our implementation of Elligator in Algorithm 3, generalizing it to the case of Montgomery curves represented by projective coefficients (see also Sect. 4.1.1).

3.2 Fixing a Leaking Branch in Onuki–Aikawa–Yamazaki–Takagi

The algorithm from [26], essentially reproduced in Algorithm 2, includes a conditional statement at Line 12 which branches on the value of the point Q computed

---

[3] The Elligator optimization is described in § 5.3 of [21]. The unoptimized constant-time version described in Algorithm 2 therein is not affected by this problem.

Algorithm 3. Constant-time projective Elligator

Input: A supersingular curve $E_{(A':C')} : C'y^2 = C'x^3 + A'x^2 + C'x$ over $\mathbb{F}_p$, and
an element $u \in \{2, \ldots, \frac{p-1}{2}\}$.
Output: A pair of points $T_+ \in E_{(A':C')}[\pi - 1]$ and $T_- \in E_{(A':C')}[\pi + 1]$.

1 $t \leftarrow A'\left((u^2 - 1)u^2 A'^2 C' + ((u^2 - 1)C')^3\right)$;
2 $a \leftarrow$ isequal$(t, 0)$;   // $t = 0$ iff $A' = 0$
3 $\alpha, \beta \leftarrow 0, u$;
4 cswap(α, β, a) ;   // $\alpha = 0$ iff $A' \neq 0$
5 $t' \leftarrow t + \alpha(u^2 + 1)$;   // $t' \neq 0$
6 $T_+ \leftarrow (A' + \alpha C'(u^2 - 1) : C'(u^2 - 1))$;
7 $T_- \leftarrow (-A'u^2 - \alpha C'(u^2 - 1) : C'(u^2 - 1))$;
8 $b \leftarrow$ Legendre_symbol(t', p) ;   // $b = \pm 1$
9 $c \leftarrow$ isequal$(b, -1)$;
10 cswap(T_+, T_-, c);
11 **return** (T_+, T_-) ;

---

at Line 10. But this value depends on the sign s of the secret exponent e_i, so the branch leaks information about the secret. We propose repairing this by always computing both $Q_0 \leftarrow [k/\ell_i]P_0$ and $Q_1 \leftarrow [k/\ell_i]P_1$ at Line 10, and replacing the condition in Line 12 with a test for $(Q_0 = \infty)$ **or** $(Q_1 = \infty)$ (and using constant-time conditional swaps throughout).[4] This fix is visible in Line 13 of Algorithm 5.

4   Optimizing Constant-Time Implementations

In this section we propose several optimizations that are compatible with both non-constant-time and constant-time implementations of CSIDH.

4.1   Isogeny and Point Arithmetic on Twisted Edwards Curves

In this subsection, we present efficient formulas in twisted-Edwards coordinates for four fundamental operations: point addition, point doubling, isogeny computation (as presented in [25]; cf. § 2.2), and isogeny evaluation (*i.e.* computing the image of a point under an isogeny). Our approach obtains a modest but still noticeable improvement with respect to previous proposals based on Montgomery representation, or hybrid strategies that propound combinations of Montgomery and twisted-Edwards representations [5, 18–20, 23].

Castryck, Galbraith, and Farashahi [5] proposed using a hybrid representation to reduce the cost of point doubling on certain Montgomery curves, by exploiting the fact that converting between Montgomery and twisted Edwards

---

[4] We also found a branch on secret data in the code provided with [21] at https://zenon.cs.hs-rm.de/pqcrypto/faster-csidh, during the 3-isogeny computation, when computing $[\ell]P = [(\ell-1)/2]P + [(\ell+1)/2]P$. This can be easily fixed by a conditional swap, without any significant impact on running time.

models can be done at almost no cost. In [23], Meyer, Reith and Campos considered using twisted Edwards formulas for computing isogeny and elliptic curve arithmetic, but concluded that a pure twisted-Edwards-only approach would not be advantageous in the context of SIDH. Bernstein, Lange, Martindale, and Panny observed in [3] that the conversion from Montgomery XZ coordinates to twisted Edwards YZ coordinates occurs naturally during the Montgomery ladder. Kim, Yoon, Kwon, Park, and Hong presented a hybrid model in [19] using Edwards and Montgomery models for isogeny computations and point arithmetic, respectively; in [18] and [20], they suggested computing isogenies using a modified twisted Edwards representation that introduces a fourth coordinate w.

To the best of our knowledge, the quest for more efficient elliptic curve and isogeny arithmetic than that offered by pure Montgomery and twisted-Edwards-Montgomery representations remains an open problem. As a step forward in this direction, Moody and Shumow [25] showed that when dealing with isogenies of odd degree $d = 2\ell - 1$ with $\ell \geq 2$, twisted Edwards representation offers a cheaper formulation for isogeny computation than the corresponding one using Montgomery curves; nevertheless, they did not address the problem of getting a cheaper twisted Edwards formulation for the isogeny evaluation operation.

4.1.1 Montgomery Curves

A Montgomery curve [24] is defined by the equation $E_{A,B} : By^2 = x^3 + Ax^2 + x$, such that $B \neq 0$ and $A^2 \neq 4$ (we often write E_A for $E_{A,1}$). We refer to [9] for a survey on Montgomery curves. When performing isogeny computations and evaluations, it is often more convenient to represent the constant A in the projective space $\mathbb{P}^1$ as $(A' : C')$, such that $A = A'/C'$. Montgomery curves are attractive because they are exceptionally well-suited to performing the differential point addition operation which computes $x(P + Q)$ from $x(P)$, $x(Q)$, and $x(P - Q)$. Equations (1) and (2) describe the differential point doubling and addition operations proposed by Montgomery in [24]:

$$X_{[2]P} = C_{24}(X_P + Z_P)^2(X_P - Z_P)^2,$$
$$Z_{[2]P} = ((X_P + Z_P)^2 - (X_P - Z_P)^2) \cdot$$
$$(C_{24}(X_P - Z_P)^2 + A_{24p}((X_P + Z_P)^2 - (X_P - Z_P)^2)) \qquad (1)$$

where $A_{24p} = A + 2C$ and $C_{24} = 4C$, and

$$X_{P+Q} = Z_{P-Q}\left[(X_P - Z_P)(X_Q + Z_Q) + (Z_P + Z_P)(X_Q - Z_Q)\right]^2$$
$$Z_{P+Q} = X_{P-Q}\left[(X_P - Z_P)(X_Q + Z_Q) - (Z_P + Z_P)(X_Q - Z_Q)\right]^2 \qquad (2)$$

Montgomery curves can be used to efficiently compute isogenies using Vélu's formulas [30]. Suppose we want the image of a point Q under an ℓ-isogeny ϕ, where $\ell = 2k + 1$. For each $1 \leq i \leq k$ we let $(X_i : Z_i) = x([i]P)$, where $\langle P \rangle = \ker \phi$. Equation (3) computes $(X' : Z') = x(\phi(Q))$ from $(X_Q : Z_Q) = x(Q)$.

$$X' = X_P \left(\prod_{i=1}^{k} \left[(X_Q - Z_Q)(X_i + Z_i) + (Z_Q + Z_Q)(X_i - Z_i) \right] \right)^2 \tag{3}$$

$$Z' = Z_P \left(\prod_{i=1}^{k} \left[(X_Q - Z_Q)(X_i + Z_i) - (Z_Q + Z_Q)(X_i - Z_i) \right] \right)^2$$

4.1.2 Twisted Edwards Curves

In [1] we see that every Montgomery curve $E_{A,B} : By^2 = x^3 + Ax^2 + x$ is birationally equivalent to a twisted Edwards curve $E_{a,d} : ax^2 + y^2 = 1 + dx^2y^2$; the curve constants are related by

$$(A, B) = \left(\frac{2(a+d)}{a-d}, \frac{4}{a-d} \right) \quad \text{and} \quad (a, d) = \left(\frac{A+2}{B}, \frac{A-2}{B} \right),$$

and the rational maps $\phi : E_{a,d} \to E_{A,B}$ and $\psi : E_{A,B} \to E_{a,d}$ are defined by

$$\phi : (x, y) \longmapsto ((1+y)/(1-y), (1+y)/(1-yx)),$$
$$\psi : (x, y) \longmapsto (x/y, (x-1)/(x+1)). \tag{4}$$

Rewriting this relationship for Montgomery curves with projective constants, $E_{a,d}$ is equivalent to the Montgomery curve $E_{(A:C)} = E_{A/C,1}$ with constants

$$A_{24p} := A + 2C = a, \qquad A_{24m} := A - 2C = d, \qquad C_{24} := 4C = a - d.$$

To avoid notational ambiguities, we write $(Y_P : T_P)$ for the $\mathbb{P}^1$ projection of the y-coordinate of the point $P \in E_{a,d}$. Let $P \in E_{(A:C)}$. In projective coordinates, the map ψ of (4) becomes

$$\psi : (X_P : Z_P) \longmapsto (Y_P : T_P) = (X_P - Z_P : X_P + Z_P) \tag{5}$$

Comparing (5) with (1) reveals that Y_P and T_P appear in the doubling formula, so we can substitute them at no cost. Replacing A_{24p} and C_{24} with their twisted Edwards equivalents a and $e = a - d$, respectively, we obtain a doubling formula for twisted Edwards YT coordinates:

$$Y_{[2]P} = e \cdot Y_P^2 \cdot T_P^2 - (T_P^2 - Y_P^2) \cdot (eY_P^2 + a(T_P^2 - Y_P^2)),$$
$$T_{[2]P} = e \cdot Y_P^2 \cdot T_P^2 + (T_P^2 - Y_P^2) \cdot (eY_P^2 + a(T_P^2 - Y_P^2)).$$

Similarly, the coordinates $Y_P, T_P, Y_Q, T_Q, Y_{P-Q}$ and T_{P-Q} appear in (2), and thus we derive differential addition formulas for twisted Edwards coordinates:

$$Y_{P+Q} = (T_{P-Q} - Y_{P-Q})(Y_P T_Q + Y_Q Z_P)^2 - (T_{P-Q} + Y_{P-Q})(Y_P T_Q - Y_Q Z_P)^2,$$
$$T_{P+Q} = (T_{P-Q} - Y_{P-Q})(Y_P T_Q + Y_Q Z_P)^2 + (T_{P-Q} + Y_{P-Q})(Y_P T_Q - Y_Q Z_P)^2.$$

The computational costs of doubling and differential addition are $4\mathbf{M} + 2\mathbf{S} + 4\mathbf{A}$ (the same as evaluating (1)) and $4\mathbf{M} + 2\mathbf{S} + 6\mathbf{A}$ (the same as (2)), respectively.

The Moody–Shumow formulas for isogeny computation [25] are given in terms of twisted Edwards YT-coordinates. It remains to derive a twisted Edwards YT-coordinate isogeny-evaluation formula for ℓ-isogenies where $\ell = 2k + 1$. We do this by applying the map in (5) to (3), which yields

$$
Y' = (T_{P-Q} + Y_{P-Q}) \cdot \left(\prod_{i=1}^{k} \left[T_Q Y_{[i]P} + Y_Q T_{[i]P} \right] \right)^2
$$

$$
- (T_{P-Q} - Y_{P-Q}) \cdot \left(\prod_{i=1}^{k} \left[T_Q Y_{[i]P} - Y_Q T_{[i]P} \right] \right)^2,
$$

$$
T' = (T_{P-Q} + Y_{P-Q}) \cdot \left(\prod_{i=1}^{k} \left[T_Q Y_{[i]P} + Y_Q T_{[i]P} \right] \right)^2
$$

$$
+ (T_{P-Q} - Y_{P-Q}) \cdot \left(\prod_{i=1}^{k} \left[T_Q Y_{[i]P} - Y_Q T_{[i]P} \right] \right)^2.
$$

The main advantage of the approach outlined here is that by only using points given in YT coordinates, we can compute point doubling, point addition and isogeny construction and evaluation at a lower computational cost. Indeed, isogeny evaluation in XZ costs $4k\mathbf{M} + 2\mathbf{S} + 6k\mathbf{A}$, whereas the above YT coordinate formula costs $4k\mathbf{M} + 2\mathbf{S} + (2k + 4)\mathbf{A}$, thus saving $4k - 4$ field additions.

4.2 Addition Chains for a Faster Scalar Multiplication

Since the coefficients in CSIDH scalar multiplications are always known in advance (they are essentially system parameters), there is no need to hide them by using constant-time scalar multiplication algorithms such as the classical Montgomery ladder. Instead, we can use shorter differential addition chains.[5]

In the CSIDH group action computation, any given scalar k is the product of a subset of the collection of the 74 small primes ℓ_i dividing $\frac{p+1}{4}$. We can take advantage of this structure to use shorter differential addition chains than those we might derive for general scalars of a comparable size. First, we pre-computed the shortest differential addition chains for each one of the small primes ℓ_i. One then computes the scalar multiplication operation $[k]P$ as the composition of the differential addition chains for each prime ℓ dividing k.

Power analysis on the coefficient computation might reveal the degree of the isogeny that is currently being computed, but, since we compute exactly one ℓ_i-isogeny for each ℓ_i per loop, this does not leak any secret information.

This simple trick allows us to compute scalar multiplications $[k]P$ using differential addition chains of length roughly $1.5\lceil \log_2(k) \rceil$. This yields a saving of about 25% compared with the cost of the classical Montgomery ladder.

---

[5] A differential addition chain is an addition chain such that for every chain element c computed as $a + b$, the difference $a - b$ is already present in the chain.

5 Removing Dummy Operations for Fault-Attack Resistance

The use of dummy operations in the previous constant-time algorithms implies that the attacker can obtain information on the secret key by injecting faults into variables during the computation. If the final result is correct, then she knows that the fault was injected in a dummy operation; if it is incorrect, then the operation was real. For example, if one of the values in Line 18 of Algorithm 2 is modified without affecting the final result, then the adversary learns whether the corresponding exponent e_i was zero at that point.

Fault injection attacks have been considered in the context of SIDH ([15,29]), but to the best of our knowledge, they have not been studied yet on dummy operations in the context of CSIDH. Below we propose an approach to constant-time CSIDH without dummy computations, making every computation essential for a correct final result. This gives us some natural resistance to fault, at the cost of approximately a twofold slowdown.

Our approach to avoiding fault-injection attacks is to change the format of secret exponent vectors $(e_1, \ldots, e_n)$. In both the original CSIDH and the Onuki et al. variants, the exponents e_i are sampled from an integer interval $[-m_i, m_i]$ centered in 0. For naive CSIDH, evaluating the action of $\mathfrak{l}_i^{e_i}$ requires evaluating between 0 and m isogenies, corresponding to either the ideal $\mathfrak{l}_i$ (for positive e_i) or $\mathfrak{l}_i^{-1}$ (for negative e_i). If we follow the approach of [26], then we must also compute $k - |e_i|$ dummy ℓ_i-isogenies to ensure a constant-time behaviour.

For our new algorithm, the exponents e_i are uniformly sampled from sets

$$\mathcal{S}(m_i) = \{e \mid e = m_i \bmod 2 \text{ and } |e| \leq m_i\},$$

i.e., centered intervals containing only even or only odd integers. The interesting property of these sets is that a vector drawn from $\mathcal{S}(m)^n$ can always be rewritten (in a non-unique way) as a sum of m vectors with entries $\{-1, +1\}$ (i.e., vectors in $\mathcal{S}(1)^n$). But the action of a vector drawn from $\mathcal{S}(1)^n$ can clearly be implemented in constant-time without dummy operations: for each coefficient e_i, we compute and evaluate the isogeny associated to $\mathfrak{l}_i$ if $e_i = 1$, or the one associated to $\mathfrak{l}_i^{-1}$ if $e_i = -1$. Thus, we can compute the action of vectors drawn from $\mathcal{S}(m)^n$ by repeating m times this step.

More generally, we want to evaluate the action of vectors $(e_1, \ldots, e_n)$ drawn from $\mathcal{S}(m_1) \times \cdots \times \mathcal{S}(m_n)$. Algorithm 4 achieves this in constant-time and without using dummy operations. The outer loop at line 3 is repeated exactly $\max(m_i)$ times, but the inner "if" block at line 5 is only executed m_i times for each i; it is clear that this flow does not depend on secrets. Inside the "if" block, the coefficients e_i are implicitly interpreted as

$$|e_i| = \underbrace{1 + 1 + \cdots + 1}_{e_i \text{ times}} + \underbrace{(1-1) - (1-1) + (1-1) - \cdots}_{m_i - e_i \text{ times}},$$

i.e., the algorithm starts by acting by $\mathfrak{l}_i^{\text{sign}(e_i)}$ for e_i iterations, then alternates between $\mathfrak{l}_i$ and $\mathfrak{l}_i^{-1}$ for $m_i - e_i$ iterations. We assume that the `sign` : $\mathbb{Z} \to \{\pm 1\}$ operation is implemented in constant time, and that $\text{sign}(0) = 1$. If one is careful to implement the isogeny evaluations in constant-time, then it is clear that the full algorithm is also constant-time.

Algorithm 4. An idealized dummy-free constant-time evaluation of the CSIDH group action.

Input: Secret vector $(e_1, \ldots, e_n) \in \mathcal{S}(m_1) \times \cdots \times \mathcal{S}(m_n)$

1    $(t_1, \ldots, t_n) \leftarrow (\text{sign}(e_1), \ldots, \text{sign}(e_n))$;   // Secret

2    $(z_1, \ldots, z_n) \leftarrow (m_1, \ldots, m_n)$;   // Not secret

3   **while** *some* $z_i \neq 0$ **do**

4   **for** $i \in \{1, \ldots, n\}$ **do**

5   **if** $z_i > 0$ **then**

6   Act by $\mathfrak{l}_i^{t_i}$;

7          $b = \text{isequal}(e_i, 0)$;

8          $e_i \leftarrow e_i - t_i$;

9          $t_i \leftarrow (-1)^b \cdot t_i$;   // Swap sign when e_i has gone past 0

10          $z_i \leftarrow z_i - 1$;

However, Algorithm 4 is only an idealized version of the CSIDH group action algorithm. Indeed, like in [21,26], it may happen in some iterations that Elligator outputs points of order not divisible by ℓ_i, and thus the action of $\mathfrak{l}_i$ or $\mathfrak{l}_i^{-1}$ cannot be computed in that iteration. In this case, we simply skip the loop and retry later: this translates into the variable z_i not being decremented, so the total number of iterations may end up being larger than $\max(m_i)$. Fortunately, if the input value u fed to Elligator is random, its output is uncorrelated to secret values[6], and thus the fact that an iteration is skipped does not leak information on the secret. The resulting algorithm is summarized in Algorithm 5.

To maintain the security of standard CSIDH, the bounds m_i must be chosen so that the key space is at least as large. For example, the original implementation [6] samples secrets in $[-5, 5]^{74}$, which gives a key space of size 11^{74}; hence, to get the same security we would need to sample secrets in $\mathcal{S}(10)^{74}$. But a constant-time version of CSIDH *à la* Onuki et al. only needs to evaluate five isogeny steps per prime ℓ_i, whereas the present variant would need to evaluate ten isogeny steps. We thus expect an approximately twofold slowdown for this variant compared to Onuki et al., which is confirmed by our experiments.

---

[6] Assuming the usual heuristic assumptions on the distribution of the output of Elligator, see [21].

Algorithm 5. Dummy-free randomized constant-time CSIDH class group action for supersingular curves over $\mathbb{F}_p$, where $p = 4 \prod_{i=1}^{n} \ell_i - 1$. The ideals $\mathfrak{l}_i = (\ell_i, \pi - 1)$, where π maps to the p-th power Frobenius endomorphism on each curve, and the vector $(m_1, \ldots, m_n)$ of exponent bounds, are system parameters. This algorithm computes exactly m_i isogenies for each ideal $\mathfrak{l}_i$.

Input: A supersingular curve E_A over $\mathbb{F}_p$, and an exponent vector $(e_1, \ldots, e_n)$ with each $e_i \in [-m_i, m_i]$ and $e_i \equiv m_i \pmod 2$.
Output: $E_B = \mathfrak{l}_1^{e_1} * \cdots * \mathfrak{l}_n^{e_n} * E_A$.

```
1   (t_1, ..., t_n) ← ( (sign(e_1)+1)/2, ..., (sign(e_n)+1)/2 ) ;          // Secret
2   (z_1, ..., z_n) ← (m_1, ..., m_n) ;                                    // Not secret
3   E_B ← E_A;
4   while some z_i ≠ 0 do
5   |   u ← Random({2, ..., (p-1)/2}) ;
6   |   (T_1, T_0) ← Elligator(E_B, u) ;          // T_1 ∈ E_B[π − 1] and T_0 ∈ E_B[π + 1]
7   |   (T_0, T_1) ← ([4]T_0, [4]T_1) ;                // Now T_0, T_1 ∈ E_B [∏_i ℓ_i]
8   |   for i ∈ {1, ..., n} do
9   |   |   if z_i ≠ 0 then
10  |   |   |   (G_0, G_1) ← (T_0, T_1) ;
11  |   |   |   for j ∈ {i+1, ..., n} do
12  |   |   |   |   (G_0, G_1) ← ([ℓ_j]G_0, [ℓ_j]G_1)
13  |   |   |   if G_0 ≠ ∞ and G_1 ≠ ∞ then
14  |   |   |   |   cswap(G_0, G_1, t_i) ;     // Secret kernel point generator: G_0
15  |   |   |   |   cswap(T_0, T_1, t_i) ;     // Secret point to be multiplied: T_1
16  |   |   |   |   (E_B, φ) ← QuotientIsogeny(E_B, G_0) ;
17  |   |   |   |   (T_0, T_1) ← (φ(T_0), φ(T_1)) ;
18  |   |   |   |   T_1 ← [ℓ_i]T_1 ;
19  |   |   |   |   cswap(T_0, T_1, t_i) ;
20  |   |   |   |   b ← isequal(e_i, 0) ;
21  |   |   |   |   e_i ← e_i + (−1)^{t_i} ;
22  |   |   |   |   t_i ← t_i ⊕ b ;
23  |   |   |   |   z_i ← z_i − 1
24  |   |   |   else if G_0 ≠ ∞ then
25  |   |   |   |   T_0 ← [ℓ_i]T_0 ;
26  |   |   |   else if G_1 ≠ ∞ then
27  |   |   |   |   T_1 ← [ℓ_i]T_1 ;
28  return B
```

6   Derandomized CSIDH Algorithms

As we stressed in Sect. 3, all of the algorithms presented here depend on the availability of high-quality randomness for their security. Indeed, the input to Elligator must be randomly chosen to ensure that the total running time is uncorrelated to the secret key. Typically, this would imply the use of a PRNG seeded with high quality true randomness that must be kept secret. An attack scenario where the attacker may know the output of the PRNG, or where the quality of PRNG output is less than ideal, therefore degrades the security of all algorithms. This is true even when the secret was generated with a high-quality PRNG if the keypair is static, and the secret key is then used by an algorithm with low-quality randomness.

We can avoid this issue completely if points of order $\prod \ell_i^{|m_i|}$, where $|m_i|$ is the maximum possible exponent (in absolute value) for ℓ_i, are available from the start. Unfortunately this is not possible with standard CSIDH, because such points are defined over field extensions of exponential degree.

Instead, we suggest modifying CSIDH as follows. First, we take a prime $p = 4 \prod_{i=1}^{n} \ell_i - 1$ such that $\lceil n \log_2(3) \rceil = 2\lambda$, where λ is a security parameter, and we restrict to exponents of the private key sampled from $\{-1, 0, 1\}$. Then, we compute two points of order $(p + 1)/4$ on the starting public curve, one in $\ker(\pi - 1)$ and the other in $\ker(\pi + 1)$, where π is the Frobenius endomorphism. This computation involves no secret information and can be implemented in variable-time; furthermore, if the starting curve is the initial curve with $A = 0$, or a public curve corresponding to a long term secret key, these points can be precomputed offline and attached to the system parameters or the public key. We also remark that even for ephemeral public keys, a point of order $p + 1$ must be computed anyway for key validation purposes, and thus this computation only slows down key validation by a factor of two.

Since we have restricted exponents to $\{-1, 0, 1\}$, every ℓ_i-isogeny in Algorithm 2 can be computed using only (the images of) the two precomputed points. There is no possibility of failure in the test of Line 12, and no need to sample any other point.

We note that this algorithm still uses dummy operations. If fault-injection attacks are a concern, the exponents can be further restricted to $\{-1, 1\}$, and the group action evaluated as in (a stripped down form of) Algorithm 5. However this further increases the size of p, as n must now be equal to 2λ.

This protection comes at a steep price: at the 128 bits security level, the prime p goes from 511 bits to almost 1500. The resulting field arithmetic would be considerably slower, although the global running time would be slightly offset by the smaller number of isogenies to evaluate.

On the positive side, the resulting system would have much stronger quantum security. Indeed, the best known quantum attacks are exponential in the size of the key space ($\approx 2^{2\lambda}$ here), but only subexponential in p (see [6,7,13]). Since our modification more than doubles the size of p without changing the size of the key space, quantum security is automatically increased. For this same reason, for security levels beyond NIST-1 (64 quantum bits of security), the size of p increases more than linearly in λ, and the variant proposed here becomes natural. Finally, parameter sets with a similar imbalance between the size of p and the security parameter λ have already been considered in the context of isogeny based signatures [11], where they provide tight security proofs in the QROM.

Hence, while at the moment this costly modification of CSIDH may seem overkill, we believe further research is necessary to try and bridge the efficiency gap between it and the other side-channel protected implementations of CSIDH.

7   Experimental Results

Tables 1 and 2 summarize our experimental results, and compare our algorithms with those of [6,21], and [26]. Table 1 compares algorithms in terms of elementary field operations, while Table 2 compares cycle counts of C implementations. All of our experiments were ran on a Intel(R) Core(TM) i7-6700K CPU 4.00 GHz machine with 16 GB of RAM. Turbo boost was disabled. The software environment was the Ubuntu 16.04 operating system and `gcc` version 5.5.

In all of the algorithms considered here (except the original [6]), the group action is evaluated using the SIMBA method (Splitting Isogeny computations into Multiple BAtches) proposed by Meyer, Campos, and Reith in [21]. Roughly speaking, SIMBA-m-k partitions the set of primes ℓ_i into m disjoint subsets S_i (batches) of approximately the same size. SIMBA-m-k proceeds by computing isogenies for each batch S_i; after k steps, the unreached primes ℓ_i from each batch are merged.

Castryck et al. We used the reference CSIDH implementation made available for download by the authors of [6]. None of our countermeasures or algorithmic improvements were applied.

Meyer–Campos–Reith. We used the software library freely available from the authors of [21]. This software batches isogenies using SIMBA-5-11. The improvements we describe in Sects. 3 and 4 were *not* applied.

Onuki et al. Unfortunately, the source code for the implementation in [26] was not freely available, so direct comparison with our implementation was impossible. Table 1 includes their field operation counts for their unmodified algorithm (which, as noted in Sect. 3, is insecure) using SIMBA-3-8, and our estimates for a repaired version applying our fix in Sect. 3. We did not apply the optimizations of Sect. 4 here. (We do not replicate the cycle counts from [26] in Table 2, since they may have been obtained using turbo boost, thus rendering any comparison invalid.)

Our Implementations. We implemented three constant-time CSIDH algorithms, using the standard primes with the exponent bounds m_i from [26, § 5.2].

MCR-style. This is essentially our version of Meyer–Campos–Reith (with one torsion point and dummy operations, batching isogenies with SIMBA-5-11), but applying the techniques of Sects. 3 and 4.

190   D. Cervantes-Vázquez et al.

Table 1. Field operation counts for constant-time CSIDH. Counts are given in millions of operations, averaged over 1024 random experiments. The counts for a possible repaired version of [26] are estimates, and hence displayed in italics. The performance ratio uses [21] as a baseline, considers only multiplication and squaring operations, and assumes $M = S$.

Implementation	CSIDH algorithm	M	S	A	Ratio
Castryck et al. [6]	Unprotected, unmodified	0.252	0.130	0.348	0.26
Meyer–Campos–Reith [21]	Unmodified	1.054	0.410	1.053	1.00
Onuki et al. [26]	Unmodified	0.733	0.244	0.681	0.67
	Repaired as in Sect. 3	*0.920*	*0.338*	*0.867*	*0.86*
This work	MCR-style	0.901	0.309	0.965	0.83
	OAYT-style	0.802	0.282	0.900	0.74
	No-dummy	1.525	0.526	1.686	1.40

Table 2. Clock cycle counts for constant-time CSIDH implementations, averaged over 1024 experiments. The ratio is computed using [21] as baseline implementation.

Implementation	CSIDH algorithm	Mcycles	Ratio
Castryck et al. [6]	Unprotected, unmodified	155	0.39
Meyer–Campos–Reith [21]	Unmodified	395	1.00
This work	MCR-style	337	0.85
	OAYT-style	300	0.76
	No-dummy	569	1.44

OAYT-style. This is essentially our version of Onuki *et al.* (using two torsion points and dummy operations, batching isogenies with SIMBA-3-8), but applying the techniques of Sects. 3 and 4.

No-dummy. This is Algorithm 5 (with two torsion points and no dummy operations), batching isogenies using SIMBA-5-11.

In each case, the improvements and optimizations of Sects. 3 and 4 are applied, including projective Elligator, short differential addition chains, and twisted Edwards arithmetic and isogenies. Our software library is freely available from

https://github.com/JJChiDguez/csidh.

The field arithmetic is based on the Meyer–Campos–Reith software library [21]; since the underlying arithmetic is essentially identical, the performance comparisons below reflect differences in the CSIDH algorithms.

Results. We see in Table 2 that the techniques we introduced in Sects. 3 and 4 produce substantial savings compared with the implementation of [21]. In particular, our OAYT-style implementation yields a 25% improvement over [21].

Since the implementations use the same underlying field arithmetic library, these improvements are entirely due to the techniques introduced in this paper. While our no-dummy variant is (unsurprisingly) slower, we see that the performance penalty is not prohibitive: it is less than twice as slow as our fastest dummy-operation algorithm, and only 44% slower than [21].

8   Conclusion and Perspectives

We studied side-channel protected implementations of the isogeny based primitive CSIDH. Previous implementations failed at being constant time because of some subtle mistakes. We fixed those problems, and proposed new improvements, to achieve the most efficient version of CSIDH protected against timing and simple power analysis attacks to date. All of our algorithms were implemented in C, and the source made publicly available online.

We also studied the security of CSIDH in stronger attack scenarios. We proposed a protection against some fault-injection and timing attacks that only comes at a cost of a twofold slowdown. We also sketched an alternative version of CSIDH "for the paranoid", with much stronger security guarantees, however at the moment this version seems too costly for the security benefits; more work is required to make it competitive with the original definition of CSIDH.

References

1. Bernstein, D.J., Birkner, P., Joye, M., Lange, T., Peters, C.: Twisted Edwards curves. In: Vaudenay, S. (ed.) AFRICACRYPT 2008. LNCS, vol. 5023, pp. 389–405. Springer, Heidelberg (2008). https://doi.org/10.1007/978-3-540-68164-9_26
2. Bernstein, D.J., Hamburg, M., Krasnova, A., Lange, T.: Elligator: elliptic-curve points indistinguishable from uniform random strings. In: 2013 ACM SIGSAC Conference on Computer and Communications Security, CCS 2013, Berlin, Germany, 4–8 November 2013, pp. 967–980 (2013)
3. Bernstein, D.J., Lange, T., Martindale, C., Panny, L.: Quantum circuits for the CSIDH: optimizing quantum evaluation of isogenies. In: Ishai, Y., Rijmen, V. (eds.) EUROCRYPT 2019. LNCS, vol. 11477, pp. 409–441. Springer, Cham (2019). https://doi.org/10.1007/978-3-030-17656-3_15
4. Beullens, W., Kleinjung, T., Vercauteren, F.: CSI-FiSh: efficient isogeny based signatures through class group computations. IACR Cryptology ePrint Archive 2019/498 (2019)
5. Castryck, W., Galbraith, S.D., Farashahi, R.R.: Efficient arithmetic on elliptic curves using a mixed Edwards-Montgomery representation. Cryptology ePrint Archive, 2008/218 (2008)
6. Castryck, W., Lange, T., Martindale, C., Panny, L., Renes, J.: CSIDH: an efficient post-quantum commutative group action. In: Peyrin, T., Galbraith, S. (eds.) ASIACRYPT 2018. LNCS, vol. 11274, pp. 395–427. Springer, Cham (2018). https://doi.org/10.1007/978-3-030-03332-3_15
7. Childs, A.M., Jao, D., Soukharev, V.: Constructing elliptic curve isogenies in quantum subexponential time. J. Math. Cryptol. 8(1), 1–29 (2014)

8. Costello, C., Longa, P., Naehrig, M.: Efficient algorithms for supersingular isogeny Diffie-Hellman. In: Robshaw, M., Katz, J. (eds.) CRYPTO 2016. LNCS, vol. 9814, pp. 572–601. Springer, Heidelberg (2016). https://doi.org/10.1007/978-3-662-53018-4_21

9. Costello, C., Smith, B.: Montgomery curves and their arithmetic - the case of large characteristic fields. J. Cryptogr. Eng. **8**(3), 227–240 (2018)

10. Couveignes, J.M.: Hard homogeneous spaces. Cryptology ePrint Archive, Report 2006/291 (2006)

11. De Feo, L., Galbraith, S.D.: SeaSign: compact isogeny signatures from class group actions. Cryptology ePrint Archive, Report 2018/824 (2018)

12. De Feo, L., Jao, D., Plût, J.: Towards quantum-resistant cryptosystems from supersingular elliptic curve isogenies. J. Math. Cryptol. **8**(3), 209–247 (2014)

13. De Feo, L., Kieffer, J., Smith, B.: Towards practical key exchange from ordinary isogeny graphs. In: Peyrin, T., Galbraith, S. (eds.) ASIACRYPT 2018. LNCS, vol. 11274, pp. 365–394. Springer, Cham (2018). https://doi.org/10.1007/978-3-030-03332-3_14

14. Decru, T., Panny, L., Vercauteren, F.: Faster SeaSign signatures through improved rejection sampling. In: Ding, J., Steinwandt, R. (eds.) PQCrypto 2019. LNCS, vol. 11505, pp. 271–285. Springer, Cham (2019). https://doi.org/10.1007/978-3-030-25510-7_15

15. Gélin, A., Wesolowski, B.: Loop-abort faults on supersingular isogeny cryptosystems. In: Lange, T., Takagi, T. (eds.) PQCrypto 2017. LNCS, vol. 10346, pp. 93–106. Springer, Cham (2017). https://doi.org/10.1007/978-3-319-59879-6_6

16. Jalali, A., Azarderakhsh, R., Kermani, M.M., Jao, D.: Towards optimized and constant-time CSIDH on embedded devices. In: Polian, I., Stöttinger, M. (eds.) COSADE 2019. LNCS, vol. 11421, pp. 215–231. Springer, Cham (2019). https://doi.org/10.1007/978-3-030-16350-1_12

17. Jao, D., De Feo, L.: Towards quantum-resistant cryptosystems from supersingular elliptic curve isogenies. In: Yang, B.-Y. (ed.) PQCrypto 2011. LNCS, vol. 7071, pp. 19–34. Springer, Heidelberg (2011). https://doi.org/10.1007/978-3-642-25405-5_2

18. Kim, S., Yoon, K., Kwon, J., Hong, S., Park, Y.H.: Efficient isogeny computations on twisted Edwards curves. Secur. Commun. Netw. **2018**, 11 (2018)

19. Kim, S., Yoon, K., Kwon, J., Park, Y.H., Hong, S.: New hybrid method for isogeny-based cryptosystems using Edwards curves. Cryptology ePrint Archive, Report 2018/1215 (2018). https://eprint.iacr.org/2018/1215

20. Kim, S., Yoon, K., Kwon, J., Park, Y.H., Hong, S.: Optimized method for computing odd-degree isogenies on Edwards curves. Cryptology ePrint Archive, Report 2019/110 (2019). https://eprint.iacr.org/2019/110

21. Meyer, M., Campos, F., Reith, S.: On Lions and elligators: an efficient constant-time implementation of CSIDH. In: Ding, J., Steinwandt, R. (eds.) PQCrypto 2019. LNCS, vol. 11505, pp. 307–325. Springer, Cham (2019). https://doi.org/10.1007/978-3-030-25510-7_17

22. Meyer, M., Reith, S.: A faster way to the CSIDH. In: Chakraborty, D., Iwata, T. (eds.) INDOCRYPT 2018. LNCS, vol. 11356, pp. 137–152. Springer, Cham (2018). https://doi.org/10.1007/978-3-030-05378-9_8

23. Meyer, M., Reith, S., Campos, F.: On hybrid SIDH schemes using Edwards and Montgomery curve arithmetic. Cryptology ePrint Archive 2017/1213 (2017)

24. Montgomery, P.L.: Speeding the Pollard and elliptic curve methods of factorization. Math. Comput. **48**, 243–264 (1987)

25. Moody, D., Shumow, D.: Analogues of Vélu's formulas for isogenies on alternate models of elliptic curves. Math. Comput. **85**(300), 1929–1951 (2016)

26. Onuki, H., Aikawa, Y., Yamazaki, T., Takagi, T.: A faster constant-time algorithm of CSIDH keeping two torsion points. In: IWSEC 2019 - The 14th International Workshop on Security (2019, to appear)

27. Rostovtsev, A., Stolbunov, A.: Public-key cryptosystem based on isogenies. Cryptology ePrint Archive, Report 2006/145 (2006)

28. Stolbunov, A.: Constructing public-key cryptographic schemes based on class group action on a set of isogenous elliptic curves. Adv. Math. Commun. **4**(2), 215–235 (2010)

29. Ti, Y.B.: Fault attack on supersingular isogeny cryptosystems. In: Lange, T., Takagi, T. (eds.) PQCrypto 2017. LNCS, vol. 10346, pp. 107–122. Springer, Cham (2017). https://doi.org/10.1007/978-3-319-59879-6_7

30. Vélu, J.: Isogénies entre courbes elliptiques. Comptes-rendu de l'académie des sciences de Paris (1971)

Post-quantum Cryptography

A Reaction Attack Against Cryptosystems Based on LRPC Codes

Simona Samardjiska[1]($\boxtimes$), Paolo Santini[2], Edoardo Persichetti[3],
and Gustavo Banegas[4,5]

[1] Radboud University, Nijmegen, The Netherlands
`simonas@cs.ru.nl`
[2] Universitá Politecnica delle Marche, Ancona, Italy
`p.santini@pm.univpm.it`
[3] Florida Atlantic University, Boca Raton, USA
`epersichetti@fau.edu`
[4] Technische Universiteit Eindhoven, Eindhoven, The Netherlands
`gustavo@cryptme.in`
[5] Chalmers University of Technology, Gothenburg, Sweden

Abstract. Rank metric is a very promising research direction for code-based cryptography. In fact, thanks to the high complexity of generic decoding attacks against codes in this metric, it is possible to easily select parameters that yield very small data sizes. In this paper we analyze cryptosystems based on Low-Rank Parity-Check (LRPC) codes, one of the classes of codes that are efficiently decodable in the rank metric. We show how to exploit the decoding failure rate, which is an inherent feature of these codes, to devise a reaction attack aimed at recovering the private key. As a case study, we cryptanalyze the recent McNie submission to NIST's Post-Quantum Standardization process. Additionally, we provide details of a simple implementation to validate our approach.

1 Introduction

It is well known that, once quantum computers of an appropriate size will be available, traditional cryptographic schemes will not be secure anymore [43]. Code-based cryptosystems are among the most promising candidates for Post-Quantum Cryptography, the area concerned with designing cryptographic primitives which will be secure in this scenario. This is evident from the recent Call for Standardization issued by NIST [37], where the number of code-based submissions is second only to that of lattice-based ones [38]. In particular, code-based schemes seem to shine as solutions for encryption and key-exchange.

This work has been supported by the European Commission through the ERC Starting Grant 805031 (EPOQUE); through the European Union's Horizon 2020 research and innovation programme under the Marie Skłodowska-Curie grant agreement No. 643161; and by Sweden through the WASP expedition project Massive, Secure, and Low-Latency Connectivity for IoT Applications.

© Springer Nature Switzerland AG 2019
P. Schwabe and N. Thériault (Eds.): LATINCRYPT 2019, LNCS 11774, pp. 197–216, 2019.
https://doi.org/10.1007/978-3-030-30530-7_10

McEliece in 1978 [27] was the first to propose a code-based encryption scheme, based on the hardness of decoding random linear codes. This NP-hard problem was exploited by selecting a binary Goppa code, for which a random-looking generator is released as public key, and encrypting a plaintext as a noisy codeword. While the private description allows for decoding (and hence decryption), the public one conveys no information about the code, and so the best attacks are generic decoding attacks such as Information-Set Decoding (ISD) [40], which are of exponential nature. This "code indistinguishability" assumption has been true for binary Goppa codes ever since, and the McEliece framework has now over 40 years of security history. However, this comes with the price of a fairly large public-key size, which can be as large as 1Mb with modern parameters [6].

The quest for obtaining compact key sizes started with investigating other families of codes (e.g. [35,44]), many of which have been shown to be insecure [30, 45]. On top of that, a popular approach is to choose *structured* codes, such as Quasi-Cyclic [5,13] or Quasi-Dyadic [31,39], which allow for a dramatic reduction in the size of the public key. However, introducing algebraic structure is not always safe, as shown in [11]. As a result, algebraic codes with an algebraic structure do not seem to be an optimal choice for cryptographic schemes.

Currently, there are two major trends for obtaining code-based schemes with small keys. The first makes use of codes defined by very sparse parity-check matrices, such as LDPC and MDPC codes [4,32], while the second is based on *rank metric* codes [12]. In this paper, we focus on the latter, and in particular, we consider the case of LRPC codes, which are in a sense a point of contact between the two. In fact, LRPC stands for Low-Rank Parity-Check, and this class of codes is characterized by a "sparse" (in the rank metric sense) parity-check matrix, and therefore it can effectively be seen as a rank-metric equivalent of LDPC/MDPC codes. As we will see, and as it is often the case for rank-metric schemes, LRPC codes share many of the aspects of their Hamming metric counterpart, including vulnerabilities.

Our Contribution. In this paper, we show how to devise a reaction attack based on observing a collection of decryption failures, which are an inherent feature for all schemes based on probabilistic decoding algorithms. These attacks become feasible when the Decoding Failure Rate (DFR) of the scheme is non-negligible, as illustrated, for the Hamming case, in a famous paper by Guo, Johansson and Stankovski [21].

The scenario behind a reaction attack is that the attacker sends a large number of encrypted messages with small modifications on the messages and then observes the reaction of the decryption of those messages (the attacker does not take into account the results of the computation). For code-based cryptography, it is common to induce a decoding failure by selecting messages with a certain property, which is the case presented in [22]. It is important to mention that in this scenario the goal of the attacker is not to recover the message, but rather the private key (or an equivalent key for decryption). In our attack, we use an approach similar to [22], in that we are interested in collecting errors that produce decoding failures. However, in our case we only need to collect a small amount of error patterns to complete the attack. We will give a justification for this nice feature, and explain how it works in detail, in the main body of the paper.

While preparing the camera ready version of this paper, we became aware of an independent work proposing a reaction attack against LRPC cryptosystems [34]. In [34], the attack requires a significantly larger amount of decryption queries and is less general, since it assumes that the adversary is free to choose the error vectors which are used for encryption.

The paper is organized as follows. We begin with preliminary notions, and notation, in Sect. 2, including an overview of LRPC cryptosystems. Our attack is described in Sect. 3, with a detailed analysis of the success probability. In Sect. 4 we discuss equivalent keys and in Sect. 5 we give a description of an attack in this case, while also investigating the possibility of applying quantum techniques to speed up the attack. As a case study, in Sect. 6 we provide the results obtained when applying our attack to McNie, one of the first round NIST submissions.

2   Preliminaries

We use capital bold letters to denote matrices, and small bold letters to denote vectors. Given a matrix $\mathbf{A}$, its entry in the i-th row and j-th column is denoted as $a_{i,j}$; in analogous way, the i-th entry of a vector $\mathbf{a}$ is denoted as a_i. The rank of a matrix $\mathbf{A}$ is denoted by $|\mathbf{A}|$.

Let q be a prime power and m be an integer; we denote with $\mathbb{F}_q$ and $\mathbb{F}_{q^m}$ the finite fields of cardinality respectively equal to q and q^m; the set of all $n \times n$ matrices over $\mathbb{F}_q$ will be denoted by $\mathcal{M}_n(\mathbb{F}_q)$, and the set of all $n \times n$ invertible matrices by $GL_n(\mathbb{F}_q)$. We denote an index set $\{1, 2, \ldots, \tau\}$ by $[1; \tau]$.

When treating codes in rank metric, a useful description can be obtained by considering each vector as a matrix.

Let $B = \{B_1, \cdots, B_m\}$ be a basis of $\mathbb{F}_{q^m}$ over $\mathbb{F}_q$, and define the function $\mathcal{F}_i : \mathbb{F}_{q^m} \to \mathbb{F}_q$ such that, for each $a \in \mathbb{F}_{q^m}$, $\mathcal{F}_i(a)$ corresponds to the i-th coefficient of a into the basis B. In other words, the following relation holds

$$a = \sum_{i=1}^{m} \mathcal{F}_i(a)B_i.$$

Let $V_n \subseteq \mathbb{F}_{q^m}^n$ be an n-dimensional subspace of $\mathbb{F}_{q^m}$; then, each vector $\mathbf{v} = \{v_i\} \in V_n$ can be represented as a matrix $\bar{\mathbf{V}} = \{v_{i,j}\} \in \mathbb{F}_q^{m \times n}$, whose entry in position (i, j) corresponds to $\mathcal{F}_i(v_j)$. In other words, the following two representations are equivalent

$$\mathbf{v} = [v_1, \cdots, v_n] \leftrightarrow \bar{\mathbf{V}} = \begin{bmatrix} \mathcal{F}_1(v_1) & \mathcal{F}_1(v_2) & \cdots & \mathcal{F}_1(v_n) \\ \mathcal{F}_2(v_1) & \mathcal{F}_2(v_2) & \cdots & \mathcal{F}_2(v_n) \\ \vdots & \vdots & \ddots & \vdots \\ \mathcal{F}_m(v_1) & \mathcal{F}_m(v_2) & \cdots & \mathcal{F}_m(v_n) \end{bmatrix}.$$

200   S. Samardjiska et al.

Using this representation, rank metric codes can be defined in a very natural and intuitive way. In particular, given two vectors $\mathbf{a}, \mathbf{b} \in \mathbb{F}_{q^m}^n$, the *rank distance* between $\mathbf{a}$ and $\mathbf{b}$ is defined as

$$\mathrm{rd}(\mathbf{a}, \mathbf{b}) = |\bar{\mathbf{A}} - \bar{\mathbf{B}}|.$$

The *rank weight* of a vector $\mathbf{a}$ is then defined as $\mathrm{wt}(\mathbf{a}) = \mathrm{rd}(\mathbf{a}, \mathbf{0}_n) = |\bar{\mathbf{A}}|$, where $\mathbf{0}_n$ denotes the length-n null vector. The *support* of a vector $\mathbf{v} \in V_n$ is denoted as $\langle \mathbf{v} \rangle$ and corresponds to the subspace generated by its entries $v_1, \cdots, v_n$. With some abuse of notation, we use $\langle V_n \rangle$ to denote the subspace generated by the vectors in V_n.

2.1 Circulant Matrices and Quasi-cyclic Codes

A *circulant matrix* is a matrix in which every row is obtained as a right cyclic shift of the previous. Equation (1) shows a circulant matrix of size[1] p.

$$\mathbf{C}_p = \begin{bmatrix} t_0 & t_1 & \cdots & t_{p-1} \\ t_{p-1} & t_0 & \cdots & t_{p-2} \\ \vdots & & \ddots & \vdots \\ t_1 & t_2 & \cdots & t_0 \end{bmatrix} \tag{1}$$

Circulant $p \times p$ matrices over $\mathbb{F}_{q^m}$ form a ring that we will denote by $\mathcal{C}_p(\mathbb{F}_{q^m})$. Its cardinality is $|\mathcal{C}_p(\mathbb{F}_{q^m})| = q^{mp}$.

Proposition 1. *Let $x^p - 1 = p_1^{\alpha_1}(x) \cdots \cdot p_\tau^{\alpha_\tau}(x)$ be the factorization of $x^p - 1$ over $\mathbb{F}_{q^m}$ into powers of irreducible factors. The number of invertible circulant matrices in $\mathcal{C}_p(\mathbb{F}_{q^m})$ is equal to $\prod_{i=1}^{\tau} (q^{m \cdot d_i \alpha_i} - q^{m \cdot d_i (\alpha_i - 1)})$, where d_i is the degree of $p_i(x)$ in the factorization of $x^p - 1$.*

Proof. It is well known that $\mathcal{C}_p(\mathbb{F}_{q^m})$ is isomorphic to $\mathbb{F}_{q^m}[x]/\langle x^p - 1 \rangle$. From the factorization $x^p - 1 = p_1^{\alpha_1}(x) \cdots \cdot p_\tau^{\alpha_\tau}(x)$ and the Chinese Remainder Theorem, $\mathbb{F}_{q^m}[x]/\langle x^p - 1 \rangle$ is isomorphic to the direct product:

$$\mathbb{F}_{q^m}[x]/\langle x^p - 1 \rangle \cong \mathbb{F}_{q^m}[x]/\langle p_1^{\alpha_1}(x) \rangle \times \cdots \times \mathbb{F}_{q^m}[x]/\langle p_\tau^{\alpha_\tau}(x) \rangle$$

The number of invertible elements in $\mathbb{F}_{q^m}[x]/\langle p_i^{\alpha_i}(x) \rangle$ is $q^{m \cdot d_i \alpha_i} - q^{m \cdot d_i (\alpha_i - 1)}$ where d_i is the degree of $p_i(x)$. Now it is easy to count the number of invertible elements in $\mathbb{F}_{q^m}[x]/\langle x^p - 1 \rangle$. It is precisely the product of the invertible elements in each $\mathbb{F}_{q^m}[x]/\langle p_i^{\alpha_i}(x) \rangle$, i.e., $\mathcal{C}_p(\mathbb{F}_{q^m}) = \prod_{i=1}^{\tau} (q^{m \cdot d_i \alpha_i} - q^{m \cdot d_i (\alpha_i - 1)})$.

Note that when $\alpha_1 = \alpha_2 = \cdots = \alpha_\tau = 1$, $\mathbb{F}_{q^m}[x]/\langle x^p - 1 \rangle$ factors into a direct product of fields, and our formula turns into $\prod_{i=1}^{\tau} (q^{m \cdot d_i} - 1)$. $\qquad \square$

---

[1] A circulant matrix can be defined as a special case of Toeplitz matrix; for more details about Toeplitz matrices see [19].

A *quasi-cyclic code* is a code with generator matrix of the form

$$
\mathbf{G} = \begin{bmatrix}
\mathbf{C}_{11} & \mathbf{C}_{12} & \cdots & \mathbf{C}_{1n_0} \\
\mathbf{C}_{21} & \mathbf{C}_{22} & \cdots & \mathbf{C}_{2n_0} \\
\vdots & & \ddots & \vdots \\
\mathbf{C}_{k_01} & \mathbf{C}_{k_02} & \cdots & \mathbf{C}_{k_0n_0}
\end{bmatrix}
\tag{2}
$$

where each matrix $\mathbf{C}_{ij}$ is a circulant matrix of the form (1).

2.2   LRPC Codes

A *Low-Rank Parity-Check (LRPC) code* C over $\mathbb{F}_{q^m}$ of length n, dimension k and rank d is described by an $(n-k) \times n$ parity-check matrix $\mathbf{H} = \{h_{i,j}\} \in \mathbb{F}_{q^m}^{(n-k) \times n}$, whose coefficients $h_{i,j}$ generate a subspace of $\mathbb{F}_{q^m}$ of dimension at most d. More precisely, each coefficient $h_{i,j}$ can be written as

$$
h_{i,j} = \sum_{l=1}^{d} h_{i,j,l} F_l, \quad h_{i,j,l} \in \mathbb{F}_q,
\tag{3}
$$

where each $F_i \in \mathbb{F}_{q^m}$, and $F = \langle F_1, F_2, \cdots, F_d \rangle$ is a $\mathbb{F}_q$ subspace of $\mathbb{F}_{q^m}$ of dimension at most d generated by the basis $\{F_1, F_2, \cdots, F_d\}$.

Decoding of LRPC Codes. Consider an LRPC code with parity-check matrix $\mathbf{H}$ of length n, dimension k and rank d, with basis $F = \{F_1, \cdots, F_d\}$. Let $\mathbf{e} = \{e_i\} \in \mathbb{F}_{q^m}^n$ be a vector of rank r, with basis $E = \{E_1, \cdots, E_r\}$. Recall that, considering the matrix representation, the vector $\mathbf{e}$ can be described as a matrix $\bar{\mathbf{E}} = \{e_{i,j}\}$, with $i \in [1;n]$, $j \in [1;r]$, such that

$$
e_i = \sum_{j=1}^{r} e_{i,j} E_j, \quad e_{i,j} \in \mathbb{F}_q.
\tag{4}
$$

Let $\mathbf{s} \in \mathbb{F}_{q^m}^{n-k}$ be the *syndrome* of $\mathbf{e}$ with respect to $\mathbf{H}$, i.e. $\mathbf{He}^\top = \mathbf{s}$. Decoding consists in recovering $\mathbf{e}$, from the knowledge of $\mathbf{s}$. A decoding procedure, specific for the case of LRPC codes, has been proposed in [14], and is shown in Algorithm 1. In this section we briefly recall its main principles, in order to provide a basic understanding of the attack procedure we propose in this paper.

Under proper conditions (which we investigate in the following), the syndrome equation can be rewritten as a linear system whose unknowns are nr scalars in $\mathbb{F}_q$. Indeed, for the i-th coordinate of $\mathbf{s}$, we have

$$
\begin{aligned}
s_i &= \sum_{j=1}^{n} h_{i,j} e_j = \sum_{j=1}^{n} \left(\sum_{l=1}^{d} h_{i,j,l} F_l \right) \left(\sum_{u=1}^{r} e_{j,u} E_u \right) \\
&= \sum_{l=1}^{d} \sum_{u=1}^{r} F_l E_u \left(\sum_{j=1}^{n} h_{i,j,l} e_{j,u} \right).
\end{aligned}
\tag{5}
$$

Then, by considering Eq. (5) for all $i \in [1; n - k]$, the syndrome equation can be rewritten as

$$\mathbf{s}' = \mathbf{A_H}\mathbf{e}'^\top, \tag{6}$$

where $\mathbf{s}' \in \mathbb{F}_q^{(n-k)rd}$, $\mathbf{A_H} \in \mathbb{F}_q^{(n-k)rd \times nr}$ and $\mathbf{e}' \in \mathbb{F}_q^{nr}$.

Essentially, the above equation corresponds to the writing of the syndrome equation in the base field $\mathbb{F}_q$. In particular, $\mathbf{s}'$ contains the coefficients of the syndrome in the basis $\{F_i E_j\}_{\substack{i \le i \le d \\ 1 \le j \le r}}$, while $\mathbf{A_H}$ and $\mathbf{e}'$ are obtained through a rewriting of $\mathbf{H}$ and $\mathbf{e}$. Then, decoding can be performed through Algorithm 1; essentially, what the decoder does is firstly recovering the support of the error vector (lines 1–5 in the algorithm), computing a basis for the found subspace (line 6) and then reconstructing the coefficients of the error vector in the selected basis (line 7).

Algorithm 1. Decoding of LRPC codes

    Input: $\mathbf{s} \in \mathbb{F}_{q^m}^{n-k}$, $\mathbf{s}' \in \mathbb{F}_q^{(n-k)rd}$, $\mathbf{A_H} \in \mathbb{F}_q^{(n-k)rd \times nr}$
    Output: $\mathbf{e}' \in \mathbb{F}_q$.

1: $S \leftarrow \langle s_1, s_2, \cdots, s_{n-k} \rangle$ ▷ *Syndrome space*
2: **for** $i \leftarrow 1$ **to** d **do**
3:      $S_i \leftarrow F_i^{-1}S$
4: **end for**
5: $E \leftarrow \bigcap_{j=1}^d S_j$ ▷ *Compute the error support*
6: $\{E_1, \cdots, E_r\} \leftarrow$ basis for E
7: Solve $\mathbf{s}' = \mathbf{A_H}\mathbf{e}'^\top$ ▷ *Find the coefficients of* $\mathbf{e}$ *in the basis* E
8: **return** $\mathbf{e}'$

Note that Algorithm 1 is characterized by a certain failure probability, which can be estimated according to the system parameters. In particular, decoding failures can happen only because of the following three events [14].

1. Case of $\text{Dim}(\langle EF \rangle) < rd$: this happens with probability $P_1 = \frac{d}{q^{m-rd}}$. (see [14, Sec. 3, Prop. 1]).
2. Case of $E \ne \bigcap_{i=1}^d S_i$: when $m > rd + 8$, this happens with probability $P_2 \ll 2^{-30}$. (see [14, Sec. 3, Remark 3]).
3. Case of $\text{Dim}(S) < rd$ this happens with probability $P_3 = \frac{1}{q^{n-k+1-rd}}$. (see [14, Sec. 5, Prop. 4]).

For parameters of practical interest, we usually have $P_1, P_2 \ll P_3$: as we describe in the following sections, this fact is crucial for the success of our attack.

2.3 LRPC Cryptosystems

The key generation, encryption and decryption of the typical LRPC cryptosystem are summarized in Fig. 1.

---

1 **Key generation:**   Choose a random LRPC code over $\mathbb{F}_{q^m}$ of low rank d with support F and parity check $(n - k) \times n$ matrix $\mathbf{H}$, generator matrix $\mathbf{G}$ and decoding matrix $\mathbf{D}_H$ which can correct errors of rank r and a random invertible $(n - k) \times (n - k)$ matrix $\mathbf{R}$.
Secret Key: the low rank matrix $\mathbf{H}$, the masking matrix $\mathbf{R}$.
Public Key: the matrix $\mathbf{G}' = \mathbf{RG}$.

2 **Encryption:**   Translate the message m into a word $\mathbf{x}$, generate $\mathbf{e} \in \mathbb{F}_{q^m}$ randomly with rank r. Compute $\mathbf{c} = \mathbf{x}\mathbf{G}' + \mathbf{e}$.

3 **Decryption:**   Compute syndrome $\mathbf{s} = \mathbf{H}\mathbf{c}^T$, recover the error vector $\mathbf{e}$ by decoding the LRPC code, then compute $\mathbf{x}\mathbf{G}' = \mathbf{c} - \mathbf{e}$ and $\mathbf{x}$.

Fig. 1. LRPC cryptosystem.

The LRPC cryptosystem described above was introduced in [14]. The authors first present the low-rank parity-check codes and their application in cryptography, and then describe a McEliece-like scheme; note that, in principle, a Niederreiter setting can be used as well.

While Fig. 1 and the LRPC cryptosystem provide a general framework for schemes based on LRPC codes, the usual setting in practical schemes is to use specific types of LRPC codes that allow shorter keys. These include Quasi-cyclic codes, as shown in [15] (and later also used in McNie [17,24] and Ouroboros-R [29]), or ideal codes (which are a generalization of LRPC codes and used in LAKE [1], Locker [2] and Rollo [28]). All of the previous cryptosystems show clear advantage over cryptosystems in the Hamming metric - for the same level of security, the keys are orders of magnitude smaller. For instance, the public key in Classic McEliece is 132 KB while Rollo-II has a public key of size 2.4 KB. Furthermore, ideal codes (with additional assumptions) have been used in the construction of the signature scheme Durandal [3] - showing once more the advantage over the Hamming metric where the construction of efficient signature schemes is still a problem.

In what follows, we describe McNie [17,24] - a first round candidate [38] to the NIST PQ crypto standardization process [37]. We will use McNie to showcase our reaction attack in Sect. 6.

McNie follows a "hybrid" framework using both McEliece and Niederreiter in the encryption process. The scheme employs QC codes with low weight parity-check matrices of the form $[\mathbf{H}_1 \, \mathbf{H}_2 \, \mathbf{H}_3]$ and $\begin{bmatrix} \mathbf{H}_1 & \mathbf{H}_2 & \mathbf{H}_3 & \mathbf{H}_4 \\ \mathbf{H}_5 & \mathbf{H}_6 & \mathbf{H}_7 & \mathbf{H}_8 \end{bmatrix}$ where $\mathbf{H}_i$ are circulant matrices. The authors refer to these codes as 3- and 4-Quasi-Cyclic codes. The key generation, encryption and decryption of McNie are summarized in Fig. 2.

Remark 1. According to the protocol specifications [17], in the general description of the scheme, the authors suggest the possibility to further use a permutation matrix $\mathbf{P}$ used to form $\mathbf{F}$ as $\mathbf{F} = \mathbf{G}'\mathbf{P}^{-1}\mathbf{H}^{\top}\mathbf{S}$. However, in the actual proposal, this matrix is set to the identity matrix, so it is never used. Therefore, we do not see a reason to use it and burden the description.

1 **Key generation:** Choose a random 3 or 4 generator QC LRPC code over
$\mathbb{F}_{q^m}$ of low rank d, parity check $(n-k) \times n$ matrix $\mathbf{H}$ and generator matrix $\mathbf{G}$.
Further, choose a random invertible $(n-k) \times (n-k)$ matrix $\mathbf{S}$ and a random
$l \times (n-k)$ matrix $\mathbf{G}'$.
Secret Key: The low rank matrix $\mathbf{H}$, and the masking matrix $\mathbf{S}$.
Public Key: The matrices $\mathbf{F} = \mathbf{G}'\mathbf{H}^\top\mathbf{S}$ and $\mathbf{G}'$.
2 **Encryption:** To encrypt a message $\mathbf{m} \in \mathbb{F}_{q^m}$, generate a random $\mathbf{e} \in \mathbb{F}_{q^m}$
of rank r. Compute $\mathbf{c}_1 = \mathbf{mG}' + \mathbf{e}$ and $\mathbf{c}_2 = \mathbf{mF}$. The ciphertext is $(\mathbf{c}_1, \mathbf{c}_2)$.
3 **Decryption:** Compute syndrome $\mathbf{s}' = \mathbf{c}_1\mathbf{H}^\top - \mathbf{c}_2\mathbf{S}^{-1} = \mathbf{eH}^\top$. Recover the
error vector $\mathbf{e}$ by decoding the LRPC code, then compute $\mathbf{mG}' = \mathbf{c}_1 - \mathbf{e}$ and
obtain $\mathbf{m}$ by solving the obtained system.

Fig. 2. The McNie cryptosystem [17,24].

3   A Reaction Attack

We are now ready to describe the details of our attack. The main idea is to exploit decoding failures caused by the syndrome $\mathbf{s}$ not generating the whole space $\langle FE \rangle$. Thus, for ease of exposition, in this section we will assume that this is the case. Later we will show that the influence of other types of decoding failures to the success of our attack is negligible, thus justifying the current assumption.

Suppose that an adversary $\mathcal{A}$ interacts with a decryption oracle $\mathcal{D}$ of an LRPC cryptosystem. He continuously sends encrypted messages to $\mathcal{D}$ and waits for the reaction from the oracle. If $\mathcal{D}$ returns failure, $\mathcal{A}$ records the error $\mathbf{e}$ that he used in the encryption of the message. $\mathcal{A}$ collects a total of t error vectors, where t is chosen appropriately. We will discuss this choice later in this section.

Let $\mathbf{e}$ be an error vector that $\mathcal{A}$ collected during his interaction with $\mathcal{D}$. We now show to use this information to recover the secret matrix $\mathbf{H}$.

Recall from Sect. 2.2, Eq. (6), that we can express the syndrome equation over the base field as $\mathbf{s}' = \mathbf{A_H}\mathbf{e}'^\top$, where $\mathbf{s}'$ contains the coefficients of the syndrome in the basis $\{F_i E_j\}_{\substack{1 \le i \le d \\ 1 \le j \le r}}$. Alternatively, directly from (5), the syndrome equation can be written in a matrix form: $\mathbf{s}$ can be written as the product between the basis $(F_1 E_1, F_1 E_2 \ldots, F_d E_r)$ and a matrix $\mathbf{\bar{A}_{H,e}} \in \mathbb{F}_q^{rd \times (n-k)}$:

$$\mathbf{s} = (F_1 E_1, F_1 E_2 \ldots, F_d E_r) \cdot \mathbf{\bar{A}_{H,e}} \qquad (7)$$

The key observation in our attack is that a decoding failure occurs when the matrix $\mathbf{\bar{A}_{H,e}}$ is not of full rank - in other words, the left kernel of the matrix $\mathbf{\bar{A}_{H,e}}$ is non-trivial. This means that there must exist (at least) one nonzero vector $\mathbf{v_e} \in \mathbb{F}_q^{rd}$, $\mathbf{v_e} \ne 0_{1 \times rd}$, such that

$$\mathbf{v_e} \cdot \mathbf{\bar{A}_{H,e}} = \mathbf{0}_{1 \times n-k}. \qquad (8)$$

Now consider our attack scenario. The adversary $\mathcal{A}$ knows the error $\mathbf{e}$ that caused the matrix $\mathbf{\bar{A}_{H,e}}$ to be of non-full rank. He, however, does not know the coefficients $\mathbf{h} = \{h_{i,j,l}\}_{\substack{1 \leq l \leq d \\ 1 \leq i \leq n-k \\ 1 \leq j \leq n}}$ of the matrix $\mathbf{H}$, and therefore he does not know the kernel vector $\mathbf{v_e}$. Setting $\bar{\mathbf{A}}_{\mathbf{e}}(\mathbf{h}) = \bar{\mathbf{A}}_{\mathbf{H},\mathbf{e}}$ to emphasize the unknown coefficients $\mathbf{h}$, we can rewrite (8) as

$$\mathbf{v_e} \cdot \bar{\mathbf{A}}_{\mathbf{e}}(\mathbf{h}) = \mathbf{0}_{1 \times n-k}. \tag{9}$$

The main step of our attack now boils down to finding the solutions to Eq. (9) in the unknown coefficients $\mathbf{h}$ of $\mathbf{H}$ and the unknown kernel vector $\mathbf{v_e}$.

Observe that we can actually use several errors $\mathbf{e}_1, \ldots, \mathbf{e}_t$ to form equations similar to Eq. (9). In these equations for each error $\mathbf{e}_i$ we introduce a new appropriate kernel element $\mathbf{v}_{\mathbf{e}_i}$. However, they all share the same unknown coefficients of the matrix $\mathbf{H}$. Thus, we can form the following system:

$$\begin{cases} \mathbf{v}_{\mathbf{e}_1} \cdot \bar{\mathbf{A}}_{\mathbf{e}_1}(\mathbf{h}) = \mathbf{0}_{1 \times n-k} \\ \mathbf{v}_{\mathbf{e}_2} \cdot \bar{\mathbf{A}}_{\mathbf{e}_2}(\mathbf{h}) = \mathbf{0}_{1 \times n-k} \\ \cdots \\ \mathbf{v}_{\mathbf{e}_t} \cdot \bar{\mathbf{A}}_{\mathbf{e}_t}(\mathbf{h}) = \mathbf{0}_{1 \times n-k} \end{cases} \tag{10}$$

The right value for t depends on several factors: the method of solving, the parameters of the system, but most notably the nature of the system. In principle, t should be big enough such that solving the system unambiguously gives the coefficients of $\mathbf{H}$. We will discuss the choice of t in the next section.

Suppose that t is chosen appropriately. Observe that system (10) is a system of bilinear equations reminiscent to the equations obtained in the MinRank problem [8]. We can thus try solve this system using similar strategies as in at least three different methods for solving MinRank - the Kernel method [18], Kipnis-Shamir method [25] and the minors method [9]. The main difference is that first, there are several polynomial matrices whose non trivial kernel needs to be found and second, all of these matrices are polynomial matrices in the same variables. At first sight, this situation bears similarities to Simultaneous MinRank [7,10] which is commonly encountered in $\mathcal{MQ}$ cryptography. However, since the different errors $\mathbf{e}_1, \mathbf{e}_2, \ldots, \mathbf{e}_t$ produce different matrices $\bar{\mathbf{A}}_{\mathbf{e}_1}(\mathbf{h}), \bar{\mathbf{A}}_{\mathbf{e}_2}(\mathbf{h}), \ldots, \bar{\mathbf{A}}_{\mathbf{e}_t}(\mathbf{h})$, it is not clear how to use the common techniques that significantly speed up the attack in $\mathcal{MQ}$ cryptosystems.

In the next subsection, we will describe in detail a Kernel method - like approach to solving system (10). A straightforward application of the other algebraic methods results in a significantly larger complexity. Therefore a deeper insight into the properties of system (10) is necessary in order to apply these efficiently.

3.1   Solving System (10) by Kernel Guessing

Suppose that the adversary $\mathcal{A}$ has collected t error vectors $\mathbf{e}_1, \mathbf{e}_2, \ldots, \mathbf{e}_t$ that cause decryption failures. As before, we assume that the corresponding matrices $\bar{\mathbf{A}}_{\mathbf{e}_1}(\mathbf{h}), \bar{\mathbf{A}}_{\mathbf{e}_2}(\mathbf{h}), \ldots, \bar{\mathbf{A}}_{\mathbf{e}_t}(\mathbf{h})$ are singular. This means that size of the kernels of these matrices is at least 1. The adversary now tries to guess the vectors $\mathbf{v}_{\mathbf{e}_i}$, such that $\mathbf{v}_{\mathbf{e}_i}$ belongs to the kernel of $\bar{\mathbf{A}}_{\mathbf{e}_i}(\mathbf{h})$ for each $i \in [1; t]$. If all vectors $\mathbf{v}_{\mathbf{e}_i}$ are correctly guessed, what remains, is to solve the obtained linear system in the unknown coefficients $\mathbf{h}$. In general, in order to obtain a unique solution we need to form at least the same number of equations as variables. For each $\mathbf{v}_{\mathbf{e}_i}$ we can form $n-k$ equations, so we need $t(n-k)$ to be at least as the number of variables. For a random LRPC code of rank d, the number of unknown coefficients of the matrix $\mathbf{H}$ is $n(n-k)d$. Hence we need:

$$t \geq nd.$$

If, in addition, the code is quasi-cyclic and its parity-check matrix is made of circulant matrices of size p, the number of unknown coefficients is $n(n-k)d/p$. In this case

$$t \geq \frac{nd}{p}. \tag{11}$$

Let us denote the probability of correctly guessing a kernel vector corresponding to an error $\mathbf{e}_i$ by $P_{\mathbf{e}_i}$. This probability clearly depends on the dimension of the kernel of $\bar{\mathbf{A}}_{\mathbf{e}_i}(\mathbf{h})$. Let us denote this dimension as $K_{\mathbf{e}_i} \geq 1$: then, we know that $|Ker(\bar{\mathbf{A}}_{\mathbf{e}_i}(\mathbf{h}))| = q^{K_{\mathbf{e}_i}}$. Then,

$$P_{\mathbf{e}_i} = \frac{q^{K_{\mathbf{e}_i}}}{q^{rd}} = q^{-(rd-K_{\mathbf{e}_i})}. \tag{12}$$

Clearly, a larger kernel of some of the matrices would make the attack faster. However, there is no way to detect whether a matrix $\bar{\mathbf{A}}_{\mathbf{e}_i}(\mathbf{h})$ associated to an error $\mathbf{e}_i$ would have a larger kernel. Therefore we must assume the worst case, i.e. a kernel of dimension 1. It remains open whether it is possible to devise a strategy to generate error vectors that induce matrices of larger kernels.

Let us denote the probability of all vectors $\mathbf{v}_{\mathbf{e}_i}$ being correctly guessed by P_t. Then

$$P_t = P_{\mathbf{e}_i}^t = q^{-(rd-1)t} \tag{13}$$

After the kernel vectors have been guessed, system (10) becomes an over-determined linear system over $\mathbb{F}_q$. Solving it gives the coefficients of $\mathbf{H}$. However, the basis F is still unknown. Luckily, knowing the coefficients of $\mathbf{H}$ turns out to be enough to find the basis F: this part is now easy and F can be obtained from sufficiently many message-ciphertext pairs and the syndrome equation. A high level description of the attack is given by Algorithm 2.

In Algorithm 2, through the procedure CollectErrors, the adversary interacts with the decryption oracle $\mathcal{D}$, by sending him encrypted messages and waiting for decryption failures. Each time there is a failure, the adversary saves the error he used, until enough errors that cause decryption failures are collected. The additional operations that the adversary performs are one encryption and one decryption of the scheme.

Once the errors have been obtained the main part of the attack can begin. Note that the collection of the errors can be done only once, and we need only a handful of errors unlike in the Hamming metric (see Sect. 3.2 for a more detailed discussion).

Algorithm 2. Reaction attack on LRPC codes

    Input: $d, t, \ell \in \mathbb{Z}$
    Output: Matrix $\mathbf{H}$ of rank d
1: $\mathbf{e}_1, \mathbf{e}_2, \ldots, \mathbf{e}_t \leftarrow$ CollectErrors(pk, $\mathcal{D}$(sk))   ▷ *Collect errors from decryption failures*
2: **repeat**
3:     $\mathbf{v}_{\mathbf{e}_1}, \mathbf{v}_{\mathbf{e}_2}, \ldots, \mathbf{v}_{\mathbf{e}_t} \leftarrow_R \mathbb{F}_q^{rd}$ ▷ *Guess kernel vectors*
4:     $\mathbf{h} \leftarrow$ SolveH($\mathbf{v}_{\mathbf{e}_1}, \mathbf{v}_{\mathbf{e}_2}, \ldots, \mathbf{v}_{\mathbf{e}_t}, \mathbf{e}_1, \mathbf{e}_2, \ldots, \mathbf{e}_t$)   ▷ *Solve system* (10)
5:     **if** $\mathbf{h} \neq \perp$ **then**
6:         $\{(\mathbf{m}_i, \mathbf{e}_i, \mathbf{c}_i)\}_{i=1}^{\ell} \leftarrow$ CollectMEC(pk) ▷ *Collect messages, errors, ciphertexts*
7:         F, success $\leftarrow$ SolveF($\mathbf{h}, \{(\mathbf{m}_i, \mathbf{e}_i, \mathbf{c}_i)\}_{i=1}^{\ell}$)   ▷ *Find basis F*
8:     **else** success $\leftarrow \perp$
9:     **end if**
10: **until** success
11: $\mathbf{H} \leftarrow$ Reconstruct($\mathbf{h}, F$)   ▷ *Reconstruct the matrix* $\mathbf{H}$
12: **return** $\mathbf{H}$

Next, the function SolveH denotes the procedure for solving system (10) for some guessed kernel elements corresponding to the obtained errors. If system (10) has a solution, then SolveH will return this solution, otherwise it will return $\perp$. This solution is then used in SolveF together with ℓ valid triplets $(\mathbf{m}_i, \mathbf{e}_i, \mathbf{c}_i)$ of messages, errors and ciphertexts generated in the procedure CollectMEC. SolveF is a procedure whose main goal is to find the basis F. However depending on the scheme, there might be other parts of the secret key sk that can be found in this procedure. The value of ℓ is also dependant on the scheme. We present an instantiation of SolveF for McNie [17] in Sect. 6.

We are now ready to state the total complexity of our attack. It is

$$Cost(\text{React}) = P_3^{-1}(Cost(\text{Enc} \wedge \text{Dec}))$$
$$+ P_t^{-1}(Cost(\text{SolveH}) + \ell Cost(\text{Enc}) + Cost(\text{SolveF})) \qquad (14)$$

where $P_3 = \frac{1}{q^{n-k+1-rd}}$ is the failure rate of the scheme (see Sect. 2.2), $P_t = q^{-(rd-1)t}$ for a d rank LRPC code and errors of rank r. In the case of random LRPC codes $t = nd$ and $Cost(\text{SolveH}) = n^3(n-k)^3 d^3$. When the code is quasi-cyclic and uses circulant matrices of size p, $t = \frac{nd}{p}$ and $Cost(\text{SolveH}) = \frac{n^3(n-k)^3 d^3}{p^3}$. As said earlier, $Cost(\text{SolveF})$ depends on the scheme, but usually, $Cost(\text{SolveF}) < Cost(\text{SolveH})$. See Sect. 6 for more details about this.

3.2 Analogies and Differences with the Hamming Metric

The cryptanalysis procedure we have described in this section resembles the one proposed by Guo et al. in [21], tailored at the McEliece cryptosystem using quasi-cyclic Moderate-Density Parity-Check (MDPC) codes [33], decoded in the Hamming metric. Essentially, these codes are a special case of Low-Density Parity-Check (LDPC) codes [16], i.e., codes which are described by a parity-check matrix that contains a low number of set entries. These codes admit efficient decoding algorithms, like the Bit Flipping (BF) decoder or some of its variants, which are all based on the sparsity of the parity-check matrix and are characterized by some intrinsic decoding failure probability which, as originally observed in [21], somehow depends on geometrical relations between the error vector and the secret parity-check matrix.

Then, reaction attacks can be mounted, by means of statistical tests on the decoding outcomes of a large number of decryption queries. In particular, these tests are used to guess the number of overlapping ones between columns in the secret key [41]; clearly, in order to achieve statistical reliability, the number of observed decryption instances (i.e., the number of queries) needs to be sufficiently large. For instance, we can consider the empirical results for the parameters that were broken in [21]: the authors used, in all successful attacks, more than 10^8 decryption queries. Considering a decoding failure probability approximately equal to 10^{-4}, this leads to a number of observed events of decoding failures in the order of 10^4.

There are clear differences between reaction attacks in the Hamming metric and the one we propose in this paper. First of all, in the rank metric case, no statistical test is needed: events of decoding failures are due (with overwhelming probability) to some rank deficiency in the syndrome, and this fact is used to establish algebraic relations like that in Eq. (9). This difference is emphasized by the fact that the number of failure events that an adversary needs to collect is significantly lower than the one that is needed for the Hamming metric case.

Additionally, in the Hamming metric case, the feasibility of reaction attacks is somehow related to the chosen decoder and to its setting [36], in the sense that modifications in the decoding procedure and/or slight variations in its setting might lead to significant differences in the attack outcome. This difference arises a question on the existence of alternative LRPC decoding techniques, and on their eventual effect on reaction attacks procedures.

Another crucial difference is represented by the fact that, for LDPC codes, only few parity-check matrices can be used to efficiently perform decoding on a given corrupted codeword. Indeed, for a given parity-check matrix $\mathbf{H}$, each matrix $\mathbf{H}' = \mathbf{WH}$, with $\mathbf{W}$ being non-singular, is again a valid parity-check matrix, but $\mathbf{W}$ preserves the density only when it is a permutation matrix. When $\mathbf{W}$ is not a permutation matrix, in fact, rows of $\mathbf{H}'$ correspond to linear combinations of rows of $\mathbf{H}$: thus, their density is, with overwhelming probability, larger than that of $\mathbf{H}$. This means that only the actual $\mathbf{H}$, or a row-permuted version of it, guarantees efficient decoding of intercepted ciphertexts. Then, when mounting a reaction attack, the adversary's goal is that of reconstructing exactly one of these matrices. In the rank metric case the number of parity-check matrices that allow for efficient decoding techniques is significantly larger - we show in the next section that any matrix of the form $\mathbf{WH}$ can be used to efficiently decode. In such a case, we speak of *equivalent keys*: this fact, as we describe in the next section, allows for significant reductions in the attack complexity.

4   Equivalent Keys in LRPC Cryptosystems

In the previous section we described the basic attack that makes use of decryption failures. Now, we dig a little deeper, and show that due to existence of particular equivalent keys, it is possible to speed up the attack by an exponential factor.

We start with a well known property of weight preservation in the rank metric. For completeness we include a proof that will be useful later on.

Proposition 2. *Let* $\mathbf{b} \in \mathbb{F}_{q^m}^n$, *and let* $\mathbf{W} \in GL_n(\mathbb{F}_q)$. *Then:*

$$\mathrm{wt}(\mathbf{b}) = \mathrm{wt}(\mathbf{b} \cdot \mathbf{W}).$$

In other words, weight is preserved under multiplication by non-singular matrices over $\mathbb{F}_q$.[2]

Proof. Let $\mathrm{wt}(\mathbf{b}) = d$. This means that $\mathbf{b}$ can be represented as $\mathbf{b} = \mathbf{F} \cdot \bar{\mathbf{B}}$, where $\mathbf{F} = (F_1, \ldots, F_d)$, and $<F_1, \ldots, F_d>$ is a basis of some d-dimensional subspace of $\mathbb{F}_{q^m}^n$, and $\bar{\mathbf{B}} \in \mathcal{M}_{d,n}(\mathbb{F}_q)$ is the (full rank) matrix representation of $\mathbf{b}$. Now

$$\mathbf{b} \cdot \mathbf{W} = \mathbf{F} \cdot \bar{\mathbf{B}} \cdot \mathbf{W} = \mathbf{F} \cdot (\bar{\mathbf{B}} \cdot \mathbf{W}).$$

Since $\mathbf{W}$ is invertible, $\bar{\mathbf{B}} \cdot \mathbf{W}$ is of full rank, i.e., $\mathrm{wt}(\mathbf{b} \cdot \mathbf{W}) = d$. □

As a direct consequence, we have the following:

Proposition 3. *Let* $\mathbf{H} \in \mathcal{M}_{n-k,n}(\mathbb{F}_{q^m})$ *be the parity check matrix of an LRPC code* $\mathcal{C}$ *of rank* d. *Let* $\mathbf{W} \in GL_{n-k}(\mathbb{F}_q)$ *be arbitrary. Then* $\mathbf{WH}$ *is a parity check matrix for the code* $\mathcal{C}$ *of the same rank* d.

Proof. Follows directly from the previous proposition, by considering the columns of $\mathbf{H}$ as vectors of weight d. □

Definition 1. *Let* $P = (KeyGen, Enc, Dec)$ *be an LRPC cryptosystem with a secret key* $\mathsf{sk} = (\mathbf{H}, \cdot)$. *We say that* P *has an equivalent key* $\mathsf{sk}' = (\mathbf{H}', \cdot')$, *if* $\mathsf{sk}' \neq \mathsf{sk}$ *and* sk' *can be used as a secrete key for* P *with equal efficiency as* sk. *In particular,* $\mathbf{H}'$ *is of the same rank as* $\mathbf{H}$ *and can be used in the decoding procedure with the same efficiency as* $\mathbf{H}$.
With some abuse of this definition, we will also say that $\mathbf{H}'$ *is an equivalent key of* $\mathbf{H}$.

As a direct consequence of Proposition 3, we have:

Corollary 1. *Let* $P = (KeyGen, Enc, Dec)$ *be an LRPC cryptosystem with a secret key* $\mathsf{sk} = (\mathbf{H}, \cdot)$ *where* $\mathbf{H} \in \mathcal{M}_{n-k,n}(\mathbb{F}_{q^m})$. *Let* $\mathbf{W} \in GL_{n-k}(\mathbb{F}_q)$ *be arbitrary. Then,* $\mathsf{sk}' = (\mathbf{WH}, \cdot)$ *is an equivalent key for* P.

---

[2] Recall that in Hamming metric, weight is preserved under multiplication by permutation matrices.

A particular equivalent key is of our interest; later we present a key recovery attack that recovers exactly such a key.

Let $\mathbf{H} \in \mathcal{M}_{n-k,n}(\mathbb{F}_{q^m})$ be the parity check matrix of an LRPC code $\mathcal{C}$ of rank d. We rewrite $\mathbf{H}$ as:

$$
\mathbf{H} = \begin{bmatrix} \sum_{i=1}^{d} h_{1,1,i}F_i & \sum_{i=1}^{d} h_{1,2,i}F_i & \cdots & \sum_{i=1}^{d} h_{1,n,i}F_i \\ \vdots & \vdots & \ddots & \vdots \\ \sum_{i=1}^{d} h_{n-k,1,i}F_i & \sum_{i=1}^{d} h_{n-k,2,i}F_i & \cdots & \sum_{i=1}^{d} h_{n-k,n,i}F_i \end{bmatrix}
$$

$$
= \sum_{i=1}^{d} \left(\begin{bmatrix} h_{1,1,i} & h_{1,2,i} & \cdots & h_{1,n,i} \\ \vdots & \vdots & \ddots & \vdots \\ h_{n-k,1,i} & h_{n-k,2,i} & \cdots & h_{n-k,n,i} \end{bmatrix} \right) F_i
$$

i.e as

$$
\mathbf{H} = \sum_{i=1}^{d} \hat{\mathbf{H}}_i \cdot F_i = \sum_{i=1}^{d} [\hat{\mathbf{H}}_{i1} | \hat{\mathbf{H}}_{i2}] \cdot F_i \tag{15}
$$

where $\hat{\mathbf{H}}_i$ is the matrix of coefficients corresponding to the basis element F_i.

Without loss of generality, assume: $\hat{\mathbf{H}}_1 = [\hat{\mathbf{H}}_{11} | \hat{\mathbf{H}}_{12}]$ where $\hat{\mathbf{H}}_{11} \in GL_{n-k}(\mathbb{F}_q)$. Then $\mathbf{H}' = \hat{\mathbf{H}}_{11}^{-1} \cdot \mathbf{H}$ is an equivalent key and can be written as:

$$
\mathbf{H}' = [\mathbf{I}_{n-k} | \hat{\mathbf{H}}_{12}'] \cdot F_1 + \sum_{i=2}^{d} [\hat{\mathbf{H}}_{i1}' | \hat{\mathbf{H}}_{i2}'] \cdot F_i \tag{16}
$$

where $\hat{\mathbf{H}}_{t1}' = \hat{\mathbf{H}}_{11}^{-1} \cdot \hat{\mathbf{H}}_{t1}$ and $\hat{\mathbf{H}}_{t2}' = \hat{\mathbf{H}}_{11}^{-1} \cdot \hat{\mathbf{H}}_{t2}$.

A crucial observation to make is that in the general case, the equivalent key $\mathbf{H}'$ is determined by $n(n-k)d - (n-k)^2$ coefficients, as opposed to $n(n-k)d$ coefficients for $\mathbf{H}$. This observation can be used to reduce the size of the private key by storing $\mathbf{H}'$ instead of $\mathbf{H}$. It can also be used to speed up our reaction attack if we recover $\mathbf{H}'$ instead of $\mathbf{H}$ because now we have less unknown coefficients, i.e., less variables in system (10). We need however to show that the collected error vectors that correspond to a secret $\mathbf{H}$ are also valid for the equivalent keys.

Proposition 4. *For an arbitrary LRPC code $\mathcal{C}$ of length n, dimension k and rank d over $\mathbb{F}_{q^m}$, with parity check matrix $\mathbf{H}$, if an error vector $\mathbf{e}$ causes a decoding failure, then the same error vector causes decoding failure for any equivalent $\mathbf{WH}$ where $\mathbf{W} \in GL_{n-k}(\mathbb{F}_q)$.*

Proof. Recall that the error vector $\mathbf{e}$ in system (10) cause the syndrome to be of non-maximal rank. By multiplying the syndrome equation by $\mathbf{W} \in GL_{n-k}(\mathbb{F}_q)$ we obtain $(\mathbf{WH}) \cdot \mathbf{e}_i^\top = \mathbf{W} \cdot \mathbf{s}^\top$, which from Proposition 2 means that the same error vectors cause syndrome of non-maximal rank for the matrix $\mathbf{WH}$. From Proposition 3 we know that $\mathbf{WH}$ is an equivalent key. $\qquad\square$

Equivalent Keys for Quasi-cyclic Codes. Note that if $\mathbf{H}$ is quasi-cyclic, then so are the matrices $\hat{\mathbf{H}}_i$ in Eq. (15). Then $\mathbf{H}' = \hat{\mathbf{H}}_{11}^{-1} \cdot \mathbf{H}$ is an equivalent key of the form (16). This key $\mathbf{H}'$ is determined by $\frac{n(n-k)d-(n-k)^2}{p}$ coefficients, as opposed to $\frac{n(n-k)d}{p}$ coefficients for $\mathbf{H}$.

5   Equivalent Key Attack on Quasi-cyclic H

In the previous section we showed that under some plausible conditions, there exists an equivalent key that is determined by less coefficients than the original one. Therefore it makes sense to look for this key in our attack. In the case of QC codes, we need $\frac{(n-k)^2}{p}$ less variables, so the number of kernel elements that we need to guess instead of (11) becomes

$$t \geq \frac{nd - (n - k)}{p}. \tag{17}$$

The gain in the probability compared to (13) is a factor of $q^{(rd-1)\frac{n-k}{p}}$, so looking for an equivalent key speeds the attack by an exponential factor.

5.1   Probability of Success

The success of the attack described above depends on two conditions being satisfied. First, recall that in Sect. 3 we assumed that all collected errors are a result of the syndrome not being of full rank. The results from Sect. 2.2 show that this is not always the case. However, as we will show shortly, this happens with significant probability, so we can conclude that the feasibility of our attack is not affected by these other types of decryption failures.

There is however one more place where the attack may fail - if we want to recover the good equivalent key from Sect. 4, the success of the attack further depends on the probability that such an equivalent As we will see later, this probability is also big, so it is safe to assume that an appropriate equivalent key exists.

Syndrome of Non-full Rank. We say that an observed decoding failure event is *useful* if it is due to the case of $\text{Dim}(S) < rd$. This happens with probability

$$\rho = \frac{P_3}{P_1 + P_2 + P_3} = \frac{1}{1 + \frac{P_1 + P_2}{P_3}}, \tag{18}$$

where the above probabilities depend on the system parameters and have been defined in Sect. 2.2. Since we typically have $P_1, P_2 \ll P_3$, we commonly have $\rho \approx 1$. Now the attack will be successful only if all of the t collected errors are useful, i.e.,

$$Pr_s = \rho^t. \tag{19}$$

Existence of Good Equivalent Key. The attack presented in Sect. 5 requires that a good equivalent key exists. Recall that in Eq. (20), we assumed that $\hat{\mathbf{H}}_{11}$ is invertible matrix of size $n - k$. Actually, note that our attack does not make a difference between the matrices $\hat{\mathbf{H}}_{l1}$, for $l \in [1; d]$, so it is enough that at least one of these is invertible. In other words, our attack will find an equivalent key of the form:

$$\mathbf{H}' = [\mathbf{I}_{n-k} | \hat{\mathbf{H}}'_{l2}] \cdot F_l + \sum_{\substack{i=2 \\ i \neq l}}^{d} [\hat{\mathbf{H}}'_{i1} | \hat{\mathbf{H}}'_{i2}] \cdot F_i \tag{20}$$

for any $l \in [1; d]$.

Since we are dealing with quasi-cyclic codes, the matrices $\hat{\mathbf{H}}_{l1}$, for $l \in [1; d]$ are block matrices of circulant matrices (block-circulant). Each of these circulant matrices can be uniquely represented by a polynomial. Now considering the determinant of the block-circulant matrix as a polynomial and assuming it behaves as a random polynomial, we can use the result from Proposition 1. Hence, the probability that the block-circulant matrix is invertible is given by:

$$Pr_c = \frac{\prod_{i=1}^{\tau} (q^{d_i \alpha_i} - q^{d_i(\alpha_i - 1)})}{q^{n-k}} \tag{21}$$

where $x^{n-k} - 1 = p_1^{\alpha_1}(x) \cdot \cdots \cdot p_\tau^{\alpha_\tau}(x)$ is the factorization over $\mathbb{F}_q$.

Now the probability that at least one of the matrices $\hat{\mathbf{H}}_{l1}$, for $l \in [1; d]$ is invertible is

$$Pr_{ek} = 1 - (1 - Pr_c)^d. \tag{22}$$

Equation (22) gives the probability that an equivalent key exists.

Remark 2. We should emphasize that forcing the matrices $\hat{\mathbf{H}}_{l1}$, for $l \in [1; d]$ to be singular in the design of the scheme does not help prevent our attack. It only requires a small modification on the equivalent key. The rest of the attack is essentially the same.

5.2   A Quantum-Enhanced Attack

Since cryptosystems based on LRPC codes are considered post-quantum, it makes sense to estimate their security against quantum-enhanced attack, using the full power of quantum computers. A second look at our attack immediately shows a possibility for a quantum speed-up using Grover's algorithm [20]. Recall that Grover's algorithm searches for an item in an unsorted database satisfying a given condition. In our attack, a huge component is represented by searching for elements in appropriate kernels (see Eq. (10)). The rest is just solving linear equations. It follows that it is straightforward to apply Grover's algorithm, and we can expect roughly a quadratic speed-up in the search phase, i.e., we can find a vector in the kernel with a number of trials which is about

$$T_e = O(\sqrt{q^{rd-1}}). \tag{23}$$

We could also think to apply a quantum algorithm for solving the linear systems like for example HHL [23]. However, in our case, there is no benefit from doing so, since HHL requires a large amount of quantum memory, and is not particularly suited for the systems that we have. Therefore, we decided to simply "Groverize" our attack. For the design of the oracle, we can reuse [42] with a small modification. The modification is that in [42] the authors use multiple variables and the cost in number of quantum gates is $2m(n^2 + 2n)$. However, we are using a linear system which means that for our attack, using an $m \times n$ matrix and a vector of length n, we have a gate complexity of mn.

6 Case Study: McNie

6.1 Recovering the Secret Key in McNie

Recall the generic structure of our attack from Algorithm 2. The two main procedures are SolveH and SolveF. The first recovers the coefficients of a key equivalent to $\mathbf{H}$ and is generic for LRPC cryptosystems. SolveF, instead, finds the secret basis F and the rest of the secret key. In the case of McNie the secret key is $\mathsf{sk} = (\mathbf{H}, \mathbf{S})$ where $\mathbf{S}$ is an invertible $(n - k) \times (n - k)$ matrix.

Recall that for McNie (see Fig. 2) it is true that:

$$\mathbf{c}_1 \mathbf{H}^\top - \mathbf{c}_2 \mathbf{S}^{-1} = \mathbf{e} \mathbf{H}^\top$$

Suppose that in SolveH we have recovered an equivalent key $\mathbf{H}' = \mathbf{T} \cdot \mathbf{H}$. Multiplying the previous equation by $\mathbf{T}^\top$ we obtain

$$\mathbf{c}_1 (\mathbf{T} \cdot \mathbf{H})^\top - \mathbf{c}_2 ((\mathbf{T}^\top)^{-1} \mathbf{S})^{-1} = \mathbf{e} (\mathbf{T} \cdot \mathbf{H})^\top$$

i.e., $\mathsf{sk}' = (\mathbf{H}', \mathbf{S}') = (\mathbf{T} \cdot \mathbf{H}, (\mathbf{T}^\top)^{-1} \mathbf{S})$ is an equivalent secret key for $\mathsf{sk} = (\mathbf{H}, \mathbf{S})$, so we can continue with recovering $\mathbf{S}'$ instead of $\mathbf{S}$. Now we can rewrite the previous equation as

$$(\mathbf{c}_1 - \mathbf{e}) \mathbf{H}'^\top = \mathbf{c}_2 \mathbf{S}'. \tag{24}$$

Notice that if we know a triple $(\mathbf{m}, \mathbf{e}, (\mathbf{c}_1, \mathbf{c}_2))$ of message, error and ciphertext (which of course anyone can generate from the public key), once the coefficients of $\mathbf{H}'$ are known, the remaining unknowns in Eq. (24) are the $(n-k)^2$ coefficients of $\mathbf{S}'$ and the d basis elements of F, all in $\mathbb{F}_{q^m}$. Furthermore, seen as a system of equations over $\mathbb{F}_{q^m}$ in these unknowns, Eq. (24) is a system of $n - k$ linear equations. Hence, by generating at least $\lceil \frac{(n-k)^2+d}{n-k} \rceil = n - k + 1$ valid triples $(\mathbf{m}_i, \mathbf{e}_i, (\mathbf{c}_1, \mathbf{c}_2)_i)$ we can form an overdetermined system in $(n-k)^2 + d$ variables. Solving this system will give the remaining parts of the secret key. Thus in the case of McNie we can define SolveF as the procedure that solves this system. Its cost is $Cost(\mathsf{SolveF}) = ((n-k)^2 + d)^3$.

Based on the results from this Section and Sects. 3 and 5 we have estimated our attack complexity for the McNie parameters given in their NIST submission [17]. The results are given in Table 1. We recall that we do not exploit any specific properties of McNie as the attack in [26] which dramatically decreases

Table 1. McNie parameters proposed to the first round of the NIST competition, complexities and success probability of our proposed attack

n	k	d	r	q	m	Dec. Failure	Security (bits)	Attack (Classical)	Attack (Quantum)	t	Success $Pr_s \cdot Pr_{ek}$
93	62	3	5	2	37	2^{-17}	128	128.8	82.8	8	$0.5 \cdot 0.8$
105	70	3	5	2	37	2^{-20}	128	139.7	83.7	8	$2^{-10} \cdot 0.74$
111	74	3	7	2	41	2^{-17}	192	188	108	8	$0.08 \cdot 0.87$
123	82	3	7	2	41	2^{-20}	192	189	109	8	$2^{-15} \cdot 0.875$
111	74	3	7	2	59	2^{-17}	256	188	108	8	$1 \cdot 0.875$
141	94	3	9	2	47	2^{-20}	256	238	134	8	$2^{-22} \cdot 0.875$
60	30	3	5	2	37	2^{-16}	128	166.5	96.5	10	$0.63 \cdot 0.67$
72	36	3	5	2	37	2^{-21}	128	168	98	10	$2^{-20} \cdot 0.75$
76	38	3	7	2	41	2^{-18}	192	228.3	128.3	10	$2^{-6} \cdot 0.875$
84	42	3	7	2	41	2^{-21}	192	229	129	10	$2^{-37} \cdot 0.623$
76	38	3	7	2	53	2^{-18}	256	228.3	128.3	10	$1 \cdot 0.875$
88	44	3	8	2	47	2^{-20}	256	259.5	144.5	10	$2^{-8} \cdot 0.875$

the security of the scheme, since our goal is that of providing a general reaction attack against LPRC cryptosystems.

We have implemented the attack using SAGE Math [46], and verified that, under the assumption that the kernel vectors have been found, an equivalent key can be successfully found.

References

1. Aragon, N., et al.: Lake. NIST Post-Quantum Cryptography Project: First Round Candidate Algorithms, December 2017
2. Aragon, N., et al.: Locker. NIST Post-Quantum Cryptography Project: First Round Candidate Algorithms, December 2017
3. Aragon, N., Blazy, O., Gaborit, P., Hauteville, A., Zémor, G.: Durandal: a rank metric based signature scheme. In: Ishai, Y., Rijmen, V. (eds.) EUROCRYPT 2019. LNCS, vol. 11478, pp. 728–758. Springer, Cham (2019). https://doi.org/10.1007/978-3-030-17659-4_25
4. Baldi, M., Chiaraluce, F., Garello, R.: On the usage of quasi-cyclic low-density parity-check codes in the McEliece cryptosystem. In: Proceedings of the First International Conference on Communication and Electronics (ICEE 2006), pp. 305–310, October 2006
5. Berger, T.P., Cayrel, P.-L., Gaborit, P., Otmani, A.: Reducing key length of the McEliece cryptosystem. In: Preneel, B. (ed.) AFRICACRYPT 2009. LNCS, vol. 5580, pp. 77–97. Springer, Heidelberg (2009). https://doi.org/10.1007/978-3-642-02384-2_6
6. Bernstein, D.J., et al.: https://classic.mceliece.org/
7. Bettale, L., Faugère, J.-C., Perret, L.: Cryptanalysis of HFE, multi-HFE and variants for odd and even characteristic. Des. Codes Crypt. **69**(1), 1–52 (2013)
8. Buss, J.F., Frandsen, G.S., Shallit, J.O.: The computational complexity of some problems in linear algebra. J. Comput. Syst. Sci. **58**(3), 572–596 (1999)

9. Courtois, N.T.: Efficient zero-knowledge authentication based on a linear algebra problem MinRank. In: Boyd, C. (ed.) ASIACRYPT 2001. LNCS, vol. 2248, pp. 402–421. Springer, Heidelberg (2001). https://doi.org/10.1007/3-540-45682-1_24

10. Faugère, J.-C., Gligoroski, D., Perret, L., Samardjiska, S., Thomae, E.: A polynomial-time key-recovery attack on MQQ cryptosystems. In: Katz, J. (ed.) PKC 2015. LNCS, vol. 9020, pp. 150–174. Springer, Heidelberg (2015). https://doi.org/10.1007/978-3-662-46447-2_7

11. Faugère, J.-C., Otmani, A., Perret, L., Tillich, J.-P.: Algebraic cryptanalysis of McEliece variants with compact keys. In: Gilbert, H. (ed.) EUROCRYPT 2010. LNCS, vol. 6110, pp. 279–298. Springer, Heidelberg (2010). https://doi.org/10.1007/978-3-642-13190-5_14

12. Gabidulin, E.M.: Theory of codes with maximum rank distance. Problemy Peredachi Informatsii 21(1), 3–16 (1985)

13. Gaborit, P.: Shorter keys for code based cryptography. In: International Workshop on Coding and Cryptography (WCC 2005), Bergen, Norway, pp. 81–91. ACM Press (2005)

14. Gaborit, P., Murat, G., Ruatta, O., Zémor, G.: Low rank parity check codes and their application to cryptography. In: Proceedings of the Workshop on Coding and Cryptography WCC, vol. 2013 (2013)

15. Gaborit, P., Ruatta, O., Schrek, J., Zémor, G.: New results for rank-based cryptography. In: Pointcheval, D., Vergnaud, D. (eds.) AFRICACRYPT 2014. LNCS, vol. 8469, pp. 1–12. Springer, Cham (2014). https://doi.org/10.1007/978-3-319-06734-6_1

16. Gallager, R.G.: Low-density parity-check codes. Ph.D. thesis, M.I.T. (1963)

17. Galvez, L., Kim, J.-L., Kim, M.J., Kim, Y.-S., Lee, N.: McNie: compact Mceliece-Niederreiter Cryptosystem. NIST Post-Quantum Cryptography Project, First Round Candidate Algorithms, December 2017

18. Goubin, L., Courtois, N.T.: Cryptanalysis of the TTM cryptosystem. In: Okamoto, T. (ed.) ASIACRYPT 2000. LNCS, vol. 1976, pp. 44–57. Springer, Heidelberg (2000). https://doi.org/10.1007/3-540-44448-3_4

19. Gray, R.M.: Toeplitz and circulant matrices: a review. Found. Trends® Commun. Inf. Theory 2(3), 155–239 (2006)

20. Grover, L.K.: A fast quantum mechanical algorithm for database search. In: Proceedings of the Twenty-Eighth Annual ACM Symposium on Theory of Computing, STOC 1996, pp. 212–219. ACM, New York (1996)

21. Guo, Q., Johansson, T., Stankovski, P.: A key recovery attack on MDPC with CCA security using decoding errors. In: Cheon, J.H., Takagi, T. (eds.) ASIACRYPT 2016. LNCS, vol. 10031, pp. 789–815. Springer, Heidelberg (2016). https://doi.org/10.1007/978-3-662-53887-6_29

22. Hall, C., Goldberg, I., Schneier, B.: Reaction attacks against several public-key cryptosystem. In: Varadharajan, V., Mu, Y. (eds.) ICICS 1999. LNCS, vol. 1726, pp. 2–12. Springer, Heidelberg (1999). https://doi.org/10.1007/978-3-540-47942-0_2

23. Harrow, A.W., Hassidim, A., Lloyd, S.: Quantum algorithm for linear systems of equations. Phys. Rev. Lett. 103(15), 150502 (2009)

24. Kim, J.-L., Kim, Y.-S., Galvez, L., Kim, M.J., Lee, N.: McNie: a code-based public-key cryptosystem. arXiv preprint arXiv:1812.05008 (2018)

25. Kipnis, A., Shamir, A.: Cryptanalysis of the HFE public key cryptosystem by relinearization. In: Wiener, M. (ed.) CRYPTO 1999. LNCS, vol. 1666, pp. 19–30. Springer, Heidelberg (1999). https://doi.org/10.1007/3-540-48405-1_2

26. Lau, T.S.C., Tan, C.H.: Key recovery attack on McNie based on low rank parity check codes and its reparation. In: Inomata, A., Yasuda, K. (eds.) IWSEC 2018. LNCS, vol. 11049, pp. 19–34. Springer, Cham (2018). https://doi.org/10.1007/978-3-319-97916-8_2
27. McEliece, R.J.: A public-key cryptosystem based on algebraic coding theory. Deep Space Netw. Prog. Rep. **44**, 114–116 (1978)
28. Melchior Aguilar, N. et al.: Locker. NIST Post-Quantum Cryptography Project: First Round Candidate Algorithms, December 2017
29. Melchior Aguilar, C., et al.: Ouroboros-R. NIST Post-Quantum Cryptography Project: First Round Candidate Algorithms, December 2017
30. Minder, L., Shokrollahi, A.: Cryptanalysis of the Sidelnikov cryptosystem. In: Naor, M. (ed.) EUROCRYPT 2007. LNCS, vol. 4515, pp. 347–360. Springer, Heidelberg (2007). https://doi.org/10.1007/978-3-540-72540-4_20
31. Misoczki, R., Barreto, P.S.L.M.: Compact McEliece keys from Goppa codes. In: Jacobson, M.J., Rijmen, V., Safavi-Naini, R. (eds.) SAC 2009. LNCS, vol. 5867, pp. 376–392. Springer, Heidelberg (2009). https://doi.org/10.1007/978-3-642-05445-7_24
32. Misoczki, R., Tillich, J.P., Sendrier, N., Barreto, P.S.: MDPC-McEliece: new McEliece variants from moderate density parity-check codes. In: IEEE International Symposium on Information Theory - ISIT 2013, pp. 2069–2073, Istambul, Turkey. IEEE (2013)
33. Misoczki, R., Tillich, J.-P., Sendrier, N., Barreto, P.S.L.M.: MDPC-McEliece: new McEliece variants from moderate density parity-check codes (2012)
34. Aragon, N., Gaborit, P.: A key recovery attack against LRPC using decryption failures. In: International Workshop on Coding and Cryptography (WCC 2019), Saint-Jacut-de-la-Mer, Norway (2019)
35. Niederreiter, H.: Knapsack-type cryptosystems and algebraic coding theory. Probl. Control. Inf. Theory **15**(2), 159–166 (1986)
36. Nilsson, A., Johansson, T., Stankovski, P.: Error amplification in code-based cryptography. IACR Trans. Cryptogr. Hardw. Embed. Syst. **2019**(1), 238–258 (2018)
37. https://csrc.nist.gov/projects/post-quantum-cryptography/post-quantum-cryptography-standardization
38. https://csrc.nist.gov/Projects/Post-Quantum-Cryptography/Round-1-Submissions
39. Persichetti, E.: Compact McEliece keys based on quasi-dyadic Srivastava codes. J. Math. Cryptol. **6**(2), 149–169 (2012)
40. Prange, E.: The use of information sets in decoding cyclic codes. IRE Trans. IT **8**, S5–S9 (1962)
41. Santini, P., Battaglioni, M., Chiaraluce, F., Baldi, M.: Analysis of reaction and timing attacks against cryptosystems based on sparse parity-check codes (2019)
42. Schwabe, P., Westerbaan, B.: Solving binary $\mathcal{MQ}$ with Grover's algorithm. In: Carlet, C., Hasan, M.A., Saraswat, V. (eds.) SPACE 2016. LNCS, vol. 10076, pp. 303–322. Springer, Cham (2016). https://doi.org/10.1007/978-3-319-49445-6_17
43. Shor, P.W.: Polynomial-time algorithms for prime factorization and discrete logarithms on a quantum computer. SIAM J. Comput. **26**(5), 1484–1509 (1997)
44. Sidelnikov, V.M.: A public-key cryptosystem based on binary Reed-Muller codes. Discrete Math. Appl. **4**(3), 191–208 (1994)
45. Sidelnikov, V.M., Shestakov, S.O.: On insecurity of cryptosystems based on generalized Reed-Solomon codes. Discrete Math. Appl. **2**(4), 439–444 (1992)
46. The Sage Developers: SageMath, the Sage Mathematics Software System (Version 8.7) (2019). https://www.sagemath.org

Lattice-Based Zero-Knowledge SNARGs for Arithmetic Circuits

Anca Nitulescu[(✉)]

Department of Computer Science, Aarhus University, Aarhus, Denmark
anca@cs.au.dk

Abstract. Succinct non-interactive arguments (SNARGs) enable verifying NP computations with substantially lower complexity than that required for classical NP verification. In this work, we construct a zero-knowledge SNARG candidate that relies only on lattice-based assumptions which are claimed to hold even in the presence of quantum computers.

Central to our construction is the notion of linear-targeted malleability introduced by Bitansky et al. (TCC 2013) and the conjecture that variants of Regev encryption satisfy this property. Then, using the efficient characterization of NP languages as Square Arithmetic Programs we build the first quantum-resilient zk-SNARG for arithmetic circuits with a constant-size proof consisting of only 2 lattice-based ciphertexts.

Our protocol is designated-verifier, achieves zero-knowledge and has shorter proofs and shorter CRS than the previous such schemes, e.g. Boneh et al. (Eurocrypt 2017).

Keywords: Lattice-based · Zero-knowledge · SNARG · Post-quantum

1 Introduction

1.1 Zero-Knowledge Arguments

Zero-knowledge arguments are cryptographic protocols between two parties, a prover P and a verifier V, in which the prover can convince the verifier about the validity of a statement without leaking any extra information beyond the fact that the statement is true.

Since their introduction in [25] zero-knowledge (ZK) proofs have been shown to be a very powerful instrument in the design of secure cryptographic protocols.

Related to efficiency and to optimization of communication complexity, it has been shown that statistically-sound proof systems are unlikely to allow for significant improvements in communication [13, 23, 24, 42]. When considering proof systems for NP this means that, unless some complexity-theoretic collapses occur, in a statistically sound proof system any prover has to communicate, roughly, as much information as the size of the NP witness. The search for ways to beat this bound motivated the study of *computationally-sound* proof systems, also called *argument systems* [15], where soundness is required to hold only against *computationally bounded* provers.

© Springer Nature Switzerland AG 2019
P. Schwabe and N. Thériault (Eds.): LATINCRYPT 2019, LNCS 11774, pp. 217–236, 2019.
https://doi.org/10.1007/978-3-030-30530-7_11

1.2   SNARG: Succinct Non-interactive Arguments

Assuming the existence of collision-resistant hash functions, Kilian [30] showed a four-message interactive argument for NP. In this protocol, membership of an instance x in an NP language can be proven with communication and verifier's running time significantly smaller than required in the classical NP verification. Argument systems of this kind are called *succinct*. A challenge, which is of both theoretical and practical interest, is the construction of non-interactive succinct arguments. Starting from Kilian's protocol that requires four messages, Micali [35] used the Fiat-Shamir heuristic [17] to construct a *one-message* succinct argument for NP whose soundness is set in the random oracle model.

In the plain model, a non-interactive argument requires the verifier V (or a trusted party) to generate a common reference string crs ahead of time and independently of the statement to be proved by the prover P. Such systems are called *succinct non-interactive arguments* (SNARGs) [22]. Several SNARGs constructions have been proposed [8,16,19,26,27,33,39], and the area of SNARGs has become popular in the last years with the proposal of constructions which introduced significant improvements in efficiency. Many of these SNARGs are also *arguments of knowledge* – so called SNARKs [7,8].

In parallel with improvements in efficiency, there has been interesting work on understanding SNARGs. An important remark is that all such constructions are based on non-falsifiable assumptions [38], a class of assumptions that is likely to be inherent in proving the security of SNARGs for general NP languages (without random oracles), as shown by Gentry and Wichs [22]. Bitansky et al. [8] proved that designated verifier SNARKs exist if and only if extractable collision-resistant hash functions exist. Bitansky et al. [9] give an abstract model of SNARKs that rely on linear encodings of field elements. Their information theoretic framework called linear interactive proofs (LIPs) capture proof systems where the prover is restricted to using linear operations in computing the expected proof. They give a generic conversion of a 2-move LIP to a publicly verifiable SNARK using pairing-based techniques or to a designated verifier SNARK using additively homomorphic encryption techniques.

1.3   SNARGs for Arithmetic Circuits

The methodology for building SNARGs common to a family of constructions, some of which represent the state of the art [16,20,27,34,39], has as a central starting point the framework based on quadratic programs introduced by Gennaro et al. in [19]. This common framework allows to build SNARGs and SNARKs for programs instantiated as boolean or arithmetic circuits.

This approach has led to fast progress towards practical verifiable computations. For instance, using span programs for arithmetic circuits (QAPs), Pinocchio [39] provides evidence that verified remote computation can be faster than local computation. At the same time, their construction is zero-knowledge, enabling the server to keep intermediate and additional values used in the computation private.

1.4   Post-quantum SNARGs

Most of the SNARGs constructed so far are based on discrete-logarithm type assumptions, that do not hold against quantum polynomial-time adversaries [41], hence the advent of general-purpose quantum computers would render insecure the constructions based on these assumptions. Efforts were made to design such systems based on quantum resilient assumptions. We note that the original protocol of Micali [35] is a zk-SNARG which can be instantiated with a post-quantum assumption since it requires only a collision-resistant hash function – however (even in the best optimized version recently proposed in [6]) the protocol does not seem to scale well for even moderately complex computations.

Some more desirable assumptions that withstand quantum attacks are the lattice assumptions [1,37]. Nevertheless, few non-interactive proof systems are built based on lattices. Some recent works that we can mention are the NIZK constructions for specific languages, like [5,31,32] and the two designated verifier SNARG constructions [10,11], designed by Boneh et al. using encryption schemes instantiated with lattices. A similar approach is used by [20] to design a designated-verifier zk-SNARK (that is a SNARG of knowledge) for boolean circuits.

We attempt to make a step forward in this direction by building a designated-verifier zk-SNARG from quantum-resilient assumptions with better efficiency and succinctness than previous such schemes.

1.5   Our Contribution

We introduce in this work a new lattice-based designated-verifier zk-SNARG.

Our scheme uses as a main building block encodings that rely on the Learning With Errors (LWE) assumption, more precisely, we employ a variant of the encryption scheme proposed by Regev in 2005 [40]. We further assume linear-only properties of this lattice encryption scheme conjectured before by [10,11].

The underlying relation of our zk-SNARG is a square arithmetic program, which is a very efficient characterization of arithmetic circuits. Square arithmetic programs are closely related to quadratic arithmetic programs [19], but use only squarings instead of arbitrary multiplications. As suggested by Groth [27] the use of squarings give nice symmetry properties and a more compact proof. This efficient language allow us to build a zk-SNARG that achieves better succinctness, CRS size and verification time than the previous similar schemes.

We provide a generalization to our scheme, in the spirit of [19,20], by using encoding schemes with certain properties. We achieve the most compact proofs known to date, consisting in just 2 lattice-based encodings and verification time in the size of the arithmetic circuit representing the statement. This contribution is of independent interest and consists in a generic framework for SNARGs from Square Arithmetic Programs (SAPs). The stronger notion of knowledge soundness (which leads to zk-SNARKs) can be achieved by replacing the linear-targeted malleability property of our encoding schemes with a stronger (extractable) assumption [9].

1.6   Related Work

Recently, in two companion papers [10,11], Boneh et al. provided the first designated-verifier SNARGs construction based on lattice assumptions.

The first paper [10] has two main results: an improvement on the LPCP construction in [9] and a construction of linear-only encryption based on LWE. The second paper [11] presents a different approach where the information-theoretic LPCP is replaced by a LPCP with multiple provers, which is then compiled into a SNARG again via linear-only encryption. The main advantage of this approach is that it reduces the overhead on the prover, achieving what they call *quasi-optimality*[1].

Then, [20] exploits the square span program language for boolean circuits in order to introduce a general-purpose framework for SNARGs that can accomodate lattice-based encodings. The main improvements over the previous lattice-based SNARGs showed by [20] are zero-knowledge property and knowledge soundness, this being the first construction of a lattice-based zk-SNARK.

1.7   Techniques and Comparison to Other SNARGs

Our new framework for building SNARGs exploits the advantages of previous proposals taking the best of these approaches. It uses the simple and efficient representation of a arithmetic circuit satisfiability problem, SAP and minimizes the proof size. Also, our scheme does need only plausible hardness assumptions for the underlying encoding scheme for proving computational soundness.

Although conceptually similar to the recent scheme by Gennaro et al. [20], our construction is designed for arithmetic circuits and achieves better properties and efficiency:

SNARG for Arithmetic Circuit Satisfiability. In contract to previous lattice-based constructions, designed for boolean circuit satisfiability, our SNARG is built for proving satisfiability of arithmetic circuits which makes it a better candidate for practical applications.

Standard results show that polynomially sized arithmetic circuits are equivalent (up to a logarithmic factor) to Turing machines that run in polynomial time, though of course the actual efficiency of computing via circuits versus on native hardware depends heavily on the application; for example, an arithmetic circuit for matrix multiplication adds essentially no overhead, whereas a boolean circuit for integer multiplication is far less efficient.

While we describe a SNARG for arithmetic circuit satisfiability (over a field $\mathbb{F} = \mathbf{Z}_p$), the problem of boolean circuit satisfiability easily reduces to arithmetic circuit satisfiability with only constant overhead (see [9] Claim A.2).

We remark also that we compare well in terms of efficiency with the quasi-optimal SNARG of [10,11] in the case of arithmetic circuit satisfiability over

---

[1] This is the first scheme where the prover does not have to compute a cryptographic group operation for each wire of the circuit, which is instead true e.g., in QSP-based protocols.

large fields ($\mathbf{Z}_p$, where $p = 2^\lambda$).[2] In this case, their proof system is no longer a SNARG (not quasi-optimally succinct).

SAP Language for Arithmetic Circuits. Our scheme exploits the simplicity of Square Arithmetic Program to optimize the size of the proofs. Due to their conceptual simplicity, SAPs offer several advantages over previous constructions for arithmetic circuits. Their reduced number of constraints lead to smaller programs, and to lower sizes and degrees for the polynomials required to represent them, which in turn reduce the computation complexity required in SNARG schemes. Notably, their simpler "square" form requires only a single polynomial to be evaluated for verification (instead of two for earlier QSPs, and three for QAP) leading to a simpler and more compact setup, smaller crs, and fewer operations required for proof and verification.

Long-Standing Assumptions. Another simplification is the use of the more general long-standing assumption of *linear-targeted malleability* of the encoding (see Sect. 5.1 for details) instead of the recent introduced *knowledge of exponent* assumptions for lattice encodings of [20]. The soundness of our SNARG is based on a plausible intractability assumption, which is in the spirit of assumptions on which previous SNARGs were based. Moreover, with minimal modifications, based on a stronger variant of the assumption, we can get a SNARK (i.e., a SNARG of knowledge) with similar complexity.

Designated-Verifier. One limitation is that our new constructions are designated-verifier, while existing constructions are publicly verifiable.

2 Definitions

2.1 Notation

Let $\lambda \in \mathbb{N}$ be the computational security parameter, and $\kappa \in \mathbb{N}$ the statistical security parameter. We say that a function is *negligible* in λ, and we denote it by negl, if it is a $f(\lambda) = \mathcal{O}(\lambda^{-c})$ for any fixed constant c. We also say that a probability is *overwhelming* in λ if it is $1 - \mathsf{negl}(\lambda)$.

When sampling uniformly at random the value a from the set S, we employ the notation $a \leftarrow_{\$} S$. When sampling the value a from the probabilistic algorithm M, we employ the notation $a \leftarrow \mathsf{M}$. We use := to denote assignment. For an n-dimensional column vector $\mathbf{a}$, we denote its i-th entry by a_i. In the same way, given a polynomial f, we denote its i-th coefficient by f_i. Unless otherwise stated, the norm $\|\cdot\|$ considered in this work is the ℓ_2 norm. We denote by $\mathbf{a} \cdot \mathbf{b}$ the dot product between vectors $\mathbf{a}$ and $\mathbf{b}$.

Unless otherwise specified, all the algorithms defined throughout this work are assumed to be probabilistic Turing machines that run in time poly - i.e., PPT. An adversary is denoted by $\mathcal{A}$.

---

[2] Quasi-optimal succinctness refers to schemes where the argument size is quasilinear in the security parameter.

2.2   Succinct Non-interactive Arguments

In this section we provide formal definitions for the notion of succinct non-interactive arguments (SNARGs).

A SNARG can be defined for a specific efficiently decidable binary relation $\mathcal{R}$. Let $\mathfrak{R}$ be a relation generator that given a security parameter λ in unary returns a polynomial time decidable binary relation $\mathcal{R}$. The relation generator may also output some side information, an auxiliary input z, which will be given to the adversary.

For pairs $(u, w) \in \mathcal{R}$ we call u the statement and w the witness. Let $L_\mathcal{R}$ be the language consisting of statements for which there exist matching witnesses in $\mathcal{R}$.

Definition 1 (zk-SNARG for NP). *An efficient prover designated-verifiable non-interactive argument for $\mathcal{R}$ is a quadruple of probabilistic polynomial algorithms $\Pi = (\mathsf{Gen}, \mathsf{P}, \mathsf{V}, \mathsf{Sim})$ such that:*

$(\mathsf{crs}, \mathsf{vrs}, \mathsf{td}) \leftarrow \mathsf{Gen}(1^\lambda, \mathcal{R})$ *the CRS generation algorithm takes as input some security parameter λ and outputs a common reference string crs, a verification state vrs, and a trapdoor td.*

$\pi \leftarrow \mathsf{P}(\mathsf{crs}, u, w)$ *the prover algorithm takes as input the crs, a statement u, and a witness w. It outputs some argument π.*

$b \leftarrow \mathsf{V}(\mathsf{vrs}, u, \pi)$ *the verifier algorithm takes as input a statement u together with an argument π, and vrs. It outputs $b = 1$ (accept) if the proof was accepted, $b = 0$ (reject) otherwise.*

$\pi \leftarrow \mathsf{Sim}(\mathsf{crs}, \mathsf{td}, u)$ *the simulator takes as input a simulation trapdoor td and a statement u together with a proof π and returns an argument π.*

In the same line of past works [16,18,20], we will assume for simplicity that crs can be extracted from the verification key vrs, and that the unary security parameter 1^λ as well as the relation $\mathcal{R}$ can be inferred from the crs.

Non-interactive proof systems are generally asked to satisfy some security properties that simultaneously protect the prover from the disclosure of the witness, and the verifier from a forged proof. We now state the security notions necessary to define a zk-SNARG:

- **Completeness.** For every relation $\mathcal{R}$, given a true statement, a honest prover P with a valid witness should convince the verifier V with overwhelming probability. More formally, for all $\lambda \in \mathbb{N}$, for all $\mathcal{R} \leftarrow \mathfrak{R}(1^\lambda)$ and for all $(u, w) \in \mathcal{R}$:

$$\Pr\left[\begin{array}{c|c} \mathsf{V}(\mathsf{vrs}, u, \pi) = 1 & (\mathsf{crs}, \mathsf{vrs}, \mathsf{td}) \leftarrow \mathsf{Gen}(1^\lambda, \mathcal{R}) \\ \wedge\ (u, w) \in \mathcal{R} & \pi \leftarrow \mathsf{P}(\mathsf{crs}, u, w) \end{array}\right] = 1 - \mathsf{negl}$$

- **Computational Soundness.** An argument system requires that no computationally bounded adversary can make an honest verifier accept a proof of a false statement $u \notin L_\mathcal{R}$. More formally, for every PPT adversarial prover $\mathcal{A}$, for any relation $\mathcal{R} \rightarrow \mathfrak{R}(1^\lambda)$ there is a negligible function negl such that:

$$\Pr\left[\begin{array}{c|c} \mathsf{V}(\mathsf{vrs}, u, \pi) = 1 & (\mathsf{crs}, \mathsf{vrs}, \mathsf{td}) \leftarrow \mathsf{Gen}(1^\lambda, \mathcal{R}) \\ \wedge\ u \notin L_\mathcal{R} & (u, \pi) \leftarrow \mathcal{A}(\mathsf{crs}) \end{array}\right] = \mathsf{negl}$$

- **Succinctness.** A non-interactive argument where the verifier runs in polynomial time in $\lambda + |u|$ and the proof size is polynomial in λ is called a preprocessing succinct non-interactive argument (SNARG). If we also restrict the common reference string to be polynomial in λ we say the non-interactive argument is a fully succinct SNARG. Bitansky et al. [8] show that preprocessing SNARKs can be composed to yield fully succinct SNARKs. The focus of this paper is on preprocessing SNARKs, where the common reference string may be long.
- **Statistical Zero-Knowledge.** An argument is zero-knowledge if it does not leak any information besides the truth of the statement. Formally, if for all $\lambda \in \mathbb{N}$, for all $\mathcal{R} \rightarrow \mathfrak{R}(1^\lambda)$, for all $(u, w) \in \mathcal{R}$ and for all PPT adversaries $\mathcal{A}$ the following two distributions are statistically close:

$$D_0 = \left[\pi_0 \leftarrow \mathsf{P}(\mathsf{crs}, u, w) : (\mathsf{crs}, \mathsf{vrs}, \mathsf{td}) \leftarrow \mathsf{Gen}(1^\lambda, \mathcal{R}) \right],$$

$$D_1 = \left[\pi_1 \leftarrow \mathsf{Sim}(\mathsf{crs}, \mathsf{td}, u) : (\mathsf{crs}, \mathsf{vrs}, \mathsf{td}) \leftarrow \mathsf{Gen}(1^\lambda, \mathcal{R}) \right].$$

Adaptive Soundness. A SNARG is called *adaptive* if the prover can choose the statement u to be proved after seeing the reference string crs and the argument remains sound.

SNARG vs. SNARK. If we replace the computational soundness with computational *Knowledge Soundness* we obtain what we call a SNARK, a succinct non-interactive argument of knowledge.

- **Knowledge Soundness.** The notion of knowledge soundness implies that there is an extractor that can compute a witness whenever the adversary produces a valid argument. The extractor gets full access to the adversary's state, including any random coins. Formally, we require that for all PPT adversaries $\mathcal{A}$ there exists a PPT extractor $\varepsilon_{\mathcal{A}}$ such that

$$\Pr \left[\begin{array}{c} \mathsf{V}(\mathsf{vrs}, u, \pi) = 1 \\ \wedge\ (u, w) \notin \mathcal{R} \end{array} \left| \begin{array}{c} (\mathsf{crs}, \mathsf{vrs}, \mathsf{td}) \leftarrow \mathsf{Gen}(1^\lambda, \mathcal{R}) \\ ((u, \pi); w) \leftarrow \mathcal{A} \| \varepsilon_{\mathcal{A}}(\mathsf{crs}) \end{array} \right. \right] = \mathsf{negl}$$

Publicly Verifiable vs. Designated Verifier. We define a SNARG such that the setup algorithm for the argument system also outputs a secret verification state vrs which is needed for proof verification. If adaptive soundness holds against adversaries that also have access to the verification state vrs, then the SNARG is called *publicly verifiable*; otherwise it is *designated verifier*. A key question that arises in the design and analysis of designated verifier arguments is whether the same common reference string can be reused for multiple proofs. Formally, this "multi-theorem" setting is captured by requiring soundness to hold even against a prover that makes adaptive queries to a proof verification oracle. If the prover can choose its queries in a way that induces noticeable correlations between the outputs of the verification oracle and the secret verification state, then the adversary can potentially compromise the soundness of the scheme. Thus, special care is needed to construct designated-verifier argument systems in the multi-theorem setting.

3 Building Blocks

3.1 Arithmetic Circuits

Informally, an arithmetic circuit consists of wires that carry values from a field $\mathbb{F}$ and connect to addition and multiplication gates.

We designate some of the input/output wires as specifying a statement and use the rest of the wires in the circuit to define a witness. This gives us a binary relation $\mathcal{R}$ consisting of statement wires and witness wires that satisfy the arithmetic circuit, i.e., make it consistent with the designated input/output wires.

3.2 Square Arithmetic Programs

We characterize NP as Square Arithmetic Programs (SAPs) over some field $\mathbb{F}$ of order $p \geq 2^{\lambda-1}$. SAPs were introduced first by Groth et al. in [28].

The main idea is to represent each gate input and each gate output as a variable. Then we may rewrite each gate as an equation in some variables representing the gate's input and output wires. These equations are satisfied only by the values of the wires that meet the gate's logical specification. By composing such constraints for all the gates in the circuit, a satisfying assignment for any arithmetic circuit can be specified first as a set of quadratic equations, then modified to a square equivalent, and finally, seen as a constraint on the span of a set of polynomials, defining the SAP for this circuit. As a consequence, the prover needs to convince the verifier that all the quadratic equations are satisfiable by finding a solution of the equivalent polynomial problem.

Definition 2 (SAP). *A Square Arithmetic Program* SAP *over the field $\mathbb{F}$ contains two sets of polynomials* $\{v_0(x), \ldots, v_m(x)\}, \{w_0(x), \ldots, w_m(x)\} \in \mathbb{F}[x]$ *and a target polynomial* $t(x)$ *such that* $\deg(v_i(x)), \deg(w_i(x)) \leq d := \deg(t(x))$ *for all* $i = 0, \ldots, m$.

We say that SAP accepts an input $a_1, \ldots, a_\ell \in \mathbb{F}$ *if and only if there exist* $\{a_i\}_{i=\ell+1}^{m} \in \mathbb{F}$ *satisfying:*

$$t(x) \; divides \; \left(v_0(x) + \sum_{i=1}^{m} a_i v_i(x)\right)^2 - \left(w_0(x) + \sum_{i=1}^{m} a_i w_i(x)\right).$$

A SAP with such a description defines the following binary relation $\mathcal{R}$, where we define $a_0 = 1$,

$$\mathcal{R} = \left\{ (\mathbf{u}, \mathbf{w}) \; \middle| \; \begin{array}{l} \mathbf{u} = (a_1, \ldots, a_{\ell_u}) \\ \mathbf{w} = (a_{\ell_u+1}, \ldots, a_m) \\[6pt] \exists h(x) \in \mathbb{F}[x], \deg(h(x)) \leq d-2 : \\ \left(\sum_{i=0}^{m} a_i v_i(x)\right)^2 = \sum_{i=0}^{m} a_i w_i(x) + h(x)t(x) \end{array} \right\}$$

3.3   Encoding Schemes

The main ingredient for an efficient preprocessing SNARG is an encoding scheme E over a field $\mathbb{F}$ with some important properties that allow proving and verifying on top of encoded values. Well-known schemes use deterministic pairing-based encodings, where the values are hidden in the exponent and the security is guaranteed by discrete logarithm type assumptions, e.g. [16,27,34,39]. A formalisation of these encoding schemes was initially introduced in [19]. Here, we recall a variant of this definition that was used for a recent SNARK construction based on lattices in [20]. This definition has the advantage that it accommodates for encodings with noise.

An encoding scheme $E = (\mathsf{K}, \mathsf{E})$ over a field $\mathbb{F}$ is composed of the following algorithms

$\mathsf{K}(1^\lambda) \to (\mathsf{pk}, \mathsf{sk})$: a key generation algorithm that outputs some secret state sk together with some public information pk.

$\mathsf{E}(a) \to C$: a (non-deterministic) encoding algorithm mapping $a \in \mathbb{F}$ to some encoding space C, such that $\{\{\mathsf{E}(a) : a \in \mathbb{F}\}$ partitions C, where $\{\mathsf{E}(a)\}$ denotes the set of the possible evaluations of the algorithm E on a.

Depending on the encoding algorithm, E will be either deterministic or not and will require either only the public information pk, or the secret state sk. For our application, it will be the case of sk. To ease notation, we will omit this additional argument.

The above algorithms must satisfy the following properties:

- d-**linearly homomorphic:** there exists a poly algorithm Eval that, given as input the public parameters pk, a vector of encodings $(\mathsf{E}(a_1), \ldots, \mathsf{E}(a_d))$, and coefficients $\mathbf{c} = (c_1, \ldots, c_d) \in \mathbb{F}^d$, outputs a valid encoding of $\mathbf{a} \cdot \mathbf{c}$ where $\mathbf{a} = (a_1, \ldots a_d)$ with probability overwhelming in λ.
- **quadratic root detection:** there exists an efficient algorithm that, given some parameter δ (either pk or sk), $\mathsf{E}(a_0), \ldots, \mathsf{E}(a_t)$, and the quadratic polynomial $\mathsf{p} \in \mathbb{F}[x_0, \ldots, x_t]$, can distinguish if $\mathsf{p}(a_1, \ldots, a_t) = 0$. With a slight abuse of notation, we will adopt the writing $\mathsf{p}(\mathsf{ct}_0, \ldots, \mathsf{ct}_t) = 0$ to denote the quadratic root detection algorithm with inputs δ, $\mathsf{ct}_0, \ldots, \mathsf{ct}_t$, and p.
- **image verification:** there exists an efficiently computable algorithm $\in$ that, given as input some parameter δ (again, either pk or sk), can distinguish if an element c is a correct encoding of a field element.

Decoding Algorithm. When using a homomorphic encryption scheme in order to instantiate an encoding scheme, we simply define the *decoding algorithm* Dec as the decryption procedure of the scheme. More specifically, since we study encoding schemes derived from encryption functions, quadratic root detection and image verification for designated-verifiers are trivially obtained by using the decryption procedure Dec together with the secret key sk.

One-Way Encodings. If such a secret state is not needed to perform the quadratic root detection, we will consider sk $=\perp$ and call it "one-way" or *publicly-verifiable* encoding. At present, the only candidates for such a "one-way" encoding scheme that we know of are based on bilinear groups, where the bilinear maps support efficient testing of quadratic degrees without any additional secret information.

4 zk-SNARG for Arithmetic Circuits

The idea of our SNARG is simple and follows the common paradigm of many well-known pairing-based constructions. The prover has to convince the verifier that it knows some polynomials, such that a division property between them holds (a solution to SAP problem). Instead of sending the entire polynomials as a proof, it evaluates them in a secret point s (hidden by the encoding) to obtain some scalar values. The verifier, instead of checking a polynomial division, has only to check a division between scalars, which makes the task extremely fast.

4.1 Framework for zk-SNARGs from SAP

In a nutshell, in order to construct succinct proofs of knowledge using our framework, one must use the following building blocks:

- an SAP, a way of "translating" the circuit satisfiability problem into a polynomial division problem, meaning that we reduce the proof of computing a circuit to the proof of a solution to this SAP problem,
- an E encoding scheme that hides scalar values, but allows linear operations on the encodings for the prover to evaluate polynomials, and some quadratic check property for the verifier to validate the proofs,
- a CRS generator that uses this encoding scheme to hide a secret random point s and all the necessary powers of s needed later by the prover to compute polynomial evaluations on s.

Our new framework for building SNARGs exploits the advantages of previous such proposals taking the best of each one. It uses the simple and efficient representation of a arithmetic circuit satisfiability problem, SAP and minimizes the proof size of our SNARG scheme. Also, our scheme does need only plausible hardness assumptions for the underlying encoding scheme for proving computational soundness.

Efficiency. The proof size is 2 encodings. The common reference string contains a description of $\mathcal{R}$ and implicitly the polynomials in SAP, a public key for an encoding scheme and $m+2d+1-\ell_u$ encodings of field elements. The verification consists of checking one quadratic equation on the encoded values.

The prover has to compute the polynomial $h(x)$. It depends on the relation how long time this computation takes; if it arises from an arithmetic circuit where each multiplication gate connects to a constant number of wires, the relation will be sparse and the computation will be linear in d. The prover also

---

$\mathsf{Gen}(1^\lambda, \mathcal{R})$

$\beta, \delta, s \leftarrow_\$ \mathbb{F}; \qquad (\mathsf{pk}, \mathsf{sk}) \leftarrow \mathsf{K}(1^\lambda)$

$\mathsf{crs} := \Big(\mathsf{SAP} = (\{v_i(x), w_i(x)\}_{i=0}^m, t(x)), \ \mathsf{pk}, \ \mathsf{E}(\delta t(s)^2), \ \mathsf{E}(\beta t(s)),$

$\qquad \{\mathsf{E}(\delta s^i)\}_{i=0}^{d-1}, \ \{\mathsf{E}(\delta s^i t(s))\}_{i=0}^{d-2}, \ \{\mathsf{E}(\delta w_i(s) + \beta v_i(s))\}_{i=\ell_u+1}^m \Big)$

$\mathsf{vrs} := \mathsf{sk}; \qquad \mathsf{td} := (\beta, \delta, s)$

$\textbf{return} \ (\mathsf{vrs}, \mathsf{crs}, \mathsf{td})$

$\mathsf{P}(\mathsf{crs}, \mathbf{u}, \mathbf{w})$

$\mathbf{u} := (a_1, \dots, a_{\ell_u})$

$\mathbf{w} := (a_{\ell_u+1}, \dots, a_m)$

$v(x) := \sum_{i=0}^m a_i v_i(x)$

$v_{\mathsf{mid}}(x) := \sum_{i>\ell_u} a_i v_i(x)$

$w(x) := \sum_{i=0}^m a_i w_i(x)$

$w_{\mathsf{mid}}(x) := \sum_{i>\ell_u} a_i w_i(x)$

$h(x) = (v(x)^2 - w(x))/t(x)$

$r \leftarrow_\$ \mathbb{F}$

$f(\mathbf{w}) := \delta w_{\mathsf{mid}}(s) + \beta v_{\mathsf{mid}}(s)$

$g(r) := r^2 \delta t(s)^2 + 2r\delta t(s) v(s) + r\beta t(s)$

$A := \mathsf{E}\big(\delta v(s) + r\delta t(s)\big)$

$B := \mathsf{E}(f(\mathbf{w}) + \delta t(s) h(s) + g(r))$

$\textbf{return} \ \pi := (A, B)$

$\mathsf{V}(\mathsf{vrs}, \mathbf{u}, \pi)$

$\pi := (A, B)$

$v_{\mathsf{in}}(x) := \sum_{i=0}^{\ell_u} a_i v_i(x)$

$w_{\mathsf{in}}(x) := \sum_{i=0}^{\ell_u} a_i w_i(x)$

$V := \mathsf{E}(\beta v_{\mathsf{in}}(s))$

$W := \mathsf{E}(\delta w_{\mathsf{in}}(s))$

Check

$A(A + \beta) = \delta(B + W + V)$

$\mathsf{Sim}(\mathsf{crs}, \mathsf{td}, \mathbf{u})$

$\mathsf{td} := (\beta, \delta, s), \quad \mu \leftarrow_\$ \mathbb{F}$

$\phi(\mathbf{u}) := \delta w_{\mathsf{in}}(s) + \beta v_{\mathsf{in}}(s)$

$A := \mathsf{E}(\delta \mu)$

$B := \mathsf{E}\big(\delta \mu^2 + \beta \mu - \phi(\mathbf{u})\big)$

$\pi := (A, B)$

Fig. 1. Framework for zk-SNARG from SAP

computes the coefficients of the representation $v(x) := \sum_{i=0}^m a_i v_i(x)$. Having all these coefficients, the prover applies $m + 2d + 1 - \ell_u$ linear homomorphic operations on the encodings from the given crs.

Besides the improvements mentioned above, one of the most remarkable features of this framework is the fact that it can accommodate for lattice-based encodings, meaning that we can use it to obtain a quantum-resilient SNARGs.

4.2 Lattice-Based Instantiation

In this section, we describe a possible encoding scheme based on learning with errors (LWE) that will be used as a building block for our post-quantum SNARG scheme.

$K(1^\lambda, \Gamma)$	$E(s, m) \to ct$	$Dec(s, (c_0, c_1)) \to m$
$s \leftarrow_\$ \mathbf{Z}_q^n$	$\mathbf{a} \leftarrow_\$ \mathbf{Z}_q^n$	$m := (\mathbf{c}_0 \cdot \mathbf{s} + c_1) \mod p$
return s	$\sigma := q\alpha; \quad e \leftarrow \chi_\sigma$	**return** m
	$ct := (-\mathbf{a}, \ \mathbf{a} \cdot \mathbf{s} + pe + m)$	

Fig. 2. An encoding scheme based on LWE.

Lattice-Based Encoding Scheme. In order to instantiate our SNARG encoding, we just use $Enc = (K, E, Dec)$ encryption scheme depicted in Fig. 2. This is the same encoding used to construct lattice-based SNARKs in [20], a slight variation of the classical LWE cryptosystem initially presented by Regev [40] and later extended in [14].

The encryption scheme Enc is described by parameters $\Gamma := (p, q, n, \alpha)$, with $q, n, p \in \mathbb{N}$ such that $(p, q) = 1$, and $0 < \alpha < 1$. In the corresponding description of our building block E, the public information is constituted by the LWE parameters $pk = \Gamma$ and an encoding of m is simply an LWE encryption of m. The LWE secret key constitutes the secret state $sk = s$ of the encoding scheme.

Basic Properties. We briefly recall the main properties Enc should satisfy as a building block in a SNARG scheme.

correctness. Let $ct = (-\mathbf{a}, \mathbf{a} \cdot \mathbf{s} + pe + m)$ be an encoding. Then ct is a valid encoding of a message $m \in \mathbf{Z}_p$ if $e < \frac{q}{2p}$.

d-**linearly homomorphicity.** Given a vector of d encodings $\mathbf{ct} \in \mathbb{Z}_q^{d \times (n+1)}$ and a vector of coefficients $\mathbf{c} \in \mathbb{Z}_p^d$, the homomorphic evaluation algorithm is defined as follows: $\mathsf{Eval}(\mathbf{ct}, \mathbf{c}) := \mathbf{c} \cdot \mathbf{ct}$.

quadratic root detection. The algorithm for quadratic root detection can be implemented using Dec and the secret key (i.e., $sk := s$): decrypt the message and evaluate the polynomial, testing if it is equal to 0.

image verification. Using the decryption algorithm Dec and sk, we can implement image verification (algorithm $\in$).

4.3 Technical Challenges

Noise growth. During the homomorphic evaluation, the noise grows as a result of the operations which are performed on the encodings. Consequently, in order to ensure that the output of Eval is a valid encoding of the expected result, we need to start with a sufficiently small noise in each of the initial encodings.

In order to bound the size of the noise, we first need a basic theorem on the tail bound of discrete Gaussian distributions due to Banaszczyk [3]:

Lemma 1 ([3]). *For any $\sigma, T \in \mathbb{R}^+$ and $\mathbf{a} \in \mathbb{R}^n$:*

$$\Pr[\mathbf{x} \leftarrow \chi_\sigma^n \ : \ |\mathbf{x} \cdot \mathbf{a}| \geq T\sigma \, \|\mathbf{a}\|] < 2 \exp(-\pi T^2). \tag{1}$$

At this point, this corollary follows:

Corollary 1. *Let $\mathbf{s} \leftarrow_{\!\!s} \mathbf{Z}_q^n$ be a secret key and $\mathbf{m} = (m_0, \ldots, m_{d-1}) \in \mathbf{Z}_p^d$ be a vector of messages. Let $\mathbf{ct}$ be a vector of d fresh encodings so that $\mathsf{ct}_i \leftarrow \mathsf{E}(\mathbf{s}, m_i)$, and $\mathbf{c} \in \mathbf{Z}_p^d$ be a vector of coefficients. If $q > 2p^2\sigma\sqrt{\frac{\epsilon d}{\pi}}$, then $\mathsf{Eval}(\mathbf{c}, \mathbf{ct})$ outputs a valid encoding of $\mathbf{m} \cdot \mathbf{c}$ under the secret key $\mathbf{s}$.*

Smudging. When computing a linear combination of encodings, the distribution of the error term in the final encoding does not result in a correctly distributed fresh encoding. The resulting error distribution depends on the coefficients used for the linear combination, and despite correctness of the decryption still holds, the error could reveal more than just the plaintext. We combine homomorphic evaluation with a technique called *noise smudging* [2,4,21], which "smudges out" any difference in the distribution that is due to the coefficients of the linear combination, thus hiding any potential information leak.

Zero-Knowledge. We now present a version of the the famous "leftover hash lemma" introduced in [29] that will be useful later when proving the zero-knowledge property of our construction. In a nutshell, it says that a random linear combination of the columns of a matrix is statistically close to a uniformly random vector, for some particular choice of coefficients.

Lemma 2 (Specialized leftover hash lemma). *Let n, p, q, d be non-negative integers. Let $A \leftarrow_{\!\!s} \mathbf{Z}_q^{n \times d}$, and $r \leftarrow_{\!\!s} \mathbf{Z}_p^d$. Then we have*

$$\Delta(A, Ar), (A, \boldsymbol{u}) \leq \frac{1}{2}\sqrt{p^{-d} \cdot q^n},$$

where Ar is computed modulo q, and $\boldsymbol{u} \leftarrow_{\!\!s} \mathbb{Z}_q^n$.

Practical Considerations. A single encoded value has size $(n+1)\log q = \widetilde{O}(\lambda)$. Therefore, as long as the prover sends only 2 encodings, the proof is guaranteed to be (quasi) succinct.

Although the scheme requires the noise terms to be sampled from a discrete Gaussian distribution, for practical purposes we can sample them from a bounded uniform distribution (see, e.g., [36] for a formal assessment of the hardness of LWE in this case).

5   Security of Our zk-SNARG

Following our framework for SAP and implementing it with the encryption scheme Enc as described above and making some modification for the zero-knowledge, we obtain a new lattice-based zk-SNARG scheme with short proofs

$$(\mathsf{pk}, \mathsf{st}, \{m_i\}, \{\mathsf{Dec}(\mathsf{ct}_j)\}) \leftarrow \mathcal{D}_0(\lambda) \qquad (\mathsf{pk}, \mathsf{st}, \{m_i\}, \{d_j\}) \leftarrow \mathcal{D}_1(\lambda)$$

$(\mathsf{pk}, \mathsf{sk}) \leftarrow \mathsf{K}(1^\lambda)$
$(\mathsf{st}, m_1, \dots, m_d) \leftarrow \mathsf{M}(1^\lambda)$
$\sigma \leftarrow (\mathsf{pk}, \mathsf{E}(m_1), \dots, \mathsf{E}(m_d))$
$\{\mathsf{ct}_j\}_{j=1}^n \leftarrow \mathcal{A}(\sigma; z)$
where $\mathsf{Dec}(\mathsf{ct}_j) \neq \perp$

$(\mathsf{pk}, \mathsf{sk}) \leftarrow \mathsf{K}(1^\lambda)$
$(\mathsf{st}, m_1, \dots, m_d) \leftarrow \mathsf{M}(1^\lambda)$
$(\mathbf{a}_1, \cdots \mathbf{a}_n, \mathbf{b}) \leftarrow \mathsf{S}(\mathsf{pk}; z)$
$\mathbf{a}_j, \mathbf{b} \in \mathbb{F}^d$
$d_j := \sum_{i=1}^d a_{ji} m_i + b_i$

Fig. 3. Distributions $\mathcal{D}_0$ and $\mathcal{D}_1$ in linear-targeted malleability.

consisting in 2 ciphertexts instead of 5 in [20]. The soundness of the resulting SNARG scheme relies on the long-standing hardness assumption of *linear targeted malleability* of the encoding scheme.

Moreover, the same construction yields a zk-SNARK (a zero-knowledge succinct non-interactive argument of knowledge) if the soundness property is replaced with a corresponding knowledge property, and the scheme E satisfies *linear-only encryption*, where the simulator is required to be efficient (i.e., PPT). For more details, we refer to [9]. Roughly, the knowledge property states that there exists an extractor such that for every linear strategy that convinces the verifier of some statement u with high probability, the extractor outputs a witness w such that $(u, w) \in \mathcal{R}$.

5.1 Hardness Assumptions

Linear-Only Encoding Schemes. A *linear-only* encoding scheme is an encoding scheme where any adversary can output a valid new encoding only if this is a linear combination of some previous encodings that the adversary had as input. At high-level, a linear-only encoding scheme does not allow any other form of homomorphism than linear operations. If we require from the adversary to actually know the coefficients of the linear combination, we assume extractable linear-only, and model this knowledge by the existence of a non-black-box polynomial time extractor.

In this work, we use the weaker notion of *linear-targeted malleability*, employed also in [9]. This is closer to the definition template of Boneh et al. [12]. In such a notion, the extractor is replaced with an efficient simulator. Relying on this weaker variant, if the simulator is allowed to be inefficient, we are only able to prove soundness of the SNARG, though not knowledge soundness as needed for SNARKs. Concretely, the linear-only property rules out any encryption scheme where ciphertexts can be sampled obliviously; instead, the weaker notion does not, and thus allows for shorter ciphertexts.

Definition 3 (Linear-Targeted Malleability, [9]). *An encoding scheme satisfies* linear-targeted malleability *property if for all* PPT *adversaries $\mathcal{A}$ and plaintext generation algorithm* M *there exists a simulator* S *such that, for any sufficiently large $\lambda \in \mathbb{N}$, any "benign" auxiliary input z the following two distributions $\mathcal{D}_0(\lambda), \mathcal{D}_1(\lambda)$ in Fig. 3 are computationally inistinguishable.*

5.2 Security Proof

Before formally proving this is a SNARG, let us give a little intuition behind the different components in the scheme (see Fig. 1). The role of β is to ensure A and B are consistent with each other in the choice of coefficients $a_0, \ldots, a_m$. In the verification equation the product $A(A + \beta)$ involves a linear dependence on β, and we will later prove that this linear dependence can only be balanced out by the term B with a consistent choice of $a_0, \ldots, a_m$ in A and B. The role of δ to make the product δB of the verification equation independent from the first product and preventing mixing and matching of elements intended for different products in the verification equation. Finally, the prover algorithm uses r to randomize the proof to get zero-knowledge.

Theorem 1. *Assuming that the scheme Enc is a linear-targeted malleable encoding scheme, the protocol given in Fig. 1 is a non-interactive zero-knowledge argument.*

Completeness. Completeness holds by direct verification.

Zero-Knowledge. To obtain a zero-knowledge protocol, we do two things: we add a smudging term to the noise of the encoding, in order to make the distribution of the final noise independent of the coefficients a_i, and we randomize the target polynomial $t(x)$ to hide the witness from the verifier. The random vectors constituting the first element of the ciphertext are guaranteed to be statistically indistinguishable from uniformly random vectors by leftover hash lemma (cf. Lemma 2).

To see that the simulated proofs are indistinguishable from the real proofs, first observe that the simulation procedure always produces verifying proofs. Next, observe that for a given instance and proof $\pi = (A, B)$ the element A uniquely determines B through the verification equation. In a real proof the random choice of r makes the value encoded in A uniformly random, and in a simulated proof the random choice of μ makes the value inside A uniformly random. So in both cases, we get the same probability distribution over the values hidden by the encodings A, B with uniformly random A and the unique matching B.

We are left with showing that after applying our encoding scheme on these values, the two proofs, the real one and the simulated one, are statistically indistinguishable.

In both worlds, the proof is a couple of encodings (A, B). Once the vrs is fixed, each encoding can be written as $(-\mathbf{a}, \mathbf{a} \cdot \mathbf{s} + pe + m)$, for some $\mathbf{a} \in \mathbb{Z}_q^n$

and some $m \in \mathbb{Z}_p$ satisfying the verification equations. Due to Lemma 2, the random vectors $\mathbf{a}$ are indistinguishable from uniformly random in both worlds. The error terms are statistically indistinguishable due to smudging techniques applied to the ciphertexts. The zero-knowledge follows from these claims, since the simulator can use re-randomization to ensure that its actual encodings (not just what is encoded) are appropriately uniform.

Computational Soundness. The linear-targeted malleability property of the encryption scheme constrains the prover to only use affine strategies. This ensures soundness for our SNARG. To check a proof, the verifier decrypts the prover's responses and checks the corresponding quadratic equation on these values.

What remains is to demonstrate that for any affine prover strategy that is able to produce a couple statement-proof $(\mathbf{u}, \pi)$ that passes the verification test, there exists the simulator S as defined in Fig. 3 that outputs a valid witness $\mathbf{w}$ for the statement $\mathbf{u}$.

For any prover algorithm $\mathcal{A}(\mathsf{crs}) \to (\mathbf{u}, \pi)$, by our linear-targeted malleability assumption the values A, B encoded in the proof $\pi = (A, B)$ are identically distributed as two simulated linear combination of some initial values $\sigma = (\delta t(s)^2, \beta t(s), \{\delta s^i\}_{i=0}^{d-1}, \{\delta s^i t(s)\}_{i=0}^{d-2}, \{\delta w_i(s) + \beta v_i(s)\}_{i=\ell+1}^m)$ encoded in the crs. More formally, we consider the simulator S that on input σ and some auxiliary input z (which corresponds to the rest of the SNARG's crs) outputs a pair of coefficients such that the resulting values c, d are indistinguishable from the values encoded by the proof π:

$(\sigma, \mathsf{st}, \mathsf{Dec}(A), \mathsf{Dec}(B)) \leftarrow \mathcal{D}_0(\lambda)$	$(\sigma, \mathsf{st}, c, b) \leftarrow \mathcal{D}_1(\lambda)$
$(\mathsf{pk}, \mathsf{sk}) \leftarrow \mathsf{K}(1^\lambda)$	$(\mathsf{pk}, \mathsf{sk}) \leftarrow \mathsf{K}(1^\lambda)$
$(\mathsf{st}, m_1, m_2, \mathbf{m}_3, \mathbf{m}_4, \mathbf{m}_5) \leftarrow \mathsf{M}(1^\lambda)$	$(\mathsf{st}, m_1, \ldots, m_n) \leftarrow \mathsf{M}(1^\lambda)$
$\sigma \leftarrow (\mathsf{pk}, \mathsf{E}(m_1), \ldots, \mathsf{E}(m_5))$	where $m_3, \ldots m_n$ is a reordering of
where $m_1 = \delta t(s)^2$, $m_2 = \beta t(s)$,	the entries in $\mathbf{m}_3, \mathbf{m}_4, \mathbf{m}_5$
$\{m_{3i} = \delta s^i\}_{i=0}^{d-1}$, $\{m_{4i} = \delta s^i t(s)\}_{i=0}^{d-2}$,	$(c', \mathbf{c}, b', \mathbf{b}) \leftarrow \mathsf{S}(\mathsf{pk}; z)$
$\{m_{5i} = \delta w_i(s) + \beta v_i(s)\}_{i=\ell+1}^m$	$c_j, b_j \in \mathbb{F}^n$
$(\mathbf{u}, \pi := (A, B)) \leftarrow \mathcal{A}(\sigma; z)$	$c := \sum_{i=1}^n c_i m_i + c'$
such that $\mathsf{V}(\mathsf{vrs}, \mathbf{u}, \pi) = 1$	$b := \sum_{i=1}^n b_i m_i + b'$

If $\mathcal{A}$ convinces the verifier to accept with probability at least $\varepsilon(\lambda)$, then, with at least $\varepsilon(\lambda) - \mathsf{negl}$ probability, the distribution on the left satisfies that $\mathsf{V}(\mathsf{vrs}, \mathbf{u}, (\mathsf{E}(c), \mathsf{E}(b))) = 1$. However, in this distribution, the generation of $(\{m_i\})$ is independent of the generation of the simulated affine function coefficients $(c', \mathbf{c}, b', \mathbf{b})$. Therefore, by averaging, there exists some $(c', \mathbf{c}, b', \mathbf{b})$ such that, with probability at least $\varepsilon(\lambda)/2$ over the choice of $\{m_i\}_i$ it holds that $\pi' = (\mathsf{E}(c), \mathsf{E}(b))$ is a valid proof for $\mathbf{u}$. We can use some basic linear algebra techniques to recombine the coefficients $(c', \mathbf{c}, b', \mathbf{b})$ and extract an actual witness $\mathbf{w} = (a_{\ell_u+1}, \ldots a_m)$ for the statements $\mathbf{u} = (a_1, \ldots a_{\ell_u})$.

Given that the number of variables and the lenght of the equation is significant we will not detail all the computations, but the intuition of how we recover these coefficients from the values c, b is the following:

We can rewrite c as

$$
c := c(\beta, \delta, s) = c_1 \delta t(s)^2 + c_2 \beta t(s) + c_3(s)\delta
$$
$$
+ c_4(s)\delta s^i t(s) + \sum_{i > \ell_u} c_{5i}\big(\delta w_i(s) + \beta v_i(s)\big)
$$

for known field elements $c_1, c_2, \{c_{5i}\}_{i > \ell_u}$ and polynomials $c_3(x), c_4(x)$ of degrees $d - 1$ and $d - 2$, respectively. We can write out $b := b(\beta, \delta, s)$ in a similar fashion from the values in σ. By the Schwartz-Zippel lemma the proof $\pi' = (c, b)$ has negligible probability to pass the check unless the verification equation $c^2 + \beta c = \delta(b + \phi(\mathbf{u}))$ holds not only for the values c, b, but for some actual polynomials $c(x_\beta, x_\delta, x_s), b(x_\beta, x_\delta, x_s)$ in indeterminates x_β, x_δ, x_s. We now view the verification equation as an equality of multivariate polynomials in x_β, x_δ, x_s and by cancelling the respective terms in this polynomial equality (for example the terms with indeterminate x_β^2, then the ones with $x_\delta x_\beta$, etc.), we eventually remain only with the terms involving powers of x_s that should satisfy:

$$
\left(\sum_{i=0}^{m} c_i v_i(x) \right)^2 = \sum_{i=0}^{m} c_i w_i(x_s) + b_h(x_s)t(x_s).
$$

This shows that $(a_{\ell_u+1}, \ldots a_m) = (c_{\ell_u+1}, \ldots c_m)$ is a witness for the statement $(a_1, \ldots a_{\ell_u})$.

Lower Bounds for SNARGs. It is an intriguing question how efficient non-interactive arguments can be and what is the minimal size of the proof. Groth showed in [27] that a pairing-based non-interactive argument with generic group algorithms must have at least two group elements in the proof. We do not have an equivalent result for lower bounds in the post-quantum setting, but recent construction aim to minimize the number of lattice-encodings in the proof and the verification overhead. Our lattice-based SNARG seems to be the most optimal to date in the size of the proof and the number of verification equations, we achieve proofs of size 2 encodings and only one verification equation.

Acknowledgements. Research founded by: the European Research Council (ERC) under the European Unions's Horizon 2020 research and innovation programme under grant agreement No 803096 (SPEC); the Danish Independent Research Council under Grant-ID DDF-6108-00169 (FoCC).

References

1. Ajtai, M.: Generating hard instances of lattice problems (extended abstract). In: Miller, G.L. (ed.) STOC, pp. 99–108. ACM (1996). http://dblp.uni-trier.de/db/conf/stoc/stoc1996.html#Ajtai96
2. Asharov, G., Jain, A., López-Alt, A., Tromer, E., Vaikuntanathan, V., Wichs, D.: Multiparty computation with low communication, computation and interaction via threshold FHE. In: Pointcheval, D., Johansson, T. (eds.) EUROCRYPT 2012. LNCS, vol. 7237, pp. 483–501. Springer, Heidelberg (2012). https://doi.org/10.1007/978-3-642-29011-4_29
3. Banaszczyk, W.: Inequalities for convex bodies and polar reciprocal lattices inRn. Discret. Comput. Geom. **13**(2), 217–231 (1995)
4. Banerjee, A., Peikert, C., Rosen, A.: Pseudorandom functions and lattices. In: Pointcheval, D., Johansson, T. (eds.) EUROCRYPT 2012. LNCS, vol. 7237, pp. 719–737. Springer, Heidelberg (2012). https://doi.org/10.1007/978-3-642-29011-4_42
5. Baum, C., Bootle, J., Cerulli, A., del Pino, R., Groth, J., Lyubashevsky, V.: Sublinear lattice-based zero-knowledge arguments for arithmetic circuits. In: Shacham, H., Boldyreva, A. (eds.) CRYPTO 2018. LNCS, vol. 10992, pp. 669–699. Springer, Cham (2018). https://doi.org/10.1007/978-3-319-96881-0_23
6. Ben-Sasson, E., Bentov, I., Horesh, Y., Riabzev, M.: Scalable, transparent, and post-quantum secure computational integrity. Cryptology ePrint Archive, Report 2018/046 (2018). https://eprint.iacr.org/2018/046
7. Bitansky, N., et al.: The hunting of the SNARK. Cryptology ePrint Archive, Report 2014/580 (2014). http://eprint.iacr.org/2014/580
8. Bitansky, N., Canetti, R., Chiesa, A., Tromer, E.: From extractable collision resistance to succinct non-interactive arguments of knowledge, and back again, pp. 326–349 (2012). https://doi.org/10.1145/2090236.2090263
9. Bitansky, N., Chiesa, A., Ishai, Y., Paneth, O., Ostrovsky, R.: Succinct non-interactive arguments via linear interactive proofs. In: Sahai, A. (ed.) TCC 2013. LNCS, vol. 7785, pp. 315–333. Springer, Heidelberg (2013). https://doi.org/10.1007/978-3-642-36594-2_18
10. Boneh, D., Ishai, Y., Sahai, A., Wu, D.J.: Lattice-based SNARGs and their application to more efficient obfuscation, pp. 247–277 (2017). https://doi.org/10.1007/978-3-319-56617-79
11. Boneh, D., Ishai, Y., Sahai, A., Wu, D.J.: Quasi-optimal SNARGs via linear multi-prover interactive proofs. Cryptology ePrint Archive, Report 2018/133 (2018). https://eprint.iacr.org/2018/133
12. Boneh, D., Segev, G., Waters, B.: Targeted malleability: homomorphic encryption for restricted computations, pp. 350–366 (2012). https://doi.org/10.1145/2090236.2090264
13. Boppana, R.B., Hastad, J., Zachos, S.: Does co-np have short interactive proofs? Inf. Process. Lett. **25**(2), 127–132 (1987). https://doi.org/10.1016/0020-0190(87)90232-8
14. Brakerski, Z., Vaikuntanathan, V.: Efficient fully homomorphic encryption from (standard) LWE, pp. 97–106 (2011). https://doi.org/10.1109/FOCS.2011.12
15. Brassard, G., Chaum, D., Crépeau, C.: Minimum disclosure proofs of knowledge. J. Comput. Syst. Sci. **37**(2), 156–189 (1988). https://doi.org/10.1016/0022-0000(88)90005-0

16. Danezis, G., Fournet, C., Groth, J., Kohlweiss, M.: Square span programs with applications to succinct NIZK arguments, pp. 532–550 (2014). https://doi.org/10.1007/978-3-662-45611-8 28

17. Fiat, A., Shamir, A.: How to prove yourself: practical solutions to identification and signature problems. In: Odlyzko, A.M. (ed.) CRYPTO 1986. LNCS, vol. 263, pp. 186–194. Springer, Heidelberg (1987). https://doi.org/10.1007/3-540-47721-7_12

18. Fuchsbauer, G.: Subversion-zero-knowledge SNARKs. In: Abdalla, M., Dahab, R. (eds.) PKC 2018. LNCS, vol. 10769, pp. 315–347. Springer, Cham (2018). https://doi.org/10.1007/978-3-319-76578-5_11

19. Gennaro, R., Gentry, C., Parno, B., Raykova, M.: Quadratic span programs and succinct NIZKs without PCPs. In: Johansson, T., Nguyen, P.Q. (eds.) EURO-CRYPT 2013. LNCS, vol. 7881, pp. 626–645. Springer, Heidelberg (2013). https://doi.org/10.1007/978-3-642-38348-9_37

20. Gennaro, R., Minelli, M., Nitulescu, A., Orrù, M.: Lattice-based zk-SNARKs from square span programs. In: Lie, D., Mannan, M., Backes, M., Wang, X. (eds.) ACM Conference on Computer and Communications Security, pp. 556–573. ACM (2018). http://dblp.uni-trier.de/db/conf/ccs/ccs2018.html#GennaroMNO18

21. Gentry, C.: Fully homomorphic encryption using ideal lattices, pp. 169–178 (2009). https://doi.org/10.1145/1536414.1536440

22. Gentry, C., Wichs, D.: Separating succinct non-interactive arguments from all falsifiable assumptions, pp. 99–108 (2011). https://doi.org/10.1145/1993636.1993651

23. Goldreich, O., Håstad, J.: On the complexity of interactive proofs with bounded communication. Inf. Process. Lett. **67**(4), 205–214 (1998). https://doi.org/10.1016/S0020-0190(98)00116-1

24. Goldreich, O., Vadhan, S., Wigderson, A.: On interactive proofs with a laconic prover. Comput. Complex. **11**(1–2), 1–53 (2002). https://doi.org/10.1007/s00037-002-0169-0

25. Goldwasser, S., Micali, S., Rackoff, C.: The knowledge complexity of interactive proof systems. SIAM J. Comput. **18**(1), 186–208 (1989)

26. Groth, J.: Short pairing-based non-interactive zero-knowledge arguments. In: Abe, M. (ed.) ASIACRYPT 2010. LNCS, vol. 6477, pp. 321–340. Springer, Heidelberg (2010). https://doi.org/10.1007/978-3-642-17373-8_19

27. Groth, J.: On the size of pairing-based non-interactive arguments. In: Fischlin, M., Coron, J.-S. (eds.) EUROCRYPT 2016. LNCS, vol. 9666, pp. 305–326. Springer, Heidelberg (2016). https://doi.org/10.1007/978-3-662-49896-5_11

28. Groth, J., Maller, M.: Snarky signatures: minimal signatures of knowledge from simulation-extractable SNARKs. In: Katz, J., Shacham, H. (eds.) CRYPTO 2017. LNCS, vol. 10402, pp. 581–612. Springer, Cham (2017). https://doi.org/10.1007/978-3-319-63715-0_20

29. Håstad, J., Impagliazzo, R., Levin, L.A., Luby, M.: A pseudorandom generator from any one-way function. SIAM J. Comput. **28**(4), 1364–1396 (1999)

30. Kilian, J.: A note on efficient zero-knowledge proofs and arguments (extended abstract), pp. 723–732 (1992). https://doi.org/10.1145/129712.129782

31. Kim, S., Wu, D.J.: Multi-theorem preprocessing NIZKs from lattices. In: Shacham, H., Boldyreva, A. (eds.) CRYPTO 2018. LNCS, vol. 10992, pp. 733–765. Springer, Cham (2018). https://doi.org/10.1007/978-3-319-96881-0_25

32. Libert, B., Ling, S., Nguyen, K., Wang, H.: Lattice-based zero-knowledge arguments for integer relations. In: Shacham, H., Boldyreva, A. (eds.) CRYPTO 2018. LNCS, vol. 10992, pp. 700–732. Springer, Cham (2018). https://doi.org/10.1007/978-3-319-96881-0_24

33. Lipmaa, H.: Progression-free sets and sublinear pairing-based non-interactive zero-knowledge arguments. In: Cramer, R. (ed.) TCC 2012. LNCS, vol. 7194, pp. 169–189. Springer, Heidelberg (2012). https://doi.org/10.1007/978-3-642-28914-9_10

34. Lipmaa, H.: Succinct non-interactive zero knowledge arguments from span programs and linear error-correcting codes. In: Sako, K., Sarkar, P. (eds.) ASIACRYPT 2013. LNCS, vol. 8269, pp. 41–60. Springer, Heidelberg (2013). https://doi.org/10.1007/978-3-642-42033-7_3

35. Micali, S.: CS proofs (extended abstracts), pp. 436–453 (1994). https://doi.org/10.1109/SFCS.1994.365746

36. Micciancio, D., Peikert, C.: Hardness of SIS and LWE with small parameters. In: Canetti, R., Garay, J.A. (eds.) CRYPTO 2013. LNCS, vol. 8042, pp. 21–39. Springer, Heidelberg (2013). https://doi.org/10.1007/978-3-642-40041-4_2

37. Micciancio, D., Regev, O.: Worst-case to average-case reductions based on Gaussian measures, pp. 372–381 (2004). https://doi.org/10.1109/FOCS.2004.72

38. Naor, M.: On cryptographic assumptions and challenges (invited talk), pp. 96–109 (2003). https://doi.org/10.1007/978-3-540-45146-46

39. Parno, B., Howell, J., Gentry, C., Raykova, M.: Pinocchio: nearly practical verifiable computation, pp. 238–252 (2013). https://doi.org/10.1109/SP.2013.47

40. Regev, O.: On lattices, learning with errors, random linear codes, and cryptography, pp. 84–93 (2005). https://doi.org/10.1145/1060590.1060603

41. Shor, P.W.: Polynomial-time algorithms for prime factorization and discrete logarithms on a quantum computer. SIAM Rev. **41**(2), 303–332 (1999). http://dblp.uni-trier.de/db/journals/siamrev/siamrev41.html#Shor99

42. Wee, H.: On round-efficient argument systems. In: Caires, L., Italiano, G.F., Monteiro, L., Palamidessi, C., Yung, M. (eds.) ICALP 2005. LNCS, vol. 3580, pp. 140–152. Springer, Heidelberg (2005). https://doi.org/10.1007/11523468_12

Compact and Simple RLWE Based Key Encapsulation Mechanism

Erdem Alkım[1], Yusuf Alper Bilgin[2,3(✉)], and Murat Cenk[3]

[1] Department of Computer Engineering, Ondokuz Mayıs University, Samsun, Turkey
erdemalkim@gmail.com
[2] Aselsan Inc., Ankara, Turkey
y.alperbilgin@gmail.com
[3] Institude of Applied Mathematics, Middle East Technical University,
Ankara, Turkey
mcenk@metu.edu.tr

Abstract. In this paper, we propose a key encapsulation scheme based on NEWHOPE and KYBER, two NIST post-quantum standardization project candidates. Our scheme is based on NEWHOPE, thus it is simple and has fast implementation while it is making use of smaller key sizes and easily changeable security level advantages of KYBER. The scheme heavily use recent advances on Number Theoretic Transform (NTT) in a way that transformation from one degree polynomial to another is easy. To make it possible, we changed the definition of component in component-wise multiplication during polynomial multiplication and show that changing security level only requires to change the size of polynomial and the definition of component. Our scheme has 11.5% smaller communication cost for the same security level comparing with NEWHOPE. In addition, it is at least 17% faster C implementation comparing with non-optimized KYBER implementation from the first round of the NIST standardization process.

Keywords: Post-quantum key encapsulation ·
Lattice-based cryptography · RLWE · NTT

1 Introduction

NIST has initiated a standardization process for quantum-safe public key algorithms including digital signatures and key encapsulation mechanisms (KEM) in 2016 [5,15]. The first round of evaluation was completed and NIST announced the second round candidates [1], which contain 17 KEMs and 9 digital signature schemes. As stated in [1,5,16], *"performance considerations will NOT play a major role in the early portion of the evaluation process."*. Therefore, the performance was not the main consideration but instead NIST considered the security and cost as primary factors in its decision. However, the significance of the implementation performance will increase and it will be one of the main criterion after the second round. Hence, the performance is more important than ever.

© Springer Nature Switzerland AG 2019
P. Schwabe and N. Thériault (Eds.): LATINCRYPT 2019, LNCS 11774, pp. 237–256, 2019.
https://doi.org/10.1007/978-3-030-30530-7_12

Among all second round candidates, 7 out of 17 KEMs and 3 out of 9 digital signature schemes are based on structured lattices. Therefore, their performance depend heavily on polynomial arithmetic in a ring of integer polynomials modulo an irreducible polynomials over the rationals denoted as $\mathbb{Z}_q/(f(x))$. In other words, polynomial arithmetic is one of the most important part of structured lattice-based post-quantum safe algorithms since the main mathematical elements of such algorithms are polynomials. The most complex and time consuming polynomial arithmetic is polynomial multiplication for such schemes. Although standard polynomial multiplication is very trivial, it consumes a lot of cpu cycles due to their quadratic complexity. There are many efficient algorithms to handle polynomial multiplication efficiently such as Number Theoretic Transform (NTT), Karatsuba or Tom-Cook multiplications. NTT, which is a special case of Fast Fourier Transform (FFT) over finite fields, has been shown to be a powerful algorithm in order to perform the polynomial multiplication over finite fields for some type of lattice-based cryptography [2,3,7,11,17]. NTT transform does not require any extra memory space, and it is highly vectorizable. That's why it is preferred by some of the lattice-based cryptographic primitives. Another reason for choosing NTT multiplication over other multiplication methods is that the random polynomials can be directly sampled in NTT domain so that one can save the cost of some forward NTTs. NewHope and Kyber are two important NIST post-quantum standardization project candidates that are utilizing NTT to handle polynomial arithmetic efficiently.

Implementing lattice-based schemes by using Single Input Multiple Data (SIMD) instructions are quite popular since NTT is easily vectorizable in this setting. NewHope is one of the fastest NTT implementation by using floating point instructions. However, these instructions work on 64 bit double values, although the coefficients of NewHope are only 14 bits. In [17], Seiler introduced the use of integer instructions with a modification of the original Montgomery reduction algorithm [14]. The integer instructions can work on 16 bit values. This is much more efficient than the floating point instructions because one 256 bit AVX2 register can hold 16 coefficients instead of just 4 coefficients. This approach can significantly speed up AVX2 implementation of NewHope. Moreover, the latest results of [3,12,19] show that with a little modification in NTT transformation during polynomial multiplication, one can reduce the size of prime. This modification is to not carry out the full NTT, but rather stop it before reaching the level of base field arithmetic. Hence, the congruence condition on the prime modulus is relaxed and a smaller prime is possible. This also means that the coefficient-wise multiplications in NTT domain are done on polynomials instead of integer coefficients. These polynomial multiplications are performed with schoolbook or Karatsuba methods.

Contributions: This paper presents a fast, compact and simple variant of NewHope called as NewHope-Compact. It makes use of the advantages of both NewHope and Kyber. The prime of NewHope is reduced to 3329 from 12289 by following the techniques used by [3,12,19]. Therefore, while the sizes of secret and public keys are almost as small as KYBER's, the security is based on the hardness of solving RLWE problem instead of module learning with errors (MLWE) problem. Consequently, instead of working with matrices or vectors of polynomials, we only deal with polynomials. Moreover, NEWHOPE has 1280 bytes ($n = 512$) or 2560 bytes ($n = 1024$) precomputed values, and these values are different while NEWHOPE-COMPACT has only 256 bytes in total and they are the same for both ($n = 512$) and ($n = 1024$). There is also no need for a bit-reversal table as in NEWHOPE whose size is 512 bytes ($n = 512$) or 1024 bytes ($n = 1024$). Therefore, even for constrained devices switching the security level is easy.

Availability of the Software: All of the software described in this paper available online at https://github.com/erdemalkim/NewHopeCompact and https://github.com/alperbilgin/NewHopeCompact.

Organization of This Paper: Sect. 2 gives an overview of NTT, and how it is used for fast polynomial multiplication. It also describes a different NTT-based polynomial multiplication approach given by [13], and recently used by [3,12]. Section 3 discusses the complexity of the revisited NTT-based polynomial multiplication algorithm. Section 4 provides our implementation details and parameter sets for NEWHOPE-COMPACT. Finally, our performance results for NEWHOPE-COMPACT and a comparison with reference (non-optimized) implementations of NEWHOPE and KYBER are presented in Sect. 5.

2   Preliminaries

2.1   Notation

Let q be a prime number, n be a power of two. The quotient ring $\mathbb{Z}/q\mathbb{Z}$ is denoted as $\mathbb{Z}_q$. q is selected in such a way that a useful primitive root of unity is available. We define $\mathcal{R} = \mathbb{Z}[X]/(X^n+1)$ as the ring of integer polynomials modulo X^n+1. Then, $\mathcal{R}_q = \mathbb{Z}_q[X]/(X^n+1)$ is defined as the ring of integer polynomials modulo $X^n + 1$ such that every coefficient is in $\mathbb{Z}_q$. Let a be a polynomial in $\mathcal{R}_q$. Then, a can be written as $a = \sum_{i=0}^{n-1} a_i X^i$ where $a_i \in \mathbb{Z}_q$.

2.2   Polynomial Multiplication Utilizing NTT

Let a, b, and $c \in \mathcal{R}_q$. If the parameters n and q are selected such that $q \equiv 1 \mod 2n$, the multiplication of $c = a \cdot b \mod (X^n + 1)$ can be calculated efficiently by utilizing NTT. The reason for the condition $q \equiv 1 \mod 2n$ is that a primitive n-th root of unity ω exists. This multiplication can be written as $c = \mathsf{NTT}^{-1}(\mathsf{NTT}(a) \circ \mathsf{NTT}(b))$ where NTT^{-1} denotes inverse NTT, $\circ$ denotes coefficient-wise multiplication. NTT and NTT^{-1} formulae are written as follows:

$$NTT(a) = \hat{a} = \sum_{i=0}^{n-1} \hat{a}_i X^i, \text{ where } \hat{a}_i = \sum_{j=0}^{n-1} a_j \omega^{ij} \mod q,$$

$$NTT^{-1}(\hat{a}) = a = \sum_{i=0}^{n-1} a_i X^i, \text{ where } a_i = \left(n^{-1} \sum_{j=0}^{n-1} \hat{a}_j \omega^{-ij}\right) \mod q.$$

The multiplication of $c = a \cdot b$ includes 2 forward NTTs, one inverse NTT, and n coefficient-wise multiplications. There are two different approaches to calculate forward NTT and inverse NTT efficiently. These are the FFT Trick and the Twisted FFT Trick which are explained in details in [10]. The FFT Trick is followed by KYBER and it leads to Cooley-Tukey butterfly [4] in forward NTT and Gentleman-Sande butterfly [6] in NTT^{-1}. On the other hand, the Twisted FFT Trick is followed by NEWHOPE and it leads to Gentleman-Sande butterfly in both forward and inverse NTT. This paper focuses on KYBER choice due to the use of signed integers which leads to faster AVX2 implementation as mentioned before. The pseudocode for NTT based on the Cooley-Tukey butterfly and NTT^{-1} based on the Gentleman-Sande butterfly are given in Algorithm 1 and Algorithm 2 respectively.

Algorithm 1. NTT based on the Cooley-Tukey butterfly

Input: A polynomial $a \in \mathcal{R}_q$ where i-th coefficient of a is denoted as $a[i]$, $0 \leq i < n$, and a precomputed table of Γ which stores $\Gamma[i] = \gamma^{brv(i)}$ where $brv(i) = \sum_{j=0}^{\log_2(n)-1}(((i >> j)\&1) << (\log_2(n) - 1 - i)$, $0 \leq i < n$.
Output: $\hat{a} \leftarrow NTT(a)$ in bit-reversed ordering.

```
 1: function NTT(a)
 2:    i ← 1
 3:    for ℓ ← n/2; ℓ ≥ 1; ℓ ← ℓ/2 do
 4:       for s ← 0; s < n; s ← s + ℓ do
 5:          g ← Γ[i]
 6:          for j ← s; j < s + ℓ; j ← j + 1 do
 7:             t ← g · a[j + ℓ] (mod q)
 8:             a[j + ℓ] ← a[j] − t (mod q)
 9:             a[j] ← a[j] + t (mod q)
10:          end for
11:          i ← i + 1
12:       end for
13:    end for
14:    return â
15: end function
```

2.3 A Different Polynomial Multiplication Approach

The standard polynomial multiplication utilizing NTT is $c = NTT^{-1}(NTT(a) \circ NTT(b))$ where $a, b,$ and $c \in \mathcal{R}_q$. This NTTs contain $k = \log_2 n$ levels where

Algorithm 2. NTT^{-1} based on the Gentleman-Sande butterfly

Input: A polynomial $c \in \mathcal{R}_q$ in bit-reversed ordering where i-th coefficient of c is denoted as $c[i]$, $0 \leq i < n$, and a precomputed table of Γ^{-1} which stores $\Gamma^{-1}[i] = \gamma^{-(brv(i)+1)}$ where $brv(i) = \sum_{l=0}^{\log_2(n)-1}(((i >> l)\&1) << (\log_2(n) - 1 - i), 0 \leq i < n$.
Output: $c \leftarrow \mathsf{NTT}^{-1}(\hat{c})$ in standard ordering.

```
 1: function NTT⁻¹(c)
 2:     i ← 0
 3:     for ℓ ← 1; ℓ < n; ℓ ← 2 · ℓ do
 4:         for s ← 0; s < n; s ← j + ℓ do
 5:             g ← Γ⁻¹[i]
 6:             for j ← s; j < s + ℓ; j ← j + 1 do
 7:                 t ← a[j]
 8:                 a[j] ← t + a[j + ℓ] (mod q)
 9:                 a[j + ℓ] ← g · (t − a[j + ℓ]) (mod q)
10:             end for
11:             i ← i + 1
12:         end for
13:     end for
14:     for j ← 0; j < n; j ← j + 1 do
15:         c[j] ← c[j]/n
16:     end for
17:     return c
18: end function
```

$n - 1$ is the degree of polynomials. Although this polynomial multiplication is very efficient, it is interesting to see that if one stops at the $(k-1)$-th level or even the $(k-2)$-th or $(k-3)$-th levels instead of applying all k levels, the multiplication of two polynomials might be faster. This is an important observation first made by [13].

KYBER: The round 2 submission of KYBER includes an update in the definition of NTT. This update corresponds to stop NTT at 7-th level instead of applying a full NTT which is 8-level. Algorithms 1 and 2 can be still used with only minor modifications. The modification in Algorithm 1 is that $(\ell \geq 1)$ condition at line 3 is replaced with $(\ell \geq 2)$ while in Algorithm 2 $(\ell \leftarrow 1)$ at line 3 is replaced with $(\ell \leftarrow 2)$, and n at lines 14 and 15 is replaced with $n/2$. These changes also affect the coefficient-wise multiplications while multiplying two polynomials in $\mathcal{R}_q$ such that they are performed on small polynomials in $\mathbb{Z}_q/(X^2 - r)$ instead of integer coefficients. The schoolbook multiplication method to multiply two coefficients in $\mathbb{Z}_q/(X^2 - r)$ is given in Algorithm 3.

A NTT-based polynomial multiplication consists of two forward NTT and one inverse NTT. By using the new approach, one can save three levels of NTT in total, two forward and one inverse. The total cost of each NTT level is $n/2$ additions, $n/2$ subtractions, and $n/2$ multiplications. Therefore, the total saving is $3n/2$ additions, $3n/2$ subtractions, and $3n/2$ multiplications. However, apart

---

Algorithm 3. Multiplication of polynomials in $\mathbb{Z}_q/(X^2 - r)$

Input: a and $b \in \mathbb{Z}_q/(X^2 - r)$ where r is a power of γ. i-th coefficient of a is denoted as $a[i]$ where $0 \le i < 2$.

Output: $c \in \mathbb{Z}_q/(X^2 - r)$.

1: **function** basemul(a, b)
2:      $c[0] \leftarrow a[1] \cdot b[1]$
3:      $c[0] \leftarrow c[0] \cdot r$ ▷ · for modular reduction
4:      $c[0] \leftarrow c[0] + (a[0] \cdot b[0])$ ▷ + for modular reduction
5:      $c[1] \leftarrow a[0] \cdot b[1]$
6:      $c[1] \leftarrow c[1] + (a[1] \cdot b[0])$
7:      **return** c
8: **end function**

---

from NTT calculations there is also coefficient-wise multiplications or polynomial multiplications according to the approach used. The standard approach has n coefficient-wise multiplications, while the new approach has polynomial multiplications which contain $n/2$ additions, $n/2$ subtractions, and $5n/2$ multiplications. Although the multiplication counts are the same in total ($5n/2$ for both), the new approach has n additions, and n subtractions less than the standard approach. Besides from this advantage, it has a more important advantage that is hidden in the definition of NTT. In order to have a ring allowing fast multiplication using NTT, schemes based on RLWE problem usually select n as a power of two such that $n = 2^k$. In order to have a primitive n-th root of unity, the prime q is selected such that $q \equiv 1 \mod 2n$. Therefore, it can be fully split, and k level NTT can be calculated efficiently. However, the new approach does not require k level NTT. Instead, $k - 1$ level is enough for polynomial multiplication in $\mathcal{R}_q$. Therefore, $n/2$-th root of unity is sufficient for the calculation, and q can be selected such that $q \equiv 1 \mod n$. If one decides to stop at another level ℓ instead of $k - 1$, then the selection of q should satisfy $q \equiv 1 \mod (n/2^{k-\ell-1})$. The degrees of the resulting polynomials after NTT will be $2^{k-\ell}$. Therefore, these polynomials will be represented in $\mathbb{Z}_q[X]/(X^{2^{k-\ell}} \pm \gamma^{brv[i]+1})$ where brv is defined as below:

$$brv(v) = \sum_{i=0}^{\ell-1} (((v >> i)\&1) << (\ell - 1 - i)).$$

Then, the polynomial multiplication is performed in $\mathbb{Z}_q[X]/(X^{2^{k-\ell}} \pm \gamma^{brv[i]+1})$. Finally, by taking ℓ level NTT^{-1}, one can get the result of the multiplication of two polynomials in $\mathcal{R}_q$.

There are two recent studies which use this polynomial multiplication approach apart from KYBER [3]. One of the similar approaches is [19]. It first represents the input degree n polynomial as two degree $n/2$ polynomials. Then, it applies $k - 1$ level NTT to both of them. The multiplication of two polynomials in their NTT domain representation is similar to the method described above. Finally, the inverse NTTs of two degree $n/2$ polynomials are taken separately. Although the approach is similar, their results is not as fast as KYBER. Their performance is even slower than the standard NTT-based multiplication approach. Another scheme that uses a similar approach is [12]. Their ring structure, $\mathbb{Z}_{7681}[X]/(X^{768}-X^{384}+1)$, is different. It is observed that this ring can be split up to $X^3 \pm r$. Therefore, 8 level NTT can be applied to the polynomials in this ring. Then, the multiplication can be performed in $\mathbb{Z}_{7681}[X]/(X^3 \pm r)$. Finally, by taking 8 level inverse NTT, one can get the result. Note that all of these approaches are given by [13] as "The Mixed Basis FFT Multiplication Algorithm" for $n = 2^k \cdot \ell$, where the cases $\ell = 1, 3, 5,$ or 7 are considered. However, if ℓ is chosen a small multiple of 2, it will be faster than the standard NTT-based multiplication approach according to their complexity analysis.

3   A Complexity Analysis of Polynomial Multiplication Methods

Standard Multiplication Utilizing NTT: n-term polynomial multiplication utilizing NTT consists of two forward NTT, one inverse NTT, and n coefficient-wise multiplications. Although this is not always the case, we assume that Cooley-Tukey, Fig. 1, and Gentleman Sande, Fig. 2, butterflies are used for forward and inverse NTT respectively.

Fig. 1. Cooley-Tukey butterfly   **Fig. 2.** Gentleman-Sande butterfly

Let's start with the computation cost of the Cooley-Tukey butterfly. As can be seen in Fig. 1, 2-term butterfly costs one multiplication, one addition, and one subtraction. Let's calculate subtraction as addition for simplicity, since $a - b$ can be written as $a + (-b)$. Therefore, the cost of 2-term 1-level NTT is one multiplication and two additions. The cost of 4-term 2-level NTT is two times of 2-term 1-level NTT, two multiplications, and four additions.

Proposition 1. *The cost of n-term NTT can be computed with the following recurrence relation:*

$$T(n) = 2 \cdot T\left(\frac{n}{2}\right) + \frac{n}{2} \cdot M + n \cdot A,$$

where $T(1) = 0$, M and A stand for multiplication and addition, and n is the number of coefficients, which it is a power of two.

Proof. Let $n = 2^k$. The computation cost of each NTT level is $n/2$ multiplications and n additions. If we divide this polynomial as two $n/2$-term polynomials, $k - 1$-level NTT is possible and each NTT levels of these polynomials costs $n/4$ multiplications and $n/2$ additions since there are $n/2$ terms. Therefore, the sum of the computation costs for each NTT levels of two $n/2$-term polynomials is equal to the cost of each NTT levels of n-term polynomial. Consequently, k-level NTT is constituted of two $(n/2)$-term $(k-1)$-level NTTs plus the last level which includes $n/2$ multiplications and n additions like all other levels.

The recursion given in Proposition 1 yields

$$T(n) = \frac{k}{2} \cdot n \cdot M + k \cdot n \cdot A,$$

where $k = \log_2 n$.

The cost of the Gentleman-Sande butterfly is equal to the cost of the Cooley-Tukey butterfly since the same number of operations are required for both of them as it can be seen from Figs. 1 and 2. Therefore, the total computation cost of multiplying two n-term polynomials in $\mathcal{R}_q$ is

$$PM(n) = 3 \cdot T(n) + n \cdot M,$$
$$= \frac{3k + 2}{2} \cdot n \cdot M + 3k \cdot n \cdot A.$$

An Analysis of $k - 1$ Level NTT then Schoolbook Multiplication: This method is described in Sect. 2.3. It requires two forward and one inverse NTTs as in the previous method. However, this time NTTs have $k - 1$ levels. Note that $2 \cdot T(n/2)$ operations are already performed up to the last level. This method just stops there and leaves the calculations required for the last level which are $n/2 \cdot M + n \cdot A$. Therefore, we need to use $2 \cdot T(n/2)$ instead of $T(n)$ in our calculations for the cost of NTT.

Proposition 2. *The multiplication of two polynomials in modulo $\mathbb{Z}_q[X]/(X^2 - r)$ costs five multiplications and two additions including modular reduction in modulo $(X^2 - r)$.*

Proof. This multiplication algorithm is given in Algorithm 3. One multiplies two polynomials in modulo $\mathbb{Z}_q[X]/(X^2 - r)$ with $(2^2 = 4)$ multiplications and one addition (computed with the formula given by [9]). The modular reduction also needs one more multiplication with r and one addition. Hence, in total it costs five multiplications and two additions.

The result of the multiplication of two small polynomials in modulo $\mathbb{Z}_q[X]/(X^2-r)$ gives us two coefficients as can be seen in Algorithm 3. Therefore, the total cost can be written as

$$
\begin{aligned}
Hybrid\text{-}SM_1(n) &= 3 \cdot 2 \cdot T\left(\frac{n}{2}\right) + \frac{1}{2}\left(5n \cdot M + 2n \cdot A\right), \\
&= \frac{3k-3}{2} \cdot n \cdot M + 3 \cdot n \cdot (k-1) \cdot A + \frac{5n}{2} \cdot M + n \cdot A, \\
&= \frac{3k+2}{2} \cdot n \cdot M + (3k-2) \cdot n \cdot A.
\end{aligned}
$$

An Analysis of $k-2$ Level NTT then Schoolbook Multiplication:

Proposition 3. *To multiply two polynomials in modulo $\mathbb{Z}_q[X]/(X^4-r)$ by using schoolbook multiplication, we need to perform 19 multiplications and 12 additions including modular reductions in modulo $(X^4 - r)$.*

Proof. This multiplication algorithm is given in Algorithm 4. The multiplication of two 4 coefficients polynomial requires $4^2 = 16$ multiplications and $3^2 = 9$ additions. Moreover, the modular reduction in modulo $(X^4 - r)$ costs three multiplications and three additions as can be seen from Algorithm 4. Therefore, the multiplication of two small polynomials in modulo $(X^4 - r)$ requires 19 multiplications and 12 additions.

Algorithm 4. Multiplication of polynomials in $\mathbb{Z}_q/(X^4 - r)$

Input: a and $b \in \mathbb{Z}_q/(X^4 - r)$ where r is a power of γ. i-th coefficient of a is denoted as $a[i]$ where $0 \le i < 2$.
Output: $c \in \mathbb{Z}_q/(X^4 - r)$.

```
 1: function basemul(a, b)
 2:     c[0] ← (a[1] · b[3]) + (a[2] · b[2]) + (a[3] · b[1])
 3:     c[0] ← c[0] · r                                          ▷ · for modular reduction
 4:     c[0] ← c[0] + (a[0] · b[0])                              ▷ + for modular reduction
 5:     c[1] ← (a[2] · b[3]) + (a[3] · b[2])
 6:     c[1] ← c[1] · r                                          ▷ · for modular reduction
 7:     c[1] ← c[1] + (a[0] · b[1]) + (a[1] · b[0])              ▷ + for modular reduction
 8:     c[2] ← a[3] · b[3]
 9:     c[2] ← c[2] · r                                          ▷ · for modular reduction
10:     c[2] ← c[2] + (a[0] · b[2]) + (a[1] · b[1]) + (a[2] · b[0])  ▷ + for modular reduction
11:     c[3] ← (a[0] · b[3]) + (a[1] · b[2]) + (a[2] · b[1]) + (a[3] · b[0])
12:     return c
13: end function
```

After the multiplication in modulo (X^4-r), we end up with four coefficients. Therefore, the total cost can be written as

$$Hybrid\text{-}SM_2(n) = 3 \cdot 4 \cdot T\left(\frac{n}{4}\right) + \frac{1}{4}\left(19n \cdot M + 12n \cdot A\right),$$

$$= \frac{3k - 6}{2} \cdot n \cdot M + 3 \cdot n \cdot (k - 2) \cdot A + \frac{19n}{4} \cdot M + 3 \cdot n \cdot A,$$

$$= \frac{6k + 7}{4} \cdot n \cdot M + (3k - 3) \cdot n \cdot A.$$

An Analysis of $k-2$ Level NTT then One-Iteration Karatsuba Multiplication: It is also possible to multiply two polynomials in modulo $\mathbb{Z}_q[X]/(X^4-r)$ by using one-iteration Karatsuba multiplication given by [18]. It requires 10 multiplications and 27 additions without modular reduction. The multiplication of two polynomials in $\mathbb{Z}_q[X]/(X^4-r)$ is given in Algorithm 5.

Algorithm 5. Multiplication of polynomials in $\mathbb{Z}_q/(X^4-r)$

Input: a and $b \in \mathbb{Z}_q/(X^4-r)$ where r is a power of γ. i-th coefficient of a is denoted as $a[i]$ where $0 \le i < 2$.
Output: $c \in \mathbb{Z}_q/(X^4-r)$.

1: **function** basemul(a, b)
2:     $d \leftarrow$ Apply Algorithm 2 of [18] to get $d = a \cdot b$ where d is a degree $2n - 2$ polynomial
3:     $c[0] \leftarrow d[0] + d[4] \cdot r$ ▷ $+$ and $\cdot$ for modular reduction
4:     $c[1] \leftarrow d[1] + d[5] \cdot r$ ▷ $+$ and $\cdot$ for modular reduction
5:     $c[2] \leftarrow d[2] + d[6] \cdot r$ ▷ $+$ and $\cdot$ for modular reduction
6:     $c[3] \leftarrow d[3]$
7:     **return** c
8: **end function**

Modular reduction requires three multiplications and three additions as in the previous method and as can be seen in Algorithm 5. Hence, it requires 13 multiplications and 30 additions including modular reductions in modulo $(X^4 - r)$. Then, the total costs of this approach can be written as

$$Hybrid\text{-}KM_2(n) = 3 \cdot 4 \cdot T\left(\frac{n}{4}\right) + \frac{1}{4}\left(13n \cdot M + 30n \cdot A\right),$$

$$= \frac{3k - 6}{2} \cdot n \cdot M + 3 \cdot n \cdot (k - 2) \cdot A + \frac{13n}{4} \cdot M + \frac{30n}{4} \cdot A,$$

$$= \frac{6k + 1}{4} \cdot n \cdot M + \left(3k + \frac{3}{2}\right) \cdot n \cdot A.$$

An Analysis of $k - 3$ Level NTT then Schoolbook Multiplication:

Proposition 4. *The multiplication in modulo $\mathbb{Z}_q[X]/(X^8-r)$ is performed with 71 multiplications and 56 additions including modular reductions in modulo $(X^8 - r)$.*

Proof. The multiplication of two degree seven polynomials require $8^2 = 64$ multiplications and $7^2 = 49$ additions. The modular reduction in modulo $(X^8 - r)$ takes seven multiplications with r and seven additions. Therefore, in total this multiplication is performed with 71 multiplications and 56 additions.

After the multiplication in modulo $\mathbb{Z}_q[X]/(X^8 - r)$, we get eight coefficients. Therefore, the total cost is

$$
\begin{aligned}
Hybrid\text{-}SM_3(n) &= 3 \cdot 8 \cdot T\left(\frac{n}{8}\right) + \frac{1}{8}\left(71n \cdot M + 56n \cdot A\right), \\
&= \frac{3k - 9}{2} \cdot n \cdot M + 3 \cdot n \cdot (k - 3) \cdot A + \frac{71n}{8} \cdot M + 7 \cdot n \cdot A, \\
&= \frac{12k + 35}{8} \cdot n \cdot M + (3k - 2) \cdot n \cdot A.
\end{aligned}
$$

An Analysis of $k - 3$ Level NTT then One-Iteration Karatsuba Multiplication: The multiplication of two degree seven polynomials costs 36 multiplications and 133 additions without modular reductions by using one-iteration Karatsuba multiplication of [18]. The modular reduction in modulo $(X^8 - r)$ of the multiplication of two degree seven polynomials requires seven multiplications and seven additions as in the previous method. Altogether it costs 43 multiplications and 140 additions with the modular reduction in modulo $(X^8 - r)$. After the multiplication, we get eight coefficients. Therefore, the total cost for this implementation is

$$
\begin{aligned}
Hybrid\text{-}KM_3(n) &= 3 \cdot 8 \cdot T\left(\frac{n}{8}\right) + \frac{1}{8}\left(43n \cdot M + 140n \cdot A\right), \\
&= \frac{3k - 9}{2} \cdot n \cdot M + 3 \cdot n \cdot (k - 3) \cdot A + \frac{43n}{8} \cdot M + \frac{140n}{8} \cdot A, \\
&= \left(\frac{12k + 7}{8}\right) \cdot n \cdot M + \left(3k + \frac{17}{2}\right) \cdot n \cdot A.
\end{aligned}
$$

The summary of all methods can be found on Table 1. Although this is not directly seen from Table 1, multiplication counts are more important than addition. Because if one uses integer words in implementation with a Montgomery reduction is definitely needed after every multiplications, the Barrett reduction might be omitted after an addition. These omitted reductions are called as lazy reductions. The number of possible joint lazy reductions increases as q decreases from the next computer word. As mentioned before, the bounds on q are looser when fewer NTT levels are applied. On the other hand, the operation counts increase when the applied NTT level number decreases. Therefore, there is a trade-off between the two. We decided to move on with $k - 2$ level for $(n = 512)$ and $k - 3$ level for $(n = 1024)$ since this enables the same q selection for both of them. Moreover, Karatsuba multiplication is preferred for NEWHOPE-COMPACT.

Table 1. The computation costs of different polynomial multiplication algorithms. The total number of multiplication and addition numbers to multiply two polynomials in $\mathcal{R}_q$.

Multiplication methods	Operations	
	Multiplications	Additions
NTT-based Multiplication	$\dfrac{12k+8}{8} \cdot n$	$3k \cdot n$
Hybrid Schoolbook-1 Multiplication	$\dfrac{12k+8}{8} \cdot n$	$(3k-2) \cdot n$
Hybrid Schoolbook-2 Multiplication	$\dfrac{12k+14}{8} \cdot n$	$(3k-3) \cdot n$
Hybrid Karatsuba-2 Multiplication	$\dfrac{12k+2}{8} \cdot n$	$\left(3k+\dfrac{3}{2}\right) \cdot n$
Hybrid Schoolbook-3 Multiplication	$\dfrac{12k+35}{8} \cdot n$	$(3k-2) \cdot n$
Hybrid Karatsuba-3 Multiplication	$\dfrac{12k+7}{8} \cdot n$	$\left(3k+\dfrac{17}{2}\right) \cdot n$

Note that applying these multiplication methods to KYBER give different computation costs, since the elements are represented as vectors or matrices of polynomials instead of just polynomials. Their polynomials are smaller. However, vector or matrix representation removes this advantage, and add an extra complexity.

4   Implementation Details

Let's recall some important parts of NEWHOPE algorithm first. Refer to [2] for full explanations.

Sampling: The secret and error terms are sampled by using the centered binomial distribution ψ_8. Sampling from ψ_8 is computed with the formula $\sum_{i=0}^{7} b_i - b_i'$ where the $b_i, b_i' \in \{0, 1\}$ are uniform independent bits. These bits are generated with SHAKE256 which generates 128 bytes of random on each call. These 128 bytes used to construct 64 coefficients, since each of them needs 16 random bits (2 bytes) to be computed. In order to generate all coefficients of a polynomial, SHAKE256 should be called 8 or 16 times for NEWHOPE512 or NEWHOPE1024 respectively.

NTT and NTT^{-1}: NEWHOPE follows the Twisted FFT Trick. Meaning that it uses Gentleman-Sande butterflies for both forward and inverse NTTs. After a full level forward NTT, which is 9 for NEWHOPE512 and 10 for NEWHOPE1024, coefficient-wise multiplication is performed. This is the standard NTT-based polynomial multiplication, and it is described in Sect. 2.2.

GenA: The public parameter **a** is generated by using this function. It takes 32 bytes random seed and generates **a** by expanding this seed with SHAKE128. This is one of the most time consuming parts of the algorithm.

Encoding and Decoding of the Secret and Public Key: The coefficients of secret and public key polynomials are encoded into a byte array. Each coefficients consists of 14 bits due to the size of the selected prime. Therefore, all coefficients can be mapped to 896 bytes (NEWHOPE512) or 1792 bytes (NEWHOPE1024). The public key also includes 32 bytes seed to generate the public parameter **a**, for a total of 928 bytes (NEWHOPE512) or 1824 bytes (NEWHOPE1024). Decoding is the reverse of this operation, mapping a byte array to a polynomial.

Encoding and Decoding of the Ciphertext: The 32 byte message is encoded into a polynomial in $\mathcal{R}_q$. Each bit of the message is encoded into $\lfloor n/256 \rfloor$ coefficients to allow robustness against errors. Then, this polynomial is encrypted. The result of the encryption has two polynomials in $\mathcal{R}_q$, the public key polynomial u and another polynomial v'. u is encoded in the same way with the public key **a**. On the other hand, v' is compressed by performing a modulus switching between modulus q and modulus 8. The total size of the ciphertext, containing u and v', after these encoding and compression is 1088 bytes (NEWHOPE512) or 2176 bytes (NEWHOPE1024).

The parameter sets of NEWHOPE are given on Table 2.

Table 2. Parameters of NEWHOPE512 and NEWHOPE1024 and derived high level properties [2]

Parameter set	NEWHOPE512	NEWHOPE1024
Dimension n	512	1024
Modulus q	12289	12289
Noise parameter k	8	8
NTT parameter γ	10968	7
Decryption error probability	2^{-213}	2^{-216}
Claimed post-quantum bit security	101	233
NIST Security Strength Category	1	5

Our first design decision is to use the FFT Trick so that Cooley-Tukey butterfly in forward NTT and Gentleman Sande butterfly in reverse NTT are used and keep the level number of NTTs at 7 and same for all n values so that the parameters modulus q, noise parameter k, and NTT parameter γ remain unchanged. This provides simplicity, and less functions are affected when the ring is changed. This makes switching from one parameter set to another and changing the security level easy. The only changing part is the multiplication of coefficients in NTT representation. NTT and NTT^{-1} functions are exactly the same for both $(n = 512)$ and $(n = 1024)$. In consequence, the precomputed powers of γ and γ^{-1} are same for both and only 256 bytes in total unlike the original NTT implementation for NEWHOPE ring which requires at least 1536 bytes for $(n = 512)$ and totally different 3072 bytes for $(n = 1024)$. There is also no need for a bit-reversal table which costs 1024 bytes $(n = 512)$ or 2048 bytes $(n = 1024)$ unlike the original NEWHOPE. In other words, the new implementation requires at least 2560 bytes memory less in total which can be very important for constrained devices. This also enables having both security level together at the same device without a memory penalty. Our level choice for NTT is 7 as mentioned before. This implies $k - 2$ level NTT approach $(n = 512)$ or $k - 3$ level NTT approach $(n = 1024)$, since the total level number is 9 or 10 respectively. Therefore, the coefficients after 7 level NTT is in fact a term of a polynomial in $\mathbb{Z}_q[X]/(X^4 \pm r)$ for $(n = 512)$ and $\mathbb{Z}_q[X]/(X^8 \pm r)$ for $(n = 1024)$ where r is a power of γ. Moreover, in order to keep NTT and NTT^{-1} functions the same for both $(n = 512)$ and $(n = 1024)$ we reorder the coefficients of input polynomials in such a way that 128-point NTT can be performed. Implementing 512-point or 1024-point NTT and stopping at 7-th level requires different implementations for $(n = 512)$ and $(n = 1024)$ since it requires two coefficients with different lengths at each butterflies. In other words, at the first level u_0 and u_{256} are needed for the first butterfly for $(n = 512)$, on the other hand u_0 and u_{512} are required for $(n = 1024)$ where $u \in \mathcal{R}_q$. The reordering starts with dividing input polynomial in 4 $(n = 512)$ or 8 $(n = 1024)$ equivalent parts. Each parts contains exactly 128 coefficients. Let $u \in \mathbb{Z}_q/(X^{512} + 1)$ and $v \in \mathbb{Z}_q/(X^{1024} + 1)$. They are divided as

$$u_a = (u_0, u_4, u_8, \cdots, u_{512-4}),$$
$$u_b = (u_1, u_5, u_9, \cdots, u_{512-3}),$$
$$u_c = (u_2, u_6, u_{10}, \cdots, u_{512-2}),$$
$$u_d = (u_3, u_7, u_{11}, \cdots, u_{512-1}),$$

$$v_a = (v_0, v_8, v_{16}, \cdots, v_{1024-8}),$$
$$v_b = (v_1, v_9, v_{17}, \cdots, v_{1024-7}),$$
$$v_c = (v_2, v_{10}, v_{18}, \cdots, v_{1024-6}),$$
$$v_d = (v_3, v_{11}, v_{19}, \cdots, v_{1024-5}),$$
$$v_e = (v_4, v_{12}, v_{20}, \cdots, v_{1024-4}),$$
$$v_f = (v_5, v_{13}, v_{21}, \cdots, v_{1024-3}),$$
$$v_g = (v_6, v_{14}, v_{22}, \cdots, v_{1024-2}),$$
$$v_h = (v_7, v_{15}, v_{23}, \cdots, v_{1024-1}).$$

After this reordering process, one can see that applying 7 level 512-point NTT to u is equivalent to applying 7 level 128-point NTT to u_a, u_b, u_c and u_d. However, the result of the latter is not equivalent to the result of the former. Instead, it is reordered just like the input. As a result, the small polynomials in NTT domain are constructed as follows

$$
\begin{aligned}
\hat{x} = (\hat{x}_0 &= u_a(0) + u_b(0) \cdot X + u_c(0) \cdot X^2 + u_d(0) \cdot X^3, \\
\hat{x}_1 &= u_a(1) + u_b(1) \cdot X + u_c(1) \cdot X^2 + u_d(1) \cdot X^3 \\
& \quad \cdot \\
& \quad \cdot \\
& \quad \cdot \\
\hat{x}_{126} &= u_a(126) + u_b(126) \cdot X + u_c(126) \cdot X^2 + u_d(126) \cdot X^3 \\
\hat{x}_{127} &= u_a(127) + u_b(127) \cdot X + u_c(127) \cdot X^2 + u_d(127) \cdot X^3),
\end{aligned}
$$

where $x_i \in \mathbb{Z}_q[X]/(X^4 \pm r)$ for $0 \leq i < 128$. A similar strategy is followed for $(n = 1024)$. The reordering process does not cost anything, because all inputs are randomly generated or distributed so one can assume that they are already reordered. Furthermore, a better vectorization is possible for AVX2 implementation by applying reordering.

Moreover, as discussed in Sect. 2.3, we can now select our q such that it satisfies $q \equiv 1 \mod (512/2^{k-(k-2)-1})$ $(n = 1024)$ or $q \equiv 1 \mod (1024/2^{k-(k-3)-1})$ $(n = 512)$ which both are equal to $q \equiv 1 \mod 256$. The smallest q that satisfies this equality is 3329. In result, we have selected our parameters as shown on Table 3. To analyze the failure probability for our parameters, we follow the approach from [3]. Moreover, the post-quantum bit security of NEWHOPE-COMPACT parameter set is estimated by using "PQSecurity.py" script provided by NEWHOPE. The result of the script is given in Table 4.

Table 3. Parameters of NEWHOPE-COMPACT512 and NEWHOPE-COMPACT1024 and derived high level properties

Parameter set	NH-COMPACT512	NH-COMPACT1024
Dimension n	512	1024
Modulus q	3329	3329
Noise parameter k	2	2
NTT parameter γ	17	17
Decryption error probability	2^{-256}	2^{-181}
Claimed post-quantum bit security	100	230
NIST Security Strength Category	1	5

The new parameter sets speed up the sampling of secret and noise polynomials. They are sampled from ψ_2 now. Sampling from ψ_2 is computed with the formula $\sum_{i=0}^{1} b_i - b_i'$. As mentioned before, the random bits are generated by using SHAKE256 which generates 128 bytes of random on each call. Different from the NEWHOPE sampling function which samples 64 coefficients on each call, we can now sample 256 coefficients at a time.

Table 4. Core hardness of NewHope-Compact512 and NewHope-Compact1024

Attack	m	b	Known classical	Known quantum	Best plausible
NewHope-Compact512: $q = 3329$, $n = 512$, $\varsigma = \sqrt{2}$					
Primal	462	381	111	101	79
Dual	465	380	111	100	78
NewHope-Compact1024: $q = 3329$, $n = 1024$, $\varsigma = \sqrt{2}$					
Primal	841	873	255	231	181
Dual	862	868	253	230	180

The new coefficients are composed of 12 bits instead of 14 bits, since q is reduced to 3329 from 12289. Therefore, all coefficients of the secret key can now be encoded as 1632 bytes ($n = 512$) or 3168 bytes ($n = 1024$). The public key which also includes 32 bytes seed is represented with 800 bytes ($n = 512$) or 1568 bytes ($n = 1024$). Moreover, the total size of the ciphertext decreases to 992 bytes ($n = 512$) or 2080 bytes ($n = 1024$). All of these mentioned sizes are summarized on Table 5.

Table 5. Sizes of public keys, secret keys and ciphertexts of NewHope (denoted as [2]) and NewHope-Compact (denoted as Ours) in bytes

Parameter set	$|pk|$		$|sk|$		$|ciphertext|$	
	[2]	Ours	[2]	Ours	[2]	Ours
512-CCA-KEM	928	800	1888	1632	1120	992
1024-CCA-KEM	1824	1568	3680	3168	2208	2080

5 Results and Comparision

Benchmark tests for all implementations are performed on an Intel Core i7-6500U Skylake processor running at 2500 MHz with Turbo Boost and Hyperthreading disabled. The operating system is Ubuntu 18.04.2 LTS with Linux Kernel 4.15.0, and all softwares are compiled with gcc-7.3.0. For comparisons, we have taken C reference (non-optimized) implementations of NewHope from https://github.com/newhopecrypto/newhope and Kyber from https://github.com/pq-cystals/kyber. We report the median of 10000 executions of the corresponding function for cycle counts.

The benchmark results for reference (non-optimized) C implementations of Kyber, NewHope and NewHope-Compact for security level 1 and 5 are given on Table 6. Our CCA-KEM implementations are 1.21 times ($n = 512$) or 1.13 times ($n = 1024$) faster, and 1.17 times ($n = 512$) or 1.26 times ($n = 1024$) faster than the corresponding implementations of [2] and [3] respectively.

We have used one-iteration Karatsuba multiplication which is mentioned in Sect. 3 as the base multiplication method in our reference C implementations. The main reason for getting a faster implementation than NEWHOPE is the size of q. Since the size of q is reduced by two bits, we can get more benefits from lazy reductions. In fact, for forward NTT, we do not need any modular reduction after an addition or a subtraction, while NEWHOPE requires a modular reduction after an addition at each odd level. On the other hand, KYBER uses the same prime. Therefore, we do not get any benefit from the lazy reductions. The difference in the cycle counts between this work and KYBER is due to the generation of the public parameter a and the difference on the constructions of the schemes.

Note that an optimized avx2 implementation of NEWHOPE-COMPACT would be more precise to compare performance results with other schemes. But that implementation is still work in progress and we left as a future work.

Table 6. Cycle counts of KYBER, NEWHOPE and NEWHOPE-COMPACT C reference (non-optimized) implementations.

Operations	CCA-KEM-512			CCA-KEM-1024		
	KYBER [3]	NEWHOPE [2]	This work	KYBER [3]	NEWHOPE [2]	This work
GEN	121 586	119 163	89 286	324 614	237 791	186 438
ENCAPS	163 996	180 193	147 045	381 360	365 240	320 787
DECAPS	197 532	203 440	176 098	431 408	417 448	394 910
Total	483 114	502 796	412 429	1 137 382	1 020 479	902 135

Thanks to its structure, KYBER is offering a parameter set for NIST security level 3. However, NEWHOPE ring needs to be changed for similar security level. Proposed NTT implementation can be easily adopt such rings, see Appendix A.

Acknowledgments. The authors are grateful to Nicolas Thériault and anonymous referees for helpful comments and discussions on drafts of this paper.

A   An Implementation for n = 768

NEWHOPE does not offer a parameter set for NIST security level 3. However, a recent observation by [12] made it possible by offering a new ring structure $\mathbb{Z}_q/(X^{768} - X^{384} + 1)$. They start with splitting this polynomial into two polynomials of the form $X^{n/2} - \zeta_1$ and $X^{n/2} - \zeta_2$ such that ζ_1 and ζ_2 are two primitive sixth root of unity and $\zeta_1 + \zeta_2 = 1$, $\zeta_1 \cdot \zeta_2 = 1$. The CRT map of this ring is as follows:

$$\mathcal{R}_q = \mathbb{Z}_q[X]/(X^{768} - X^{384} + 1) \rightarrow$$
$$\mathbb{Z}_q[X]/(X^{384} - \zeta_1) \times \mathbb{Z}_q[X]/(X^{384} - \zeta_2)$$

Let $f \in \mathcal{R}_q$. Then, in order to get the coefficients after the first level, we need to compute:

$$g = f \mod (X^{n/2} - \zeta_1), h = f \mod (X^{n/2} - \zeta_2)$$

We know that $\zeta_2 = 1 - \zeta_1$. Therefore, instead of computing $h = f \mod (X^{n/2} - \zeta_2)$ we can compute $h = f \mod (X^{n/2} + 1 - \zeta_1)$. Therefore, the burden of multiplication with ζ_2 to perform the modular reduction is removed. We can benefit from the already computed product with ζ_1. After this trick is applied, it turns out that a standard NTT can be performed. We have 7-level NTT left. We know that $\zeta_1^6 \equiv 1 \mod q$. To be able to perform 7-level NTT by using ζ_1, $\gamma^{128} \equiv \zeta_1 \mod q$ is needed. Then, q needs to satisfy $q \equiv 1 \mod 768$. The smallest q that satisfies this condition is 7681. That's why, [12] selects q as 7681 and γ such that it satisfies $\gamma^{128} \equiv \zeta_1 \mod 7681$. This also implies that $\gamma^{640} \equiv \zeta_2 \mod 7681$, since $\zeta_1^5 = \zeta_2$. After NTT, there are 256 polynomials of degree 3 in $\mathbb{Z}_q[X]/(X^3 \pm r)$.

In order to keep our total NTT level the same for all of our implementations, we changed the parameters of [12]. Our algorithm for $n = 512$ and $n = 1024$ has 7-level NTT. Therefore, in order to use 7-level NTT q needs to satisfy $q \equiv 1 \mod 384$ so that $\gamma^{64} \equiv \zeta_1 \mod q$ exits. We cannot use 3329, since $3329 \neq 1 \mod 384$. The smallest such q is 3457. However, 3457 cannot be used for other rings $\mathbb{Z}_q/(X^{512} + 1)$ and $\mathbb{Z}_q/(X^{1024} + 1)$, because 256-th root of unity does not exits ($3457 \neq 1 \mod 256$) so there is no γ such that $\gamma^{256} = 1$ and 7-level NTT is not possible. Therefore, we have selected our parameters for $n = 768$ as $q = 3457$, noise parameter $k = 2$. By using the "PQSecurity.py" script provided by NEWHOPE, the post-quantum bit-security is estimated as 163. The result of this script is given in Table 7. Therefore, it achieves NIST security level 3.

Table 7. Core hardness of NEWHOPE-COMPACT768

Attack	m	b	Known classical	Known quantum	Best plausible
NEWHOPE-COMPACT768: $q = 3457$, $n = 768$, $\varsigma = \sqrt{2}$					
Primal	655	620	181	164	128
Dual	667	617	180	163	128

Although there are different approaches like [8] to analyze the failure probability for our parameters, we follow the approach from [3]. But because the underlying ring has trinomial quotient, each coefficients of the result of multiplication becomes a sum of $\frac{n}{2}$ multiplication of elements in the form of $ab + b'(a + a')$, where a, a', b, b' from ψ_2. Although some coefficients of the result are of the form $ab + ab'$ in their sum, we use the first form for simplicity, which is also suggested in [12]. Thus, the result is a sum of $\frac{n}{2}$ multiplication of the form of $ab + b'(a + a')$. This computation gave us 2^{-170} failure probability for $n = 768$.

The sizes of public key, secret key, and ciphertext when q is selected as 3457 are 1184 bytes, 2400 bytes and 1568 bytes respectively.

Benchmark results for our C implementation can be found on Table 8. It is 1.18 times faster than non-optimized reference implementation of KYBER.

Table 8. Cycle counts of KYBER and NEWHOPE C reference (non-optimized) implementation

Operations	CCA-KEM-768		
	KYBER [3]	NEWHOPE [2]	This work
GEN	208 826	-	137 960
ENCAPS	254 838	-	228 976
DECAPS	294 748	-	277 814
Total	758 412	-	644 750

References

1. Alagic, G., et al.: Status report on the first round of the NIST post-quantum cryptography standardization process. National Institute for Standards and Technology Internal Report 8240 (2019). https://doi.org/10.6028/NIST.IR.8240
2. Alkim, E., et al.: NewHope - algorithm specifications and supporting documentation (version 1.02). NIST Post-Quantum Cryptography Standardization Process (2019). https://newhopecrypto.org/
3. Avanzi, R., et al.: CYRYSTALS-Kyber - algorithm specifications and supporting documentation (version 2.0). NIST Post-Quantum Cryptography Standardization Process (2019). https://pq-crystals.org/kyber/
4. Cooley, J.W., Tukey, J.W.: An algorithm for the machine calculation of complex fourier series. Math. Comput. **19**(90), 297–301 (1965)
5. National Institute for Standards and Technology. Submission requirements and evaluation criteria for the postquantum cryptography standardization process. official call for proposals. NIST Post-Quantum Cryptography Standardization Process, December 2019. http://csrc.nist.gov/groups/ST/post-quantum-crypto/documents/call-for-proposals-final-dec-2016.pdf
6. Gentleman, W.M., Sande, G. Fast fourier transforms: for fun and profit. In: Proceedings of the 7–10 November 1966, Fall Joint Computer Conference, AFIPS 1966 (Fall), pp. 563–578. ACM, New York (1966)
7. Güneysu, T., Oder, T., Pöppelmann, T., Schwabe, P.: Software speed records for lattice-based signatures. In: Gaborit, P. (ed.) PQCrypto 2013. LNCS, vol. 7932, pp. 67–82. Springer, Heidelberg (2013). https://doi.org/10.1007/978-3-642-38616-9_5
8. Hamburg, M.: Post-quantum cryptography proposal: ThreeBears. NIST Post-Quantum Cryptography Standardization Process (2019). https://www.shiftleft.org/papers/threebears/
9. İlter, M.B., Cenk, M.: Efficient big integer multiplication in cryptography. International Journal of Information Security Science **6**(4), 70–78 (2017)
10. Bernstein, D.J.: Multidigit multiplication for mathematicians, September 2001

11. Longa, P., Naehrig, M.: Speeding up the number theoretic transform for faster ideal lattice-based cryptography. In: Foresti, S., Persiano, G. (eds.) CANS 2016. LNCS, vol. 10052, pp. 124–139. Springer, Cham (2016). https://doi.org/10.1007/978-3-319-48965-0_8

12. Lyubashevsky, V., Seiler, G.: NTTRU: truly fast NTRU using NTT. IACR Trans. Cryptogr. Hardw. Embed. Syst. **2019**(3), 180–201 (2019)

13. Moenck, R.T.: Practical fast polynomial multiplication. In: Proceedings of the Third ACM Symposium on Symbolic and Algebraic Computation, SYMSAC 1976, pp. 136–148. ACM, New York (1976)

14. Montgomery, P.L.: Modular multiplication without trial division. Math. Comput. **44**(170), 519–521 (1985). http://www.ams.org/journals/mcom/1985-44-170/S0025-5718-1985-0777282-X/S0025-5718-1985-0777282-X.pdf

15. Moody, D.: Post-quantum cryptography: NIST's plan for the future. In: PQCrypto 2016 Conference, Fukuoka, Japan, 23–26 February 2016, February 2016. https://pqcrypto2016.jp/data/pqc2016_nist_announcement.pdf

16. Moody, D.: Round 2 of the NIST PQC "competition" what was NIST thinking? In: PQCrypto 2019 Conference, 8–10 May 2019, Chongqing, China, May 2019. https://csrc.nist.gov/CSRC/media/Presentations/Round-2-of-the-NIST-PQC-Competition-What-was-NIST/images-media/pqcrypto-may2019-moody.pdf

17. Seiler, G.: Faster AVX2 optimized NTT multiplication for Ring-LWE lattice cryptography. Cryptology ePrint Archive, Report 2018/039 (2018). https://eprint.iacr.org/2018/039

18. Weimerskirch, A., Paar, C.: Generalizations of the Karatsuba algorithm for efficient implementations. Cryptology ePrint Archive, Report 2006/224 (2006). https://eprint.iacr.org/2006/224

19. Zhou, S., et al.: Preprocess-then-NTT technique and its applications to KYBER and NEWHOPE. In: Guo, F., Huang, X., Yung, M. (eds.) Inscrypt 2018. LNCS, vol. 11449, pp. 117–137. Springer, Cham (2019). https://doi.org/10.1007/978-3-030-14234-6_7

Signatures and Protocols

How to Sign with White-Boxed AES

Marc Fischlin[1(✉)] and Helene Haagh[2]

[1] Technische Universität Darmstadt, Darmstadt, Germany
marc.fischlin@cryptoplexity.de
[2] Aarhus University, Aarhus, Denmark

Abstract. We investigate the possibility to use obfuscated implementations of the Advanced Encryption Standard AES ("white-boxed AES") to devise secure signature schemes. We show that the intuitive idea to use AES-based message authentication codes to sign, and the white-boxed implementation to verify, fails in general. This underlines that providing a secure white-box implementation is only the first step and that using it securely as a component in cryptographic protocols may be harder than originally thought. We therefore provide secure signature schemes based on white-boxed AES and on random oracles, as well as stateful and stateless constructions without random oracles. All our solutions are shown to be secure for reasonable parameters.

1 Introduction

White-box cryptography aims at hiding the secrets in cryptographic algorithms [13,14]. It can be seen as a special case of obfuscation where the goal is to obfuscate secret-key algorithms. The most prominent example is to white-box AES in order to thwart leakage of the secret key from the code of the Advanced Encryption Standard (AES).

Since its introduction [13,14], the idea of white-boxing AES has received quite some attention from the engineering's perspective. In an arms race there have been several attempts in the academic literature to construct secure solutions for white-boxing AES [12,14,30,39], which have subsequently been broken [9–11,17,18,20,23,24,27,29,34]. This indicates that devising secure white-box AES implementations is challenging.

1.1 The Quest for Securely White-Boxing AES

Driven by the importance and the vast potential applications, the search for secure white-boxing solutions continues. For example, Peeters [31] lists companies like Arxan or Irdeto providing commercial white-boxed primitives, and other companies like Apple and Microsoft using such primitives. In the academic community, CHES 2016 held a "Capture the Flag" event[1] about white-box AES

---

[1] https://ctf.newae.com.

© Springer Nature Switzerland AG 2019
P. Schwabe and N. Thériault (Eds.): LATINCRYPT 2019, LNCS 11774, pp. 259–279, 2019.
https://doi.org/10.1007/978-3-030-30530-7_13

challenges. The European project Ecrypt-CSA started another WhiBoX competition in 2017, albeit the security of the winning submission lasted only 28 days.[2] The second edition of the WhiBoX competition has just started.[3] In search for constructions there have also been proposal to use hardware components ("gray boxing"), although known attacks may still work (see, e.g., [10,36]). Similarly, Banik et al. [3] analyze additional external software measures to support whiteboxing and show that most solutions so far fail to strengthen the design, but they also discuss potential countermeasures.

As discussed in [33] another option is to investigate the possibility to borrow techniques and solutions considered mainly in theory so far. There, formal notions for obfuscation have been introduced in the seminal paper by Barak et al. [4]. Starting with the obfuscator candidate by Garg et al. [22] there has been a growing interest in the cryptographic community to derive obfuscators (e.g., see [1,2] for a few recent proposals which have not been broken yet). The goal is to build obfuscators with rigorous security guarantees based on sound foundations and, ideally, also for arbitrary programs.

White-boxing AES (WB-AES) on the one hand is easier than devising general-purpose obfuscators, since one "merely" needs to protect a specific program. On the other hand, the meanwhile prevalent notion of indistinguishability obfuscation (iO) [4] in the crypto community aims at hiding how a function is computed and is thus not immediately applicable to WB-AES. The notion of virtual black-box (VBB) obfuscation [4], which says that the obfuscated program hides everything except for input/output behavior, at first seems to be much closer in spirit to the sought-after goal behind white boxing. The VBB notion has been shown to be unachievable in general, though [4]. Still, it is unclear if this impossibility result for general-purpose VBB obfuscation applies to the AES case (see, for example, the discussion in [33]). Eventually, theoretical approaches for obfuscation may thus lead to secure white-boxing solutions for AES.

1.2   Signing with WB-AES

Here we investigate the dual problem to designing secure implementations, and address the question how we can *use* a WB-AES implementation. This study of applications will provide helpful and important information for the future development of secure white-box implementations. These studies will help establish what kind of security guarantees an implementation need to achieve in order to realize these applications. When white-box cryptography was introduced in 2003 there was an apparent absence of well-defined security goals. It is believed that this absence is a significant factor in the break of several white-box implementations [19]. In the last decade, research on white-box cryptography has moved towards investigating and determining different security goals of whitebox implementations [19,37] that will be helpful in the development of secure implementations. We believe that a thorough investigation of how white-box

---

[2] https://whibox.cr.yp.to/.
[3] https://whibox.cyber-crypt.com/.

implementations can be used, will help us learn more about the security requirements, and hopefully bring us even closer to the goal of a secure white-box implementation. In this paper, we are especially interested in the fundamental question: how to use WB-AES implementations for devising secure signature schemes and what security guarantees do we achieve?

Signing with WB-AES may come in two flavors: The first one is to turn a message authentication code (MAC) into a signature scheme by using WB-AES in the verification step. This is for example proposed by [25] and allows fast signing through AES_K, e.g., on a resource-limited device, whereas verification is performed with the slower white-box version of the inverse AES_K^{-1}. The other deployment option of WB-AES, usually discussed in connection with NFC payment systems, e.g., [28], is to use the white-boxed variant instead on the weak device. This should harden leakage of the secret key via attacks against the device. From a cryptographic point of view, the latter case is still a MAC, though, only that the secret key is better protected in practice. We are interested here in the former challenge to turn a MAC into a signature scheme.

Note that it is in principle possible to use general obfuscation techniques to build secure signature schemes from symmetric primitives [32,35]. This, however neglects that AES is the prevalent standard for symmetric encryption schemes and that it is already available in many devices, potentially even supported by hardware accelerators. Our goal here is to start with the pragmatic assumption that we are given a secure WB-AES implementation and build a secure scheme from this, where the signer like a constrained device can use the handy AES implementation to sign and the verifier, e.g., a powerful server, uses the obfuscated version to verify. In fact, our results also allow to take a more fine-grained view on the desirable security properties of a WB-AES implementation.

The security proofs for our signature schemes will be based on two hardness problems for WB-AES, both saying that the adversary cannot predict AES values. This should hold even if the adversary receives the obfuscated program WBAES_K^{-1} as input and being allowed to adaptively query an AES_K oracle on other values. For the first notion, the adversary has to predict the value for a random challenge. This unpredictability property is dual to the one-wayness property in [19], and similar to other notions that has been considered in the literature, e.g. the setting of adaptive trapdoor permutations [26]. In the other case, the correlation-intractability case, the adversary may find all AES values for a set of adversarial chosen, but related inputs (e.g. the adversary has to determine the AES values of the strings $r||00, r||01, r||10, r||11$ for an adversarial chosen r of 126 bits). Note that the adversary will trivially be able to break an requirement of finding the AES value of an adversarial chosen 128 bits string, since he has access to the program WBAES_K^{-1} (i.e. choose a random 128 bits string r and output $\mathsf{WBAES}_K^{-1}(r)$). Thus, we need to harden the challenge as in the unpredictability and correlation-intractability properties.

We discuss the hardness of the latter correlation-intractability problem by relating it to the unpredictability problem and discussing generic attacks. Especially the relation between unpredictability and correlation intractability dis-

262   M. Fischlin and H. Haagh

plays a noteworthy aspect: In some cases one can transform white-boxing algorithms for one block cipher into solutions for another cipher, such that the new white-boxing construction preserves security but shows an "if-then-else" structure on the outside. The remarkable point here is that this signals that the full power of VBB obfuscation (or even indistinguishability obfuscation), which are supposed to hide such a structure, may not be necessary for these assumptions to hold for block ciphers.

1.3 White-Boxing CBC-MAC Is Insecure

Our first result emphasizes that the challenge addressed in this paper here is far from moot and that intuitive ideas fail. Joye [25] suggested to turn a MAC into a signature scheme, by using the WB-AES version for verification. This assumes, of course, that verification of a MAC computed with AES_K can be carried out by calling the white-boxed inverse WBAES_K^{-1}. Natural candidates satisfying this property are CBC-MACs.

Unfortunately, as we show, the resulting signature scheme from CBC-MAC becomes insecure. One can easily break the scheme with probability 1 by making a few calls to the signing oracle. This problem appears both for (fixed-length) input messages as well as for messages hashed with a collision-resistant hash function. This indicates that turning AES-based MACs into signatures via white-boxing requires more care.

We also discuss the possibility to show security of CBC-MACs with WB-AES when we assume that the hash function, with which the message is first hashed, behaves like a random oracle. If one is merely interested in selective unforgeability, where the adversary needs to forge a signature for a given message, we obtain a reasonable security bound assuming the unpredictability of AES values for random inputs. For existential forgeries, however, the birthday bound strikes, introducing a term $q_R^2 \cdot 2^{-128}$ for the number q_R of random oracle queries and the (limited) block size of 128 for AES. The resulting security guarantee appears to be too weak for practical considerations.

1.4 Secure Signatures Based on WB-AES

If one adopts the viewpoint that WBAES_K^{-1} and AES_K act as a public one-way permutation and its trapdoor inverse, then it seems that one can straightforwardly apply known signature scheme construction from trapdoor permutations [7,26]. However, such *full domain hash* signatures embed the entire hash value into the domain of the trapdoor permutation, whereas the output size of modern hash functions exceeds the input size of AES—and we cannot simply truncate the hash value to 128 bits without sacrificing reasonable security margins. Plus, the hash function in full domain hash schemes is usually modeled as a programmable random oracle whereas we also give constructions in the non-programmable random oracle model and in the standard model. Bellare and Micali [6] gave a standard-model solution using trapdoor permutations, but the scheme is quite expensive in terms of storage, communication, and computation; certainly more expensive than our solutions in the standard model.

In conclusion, the fixed block size of 128 for AES poses the main challenge for deriving secure solutions. As we have seen, chaining outputs via CBC in general does not result in secure schemes (in the standard model) or merely gives loose bounds (in the random oracle model). We therefore use a different chaining strategy, where we compute the input to the next AES evaluation by calling the hash function on the previous AES value and the original message. We call this the random-oracle-chaining (ROChainSign) construction.

We show that the ROChainSign construction yields decent security bounds. The bound now has a quadratic factor $q_S^2 \cdot 2^{-128}$, too, but this time it is based on the number q_S of *signature* queries. In practice, this number should be much smaller than the number of hash evaluations which the adversary can carry out locally. In addition, we work in the non-programmable random oracle model but require the aforementioned correlation intractability property. For reasonable parameter choices, the signatures of the ROChainSign construction are of roughly 2,000 bits.

Finally, we give two solutions in the standard model, without random oracles, and with tight reductions to the correlation-intractability problem. This comes at the cost of larger signatures of approximately 8,000 bits. The first solution is stateful and uses a counter, the second one replaces the counter by nonces, resulting in slightly larger signatures.

We note that, in this version, most of the proofs had to be omitted for space reasons. If possible, the main proof idea is sketched, though.

2 Preliminaries

For $n \in \mathbb{N}$ let $[n]$ denote the set $\{1, \ldots, n\}$. By $x \| y$ we denote the concatenation of two bit strings $x, y \in \{0,1\}^*$. We occasionally interpret a bit string $x = x_1 \| \ldots \| x_n \in \{0,1\}^n$ as an integer $x = \sum_{i=0}^{n-1} 2^i x_{n-i}$ and vice versa. We denote by $x \leftarrow_\$ S$ that x is drawn uniformly at random from the set S, and by $x \leftarrow \mathsf{Alg}(\cdot)$ that x is the result after running algorithm Alg on some inputs.

2.1 White-Boxing AES

White-boxing AES is concerned with obfuscated implementations of the AES encryption or decryption algorithm. Following the work of Delerablée et al. [19], we consider a possibly probabilistic AES_K obfuscator (or compiler) $\mathcal{WB}$ that takes as input the security parameter κ and a key $K \in \{0,1\}^{128}$, and outputs a white-box implementation of the AES decryption algorithm (WB-AES implementation, for short)

$$\mathsf{WBAES}_K^{-1} \leftarrow \mathcal{WB}(1^\kappa, K)$$

such that $\mathsf{WBAES}_K^{-1}(x) = \mathsf{AES}_K^{-1}(x)$ for all $x \in \{0,1\}^{128}$.[4]

---

[4] Note that this can also be defined for AES with key size 192 and 256 bits. We stick here, and throughout, to 128-bit keys for sake of simplicity.

We remark that AES_K is of course a block cipher of fixed input and output length. The obfuscator, on the other hand, may use arbitrary cryptographic tools to construct the program WBAES_K^{-1}, such that we hand it an extra security parameter κ. We usually neglect the efficiency of the obfuscator $\mathcal{WB}$ since practical considerations (code size, run time, etc.) have a major impact, and we are mainly interested in the security of the given program WBAES_K^{-1}. We discuss such security properties later in Sect. 4.

Note also that we define the obfuscator to output the white-boxed implementation of the inverse to AES_K. The reason is that we are concerned with AES used within a signature scheme, where the signing (on a ressource-constrained device) is done via AES encryption and verification (on a more powerful terminal) via AES decryption. One could also look at it the other way round and all our definitions and results could be easily adapted.

2.2 Signature Schemes

A signature scheme is defined by the following algorithms.

Key Generation: The Gen algorithm on input the security parameter 1^κ outputs a signing key sk and a verification key vk.
Signing: The Sign algorithm on input a signing key sk and a message m outputs a signature σ.
Verification: The Ver algorithm on input a verification key vk, a message m and a signature σ, outputs a bit $b \in \{0,1\}$.

Completeness demands that for any security parameter κ, any key pair $(sk, vk) \leftarrow \mathsf{Gen}(1^\kappa)$, any message m, and any signature $\sigma \leftarrow \mathsf{Sign}(sk, m)$ we always have $\mathsf{Ver}(vk, m, \sigma) = 1$.

All the constructions presented in this paper follow a basic structure, where the verification key $vk = \mathsf{WBAES}_K^{-1}$ is a WB-AES implementation. Thus, the verification of signature σ will consist of undoing the AES computations presented in σ using the WB-AES implementation, and comparing it with the inputs to the AES computation used in the signing phase (which can easily be reconstructed from the message and the signature). This means that the completeness of the presented signature schemes, trivially, follows from an inspection of the algorithms.

We consider the adaptive-chosen message attack model, where the adversary is given access to a signing oracle that produces signatures on adversarial chosen messages. The oracle is initialized with the signing key sk generated according to $(sk, vk) \leftarrow \mathsf{Gen}(1^\kappa)$. Each message in the signature requests is chosen adaptively, based on the previous answers. Furthermore, we consider two different goals of the adversary. In a *selective-forgery* attack the adversary should produce a forgery for a given message (chosen uniformly at random). In an *existential-forgery* attack the adversary can adaptively choose the message for which it tries to create a forgery.

3   On the Insecurity of CBC-Signatures

Given a white-box implementation of AES a straightforward attempt to sign securely is to compute a message authentication code σ via CBC mode. To verify one performs the CBC computations "backwards" via the (public) WBAES_K^{-1} algorithm. We show that, contrary to some believes, this does not yield a secure signature scheme. Put differently, a MAC scheme in general does not yield a secure signature scheme when using white boxing.

3.1   CBC-Signatures

We first introduce CBC-signatures for fixed input lengths, aligned to a multiple of the block length 128 of AES. We note that CBC provides a secure MAC for fixed-length messages [5].

Construction 1. *Let $\kappa \in \mathbb{N}$ be the security parameter, let $\ell \in \mathbb{N}$ be the number of blocks, and $n = 128 \cdot \ell$ be the fixed input length for messages. Let $\mathsf{CBCSign} = (\mathsf{Gen}, \mathsf{Sign}, \mathsf{Ver})$ be a signature scheme defined by the following algorithms.*

Key Generation: Let the signing key $sk = K \in \{0,1\}^{128}$ be an AES key, and let the verification key $vk = \mathsf{WBAES}_K^{-1} \leftarrow \mathcal{WB}(1^\kappa, K)$ be a WB-AES implementation of AES_K.

Signing: On input a signing key sk and a message $m \in \{0,1\}^n$, parse the message as $m = m_1||\cdots||m_\ell$ such that $m_i \in \{0,1\}^{128}$. Then output

$$\sigma \leftarrow \mathsf{AES}_K(\cdots(\mathsf{AES}_K(\mathsf{AES}_K(m_1) \oplus m_2) \cdots) \oplus m_\ell).$$

Verification: On input a verification key vk, a message $m \in \{0,1\}^n$, and a signature σ, parse the message as $m = m_1||\cdots||m_\ell$ such that $m_i \in \{0,1\}^{128}$. Then check that

$$m_1 = \mathsf{WBAES}_K^{-1}(\cdots(\mathsf{WBAES}_K^{-1}(\mathsf{WBAES}_K^{-1}(\sigma) \oplus m_\ell) \cdots) \oplus m_2).$$

3.2   Attacking CBC-Signatures

For simplicity, we describe our attack for messages of two AES blocks ($= 256$ bits).

Proposition 1 (Insecurity of CBC-Signatures). *If $n = 256$, then the signature scheme $\mathsf{CBCSign}$ is not secure against selective forgeries under chosen message attack.*

Proof. An adversary $\mathcal{A}$ is given $vk = \mathsf{WBAES}_K^{-1}$ and a message $m^* = m_1^*||m_2^* \in \{0,1\}^{256}$ for which it is supposed to create a forgery σ^*. The adversary $\mathcal{A}$ queries the following messages to the signing oracle:

1. query for message $m_1^*||x_1$, where $x_1 \neq m_2^*$. The signing oracle returns $\sigma_1 = \mathsf{AES}_K(\mathsf{AES}_K(m_1^*) \oplus x_1)$, which allows $\mathcal{A}$ to recover $y_1 = \mathsf{WBAES}_K^{-1}(\sigma_1) \oplus x_1 = \mathsf{AES}_K(m_1^*)$.

2. query for message $x_2||0^{128}$, where $x_2 \neq m_1^*$. The signing oracle returns $\sigma_2 = \mathsf{AES}_K(\mathsf{AES}_K(x_2) \oplus 0^{128})$, which allows $\mathcal{A}$ to recover $y_2 = \mathsf{WBAES}_K^{-1}(\sigma_2) = \mathsf{AES}_K(x_2)$.
3. query for message $x_2||(y_1 \oplus m_2^* \oplus y_2)$. The signing oracle returns the signature

$$
\begin{aligned}
\sigma_3 &= \mathsf{AES}_K(\mathsf{AES}_K(x_2) \oplus (y_1 \oplus m_2^* \oplus y_2)) \\
&= \mathsf{AES}_K(\mathsf{AES}_K(x_2) \oplus \mathsf{AES}_K(m_1^*) \oplus m_2^* \oplus \mathsf{AES}_K(x_2)) \\
&= \mathsf{AES}_K(\mathsf{AES}_K(m_1^*) \oplus m_2^*)
\end{aligned}
$$

Thus, $\mathcal{A}$ can return $\sigma^* = \sigma_3$ as the signature for message m^*. Furthermore, since $x_1 \neq m_2^*$ and $x_2 \neq m_1^*$ neither signature query equals $m_1^*||m_2^*$. Hence $\mathcal{A}$ produces a valid forgery for the given message with probability 1. □

Note that if $n = 128$, then the signature consist of a single AES encryption, i.e., the signature on message m is given by $\sigma = \mathsf{AES}_K(m)$. In this case, the signature scheme CBCSign is secure *against selective forgery* for random messages, since this is precisely the unpredictability property of the white-box implementation which we discuss in the next section. On the other hand, the scheme is still not secure *against existential forgeries*, since given the white-box implementation WBAES_K^{-1} the adversary can pick some σ, then compute $m = \mathsf{WBAES}_K^{-1}(\sigma)$, such that σ would constitute a valid signature for m.

Let us briefly point to the step which allows the adversary against the signature scheme to produce a forgery, whereas CBC-MAC would still be unforgeable: The difference shows when our adversary exploits the availability of WBAES_K^{-1} which allows it to undo the final step of the CBC computation. In the MAC case, obtaining such intermediate values is infeasible.

3.3   Extensions

Joye [25] suggests, to achieve non-repudiation, to hash the message before handing it over to the MAC algorithm. Here we argue that using a collision-resistant hash function H does not work in general. Suppose for sake of concreteness that we take the hash function to be

$$
\mathsf{H}(m_1||m_2) = \mathsf{H}'(m_1)||m_2
$$

for $m_1 \in \{0,1\}^*$, $m_2 \in \{0,1\}^{128}$, and some collision-resistant hash function $\mathsf{H}' : \{0,1\}^{\geq 128} \to \{0,1\}^{128}$.[5]

Now suppose that we build CBC-Signatures but where we first apply the hash function H to the message. Then our adversary $\mathcal{A}$ proceeds analogously to the attack against selective forgery in the hash-free version. Given $m^* = m_1^*||m_2^* \in \{0,1\}^{256}$ it first asks to see a signature for message $m_1^*||x_1$ for $x_1 \neq m_2^*$, then for

---

[5] Asking for collision resistance for 128-bit outputs seems to be moot. It is owned to the limited block size of AES. Still, the example here shows that there are fundamental problems with the general approach and the attack strategy applies also for larger block sizes of, say, 256 bits.

$x_2 || 0^{128}$ for $x_2 \neq m_1^*$, and finally for $x_2 || (y_1 \oplus m_2^* \oplus y_2)$. From this is it easy to compute

$$\sigma^* = \mathsf{AES}_K(\mathsf{AES}_K(\mathsf{H}'(m_1^*)) \oplus m_2^*),$$

which is a valid signature for m^*. As long as $\mathsf{H}'(x_2) \neq \mathsf{H}'(m_1^*)$ for $x_2 \neq m_1^*$ this is a valid forgery.

4 WBAES Security Assumptions

We give two security assumptions about the white-boxed implementation. One says that predicting the value $\mathsf{AES}_K(r)$ at a random position r is infeasible, even if one receives the implementation WBAES_K^{-1} and sees values $\mathsf{AES}_K(x)$ at other inputs x. The other property says that one should not be able to compute the correlated values $\mathsf{AES}_K(r_0), \mathsf{AES}_K(r_1), \ldots$ for a self-chosen r_0 and correlated $r_1, r_2, \ldots$, e.g., all values may coincide on all but a few bits. We then relate the two assumptions, showing that for some relations correlation intractability is a strictly stronger requirement than unpredictability. Finally, as a sanity check, we argue that both assumptions hold if the adversary does not take advantage of the code of the white-boxed AES but generically uses this input only in a black-box way to compute inverses.

4.1 Defining Unpredictability

Our unpredictability notion states that given a white-box implementation of the AES decryption algorithm you cannot compute the AES encryption of a predefined message. This unpredictability property is similar to the one-wayness property defined by Delerablée et. al [19]. The main difference between the two properties is that in the one-wayness game the adversary is given a white-box implementation of the AES *encryption* algorithm, then his goal is to determine the message that maps to a predefined AES ciphertext. Thus, the one-wayness property states that given a white-box implementation of a function, you cannot invert it to get the preimage, while the unpredictability property states that given a white-box implementation of the inverse function you cannot predict the image.

Definition 1 (Unpredictability). *Let $\kappa \in \mathbb{N}$ be the security parameter, and let $q \in \mathbb{N}$. Assume we are given a white-box compiler $\mathcal{WB}$. Consider the following game between a challenger and an adversary $\mathcal{A}$:*

Game Definition
1. $K \leftarrow_\$ \{0,1\}^{128}$;
2. $\mathsf{WBAES}_K^{-1} \leftarrow \mathcal{WB}(1^\kappa, K)$;
3. $r \leftarrow_\$ \{0,1\}^{128}$;
4. $c \leftarrow \mathcal{A}^{\mathsf{AES}_K(\cdot)}(\mathsf{WBAES}_K^{-1}, r)$;

The adversary $\mathcal{A}$ wins the game if $c = \mathsf{AES}_K(r)$, and for all queries x to the oracle $\mathcal{O}$ it holds that $x \neq r$.

We say that a WB-AES implementation is unpredictable *if for all PPT adversaries $\mathcal{A}$ that make at most q oracle queries, the advantage of $\mathcal{A}$ is*

$$\mathsf{Adv}_{\mathcal{A}}^{\mathsf{UP}}(\kappa, q) = \Pr\left[\mathcal{A} \text{ wins the unpredictability game}\right] \leq \mathsf{negl}(\kappa)$$

There is a trivial strategy to attack the unpredictability property, without making any AES_K queries at all. Namely, starting with $c = 0^{128}$ incrementally pick the next c, compute $\mathsf{WBAES}_K^{-1}(c)$, and check if this matches the challenge value r. If one considers a still reasonable number of 2^{64} trials then the probability that the adversary predicts $\mathsf{AES}_K(r)$ is roughly 2^{-64} with this strategy. However, this bound has immediate consequences for signature schemes based on unpredictability. To clarify this, we give an example of a simple signature scheme that on the surface seems to have a good security bound.

Consider the following signature scheme, where one hashes the message with a random oracle and truncates the output to 128 bits. Then one applies AES_K to this value to derive the signature σ. There is a straightforward reduction for this signature scheme to the unpredictability game, using the security reduction for the FDH signature scheme for trapdoor permutations [7]. In particular that reduction never queries the AES_K oracle but uses the WB-AES implementation WBAES_K^{-1} to answer all signature and random oracle queries.

Following [7], the bound for the security of the signature scheme above (with respect to existential forgeries) for q_S signature and q_R random oracle queries is then given by $q_R \cdot \mathsf{Adv}_{\mathcal{B}}^{\mathsf{UP}}(0)$. Unfortunately, since it seems reasonable to assume that $\mathsf{Adv}_{\mathcal{B}}^{\mathsf{UP}}$ can be in the order of 2^{-64} (from the above trivial attack strategy on the unpredictability property), the factor q_R may trivialize the security bound for the signature scheme. An improved bound by Coron [15] for full domain hash signatures yields the advantage of approximately $q_s \cdot \mathsf{Adv}_{\mathcal{B}}^{\mathsf{UP}}(0)$ for our scheme here. Even though the number q_S of signature generations is usually smaller than the number q_R of hash queries, this bound may still be too loose, e.g., if q_S can be in the order of 2^{30}.

Another disadvantage of both bounds is that they inherently rely on the programmability of the random oracle. In the proof the reduction injects suitable values in the adversary's random oracle queries in order to break the unpredictability (or one-wayness) of the underlying problem. Fischlin et al. [21] later showed that this strong programmability property cannot be replaced by weaker notions for full domain hash signatures.

It is tempting to assume that a randomized version of the above scheme would yield better bounds. One option could be to use an adaptation of the PSS signature scheme [8] as a randomized version of FDH signatures, and which provides an almost tight reduction to the underlying problem. Translating the bound to our setting we would obtain a bound of roughly $\mathsf{Adv}_{\mathcal{B}}^{\mathsf{UP}}(0) + (q_S + q_R)^2 \cdot 2^{-64}$ where, again, the number of hash queries q_R may trivialize this bound. This is also true for the alternative bound for PSS by Coron [16] which still has at least a term $\mathsf{Adv}_{\mathcal{B}}^{\mathsf{UP}}(0) + (q_S + q_R)^2 \cdot 2^{-128}$ in our setting.

4.2   Defining Correlation Intractability

We state correlation intractability for general R-ary relations $\mathcal{R} \subseteq (\{0,1\}^{128})^R$, demanding that the adversary is able to predict the AES values for $r_0, \ldots, r_{R-1}$ with $\mathcal{R}(r_0, \ldots, r_{R-1}) = 1$, without having queried the AES_K oracle for any of the r_i's. An example relation $\mathcal{R}$ is the one where $r_0, \ldots, r_3$ coincide on the leading 126 bits and differ only in the last two bits, which equal the index $00, \ldots, 11$ in binary. This relation has a special property, stating that for each $r \in \{0,1\}^{128}$ there is a unique and efficiently computable sequence $r_0, \ldots, r_{R-1}$ such that $\mathcal{R}(r_0, \ldots, r_{R-1}) = 1$ and a unique i such that $r = r_i$. We call such relations *partitioning* and denote the unique vector of matching values $r_0, r_1, \ldots, r_{R-1}$ to r as $\mathsf{clust}(r)$.

Definition 2 (Correlation Intractability). *Let $\kappa \in \mathbb{N}$ be the security parameter, and let $q \in \mathbb{N}$. Let $\mathcal{R} \subseteq (\{0,1\}^{128})^R$ be an efficiently computable R-ary relation. Assume we are given a white-box compiler $\mathcal{WB}$. Consider the following game between a challenger and an adversary $\mathcal{A}$:*

Game Definition
1. $K \leftarrow_\$ \{0,1\}^{128}$;
2. $\mathsf{WBAES}_K^{-1} \leftarrow \mathcal{WB}(1^\kappa, K)$;
3. $(r_0, \ldots, r_{R-1}, c_0, \ldots, c_{R-1}) \leftarrow \mathcal{A}^{\mathsf{AES}_K(\cdot)}(\mathsf{WBAES}_K^{-1})$;

   The adversary $\mathcal{A}$ wins the game if $c_i = \mathsf{AES}_K(r_i)$ for all i, and $\mathcal{R}(r_0, \ldots, r_{R-1}) = 1$, and for all queries x to the oracle AES_K it holds that $x \notin \{r_0, \ldots, r_{R-1}\}$.
   We say that a WB-AES implementation is correlation intractability *for relation $\mathcal{R}$ if for all PPT adversaries $\mathcal{A}$ that make at most q oracle queries, the advantage of $\mathcal{A}$ is*

$$\mathsf{Adv}_{\mathcal{A}, \mathcal{R}}^{\mathsf{CI}}(\kappa, q) = \Pr\left[\mathcal{A} \text{ wins the } \mathcal{R} \text{-correlation-intractability game}\right] \leq \mathsf{negl}(\kappa)$$

   Consider a simple example of a binary relation $\mathcal{R}$ which contains pairs $(r||0, r||1)$. The correlation intractability property captures that, even though it is easy to produce r_0 and $c_0 = \mathsf{AES}_K(r_0)$ given WBAES_K^{-1} (i.e., choose a random c_0 and compute $r_0 = \mathsf{WBAES}_K^{-1}(c_0)$), then it is unclear how to get $c_1 = \mathsf{AES}_K(r_1)$ without querying the AES_K oracle about r_1. This example also shows that it is in general necessary to exclude AES_K queries for any of the values $r_0, \ldots, r_{R-1}$.
   The correlation intractability assumption allows the adversary to choose the pre-image r_0 (from which $r_1, \ldots, r_{R-1}$ are determined for a partitioning relation). For R-ary relations for small values of R this usually allows the adversary to mount a collision attack. For example, consider again the binary relation $\mathcal{R}$ consisting of pairs $(r||0, r||1)$. In this case the adversary may continuously sample random c, apply $\mathsf{WBAES}_K^{-1}(c)$, and check for a collision among the leading 127 bits of all the values. We expect to find a solution after roughly 2^{64} trials, in

which case the values differ in the last bit with probability $\frac{1}{2}$. This would yield a solution for the correlation intractability problem.

For the R-ary extension of the above relations a collision attack finds an R-fold collision after approximately $2^{128(R-1)/R}$ trials with probability $\frac{1}{R!}$, where we ignore that the truncated r values are of size slightly less than 128 bits. The probability of having a collision after q trials is approximately $q^R \cdot 2^{-128(R-1)}$. See for instance [38]. This effort may only be infeasible for $R \geq 4$ for AES; for smaller values of R it may still give reasonable security guarantees for block ciphers with larger input and output size.

In contrast, it is unclear how to use a collision-finder to solve the unpredictability problem. Therefore, an alternative to increasing the arity R of the relation for correlation intractability may therefore be to combine the notions. That is, ask the adversary to predict $\mathsf{AES}_K(r_0)$ *for a given random* r_0 and to also find the AES value for a related value r_1, without querying the AES_K oracle about either of the values, of course. For partitioning relations this can be seen as the task of predicting the images of two random (but correlated) inputs. For the security proofs of our signature schemes, however, we still need to give the adversary the possibility to determine r_0, and therefore use the plain correlation intractability with $R \geq 4$.

4.3 Relationship •

We can show that correlation intractability for partitioning binary relations is at least as hard as unpredictability. For arbitrary block ciphers and general relations of arbitrary arity this is not known to hold anymore. The proofs of the following statements are omitted for space reasons.

Proposition 2. *If* WBAES_K^{-1} *is correlation intractable for a partitioning 2-ary relation* $\mathcal{R}$, *then* WBAES_K^{-1} *is also unpredictable.*

The idea is that we can pick a random c, compute $r = \mathsf{WBAES}_K^{-1}(c)$, and then run the predictor on the partitioning counterpart r' to r (which is also random). If we get a correct answer we also have a solution for the correlation intractability problem.

As for the converse direction and the question if unpredictability implies correlation intractability, it is easy to devise a block cipher which is unpredictable but not correlation intractable (for binary relations). For AES it is an open question whether or not this implication holds.

Proposition 3. *Assume that there exists a block cipher* BC' *and obfuscator* $\mathcal{WB}'$ *which are unpredictable. Then there exists a block cipher* BC *with obfuscator* $\mathcal{WB}$, *which is unpredictable, but such that for any obfuscator the block cipher is easy to correlate for the binary common-prefix relation.*

The idea is to tweak the unpredictable cipher BC' into a block cipher BC which maps 0^n and $0^{n-1}1$ into themselves, and to also argue that the white-boxing can be adapted from BC' to BC. Since a random input r will most likely not hit such exceptional cases, the cipher BC inherits unpredictability. But the values $0^n, 0^{n-1}1$ easily give a solution to the correlation intractability game.

For relations with larger arities than $R = 2$ the implication from Proposition 2 in general—for arbitrary block ciphers—no longer holds. Again it is an open question whether the implication holds for AES when $R > 2$.

Proposition 4. *Assume that there exists a block cipher* BC′ *with obfuscator* WB′ *which is correlation-intractable for the binary common-prefix relation. Then there exists a block cipher* BC *with obfuscator* WB, *which is correlation intractable for the quaternary common-prefix relation, but such that for any obfuscator the block cipher is easy to predict.*

The idea here is to change BC′ into a cipher BC which maps half of the inputs to the same output value. Predicting with probability $1/2$ is then easy, but solving correlation intractability for BC for four values requires to solve the problem for BC′ for at least two (non-tweaked) values.

4.4   Generic Security of the Assumptions

One can argue that the above assumptions are true if AES is a strong PRP and the adversary does not receive the WB-AES implementation as input but instead gets oracle access to AES_K^{-1}. Note that such a result means that the adversary, in order to refute the assumptions, must somehow take advantage of the code of the WB-AES implementation and cannot generically break the security. The formal treatment is omitted for space reasons.

5   CBC-Signatures with Random Oracles

In Sect. 3 we showed that the trivial construction of using AES in CBC mode is not a secure signature scheme. In this section we will show that, switching to the stronger assumption that the hash function behaves like a random oracle, we get a secure signature scheme in the ROM. Noteworthy, the derived security bound in the existential unforgeability game is rather tenuous given the current block size of AES of 128 bits. Still, the approach is valid and would yield stronger bounds for block ciphers with larger input size. We also show better bounds for AES for *selective* forgeries where the adversary has to forge a signature for a given message.

We note that in all constructions we use a single-keyed WB-AES implementation. The reason is that using multiple keys may stress the storage capacity, both on the signer's side and in particular on the verifier's side with the white-boxed versions. Also, it seems to us that domain separation, e.g., in the form of using $\mathsf{AES}_K(0||\cdot)$, $\mathsf{AES}_K(1||\cdot)$, would most times be a viable alternative to two keys anyway.

5.1 Construction

We first assume below for sake of concreteness that the hash function has 256 bits output size. The construction and the proof easily carries over to other multiples of 128, as discussed briefly after the theorem.

Construction 2. *Let $\kappa \in \mathbb{N}$ be the security parameter and let $\mathcal{H} : \{0,1\}^* \rightarrow \{0,1\}^{256}$ be a random oracle. Let* ROCBCSign $=$ (Gen, Sign, Ver) *be a signature scheme defined by the following algorithms.*

Key Generation: Let the signing key $sk = K \in \{0,1\}^{128}$ be an AES key, and let the verification key $vk = \mathsf{WBAES}_K^{-1} \leftarrow \mathcal{WB}(1^\kappa, K)$ be a WB-AES implementation.

Signing: On input a signing key sk and a message $m \in \{0,1\}^*$, compute $h = \mathcal{H}(m) \in \{0,1\}^{256}$ and parse $h = h_1 \| h_2$ such that $h_1, h_2 \in \{0,1\}^{128}$. Then output

$$\sigma \leftarrow \mathsf{AES}_K(\mathsf{AES}_K(h_1) \oplus h_2).$$

Verification: On input a verification key vk, a message $m \in \{0,1\}^*$, and a signature σ. Compute $h = h_1 \| h_2 = \mathcal{H}(m)$ and check that

$$h_1 = \mathsf{WBAES}_K^{-1}(\mathsf{WBAES}_K^{-1}(\sigma) \oplus h_2).$$

5.2 Existential Forgeries

For selective forgeries we can show a security bound of

$$\mathsf{Adv}_{\mathcal{A}}^{\mathsf{SF}}(\kappa, q_R, q_S) \leq 2 \cdot (q_R + q_S) \cdot 2^{-128} + \mathsf{Adv}_{\mathcal{B}}^{\mathsf{UP}}(\kappa, 2q_S).$$

For existential forgeries, however, the bound becomes significantly more loose:

Theorem 1. *Let $\kappa \in \mathbb{N}$ be the security parameter. For any adversary $\mathcal{A}$ that can produce a existential forgery for the* ROCBCSign *scheme with q_R queries to the random oracle and q_S signature queries, there exists an adversary $\mathcal{B}$ for the unpredictability property of the WB-AES implementation, such that the advantage of $\mathcal{A}$ is*

$$\mathsf{Adv}_{\mathcal{A}}^{\mathsf{EF}}(\kappa, q_R, q_S) \leq 2^{-256} + 2q_R \cdot (q_R + q_S) \cdot 2^{-128} + q_R \cdot \mathsf{Adv}_{\mathcal{B}}^{\mathsf{UP}}(\kappa, 2q_S).$$

The proof is again omitted for space reasons.

The bound in the case of existential unforgeability is delicate: If we assume that q_R can be in the order of $q_R = 2^{64}$, then both the factors $q_R^2 \cdot 2^{-128}$ and $q_R \cdot \mathsf{Adv}_{\mathcal{B}}^{\mathsf{UP}}(\kappa, 2q_S)$ can be close to 1, such that the overall bound becomes meaningless.

6 Construction via Random-Oracle-Chaining

In this section we provide a random-oracle based solution with short signatures, consisting of eight AES blocks, and with improved security bounds in the non-programmable random oracle model. The bound follows from the correlation intractability for the quaternary common-prefix relation $\mathcal{R}(r_{00}, r_{01}, r_{10}, r_{11}) = 1$ iff there exists r such that $r_{ab} = r||ab$ for any bit combination $a, b \in \{0, 1\}$.

The construction idea is to chain the AES computations, but not via CBC mode, but by deploying the random oracle $\mathcal{H}$. The first AES computation is carried out by hashing the message m to $x||y = \mathcal{H}(0||m)$, where x are the leading 125 bits. Apply AES_K to the four values $x||000, \ldots, x||011$, and then hash again as $X||Y = \mathcal{H}(1||\text{AES}_K(x||000)||\ldots||\text{AES}_K(x||011)||m)$, but including again the entire message in the second hash computation. Apply AES again to the X part with suffixes $100, \ldots, 110$. The final signature is then given by the eight values $(\text{AES}_K(x||000), \ldots, \text{AES}_K(x||011), \text{AES}_K(X||100), \ldots, \text{AES}_K(X||111))$.

We give a more general presentation of the scheme with a R-ary partitioning relations $\mathcal{R}$ for arbitrary R. Recall that for a string r we denote by $\text{clust}(r)$ the (unique) vector of values $r_0, \ldots, r_{R-1}$ such that the relation holds. We let $\text{AES}_K(\text{clust}(r))$ denote the vector where we apply AES_K to each component of $\text{clust}(r)$ and analogously for WBAES_K^{-1}. If used as input to the hash function we assume that it is converted into a string via standard concatenation of all fixed-size entries.

Construction 3. *Let $\kappa \in \mathbb{N}$ be the security parameter and let $\mathcal{R}$ be the R-ary common-prefix relation. Let ρ be the smallest integer such that $2^\rho \geq R$. Let $\mathcal{H} : \{0,1\}^* \to \{0,1\}^{\geq 128 - \rho - 1}$ be a random oracle. Define the signature scheme $\text{ROChainSign} = (\text{Gen}, \text{Sign}, \text{Ver})$ by the following algorithms:*

Key Generation: Let the signing key $sk = K \in \{0,1\}^{128}$ be an AES key, and let the verification key $vk = \text{WBAES}_K^{-1} \leftarrow \mathcal{WB}(1^\kappa, K)$ be a WB-AES implementation.

Signing: On input a signing key sk and a message $m \in \{0,1\}^*$, compute $x||y = \mathcal{H}(0||m)$ where $x \in \{0,1\}^{127-\rho}$. Compute $\Sigma_0 = \text{AES}_K(\text{clust}(x||0^{\rho+1}))$, and then $X||Y = \mathcal{H}(1||\Sigma_0||m)$ where $X \in \{0,1\}^{127-\rho}$. Finally derive $\Sigma_1 = \text{AES}_K(\text{clust}(X||10^\rho))$. Output $\sigma = (\Sigma_0, \Sigma_1)$ as the signature to m.

Verification: On input a verification key vk, a message $m \in \{0,1\}^*$, and a signature $\sigma = (\Sigma_0, \Sigma_1)$, compute $x||y = \mathcal{H}(0||m)$ and $X||Y = \mathcal{H}(1||\Sigma_0||m)$. Finally check that $\text{clust}(x||0^{\rho+1}) = \text{WBAES}_K^{-1}(\Sigma_0)$ and that $\text{clust}(X||10^\rho) = \text{WBAES}_K^{-1}(\Sigma_1)$ for all entries.

Theorem 2. *Let $\kappa \in \mathbb{N}$ be the security parameter, and let $\mathcal{R}$ be the R-ary common-prefix relation. Let ρ be the smallest integer such that $2^\rho \geq R$. For any adversary $\mathcal{A}$ that can produce an existential forgery for the ROChainSign scheme with q_S queries to the signature oracle, there exists an adversary $\mathcal{B}$ for the correlation intractability property of the WB-AES implementation, such that the advantage for $\mathcal{A}$ is*

$$\text{Adv}_{\mathcal{A}}^{\text{EF}}(\kappa, q_R, q_S) \leq 3 \cdot 2^{-128} + q_S^2 \cdot 2^{-115+\rho} + 2 \cdot \text{Adv}_{\mathcal{B},\mathcal{R}}^{\text{CI}}(\kappa, 2R \cdot q_S),$$

where $q_R \leq 2^{127-\rho}$.

The proof idea is to show that the bound $q_R \leq 2^{127-\rho}$ on the number of random oracle queries provides an upper bound on the number of hash collisions for each message appearing in one of the q_S signature queries. The bound guarantees, via the occupancy problem, that these are at most 2^6 collisions for each signed message, with overwhelming probability. If the adversary would make further first-stage hash queries with other valid tuples Σ_0 then it would immediately break correlation intractability. But the probability that any of these at most $2^6 \cdot q_S$ messages with a known first-stage hash value also collides in the second hash step is at most $q_S^2 \cdot 2^{-115+\rho}$. This means that the adversary would again need to find fresh values Σ_1 and break correlation intractability for a forgery.

7   Constructions via Input Encoding

In this section we present two constructions of secure signature schemes based on a correlation intractable white-box implementation of AES. The main idea of the constructions is to split the message in blocks of size $B \leq 128$, e.g., $B = 64$, and concatenate each of these message blocks with some signature-specific information that entangles the different AES evaluations. Natural candidates for the encodings for the message blocks are a signature-based counter or a nonce, and the block number of the processed message.

We discuss a counter-based (and thus stateful) solution as well as a state-free version where a nonce is used instead of the counter, but with longer signatures. Both constructions provide adequate security bounds based on correlation intractability for the common-prefix relation. One advantage of the constructions is that they are random-oracle free. On the downside, both schemes provide larger signatures of a few kilobytes each. For space reasons we present here only the counter-based solution.

In the constructions below we assume that messages are hashed first with a collision-resistant hash function; we do not need to model the hash function as a random oracle. With the common hash functions this results in messages of 256, 384, or 512 bits. We omit mentioning the hashing step for sake of a simpler presentation and assume that messages have a fixed size.

The high-level idea of the construction is to use a public counter ctr to make the AES evaluations unique for each signature, preventing the attacker to forge a signature by combining information from different signatures. Given a message $m \in \{0,1\}^{B \cdot \ell}$ consisting of ℓ messages blocks each of size B, we use a local block counter $i = 0, 1, \ldots, \ell - 1$ to ensure that an attacker cannot create a forgery by changing the order of the message blocks. The input encoding for the i-block is given by $m_i||i||\text{ctr}$, where the reader may think for sake of concreteness that messages are of 256 bits and we pick $B = 64$ and $\ell = 4$.

To enable a reduction to the correlation intractability to the R-ary common-prefix relation $\mathcal{R}$ we also reserve some bits for the R distinct suffixes for vectors in the relation in the encoding. We will append all combinations of ρ bits (with $2^\rho \geq R$) to the encoding. Then we evaluate AES on each of these $R \cdot \ell$ blocks.

Concretely, given a message $m \in \{0,1\}^{B \cdot \ell}$ with $m_i \in \{0,1\}^B$ and the R-ary common-prefix relation (e.g., $R = 4$), let ρ be the smallest integer such that

$2^\rho \geq R$. Let λ be the smallest integer such that $2^\lambda \geq \ell$ and assume that ctr can be represented with at most $\gamma := 128 - B - \lambda - \rho$ bits. For example, if $B = 64$, $\ell = 4$ and $R = 4$ the space for the counter value is $\gamma = 60$, allowing to sign up to 2^{60} messages.

The signature will consist of the value of the counter ctr and the $R \cdot \ell$ AES evaluations on the inputs

$$(m_i\|i\|\text{ctr}\|j)_{i=0,1,\ldots,\ell-1,\ j=0,1,\ldots,R-1}$$

where integers $i = 0, 1, \ldots, \ell - 1$ for the block number are encoded with λ bits, integers $j = 0, 1, \ldots, R - 1$ for the relation $\mathcal{R}$ are encoded with ρ bits, and the counter value ctr is encoded with γ bits. Note that each sequence $(m_i\|i\|\text{ctr}\|j)_{j=0,1,\ldots,R-1}$ for fixed i is a valid solution for the correlation intractability property for the common-prefix relation. In the construction we re-use the notation from Sect. 6 and let $\text{AES}_K(\text{clust}(r))$ denote the vector, where we apply AES_K to each entry in the vector $\text{clust}(r)$ (and likewise for WBAES_K^{-1}).

Construction 4. *Let $\kappa \in \mathbb{N}$ be the security parameter and let $\mathcal{R}$ be the R-ary common-prefix relation. Let ρ be the smallest integer such that $2^\rho \geq R$. Let $B \in \mathbb{N}$ be the size of each message block, and let $\ell \in \mathbb{N}$ be the number of message blocks, such that $n = B \cdot \ell$ is the fixed input length for messages. Let λ be the smallest integer such that $2^\lambda \geq \ell$. Then define $\gamma := 128 - B - \lambda - \rho$.*

Let $\text{CountSign} = (\text{Gen}, \text{Sign}, \text{Ver})$ be a signature scheme defined by the following algorithms:

Key Generation: Let the signing key $sk = K \in \{0,1\}^{128}$ be an AES key, and let the verification key $vk = \text{WBAES}_K^{-1} \leftarrow \mathcal{WB}(1^\kappa, K)$ be a WB-AES implementation. Let $\text{ctr} = 0^\gamma$ be the counter.

Signing: On input a signing key sk and a message $m \in \{0,1\}^n$, parse the message as $m = m_0\|\cdots\|m_{\ell-1}$ such that $m_i \in \{0,1\}^B$. For $i = 0, 1, \ldots, \ell - 1$ compute

$$\Sigma_i \leftarrow \text{AES}_K(\text{clust}(m_i\|i\|\text{ctr}\|0^\rho)).$$

Finally, output $\sigma = (\Sigma_0, \ldots, \Sigma_{\ell-1}, \text{ctr})$, and update the counter to $\text{ctr} \leftarrow \text{ctr} + 1$.

Verification: On input a verification key vk, a message $m \in \{0,1\}^n$, and a signature $\sigma = (\Sigma_0, \ldots, \Sigma_{\ell-1}, \text{ctr})$, parse the message as $m = m_0\|\cdots\|m_{\ell-1}$ such that $m_i \in \{0,1\}^B$, and for all $i = 0, 1, \ldots, \ell - 1$ check that

$$\text{clust}(m_i\|i\|\text{ctr}\|0^\rho) = \text{WBAES}_K^{-1}(\Sigma_i).$$

Theorem 3. *Let $\kappa \in \mathbb{N}$ be the security parameter and let $\mathcal{R}$ be the R-ary common-prefix relation. Let ℓ be the number of message blocks. For any adversary $\mathcal{A}$ that can produce an existential forgery for the CountSign scheme with q_S queries to the signature oracle, there exists an adversary $\mathcal{B}$ for the correlation-intractability property with relation $\mathcal{R}$ of the WB-AES implementation, such that the advantage for $\mathcal{A}$ is*

$$\text{Adv}_{\mathcal{A}}^{\text{EF}}(\kappa, q_S) \leq \text{Adv}_{\mathcal{B},\mathcal{R}}^{\text{CI}}(\kappa, R \cdot \ell \cdot q_S).$$

Note, that this scheme give us a tight security bound and allows us to sign 2^γ messages. However, a signature requires $R \cdot \ell$ AES invocations and produces signatures of size $R \cdot \ell \cdot 128 + \gamma$ bits (i.e. the signature consist of the γ bit counter and ℓ vectors $\Sigma_0, \ldots, \Sigma_{\ell-1}$ which each consist of R AES values). As a concrete example, consider a relation with arity $R = 4$ and messages of size $n = 256$ bits with a block size of $B = 64$ bits. Then we have $\rho = 2$, $\ell = 4$, $\lambda = 2$, and $\gamma = 128 - 64 - 2 - 2 = 60$. In this setting the CountSign construction yields signatures of size 2108 bits and we can sign 2^{60} messages.

8   Conclusion

Our results show that the limited block size of AES of 128 causes some challenges when devising signature schemes from WB-AES, due to the fact that outputs of a collision-resistant hash function do not fit into single blocks. This suggests that switching to block ciphers with larger size may ease the problem. For example, Rijndael supports larger blocks. Also, when potentially designing new, "whiteboxing friendly" block ciphers, larger sizes should be considered an option, too. For the moment, however, AES will most likely be the primary candidate because of its wide availability and since it is standardized.

Another implication from the security bounds and the generic attacks on the underlying problems is that it may be advantageous in some scenarios to deliberately make WBAES_K^{-1} evaluations *slow*. This limits the number of evaluation of WBAES_K^{-1} the adversary can perform in a period of time, aggravating for example collision finding strategies. Similar ideas appear in the domain of password-based hashing where iterative verification should slow down attacks.

Acknowledgments. This work has been [co-]funded by the DFG as part of project P2 within the CRC 1119 CROSSING, and the Danish Independent Research Council under Grant-ID DFF-6108-00169 (FoCC).

References

1. Agrawal, S.: New methods for indistinguishability obfuscation: bootstrapping and instantiation. IACR Cryptology ePrint Archive 2018, 633 (2018)
2. Ananth, P., Jain, A., Khurana, D., Sahai, A.: Indistinguishability obfuscation without multilinear maps: iO from LWE, bilinear maps, and weak pseudorandomness. IACR Cryptology ePrint Archive 2018, 615 (2018)
3. Banik, S., Bogdanov, A., Isobe, T., Jepsen, M.B.: Analysis of software countermeasures for whitebox encryption. IACR Trans. Symmetric Cryptol. **2017**(1), 307–328 (2017)
4. Barak, B., et al.: On the (im)possibility of obfuscating programs. J. ACM **59**(2), 6:1–6:48 (2012)
5. Bellare, M., Kilian, J., Rogaway, P.: The security of the cipher block chaining message authentication code. J. Comput. Syst. Sci. **61**(3), 362–399 (2000)
6. Bellare, M., Micali, S.: How to sign given any trapdoor permutation. J. ACM **39**(1), 214–233 (1992)

7. Bellare, M., Rogaway, P.: Random oracles are practical: a paradigm for designing efficient protocols. In: Proceedings of the 1st ACM Conference on Computer and Communications Security, CCS 1993, pp. 62–73. ACM (1993)

8. Bellare, M., Rogaway, P.: The exact security of digital signatures-how to sign with RSA and Rabin. In: Maurer, U. (ed.) EUROCRYPT 1996. LNCS, vol. 1070, pp. 399–416. Springer, Heidelberg (1996). https://doi.org/10.1007/3-540-68339-9_34

9. Billet, O., Gilbert, H., Ech-Chatbi, C.: Cryptanalysis of a white box AES implementation. In: Handschuh, H., Hasan, M.A. (eds.) SAC 2004. LNCS, vol. 3357, pp. 227–240. Springer, Heidelberg (2004). https://doi.org/10.1007/978-3-540-30564-4_16

10. Alpirez Bock, E., Brzuska, C., Michiels, W., Treff, A.: On the ineffectiveness of internal encodings - revisiting the DCA attack on white-box cryptography. In: Preneel, B., Vercauteren, F. (eds.) ACNS 2018. LNCS, vol. 10892, pp. 103–120. Springer, Cham (2018). https://doi.org/10.1007/978-3-319-93387-0_6

11. Bos, J.W., Hubain, C., Michiels, W., Teuwen, P.: Differential computation analysis: hiding your white-box designs is not enough. In: Gierlichs, B., Poschmann, A.Y. (eds.) CHES 2016. LNCS, vol. 9813, pp. 215–236. Springer, Heidelberg (2016). https://doi.org/10.1007/978-3-662-53140-2_11

12. Bringer, J., Chabanne, H., Dottax, E.: White box cryptography: another attempt. Cryptology ePrint Archive, Report 2006/468 (2006). http://eprint.iacr.org/2006/468

13. Chow, S., Eisen, P., Johnson, H., van Oorschot, P.C.: A white-box DES implementation for DRM applications. In: Feigenbaum, J. (ed.) DRM 2002. LNCS, vol. 2696, pp. 1–15. Springer, Heidelberg (2003). https://doi.org/10.1007/978-3-540-44993-5_1

14. Chow, S., Eisen, P., Johnson, H., Van Oorschot, P.C.: White-box cryptography and an AES implementation. In: Nyberg, K., Heys, H. (eds.) SAC 2002. LNCS, vol. 2595, pp. 250–270. Springer, Heidelberg (2003). https://doi.org/10.1007/3-540-36492-7_17

15. Coron, J.-S.: On the exact security of full domain hash. In: Bellare, M. (ed.) CRYPTO 2000. LNCS, vol. 1880, pp. 229–235. Springer, Heidelberg (2000). https://doi.org/10.1007/3-540-44598-6_14

16. Coron, J.-S.: Optimal security proofs for PSS and other signature schemes. In: Knudsen, L.R. (ed.) EUROCRYPT 2002. LNCS, vol. 2332, pp. 272–287. Springer, Heidelberg (2002). https://doi.org/10.1007/3-540-46035-7_18

17. De Mulder, Y., Roelse, P., Preneel, B.: Cryptanalysis of the Xiao – Lai white-box AES implementation. In: Knudsen, L.R., Wu, H. (eds.) SAC 2012. LNCS, vol. 7707, pp. 34–49. Springer, Heidelberg (2013). https://doi.org/10.1007/978-3-642-35999-6_3

18. De Mulder, Y., Wyseur, B., Preneel, B.: Cryptanalysis of a perturbated white-box AES implementation. In: Gong, G., Gupta, K.C. (eds.) INDOCRYPT 2010. LNCS, vol. 6498, pp. 292–310. Springer, Heidelberg (2010). https://doi.org/10.1007/978-3-642-17401-8_21

19. Delerablée, C., Lepoint, T., Paillier, P., Rivain, M.: White-box security notions for symmetric encryption schemes. In: Lange, T., Lauter, K., Lisoněk, P. (eds.) SAC 2013. LNCS, vol. 8282, pp. 247–264. Springer, Heidelberg (2014). https://doi.org/10.1007/978-3-662-43414-7_13

20. Derbez, P., Fouque, P., Lambin, B., Minaud, B.: On recovering affine encodings in white-box implementations. IACR Trans. Cryptogr. Hardw. Embed. Syst. **2018**(3), 121–149 (2018)

21. Fischlin, M., Lehmann, A., Ristenpart, T., Shrimpton, T., Stam, M., Tessaro, S.: Random oracles with(out) programmability. In: Abe, M. (ed.) ASIACRYPT 2010. LNCS, vol. 6477, pp. 303–320. Springer, Heidelberg (2010). https://doi.org/10.1007/978-3-642-17373-8_18

22. Garg, S., Gentry, C., Halevi, S., Raykova, M., Sahai, A., Waters, B.: Candidate indistinguishability obfuscation and functional encryption for all circuits. In: 54th Annual IEEE Symposium on Foundations of Computer Science, FOCS 2013, Berkeley, CA, USA, 26–29 October 2013, pp. 40–49 (2013)

23. Goubin, L., Paillier, P., Rivain, M., Wang, J.: How to reveal the secrets of an obscure white-box implementation. Cryptology ePrint Archive, Report 2018/098 (2018). http://eprint.iacr.org/2018/098

24. Jacob, M., Boneh, D., Felten, E.: Attacking an obfuscated cipher by injecting faults. In: Feigenbaum, J. (ed.) DRM 2002. LNCS, vol. 2696, pp. 16–31. Springer, Heidelberg (2003). https://doi.org/10.1007/978-3-540-44993-5_2

25. Joye, M.: On white-box cryptography. In: Elçi, A., Ors, S.B., Preneel, B. (eds.) Security of Information and Networks, pp. 7–12. Trafford Publishing, Bloomington (2008)

26. Kiltz, E., Mohassel, P., O'Neill, A.: Adaptive trapdoor functions and chosen-ciphertext security. In: Gilbert, H. (ed.) EUROCRYPT 2010. LNCS, vol. 6110, pp. 673–692. Springer, Heidelberg (2010). https://doi.org/10.1007/978-3-642-13190-5_34

27. Lepoint, T., Rivain, M., De Mulder, Y., Roelse, P., Preneel, B.: Two attacks on a white-box AES implementation. In: Lange, T., Lauter, K., Lisoněk, P. (eds.) SAC 2013. LNCS, vol. 8282, pp. 265–285. Springer, Heidelberg (2014). https://doi.org/10.1007/978-3-662-43414-7_14

28. Mastercard: Mastercard mobile payment SDK. Version 2.0, January 2017. https://developer.mastercard.com/

29. Michiels, W., Gorissen, P., Hollmann, H.D.L.: Cryptanalysis of a generic class of white-box implementations. In: Avanzi, R.M., Keliher, L., Sica, F. (eds.) SAC 2008. LNCS, vol. 5381, pp. 414–428. Springer, Heidelberg (2009). https://doi.org/10.1007/978-3-642-04159-4_27

30. Muir, J.A.: A tutorial on white-box AES. Cryptology ePrint Archive, Report 2013/104 (2013). http://eprint.iacr.org/2013/104

31. Peeters, M.: Challenges in white-box cryptography. In: Early Symmetric Crypto 2015 (2015). https://www.cryptolux.org/mediawiki-esc2015/index.php/ESC_2015

32. Ramchen, K., Waters, B.: Fully secure and fast signing from obfuscation. In: Proceedings of the 2014 ACM SIGSAC Conference on Computer and Communications Security, pp. 659–673. ACM (2014)

33. Rivain, M., Pailler, P.: White-box cryptography – new challenges and research directions. ECRYPT CSA Report D1.3, September 2016. www.ecrypt.eu.org/csa/documents/

34. Rivain, M., Wang, J.: Analysis and improvement of differential computation attacks against internally-encoded white-box implementations. IACR Trans. Cryptogr. Hardw. Embed. Syst. 2019(2), 225–255 (2019)

35. Sahai, A., Waters, B.: How to use indistinguishability obfuscation: deniable encryption, and more. In: Symposium on Theory of Computing, STOC 2014, New York, NY, USA, 31 May–03 June 2014, pp. 475–484. ACM (2014)

36. Sasdrich, P., Moradi, A., Güneysu, T.: White-box cryptography in the gray box. In: Peyrin, T. (ed.) FSE 2016. LNCS, vol. 9783, pp. 185–203. Springer, Heidelberg (2016). https://doi.org/10.1007/978-3-662-52993-5_10

37. Saxena, A., Wyseur, B., Preneel, B.: Towards security notions for white-box cryptography. In: Samarati, P., Yung, M., Martinelli, F., Ardagna, C.A. (eds.) ISC 2009. LNCS, vol. 5735, pp. 49–58. Springer, Heidelberg (2009). https://doi.org/10.1007/978-3-642-04474-8_4

38. Suzuki, K., Tonien, D., Kurosawa, K., Toyota, K.: Birthday paradox for multi-collisions. In: Rhee, M.S., Lee, B. (eds.) ICISC 2006. LNCS, vol. 4296, pp. 29–40. Springer, Heidelberg (2006). https://doi.org/10.1007/11927587_5

39. Xiao, Y., Lai, X.: A secure implementation of white-box AES. In: 2009 2nd International Conference on Computer Science and its Applications, pp. 1–6, December 2009

The Simplest Multi-key Linearly Homomorphic Signature Scheme

Diego F. Aranha[1,2(✉)] and Elena Pagnin[1]

[1] Aarhus University, Aarhus, Denmark
dfaranha@eng.au.dk, elena@cs.au.dk
[2] University of Campinas, Campinas, Brazil

Abstract. We consider the problem of outsourcing computation on data authenticated by different users. Our aim is to describe and implement the simplest possible solution to provide data integrity in cloud-based scenarios. Concretely, our multi-key linearly homomorphic signature scheme (mklhs) allows users to upload signed data on a server, and at any later point in time any third party can query the server to compute a linear combination of data authenticated by different users and check the correctness of the returned result. Our construction generalizes Boneh et al.'s linearly homomorphic signature scheme (PKC'09 [7]) to the multi-key setting and relies on basic tools of pairing-based cryptography. Compared to existing multi-key homomorphic signature schemes, our mklhs is a conceptually simple and elegant direct construction, which trades-off privacy for efficiency. The simplicity of our approach leads us to a very efficient construction that enjoys significantly shorter signatures and higher performance than previous proposals. Finally, we implement mklhs using two different pairing-friendly curves at the 128-bit security level, a Barreto-Lynn-Scott curve and a Barreto-Naehrig curve. Our benchmarks illustrate interesting performance trade-offs between these parameters, involving the cost of exponentiation and hashing in pairing groups. We provide a discussion on such trade-offs that can be useful to other implementers of pairing-based protocols.

Keywords: Multi-key homomorphic signatures ·
Cryptographic pairings · Efficient software implementation

1 Introduction

Outsourcing tasks and data is an increasing need in today's society. A common paradigm is to collect data, store and process it on remote servers and finally return an aggregated result. As an example, consider a fitness program where devices upload user data to a remote server, a service provider computes on the outsourced data and informs users with statistics on their average heartbeat rates, running speed and so on. The very same pattern applies also to a wide range of data coming from medical, financial or general measurement

© Springer Nature Switzerland AG 2019
P. Schwabe and N. Thériault (Eds.): LATINCRYPT 2019, LNCS 11774, pp. 280–300, 2019.
https://doi.org/10.1007/978-3-030-30530-7_14

sources. Recent scandals have taught us that users should not blindly rely on *the cloud* or *trust* service providers not to misbehave. Therefore, to fully enjoy the benefits of cloud-based solutions users must be able to somehow "protect" the tasks and data they outsource. To this end, researchers developed specific tools for retaining privacy, ensuring correctness and other desirable properties, such as Private Information Retrieval (PIR), Verifiable delegation of Computations (VC), (Fully) Homomorphic Encryption (FHE) and Signatures (FHS), to mention a few.

This work focuses on a special subset of Homomorphic Signature schemes, namely Multi-Key Homomorphic Signatures (MKHS). In a nutshell, a MKHS scheme enables a set of multiple signers to independently authenticate their data, upload data and signatures to a remote server, let any third party (usually the server) carry out sensible computations and output a "combined" signature vouching for the correctness of the outcome of the computation, even when this was carried on data authenticated by different users. We remark that, in this model, after uploading the authenticated data, the signers are not required to interact with the cloud or the verifier. While MKHS do not guarantee privacy of the outsourced data, they target integrity of the information the server provides to the verifiers. In more detail, homomorphic signatures are a valid defense against malicious manipulation of data since they not only guarantee that the data used in the computation was authenticated by each signer involved but also that the output of the computation is correct. In other words, the "combined" signature can be used to verify that what the cloud outputs to the verifier is indeed the answer to the desired computation on the database (and not some random authenticated record). Existing MKHS constructions are based on lattice techniques [13], zero-knowledge succinct non-interactive arguments of knowledge (zk-SNARK) [23], or creative yet convoluted compilers [14, 26]. In this work, we take multi-key homomorphic signatures as a case of study and propose a new scheme that we consider conceptually simpler than all existing proposals.

Our Contribution. We aim to provide a MKHS scheme that is simpler to understand and thus can be seen as an easy way to introduce this fairly new research area. Our scheme, mklhs, allows to authenticate data signed by independent signers in a concise way and also to authenticate the result of a linear combination of data signed with different secret keys. While we are restricted to linear functions only, our signatures are shorter than all existing constructions. Despite the lack of full-fledged properties, such as full homomorphism or context hiding, mklhs has desirable characteristics including better succinctness and performance than previous proposals and relying entirely on standard assumptions (Random Oracle Model). Our scheme is inspired by the signature scheme by Boneh *et al.* [7] for signing a vector space in linear network coding scenarios. We remove the tools that are network-coding related and use a simple trick to obtain the multi-key features. While this technique is known and implicitly used in other works (*e.g.*, [13,26]), here we make a clear explanation of it and show that a natural application of this technique already brings with a non-trivial construction. Performance-wise, mklhs only requires operations in the base curve for computing signatures or evaluating functions over authenticated data, while signature verification requires a product of pairings. We implement mklhs using pairings defined over elliptic curves using two sets of parameters at the current 128-bit security level: a Barreto-Lynn-Scott [5] curve with embedding degree 12 over a 381-bit prime field (BLS12-381) used in ZCash [25], and a Barreto-Naehrig [6] curve defined over a 382-bit field (BN-382). Our implementations illustrate trade-offs among parameters which can be useful to other instantiations of pairing-based protocols. To the best of our knowledge, this constitutes the first concrete implementation of multi-key homomorphic signature schemes.

Related Work. The notion of homomorphic signature schemes (HS) was introduced by Johnson *et al.* in [20], together with a security model for HS and a concrete construction for redactable signatures. Intuitively, this first example of HS allows to erase part of the message as an homomorphic operation: given a message m and a signature σ of m, anyone can derive from σ a new signature σ' for any message m' obtained after redacting m. Subsequent proposals extended the kind of operations supported by HS. The main bulk of work comes with constructions of linearly homomorphic signatures for linear network coding [3,7,8,10]. More recently, Catalano *et al.* [11] address the question of HS for higher degree functions and show applications to efficient verifiable computation of polynomial functions. The first construction of (leveled) fully homomorphic signatures (FHS) is due to Gorbunov *et al.* [18]. The scheme presented in [18] is a lattice-based HS capable of evaluating arbitrary boolean circuits of bounded polynomial depth over signed data. However, none of the aforementioned schemes support computations on data signed by multiple clients.

Agrawal *et al.* [1] expand the horizon of applications by considering *multi-source* signatures in the context of network coding. A few years later, Fiore *et al.* [13] formalize the concept of multi-key homomorphic authenticators and provided the first constructions of a multi-key homomorphic signature scheme (MKHS) and of a multi-key homomorphic MAC. The MKHS in [13] is designed for boolean circuits of bounded depth and can be seen as a (non-trivial) extension of the FHS scheme in [18]. A limitation of this work is that the proposed MKHS scheme is not unforgeable if corrupted parties take part to the computation. Lai *et al.* [23] address this issue and show that MKHS unforgeable under corruption can be constructed using zk-SNARKs and indeed must rely on non-falsifiable assumptions. Fiore and Pagnin [14] put forward a generic compiler to empower any single-key FHS with multi-key features without adding any security assumptions on top of the ones required by the base scheme. While the intuition behind this compiler is quite simple, its formal description gets quickly entangled. Schabhüser *et al.* [26] recently proposed another generic compiler to obtain multi-key *linearly* homomorphic authenticators from any signature or MAC scheme. Their technique relies on asymmetric bilinear groups, is based on standard assumptions only, and achieves the non-trivial property of context hiding. In a nutshell, homomorphic signatures that are context hiding guarantee the privacy of the data input to the homomorphic evaluation, as evaluated authenticators do not leak any information about the input messages.

Our scheme provides the first direct construction of a multi-key linearly homomorphic signature scheme that is not based on a compiler. Albeit lacking context hiding, our proposal is the simplest and most intuitive HS to enjoy multi-key features up to date. Suitable application scenarios are contexts involving public data where authenticity is preferable to confidentiality, e.g., processing pollution values recorded by sensors scattered around the city, simple statistic on public data such as weather forecast, among others. Moreover, compared to [26], we achieve concretely better succinctness: while the asymptotic bound is the same for both ($\mathcal{O}(t)$, for t signers involved in the computation), the constants hidden by the big-oh notation differ considerably. In terms of performance, our implementations show that mklhs outperforms [26] in all protocol operations (see Sect. 4 for further details).

2 Preliminaries

In this section, we recall the fundamental definitions of bilinear pairings and multi-key homomorphic signatures. In what follows, we use *choosing at random* or *randomly choosing* to refer to sampling from the given set according to the uniform distribution. In addition, we write $\mathsf{poly}(\lambda)$ to denote a polynomial function in the variable λ, and ε a negligible function (*i.e.*, $\varepsilon(\lambda) < 1/\mathsf{poly}(\lambda)$, for any function poly and large enough values of λ).

2.1 Bilinear Pairings and Security Assumptions

An *admissible bilinear pairing* is a non-degenerate efficiently-computable map $e : \mathbb{G}_1 \times \mathbb{G}_2 \to \mathbb{G}_T$ defined over groups of prime order q. For efficiency, we assume here an *asymmetric* pairing constructed over an ordinary pairing-friendly curve with embedding degree k. In practice, groups $\mathbb{G}_1$ and $\mathbb{G}_2$ are then chosen as subgroups of points in elliptic curves E and d-degree twist E' defined over a finite field $\mathbb{F}_p$ and its extension $\mathbb{F}_{p^{k/d}}$, respectively, and $\mathbb{G}_T$ is a subgroup of the multiplicative group of the related finite field $\mathbb{F}_{p^k}^*$.

The core property of the map e is linearity in both arguments, allowing the construction of novel cryptographic schemes with security relying on the hardness of the *Discrete Logarithm Problem* (DLP) in $\mathbb{G}_1, \mathbb{G}_2$ and $\mathbb{G}_T$. Security of pairing-based protocols typically relies directly or indirectly on the hardness of solving the *Bilinear Diffie-Hellman* problem (BDHP) of computing $e(g,h)^{abc}$ given $g, g^a, g^b, g^c, h, h^a, h^b, h^c$ for $g \in \mathbb{G}_1$, $h \in \mathbb{G}_2$ and $a, b, c \in \mathbb{Z}_q^*$. The security of our particular scheme depends on the hardness of the *co-Computational Diffie-Hellman* problem (co-CDH) in the bilinear setting:

Definition 1 (co-CDH). *Given $g \in \mathbb{G}_1$ and $h, h^x \in \mathbb{G}_2$, compute $g^x \in \mathbb{G}_1$.*

2.2 Multi-key Homomorphic Signatures

The seminal notions of homomorphic signatures consider only authenticated data and a function to be evaluated on the data and the signatures. While this is a direct approach, more recent work on homomorphic authenticators and especially on multi-key variations thereof points out the need to authenticate data "in a context". Intuitively, we are not interested in verifying that a certain value m is the output of function f on *some* authenticated data, but rather that m is the output of f on *precisely* the data asked to be computed on. This linkability property allows us to put the values into a well-defined context. The cryptographic artifact that is used to formalize the intuition above is called a *labeled program*.

Definition 2 (Labeled Programs [17]). *A labeled program $\mathcal{P}$ is a tuple of form $(f, \ell_1, \ldots, \ell_n)$ where f is a function $f : \mathcal{M}^n \rightarrow \mathcal{M}$ that takes as input n messages and returns a single value, while $\ell_1, \ldots, \ell_n \in \{0,1\}^*$ are the n labels that identify each input of f.*

In this work, we follow the mainstream approach to include the identity of users in the labels. A meaningful definition of multi-key HS requires the signatures to be verified with respect to the set of keys used to sign the inputs to the computation. Our labels are of the form $\ell = (\mathsf{id}, \tau)$ where id is a user's identifier (we often refer to it as identity) and τ is a tag, a string used to uniquely identify a data item from user id. As a general rule, n denotes the number of inputs to the labeled program (essentially the number of messages involved in the computation), while t denotes the number of distinct entities contributing with data to the computation. Therefore it holds that $n \geq t$. For further details we refer the reader to [13, 14, 17].

Next, we present the definition of multi-key homomorphic signatures. For completeness, we include dataset identifiers Δ in the general definitions, even though these will be dropped in our construction (where they can trivially be included into the tags as shown in [13]). Intuitively, dataset identifiers enable users to authenticate data on different databases, or to sign a new message under the same label (but for a different Δ).

Definition 3 (Multi-Key Homomorphic Signatures [13]). *A multi-key homomorphic signature scheme* MKHS *is a tuple of five PPT algorithms* MKHS $=$ (Setup, KeyGen, Sign, Eval, Verify) *defined as follows.*

Setup(1^λ): *The setup algorithm takes as input the security parameter and outputs some public parameters* pp *including a description of an identity space* ID, *a tag space* $\mathcal{T}$ *a message space* $\mathcal{M}$ *and a set of admissible functions* $\mathcal{F}$.

KeyGen(pp): *The key generation algorithm takes as input the public parameters and outputs a pair of keys (*sk,pk*) to which is associated an identity* id.

Sign(sk, Δ, ℓ, m): *The sign algorithm takes as input a secret key* sk, *a dataset identifier* Δ, *a label* $\ell = (\mathsf{id}, \tau)$ *for the message* m, *and it outputs a signature* σ.

Eval($\mathcal{P}$, $\{\mathsf{pk}_{\mathsf{id}}\}_{\mathsf{id} \in \mathcal{P}}$, $\sigma_1, \ldots, \sigma_n$): *The evaluation algorithm takes as input a labeled program* $\mathcal{P} = (f, \ell_1, \ldots, \ell_n)$ *a set of public-keys and signatures, and outputs an homomorphic signature* σ.

Verify($\mathcal{P}, \Delta, \{\mathsf{pk}_{\mathsf{id}}\}_{\mathsf{id} \in \mathcal{P}}, m, \sigma$): *The verification algorithm takes as input a labeled program $\mathcal{P}$, a dataset identifier Δ, the set of public keys defined by the labels in $\mathcal{P}$, a message m and an homomorphic signature σ. It outputs 0 (reject) or 1 (accept).*

In this work, we consider a special family of MKHS, namely schemes that support evaluation of solely linear functions. When referring to MKHS schemes we give for granted that the construction satisfies the properties of authentication correctness, evaluation correctness and compactness described below.

Authentication Correctness. Intuitively, this property states that every signature output by the Sign algorithm for a message m and label ℓ verifies successfully, with overwhelming probability, against m, ℓ and labeled program $\mathcal{I}$ corresponding to the identity function for label ℓ. Formally, a multi-key homomorphic signature satisfies authentication correctness if for all public parameters $\mathsf{pp} \leftarrow \mathsf{Setup}(1^\lambda)$, any database identifier Δ, any key pair $(\mathsf{sk}_{\mathsf{id}}, \mathsf{pk}_{\mathsf{id}}) \leftarrow \mathsf{KeyGen}(\mathsf{pp})$, any label $\ell = (\mathsf{id}, \tau) \in \mathsf{ID} \times \mathcal{T}$, any message $m \in \mathcal{M}$ and any signature $\sigma \leftarrow \mathsf{Sign}(\mathsf{sk}, \Delta, \ell, m)$, it holds that

$$\Pr\left[\mathsf{Verify}(\mathcal{I}_\ell, \Delta, \mathsf{pk}, m, \sigma) = 1\right] \geq 1 - \varepsilon \ .$$

Evaluation Correctness. Intuitively, this property states that if the signatures input to the Eval algorithm satisfy authentication correctness, then Eval outputs signatures that, with overwhelming probability, verify successfully for the appropriate value m and labeled program $\mathcal{P}'$ (seen as the composition of multiple labeled programs). Formally, a multi-key homomorphic signature satisfies evaluation correctness if

$$\Pr\left[\mathsf{MKHS.Verify}(\mathcal{P}', \Delta, \{\mathsf{pk}_{\mathsf{id}}\}_{\mathsf{id} \in \mathcal{P}'}, m', \sigma') = 1\right] \geq 1 - \varepsilon \ ,$$

where the equality holds for a fixed description of the public parameters $\mathsf{pp} \leftarrow \mathsf{Setup}(1^\lambda)$, an arbitrary set of honestly generated keys $(\mathsf{sk}_{\mathsf{id}}, \mathsf{pk}_{\mathsf{id}}) \leftarrow \mathsf{KeyGen}(\mathsf{pp})$, a function $f : \mathcal{M}^n \to \mathcal{M}$, any dataset Δ, and any set of program/message/signature triples $\{(\mathcal{P}_i, m_i, \sigma_i)\}_{i \in [n]}$ such that $\mathsf{Verify}(\mathcal{P}_i, \Delta, \{\mathsf{pk}_{\mathsf{id}}\}_{\mathsf{id} \in \mathcal{P}_i}, m_i, \sigma_i) = 1$ for all $i \in [n]$, and $m' = g(m_1, \ldots, m_n)$, $\mathcal{P}' = g(\mathcal{P}_1, \ldots, \mathcal{P}_n)$, and $\sigma' \leftarrow \mathsf{Eval}(\mathcal{P}, \{\mathsf{pk}_{\mathsf{id}}\}_{\mathsf{id} \in \mathcal{P}_i}, \{\sigma_i\}_{i \in [n]})$.

Succinctness. This is a crucial property for MKHS as it rules out trivial constructions. One could define a MKHS scheme by using a standard (non-homomorphic) signature scheme, and set the Eval procedure to simply append the input signatures (and corresponding messages). Now, all the workload drops on the Verify algorithm, that checks the authentication correctness of each individual signature and its message, and afterwards performs the desired computation on the authenticated messages. What makes such a solution unattractive is that (i) the verifier needs to check the validity of n signatures (where n is the number of inputs to the function it wishes to evaluate) and (ii) the verifier essentially needs to compute the function itself. The succinctness property guarantees that the verifier only needs to perform *one* signature verification. Intuitively, this means that the size of the signature output by Eval for a labeled program $\mathcal{P}$ should be significantly smaller than n, the input size of $\mathcal{P}$, concretely, it should depend at most logarithmically in n, and linearly in the number of signers involved in the computation. More formally, a multi-key homomorphic signature is succinct if the signature $\sigma \leftarrow \mathsf{Eval}(\mathcal{P}, \{\mathsf{pk}_{\mathsf{id}}\}_{\mathsf{id} \in \mathcal{P}_i}, \{\sigma_i\}_{i \in [n]})$ has size $|\sigma| = \mathsf{poly}(\lambda, t, \log n)$ where λ denotes the security parameter of the scheme, $t = |\mathsf{id} \in \mathcal{P}|$ denotes the number of distinct identities involved in the computation and n is the total number of inputs to $\mathcal{P}$.

Security. Finally, we present the security notion for multi-key homomorphic signatures. Our definition is equivalent to the one provided by Fiore *et al.* [13], however, we split the authentication query phase into two phases: a identity query one and a sign phase to improve readability and avoid long listing sub-cases.

Definition 4 (Homomorphic Unforgeability Under Chosen Message Attack security experiment – HUFCMA).

Setup. *The challenger $\mathscr{C}$ runs* $\mathsf{pp} \leftarrow \mathsf{Setup}(1^\lambda)$ *and returns* pp *to the adversary $\mathscr{A}$. In addition, $\mathscr{C}$ initiates three empty lists, the first one to keep track of already generated identities $L_{ID} \leftarrow \varnothing$, the second one for bookkeeping the dataset/labels/messages that will sign during the game $L_\sigma \leftarrow \varnothing$, and the third one for corrupted identities $L_{\mathsf{corr}} \leftarrow \varnothing$.*

Identity Queries. *The adversary can adaptively submit identity queries of the form* $\mathsf{id} \in \mathsf{ID}$. *Whenever* $\mathsf{id} \notin L_{ID}$, *it means that this is the first query with identity* id, *and $\mathscr{C}$ generates new keys for this identity by running* $(\mathsf{sk}, \mathsf{pk}) \leftarrow \mathsf{KeyGen}(\mathsf{pp})$. *Then it numbers the identity as* id_d, *where* $d = |L_{ID}| + 1$, *and adds* id_d *to the list of already generated identities* $L_{ID} \leftarrow L_{ID} \cup \{(\mathsf{id}, d, \mathsf{sk}, \mathsf{pk})\}$. *Finally, the challenger returns to $\mathscr{A}$ the public key* pk. *Whenever* $\mathsf{id} \in L_{ID}$ *the challenger interprets the query as a corruption query, so it updates the list of corrupted parties* $L_{\mathsf{corr}} \leftarrow L_{\mathsf{corr}} \cup \mathsf{id}$ *and retrieves the handle of information containing* id *from* L_{ID}, *i.e.,* $(\mathsf{id}, d, \mathsf{sk}, \mathsf{pk})$. *Finally, the challenger returns to $\mathscr{A}$ the secret key* sk *corresponding to the queried identity.*

Sign Queries. *The adversary can adaptively submit queries of the form* (Δ, ℓ, m), *where Δ is a database identifier,* $\ell = (\mathsf{id}, \tau)$ *is a label in* $\mathsf{ID} \times \mathcal{T}$ *and* $m \in \mathcal{M}$ *is a message. The challenger ignores the query whenever* $(\Delta, \ell, \cdot) \in L_\sigma$, *i.e., the adversary has already asked a signature for label ℓ in the dataset Δ; or* $(\mathsf{id}, \cdots) \notin L_{ID}$, *i.e., the identity specified in* $\ell = (\mathsf{id}, \tau)$ *has not yet been generated. Otherwise, the challenger computes* $\sigma \leftarrow \mathsf{Sign}(\mathsf{sk}_{\mathsf{id}}, \Delta, \ell, m)$, *updates the list* $L_\sigma \leftarrow L_\sigma \cup (\Delta, \ell, m)$ *and returns σ to the adversary.*

Forgery. *At the end of the game, the adversary $\mathscr{A}$ outputs a tuple*

$$(\mathcal{P}^*, \Delta^*, \{\mathsf{pk}_{\mathsf{id}}^*\}_{\mathsf{id} \in \mathcal{P}^*}, m^*, \sigma^*).$$

The experiment outputs 1 *if the tuple returned by $\mathscr{A}$ is a forgery (defined below), and* 0 *otherwise.*

Definition 5. *A* MKHS *scheme is said to be* unforgeable *if, for every PPT adversary $\mathscr{A}$, its advantage in winning the security game (HUFCMA) described before is negligible in the security parameter of the scheme, formally:*

$$\mathsf{Adv}_{\mathsf{MKHS},\mathscr{A}}[\lambda] = \Pr[\mathscr{A} \text{ wins the HUFCMA game for MKHS}(\lambda) = 1] \leq \varepsilon.$$

Definition 6 (Forgery). *We consider an execution of HUFCMA where* $(\mathcal{P}^*, \Delta^*, \{\mathsf{pk}^*_{\mathsf{id}}\}_{\mathsf{id} \in \mathcal{P}^*}, m^*, \sigma^*)$ *is the tuple returned by $\mathscr{A}$ at the end of the experiment. Let $\mathcal{P}^* = (f^*, \ell_1^*, \ldots, \ell_n^*)$. The adversary outputs a successful forgery if*

$$\mathsf{Verify}(\mathcal{P}^*, \Delta^*, \{\mathsf{pk}^*_{\mathsf{id}}\}_{\mathsf{id} \in \mathcal{P}^*}, m^*, \sigma^*) = 1$$

and at least one of the following conditions hold:
   Type-1 Forgery: *the database Δ^* was never initialized during the game, i.e., $(\Delta^*, \cdot, \cdot) \notin L_\sigma$.*
   Type-2 Forgery: *for all* $\mathsf{id} \in \mathcal{P}^*$, $\mathsf{id} \notin L_{\mathsf{corr}}$ *and* $(\Delta^*, \ell_i^*, m_i) \in L_\sigma$ *for all* $i \in [n]$, *but* $m^* \neq f^*(m_1, \ldots, m_n)$.
   Type-3 Forgery: *there exists (at least) one index $i \in [n]$ such that ℓ_i^* was never queried, i.e., $(\Delta^*, \ell_i^*, \cdot) \notin L_\sigma$ and $\mathsf{id}_i \notin L_{\mathsf{corr}}$ is a non-corrupted identity.*

In all forgery types, the adversary tampers with the result of the computation by creating a signature σ^* that verifies an incorrect or un-initialized value m^*. More precisely, type-1 forgeries model cross-database attacks and are relevant only to constructions that consider multiple datasets. Type-2 forgeries model attack scenarios where the adversary intents to authenticate a value m^* that is not the correct output of $\mathcal{P}^*$ when executed over previously signed data. It is important to notice that all label-message pairs have been queried during the game. In contrast, type-3 forgeries model attack scenarios where at least one of the inputs to the labeled program $\mathcal{P}^*$ has never been initialized during the security game. In such cases, the adversary has no access to the signature of a message for a certain label ℓ_i^*. Thus, $\mathscr{A}$ has the freedom to choose a value m_i^* for the i-th input to the computation, conditioned to forging a valid signature for (ℓ_i^*, m_i^*).
   In this work we want to provide a construction of a multi-key linearly homomorphic signature scheme that is as simple and intuitive as possible. To this end, we do not consider multiple datasets, and thus ignore database identifiers and type-1 forgeries.

3   Our Construction

We propose mklhs, a linearly homomorphic signature scheme that supports computations on data authenticated by different secret keys. Compared to existing constructions [26], our proposal is conceptually simpler and more direct.
   Our scheme is inspired by the linearly homomorphic signature scheme by Boneh *et al.* [7] for signing vector spaces in the context of linear network coding. Concretely, we remove all of the network-coding related machinery from [7] and modify the resulting scheme to accommodate for homomorphic computations

on signatures generated using different secret keys. The joint signature results unforgeable under the co-CDH assumption and achieves better succinctness (in terms of number of entries) than [26] and [13]. Similarly to [7], we work with Type-2 pairings for clarity and convenience. This gives us a homomorphism φ from $\mathbb{G}_2$ to $\mathbb{G}_1$ that plays a central role in our security proof. However, standard tools from the literature can be used to adapt the security proof to the more efficient Type-3 pairing setting by tweaking the hardness assumption [12]. A hash function $H : \{0,1\}^* \to \mathbb{G}_1$ will also be needed to embed labels in the signatures.

3.1   Intuition

The main algorithms of our construction are detailed in Fig. 1. In what follows, we provide an intuitive description. Our signatures are obtained by hashing the label corresponding to the desired message to a group element in $\mathbb{G}_1$. Subsequently, we multiply this group element by the generator of the elliptic curve group to the power of the message. Finally, we wrap the result by exponentiating to the secret key. For security, we also need to append the message to the signatures. While this approach precludes us from achieving context hiding features, it does not go against the basic requirements of a signature scheme, namely guaranteeing data integrity and not confidentiality. The homomorphic evaluation of signatures follows the same aggregation style as [7], with an additional routine to take care of the second component of the input signatures. In detail, for every distinct identity that contributed to the computation with a signature, we identify all of the partial inputs of this identity and homomorphically combine them into one single component. Finally, for verification, we perform two consistency checks: first we make sure that the contribution provided by each signer actually adds up to all the target message (line 3); then we check that each signer's contribution verifies, in a batch manner (lines 5 and 6).

The **Organize** subroutine used by the evaluation and verification algorithms is formalized in the pseudocode to the right. Given as input a set of elements each containing an identity identifier (*e.g.,* the signatures or the labels), it identifies what are the different identities, re-labels them according to the order of appearance, and outputs the ordered set of identities as well as sets of indexes corresponding to the element connected to each identity. Essentially, it translates statements like "without loss of generality, we assume that the input signatures are grouped per-user and that the identities involved have indexes from 1 to t".

$\text{Organize}(a_1, \dots, a_n)$
1 : $\text{OrdID} \leftarrow \varnothing, j \leftarrow 0, t \leftarrow 0$
2 :   **for** $i \in [n]$
3 :   **parse** $a_i = (\text{id}_i, *)$
4 :   **if** $\text{id}_i \notin \text{OrdID}$
5 : $j \leftarrow |\text{OrdID}| + 1$
6 : $\tilde{\text{id}}_j \leftarrow \text{id}_i$
7 : $\text{OrdID} \leftarrow \text{OrdID} \cup \{\tilde{\text{id}}_j\}$
8 : $t \leftarrow |\text{OrdID}|$
9 :   **for** $j \in [n]$
10 : $\mathsf{l}_j \leftarrow \varnothing$
11 :   **if** $\text{id}_i == \tilde{\text{id}}_j$
12 : $\mathsf{l}_j \leftarrow \mathsf{l}_j \cup \{i\}$
return $(t, \text{OrdID}, \mathsf{l}_1, \dots, \mathsf{l}_t)$.

3.2   Security Analysis

The security of our scheme is supported by the main theorem below.

Setup(1^λ)

1 : $\mathcal{G} \leftarrow \mathsf{BilinGroup}(\lambda)$

2 :   **define sets:**

    $\mathsf{ID}, \mathcal{T} \subseteq \{0,1\}^k$

3 : $\mathcal{M} \subseteq \mathbb{Z}_q$

    return $\mathsf{pp} \leftarrow (\mathcal{G}, \mathsf{ID}, \mathcal{M}, \mathcal{T})$.

KeyGen(pp)

1 : $\mathsf{id} \xleftarrow{\$} \mathsf{ID}$

2 : $\mathsf{sk_{id}} \xleftarrow{\$} \mathbb{Z}_q^*$

3 : $\mathsf{pk_{id}} = g_2^{\mathsf{sk_{id}}} \in \mathbb{G}_2$

    return $(\mathsf{sk_{id}}, \mathsf{pk_{id}}, \mathsf{id})$.

Sign($\mathsf{sk_{id}}, \ell, m$)

1 : $\gamma = (H(\ell) \cdot g_1^m)^{\mathsf{sk_{id}}}$

2 : $\mu = m$

    return $\sigma = (\mathsf{id}, \gamma, \mu)$.

Eval($f, \sigma_1, \dots, \sigma_n$)

1 :   **parse** $f = (f_1, \dots, f_n) \in \mathbb{Z}_q^n$

2 :   **parse** $\sigma_i = (\mathsf{id}_i, \gamma_i, \mu_i) \in \mathsf{ID} \times \mathbb{G}_1 \times \mathbb{Z}_q$

3 : $\gamma = \prod_{i=1}^{n} \gamma_i^{f_i}$

4 : $out \leftarrow \mathbf{Organize}(\sigma_1, \dots, \sigma_n)$

5 :   **parse** $out = (t, \mathsf{OrdID}, \mathsf{I}_1, \dots, \mathsf{I}_t)$

6 :   **for** $j \in [t]$

    $\mu_j = \sum_{i \in \mathsf{I}_j} f_i \cdot \mu_i$.

    return $\sigma = (\gamma, \mu_1, \dots, \mu_t)$.

Verify($\mathcal{P}, \{\mathsf{pk_{id}}\}, m, \sigma$)

1 :   **parse** $\mathcal{P} = (f, \ell_1, \dots, \ell_n) \in \mathbb{Z}_q^n \times (\mathsf{ID} \times \mathcal{T})^n$

2 :   **parse** $\sigma = (\gamma, \mu_1, \dots, \mu_t) \in \mathbb{G}_1 \times \mathbb{Z}_q^t$

3 : $ver_1 \leftarrow \mathbf{Boolean} \left[m == \sum_{k=1}^{t} \mu_k \right]$

4 : $out \leftarrow \mathbf{Organize}(\ell_1, \dots, \ell_n)$

5 :   **parse** $out = (t, \mathsf{OrdID}, \mathsf{I}_1, \dots, \mathsf{I}_t)$

6 : $c = \prod_{j=1}^{t} e(g_1^{\mu_j} \cdot \prod_{i \in \mathsf{I}_j} H(\ell_i)^{f_i}, \ \mathsf{pk}_{\bar{\mathsf{id}}_j})$

7 : $ver_2 \leftarrow \mathbf{Boolean}\, [e(\gamma, g_2) == c]$

    return Boolean $[ver_1 \wedge ver_2]$

Fig. 1. Our mklhs construction.

Theorem 1. *The* mklhs *scheme is secure in the random oracle model assuming that the co-CDH problem is computationally infeasible. In detail, let $\mathscr{A}$ be a probabilistic polynomial-time adversary in the security experiment (HUFCMA) described in Sect. 2.2, then its advantage is bounded by*

$$\mathsf{Adv}_{\mathsf{mklhs}, \mathscr{A}}[\lambda] \leq \frac{1}{2} \cdot \left[R_H + Q_{\mathsf{id}} \cdot \mathsf{Adv}_{\mathscr{B}}^{\mathsf{coCDH}[\lambda]} \right].$$

where $\mathscr{B}$ is a polynomial-time algorithm that solves a co-CDH instance with probability $\mathsf{Adv}_{\mathscr{B}}^{\mathsf{coCDH}}[\lambda]$, $R_H = \frac{1}{\mathsf{poly}(\lambda)}$ is determined by the prime number q corresponding to the order of the group $\mathbb{G}_1$ (the range of the hash function) and $Q_{\mathsf{id}} = \mathsf{poly}(\lambda)$ is the total number of identities generated during the game.

The proof flow works as follows. We begin by ruling out corruption queries using the generic result by Fiore *et al.* on the equivalence between multi-key homomorphic authenticators secure against adversaries that make *no corruption* queries and secure against adversaries that make *non-adaptive* corruption queries (Proposition 1 in [13]). Next, we consider an adversary that outputs type-3 forgeries and show that it can only succeed with a negligible probability of $R_H = \frac{1}{q} = \frac{1}{\mathsf{poly}(\lambda)}$ corresponding to randomly guessing $H(\ell^*)$, the output of the hash function on the un-queried label. Finally, we exhibit a reduction from type-2 forgeries to the co-CDH problem that combines techniques for multi-key settings with a clever embedding of the co-CDH challenge into our signature scheme. In particular, modulo the multi-key factor, our reduction is conceptually simpler and more efficient (less probability to abort) than the one used in [7]. This improvement is mainly due to a technical choice: separating hash queries from sign queries, namely our adversary can perform hash queries only after the sign-query phase is over. In this way, we avoid to abort every time the reduction could not program the hash function (as it happens in [7]).

In light of the generic equivalence stated by Fiore *et al.* in Proposition 1 [13], we ignore corruption queries during the security game. Therefore, our initial game is the security game between the adversary $\mathscr{A}$ the challenger $\mathscr{C}$ described at the end of Sect. 2.2, where no corruptions are allowed, hash queries happen after the signing query phase and forgeries follow the Definition 6. We prove the security of our scheme in 2 steps:

(1) we bound the success probability of any PPT adversary that outputs **type-3** forgeries to $\frac{1}{q}$;
(2) for any PPT adversary that outputs **type-2** forgeries we show a reduction to a co-CDH instance with factor $\frac{1}{Q_{\mathsf{id}}}$ where Q_{id} is the total number of identities generated during the game (this loss is common to all multi-key homomorphic signatures schemes to date [13,26]).

Type-3 Forgeries. Let $\mathscr{A}$ be a **type-3** forger. By definition, the adversarial output $(\mathcal{P}^*, m^*, \sigma^*)$ contains a label $\ell^* \in \mathcal{P}^*$ for which no signature or hash query has been performed. This means that in order to verify $(\mathcal{P}^*, m^*, \sigma^*)$ the challenger needs to generate a value for $H(\ell^*)$ on-the-fly. Since $\mathscr{C}$ acts as a Random Oracle on hash queries, the probability that the adversary outputs a valid type-3 forgery is at most equal to the probability of randomly guessing the value $H(\ell^*) \in \mathbb{G}_1$, *i.e.*, R_H. Thus

$$\mathsf{Prob}[\mathscr{A} \text{ outputs a valid type-3 forgery }] \leq R_H = \frac{1}{q}.$$

Given that $|\mathbb{G}_1| = q$ is a $\mathsf{poly}(\lambda)$-bit prime, we can make the above probability arbitrarily small.

Type-2 Forgeries. Now consider the case of $\mathscr{A}$ be a **type-2** forger. We define a reduction $\mathscr{B}$ that turns any type-2 forger (against a specific identity) into solutions of an instance of the co-CDH problem. We recall that we require $\mathscr{A}$ to perform all sign queries before any hash query. In particular, after the first hash query $\mathscr{A}$ is no longer allowed to request new signatures.

Concretely, $\mathscr{B}$ takes as input a bilinear group $\mathcal{G} = (\mathbb{G}_1, \mathbb{G}_2, \mathbb{G}_T, q, e, \varphi)$, two generators $g_1 \in \mathbb{G}_1$, $g_2 \in \mathbb{G}_2$ and a point $h = g_2^x \in \mathbb{G}_2$. The goal of the reduction is to output an element $\omega \in \mathbb{G}_1$ such that $\omega = g_1^x$. Algorithm $\mathscr{B}$ simulates Setup, KeyGen, Sign and the hash function H of mklhs as follows.

Setup: $\mathscr{B}$ utilizes the group homomorphism φ to identify the image of g_2 in $\mathbb{G}_1$, i.e., $\varphi(g_2) \in \mathbb{G}_1$. Then, $\mathscr{B}$ sets $\tilde{g}_1 = g_1^{\tilde{s}} \varphi(g_2)^{\tilde{t}}$ for randomly chosen $\tilde{s}, \tilde{t} \xleftarrow{\$} \mathbb{Z}_q$, and outputs the bilinear group $\mathcal{G}$ and the generators $\tilde{g}_1, g_2$. In addition, $\mathscr{B}$ chooses an index $\tilde{j} \xleftarrow{\$} [Q_{id}]$ as a guess that $\mathscr{A}$ will make a type-2 forgery against the $\tilde{j}$-th identity in the system. We will refer to this special identity as the *target identity*. Finally, $\mathscr{B}$ initializes three empty lists L_{ID}, L_H and L_σ to track $\mathscr{A}$'s identity, hash and signature queries respectively.

Identity Query: on input a query of the form $id \in ID$, $\mathscr{B}$ checks if $id \in L_{ID}$ in which case it ignores the query. Otherwise, this is the first query with identity id. Let $i - 1$ be the number of identities already present in L_{ID}, if $i \in [Q_{id}] \setminus \tilde{j}$ the reduction produces a fresh pair of keys, when $i = \tilde{j}$ the reduction embeds h as the challenge public key. In detail, for $i \neq \tilde{j}$ the reduction creates a new user by choosing a random $sk_i \xleftarrow{\$} \mathbb{Z}_q$, adding $(id, i, sk_i, pk_i = g_2^{sk_i})$ to L_{ID} and returning pk_{id}. For $i = \tilde{j}$ the reduction stores $(\tilde{id}, \tilde{j}, \cdot, pk_{\tilde{j}} = h)$ in L_{ID} and returns its co-CDH challenge piece $h \in \mathbb{G}_2$.

Sign Query: on input a query of the form (ℓ, m), $\mathscr{B}$ checks whether $\mathscr{A}$ already queried the label (possibly on a different message), i.e., $(\ell, \cdot) \in L_\sigma$, or the identity in $\ell = (id, \tau)$ has not yet been generated, i.e., $(id, \cdot, \cdot, \cdot) \notin L_{ID}$. The reduction ignores the query if any of the two conditions above is met. Otherwise, there are three possible scenarios:

(a) this is the first sign query for the identity id and $id \neq \tilde{id}$,
(b) identity $id \neq \tilde{id}$ was already queried in combination to another label ℓ',
(c) the queried identity is the target identity, i.e., $id = \tilde{id}$.

So long $i \neq \tilde{j}$, the reduction can retrieve (id, i, sk_i, pk_i) from L_{ID} and sign in a perfect manner using sk_i. Concretely, in case (a) this is the first sign query for the identity id, $\mathscr{B}$ chooses two random values $s_{id}, t \xleftarrow{\$} \mathbb{Z}_q$ and sets

$$H(\ell) = g_1^{-s_{id} \cdot m} \cdot \varphi(g_2)^t \tag{1}$$
$$\gamma = (H(\ell) \cdot \tilde{g}_1^m)^{sk_i} \tag{2}$$
$$\mu = m. \tag{3}$$

In case (b), $\mathscr{B}$ retrieves the identity's s_{id} value from an existing record in L_H with $\ell' = (id, \tau')$ and computes (1), (2), (3) for a random $t \xleftarrow{\$} \mathbb{Z}_q$. In case (c), i.e., when $i = \tilde{j}$, the reduction can perfectly simulate the signature thanks to the special generator $\tilde{g}_1$ created in the setup phase. In detail, $\mathscr{B}$ chooses a random $t \xleftarrow{\$} \mathbb{Z}_q$, uses $\tilde{s}$ as the target identity's "random" $s_{\tilde{id}}$ value and computes

$$H(\ell) = g_1^{-\tilde{s}\cdot m} \cdot \varphi(g_2)^t \tag{4}$$

$$\gamma = \varphi(h)^{t+\tilde{t}\cdot m} \tag{5}$$

$$\mu = m. \tag{6}$$

where we recall that $h = \mathsf{pk}_{\tilde{j}} \in \mathbb{G}_2$ was given to $\mathcal{B}$ by the co-CDH challenger.

In all cases, $\mathcal{B}$ does some bookkeeping by storing $(\ell, s_{\mathsf{id}}, t)$ in L_H and (ℓ, m, σ) in L_σ. Finally, $\mathcal{B}$ returns $\sigma = (\gamma, \mu)$ as the answer to $\mathcal{A}$'s sign query.

Hash Query: let (ℓ) denote $\mathcal{A}$'s input to the hash oracle with $\ell = (\mathsf{id}, \tau)$. There are three possible scenarios:

(a) this is the first hash query for the identity id and $\mathsf{id} \neq \tilde{\mathsf{id}}$,
(b) identity $\mathsf{id} \neq \tilde{\mathsf{id}}$ was already queried in combination to another label ℓ',
(c) the queried identity is the target identity, *i.e.*, $\mathsf{id} = \tilde{\mathsf{id}}$.

In the first case, (a), our reduction chooses two random values $s_{\mathsf{id}}, t \xleftarrow{\$} \mathbb{Z}_q$ and sets $H(\ell) = g_1^{-s_{\mathsf{id}}\cdot m}\varphi(g_2)^t$. To ensure consistency, in case (b), our reduction retrieves s_{id} from any of the previous hash queries on id present in L_H and computes $H(\ell) = g_1^{-s_{\mathsf{id}}\cdot m}\varphi(g_2)^t$ for a random $t \xleftarrow{\$} \mathbb{Z}_q$. In the last case, (c), our reduction uses the randomness generated during the setup phase and sets $s_{\tilde{\mathsf{id}}} = \tilde{s}$, $t \xleftarrow{\$} \mathbb{Z}_q$ and computes $H(\ell) = g_1^{-\tilde{s}\cdot m}\varphi(g_2)^t$.

In all cases, $\mathcal{B}$ stores $(\ell, s_{\mathsf{id}}, t)$ in L_H and returns $H(\ell) \in \mathbb{G}_1$.

It is easy to see that $\mathcal{B}$ simulates the security game in a perfect way, as we show at the end of this section. Assuming for now that the simulation works fine, we demonstrate how to extract a solution to the co-CDH problem from a type-2 forgery. Let $(\mathcal{P}^*, m^*, \sigma^*)$ be the output of the algorithm $\mathcal{A}$ at the end of its interaction with $\mathcal{B}$. Since we are dealing with a type-2 forger it must be the case that the labeled program $\mathcal{P}^* = (f^*, \ell_1, \ldots, \ell_n)$ is well-defined and

$$\begin{cases} \mathsf{Verify}(\mathcal{P}^*, \{\mathsf{pk}_i\}_{i\in\mathcal{P}^*}, m^*, \sigma^*) = 1 \\ m^* \neq f^*(m_1, \ldots, m_t) \end{cases}$$

where m_i is the message queried by $\mathcal{A}$ for the label ℓ_i during the interaction with $\mathcal{B}$. Without loss of generality, we assume the identities involved in $\mathcal{P}^*$ be $\mathsf{id}_1, \mathsf{id}_2, \ldots, \mathsf{id}_t$ and the messages be ordered per-party. In particular, the first $k_1 > 0$ messages belong to id_1, the subsequent $k_2 > 0$ messages belong to id_2 and so on, so that $\sum_{i=1}^{t} k_i = n$ (the number of inputs to f). Define f_i^* to be the labeled program $\mathcal{P}^*$ restricted to the inputs (labels) of identity id_i, so that $f^* = f_1^* + f_2^* + \ldots + f_t^*$ and $k = \sum_{i=1}^{k_{\tilde{j}}-1} k_i$ to be the last index before the messages by $\mathsf{id}_{\tilde{j}}$ are input. Our reduction $\mathcal{B}$ looks for type-2 forgeries against the user $\mathsf{id}_{\tilde{j}}$, i.e, forgeries that satisfy

$$\begin{cases} \mathsf{id}_{\tilde{j}} \in \mathcal{P}^* \\ \mu_{\tilde{j}} \neq f_{\tilde{j}}^*(m_{k+1}, \ldots, m_{k+k_{\tilde{j}}}) \end{cases}$$

The above conditions ensure that the identity $\tilde{j}$ used to embed the co-CDH challenge is present in the labeled program *and* that the corresponding entry in

σ^* is a type-2 forgery. The reduction aborts every time at least one condition is not satisfied (this happens with probability $\frac{1}{Q_{id}}$ corresponding to the event $\mathscr{B}$ made the wrong guess for the target identity). Otherwise, $\mathscr{B}$ extracts its output to the co-CDH challenger from the type-2 forgery against $\text{id}_{\bar{j}}$ as follows. First, $\mathscr{B}$ removes from $\sigma^* = (\gamma^*, \mu_1^*, \ldots, \mu_t^*)$ the contributions by all other parties and the parts of the forgery that depend $\varphi(h)$:

$$K_0 = \frac{\gamma^*}{\prod_{j \in [t] \setminus \bar{j}} \left(\prod_{i=k_{j-1}+1}^{k_j} H(\ell_i)^{f_i} \right)^{\text{sk}_j} \cdot \tilde{g}_1^{\mu_{\bar{j}}^* \cdot \text{sk}_{\bar{j}}}} \cdot \frac{1}{\prod_{i=k+1}^{k_{\bar{j}}} \varphi(h)^{t_i} \cdot \varphi(h)^{\bar{t} \cdot \mu_{\bar{j}}^*}}$$

Note that the left most denominator removes from γ^* all contributions by the identities $\text{id}_i \neq \text{id}_{\bar{j}}$. The right most denominator is constructed with the randomness values present in L_H for the labels related to $\text{id}_{\bar{j}}$ and the messages m_i that were queried together with those labels and stored in L_σ (note that the m_i exist since this is a type-2 forgery). Let $y = \tilde{s} \cdot (\mu_{\bar{j}}^* - f_{\bar{j}}^*(m_{k+1}, \ldots, m_{k+k_{\bar{j}}}))$ then $\mathscr{B}$ output to its co-CDH challenger is

$$K_1 = K_0^{\left(\frac{1}{y}\right)}.$$

It is straightforward to check that $K_1 = g_1^x$. The way we extract the co-CDH solution is indeed a generalization of Boneh *et al.*'s technique [7] to multi-key signatures. Thus, our reduction transforms type-2 forgeries into a solution to the co-CDH problem unless it aborts, which leads us to

$$\text{Adv}_{\mathscr{B}}^{\text{co-CDH}}(\lambda) \geq \frac{1}{Q_{id}} \cdot \text{Prob}[\mathscr{A} \text{ outputs a valid type-2 forgery }].$$

Combining the bounds we proved on type-3 and type-2 forgeries we obtain:

$$\text{Adv}_{\text{mklhs}, \mathscr{A}}(\lambda) \leq \frac{1}{2} \cdot \left[R_H + Q_{id} \cdot \text{Adv}_{\mathscr{B}}^{\text{co-CDH}}(\lambda) \right],$$

that proves the security of our mklhs scheme.

Correctness of the Simulation. In what follows we argue that our reduction simulates the answers to signatures and hash queries in a perfect way.

First, we observe that the element $\tilde{g}_1$ constructed by $\mathscr{B}$ is a generator of $\mathbb{G}_1$ with overwhelming probability and that $\text{pk}_{\bar{j}} = h$ is distributed identically to the public key produced by the real KeyGen algorithm.

Second, the responses to all hash queries are uniformly random in $\mathbb{G}_1$, thus simulate the behavior of any cryptographic hash function. Indeed it is possible to rewrite $H(\ell)$ as

$$H(\ell) = g_1^{-s_{id} \cdot m} \cdot \varphi(g_2)^t = g_1^{-s_{id} \cdot m + t \cdot r}$$

where r is a fixed, unknown, value that depends on the homomorphism φ. Clearly, the $(t \cdot r)$ component in the exponent ensures that the hash values fall back to the uniform distribution.

Third, on all identities other than the target $\mathsf{id}_{\tilde{\jmath}}$ our reduction behaves as in the real scheme.

Finally, we prove that the signatures output by $\mathscr{B}$ for the target identity $\mathsf{id}_{\tilde{\jmath}}$ are identical to the signatures that would be output by the real Sign algorithm given the public key $\mathsf{pk}_{\tilde{\jmath}} = h$, the public parameters output by $\mathscr{B}$ and the answers to hash queries produced by our reduction. In detail, it suffices to show that, for every pair of label and message the simulated signature output by the $\mathscr{B}$ algorithm equals the real signature on ℓ and m, i.e., the output of $\mathsf{Sign}(\mathsf{sk}_{\tilde{\jmath}}, \ell, m)$ as in Fig. 1. We show the equality only for the γ part of the signature, as the μ part is trivial. By construction, the output of Sign on the given inputs is:

$$
\begin{aligned}
(H(\ell) \cdot \tilde{g}_1^m)^{\mathsf{sk}_{\tilde{\jmath}}} &= \left(g_1^{-\tilde{s} \cdot m} \varphi(g_2)^t \cdot \left[g_1^{\tilde{s}} \varphi(g_2)^{\tilde{t}} \right]^m \right)^{\mathsf{sk}_{\tilde{\jmath}}} \\
&= \left(g_1^{-\tilde{s} \cdot m + \tilde{s} \cdot m} \cdot \varphi(g_2)^{t + \tilde{t} \cdot m} \right)^{\mathsf{sk}_{\tilde{\jmath}}} \\
&= \varphi(h)^{t + \tilde{t} \cdot m}
\end{aligned}
$$

where the left-hand-side is the real signature and the final right-hand-side term is the simulated one.

4   Performance Evaluation

Our proposed scheme is well-tailored to asymmetric pairings, as most operations happen in $\mathbb{G}_1$. Key generation is the only important operation involving arithmetic in $\mathbb{G}_2$, but it is assumed to happen offline and only once per user. In detail, it requires just one fixed-base exponentiation in $\mathbb{G}_2$ involving the generator g_2 and the private key. Computing a signature involves hashing the label to $\mathbb{G}_1$, performing a fixed-based exponentiation of a generator $g_1 \in \mathbb{G}_1$ to compute g_1^m, a point addition to compute $H(\ell) \cdot g_1^m$, and a variable-base exponentiation using the private key to finally compute $(H(\ell) \cdot g_1^m)^{\mathsf{sk}}$. Hence, hashing to $\mathbb{G}_1$ and variable-base exponentiations dominate the execution time for generating signatures. The performance-critical operation in the homomorphic evaluation of mklhs is the multi-exponentiation in $\mathbb{G}_1$ that corresponds to the computation of $\gamma = \prod_{i=1}^n \gamma_i^{f_i}$. Finally, verifying a multi-key homomorphic signature for computations involving t signers involves mostly hashing to $\mathbb{G}_1$, fixed-base exponentiations in $\mathbb{G}_1$ and a product of t pairings.

4.1   Implementation

We implemented mklhs within the RELIC library [2] using two sets of supported parameters at the 128-bit security level. The first choice is the curve BLS12-381 with embedding degree $k = 12$ and 255-bit prime-order subgroup used in the ZCash cryptocurrency [25]. The second choice is a prime-order BN curve defined over a 382-bit field (BN-382). These choices are motivated by the recent attacks against the DLP over $\mathbb{G}_T$ [22] and are supported by the analysis in [24].

Although recent analysis has point out that even larger parameters may be needed for 128-bit security [4], our main performance observations should still hold. The two curves are defined over a prime field $\mathbb{F}_p$ such that $p \equiv 3 \pmod 4$, providing an efficient towering for representing $\mathbb{F}_{p^k}$ and efficient extraction of square roots. RELIC provides Assembly acceleration for Intel 64-bit platforms for both curves using a shared codebase, which means that finite field arithmetic is implemented using essentially the same techniques, allowing for fair comparisons across different curves and protocols. The resulting code is publicly available in the library repository.

The top two blocks of Table 1 list the curves parametrization, while the bottom block displays the concrete instantiation of z_0 used in our evaluation. Both curves have the same format $E : y^2 = x^3 + b$ when represented in short Weierstraß equation, therefore the same arithmetic optimizations apply to both curves. A significant difference comes with the length of parameters, such as the group size q and cofactor $h = \#E/q$, which offer interesting performance trade-offs: hashing and membership testing in $\mathbb{G}_1$ are faster on the BN curve due to the prime order (no need to clear cofactors); while exponentiations are more efficient on the BLS12 curve due to shorter exponents. We could consider using the short exponent optimization for the BN curve, but these would violate security assumptions about the distribution of exponents.

Table 1. Parametrization and concrete parameters for the BN and BLS12 pairing-friendly curves used in our implementation.

BN curves: $k = 12$, $\rho \approx 1$				
$p(z)$	$36z^4 + 36z^3 + 24z^2 + 6z + 1$			
$q(z)$	$36z^4 + 36z^3 + 18z^2 + 6z + 1$			
$t(z)$	$6z^2 + 1$			
BLS12 curves: $k = 12$				
$p(z)$	$(z - 1)^2(z^4 - z^2 + 1)/3 + z$			
$q(z)$	$z^4 - z^2 + 1$			
$t(z)$	$z + 1$			
E	b	z_0	$\lceil \log_2 p \rceil$	$\lceil \log_2 q \rceil$ $\lceil \log_2 h \rceil$
BN-382	2	$-(2^{94} + 2^{78} + 2^{67} + 2^{64} + 2^{48} + 1)$	382	382 1
BLS12-381	4	$-(2^{63} + 2^{62} + 2^{60} + 2^{57} + 2^{48} + 2^{16})$	381	255 126

We also took side-channel resistance into consideration. The most critical procedure in our protocol from the point of view of implementation security is the signature generation. This is due to the fact that all other recurrent procedures are publicly evaluated and do not involve secret or sensitive information. In the signature generation, the fixed-base exponentiation does not need counter measures because messages are assumed to be public. Therefore, the variable-base exponentiation involving sk is the only operation requiring protection from side-channel leakage. Our pairing-friendly curves support efficient endomorphisms that we exploit to speed up the exponentiation [16]. Moreover, we combine the GLV scalar decomposition method for the private key [16] with the constant-time exponentiation based on regular recoding of exponents [21] to implement a side-channel resistant signing procedure. The GLV decomposition process was implemented in variable time and is assumed to be executed during key generation, after which only the subscalars are needed. The constant-time implementation of exponentiation has the typical constant-time countermeasures, with lookup in precomputed tables performed by linear scanning across the entire table and branchless programming to replace all branches with logical operations.

Hashing to pairing groups is commonly implemented using a heuristic try-and-increment approach, where the string is hashed to the x-coordinate of a point and incremented until a suitable y-coordinate is found after extracting a square root using the curve equation. The point (x, y) is then multiplied by the curve cofactor to guarantee that the resulting point is in the right q-order subgroup. A problem with this approach is that it lacks any proper guarantees about the output distribution. In particular, it does not satisfy the requirements of a random oracle assumed in our scheme. We instead employ a Shallue–van de Woestijne (SW) [27] encoding of strings that is indifferentiable from a random oracle. Concretely, we employ versions of the approach customized to pairing-friendly curves belonging to the BN [15] and BLS12 families [28]. For BLS12 curves, we implemented the simpler version recently proposed in [28] with the optimization of replacing the cofactor multiplication inside hashing by the value $(1 - z_0)$ with low Hamming weight. Homomorphic evaluation of linear functions over signatures was implemented with standard binary multi-exponentiation techniques, because the coefficients are assumed to be small. We implemented products of pairings using the conventional interleaving techniques to eliminate point doublings in the pairing computation and share the final exponentiation [19].

For comparison to the related work by Schabhüser et al. [26], we also implemented their scheme under similar constraints. This protocol requires an underlying conventional signature algorithm, for which we chose the pairing-based Boneh-Lynn-Schacham (BLS) [9] short signature scheme to rely on the same set of parameters. Computation of BLS signatures was implemented in constant-time in the same way as mklhs, because it depends on the secrecy of a long-term key. All other operations were implemented in variable-time for better performance, since they rely only on public or ephemeral data.

4.2   Experimental Results and Discussion

We benchmarked our implementation on a high-end Intel Core i7-6700K Skylake processor running at 4.0 GHz. We turned off HyperThreading and TurboBoost to reduce noise in the benchmarks. The benchmarking dataset was created by generating 10 different users, who sign 16 individual messages each using 16 different labels. These signatures are collected by a third party, which homomorphically evaluates a linear function f composed of 16 random 32-bit integer coefficients across all signatures. The resulting multi-key signature is then verified. Each procedure is executed 10^4 times and the timings for mklhs and Schabhüser *et al.* instantiated both with curves BN-382 and BLS12-381 are presented in Table 2. The figures are amortized per user, so similar performance improvements are expected for datasets of different size.

Table 2. Efficiency comparison of our mklhs with Schabhüser *et al.*'s scheme. We display execution times in clock cycles (cc) for each of the main algorithms in the protocols. The dataset includes homomorphic evaluation and verification of 16 signatures computed by 10 users each. Figures represent the average of 10^4 executions, and fastest timings are typeset in **bold**. Timings for signature computation refer to individual signatures, and timings for homomorphic evaluation and verification are amortized per user. Individual and combined signature sizes are also displayed for reference, assuming point compression of $\mathbb{G}_1$ and $\mathbb{G}_2$ elements.

| | Protocol | | | |
| | Schabhüser *et al.* [26] | | mklhs | |
Operation	BN-382	BLS12-381	BN-382	BLS12-381
Key Generation (cc)	42,071,481	28,575,291	879,258	**592,454**
Signature computation (cc)	5,643,798	4,137,016	1,552,369	**1,257,424**
Homomorphic Evaluation (cc)	3,346,135	3,349,471	666,542	**661,664**
Verification (cc)	14,702,224	12,770,063	10,814,364	**10,710,053**
Individual signature (bytes)	384	384	96	80
Combined sigs for t signers (bytes)	$144 + 240t$	$144 + 240t$	$48(1 + t)$	$48 + 32t$

Our scheme is clearly more efficient than Schabhüser *et al.* and trades off advanced security properties (such as context hiding) in favor of performance and compactness. Computing an individual signature in mklhs is more than 3 times faster than in [26]. The homomorphic evaluation of mklhs is also much more efficient (around 5 times faster), since it does not require exponentiations in $\mathbb{G}_2$ to preserve the homomorphism. Verification is up to 26% faster in our proposal, depending on curve choice. Comparing the two curves in mklhs, we have the following observations. Key generation and signing are faster on BLS12-381 due to shorter exponents. BN-382 becomes competitive for homomorphic evaluation with same-length coefficients, and verification due to faster hashing but slower exponentiations. Protocols relying heavier on hashing are expected to further benefit from choosing BN-382 as the underlying pairing-friendly curve.

5   Conclusion

We presented mklhs, a novel multi-key linearly homomorphic signature scheme that addresses the problem of outsourcing computation on data authenticated by independent users. Our construction relies solely on standard assumptions (co-CDH and ROM), is conceptually simpler than existing proposals, and enjoys the most succinct signatures up to date with just 1 element in $\mathbb{G}_1$ and t elements in $\mathbb{Z}_q$ (t is the number of distinct signers). In addition, mklhs is the first direct construction of a multi-key linearly homomorphic signature scheme not based on a compiler. We use standard tools of pairing-based cryptography and design extremely efficient algorithms for signing, combining and verifying.

Compared to existing schemes, our mklhs scheme substantially improves execution times for most relevant operations in a multi-key homomorphic signature scheme, outperforming existing proposals by several times. Valuable pointers to further improvement include designing a context hiding version of mklhs and extending homomorphic computations to a wider and more expressive set of functions. From the implementation point of view, instantiating the scheme with other parameters would also allow a better view of performance trade-offs across different curves.

Acknowledgments. This work was partly funded by: the European Research Council (ERC) under the European Unions's Horizon 2020 research and innovation programme under grant agreement No 669255 (MPCPRO); and the Concordium Blockchain Research Center at Aarhus University, Denmark. The first author is also affiliated to the DIGIT Centre for Digitalisation, Big Data and Data Analytics at Aarhus University.

References

1. Agrawal, S., Boneh, D., Boyen, X., Freeman, D.M.: Preventing pollution attacks in multi-source network coding. In: Nguyen, P.Q., Pointcheval, D. (eds.) PKC 2010. LNCS, vol. 6056, pp. 161–176. Springer, Heidelberg (2010). https://doi.org/10.1007/978-3-642-13013-7_10
2. Aranha, D.F., Gouvêa, C.P.L.: RELIC is an Efficient LIbrary for Cryptography. https://github.com/relic-toolkit/relic
3. Attrapadung, N., Libert, B., Peters, T.: Efficient completely context-hiding quotable and linearly homomorphic signatures. In: Kurosawa, K., Hanaoka, G. (eds.) PKC 2013. LNCS, vol. 7778, pp. 386–404. Springer, Heidelberg (2013). https://doi.org/10.1007/978-3-642-36362-7_24
4. Barbulescu, R., Duquesne, S.: Updating key size estimations for pairings. J. Cryptol. (2018, to appear). https://link.springer.com/article/10.1007%2Fs00145-018-9280-5
5. Barreto, P.S.L.M., Lynn, B., Scott, M.: Constructing elliptic curves with prescribed embedding degrees. In: Cimato, S., Persiano, G., Galdi, C. (eds.) SCN 2002. LNCS, vol. 2576, pp. 257–267. Springer, Heidelberg (2003). https://doi.org/10.1007/3-540-36413-7_19
6. Barreto, P.S.L.M., Naehrig, M.: Pairing-friendly elliptic curves of prime order. In: Preneel, B., Tavares, S. (eds.) SAC 2005. LNCS, vol. 3897, pp. 319–331. Springer, Heidelberg (2006). https://doi.org/10.1007/11693383_22
7. Boneh, D., Freeman, D., Katz, J., Waters, B.: Signing a linear subspace: signature schemes for network coding. In: Jarecki, S., Tsudik, G. (eds.) PKC 2009. LNCS,

vol. 5443, pp. 68–87. Springer, Heidelberg (2009). https://doi.org/10.1007/978-3-642-00468-1_5

8. Boneh, D., Freeman, D.M.: Linearly homomorphic signatures over binary fields and new tools for lattice-based signatures. In: Catalano, D., Fazio, N., Gennaro, R., Nicolosi, A. (eds.) PKC 2011. LNCS, vol. 6571, pp. 1–16. Springer, Heidelberg (2011). https://doi.org/10.1007/978-3-642-19379-8_1

9. Boneh, D., Lynn, B., Shacham, H.: Short signatures from the weil pairing. In: Boyd, C. (ed.) ASIACRYPT 2001. LNCS, vol. 2248, pp. 514–532. Springer, Heidelberg (2001). https://doi.org/10.1007/3-540-45682-1_30

10. Catalano, D., Fiore, D., Warinschi, B.: Efficient network coding signatures in the standard model. In: Fischlin, M., Buchmann, J., Manulis, M. (eds.) PKC 2012. LNCS, vol. 7293, pp. 680–696. Springer, Heidelberg (2012). https://doi.org/10.1007/978-3-642-30057-8_40

11. Catalano, D., Fiore, D., Warinschi, B.: Homomorphic signatures with efficient verification for polynomial functions. In: Garay, J.A., Gennaro, R. (eds.) CRYPTO 2014. LNCS, vol. 8616, pp. 371–389. Springer, Heidelberg (2014). https://doi.org/10.1007/978-3-662-44371-2_21

12. Chatterjee, S., Menezes, A.: On cryptographic protocols employing asymmetric pairings–the role of ψ revisited. Discrete Appl. Math. **159**(13), 1311–1322 (2011)

13. Fiore, D., Mitrokotsa, A., Nizzardo, L., Pagnin, E.: Multi-key homomorphic authenticators. In: Cheon, J.H., Takagi, T. (eds.) ASIACRYPT 2016. LNCS, vol. 10032, pp. 499–530. Springer, Heidelberg (2016). https://doi.org/10.1007/978-3-662-53890-6_17

14. Fiore, D., Pagnin, E.: Matrioska: a compiler for multi-key homomorphic signatures. In: Catalano, D., De Prisco, R. (eds.) SCN 2018. LNCS, vol. 11035, pp. 43–62. Springer, Cham (2018). https://doi.org/10.1007/978-3-319-98113-0_3

15. Fouque, P.-A., Tibouchi, M.: Indifferentiable hashing to barreto–naehrig curves. In: Hevia, A., Neven, G. (eds.) LATINCRYPT 2012. LNCS, vol. 7533, pp. 1–17. Springer, Heidelberg (2012). https://doi.org/10.1007/978-3-642-33481-8_1

16. Gallant, R.P., Lambert, R.J., Vanstone, S.A.: Faster point multiplication on elliptic curves with efficient endomorphisms. In: Kilian, J. (ed.) CRYPTO 2001. LNCS, vol. 2139, pp. 190–200. Springer, Heidelberg (2001). https://doi.org/10.1007/3-540-44647-8_11

17. Gennaro, R., Wichs, D.: Fully homomorphic message authenticators. In: Sako, K., Sarkar, P. (eds.) ASIACRYPT 2013. LNCS, vol. 8270, pp. 301–320. Springer, Heidelberg (2013). https://doi.org/10.1007/978-3-642-42045-0_16

18. Gorbunov, S., Vaikuntanathan, V., Wichs, D.: Leveled fully homomorphic signatures from standard lattices. In: Proceedings of the Forty-seventh Annual ACM Symposium on Theory of Computing, pp. 469–477. ACM (2015)

19. Granger, R., Smart, N.P.: On computing products of pairings. IACR Cryptology ePrint Archive, 2006/172 (2006)

20. Johnson, R., Molnar, D., Song, D., Wagner, D.: Homomorphic signature schemes. In: Preneel, B. (ed.) CT-RSA 2002. LNCS, vol. 2271, pp. 244–262. Springer, Heidelberg (2002). https://doi.org/10.1007/3-540-45760-7_17

21. Joye, M., Tunstall, M.: Fault Analysis in Cryptography, vol. 147. Springer, Heidelberg (2012). https://doi.org/10.1007/978-3-642-29656-7

22. Kim, T., Barbulescu, R.: Extended tower number field sieve: a new complexity for the medium prime case. In: Robshaw, M., Katz, J. (eds.) CRYPTO 2016. LNCS, vol. 9814, pp. 543–571. Springer, Heidelberg (2016). https://doi.org/10.1007/978-3-662-53018-4_20

23. Lai, R.W.F., Tai, R.K.H., Wong, H.W.H., Chow, S.S.M.: Multi-key homomorphic signatures unforgeable under insider corruption. In: Peyrin, T., Galbraith, S. (eds.) ASIACRYPT 2018. LNCS, vol. 11273, pp. 465–492. Springer, Cham (2018). https://doi.org/10.1007/978-3-030-03329-3_16

24. Menezes, A., Sarkar, P., Singh, S.: Challenges with assessing the impact of NFS advances on the security of pairing-based cryptography. In: Phan, R.C.-W., Yung, M. (eds.) Mycrypt 2016. LNCS, vol. 10311, pp. 83–108. Springer, Cham (2017). https://doi.org/10.1007/978-3-319-61273-7_5

25. Sasson, E.B., et al.: Zerocash: decentralized anonymous payments from Bitcoin. In: 2014 IEEE Symposium on Security and Privacy, pp. 459–474. IEEE (2014)

26. Schabhüser, L., Butin, D., Buchmann, J.: Context hiding multi-key linearly homomorphic authenticators. In: Matsui, M. (ed.) CT-RSA 2019. LNCS, vol. 11405, pp. 493–513. Springer, Cham (2019). https://doi.org/10.1007/978-3-030-12612-4_25

27. Shallue, A., van de Woestijne, C.E.: Construction of rational points on elliptic curves over finite fields. In: Hess, F., Pauli, S., Pohst, M. (eds.) ANTS 2006. LNCS, vol. 4076, pp. 510–524. Springer, Heidelberg (2006). https://doi.org/10.1007/11792086_36

28. Wahby, R.S., Boneh, D.: Fast and simple constant-time hashing to the BLS12-381 elliptic curve. Cryptology ePrint Archive, Report 2019/403 (2019). https://eprint.iacr.org/2019/403

Efficient Fair Multiparty Protocols Using Blockchain and Trusted Hardware

Souradyuti Paul[1] and Ananya Shrivastava[2(✉)]

[1] Indian Institute of Technology Bhilai, Raipur, India
souradyuti@iitbhilai.ac.in
[2] Indian Institute of Technology Gandhinagar, Gandhinagar, India
ananya.shrivastava@iitgn.ac.in

Abstract. In ACM CCS'17, Choudhuri *et al.* designed two *fair* public-ledger-based multi-party protocols (in the malicious model with *dishonest* majority) for computing an arbitrary function f. One of their protocols is based on a trusted hardware enclave $\mathcal{G}$ (which can be implemented using Intel SGX-hardware) and a public ledger (which can be implemented using a blockchain platform, such as Ethereum). Subsequently, in NDSS'19, a stateless version of the protocol was published. This is the first time, (a certain definition of) *fairness* – that guarantees either all parties learn the final output or nobody does – is achieved without any monetary or computational penalties. However, these protocols are *fair*, if the underlying *core MPC component* guarantees both *privacy* and *correctness*. While *privacy* is easy to achieve (using a secret sharing scheme), *correctness* requires expensive operations (such as ZK proofs and commitment schemes). We improve on this work in three different directions: *attack*, *design* and *performance*.

Our first major contribution is building practical attacks that demonstrate: if *correctness* is not satisfied then the *fairness* property of the aforementioned protocols collapse. Next, we design two new protocols – stateful and stateless – based on public ledger and trusted hardware that are: resistant against the aforementioned attacks, and made several orders of magnitude more efficient (related to both time and memory) than the existing ones by eliminating ZK proofs and commitment schemes in the design.

Last but not the least, we implemented the *core MPC part* of our protocols using the SPDZ-2 framework to demonstrate the feasibility of its practical implementation.

Keywords: Blockchain · Fairness · Multi-party computation

1 Introduction

BACKGROUND. In a secure *multiparty computation* (MPC), a set of mutually distrusting parties can jointly execute an algorithm (or a program) without revealing their individual secrets. The notion of MPC was introduced in the seminal

© Springer Nature Switzerland AG 2019
P. Schwabe and N. Thériault (Eds.): LATINCRYPT 2019, LNCS 11774, pp. 301–320, 2019.
https://doi.org/10.1007/978-3-030-30530-7_15

work of Yao in 1982 [22], and since then its applicability has grown from strength to strength. Multiparty protocols are used in, among others, various day-to-day applications such as Blockchain, e-auction, e-voting, e-lottery, smart contracts, privacy-preserving data mining, IoT-based applications, cloud-computing, grid computing, and identity/asset management [12,19].

For real-life deployment, a multiparty protocol should have the *fairness* property that should guarantee: either all the parties learn the final output or nobody does. While unconditional fairness is impossible to achieve [9], based on the use cases, several weaker variants of this property have been proposed. For an elaborate discussion on this, see [6].

In [8], for the first time, a *fair* multiparty protocol in the malicious model with the dishonest majority has been proposed that depends *neither* on monetary *nor* computational penalties.[1] This protocol can be implemented using the existing (and easily available) infrastructure, such as Blockchain, Google's CT log and Intel SGX [1,10,19]. While this is an important piece of result with significant practical implications, there is still room for improvement.

MOTIVATION. We start with the fact that the protocols described in [8,16] (denote them by Π) essentially consist of three generic components – a public ledger BB (a.k.a. bulletin board), a protective memory region $\mathcal{G}$ (a.k.a. enclave), and an *underlying* multi-party protocol π (modeled in Fig. 1).[2] We observe that the security of Π is proved (in the malicious model with *dishonest* majority) under the condition that π supports the *privacy* of the individual secrets, and the *correctness* of the output. While *privacy* is ensured using a *secret-sharing* scheme [21], achieving *correctness* of output requires expensive operations such as ZKP and commitment schemes [11,14]. We now ask the following questions:

1. *Can we break the fairness property of the protocols described in [8,16], if π is allowed to output an incorrect value?*
2. *If the answer to the previous question is yes, can we design a new protocol Γ, which is fair as well as efficient even when π is allowed to output an incorrect value?*

We now show that answers to the above questions are indeed in the affirmative.

OUR CONTRIBUTION. Our first contribution is showing concrete attacks on the protocols described in CGJ+ and KMG [8,16], when the underlying protocol π allows incorrect output to be returned (formalized in Definition 4).

Next, we design a new protocol Γ based on public ledger and trusted hardware (see Fig. 1 and Sect. 5), and prove that it is *fair*, even if π returns an incorrect value. We extended our work to design a stateless version of Γ, namely Υ, and also prove its *fairness*.

---

[1] See [6] and [7] for description of monetary and computational (a.k.a. Δ-fairness) penalties.

[2] $\mathcal{G}$ is implemented using Intel SGX hardware.

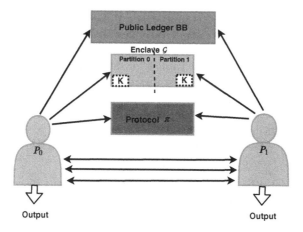

Fig. 1. Generic structure of the protocols of Table 1: public ledger BB, enclave $\mathcal{G}$, and the underlying core MPC component π. K is the (identical) symmetric key stored in all partitions of the (tamper-resistant) hardware enclave $\mathcal{G}$. Arrowhead denotes the direction in which a query is submitted. Thick arrowhead denotes the release of output.

Table 1. Comparison of multiparty protocols following the framework of Fig. 1. Cryptographic primitives: SSS = Shamir's secret sharing, MAC = Message authentication code, ZKPoPK = Zero-knowledge proof of plaintext knowledge, Comm. = CS.Com, Enc. = AE.Enc, Dec. = AE.Dec, OWF = One-way function, and PRF = Pseudo-random function. Here, $k =$ size of encryption and $\lambda =$ security parameter.

Protocol	Stateful/ Stateless	Primitives used in π	ZKPoPK amortized compl.	π security		# of var. in $\mathcal{G}$	# of calls in $\mathcal{G}$	Ref.
				Definition 3	Definition 4			
Π	Stateful	SSS + AE + MAC + ZKPoPK	$O(k+\lambda)$ bits	Fair	Attack	13	Comm.: 1 Enc.: 1 Dec.: 2 OWF: 2	[8]
Γ	Stateful	SSS + AE	0 bits	Fair	Fair	8	Comm.: 0 Enc.: 1 Dec.: 2 OWF: 0	Section. 5
KMG	Stateless	SSS + AE + MAC + ZKPoPK	$O(k+\lambda)$ bits	Fair	Attack	2	Comm.: 2 Encr.: 2 Dec.: 3 OWF: 2 PRF: 2 Hash: 3	[16]
Υ	Stateless	SSS + AE	0 bits	Fair	Fair	2	Comm.: 1 Enc.: 2 Dec.: 3 OWF: 0 PRF: 2 Hash: 3	Section. 5

Finally, we establish that our protocols are not only better secure than the existing ones, they also require fewer variables and cryptographic operations in the hardware enclave, not to mention the elimination of the expensive ZK proofs and the commitment scheme (see Table 1 for details).

We conclude with an open question regarding how our strategy can be adapted to design a *fair* and *efficient* protocol based on witness encryption (rather than any protective hardware enclave), where the internal component π is allowed to release incorrect values.

Our results have been applied to 2-party protocols, nevertheless, they can be easily generalized to n-party protocols (with $n > 2$).

RELATED WORK. In the beginning of this section, we briefly discussed the works of Yao and Cleve [9,22]. Other than them, we mentioned [8,16] that form the basis of our work in this paper. In addition, the following papers, similar to ours, deal with the many other variants of the fairness property [4–6,17,18].

ORGANIZATION. We start with the overview of our main results in Sect. 2. In Sect. 3 we describe various security properties of a multiparty protocol as preliminaries. Thereafter, in Sect. 4, we design the fairness attacks on several constructions in [8,16] under various realistic scenarios. We present the full description of our protocols along with their security proofs in Sect. 5. Then, we discuss the feasibility of practical implementation our protocols in Sect. 6. Finally, we conclude with an open problem in Sect. 7.

2   Overview of the Main Results

We improve on the existing works of [8,16] on three different directions: attack, design and performance.

ATTACK. We mount a *fairness* attack on the protocols described in [8,16], where the underlying protocol π returns an *incorrect* encryption of the function $f(\cdot)$ to the honest party P_0 (see Fig. 1), but it returns the correct encryption to the dishonest party P_1. Also note that, in these protocols, the parties are supplied with a protective memory region, known as enclave $\mathcal{G}$, which nobody can tamper with. In addition, there is a public ledger BB that generates an authentication *tag*, given a random string. The gist of the attack is as follows (see Sect. 4 for details).

The protocols of [8,16], denoted Π, essentially consist of three components $\Pi = \Pi_2 \circ \pi \circ \Pi_1$. As usual, P_i stores (x_i, k_i) as its secret. The first component Π_1 executes the Diffie-Hellman protocol to store the symmetric key $K = (k_0, k_1)$ in the enclave $\mathcal{G}$. The second component π computes the encryption of f using (k_0, k_1). Finally, the third component Π_2 decrypts f by submitting to $\mathcal{G}$ the random strings (a.k.a. *release tokens*) and the corresponding *tags* of *all the parties* obtained from the public ledger BB. Finally, the enclave $\mathcal{G}$ computes f, *only if* the *release tokens* and the corresponding *tags* of *all the parties* are valid. Our attack exploits the crucial fact that the *release tokens* are generated independently of the ciphertext, enabling the dishonest party P_1 with the correct output from π, to obtain from BB the correct *release token* and the corresponding *tag* of the honest party P_0 as well. The attack works because P_0 submits to BB his correct *release token,* without realizing that it received an incorrect encryption from π.

DESIGN. Next, using the lesson learnt from the aforementioned *fairness* attack on Π, we now design a new *fair* protocol Γ, which works even if the internal component π returns an incorrect value. We reiterate that the origin of the attack in Π is the *release tokens* being generated independently of the ciphertext. Therefore, our cardinal observation is as follows:

> We remove the *release token* altogether from the protocol and generate a *tag* from BB using the ciphertext directly. Now, the enclave $\mathcal{G}$ decrypts in the following way: it computes f *only if* the ciphertext and the *tag* submitted by a party are both authenticated. (The full details of Γ can be found in Sect. 4.)

Now, we briefly explain why Γ is a *fair* protocol. Suppose, P_0 and P_1 receive incorrect and correct outputs from π. Then, as soon as P_1 posts the ciphertext to BB, it immediately becomes available to P_0 as well, enabling him to obtain f from $\mathcal{G}$ by submitting the correct ciphertext-*tag* pair. Thus, *fairness* is preserved.[3]

At a very high level, we achieved security as well as the improved performance of Γ by weakening the security property of the underlying sub-protocol π (thereby achieving high performance), while rescuing this lost security by better exploiting the existing hardware enclave $\mathcal{G}$ without any performance penalty.

Similar techniques can be used to construct a stateless version of Γ, denoted Υ. The full details are given in Sect. 5.

PERFORMANCE. In our new protocol Γ, we obtain reduction in costs, mainly, due to the following two factors: the inner protocol π is now stripped of the expensive functionalities ZK proofs and commitment schemes; the enclave $\mathcal{G}$ now works without commitments and one-way functions. The various details can be found in Table 1.

3   Preliminaries

3.1   Cryptographic Primitives

Due to space constraints, we refer the reader to [13] and [20] for the rigorous definitions of various well-known cryptographic schemes used in our constructions, namely, secret sharing scheme SSS, message authentication code MAC, one-way function OWF, pseudorandom function PRF, collision-resistant hash function H, signature $\Sigma = (\Sigma.\mathsf{Gen}, \Sigma.\mathsf{Sign}, \Sigma.\mathsf{Verify})$, and commitment CS $= (\mathsf{CS.Setup}, \mathsf{CS.Com}, \mathsf{CS.Open})$. For Authentication scheme (with public verification) AS $= (\mathsf{AS.Gen}, \mathsf{AS.Tag}, \mathsf{AS.Verify})$, and authenticated encryption

---

[3] If P_1 posts an incorrect ciphertext to BB then he himself gets a wrong tag from BB, preventing him from obtaining the f from $\mathcal{G}$.

AE = (AE.Gen, AE.Enc, AE.Dec), we refer the reader to [8]. Because of their critical nature in our protocol, we describe the following functionalities in detail.

Public Ledger (Bulletin Board BB). A *Bulletin Board* BB is a publicly verifiable database that allows parties to update arbitrary strings on it [8]. These strings of the BB are called *release tokens*. When a party submits a *release token* ρ to the BB, it returns an authentication tag σ corresponding to ρ, and an index to the database t. The σ is the proof of the submission of ρ by the party.

It is a 3-tuple of algorithms, BB = {BB.getCurrCount, BB.post, BB.getCont}.

- BB.getCurrCount() returns the current index t.
- On given a *release token* ρ, BB.post(ρ), computes the authentication tag $\sigma = $ AS.Tag(t, ρ) and its corresponding index t and returns (σ, t) to the posting party.
- On given the index t', BB.getCont(t') returns (σ, ρ) corresponding to t', if t' is less than or equal to the current index t of BB. Otherwise it returns $\bot$.
- AS.Verify($\sigma, (t, \rho)$) returns 1, if the triplet (σ, t, ρ) is correct.

Enclaves $\mathcal{G}$ and $\mathcal{G}'$. They are the private regions of memory for running programs. An *enclave* provides *confidentiality* and *integrity* of a program in the presence of adversarial environment. This can establish a secure channel with other *enclaves*, as well as can remotely *attest* to its correct functioning [10]. An enclave can be practically implemented using Intel SGX-hardware.

STATEFUL ENCLAVE $\mathcal{G}$. It is a 4-tuple of algorithms $\mathcal{G} = (\mathcal{G}.\Sigma, \mathcal{G}.\text{getpk}, \mathcal{G}.\text{install}, \mathcal{G}.\text{resume})$ associated with a state State. We describe the individual algorithms and state as follows.

- $\mathcal{G}.\Sigma$ is a signature scheme with security parameter 1^λ. $\mathcal{G}.\Sigma.Gen(1^\lambda)$ generates the pair of signing and verification keys (msk, mpk), and stores it locally.
- $\mathcal{G}.\text{getpk}()$ returns a copy of mpk.
- $\mathcal{G}.\text{install}(\cdot)$: On input a party P, and the program prog, it does the following:
  1. generate enclave-id: $eid \xleftarrow{\$} \{0,1\}^\lambda$
  2. store in enclave: $T[eid, P] := (\text{prog}, 0)$
  3. return eid
- $\mathcal{G}.\text{resume}(\cdot)$: On input a party P, the enclave-id eid, and the input inp, it does the following:
  1. If $T[eid, P] \neq \emptyset$ then (prog, mem) $:= T[eid, P]$
     else abort.
  2. (outp, mem) := prog(inp, P, mem)
  3. update enclave: $T[eid, P] := (\text{prog}, \text{mem})$
  4. signature generation: $sig \leftarrow \mathcal{G}.\Sigma.\text{Sign}(\text{msk}, \underbrace{eid, \text{prog}, \text{outp}}_{\text{message}})$
  5. return (outp, sig)
- The state State is defined to be $S \cup T$, where $S = (\text{msk}, \text{mpk})$. Initially, T and S are empty sets.

STATELESS ENCLAVE $\mathcal{G}'$. Unlike the stateful $\mathcal{G}$, as described above, here there is no persistent storage; nevertheless, the parties maintain a state in the encrypted form outside of $\mathcal{G}'$ (for more details see [16]). We model it as a 2-tuple of algorithms $\mathcal{G}' = (\mathcal{G}'.\mathsf{Setup}, \mathcal{G}'.\mathsf{execute})$ as follows [16].

- $\mathcal{G}'.\mathsf{Setup}(\cdot)$: On input the security parameter 1^λ:
  1. generates secret key for *enclave*: $K \leftarrow \{0,1\}^\lambda$
  2. generates public commitment parameter: $\mathsf{pp} \leftarrow \mathsf{CS.Setup}(1^\lambda)$
  3. generates signing and verification key pair: $(\mathsf{msk}, \mathsf{mpk}) \leftarrow \Sigma.Gen(1^\lambda)$
  4. returns $(\mathsf{mpk}, \mathsf{pp})$
- $\mathcal{G}'.\mathsf{execute}(\cdot)$: On input program prog, round l, encrypted *previous state* S_{l-1}, program input I_l, random number r_l, commitment value C_l, BB's index t_l, and authentication tag σ_l, it does the following (initially, $l = 0$, $S_0 = \emptyset$):
  1. Check if $\mathsf{Verify}_{\mathsf{BB}}(C_l, t_l, \sigma_l) \neq 1$ then return $\perp$
  2. Check if $C_l \neq \mathsf{CS.Com}(\mathsf{pp}, \mathsf{prog}, l, S_{l-1}, I_l, r_l)$ then return $\perp$
  3. If $l > 1 \wedge S_{l-1} = \emptyset$ then return $\perp$
  4. Compute $(l-1)$th round encryption key $k_{l-1} \leftarrow \mathsf{PRF}(K, t_{l-1})$
  5. $(s_{l-1}, h) \leftarrow \mathsf{AE.Dec}(k_{l-1}, S_{l-1})$
  6. Check if $(s_{l-1}, h) = \perp$ then return $\perp$
  7. Check if $h \neq \mathsf{H}(\mathsf{prog}\|l-1)$ then return $\perp$
  8. Compute random number and l^{th} round encryption key: $(k_l, r'_l) \leftarrow \mathsf{PRF}(K, t_l)$
  9. Execute program and determine: $(s_l, \mathsf{out}_l) \leftarrow \mathsf{prog}(s_{l-1}, I_l, r'_l)$
  10. If $(s_l, \mathsf{out}_l) = \perp$ then return $\perp$
  11. Encrypt state: $S_l \leftarrow \mathsf{AE.Enc}\Big(k_l, s_l\|\mathsf{H}(\mathsf{prog}\|l)\Big)$
  12. Signature generation: $sig_l \leftarrow \Sigma.\mathsf{Sign}(\mathsf{msk}, \underbrace{\mathsf{pp}, \mathsf{prog}, \mathsf{out}_l}_{\text{message}})$
  13. return $(S_l, \mathsf{out}_l, sig_l)$.

Enclave-Ledger Interaction (ELI). An ELI is a 3-tuple of algorithms, $\mathsf{ELI} = (\mathsf{ELI.Setup}, \mathsf{ELI.ExecEnc}, \mathsf{ELI.ExecApp})$, that allows a party to securely communicate with the enclave $\mathcal{G}'$ and the public ledger BB [16]. The algorithmic descriptions of $\mathsf{ELI.Setup}$ and $\mathsf{ELI.ExecEnc}$ are identical to that of $\mathcal{G}'.\mathsf{Setup}$ and $\mathcal{G}'.\mathsf{execute}$. We now describe the algorithm $\mathsf{ELI.Exec}$ as follows.

- $\mathsf{ELI.Exec}(\cdot)$: On input security parameter 1^λ, public commitment parameter pp, program prog, round l, encrypted previous state S_{l-1}, and input I_l, it does the following.
  1. If $I_l = \perp$ then return $\perp$
  2. Choose random number: $r_l \leftarrow \{0,1\}^\lambda$
  3. Compute commitment on input values: $C_l \leftarrow \mathsf{CS.Com}(\mathsf{pp}, \mathsf{prog}, l, S_{l-1}, I_l, r_l)$
  4. Invokes $\mathsf{BB.Post}(C_l)$ to receive (t_l, σ_l)
  5. Invokes $\mathsf{ELI.ExecEnc}(\mathsf{prog}, l, S_{l-1}, I_l, r_l, C_l, t_l, \sigma_l)$ to receive $(S_l, \mathsf{out}_l, sig_l)$.

Definition 1 ([16]). *A protocol ELI is said to be secure, if for every non-uniform p.p.t. adversary $\mathcal{A}$, security parameter 1^λ, and non-negative integer n in the real world, there exists a non-uniform p.p.t. simulator $\mathcal{S}$ in the ideal world such that,*

$$IDEAL(\mathcal{S}, 1^\lambda, n) \stackrel{c}{\equiv} REAL(\mathcal{A}, 1^\lambda, n)$$

The IDEAL(·) and REAL(·) are described in [16].

Theorem 1 ([16]). *Suppose the following assumptions hold good: the commitment scheme CS is secure; the authenticated encryption scheme AE is INT-CTXT secure; the authentication scheme AS is unforgeable; the hash function H is collision-resistant; and PRF is pseudorandom. The ELI satisfies Definition 1.*

3.2 Security Properties

Consider a set of parties $\mathcal{P} = \{P_0, P_1\}$ executing a protocol π for computing a function f on x_0 and x_1; x_0 and x_1 are chosen according to some distributions from the sets X_κ and Y_κ, where κ is the security parameter. W.l.g., we assume P_0 and P_1 are the honest and corrupt parties respectively in the *real* world. $\mathcal{H}$ and P_1 are the honest and corrupt parties in the *ideal* world. Other than them, we will be using two more entities, attacker $\mathcal{A}$ and a simulator $\mathcal{S}$, *that control the corrupt party P_1 in the *real* and the *ideal* worlds. Now, P_1 has input x_1; both $\mathcal{H}$ and P_0 has x_0; $\mathcal{A}$ and $\mathcal{S}$ have x_1, and the auxiliary input[4] $z \in \{0, 1\}^*$.

The adversary $\mathcal{A}$'s view consists of the following: the input of $\mathcal{A}$, the values sent to and received from P_0, and the content of its internal random tape. Similarly, the views of P_0 and $\mathcal{H}$ can be defined. The view of the simulator is a function of $(x_1, z, f(x_0, x_1), \kappa)$. The outputs of P_0, $\mathcal{H}$, $\mathcal{A}$ and $\mathcal{S}$ can be computed from there respective views.

($\mathcal{G}$, **BB**)-*Fairness* with Abort. Unconditional fairness is impossible to achieve [9]; ($\mathcal{G}$, BB)-*fairness with abort* is a variant of it. If a protocol – which is built on enclave $\mathcal{G}$, and the *Bulletin Board* BB – has ($\mathcal{G}$, BB)-*fairness with abort* property then it is guaranteed that either all parties learn the final output or nobody does; the privacy property is preserved implicitly as well. We formally define this property in the spirit of semantic security which is based on designing appropriate *real* and *ideal* worlds. The pictorial description of the *ideal* and *real* worlds is given in Fig. 2.

The ideal world. Here, F is the trusted party. Also, the view of $\mathcal{S}$, and the output of $\mathcal{H}$ are denoted by view and $out_\mathcal{H}$ respectively. Let $IDEAL^{\text{SB-FAIR}}_{f(x_0,x_1),\mathcal{S}(x_1,z)}$ (x_0, x_1, κ) denote $out_\mathcal{H}\|$view. Here, $\mathcal{S}$ has access to the honest oracles: the enclave $\mathcal{G}$ and the public ledger BB in a similar fashion as described in [16]. The instructions executed in the *ideal* world are described below.

1. $\mathcal{H}$ sends x_0 to F. Depending on x_1 and the auxiliary information z, $\mathcal{S}$ sends x_1' to F, where $|x_1'| = |x_1|$.

---

[4] The auxiliary input is derived by the adversary (as well as the simulator) from the previous executions of the protocol.

2. F returns $f(x_0, x_1')$ to $\mathcal{S}$.

3. $\mathcal{S}$ sends either *continue* or *abort* to F, depending on its view.

4. If $\mathcal{S}$ sends *abort* to F, then F, in turn, sends *abort* to $\mathcal{H}$. If $\mathcal{S}$ sends *continue* to F, then F returns $f(x_0, x_1')$ to $\mathcal{H}$.

5. $\mathcal{H}$ outputs, $\text{out}_{\mathcal{H}}$, which is whatever it obtained from F; P_1 outputs nothing; and $\mathcal{S}$ outputs out, which is a function of view.

The real world. Let $REAL^{\text{SB-FAIR}}_{\pi, \mathcal{A}(x_1, z)}(x_0, x_1, \kappa)$ denote $\text{out}_0 \| \text{view}_{\mathcal{A}}$, where out_0 denote output of P_0, and $\text{view}_{\mathcal{A}}$ denote $\mathcal{A}$'s view. P_0 and P_1 execute π which consists of two honest oracles: $\mathcal{G}$ and BB. Throughout the execution of π, as before, $\mathcal{A}$ sends messages on behalf of P_1, while P_0 *correctly follows the protocol instructions*. Finally, P_0 outputs out_0; P_1 outputs nothing; and $\mathcal{A}$ outputs $\text{out}_{\mathcal{A}}$, which is a function of $\text{view}_{\mathcal{A}}$.

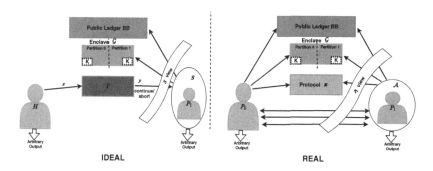

Fig. 2. Execution of *ideal* and *real* worlds of $(\mathcal{G}, \mathsf{BB})$-*Fairness* with abort. Arrowhead denotes the direction in which a query is submitted. Thick arrowhead denotes the release of output.

Definition 2. *A protocol π is said to* securely compute f with $(\mathcal{G}, \mathsf{BB})$-fairness with abort, *if for every non-uniform PPT adversary $\mathcal{A}$ in the real world, there exists a non-uniform PPT simulator $\mathcal{S}$ in the* ideal world *such that*

$$IDEAL^{\text{SB-FAIR}}_{f(x_0, x_1), \mathcal{S}(x_1, z)}(x_0, x_1, \kappa) \overset{c}{\equiv} REAL^{\text{SB-FAIR}}_{\pi, \mathcal{A}(x_1, z)}(x_0, x_1, \kappa),$$

for all $(x_0, x_1) \in X_k \times Y_k, z \in \{0, 1\}^*, \kappa \in \mathbb{N}$.

Privacy-and-Correctness with Abort. If a protocol has *privacy-and-correctness with abort* property then it guarantees that the honest party: (1) does not reveal its secret (privacy), and (2) outputs the correct value or $\perp$.

The ideal world. Let $IDEAL^{\text{PRV-CORR}}_{f(x_0, x_1), \mathcal{S}(x_1, z)}(x_0, x_1, \kappa)$ denote $\text{out}_{\mathcal{H}} \| \text{view}$. The instructions of the ideal world are identical to that of $(\mathcal{G}, \mathsf{BB})$-*fairness with abort*.

The real world. Let $REAL^{\text{PRV-CORR}}_{\pi, \mathcal{A}(x_1, z)}(x_0, x_1, \kappa)$ denote $\text{out}_0 \| \text{view}_{\mathcal{A}}$. P_0 and P_1 execute π without any trusted party. Throughout the execution of π, $\mathcal{A}$ sends messages on behalf of P_1, while P_0 *correctly follows the protocol instructions*. Finally,

P_0 outputs out_0; P_1 outputs nothing; and $\mathcal{A}$ outputs $\mathsf{out}_{\mathcal{A}}$, which is a function of $\mathsf{view}_{\mathcal{A}}$.

Definition 3. *A protocol* π *is said to* securely compute f *with privacy-and-correctness with abort, if for every non-uniform PPT adversary* $\mathcal{A}$ *in the* real world, *there exists a non-uniform PPT simulator* $\mathcal{S}$ *in the* ideal world *such that*

$$\mathrm{IDEAL}^{\mathrm{PRV\text{-}CORR}}_{f(x_0,x_1),\mathcal{S}(x_1,z)}(x_0,x_1,\kappa) \stackrel{c}{\equiv} \mathrm{REAL}^{\mathrm{PRV\text{-}CORR}}_{\pi,\mathcal{A}(x_1,z)}(x_0,x_1,\kappa),$$

for all $(x_0,x_1) \in X_k \times Y_k, z \in \{0,1\}^*, \kappa \in \mathbb{N}$.

Privacy Property. If a protocol has *privacy* property then it guarantees that the honest party does not reveal its secret. Note that this is a weaker property (and therefore, easy to achieve) than Definition 3.

The ideal world. Let $IDEAL^{\mathrm{PRV}}_{f(x_0,x_1),\mathcal{S}(x_1,z)}(x_0,x_1,\kappa)$ denote the view whose instructions are described below.
1. $\mathcal{H}$ sends x_0 to F. Depending on x_1 and the auxiliary information z, $\mathcal{S}$ sends x'_1 to F, where $|x'_1| = |x_1|$.
2. F returns $f(x_0,x'_1)$ to $\mathcal{H}$ and $\mathcal{S}$.
3. $\mathcal{H}$ outputs $\mathsf{out}_{\mathcal{H}}$; P_1 outputs nothing; and $\mathcal{S}$ outputs out, which is a function of view.

The real world. Let $REAL^{\mathrm{PRV}}_{\pi,\mathcal{A}(x_1,z)}(x_0,x_1,\kappa)$ denote $\mathsf{view}_{\mathcal{A}}$. The P_0 and P_1 execute π without any trusted party. Throughout the execution of π, $\mathcal{A}$ sends messages on behalf of P_1, while P_0 *correctly follows the protocol instructions*. Finally, P_0 outputs out_0; P_1 outputs nothing; and $\mathcal{A}$ outputs $\mathsf{out}_{\mathcal{A}}$, which is a function of $\mathsf{view}_{\mathcal{A}}$.

Definition 4. *A protocol* π *is said to* securely compute f *with privacy property, if for every non-uniform PPT adversary* $\mathcal{A}$ *in the* real world, *there exists a non-uniform PPT simulator* $\mathcal{S}$ *in the* ideal world *such that*

$$\mathrm{IDEAL}^{\mathrm{PRV}}_{f(x_0,x_1),\mathcal{S}(x_1,z)}(x_0,x_1,\kappa) \stackrel{c}{\equiv} \mathrm{REAL}^{\mathrm{PRV}}_{\pi,\mathcal{A}(x_1,z)}(x_0,x_1,\kappa),$$

for all $(x_0,x_1) \in X_\kappa \times Y_\kappa, z \in \{0,1\}^*, \kappa \in \mathbb{N}$.

4   Fairness Attacks on CGJ+ and KMG Protocols

The protocol of CGJ+ which is based on an enclave $\mathcal{G}$ (implemented using SGX-hardware) is now denoted by Π. The description of Π is given in Fig. 3. The Π works in $(\pi,\mathcal{G},\mathsf{BB})$-hybrid model, where π is a 2-party protocol computing the *encryption* of the given function $f(\cdot)$. Note that $\mathcal{G}$ and BB have already been described. Below we give the description of π.

$$\Pi[\Delta t, \pi, \mathsf{BB}, \mathcal{G}, \lambda, \mathcal{P}]$$

Input: For all $i \in \{0,1\}$, P_i inputs x_i.
Output: Both P_0 and P_1 output either $f(x_0, x_1)$ or $\bot$.
[If π is replaced by π_0 then P_1 outputs $f(x_0, x_1)$, and P_0 outputs $f'(x_0, x_1) \neq f(x_0, x_1)$.]

1. **[Setting up parameters (Offline)]** For all $i \in \{0,1\}$:
   (a) P_i samples the *release token* $\rho_i \xleftarrow{\$} \{0,1\}^\lambda$, key share $k_i \xleftarrow{\$} \{0,1\}^\lambda$, and random number share $r_i \xleftarrow{\$} \{0,1\}^\lambda$ **[used in Steps 5 and 8]**.
   (b) P_i invokes BB.getCurrCount() to obtain the current index t_i **[used in Step 6]**.

2. **[Exchange of enclaves' verification-keys (Offline+Online)]** For all $i \in \{0,1\}$, P_i invokes $\mathcal{G}$.getpk() to receive mpk_i which is then sent to P_j **[used in Steps 4 and 6]**.

3. **[Install prog in enclave (Offline)]** For all $i \in \{0,1\}$, party P_i invokes $\mathcal{G}$.install(prog[$\Delta t, \mathsf{vk_{BB}}, \mathcal{P}, i$]) and receives output eid_i **[used in Steps 4-7, 9(a) and 10]**.

4. **[Diffie-Hellman key-exchange by enclaves (Offline+Online)]** For all $i \in \{0,1\}$: P_i invokes $\mathcal{G}$.resume(eid_i, keyex) to receive $(g^{a_i}, sig_i^{(1)})$, and *broadcasts* $(eid_i, g^{a_i}, sig_i^{(1)})$; P_i checks, if $\mathcal{G}.\Sigma.\mathsf{Ver}_{\mathsf{mpk}_j}((eid_j, \mathsf{prog}[\Delta t, \mathsf{vk_{BB}}, \mathcal{P}, j], g^{a_j}), sig_j^{(1)}) = 1$ then continue, else abort. (Thus, a secure channel is established between the enclaves using Diffie-Hellman key.) **[used in Steps 6 and 7]**

5. **[Enclave stores (ρ_i, k_i, r_i) and returns each party's commitments (Offline)]** For all $i \in \{0,1\}$, P_i invokes $\mathcal{G}$.resume(eid_i, init, ρ_i, k_i, r_i) and receives $(com_{ii}, sig_i^{(2)})$. (The commitment com_{ii} on key share is used as one of the inputs in MPC protocol to ensure *correctness* property.) **[used in Steps 6 and 8]**

6. **[Enclave stores t_i and returns ciphertext (Offline+Online)]** For all $i \in \{0,1\}$: P_i invokes $\mathcal{G}$.resume(eid_i, send, g^{a_j}, t_i) to receive $(ct_i, sig_i^{(3)})$ which is then sent to P_j; P_i checks if $\mathcal{G}.\Sigma.\mathsf{Ver}_{\mathsf{mpk}_j}((eid_j, \mathsf{prog}[\Delta t, \mathsf{vk_{BB}}, \mathcal{P}, j], ct_{ij}), sig_j^{(3)}) = 1$ then continue, else abort **[used in Step 7]**.

7. **[Obtaining each other's commitments (Offline)]** For all $i \in \{0,1\}$: P_i invokes $\mathcal{G}$.resume(eid_i, receive, ct_{ji}) and receives $(com_{ji}, sig_i^{(4)})$, where com_{ji} is the 4th component in the decryption of ct_{ji} under secret key sk_{ji} (Here $\mathsf{sk}_{ji} = \mathsf{sk}_{ij}$). (Note that in this step both the enclave stores other parties secret values securely.) **[used in Step 8 and 9(a)]**

8. **[Execute π to obtain encryption of $f(\cdot)$ (Online)]** The a denotes π's output (see Sect. 4) **[used in Step 10]**.

9. **[Parameters required to obtain $f(\cdot)$ by decryption (Offline+Online)]**
   (a) For all $i \in \{0,1\}$, P_i invokes $\mathcal{G}$.resume(eid_i, getParams) and receives $(T, y, sig_i^{(5)})$, where $T = \max(t_0, t_1)$ and $y = \mathsf{OWF}(\rho_0 \oplus \rho_1)$ **[used in Step 9(b)]**.
   (b) For all $i \in \{0,1\}$, P_i sends ρ_i to P_j, and receives (ρ_j, t, σ) from BB. Here, T and y are used for verification of ρ_j and t. (see [8] for details) **[used in Step 10]**.

10. **[Computing $f(\cdot)$ by decryption (Offline)]** For all $i \in \{0,1\}$, P_i invokes $\mathcal{G}$.resume(eid_i, output, $a, \rho_0 \oplus \rho_1, t, \sigma$) to receive $f(\cdot)$.

Fig. 3. Algorithmic description of Π in $(\pi, \mathcal{G}, \mathsf{BB})$-hybrid model. In all the cases, $j = 1 - i$. The program prog is described in Appendix A. It is parameterized by: cut-off time Δt (which is $poly(\lambda)$), a 2-party protocol π, a *Bulletin Board* BB, an enclave $\mathcal{G}$, the security parameter 1^λ, and a set of parties $\mathcal{P} = \{P_0, P_1\}$. The orange colored steps in the algorithm represent the local computation done by a party. The purple colored step in the algorithm represents the communication among the parties and BB. (Color figure online)

DESCRIPTION OF π: It is a 2-party protocol that computes an *encryption* of the given function $f(x_0, x_1)$. Concretely:

$$\pi\left(\{x_i, k_i, com_{0,i}, com_{1,i}\}_{i \in \{0,1\}}\right) \stackrel{\text{def}}{=} a = \begin{cases} ct', & \text{if } P_1 \text{ is } malicious \\ ct, & \text{otherwise.} \end{cases}$$

Here, the private input x_i, and the key share k_i are generated by P_i; $com_{j,i} = $ CS.Com(k_j, r_j), which is commitment of k_j computed by P_j and given to P_i. Also, $ct = $ AE.Enc$\left(\oplus_{i=0}^{1} k_i, f(x_0, x_1)\right)$, and $ct' \neq ct$.

We recall that such a π which is secure in terms of *privacy-and-correctness with abort* in the malicious model with dishonest majority – as defined in Definition 3 – can be obtained in the following way: first design a *privacy* secure semi-honest multi-party protocol π_0, and then execute the GMW compiler on input π_0 to obtain π [15].[5] For such a π, $ct' = \perp$.

The components of π are: (1) (n, n)-*secret sharing* scheme; (2) AE scheme; (3) ZK proofs; and (4) CS scheme. The π inherits: (1) and (2) from π_0 which ensures *privacy*; it inherits (3) and (4) from the GMW compiler which ensures *correctness* [14].   □

DESCRIPTION OF Π (see Fig. 3): It is a 2-party protocol such that:

$$\Pi(x_0, x_1) \stackrel{\text{def}}{=} \begin{cases} f'(x_0, x_1), & \text{if } P_1 \text{ is malicious} \\ f(x_0, x_1), & \text{otherwise.} \end{cases}$$

Here $f(\cdot)$ is an arbitrary function and $f'(\cdot) \neq f(\cdot)$. From the standpoint of design, Π can be seen as the composition of the following 3 sub-protocols, all executed by the parties (P_0, P_1); note that each P_i is inherently supplied with an enclave $\mathcal{G}_i$:

$$\Pi = \Pi_2 \circ \pi \circ \Pi_1.$$

The Π_1 securely stores the *internally generated* symmetric key $K = (k_0, k_1)$ (and various other auxiliary data) inside the enclave $\mathcal{G} = (\mathcal{G}_0, \mathcal{G}_1)$ using Diffie-Hellman key-exchange.[6] It returns k_i along with the commitment values $(com_{0,i}, com_{1,i})$ on (k_0, k_1) to P_i to be used in the next stage π. The description of Π_1 is in steps 1–7.

The second stage π – which is invoked in step 8 – has already been described in detail. It returns the symmetric encryption of f using (k_0, k_1) to all the parties to be used for the next stage Π_2. At this point, there are two possible cases – P_0 receives either $\perp$ (case 1), or the correct encryption of f (case 2). In the former case, P_0 stops execution, while in the latter, both the parties (P_0, P_1) start executing the final stage Π_2.

The final stage Π_2 returns f after decrypting the output of π inside the enclave $\mathcal{G}$, using the various data generated in Π_1. It also uses the *release tokens*

---

[5] Another way of designing π is by using SPDZ directly [11].
[6] Note that none of the parties know the key K; P_i knows only k_i.

and the corresponding *tags* of *both the parties* obtained from BB. Note that any enclave in $\mathcal{G}$ would *never* decrypt, if any of the following five checks fails: the *release tokens* are incorrect; any pair of the *release-tokens-tags* is invalid; the authentication of the ciphertext fails; and the input is supplied after the cut-off time Δt. Otherwise, it would allow the dishonest party P_1 to obtain f using $\mathcal{G}_1$, while the honest party P_0 is unable to obtain it, due to the occurrence of case 1 as above, or due to aborting the protocol after waiting for a time longer than Δt; in either case it violates the *fairness* property. It is easy to observe that any attempt to attack the *fairness* property when case 2 has occurred can also be prevented by these aforementioned five checks. The description of Π_2 is in steps 9–10. In [8], it has been proved that if π satisfies the *privacy-and-correctness with abort* property (Definition 3), then Π satisfies $(\mathcal{G}, \mathsf{BB})$-*fairness with abort* (Definition 2).

ATTACK ON Π WHEN π IS REPLACED BY π_0: It is obvious from the previous discussion that π is more expensive than π_0, although the input and output for both of them are identical. We note that, π_0 preserves *privacy* in the malicious model with dishonest majority, but may not guarantee *correctness* [14]. Now we show that setting $\pi = \pi_0$, immediately leads to a *fairness* attack in Π. The attack works as follows: suppose $\pi = \pi_0$; and the honest party P_0 receives incorrect ciphertext $ct' \neq \perp$ (see step 8), however, the dishonest party P_1 receives the correct output ct. Since, no parties receive $\perp$ from π, they post the *release tokens* to get the *tags* from BB (step 9(b)). Now, P_0 invokes $\mathcal{G}_0$ by supplying the incorrect ciphertext ct' (along with all the *release tokens* and the *tags*) only to receive $\perp$, while P_1 receives the correct $f(\cdot)$. The *fairness* attack is now complete. □

ATTACKS ON WE-BASED CGJ+ AND KMG PROTOCOLS: In WE-based CGJ+, the enclave $\mathcal{G}$ is replaced with a witness encryption WE; in KMG, the state is stored by the parties, while the enclaves are stateless; nevertheless, both of them use π as described above. The attack follows from the fact that the last two steps of these protocols constitute a sub-protocol which is identical to the third stage of Π, namely, Π_2. We note that the aforementioned *fairness* attack on Π takes place inside the sub-protocol Π_2. From this observation, the similar attacks on WE-based CGJ+ and KMG protocols follow.

5 New Constructions

In this section, we design two new protocols – more efficient than the existing ones – that are also *fair* in the malicious model with dishonest majority. Our first protocol, denoted Γ (see Fig. 4), works in $(\pi', \mathcal{G}, \mathsf{BB})$-hybrid model, where π' is a 2-party protocol computing the *encryption* of the given function $f(\cdot)$. Following is the description of π'.

DESCRIPTION OF π': It is a 2-party protocol that computes an *encryption* of the given function $f(x_0, x_1)$. Concretely:

$$\pi'\left(\{x_i, k_i\}_{i \in \{0,1\}}\right) \overset{def}{=} a = \begin{cases} ct', & \text{if } P_1 \text{ is } malicious \\ ct, & \text{otherwise.} \end{cases}$$

We can design such a π' – which is *privacy* secure in the malicious model with dishonest majority (as defined in Definition 4) – using known techniques in the existing literature [14]. The cryptographic components used in π' are: an (n, n)-*secret sharing* scheme and an AE scheme. Therefore, the differences between π (of protocol Π) and π' are the following: (1) the input size is less since we do not have the commitments; (2) removed are the expensive components ZK proofs and CS scheme; (3) while π is secure under *privacy-and-correctness with abort* in the malicious model with dishonest majority, π' is only *privacy* secure in the same setting. $\qquad\square$

DESCRIPTION OF Γ: The Γ is a composition of 3 sub-protocols:

$$\Gamma = \Gamma_2 \circ \pi' \circ \Gamma_1.$$

The Γ_1 securely stores the *internally generated* symmetric key $K = (k_0, k_1)$ (and various other auxiliary data) inside the enclave $\mathcal{G} = (\mathcal{G}_0, \mathcal{G}_1)$ using Diffie-Hellman key-exchange. It returns k_i to P_i to be used in the next stage π'. Unlike Π_1, the execution of Γ_1 does not require the following components: the release tokens ρ_i's, the commitments of the key-shares $com_{j,i}$'s and the OWF inside the enclave $\mathcal{G}$ (see Appendix A for more details). The description of Γ_1 is in steps 1–7.

The second stage π' – which is invoked in step 8 – has already been described in detail. It returns the symmetric encryption of f using (k_0, k_1) to all the parties to be used for the next stage Γ_2. At this point, there are two possible cases – P_0 receives either ct' ($\neq ct$) (case 1), or the correct encryption of f (case 2). Unlike in π, in both the cases, the parties (P_0, P_1) start executing the final stage Γ_2.

The final stage Γ_2 returns f after decrypting the output of π' inside the enclave $\mathcal{G}$, using the various data generated in Γ_1 along with the data obtained from BB. The protocol works as follows: Each party directly posts the ciphertext obtained in π' to BB, and gets the corresponding *tag*. Finally, each party submits the ciphertext-*tag* pair to the enclave $\mathcal{G}$ to obtain the correct f. The enclave would never decrypt, if any of the following three checks fails: the ciphertext-*tag* pair is invalid; the authentication of the ciphertext fails; and the input is supplied after the cut-off time Δt. Otherwise, it would allow the dishonest party P_1 to obtain f using $\mathcal{G}_1$, while the honest party P_0 is unable to obtain it, due to the occurrence of case 1 as above, or due to aborting the protocol after waiting for a time longer than time Δt; in either case it violates the *fairness* property. The description of Γ_2 is in steps 9–10. The differences between Γ_2 and Π_2 are the following: (1) we post the ciphertext (as opposed to the *release tokens*) to BB; and (2) consequently, the *release tokens* verification inside the enclave $\mathcal{G}$ are eliminated. The *fairness* property of Γ as argued so far is formalized in the following theorem.

$$\Gamma[\Delta t, \pi', \mathsf{BB}, \mathcal{G}, \lambda, \mathcal{P}]$$

Input: For all $i \in \{0,1\}$, P_i inputs x_i.

Output: Both P_0 and P_1 output either $f(\cdot)$ or $\perp$.

1. **[Setting up parameters (Offline)]** For all $i \in \{0,1\}$:
   (a) P_i samples key share $k_i \xleftarrow{\$} \{0,1\}^\lambda$ [used in Steps 5 and 8].
   (b) P_i invokes BB.getCurrCount() to obtain the current index t_i [used in Step 6].

2. **[Exchange of enclaves' verification-keys (Offline+Online)]** For all $i \in \{0,1\}$, P_i invokes $\mathcal{G}$.getpk() to receive mpk_i which is then sent to P_j [used in Steps 4 and 6].

3. **[Install prog' in enclave (Offline)]** For all $i \in \{0,1\}$, party P_i invoke $\mathcal{G}$.install(prog'$[\Delta t, \mathsf{vk_{BB}}, \mathcal{P}, i]$) and receives output eid_i [used in Steps 4 and 9-10].

4. **[Diffie-Hellman key-exchange by enclaves (Offline+Online)]** For all $i \in \{0,1\}$: P_i invokes $\mathcal{G}$.resume(eid_i, keyex) to receive $(g^{a_i}, sig_i^{(1)})$, and *broadcasts* $(eid_i, g^{a_i}, sig_i^{(1)})$; P_i checks if $\mathcal{G}.\Sigma.\mathsf{Ver}_{\mathsf{mpk}_j}((eid_j, \mathsf{prog}'[\Delta t, \mathsf{vk_{BB}}, \mathcal{P}, j], g^{a_j}), sig_j^{(1)}) = 1$ then continue, else abort. (Thus, a secure channel is established between the enclaves using Diffie-Hellman key.) **[used in Steps 6 and 7]**

5. **[Enclave stores own key-share k_i (Offline)]** For all $i \in \{0,1\}$, P_i invokes $\mathcal{G}$.resume(eid_i, init, k_i) [used in Step 6].

6. **[Enclave stores t_i and returns ciphertext (Offline+Online)]** For all $i \in \{0,1\}$: P_i invokes $\mathcal{G}$.resume(eid_i, send, g^{a_j}, t_i) to receive $(ct_{ij}, sig_i^{(3)})$ which is then sent to P_j; P_i checks if $\mathcal{G}.\Sigma.\mathsf{Ver}_{\mathsf{mpk}_j}((eid_j, \mathsf{prog}'[\Delta t, \mathsf{vk_{BB}}, \mathcal{P}, j], ct_{ij}), sig_j^{(3)}) = 1$ then continue, else abort **[used in Step 7]**.

7. **[Enclave stores other's key-share k_j (Offline)]** For all $i \in \{0,1\}$, P_i invokes $\mathcal{G}$.resume(eid_i, receive, ct_{ji}). If $\mathcal{G}$ returns $\perp$ then P_i abort, else continue. [Note that in this step both the enclave stores other parties secrets securely.] **[used in Step 8 and 9]**

8. **[Execute π' to obtain encryption of $f(\cdot)$ (Online)]** The a denotes π' output (see Sect. 5) **[used in Step 10]**.

9. **[Enclave returns BB's index T (Offline)]** For all $i \in \{0,1\}$, P_i invokes $\mathcal{G}$.resume(eid_i, getParams) and receives $(T, sig_i^{(5)})$ [used in Step 10].

10. **[Obtaining parameters and computing $f(\cdot)$ (Online+Offline)]** For all $i \in \{0,1\}$, P_i posts a to BB and receives (t, σ) from it. Finally, P_i invokes $\mathcal{G}$.resume(eid_i, output, a, t, σ), and receives $f(x_0, x_1)$.

Fig. 4. Description of Γ in $(\pi', \mathcal{G}, \mathsf{BB})$-hybrid model. In all the cases, $j = 1 - i$. The program prog' is described in Appendix A. It is parameterized by: a cut-off time Δt (which is $poly(\lambda)$), a 2-party protocol π', a *Bulletin Board* BB, an enclave $\mathcal{G}$, the security parameter 1^λ, and a set of parties $\mathcal{P} = \{P_0, P_1\}$. The orange colored steps in the algorithm represent the local computation done by a party. The purple colored steps in the algorithm represent the communication among the parties and the BB. (Color figure online)

Theorem 2. *Suppose the following assumptions hold good: the signature scheme Σ is existentially unforgeable under chosen message attack; the authenticated encryption scheme AE is INT-CTXT secure; the authentication scheme AS is unforgeable; the DDH assumption is valid in the underlying algebraic group $\mathbb{Z}_p$; and π' is secure under Definition 4. The protocol Γ – as described in Fig. 4 – satisfies Definition 2 in the $(\pi', \mathcal{G}, \mathsf{BB})$-hybrid model.*

Proof Sketch. We first sketch the simulator $\mathcal{S}$, and prove that Γ is simulatable, that is, for all PPT adversary $\mathcal{A}$, the execution of Γ in the $(\pi', \mathcal{G}, \mathsf{BB})$-hybrid world and the simulated execution in the ideal world are indistinguishable. Briefly, in order to ensure *fairness*, $\mathcal{S}$ needs to simulate the following abort conditions of the real world: (1) If P_1 aborts immediately after receiving the output without P_0 getting it, then $\mathcal{S}$ sends abort to F, and continues to execute. If P_1 queries $\mathcal{G}$ for the output on a valid authentication tag, then $\mathcal{S}$ aborts; (2) if P_1 does not post correct ct_1 (i.e. the ciphertext is not the same as received from $\pi'(\cdot)$) during the interval T and $T + \Delta t$, but queries $\mathcal{G}$ for the output on a valid authentication tag, then $\mathcal{S}$ sends abort to F and aborts. □

A New Stateless Protocol Υ. We now design a stateless protocol Υ which is more efficient than the KMG stateless protocol [16]; although, both achieve *fairness* in the malicious model with dishonest majority.

We design Υ by making changes to Γ which is described in Fig. 4: First, we replace $\mathcal{G}$ with ELI (see Sect. 3); inside ELI we use $\widetilde{\mathsf{prog}}$ instead of prog' (see Appendix A). The difference between $\widetilde{\mathsf{prog}}$ and prog' is that the stored state in prog' is first *encrypted* which is then returned to the parties, along with the output of the function invoked. Therefore, the security of Υ follows from the security of Γ, which is formalized in the theorem below.

Since KMG is derived from Π in the same way Υ is derived from Γ, Υ is more efficient than KMG because Γ is more efficient than Π.

Theorem 3. *Suppose the following assumptions hold good: the signature scheme Σ is existentially unforgeable under chosen message attack; the authenticated encryption scheme AE is INT-CTXT secure; the authentication scheme AS is unforgeable; the hash function H is collision-resistant; PRF is pseudorandom; the DDH assumption is valid in the underlying algebraic group $\mathbb{Z}_p$; π' is secure under Definition 4; and ELI is secure under Definition 1. The Υ satisfies Definition 2 in the $(\pi', \mathsf{ELI}, \mathsf{BB})$-hybrid model.*

Proof Sketch. We first divide the simulator $\mathcal{S}$ into two parts: (i) simulation for real-world interaction between party P_1 and ELI, and (ii) simulation for real-world interaction between P_0 and P_1. For case (i), the security follows directly from Theorem 1 (as described in Sect. 3.1). For case (ii), the proof is obtained from Theorem 2. Together, (i) and (ii) complete the proof of the theorem. □

6   Feasibility of Implementing Our Protocols

In this section, we describe the feasibility of implementing Γ and Υ (as described in Sect. 5). We will describe the implementation details for Γ; Υ can be implemented in a similar way.

The Γ consists of three components: the *Bulletin Board* BB implemented using Bitcoin, π' implemented using the SPDZ-2 framework, and an enclave $\mathcal{G}$ implemented using Intel SGX. The details are given below.

Bitcoin as a Bulletin Board. We are adapting the implementation of CGJ+ bulletin board for our construction. We can use the Bitcoin testnet which has a zero-value currency, but the functions are similar to that of the Bitcoin main network. The testnet also allows faster block generation and easier sandbox-ing. For our implementation, we will use Bitcoin script that supports a spe-cial instruction named OP_RETURN, which allows a creator of a transaction to include up to 40 bytes of arbitrary data into a transaction. We can implement BB.post($\cdot$) in the following way: each party broadcasts a transaction, namely Tx, by including OP_RETURN$\|$"ct" in the output script, and the authentication tag $\sigma = B\|B_1\|\cdots\|B_6$, where B denotes the block containing Tx; and $B_1,\cdots,B_6$ denote six consecutive blocks after B in the consensus chain. In order to verify σ, one can simply check that the blocks $B\|B_1\|\cdots\|B_6$ exist in the Blockchain.

Implementing π' Using SPDZ-2. We have implemented the inner MPC com-ponent $\pi'(\cdot)$ in SPDZ-2 framework [2], where $f(\cdot)$ is Yao's circuit, and the encryp-tion circuit is the AES. The SPDZ-2 is an MPC protocol that computes arbitrary function in the presence of a malicious adversary. The computation is done in two phases: an offline phase, where a party generates the preprocessed data, and an online phase where parties perform the actual computation.

We implemented millionaire's protocol to demonstrate the proof-of-concept of our results. We first fixed the offline phase parameters, which are then converted into SPDZ-2 format. Finally, these parameters were stored in their respective data files. Then, we executed the code for Yao's millionaire's protocol (embedded with the AES circuit) with the number of parties $n = 2, 3, \ldots, 6$. Then, we ran 50 trials with as many distinct keys, and benchmarked the running times by computing their average. We have plotted the results in Fig. 5. We observed that the running time to execute the online phase increases with the number of parties, most likely because the total size of the key shares increases with n. However, it still adds only a fraction of a second; therefore, we conclude that π' is feasible to implement. Our implementation of π' differs from that of π of CGJ+ in the following way: π''s input does not contain commitments; π''s instructions do not have the commitment schemes and the ZK proofs.

Implementing Enclave $\mathcal{G}$ Using Intel SGX-Hardware. To implement $\mathcal{G}$, we adapt the existing SGX-BB client called Obscuro [3] that provides the interface to execute the program prog$'$ inside the enclave. The Obscuro client is invoked by both P_0 and P_1, and it returns the respective enclave id's to both the parties. The parties then interact with the client to store the secret values inside it. Finally, it returns T to both the parties. After the successful execution of π', each party sends the received ciphertext along with the *tag* to the client by invoking the respective function securely residing inside it. The program then returns the function output $f(\cdot)$ upon successful verification of all the credentials. Our enclave implementation of $\mathcal{G}$ differs from that in [8] in the following way: the stored program for our enclave is prog$'$, where in their case it is prog (see Appendix A for details).

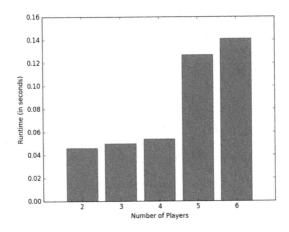

Fig. 5. Runtime of the online phase of the Yao's millionaire protocol embedded with the AES circuit vs. the number of players, implemented using the SPDZ-2 framework.

7   Conclusion

This paper has demonstrated attacks on the *fairness* properties of the various multiparty protocols described in [8,16]; these attacks are *only* effective, if we weaken the security of their underlying sub-protocol. We provide techniques to avoid these attacks (even if the sub-protocols are weak). These techniques not only make our new protocols more secure, but also boost their performances, both with respect to memory and the number of operations. A possible future work will be extending this techniques to design highly efficient fair multi-party protocols based on witness-based encryption, instead of on the trusted hardware.

Acknowledgment. Second author is supported by a research fellowship generously provided by Tata Consultancy Services (TCS). We thank the anonymous reviewers for their constructive comments.

A   Program **prog** and **prog'** for $\mathcal{G}$

The algorithmic description of prog and prog' is given in Fig. 6.

$$\text{prog'} \boxed{\text{prog}} [\Delta t, \text{vk}_{\text{BB}}, \mathcal{P}, i]$$

1. If inp = (keyex) then:
   (a) Choose $a_i \xleftarrow{\$} \mathbb{Z}_p$
   (b) return g^{a_i}, where g is the primitive root modulo p
2. If inp = (init, k, $\boxed{\rho, r}$) then:
   (a) $k_i := k$, $\boxed{\rho_i := \rho, k_i := k, r_i := r}$
   (b) $\boxed{com_{i,i} := \text{CS.Com}(k_i, r_i)}$
   (c) $\boxed{\text{return } com_{i,i}}$
3. If inp = (send, g^{a_j}, t) then:
   (a) $t_i = t$
   (b) $\text{sk}_{ij} = (g^{a_j})^{a_i} \bmod p$
   (c) $ct_{ij} := \text{AE.Enc}_{\text{sk}_{ij}}(k_i, t_i, \boxed{\rho_i})$
       (Here, $com_{i,j} = com_{i,i}$)
   (d) return ct_{ij}
4. If inp = (receive, ct_{ji}) then:
   (a) assert init and send
   (b) $(k_j, t_j, \boxed{\rho_j, com_{j,i}}) := \text{AE.Dec}_{\text{sk}_{ij}}(ct_{ji})$
   (c) If $(k_j, t_j, \boxed{\rho_j, com_{j,i}}) = \bot$ then return $\bot$

   $\boxed{\text{else return } com_{j,i}}$

5. If inp = (getParams) then:
   (a) assert init, send and receive
   (b) $T \quad := \qquad \max(t_0, t_1)$,
       $\boxed{y := \text{OWF}(\rho_0 \oplus \rho_1)}$
   (c) $K := (k_0 \oplus k_1)$
   (d) return T, $\boxed{y}$
6. If inp = (output, ct, t, σ, $\boxed{\rho}$) then:
   (a) assert getParams
   (b) If $t \notin \{T, \cdots, T + \Delta t\}$ then return $\bot$
   (c) If $\text{Ver}_{\text{vk}_{\text{BB}}}(t, ct, \sigma) \neq 1$ then return $\bot$
   (d) $\boxed{\text{If OWF}(\rho) \neq y \text{ then return } \bot}$
   (e) $out := \text{AE.Dec}_K(ct)$
   (f) If $out \neq \bot$ then return out

Fig. 6. Algorithmic descriptions of prog and prog'. We get prog' by removing the boxed statements of prog. Here, $j = 1 - i$. It is parameterized by: a cut-off time Δt, the verification key vk$_{\text{BB}}$ of *Bulletin Board*, a set of parties $\mathcal{P} = \{P_0, P_1\}$, and the party index i. It uses the following primitives: commitment Com, the authenticated encryption scheme AE, a one-way function OWF, and the *Bulletin Board* BB (see Sect. 3 for more details). Here, the state variables are marked blue, and the variables that are not stored locally are marked purple. (Color figure online)

References

1. Certificate transparency. https://www.certificate-transparency.org/. Accessed 25 Feb 2019
2. SPDZ, MASCOT, and Overdrive offline phases Github (2017). https://github.com/bristolcrypto/SPDZ-2
3. Obscuro. Github (2017). https://github.com/BitObscuro/Obscuro
4. Andrychowicz, M., Dziembowski, S., Malinowski, D., Mazurek, L.: Fair two-party computations via bitcoin deposits. In: Böhme, R., Brenner, M., Moore, T., Smith, M. (eds.) FC 2014. LNCS, vol. 8438, pp. 105–121. Springer, Heidelberg (2014). https://doi.org/10.1007/978-3-662-44774-1_8
5. Bahmani, R., et al.: Secure multiparty computation from SGX. In: Kiayias, A. (ed.) FC 2017. LNCS, vol. 10322, pp. 477–497. Springer, Cham (2017). https://doi.org/10.1007/978-3-319-70972-7_27

6. Bentov, I., Kumaresan, R.: How to use bitcoin to design fair protocols. In: Garay, J.A., Gennaro, R. (eds.) CRYPTO 2014. LNCS, vol. 8617, pp. 421–439. Springer, Heidelberg (2014). https://doi.org/10.1007/978-3-662-44381-1_24

7. Boneh, D., Naor, M.: Timed commitments. In: Bellare, M. (ed.) CRYPTO 2000. LNCS, vol. 1880, pp. 236–254. Springer, Heidelberg (2000). https://doi.org/10.1007/3-540-44598-6_15

8. Choudhuri, A.R., Green, M., Jain, A., Kaptchuk, G., Miers, I.: Fairness in an unfair world: fair multiparty computation from public bulletin boards. In: Proceedings of the 2017 ACM SIGSAC Conference on Computer and Communications Security, pp. 719–728. ACM (2017)

9. Cleve, R.: Limits on the security of coin flips when half the processors are faulty. In: Proceedings of the Eighteenth Annual ACM Symposium on Theory of Computing, pp. 364–369. ACM (1986)

10. Costan, V., Devadas, S.: Intel SGX explained. In: IACR Cryptology ePrint Archive, vol. 2016, no. 086, pp. 1–118 (2016)

11. Damgård, I., Keller, M., Larraia, E., Pastro, V., Scholl, P., Smart, N.P.: Practical covertly secure MPC for dishonest majority – Or: breaking the SPDZ limits. In: Crampton, J., Jajodia, S., Mayes, K. (eds.) ESORICS 2013. LNCS, vol. 8134, pp. 1–18. Springer, Heidelberg (2013). https://doi.org/10.1007/978-3-642-40203-6_1

12. Du, W., Atallah, M.J.: Secure multi-party computation problems and their applications: a review and open problems. In: Proceedings of the 2001 Workshop on New Security Paradigms, pp. 13–22. ACM (2001)

13. Goldreich, O.: Foundations of Cryptography: Basic Tools, vol. 1. Cambridge University Press, Cambridge (2007)

14. Goldreich, O.: Foundations of Cryptography: Basic Applications, vol. 2. Cambridge University Press, Cambridge (2009)

15. Goldreich, O., Micali, S., Wigderson, A.: How to play any mental game. In: Proceedings of the Nineteenth Annual ACM Symposium on Theory of Computing, pp. 218–229. ACM (1987)

16. Kaptchuk, G., Green, M., Miers, I.: Giving state to the stateless: augmenting trustworthy computation with ledgers. In: 26th Annual Network and Distributed System Security Symposium, NDSS (2019)

17. Kiayias, A., Zhou, H.-S., Zikas, V.: Fair and robust multi-party computation using a global transaction ledger. In: Fischlin, M., Coron, J.-S. (eds.) EUROCRYPT 2016. LNCS, vol. 9666, pp. 705–734. Springer, Heidelberg (2016). https://doi.org/10.1007/978-3-662-49896-5_25

18. Kumaresan, R., Moran, T., Bentov, I.: How to use bitcoin to play decentralized poker. In: Proceedings of the 22nd ACM SIGSAC Conference on Computer and Communications Security, pp. 195–206. ACM (2015)

19. Nakamoto, S.: Bitcoin: a peer-to-peer electronic cash system. Consulted 1(2012), 28 (2008)

20. Rogaway, P., Bellare, M., Black, J.: OCB: a block-cipher mode of operation for efficient authenticated encryption. ACM Trans. Inf. Syst. Secur. (TISSEC) 6, 365–403 (2003)

21. Shamir, A.: How to share a secret. Commun. ACM 22, 612–613 (1979)

22. Yao, A.C.-C.: Protocols for secure computations. In: FOCS, pp. 160–164. IEEE (1982)

Implementation

Efficient Cryptography on the RISC-V Architecture

Ko Stoffelen$^{(\boxtimes)}$

Digital Security Group, Radboud University, Nijmegen, The Netherlands
k.stoffelen@cs.ru.nl

Abstract. RISC-V is a promising free and open-source instruction set architecture. Most of the instruction set has been standardized and several hardware implementations are commercially available. In this paper we highlight features of RISC-V that are interesting for optimizing implementations of cryptographic primitives. We provide the first optimized assembly implementations of table-based AES, bitsliced AES, ChaCha, and the Keccak-$f[1600]$ permutation for the RV32I instruction set. With respect to public-key cryptography, we study the performance of arbitrary-precision integer arithmetic without a carry flag. We then estimate the improvement that can be gained by several RISC-V extensions. These performance studies also serve to aid design choices for future RISC-V extensions and implementations.

Keywords: RISC-V · AES · ChaCha · Keccak ·
Arbitrary-precision arithmetic · Software optimization

1 Introduction

The RISC-V project started out in 2010 as a research project at the University of California, Berkeley. The goal was to design an open-source reduced instruction set that was free and practical to use by academics and industry. Today, it comprises a foundation[1] with well over two hundred member organizations, including major industry partners such as Google, Qualcomm, and Samsung. The fact that many large companies are joining this efforts indicates that RISC-V might await a bright future. In particular, no longer having to pay any license fees makes it an attractive alternative and a serious competitor to ARM microcontrollers.

Together, the foundation's members developed a specification for the RISC-V instruction set architecture [RIS17]. RISC-V targets both embedded 32-bit devices and larger 64-bit and even 128-bit devices. While some parts of the specification are still in development, the most important parts have been frozen such that hardware and software could be implemented. Compilers, debuggers, and software libraries with RISC-V support have been around for several years[2].

---

[1] https://riscv.org/.
[2] https://riscv.org/software-status.

© Springer Nature Switzerland AG 2019
P. Schwabe and N. Thériault (Eds.): LATINCRYPT 2019, LNCS 11774, pp. 323–340, 2019.
https://doi.org/10.1007/978-3-030-30530-7_16

Commercial boards with fully functional RISC-V SoCs have been available for sale since 2016[3].

There exist several open-source RISC-V CPU designs designed to be easily extensible. This makes the platform an ideal candidate for software-hardware co-design, as was exemplified by a recent implementation of the hash-based signature scheme XMSS [WJW+18]. The underlying hash-function, SHA-256, was implemented in hardware to increase the performance of the full signature scheme. However, it is not always possible to 'simply' add a hardware co-processor of a required cryptographic primitive. In practice, one may have to deal with whatever hardware is available or a developer might lack the capabilities to modify a hardware implementation. More importantly, adding a co-processor to an ASIC will most likely increase the production cost of that chip. In order to make any trade-off decision for software-hardware co-design meaningful, some numbers need to exist to have an idea about the cost of software implementations. To the best of our knowledge, we are the first to provide such numbers for cryptographic primitives.

We explain how AES-128, ChaCha20, and Keccak-f[1600] can be implemented efficiently on RISC-V and we optimize 32-bit RISC-V assembly implementations. We also study the speed of arbitrary-precision addition, schoolbook multiplication, and Karatsuba multiplication for unique and redundant or reduced-radix integer representations. We then draw a parallel to the ARM Cortex-M line of microcontrollers and we show how architectural features such as the availability of native rotation instructions, a carry flag, and the number of available registers impact the performance of these primitives. We continue by estimating what the performance would be if a RISC-V core were to be extended with these features.

In Sect. 2 we first explain details about the RISC-V instruction set and our benchmarking platform. Sections 3, 4, and 5 cover implementation strategies that are specific to AES, ChaCha, and Keccak, respectively. Arbitrary-precision integer arithmetic is discussed in Sect. 6. Finally, in Sect. 7 we compare the relative performance of cryptographic primitives to that on the ARM Cortex-M4 and estimate what the performance would be with RISC-V extensions for several architectural features.

Our software implementations are open-source and placed into the public domain. They are available at https://github.com/Ko-/riscvcrypto.

2   The RISC-V Architecture

The RISC-V instruction set architecture (ISA) specification is split into a user-level ISA and a privileged ISA. The privileged ISA specifies instructions and registers that are useful when creating, for example, operating systems, but for our purpose we only need to consider the user-level ISA. The user-level ISA is divided in a base ISA and in several standardized extensions that are discussed

---

[3] https://www.sifive.com/boards/hifive1.

in Sect. 2.2. At the time of writing, the base ISAs for 32-bit and 64-bit machines, called RV32I and RV64I respectively, have been frozen at version 2.0. A base ISA for 128-bit machines (RV128I) and a smaller 32-bit variant with fewer registers (RV32E) still have draft status. In this work we focus on the 32-bit RV32I instruction set.

2.1   The RV32I Base Instruction Set

RV32I specifies 32 32-bit registers named x0 to x31. However, not all of them can be used freely. The registers have aliases that makes their purpose more clear. For example, x0 is also known as zero: writes to it are ignored and it always reads as the value 0. The others are: ra (return address, x1), sp (stack pointer, x2), gp (global pointer, x3), tp (thread pointer, x4), a0-a7 (function arguments and return value), s0-s11 (saved registers), and t0-t6 (temporary registers). That means that 27 registers can be used without complications and maybe a few more depending on the environment. Only sp and s0-s11 are callee-saved.

As a true RISC, the number of available instructions is fairly limited. We therefore include a concise but complete overview in this section. All instructions are described in more detail in the official specification [RIS17].

Arithmetic and bitwise instructions have three register operands, or two register operands and a sign-extended 12-bit immediate, denoted by the I suffix. The following self-explanatory instructions are available: ADD, ADDI, SUB, AND, ANDI, OR, ORI, XOR, and XORI. There is no SUBI, because that is just an ADDI with a negative immediate. Similarly, there is no real NOT instruction, because it can be implemented with XORI and −1 as immediate. NOT is recognized as a pseudo-instruction by assemblers.

Regarding shifts, the following instructions exist: SLL, SLLI, SRL, SRLI, SRA, and SRAI. These naming convention that is used here is Shift (Left or Right) (Logical or Arithmetic) (Immediate). Note that the base ISA does not specify a rotation instruction.

To load a value from memory, LW, LH, LHU, LB, and LBU can be used. The W stands for word (32 bits), the H for half-word (16 bits), and the B for byte (8 bits). With LH and LB, the value is assumed to be signed and will therefore be sign-extended to a 32-bit register. LHU and LBU are their unsigned counterparts that perform zero-extension instead of sign-extension. To store a register value to memory, one can use SW, SH, and SB. For all load and store instructions, the base address needs to be in a register. An immediate offset can be specified in the instruction. For example, LW a1, 4(a0) loads a word from a0 + 4 in a1. It is not possible to specify the offset in a register or to automatically increment/decrement the address.

The JAL and JALR instructions specify unconditional jumps. The target address can be specified relative to the program counter (JAL) or as an absolute address in a register (JALR). On the other hand, BEQ, BNE, BLT, BLTU, BGE, and BGEU denote conditional jumps based on a comparison. Their first two operands are registers of which the values are compared. The U suffix denotes that the operands are interpreted as unsigned values for the comparison. The third operand specifies the destination address relative to the program counter.

It is also possible to compare without branching. The SLT, SLTU, SLTI, and SLTIU instructions set a destination register to one if the second operand (a register) is less than (signed or unsigned) the third operand (either a register or an immediate). Otherwise, the destination register is set to zero.

The LUI (load upper immediate) and AUIPC (add upper immediate to program counter) instructions can be used to set values larger than 12 bits in a register.

Finally, for the sake of completeness, there are specialized instructions to deal with synchronization (FENCE and FENCE.I), to deal with control and status registers (6 CSR* variants), to call an operating system (ECALL) and to signal debuggers (EBREAK). We will not use them, except for reading a cycle counter.

2.2   Standardized Extensions

A RISC-V core has to implement a base ISA, and optionally it can implement one or several standardized extensions to the instruction set. Most extensions are denoted by a single letter. The extensions with a frozen specification are M (with instructions for integer multiplication/division), A (atomic instructions), F (single-precision floating point), D (double-precision floating point), Q (quad-precision floating point), and C (compressed instructions).

Other extensions, such as those for bit manipulation, vector instructions, and user-level interrupts still have draft status. To the best of our knowledge the extensions in draft status have not yet been implemented by any commercially available core[4].

2.3   Benchmarking Platform

We use a HiFive1 development board as our benchmarking platform, as they are relatively easily available. This contains the FE310-G000 SoC [SiF17] with an E31 core [SiF18]. The core implements the RV32IMAC instruction set, i.e., the RV32I base ISA with the extensions for multiplication/division, atomic instructions, and compressed instructions. Of these, only the M extension is relevant to us.

The RISC-V specification does not specify how long instructions take to execute or what kinds of memory are available. This is left open to the hardware core implementer. Benchmarks across different RISC-V cores therefore need to be compared with caution. To provide more insight, we briefly describe some characteristics of this particular RISC-V core.

The E31 is designed as a 5-stage single-issue in-order pipelined CPU that runs at 320+ MHz, although the PLL clock generator has an output of at most 384 MHz. The core has support for up to 64 KiB of DTIM memory that is used as RAM, but the HiFive1 only has 16 KiB. Outside of the core, there is another

---

[4] https://riscv.org/risc-v-cores.

16 MB of QSPI flash memory. To accelerate instruction fetches from the flash memory, the E31 comes with 16 KiB of 2-way instruction cache.

Most instructions have a result latency of a single cycle. There are a few exceptions. For example, word-loads have a result latency of 2 cycles with a cache hit. With a cache miss, it highly depends on the relative clock frequency of the flash controller compared to the core. Half-word-loads and byte-loads have a result latency of 3 cycles in the event of a cache hit. Misaligned DTIM accesses are not allowed and result in a trap signal.

The E31 has an elaborate branch predictor, consisting of a branch target buffer, a branch history buffer, and a return address stack. Correctly predicted branches should suffer no penalty, while wrong guesses receive a penalty of 3 cycles.

The RISC-V specification describes a 64-bit increasing cycle counter that is accessible through two CSR registers. This can be used for accurate benchmarking of code. We aim to unroll the code as much as possible as long as the code still fits in the instruction cache. Tables and constants are stored in the DTIM memory. This way, we manage to get very consistent measurements. Occasionally, a measurement ends up taking much longer than expected. These outliers are ignored.

3   AES

32-bit software implementations of AES usually fall into two categories, depending on whether it it safe to use table lookups or not. The fastest encryption implementations *for a single block* use the idea that the various steps of the round function can be combined in large lookup tables, usually called T-tables [DR02]. However, this type of implementation is known to be vulnerable to cache-based timing attacks [Ber05a, OST06]. A CPU cache can leak information about which memory address has been accessed during a computation. When this memory address depends on a secret intermediate value as is the case with the T-table approach, it can be used to extract secret information.

When *multiple blocks* can be processed in parallel (e.g., in CTR or GCM mode) and the CPU registers are large enough to accommodate multiple blocks, bitsliced implementations can be more efficient [KS09, Kön08]. This type of AES implementation has the additional advantage that lookup tables are easily avoidable, allowing a careful implementer to make it resistant against timing attacks.

Our particular benchmarking platform does not have a data cache. Therefore, it *should* be safe to use a table-based AES implementation on this device. However, this might not be the case on other RISC-V platforms. Table-based implementations might also demand an unreasonable amount of memory on small embedded RISC-V-based devices. This is why we treat both implementation categories.

3.1 Table-Based Implementations

At Indocrypt 2008, Bernstein and Schwabe explained how to optimize table-based AES implementations for a variety of CPU architectures [BS08]. They describe a baseline of 16 shift instructions, 16 mask instructions, 16 load instructions for table lookups, 4 load instructions for round keys, and 16 xor instructions per AES round, plus 16 additional mask instructions in the last round and 4 additional round-key loads and 4 xor instructions for the initial AddRoundKey. This baseline excludes the cost of loading the input into registers, writing the output back to memory, and some overhead such as setting the address of the lookup table in a register and storing callee-save registers on the stack when necessary. They then continue by listing various architecture-dependent optimizations.

On RISC-V, very few of these techniques are possible, which is no surprise given that the instruction set is intentionally kept very simple. The LBU byte load instruction allows to save 4 mask instructions in the final round. On the other hand, the baseline count assumes that it is possible to load from an address specified by a base value in one register and an offset in another register. While this holds for many architectures, it is not true for RISC-V. Instead, the full address needs to be explicitly computed each time. This means that we require 16 extra ADD instructions per round.

With round-key recomputation, only 14 round-key words have to be stored and loaded instead of 44. This saves 30 SW instructions in the key expansion, but more importantly, it allows to swap 30 LW instructions for 30 XOR instructions at the cost of using 4 extra registers of which their values need to be saved on the stack. We expected this to improve performance for encryption on our platform. However, it turned out that this was not the case so we did not employ this technique.

There is more that can be done with the free registers that are available. Some of the round keys could also be cached in registers such that they do not have to be loaded for every block when encrypting multiple blocks. However, to keep the implementation as versatile as possible, we decided not to do this and to encrypt just a single block. This makes it possible to straightforwardly build any mode around it.

Result. We implemented and optimized the AES-128 key expansion and encryption algorithms. Both use the same 4 KiB lookup table. Key expansion finishes in 340 cycles and requires no stack memory. Encryption of a single 16-byte block is performed in 912 clock cycles. This uses 24 bytes on the stack to store callee-save registers.

3.2 Bitsliced Implementations

With bitsliced AES implementations, the internal parallelism in the SubBytes step usually means that the AES state is represented in such a way that a register is made to contain the ith bit of every byte of the state. This means that 8 registers are needed to represent the AES state, but then only 16 bits in the register are used, which is suboptimal. However, when multiple AES blocks can be processed in parallel, they can be stored in the same registers in order to process them simultaneously. Especially when the registers are large, this yields very high throughputs [KS09].

We implement an optimized bitsliced implementation of AES-128 in CTR mode. With 32-bit registers, only 2 blocks can be processed in parallel. The implementation is inspired by an earlier implementation optimized for the ARM Cortex-M4 architecture [SS16].

For the most expensive operation, SubBytes, we use the smallest known circuit by Boyar and Peralta of 113 gates [BP10]. On the Cortex-M4, this could not be implemented directly because there were not enough registers available. With RV32I, carefully rearranging the instructions permits not having to spill any intermediate value to the stack. We can therefore implement SubBytes in exactly 113 single-cycle bitwise instructions.

ShiftRows with a 'regular' state representation uses rotations over the full rows of the AES state that are stored in registers. The equivalent for the bitsliced state representation requires to do rotations within a byte of a register, which is trickier to implement. The RV32I base ISA does not offer convenient instructions to do this or to extract bits from a register. It therefore has to be implemented by simply masking out a group of bits, shifting them to their correct position and inserting them in a result register. This takes 6 OR instructions, 7 AND(I) instructions and 6 shift instructions per state register. There are 8 state register, so this has to be done 8 times for one AES round.

On the Cortex-M4, MixColumns could be implemented with just 27 xor instructions, heavily using the fact that one operand could be rotated for free. RISC-V, however, does not have a native rotation instruction in the base ISA at all. Therefore the rotation has to be implemented with two shifts and an OR instruction. We study the impact of rotation instructions in more detail in Sect. 7.2. In total, our MixColumns implementation uses 27 XOR instructions and 16 rotations.

The other parts of the implementation are straightforward or are very similar to the Cortex-M implementation [SS16].

Result. Key expansion and conversion of all round keys to the bitsliced format takes 1239 clock cycles and 16 stack bytes. For benchmarking encryption, we selected a fixed plaintext size of 4096 bytes. This can be encrypted or decrypted with AES-128-CTR in 509622 cycles, or at 124.4 cycles per byte. 60 stack bytes are used to store callee-save registers and copies of a few other values.

4   ChaCha

ChaCha is a family of stream ciphers based on Salsa20 [Ber08]. It is known for its high speed in software and together with a message authentication code called Poly1305 it is used in TLS and OpenSSH [Ber05b, LCM+16, NL18].

ChaCha starts by loading constants, a 256-bit key, a 96-bit nonce, and a 32-bit counter into a 512-bit state. With RV32I, there are enough registers to keep the full state in registers during the whole computation. ChaCha20 is the most commonly used ChaCha variant that performs 20 rounds. Every round contains 4 quarter-rounds and every quarter-round consist of 4 additions, 4 xors, and 4 rotations. Because the RV32I base ISA lacks rotation instructions, every rotation has to be replaced by 2 shift instructions and an OR instruction. In total we require 20 single-cycle instructions to implement the ChaCha quarter-round.

The other parts are straightforward. As long as the input to the stream cipher is longer than 64 bytes, we generate the key-stream and xor it with the input in blocks of 64 bytes. If the input length is not divisible by 64 bytes, there will be some bytes remaining that still need to be encrypted. For those, another 64 bytes of key-stream is generated. These are xored with the input first per word (4 bytes) and finally per byte.

4.1 Result

Our implementation of the complete Chacha20 stream cipher requires 32 bytes in the DTIM memory to store constants and another 40 bytes on the stack to store callee-save registers. We benchmark speed with the same fixed input size of 4096 bytes as we used for the bitsliced AES-128-CTR implementation. This can be encrypted or decrypted in 114365 clock cycles, or at 27.9 cycles per byte.

5 Keccak

The Keccak-f family of permutations was designed in the course of the SHA-3 competition [BDPA08]. The Keccak-f[1600] instance is now at the core of the SHA-3 hash functions and the SHAKE extendable output functions standardized by NIST [NIS15]. It it also used in various other cryptographic functions. An optimized implementation of the Keccak-f[1600] permutation therefore benefits all those schemes. In the *Keccak implementation overview* a number of implementation techniques are discussed, including those relevant to 32-bit software implementations [BDP+12].

5.1 Efficient Scheduling

The permutation operates on a relatively large state of 1600 bits. Having the RV32I architecture in mind, this state is clearly too large to be able to contain the full state in registers. It is therefore required to swap parts between memory and registers during the computation. Loads from memory and stores to memory are relatively expensive, so for an efficient implementation it is important to keep the number of loads and stores at a manageable level.

The permutation iterates a round function consisting of the steps θ, ρ, π, χ, and ι. The first four steps each process the full state. Computing them one by one would therefore use many loads and stores. The designers described a technique to merge the computation of these steps such that only two passes over the full state are required per round. This is explained in detail in the implementation overview document [BDP+12]. We follow the same approach for our RISC-V implementation.

5.2 Bit Interleaving

The state is structured as 5×5 64-bit lanes. On a 32-bit architecture, one could simply split the lanes into two halves that are stored in separate registers, but it is more efficient to interleave the bits. The bits with an 'even' index are then stored in one register and those with an 'odd' index in another. The lane-wise translations in θ and in ρ then become 32-bit rotations. It has been mentioned before that the RV32I base ISA does not contain rotation instructions.

In fact, with both approaches a lane-wise translation costs 6 single-cycle instructions. The difference is that with the interleaved representation, for translation offsets of 1 or -1 only a single register has to be rotated. Those then only cost 3 single-cycle instructions. Because this is the case for 6 out of 29 lane translations per round, bit interleaving still provides a nice improvement.

5.3 Lane Complementing

The χ step computes 5 XOR, 5 AND, and 5 NOT (64-bit) operations on the lanes of every plane of the state. There are 5 such planes and we only have 32-bit instructions, so in total χ requires 50 XOR instructions, 50 AND instructions, and 50 XORI instructions with -1 as immediate per round. The number of XORI instructions can be reduced to 10 by representing certain lanes by their complement and by changing some AND instructions into OR instructions. This comes at the cost of applying a mask at the beginning and at the output of Keccak-f. This technique is also described in more detail in the implementation overview document [BDP+12]. This is a useful technique on the RISC-V, because there is no instruction that combines an AND with a NOT of one of its operands, as is the case on some other architectures.

5.4 Result

Our RISC-V implementation is inspired by the fastest Cortex-M3/M4 implementation known to us, which is the KeccakP-1600-inplace-32bi-armv7m-le implementation in the eXtended Keccak Code Package[5]. The main differences are that we add lane complementing and that we keep more variables in registers instead of having to store them on the stack.

Memory-wise our implementation requires 192 bytes in the DTIM memory for the round constants and 20 bytes on the stack. To benchmark speed, we measure a single execution of the permutation from the instruction cache. This takes 13774 clock cyles, or 68.9 cycles per byte.

---

[5] https://github.com/XKCP/XKCP.

6   Arbitrary-Precision Arithmetic

Arbitrary-precision arithmetic on integers, also called big-integer arithmetic, is a core component of public-key cryptographic systems such as RSA and elliptic-curve cryptography. We consider addition and two multiplication algorithms, schoolbook and Karatsuba multiplication. The multiplication algorithms make heavy use of the RISC-V M extension. This provides a 32×32-bit multiplier and the MUL and MULHU instructions, among some others that we will not use. MUL gives the lower 32 bits of the 64-bit multiplication result, MULHU the higher 32 bits, interpreting its operands both as unsigned values. On the E31, they each have a result latency of 2 clock cycles.

6.1   Carries and Reduced-Radix Representations

An arbitrarily large integer is usually represented as a vector of CPU words. The part of the integer that fits in a single CPU word is called a *limb*. Arithmetic on arbitrary-precision integers then translates to an algorithm that performs arithmetic with the limbs, as those are the only units that a CPU can work with.

The addition of two limbs may result in an overflow. On most CPU architectures, whether an overflow occurred is stored in a carry flag. This can then subsequently be used in an add-with-carry operation.

RISC-V, however, does not specify the existence of a carry flag. Instead, the carry needs to be explicitly computed every time. The SLTU instruction (set less than unsigned) is very useful for this. Let $r = a + b$, where r, a, and b are unsigned 32-bit values. Then the addition produces a carry c whenever $r < a$ (or $r < b$). In assembly, this can be implemented with ADD r, a, b; SLTU c, r, a.

This explicit carry handling can be the cause of a significant overhead. One way to avoid this is by guaranteeing that a carry will not occur. This is possible by using a reduced-radix representation, also known as a redundant integer representation. Instead of the full 32 bits, one can use the least significant k bits of every limb, such that the most significant $32 - k$ bits are zero at the start. This *radix-2^k representation* requires more limbs to store an integer of the same bit length, but the advantage is that one can do one or even many additions without producing a carry. The carries are accumulated in the most significant $32 - k$ bits of the same limb. Only in the end they may need to be added to the next limb to get back to a unique integer representation.

What is more efficient is highly application-dependent, as that determines how many and which operations are computed on the integers. We aim to keep this generic by studying the performance of both types of addition and multiplication algorithms for an arbitrary number of limbs, without specifying a precise radix.

6.2   Addition

Arbitrary-precision addition is a simple operation that consists of a carry chain for full-limb (radix-2^{32}) integer representations. The operands are added limbwise, where every such addition may result in an overflow that has to be carried to the next limb.

Figure 1 shows how both reduced and full representations compare. It appears that carry handling is a significant part of the computational effort. A reduced-radix representation is approximately 37% faster than a non-redundant representation. However, one should note that with a reduced-radix representation, more limbs will be required. For example, it is fairer to compare the reduced-radix representation with 12 limbs to the full-radix representation with 10 limbs, when only 27 bits are used in every limb, i.e., in radix 2^{27}. The cost of carrying at the end to get back to a unique representation also needs to be taken into account.

Still, it appears that reduced-radix representations can be beneficial when multiple additions have to be computed.

Figure 1 also shows the estimated cost of full-limb addition if there were a carry flag and add-with-carry operation. This is discussed in Sect. 7.4.

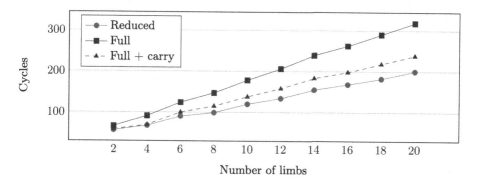

Fig. 1. Performance of arbitrary-precision addition.

6.3   Schoolbook Multiplication

Many algorithms exist to implement arbitrary-precision multiplication. One of the simplest ones is called schoolbook multiplication. With the schoolbook multiplication method multiplying two n-limb integers takes n^2 single-limb (in our case: 32×32-bit) multiplications.

A non-reduced representation still has to perform some carry handling, but the cost of this is much less significant with multiplication compared to addition, as can be seen in Fig. 2. Schoolbook multiplication with reduced-radix representations is only 8% faster than multiplication with non-reduced representations.

And because more limbs will be required, there is actually very little advantage to using a reduced-radix representation.

This can be explained by the fact that the LW, SW, MUL, and MULHU instructions take more CPU cycles compared to the simpler bitwise and arithmetic instructions. A reduced-radix representation does not avoid this more significant part of the cost of the inner loop of the algorithm.

6.4 Karatsuba Multiplication

The Karatsuba algorithm was the first multiplication algorithm that was discovered that has a lower asymptotic time complexity than $\mathcal{O}(n^2)$ [KO63]. Instead, it can recursively multiply arbitrary-precision integers in $\mathcal{O}(n^{\log_2 3})$. It succeeds in this by effectively trading an n-limb multiplication for 3 $\frac{n}{2}$-limb multiplications and several additions.

The details of the Karatsuba multiplication algorithm have been extensively covered in other works. It is used in many implementations of cryptographic schemes, most notably for RSA [SV93] and elliptic-curve cryptography [BCL14, DHH+15,FA17], but also for more recent lattice-based [KRS19] and isogeny-based [SLLH18] post-quantum cryptography.

We implement a single level of subtractive Karatsuba that multiplies two equal-length operands with an even number of limbs. This restriction is only there to simplify the performance analysis by being able to omit a few implementation details for dealing with special cases. The case of equal-length operands with an even number of limbs is also in fact the most common scenario in cryptography, which is why it is not even necessarily a relevant restriction.

Figure 2 shows that even for a very small number of limbs, the Karatsuba multiplication algorithm is already faster than schoolbook multiplication. This is not obvious, as the cost of the extra additions and constants in the complexity typically imply a certain threshold where Karatsuba starts to perform better.

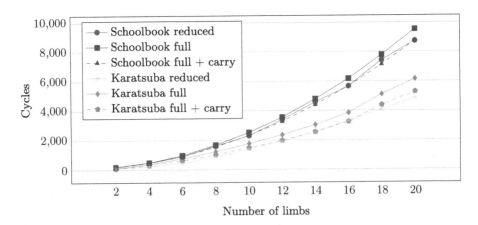

Fig. 2. Performance of arbitrary-precision multiplication.

The gap between reduced-radix representations and non-reduced or full-limb representations is slightly larger than with schoolbook multiplication, which can be partially explained by the extra additions that need to be computed. Its difference is now approximately 21%. Whether this suffices to make a reduced-radix representation more efficient in practice is hard to conclude from this data. It will depend on the specific application.

7 Extending RISC-V and Discussion

7.1 Speed Comparison with ARM Cortex-M4

The RISC-V platform that we used has similarities with the ARM Cortex-M family of microcontrollers. Both have 32-bit architectures and are designed for cheap embedded applications. The main difference is that ARM microcontrollers have a richer (proprietary) instruction set. For example, rotations are first-class citizens in the ARMv7-M instruction set and can even be combined with arithmetic instructions in a single CPU cycle. The architecture also provides nicer bit-extraction instructions, a carry flag and a single-cycle add-with-carry. On the other hand, RV32I comes with more registers, which may benefit cryptographic primitives that have a larger state. This can save a lot of overhead of having to spill values to the stack.

At first sight, it is unclear which weighs more heavily. We therefore compare the relative performance of our optimized cryptographic primitives with their counterpart on the Cortex-M4. There already exist AES, ChaCha20, and Keccak-f[1600] assembly implementations optimized for that platform.

Table 1. Comparison between the E31 (RV32IMAC) and the Cortex-M4.

Scheme	Cortex-M4		E31/RV32IMAC	
	Cycles	Cycles/byte	Cycles	Cycles/byte
Table AES-128 key schedule	254.9 [SS16]		340	
Table AES-128	644.7 [SS16]	40.3	912	57.0
Bitsliced AES-128 key schedule	1033.8 [SS16]		1239	
Bitsliced AES-128-CTR	414617.6*	101.2 [SS16]	509622*	124.4
ChaCha20 encrypt	56934.4*	13.9 [HRS16]	114365*	27.9
Keccak-f[1600] permute	12969†	64.8	13774	68.9

*When encrypting 4096 bytes.
†We benchmarked `KeccakP1600_Permute_24rounds` from https://github.com/XKCP/ XKCP/blob/master/lib/low/KeccakP-1600/Optimized32biAsmARM/KeccakP-1600- inplace-32bi-armv7m-le-gcc.s on an STM32F407.

Table 1 provides the exact numbers, while Fig. 3 visualizes their relative speed. It can be seen that all schemes require more cycles with the RV32I architecture. Of course, this does not directly relate to speed in practice, as we do not take the different CPU clock frequencies into account. It shows that all schemes use instructions that can be computed in a single cycle on the Cortex-M4, but not with RV32I. Relatively, it appears that ChaCha20 has the largest disadvantage because of this. For this scheme, the lack of rotation instructions seems to outweigh the possibility to keep the full state in registers without spilling to the stack, something that is necessary on the Cortex-M4. When the algorithms are compared to each other, their differences remain very similar with the RV32I instruction set architecture.

7.2   The RISC-V B Extension

The RISC-V foundation reserved the B extension for bit manipulation instructions. In 2017 there was an active working group that would develop a specification for the B extension. However, apparently the working group dissolved in November 2017 for bureaucratic reasons[6]. An independent fork was developed outside of the RISC-V foundation, which was merged back and made official again in March 2019.

The latest V0.37 draft specification adds 37 new instructions[7]. While it is unknown which will be used in the end, it is likely that this will include some type of rotation, byte shuffle, and bit-extraction instructions. The current specification also includes an and-with-complement instruction. This would imply that lane complementing would no longer be advantageous for Keccak-$f[1600]$.

We estimate the impact that this extension will have, focussing on rotations. For each scheme, we counted all instruction sequences that could be replaced by a rotation instruction. Our table-based AES does not use rotations, while the bitsliced AES implementations uses 144 of them. ChaCha20 uses 320 rotation instructions and Keccak-$f[1600]$ 1248.

Assuming that the rotation would be possible in a single cycle, we then calculated how many CPU cycles would be saved by having this instruction. The results can be seen in Table 2 and Fig. 3. For Keccak-$f[1600]$ and especially for ChaCha20, rotations are a significant part of their computational cost. From Fig. 3 it is clear that with rotations, the Keccak-$f[1600]$ permutation can be computed in fewer cycles than on the Cortex-M4. This is due to the fact that more registers are available.

Table 2. Estimated improvement with a rotation instruction.

Scheme	Rotations	Improvement	Cycles/byte
Table-based AES	0	0.0%	57.0
Bitsliced AES	144	7.0%	115.7
ChaCha20	320	35.8%	17.9
Keccak-$f[1600]$	1248	18.1%	56.4

---

[6] https://groups.google.com/forum/#!forum/riscv-xbitmanip.
[7] https://github.com/riscv/riscv-bitmanip.

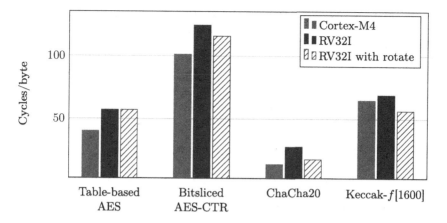

Fig. 3. Speed of cryptographic primitives.

7.3 Number of Registers

We already discussed some consequences of the large number of registers that are available on the performance of these implementations. Especially ChaCha and Keccak-f[1600], but also the bitsliced AES implementation, benefit from having to spill fewer intermediate values to the stack. It is noteworthy to mention that the RV32E instruction set, which is nearing its completion and which is intended to target embedded devices, will most likely decrease the number of registers from 32 back to 16 [RIS17]. This will set back the performance of aforementioned schemes, but this may be compensated by supporting the B extension with a rotation instruction.

7.4 Carry Flag

In Sect. 6 we studied the performance of arbitrary-precision addition and multiplication with and without reduced-radix integer representations. We now estimate how full-limb representations would perform if an RV32I core was extended with a carry flag and an add-with-carry instruction. We assume that this instruction would have a result latency of a single CPU clock cycle, similar to a regular addition instruction.

For addition, 4 cycles per limb would be saved in our implementation. We then subtracted $4n$ cycles from the full-radix addition results, where n is the number of limbs. The result can be seen in Fig. 1. As is to be expected, addition with this instruction is almost as fast as reduced-radix representation, the only difference being the top (most significant) limb that gets set.

With schoolbook multiplication $2n^2$ cycles are subtracted, as we can save 2 cycles in the inner loop with the add-with-carry instruction, which is executed n^2 times. For Karatsuba multiplication we computed that the add-with-carry instruction would save $27\frac{n}{2} + 6\left(\frac{n}{2}\right)^2$ cycles. The quadratic term comes from the cycles that are saved with the schoolbook multiplications and the linear part from the cycles that are saved with additions. Figure 2 contains plots for both estimates. With an add-with-carry instruction both schoolbook and Karatsuba multiplication would be approximately as fast as their reduced-radix counterparts. The reduced-radix implementations use more limbs and still need to carry at the end, so it is appears that an add-with-carry instruction completely compensates for any advantage that a reduced-radix implementation might give.

8 Conclusion

We showed how AES, ChaCha, and Keccak-f can be implemented efficiently on the 32-bit variant of the promising open-source RISC-V architecture. We also showed how arbitrary-precision addition and multiplication can be implemented and studied the performance of all these primitives. As the RISC-V is an open design intended to be extensible, we showed for several features, such as a rotation instruction and an add-with-carry instruction, how much improvement exactly could be gained by adding these features. These numbers are essential for making reasonable trade-offs in software-hardware co-design and we hope that they will be found useful by a wide audience.

References

[BCL14] Bernstein, D.J., Chuengsatiansup, C., Lange, T.: Curve41417: Karatsuba revisited. In: Batina, L., Robshaw, M. (eds.) CHES 2014. LNCS, vol. 8731, pp. 316–334. Springer, Heidelberg (2014). https://doi.org/10.1007/978-3-662-44709-3_18

[BDP+12] Bertoni, G., Daemen, J., Peeters, M., Van Assche, G., Van Keer, R.: Keccak implementation overview, May 2012. https://keccak.team/files/Keccak-implementation-3.2.pdf

[BDPA08] Bertoni, G., Daemen, J., Peeters, M., Van Assche, G.: Keccak sponge function family main document. NIST SHA-3 Submission, October 2008. https://keccak.team/obsolete/Keccak-main-1.0.pdf

[Ber05a] Bernstein, D.J.: Cache-timing attacks on AES, April 2005. https://cr.yp.to/antiforgery/cachetiming-20050414.pdf

[Ber05b] Bernstein, D.J.: The Poly1305-AES message-authentication code. In: Gilbert, H., Handschuh, H. (eds.) FSE 2005. LNCS, vol. 3557, pp. 32–49. Springer, Heidelberg (2005). https://doi.org/10.1007/11502760_3

[Ber08] Bernstein, D.J.: ChaCha, a variant of Salsa20. In: The State of the Art of Stream Ciphers - SASC, January 2008. https://cr.yp.to/chacha/chacha-20080120.pdf

[BP10] Boyar, J., Peralta, R.: A new combinational logic minimization technique with applications to cryptology. In: Festa, P. (ed.) SEA 2010. LNCS, vol. 6049, pp. 178–189. Springer, Heidelberg (2010). https://doi.org/10.1007/978-3-642-13193-6_16

[BS08] Bernstein, D.J., Schwabe, P.: New AES software speed records. In: Chowdhury, D.R., Rijmen, V., Das, A. (eds.) INDOCRYPT 2008. LNCS, vol. 5365, pp. 322–336. Springer, Heidelberg (2008). https://doi.org/10.1007/978-3-540-89754-5_25

[DHH+15] Düll, M., et al.: High-speed Curve25519 on 8-bit, 16-bit, and 32-bit micro-controllers. Des. Codes Crypt. **77**(2), 493–514 (2015)

[DR02] Daemen, J., Rijmen, V.: The Design of Rijndael: AES - The Advanced Encryption Standard. Information Security and Cryptography. Springer, Heidelberg (2002)

[FA17] Fujii, H., Aranha, D.F.: Curve25519 for the Cortex-M4 and beyond. In: Lange, T., Dunkelman, O. (eds.) LATINCRYPT 2017. LNCS, vol. 11368, pp. 109–127. Springer, Cham (2019). https://doi.org/10.1007/978-3-030-25283-0_6

[HRS16] Hülsing, A., Rijneveld, J., Schwabe, P.: ARMed SPHINCS - computing a 41 KB signature in 16 KB of RAM. In: Cheng, C.-M., Chung, K.-M., Persiano, G., Yang, B.-Y. (eds.) PKC 2016. LNCS, vol. 9614, pp. 446–470. Springer, Heidelberg (2016). https://doi.org/10.1007/978-3-662-49384-7_17

[KO63] Karatsuba, A., Ofman, Y.: Multiplication of multidigit numbers on automata. Soviet Phys. Doklady **7**, 595–596 (1963). Translated from Doklady Akademii Nauk SSSR 145(2), 293–294 (1962)

[Kön08] Könighofer, R.: A fast and cache-timing resistant implementation of the AES. In: Malkin, T. (ed.) CT-RSA 2008. LNCS, vol. 4964, pp. 187–202. Springer, Heidelberg (2008). https://doi.org/10.1007/978-3-540-79263-5_12

[KRS19] Kannwischer, M.J., Rijneveld, J., Schwabe, P.: Faster multiplication in $\mathbb{Z}_{2^m}[x]$ on Cortex-M4 to speed up NIST PQC candidates. In: Deng, R.H., Gauthier-Umaña, V., Ochoa, M., Yung, M. (eds.) ACNS 2019. LNCS, vol. 11464, pp. 281–301. Springer, Cham (2019). https://doi.org/10.1007/978-3-030-21568-2_14

[KS09] Käsper, E., Schwabe, P.: Faster and Timing-attack resistant AES-GCM. In: Clavier, C., Gaj, K. (eds.) CHES 2009. LNCS, vol. 5747, pp. 1–17. Springer, Heidelberg (2009). https://doi.org/10.1007/978-3-642-04138-9_1

[LCM+16] Langley, A., Chang, W.-T., Mavrogiannopoulos, N., Strombergson, J., Josefsson, S.: Internet Engineering Task Force. RFC 7905: ChaCha20-Poly1305 Cipher Suites for Transport Layer Security (TLS), June 2016. https://tools.ietf.org/html/rfc7905

[NIS15] NIST. SHA-3 standard: permutation-based hash and extendable-output functions. FIPS 202, August 2015. https://nvlpubs.nist.gov/nistpubs/FIPS/NIST.FIPS.202.pdf

[NL18] Nir, Y., Langley, A.: Internet Research Task Force. RFC 8439: ChaCha20 and Poly1305 for IETF Protocols, June 2018. https://tools.ietf.org/html/rfc8439

[OST06] Osvik, D.A., Shamir, A., Tromer, E.: Cache attacks and countermeasures: the case of AES. In: Pointcheval, D. (ed.) CT-RSA 2006. LNCS, vol. 3860, pp. 1–20. Springer, Heidelberg (2006). https://doi.org/10.1007/11605805_1

[RIS17] RISC-V Foundation. The RISC-V Instruction Set Manual, Volume 1: User-Level ISA, Document Version 2.2, May 2017. https://content.riscv.org/wp-content/uploads/2017/05/riscv-spec-v2.2.pdf

[SiF17] SiFive, Inc.: SiFive FE310-G000 Manual, v2p3, October 2017. https://sifive.cdn.prismic.io/sifive/4d063bf8-3ae6-4db6-9843-ee9076ebadf7_fe310-g000.pdf

[SiF18] SiFive, Inc.: SiFive E31 Core Complex Manual, v2p0, June 2018. https://sifive.cdn.prismic.io/sifive/b06a2d11-19ea-44ec-bf53-3e4c497c7997_sifive-e31-manual-v2p0.pdf

[SLLH18] Seo, H., Liu, Z., Longa, P., Hu, Z.: SIDH on ARM: faster modular multiplications for faster post-quantum supersingular isogeny key exchange. IACR Trans. Cryptogr. Hardw. Embed. Syst. **2018**(3), 1–20 (2018). https://tches.iacr.org/index.php/TCHES/article/view/7266

[SS16]   Schwabe, P., Stoffelen, K.: All the AES you need on Cortex-M3 and M4. In: Avanzi, R., Heys, H. (eds.) SAC 2016. LNCS, vol. 10532, pp. 180–194. Springer, Cham (2017). https://doi.org/10.1007/978-3-319-69453-5_10

[SV93]   Shand, M., Vuillemin, J.: Fast implementations of RSA cryptography. In: Proceedings of IEEE 11th Symposium on Computer Arithmetic, pp. 252–259, June 1993

[WJW+18] Wang, W., et al.: XMSS and embedded systems - XMSS hardware accelerators for RISC-V. Cryptology ePrint Archive, Report 2018/1225 (2018). https://eprint.iacr.org/2018/1225

Fast White-Box Implementations of Dedicated Ciphers on the ARMv8 Architecture

Félix Carvalho Rodrigues[(✉)], Hayato Fujii, Ana Clara Zoppi Serpa,
Giuliano Sider, Ricardo Dahab, and Julio López

Institute of Computing, University of Campinas (Unicamp),
Campinas, SP, Brazil
{felix.rodrigues,hayato.fujii,rdahab,jlopez}@ic.unicamp.br,
{ra146271,ra165880}@students.ic.unicamp.br

Abstract. Dedicated white-box ciphers concern the design of algorithms that withstand secret (key) extraction while executing in an insecure, fully explorable environment. This work presents strategies to efficiently implement on software three families of dedicated white-box ciphers targeted towards the ARMv8 architecture with NEON vector instructions. We report results of our white box implementations for the dedicated ciphers SPACE, WEM and SPNBox on four different ARMv8 CPU cores. In most cases, our optimized implementations improve the performance when compared with the best known implementations. For the cipher SPNbox-16 we propose a faster method for its matrix multiplication layer and discuss the impact on performance.

Keywords: White-Box Cryptography · SPACE · WEM · SPNbox

1 Introduction

With the trend on content consumption based on mobile devices, new security paradigms must be built and evaluated considering this scenario, specially when attackers may have full control over the executing hardware.

White-box cryptography concerns the design and secure implementation of cryptographic algorithms running in untrusted environments, where the attacker has access to the implementation and has control of the execution environment (such as CPU control and full memory access), not excluding the possibility of performing side-channel analysis, such as fault attacks. The concept was introduced in 2003 [10], via a software implementation of the AES cipher without explicitly showing a secret key. However, that white-box implementation was shown to be susceptible to practical attacks [3], and new proposals of white-box AES implementations were also successfully attacked [1,18].

This research was supported by Samsung Eletrônica da Amazônia Ltda., via project "White-Box Cryptography", within the scope of the Informatics Law No. 8248/91.

P. Schwabe and N. Thériault (Eds.): LATINCRYPT 2019, LNCS 11774, pp. 341–363, 2019.
https://doi.org/10.1007/978-3-030-30530-7_17

These attacks have prompted efforts to design new symmetric ciphers, which take into account white-box threats from the start. Most current proposals focus not only on ensuring that discovering the protected secret key is infeasible, but also on mitigating possible *code lifting* attacks, in which the attacker extracts the cryptographic implementation itself to use it as an oracle, duplicating the functionality of the cipher.

While standard security solutions, such as the ones based on black-box implementations of the AES cipher, have great performance on ARM-powered devices due to hardware support, white-box versions of the same ciphers run a great deal slower, mostly due to their structure and the lack of hardware acceleration. Thus, new white-box ciphers must be designed and implemented around the capabilities of CPUs in order to attain a performance at least comparable to non-hardware-optimized black-box ciphers. In this work we present results regarding the performance of the SPACE, SPNbox and the WEM family of ciphers, specifically on the software implementation of such ciphers using the ARMv8 platform and its cryptographic instructions.

Related Work. The first dedicated white-box cipher was proposed in 2014 [4]. Its design was based on an *ASASA* structure, and its security relied on the hardness of decomposing its layers. Subsequent cryptanalysis revealed possible vulnerabilities in this structure [5].

Bogdanov et al. [7] introduced the SPACE family of dedicated block ciphers, with a focus on using proven standard cryptographic primitives to guarantee their security. The SPNbox proposal [8] can be seen as an evolution of SPACE, using a less conservative design intent on making white-box implementations more practical. More recently, further improvements were proposed for the SPNbox design in order to speed up decryption in the black-box setting [11]. In another proposal [9], the WEM family of ciphers is presented, based on the Even-Mansour scheme, where the secret key layers are replaced by secret incompressible *S*-boxes. The WhiteBlock block cipher [13] is similar to the WEM design as it uses a standard block cipher as a public permutation between each *S*-box layer, differing mostly on how the *S*-box layer is constructed. Its main contribution is in providing a more rigorous proof of its security goals when compared to other dedicated ciphers. In [6], Bock et al. propose an incompressible white-box encryption scheme using one-way permutation assumptions, based on pseudo-random functions.

Existing performance measures of these ciphers cannot be directly compared since different computer platforms were used. In addition, there is no ARM implementation of these ciphers in the public domain.

In the context of cryptographic implementations in the ARM architecture, most works focus on standard (black-box) block ciphers and modes of operation, such as the AES block cipher and the Galois Counter Mode (GCM) of operation [14]. There are AES implementations for ARM processors protected against cache-timing side-channel attacks without relying on hardware cryptographic instructions with an acceptable level of performance [2,17]. Newer proposals, such as the Salsa20 stream cipher, were also implemented using the same platform, with better efficiency than AES implementations [2].

Contributions. This work presents white-box implementations of proposed SPACE, SPNbox and WEM instantiations on the ARMv8 architecture. We describe a few different optimization strategies, and use them for all dedicated ciphers analyzed. Furthermore, novel approaches regarding SPNbox in the white-box setting implementations are shown, impacting on the cost of finite field matrix multiplication in its diffusion layer, as well as showing a constant time implementation for one of its variants. Finally, we compare the performance numbers of our implementations executing on different ARMv8 platforms, presenting the best known results of SPACE and WEM implementations and a comparison of our SPNbox implementation against previous results, showing how some discrepancies might explain differences in performance.

Paper Organization. In Sect. 2, we introduce some preliminary white box concepts, such as incompressibility. Section 3 gives an overview of the dedicated white-box block ciphers SPACE, SPNbox and WEM families. Section 4 details the implementation aspects, briefly presenting the ARMv8 architecture, and describing optimization strategies for the analyzed ciphers, while Sect. 5 presents performance results and comparisons between the implemented ciphers. Finally, Sect. 6 presents our final remarks.

2   Preliminaries

A symmetric encryption scheme is a tuple $\mathcal{E} = (\mathcal{K}, \mathcal{M}, \mathcal{C}, G, E, D)$, where $\mathcal{K}, \mathcal{M}$ and $\mathcal{C}$ are the set of possible keys, plaintexts (messages) and ciphertexts, respectively, while G, E and D are the functions for key generation, encryption and decryption, respectively. For any $k \in \mathcal{K}, m \in \mathcal{M}$, $D(E(m, k), k)$ must be equal to m. Note that we alternatively use $E(m)$ or $E_k(m)$ to denote encryption (similarly for decryption), when the context is clear. A white-box compiler $C_{\mathcal{E}}$ takes a symmetric encryption scheme $\mathcal{E}$, a key $k \in \mathcal{K}$, a nonce r (optionally) and returns a compiled white-box program $C_{\mathcal{E}}(k, r) = [E_k]$.

Any secure compiler must strive for the main security goal of *unbreakability*: given a program $[E_k]$, the secret key k embedded in $[E_k]$ must not be discovered efficiently by any adversary. Once such goal is obtained, additional security goals may be addressed. Among the most important is the notion of *incompressibility*, which aims at mitigating *code lifting* attacks, where an attacker simply extracts the whole implementation, using it instead of attempting to extract its embedded secret key. In [7], the term *space hardness* is used to measure this incompressibility notion, further dividing it into weak and strong space hardness. In the weak notion, an adversary should not have the capacity to encrypt or decrypt messages at will with less than M bits of the compiled cipher's code, while in the strong, he should not have the capacity to decipher any messages even when having access to M bits of the code. All ciphers studied in this work use the concept of weak space hardness as their main incompressibility guarantee.

Definition 1 (Weak (M, Z)–space hardness [7]). *Given an encryption scheme $\mathcal{E}$, a white-box compiler $C_{\mathcal{E}}$ is weakly (M, Z)–space hard if it is infeasible for an adversary $\mathcal{A}$ to encrypt (or decrypt) a randomly drawn plaintext (or*

344 F. C. Rodrigues et al.

ciphertext) with probability greater than 2^{-Z}, given access to M bits from $[E_k]$ (or $[D_k]$).

The dedicated white-box ciphers contemplated in this work (and all current proposals in the literature) focus solely on these two security goals, and thus do not achieve other possible notions such as *one-wayness* and *traceability* [19].

3 Dedicated Ciphers

In this section, we describe three families of dedicated white-box block ciphers: SPACE, SPNbox and WEM.

3.1 The SPACE Family

The SPACE family of block ciphers was one of the first proposed dedicated ciphers [7]. It adopts a conservative design, ensuring that its security against key extraction relies on the security of an underlying standard block cipher in the black-box model. It uses an unbalanced Feistel network construction, where a round function is applied to a portion of n_{in} bits of the full 128-bit input. The value of n_{in} determines the different instantiations of the cipher. The designers recommend instantiations with n_{in} equal to $8, 16, 24$ or 32.

In the SPACE-n_{in} encryption, the state of the cipher is updated by applying the Feistel round function to the first n_{in}-bit line of the state, and XORing the $(n - n_{in})$-bit output with the other lines, where n is the block size. The result is then concatenated with the first line. This is repeated for a number R of rounds. Let $l = \frac{n}{n_{in}}$ and $n_{out} = n - n_{in}$. The transformation for round $r = 0, 1, \ldots, R$ is given by the expression $X^{r+1} = (F_{n_{in}}(x_0^r) \oplus r \oplus (x_1^r||x_2^r|| \ldots ||x_{l-1}^r))||x_0^r$, where $||$ is the concatenation operator and $F_{n_{in}} : \{0,1\}^{n_{in}} \to \{0,1\}^{n_{out}}$ is the Feistel function computing $F_{n_{in}}(x) = msb_{n_{out}}(E_k(0||x))$. Here, $msb_i(x)$ denotes the i most significant bits of x and E_k represents a standard block cipher (e.g. AES).

Figure 1a shows the Feistel round structure, while Fig. 1b details an instantiation using AES-128 as the round function. The dashed line encloses the computation of the round function, which is performed by a lookup table in the white-box environment.

In the white-box implementation of the cipher for a fixed key k, the round cipher function is implemented as a lookup table $T : \{0,1\}^{n_{in}} \to \{0,1\}^{n_{out}}$. As a result, the key k becomes enmeshed with the output of the block cipher into a lookup table of size $2^{n_{in}} \cdot n_{out}$ bits. As a consequence, the table size varies greatly depending on n_{in}. For SPACE-8, a total of 2^8 entries of 14 bytes are needed, while for SPACE-32 the lookup table requires $2^{32} \times 12$ bytes.

The recommended number of rounds differs depending on n_{in}. For SPACE-8, the authors recommend at least 300 rounds, while the recommended number for the other sizes is at least 128 rounds. This elevated number of rounds is necessary to ensure a high level of space hardness, which ensures incompressibility.

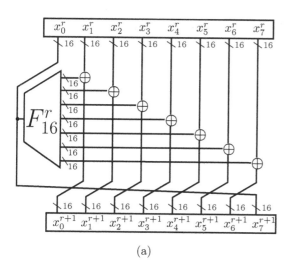

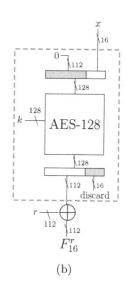

(a)   (b)

Fig. 1. In (a), the round r transformation for SPACE-16, operating on $(x_0^r, \ldots, x_7^r)$. In (b), the round r Feistel function for SPACE-16, F_{16}^r, is shown instantiated with AES-128 as the block cipher E_k.

3.2   The SPNbox Family

A new family of block ciphers called SPNbox [8] was presented as an improvement regarding the SPACE proposal. Its design allows greater opportunities for pipelining and parallelism in relation to their previous proposal, since it is based on a nested substitution-permutation network (SPN) that uses a small SPN block cipher as a key dependent S-box in its confusion layer.

The SPNbox proposal defines its instantiations based on a parameter n_{in}. A SPNbox-n_{in} cipher is composed of three main layers for each round: a non-linear layer, based on a small block cipher where parameter n_{in} determines its block size, in bits; a linear layer and an affine layer. Only the non-linear layer is changed in a white-box implementation, where it is implemented as an incompressible lookup table. The suggested instantiations of the cipher are SPNbox-8, SPNbox-16, SPNbox-24, and SPNbox-32.

Let n be the block size of the cipher, k the size of the key, R the number of rounds of the cipher, and $R_{n_{in}}$ the number of rounds of the inner SPN cipher (the S-box). We write the state of the cipher after r rounds as $X^r = (x_0^r, x_1^r, \ldots, x_{t-1}^r)$, with $t = \frac{n}{n_{in}}$ as the number of elements of the state. In this notation, X^0 is the plaintext and X^R is the ciphertext. Each element x_i^r has n_{in} bits and is interpreted as an element of the binary field $GF(2^{n_{in}})$, where the irreducible polynomial $p(x)$, for each instantiation of SPNbox-n_{in}, is given as follows: for SPNbox-8, SPNbox-16, SPNbox-24, and SPNbox-32, they are respectively, $p(x) = x^8 + x^4 + x^3 + x + 1$ (the same used in AES), $p(x) = x^{16} + x^5 + x^3 + x + 1$, $p(x) = x^{24} + x^4 + x^3 + x + 1$, and $p(x) = x^{32} + x^7 + x^3 + x^2 + 1$.

While SPNbox-8, SPNbox-16 and SPNbox-32 use a block size of $n = 128$ bits, SPNbox-24 uses a block size of 120 bits; therefore, it processes $t = 5$ elements in the state. In all cases, the key is fed to a generic key derivation function, KDF, to generate the $n_{in} \cdot (R_{n_{in}} + 1)$ bits of key material that will be used in the S-box:

$$(k_0, k_1, \ldots, k_{R_{in}}) = \text{KDF}(k, n_{in} \cdot (R_{n_{in}} + 1)). \tag{1}$$

Since SPNbox is an SPN cipher, it alternates the application of a confusion layer—in this case, the key dependent S-box—and a diffusion layer—a linear transformation with good mixing properties represented by an MDS matrix. We can describe the cipher succinctly by using the following expression [8]:

$$X^R = (\bigcirc_{r=1}^{R} (\sigma^r \circ \theta \circ \gamma))(X^0).$$

A single round transformation is characterized by the application of the non-linear layer, γ, followed by the linear layer, θ; σ^r is simply the addition of a round constant.

The γ transformation can be described as $t = \frac{n}{n_{in}}$ parallel applications of the SPN S-box, $S_{n_{in}}$:

$$\gamma : GF(2^{n_{in}})^t \rightarrow GF(2^{n_{in}})^t, (x_0, \ldots, x_{t-1}) \mapsto (S_{n_{in}}(x_0), \ldots, S_{n_{in}}(x_{t-1})).$$

Here, $S_{n_{in}}$ is a key-dependent miniature n_{in}-bit block cipher that operates on $l = \frac{n_{in}}{8}$ elements of one byte each. We denote its state after the application of j rounds by $Y^j = (y_0^j, \ldots, y_{l-1}^j)$, and describe its operation by the expression

$$S_{n_{in}} : GF(2^8)^l \rightarrow GF(2^8)^l, S_{n_{in}}(x) = ((\bigcirc_{j=1}^{R_{n_{in}}} (AK^j \circ MC_{n_{in}} \circ SB)) \circ AK^0)(x).$$

In this notation, the function AK^j refers to XOR addition of the jth key obtained from the key expansion shown in Eq. 1. Before the application of the first round, AK^0 is applied as a pre-whitening step, from which we obtain Y^0. Then, $R_{n_{in}}$ iterations of the cipher are applied.

The function $MC_{n_{in}}$ refers to multiplication by an *Maximum Distance Separable* (MDS) matrix based on the MixColumns matrix from AES. An MDS matrix can be (broadly) seen as representing a linear transformation over a finite field which guarantees maximal diffusion [15]. If we take the state of the inner block cipher to be a row vector of l elements of $GF(2^8)$ as specified above, $MC_{n_{in}}$ can be described as post-multiplication of the state (vector) by an $l \times l$ matrix with elements in $GF(2^8)$:

$$MC_{32} = \begin{bmatrix} 2 & 1 & 1 & 3 \\ 3 & 2 & 1 & 1 \\ 1 & 3 & 2 & 1 \\ 1 & 1 & 3 & 2 \end{bmatrix}, MC_{24} = \begin{bmatrix} 2 & 1 & 1 \\ 3 & 2 & 1 \\ 1 & 3 & 2 \end{bmatrix}, MC_{16} = \begin{bmatrix} 2 & 1 \\ 3 & 2 \end{bmatrix}$$

Note that MC_{32} is the MixColumns matrix from AES, while MC_{24} and MC_{16} are truncations of it. MC_8 is defined to be the identity mapping. Finally, to

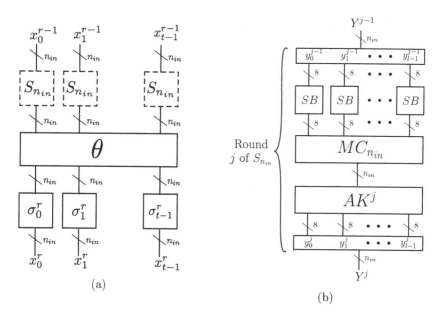

(a)

(b)

Fig. 2. In (a), the round r of a generic SPNbox-n_{in}, $1 \le r \le R$. In (b), the round j of a generic SPNbox-n_{in} inner cipher.

complete the specification of the inner SPN cipher, SB is simply defined to be the application of the AES S-box to each byte of the state. Figure 2b illustrates the components for a single round j of the inner cipher, $S_{n_{in}}$, while Fig. 2a presents the blueprint for a single round r of a generic SPNbox-n_{in} cipher, $1 \le r \le R$.

The θ transformation is performed by multiplying the state X^r of the cipher, given as a row vector of t elements in $GF(2^{n_{in}})$, by a $t \times t$ MDS matrix $M_{n_{in}}$ with elements in $GF(2^{n_{in}})$:

$$\theta : GF(2^{n_{in}})^t \to GF(2^{n_{in}})^t, (x_0^r, \cdots, x_{t-1}^r) \mapsto (x_0^r, \cdots, x_{t-1}^r) \cdot M_{n_{in}}.$$

The matrices are given by

$$M_{32} = had(1, 2, 4, 6), \ M_{24} = cir(1, 2, 5, 3, 4),$$
$$M_{16} = had(01, 03, 04, 05, 06, 08, 0B, 07) , \text{ and}$$
$$M_8 = had(08, 16, 8A, 01, 70, 8D, 24, 76, A8, 91, AD, 48, 05, B5, AF, F8),$$

where $cir(e_0, \ldots, e_{k-1})$ denotes a $k \times k$ circulant matrix with elements e_0 to e_{k-1} in the top row, and $had(e_0, \ldots, e_{k-1})$ denotes a $k \times k$ (finite field) Hadamard matrix – that is, one whose elements $M_{i,j} = e_i \oplus e_j$, for $0 \le i < k, 0 \le j < k$, in which k is a power of 2. All the elements given above are hexadecimal numbers that represent a polynomial in the corresponding finite field.

The σ^r transformation simply adds a round dependent constant to each element of the state, with

$$\sigma^r : GF(2^{n_{in}})^t \to GF(2^{n_{in}})^t, (x_0^r, \ldots, x_{t-1}^r) \mapsto (x_0^r \oplus \sigma_0^r, \ldots, x_{t-1}^r \oplus \sigma_{t-1}^r),$$

where $\sigma_i^r = (r-1) \cdot t + i + 1$, for $1 \leq r \leq R$, $0 \leq i \leq t - 1$.

While the authors suggest using $R = 10$ rounds for the outer SPN cipher, the recommended number of rounds for the inner SPN cipher depends on n_{in}: they suggest setting $R_8 = 64, R_{16} = 32, R_{24} = 20$, and $R_{32} = 16$ to provide resistance against cryptanalytic attacks.

In the white-box environment, the inner SPN cipher, $S_{n_{in}}$, is implemented as a lookup table. As a result, depending on the availability of storage space and on the desired space-hardness of the implemented cipher, implementers may choose between four different variants: SPNbox-8 with $2^8 \cdot 1$ bytes, SPNbox-16 with $2^{16} \cdot 2$ bytes (64 KiB), SPNbox-24 with $2^{24} \cdot 3$ bytes (48 MiB), and SPNbox-32 with $2^{32} \cdot 4$ bytes (16 GiB) of lookup table space.

3.3   The White-Box Even-Mansour Family

The White-Box Even-Mansour (WEM) [9] family of specialized white-box block ciphers is based on the well known iterated Even-Mansour construction. The encryption function is defined as $EM_{k_0,k_1}(x) = k_1 \oplus P(k_0 \oplus x)$, for $x \in \{0,1\}^n$, where k_0 and k_1 are independent n-bit secret keys, P is an n-to-n permutation and x is an n-bit plaintext. A known-plaintext attack on this construction has $\Omega(2^n)$ workload [12], defining the security level of the EM cipher to be $2^{n/2}$. To improve it, iterations (or rounds) of the construction are proposed. For a variant of this cipher using the same key in all rounds (i.e., $k_0 = k_1 = \ldots = k_t$), no attack faster than $2^n/n$ steps is known, even for a 2-round EM (2EM). In a black-box scenario, WEM's security is related to well known ciphers, most notably the AES and iterated Evan-Mansour encryption schemes [9].

The WEM algorithm uses the Evan-Mansour construction as its base, replacing the key additions with incompressible, large key dependent S-boxes. Furthermore, it uses a standard block cipher (in practice the AES) as its permutation function. Several parameters are used to define a practical instance of the cipher: n denotes the block size of the cipher, m denotes the size of the incompressible S-box, requiring n to be divisible by n. The number of rounds is given by t, while E denominates the underlying block cipher used (e.g., AES), with d being the number of rounds of E (keyed with zeroes) that is used in each round of the cipher.

Figure 3a illustrates WEM when $n = 128$, $m = 16$, $t = 2$, $E = $ AES-128, $d = 5$. The main secret key k is embedded into the S-boxes. To generate them, a secure environment must be used to execute two steps: a long sequence of random bits is generated depending on the secret key k; then, the sequence is used as a way to provide random numbers to a shuffler (such as the Fisher-Yates algorithm [16]) which permutes a sequence $(0, 1, \ldots, 2^m - 1)$ to form an m-to-m S-box. Figure 3b illustrates the shuffling method. In the white-box model, the

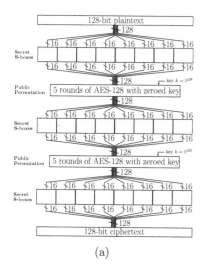

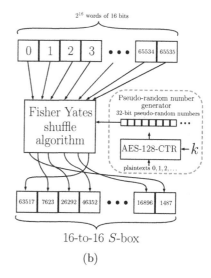

(a)   (b)

Fig. 3. The full instance WEM (128, 16, 2, AES-128, 5) is shown in (a), while the 16-to-16 S-box generation is shown in (b).

workload to extract the key used in the generation of the S-boxes is reduced to breaking the AES-CTR encryption scheme in the black-box model. Even if an adversary extracts all the S-boxes and reverses the shuffling, only a few pairs of plaintext and ciphertext will be known, which are not useful for recovering the original secret key.

The authors of WEM recommend using the WEM-16 cipher, which is WEM using parameters $n = 128$, $m = 16$, $t = 12$, $E = AES$-128 and $d = 5$. This instance requires 104 S-boxes, each having 2^{16} entries of 16 bits.

4 White-Box Implementation

Several techniques and methods were used on the implementation of the different ciphers. First, we provide an overview on the ARMv8-A architecture, briefly describing its most relevant aspects to our work. Then, we summarize our two different approaches for implementing the dedicated ciphers: one focused on instruction pipeline optimization (n-way) and another focused on minimizing cache misses (H-way). Finally, we give a detailed overview of how to efficiently implement the SPNbox-8 and SPNbox-16 ciphers.

4.1 The ARMv8-A Architecture

The ARMv8 architecture is a reduced instruction set computer (RISC) employing a load-store architecture. Specifically, the ARMv8-A architecture profile is targeted towards complex computer application areas such as servers, mobile and infotainment devices. The Cortex-A53, A57, A55, and A75 are examples of CPU cores that implement the ARMv8-A profile. These CPU cores have a different number of pipeline stages to execute *microoperations* generated in the decoding phase, allowing the execution of multiple operations in parallel if they do not conflict each other. Both Cortex-A57 and A75 are capable of executing instructions in an out-of-order fashion, while Cortex-A53 and A55 are in order.

The ARMv8-A profile introduces, in comparison to the older ARMv7-A architecture profile, 64-bit processing capabilities. In the 64-bit processing mode, the A64 instruction set is supported, permitting operations on 64-bit-wide registers. The CPU is equipped with a bank of 31 general purpose registers (x0 to x30) in addition to the dedicated stack pointer (sp) and zero (zr) registers. In addition to the native AArch64 mode, the NEON engine is present on CPU cores implementing the ARMv8-A profile. This engine is an advanced Single Instruction-Multiple Data (SIMD) unit, designed towards multimedia applications but also useful in scientific and high performance computing. In this unit, a separate set of 32 registers, each one 128-bit wide, can be used. Each 128-bit register can be interpreted as 16 bytes, 8 halfwords (of 16 bits), 4 words (of 32 bits), 2 doublewords (of 64 bits) or a 128-bit quadword.

NEON instructions are decoded and forwarded to the NEON unit using the same fetch and decode pipeline units running native instructions. Cortex-A55 and A57 CPU cores dispatch those microoperations into two NEON 5-stage pipelines. Memory-related operations share the load and store units used in native instructions. On the Cortex-A75, an additional decode stage is required before handling operations over two, 8-long NEON stages. Alongside those two, a dedicated load/store NEON line is present, in addition to the pair of shared native load/store lines. The NEON unit has special instructions to support permutations and byte substitutions, common operations in a block cipher:

Table Lookup and Table Lookup, Extended (tbl/tbx). This instruction builds a new vector based on an index vector, looking up a table residing in one up to four registers, effectively being a bytewise table lookup. The tbl instruction can be repurposed to work as an arbitrary byte permutation if a single source vector is used as a table, at the cost of setting up the permutation.

Vector Extract (ext). Extracts bytes from a pair of source vectors. The resulting vector combines the most significant bytes from the first operand and least significant bytes of the second. This instruction can also be used to execute byte rotations on a 128-bit vector, as well as to execute left and right byte shifts.

Reverse (rev). Reverses the order of the elements within a vector. Depending on the interpretation of a 128-bit register, this instruction can be used to reverse the order of bytes (from little endian order to big endian and vice-versa) to reverse the order of the 64-bit high and lower parts of a 128-bit vector.

Cryptographic Extension. CPU manufacturers may also include the cryptographic extension on ARM CPU cores. This extension adds new instructions on the SIMD unit to provide hardware-accelerated operations used in the AES (both encryption and decryption operations) algorithm and the hash functions

SHA-1, SHA-224 and SHA-256. Of interest, we note the instructions `aese` and `aesmc`, which together perform a full round of the AES cipher.

4.2   Maximizing Instruction Pipeline Versus Cache Hits

Here we outline our two main optimization strategies, which are used for all dedicated ciphers, using the CTR mode of operation. The first is a traditional strategy based on processing a small number of blocks in parallel, while the latter extends this notion to process all input in a parallel manner, with the aim of improving cache usage, but at the cost of additional space.

Instruction Pipeline Optimization (n-way). Ciphers employing simpler operations, such as logical, arithmetical or bit manipulation ones, have shown speedups in 2, 4, 8 or 16-way implementations. In these versions, instead of processing each block sequentially, multiple blocks are processed in an interleaved manner, in order to better utilize the hardware instruction pipeline and eliminate data dependency hazards between instructions. When using such optimization strategies, care must be taken to ensure no register spill occurs. A *register spill* happens when the compiler is unable to allocate all coded variables into registers, requiring extra memory operations to manage the various variables at different parts of the machine code. These implementations are referred in this work as *"n-way"*, where n indicates how many 128-bit blocks are processed in parallel.

Memory Coverage Optimization (H-way). Due to the incompressible nature of the lookup tables used on the studied ciphers, one may not hope to improve locality for the usage of a single table. However, due to the difference regarding how much data is brought to cache on each cache miss and the small amount of data required by each load operation, an approach where a lookup table is used as much as possible before other operations replace its content from cache may end up better utilizing the underlying hardware.

With the required ROM size for storing the precomputed tables of dedicated white-box ciphers in mind, a horizontal version of the CTR mode for the ciphers was implemented in order to take advantage of the CPU caches – namely, the usually larger L2 cache. In this type of optimization, cache hit ratio is prioritized and the CTR implementation is completed in layers. For a message of size n, first all necessary counters (i.e. the input for the cipher) are created with a given IV. Then, for the first round of the cipher, the whole input goes through its substitution layer, keeping as much of its lookup table in local cache memory as possible. After the substitution layer is completed, subsequent layers are computed, and the process repeats for the other rounds.

This approach can have a few advantages when compared to maximizing the instruction pipeline. The main advantage occurs when multiple large lookup tables are used, as with this approach the implementer can schedule all operations for a single table in sequence, guaranteeing that the table remains as much as possible in the cache for the whole period it is utilized. Another possible advantage occurs when traditional n-way implementations waste cycles waiting for load operations to complete, which may happen due to further optimizations in other areas (especially for a small n) of the cipher or very slow memory access.

Note however that such implementation requires the storage of each intermediary value in memory, which can be costly. Furthermore, when using a single incompressible lookup table, both approaches are expected to achieve the same amount of cache misses. Thus, care and experimentation must be taken when considering which approach is better for any particular hardware configuration. These horizontal implementations are referred to as "H-way".

Usage in SPACE and WEM Implementations. While we applied the mentioned general strategies throughout all implementations, each cipher implementation has its own distinct details. Here, we expand on their usage for the SPACE and WEM family, while Sect. 4.3 delves deeper into the SPNbox family.

For the SPACE implementations, each benefit from the memory pipeline, as multiple table lookups may be executed. Those tables hold the results of AES encryption of 8 or 16 bits using a secret key. Each 120 or 112-bit lookup value is padded with 0s to fill a 128-bit word to avoid memory alignment issues. Here the horizontal implementation appears to not be the best suitable approach, since it has few NEON instructions, and its single large lookup table is expected to remain (partially) in the cache the same amount in both strategies.

For the WEM family, we implemented a WEM-16 version as a mix of both pipeline and cache-oriented strategies. As an attempt to better utilize the L2 cache on lower spec hardware, we implemented each 16-to-16 lookup table as two 16-to-8 tables, in a "half-word" substitution table strategy. This can increase the cache-hit ratio by ensuring that the smaller table fits completely in cache layers closer to the CPU, instead of the slower, more distant layers of memory.

4.3   Optimizing the SPNbox Family

Regarding the SPNbox family of ciphers, we implemented two versions, SPNbox-16 and SPNbox-8. As seen in Sect. 3.2, the SPNbox cipher has three main layers: a substitution layer γ, a permutation layer θ comprising a matrix multiplication, and a round constant addition layer σ. The γ layer must be implemented as table lookups in the white-box context, while the round constant addition can be accomplished by a simple XOR operation using NEON instructions. The θ layer, however, is significantly more complex.

For SPNbox-8, in the θ layer the state is multiplied in $GF(2^8)$ by the matrix

$$M_8 = had(08, 16, 8A, 01, 70, 8D, 24, 76, A8, 91, AD, 48, 05, B5, AF, F8),$$

while for SPNbox-16 the state is multiplied in $GF(2^{16})$ by the matrix

$$M_{16} = had(01, 03, 04, 05, 06, 08, 0B, 07),$$

where $had(e_0, \ldots, e_{k-1})$ denotes a $k \times k$ Hadamard matrix and all binary polynomial coefficients are represented as hexadecimal values.

For both SPNbox-8 and SPNbox-16, we implemented three versions of the cipher, differing mostly on how they approach the θ diffusion layer: a version processing a single block at a time using NEON instructions, a version with multiple blocks processed simultaneously and a version based on lookup tables for both the γ and θ layers. Furthermore, for the version with multiple blocks processed simultaneously, we also implemented a version where all blocks are processed in a horizontal fashion, i.e. where each layer for each round is processed for all blocks before the next layer or round. Finally, we also show a way to achieve a constant-time implementation of the SPNbox-8 cipher, by combining tbl/tbx instructions with a horizontal implementation.

Finite Field Arithmetic with NEON Instructions. Here we implement the matrix multiplication as a series of multiplications and permutations using NEON instructions in constant-time. We can perform a polynomial multiplication of the state by x in $GF(2^{16})$ (e.g. a *doubling operation*) in constant-time by using the following four NEON instructions, as shown below for SPNbox-16:

```
sshr   v2.8h,v0.8h, #15
shl    v0.8h,v0.8h, #1
and    v2.8h,v1.8h,v2.8h
eor    v0.8h,v0.8h,v2.8h
```

where the NEON register v0 represents the state, with eight 16-bit polynomials in $GF(2^{16})$, while register v1 must have eight copies of the value $0x002B$. It exploits sshr, which performs a signed right shift operation, effectively creating a vector where each word is either all zeros or all ones depending on the last bit of the state word.

For SPNbox-16, given a state S, we can perform the multiplication of M_{16} as a series of additions and doubling operations in $GF(2^{16})$, followed by permutations on the state. Let $T_i(S)$ be the state multiplied by the polynomial represented by i. We can build $T_2(S)$, $T_4(S)$ and $T_8(S)$ by using the code shown previously. Then, we can use these values to build $T_1(S), T_3(S), T_5(S), T_6(S), T_7(S)$ and $T_B(S)$ as additions in $GF(2^{16})$, i.e. using XOR operations.

Finally, the result is obtained by adding several permutations of $T_i(S)$:

$$S = T_1(S) \oplus P_1(T_3(S)) \oplus P_2(T_4(S)) \oplus P_3(T_5(S))$$
$$\oplus\ P_4\Big(T_6(S) \oplus P_1(T_8(S)) \oplus P_2(T_B(S)) \oplus P_3(T_7(S))\Big).$$

Here, permutations P_1, P_2, P_3 and P_4 are given by:

$$P_1(X) = (x_1, x_0, x_3, x_2, x_5, x_4, x_7, x_6), \quad P_2(X) = (x_2, x_3, x_0, x_1, x_6, x_7, x_4, x_5),$$
$$P_3(X) = (x_3, x_2, x_1, x_0, x_7, x_6, x_5, x_4), \quad P_4(X) = (x_4, x_5, x_6, x_7, x_0, x_1, x_2, x_3),$$

where $X = (x_0, x_1, x_2, x_3, x_4, x_5, x_6, x_7)$ is an eight element vector. These permutations can be efficiently computed by NEON instructions, namely rev32, rev64 and ext.

Transposed Multiple Blocks Multiplication. Building upon the previous method, we can avoid the necessity of performing permutations in each round by processing simultaneously 8 blocks of 128-bits for SPNbox-16 or 16 blocks for SPNbox-8. Again, we detail the idea by using SPNbox-16 as an example. Let $S_i = (s_{i0}, \ldots, s_{i7})$ be the state for block i, for $i = 0, \ldots, 7$. We can see such collection of blocks as an 8 by 8 matrix S of 16-bit values. Let S' be the transposed S matrix. Then we can calculate $R = (R_0, \ldots, R_7)$ as follows:

$$R_i = T_{a_{i,0}}(S'_0) \oplus T_{a_{i,1}}(S'_1) \oplus T_{a_{i,2}}(S'_2) \oplus T_{a_{i,3}}(S'_3)$$
$$\oplus \, T_{a_{i,4}}(S'_4) \oplus T_{a_{i,5}}(S'_5) \oplus T_{a_{i,6}}(S'_6) \oplus T_{a_{i,7}}(S'_7),$$

where $i \in [0, 7]$ and $a_{i,j}$ is the element in row i, column j of matrix M_{16}.

The result for $S_i \times M_{16}$ will therefore be stored in $R_{0i}, R_{1i}, \ldots, R_{7i}$. At the end of the 8-block encryption, one can simply transpose the result when storing to memory. Additionally, processing multiple blocks of the input allows one to use advantageous properties of binary fields, particularly the fact that consecutive sums cancel out, to further optimize the number of multiplications and additions necessary to calculate R. Let S_{ij} be the sum (in $GF(2^{16})^8$) of vectors S'_i and S'_j. Then, R can be rewritten as:

$$R_0 = S'_0 \oplus x^3(S_{56}) \oplus x^2(S_{23} \oplus S_{47}) \oplus x(S_{14} \oplus S_{67}) \oplus S_{13} \oplus S_{67},$$
$$R_1 = S'_1 \oplus x^3(S_{47}) \oplus x^2(S_{23} \oplus S_{56}) \oplus x(S_{05} \oplus S_{67}) \oplus S_{02} \oplus S_{67},$$
$$R_2 = S'_2 \oplus x^3(S_{47}) \oplus x^2(S_{01} \oplus S_{56}) \oplus x(S_{36} \oplus S_{45}) \oplus S_{13} \oplus S_{45},$$
$$R_3 = S'_3 \oplus x^3(S_{56}) \oplus x^2(S_{01} \oplus S_{47}) \oplus x(S_{27} \oplus S_{45}) \oplus S_{02} \oplus S_{45},$$
$$R_4 = S'_4 \oplus x^3(S_{12}) \oplus x^2(S_{03} \oplus S_{67}) \oplus x(S_{05} \oplus S_{23}) \oplus S_{23} \oplus S_{57},$$
$$R_5 = S'_5 \oplus x^3(S_{03}) \oplus x^2(S_{12} \oplus S_{67}) \oplus x(S_{14} \oplus S_{23}) \oplus S_{23} \oplus S_{46},$$
$$R_6 = S'_6 \oplus x^3(S_{03}) \oplus x^2(S_{12} \oplus S_{45}) \oplus x(S_{01} \oplus S_{27}) \oplus S_{01} \oplus S_{57},$$
$$R_7 = S'_7 \oplus x^3(S_{12}) \oplus x^2(S_{03} \oplus S_{45}) \oplus x(S_{01} \oplus S_{36}) \oplus S_{01} \oplus S_{46}.$$

This allows us to reduce the number of additions by precomputing the values S_{ij} which are used multiple times. However, we can further minimize the number of multiplications and additions. Each R_i can be computed as a combination of multiple R_j, for $0 \leq i, j \leq 7$. We use this fact to build intermediate vectors R_{01} and R_{45}, where $R_{ij} = R_i \oplus R_j$:

$$R_{01} = S_{01} \oplus x^3(S_{56} \oplus S_{47}) \oplus x^2(S_{47} \oplus S_{56}) \oplus x(S_{14} \oplus S_{05}) \oplus S_{13} \oplus S_{02},$$
$$R_{45} = S_{45} \oplus x^3(S_{12} \oplus S_{03}) \oplus x^2(S_{12} \oplus S_{03}) \oplus x(S_{14} \oplus S_{05}) \oplus S_{57} \oplus S_{46}.$$

Note that the computation can be efficiently implemented by storing in NEON registers the value $S_{0\ldots k}$, which represents the sum of all S_j, for $j \in [0, k]$, as well as a few intermediate sums $K_0 = x(S_{0123}), K_1 = x(S_{4567})$ and $K_2 = x(S_{0\ldots7})$. We can build R_0 and R_4 as already shown, while R_1 and R_5 use R_{01} and R_{45} for its computation. Let $R_{01} = S_{01} \oplus x^2 K_1 \oplus x(K_1 \oplus S_{0514}) \oplus S_{0123}$ and $R_{45} = x^2(K_2 \oplus S_{0\ldots7}) \oplus S_{0\ldots7} \oplus S_{0145} \oplus R_{01}$. Then, $R_1 = R_{01} \oplus R_0$ and

$R_5 = R_{45} \oplus R_4$. Finally, we can use these computed vectors to help build the remaining ones. First we build $R_{0123} = R_0 \oplus R_1 \oplus R_2 \oplus R_3 = S_{0123} \oplus K_2$ and $R_{4567} = R_4 \oplus R_5 \oplus R_6 \oplus R_7 = S_{4567} \oplus K_2$. Then, R_{12}, R_{56}, R_{03} and R_{47} are computed:

$$R_{12} = S_{12} \oplus x(K_0 + S_{0347}) + S_{0...7}, \qquad R_{03} = R_{0123} \oplus R_{12},$$
$$R_{56} = S_{56} \oplus x(K_1 + S_{0347}) + S_{0...7}, \qquad R_{47} = R_{4567} \oplus R_{56}.$$

The final values R_2, R_3, R_6 and R_7 are obtained by simply subtracting (XOR operations) from these intermediate values the already computed R_0, R_1, R_4, R_5.

Matrix Multiplication as Lookup Tables. While the amount of NEON instructions to perform a matrix multiplication for SPNbox-16 is relatively small, the same is not true for the SPNbox-8 cipher. By increasing the size of the implementation, we can speed up the matrix computation by pre-computing its results as a lookup table. Clearly, one cannot build a 128-to-128 bit lookup table computing the whole operation, however we can decompose the matrix multiplication $M \times S^T$ into several column multiplications, as is shown here for the M_{32} matrix (used in SPNbox-32):

$$\begin{bmatrix} 1 & 2 & 4 & 6 \\ 2 & 1 & 6 & 4 \\ 4 & 6 & 1 & 2 \\ 6 & 4 & 2 & 1 \end{bmatrix} \begin{bmatrix} s_0 \\ s_1 \\ s_2 \\ s_3 \end{bmatrix} = s_0 \begin{bmatrix} 1 \\ 2 \\ 4 \\ 6 \end{bmatrix} \oplus s_1 \begin{bmatrix} 2 \\ 1 \\ 6 \\ 4 \end{bmatrix} \oplus s_2 \begin{bmatrix} 4 \\ 6 \\ 1 \\ 2 \end{bmatrix} \oplus s_3 \begin{bmatrix} 6 \\ 4 \\ 2 \\ 1 \end{bmatrix}.$$

By doing this, we can implement the θ layer as a series of lookups in n-to-128 bit tables, where n is the size of the inner block (e.g., 8 for SPNbox-8). Note that we can choose whether to implement the whole multiplication as only lookup tables, or use a single lookup table and perform the necessary permutations (or even a mix of the two, implementing a few lookup tables and a few permutations).

Now, since both γ and θ layers are implemented as lookup tables, we can compose them, further minimizing the number of table lookups needed to encrypt a block. This approach proves to be beneficial when cache size is not a limitation, i.e., when the all new n-to-128 bit lookup tables fit into the cache.

A Constant Time SPNbox-8 Implementation. In order for an SPNbox-8 cipher implementation to run in constant time, one must make sure that lookup table accesses are constant time operations. For SPNbox-8, this can be accomplished efficiently by keeping the whole lookup table in 16 NEON registers, using four `ld1` operations, and then use four `tbl` instructions to execute each table lookup. One way to achieve this is to first apply an XOR operation between the state and masks $[0x40, \ldots, 0x40], [0x08, \ldots, 0x80]$, and $[0xC0, \ldots, 0xC0]$, storing the results in registers `v1`, `v2` and `v3`. Then, assuming the table is loaded in registers `v16` to `v31`, do the following:

```
tbl v0.16b, {v16.16b, v17.16b, v18.16b, v19.16b}, v0.16b
tbl v1.16b, {v20.16b, v21.16b, v22.16b, v23.16b}, v1.16b
tbl v2.16b, {v24.16b, v25.16b, v26.16b, v27.16b}, v2.16b
tbl v3.16b, {v28.16b, v29.16b, v30.16b, v31.16b}, v3.16b
```

The lookup table access for 16 bytes can then be obtained by adding the registers v0, v1, v2 and v3 in $GF((2^8)^{16})$. An alternative is to use a combination of tbl or tbx instructions to execute each table lookup by subtracting from the state between tbl/tbx. Such usage is present on the Linux Kernel AES implementation geared towards ARMv8 CPUs without cryptographic extensions. Since this setup requires a large number of registers, a horizontal implementation alleviates this restriction by allowing the reuse of these registers for the constant time finite field operations after each γ layer is completed. Performance wise, the constant time implementation is 40% to 50% slower compared to the best implementations on higher-end platforms; numbers are shown on the SPNbox8-Hway implementation on Table 1.

5 Results

In this section we present the performance measures of all implemented dedicated ciphers, along with a black-box AES implementation using ARMv8 cryptographic instructions and one relying only on NEON instructions, similar to the one implemented in the Linux kernel[1].

5.1 Experimental Setup

Performance measurements were taken using the system call perf_event_open available in the Linux Kernel, configured to read the CPU cycles spent to run an encryption method. Current perf implementations take advantage of using hardware performance counters; in particular, on CPUs implementing the ARMv8 ISA, the Performance Monitoring Unit (PMU) is present as an obligatory block of the CPU core. The perf subsystem, while requiring context switches between user and kernel code thus bringing some overhead, takes those factors in account and gives precise count of CPU cycles spent of the code under profiling.

On the hardware side, four different ARMv8 cores were used to run the experiments: the first two present in Samsung Galaxy S6 (SM-G920I) devices and the latter present in Samsung Galaxy S9 (SM-G9600) devices.

Cortex-A53. Exynos7420 Cortex-A53 core clocked at 1500 MHz, equipped with 256 KiB of L2 cache shared across all A53 cores;

Cortex-A57. Exynos7420 Cortex-A57 core clocked at 2100 MHz, equipped with 2 MiB of L2 cache shared across all A55 cores;

Cortex-A55. SDM845 Cortex-A55 core clocked at 1766 MHz, equipped with 128 KiB of L2 cache for each core and 2 MiB of shared L3 cache;

Cortex-A75. SDM845 Cortex-A75 core clocked at 2803 MHz, equipped with 256 KiB of L2 cache for each core and 2 MiB of shared L3 cache;

---

[1] See: https://git.kernel.org/pub/scm/linux/kernel/git/torvalds/linux.git/tree/arch/arm64/crypto/aes-neon.S.

All frequency scaling and CPU shutdown features were disabled and the CPUs were clocked at their maximum supported frequencies by setting the Linux frequency scaling governor to performance. Performance was measured only for the white-box versions of the ciphers. Secret S-box (lookup tables) precomputation can be done away from the consumer platforms and, thus, all tests shown assume tables are already precomputed.

Ciphers were cross-compiled to the Android platform using clang version 8.0.2 for all cores with flag -O3 enabled, as recommended by Google[2]. The performance test was done using the CTR mode of operation to encrypt messages of size 2KiB for 2^{15} iterations in which each iteration takes as input the output of the previous one; the first message was sampled from /dev/urandom. Table 1 shows the complete test results, while Fig. 4 illustrates the comparison for the Cortex-A57 and A75.

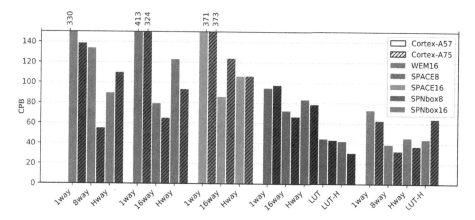

Fig. 4. Average performance (cpb) for all implementations in the Cortex-A57 and A75 cores (lower is better).

We show a pipeline-optimized version (either 8 or 16 way), a cache-optimized version ("Hway", see Sect. 4.2), and a single block version (equivalent to a "1-way" version). Pipeline-oriented versions were built on the fact that there are 32 NEON registers, hence avoiding register spilling and penalties associated with it. For the SPNbox cipher, we additionally present a version using lookup tables as a way to speed up the θ and γ layers, here referred as the "LUT" version (see Sect. 4.3 for more details on this implementation). The pipelined version for SPNbox refers to the transposed variant as described in Sect. 4.3. The SPNbox-8-Hway version also refers to the constant time white-box implementation described in Sect. 4.3. On the WEM-16 cipher, we additionally present an implementation of the "half-word" substitution table ("Half"), as described in Sect. 4.2.

---

[2] See: https://android.googlesource.com/platform/ndk/+/refs/heads/ndk-r13-release /CHANGELOG.md.

358   F. C. Rodrigues et al.

Table 1. Measured performance (in cycles per byte) of dedicated ciphers in CTR mode of operation for messages of 2048 bytes. The "# Loads" column shows the quantity of loads/table lookups needed to cipher a single 128-bit block.

Implementation	Lookup tables		Average performance (cpb)			
	Size (KiB)	# Loads	A53	A55	A57	A75
AES128-Crypto	—	—	**1.21**	**1.20**	**0.95**	**0.91**
AES128-Asm	0.25	—	21.95	21.94	24.31	21.59
SPACE8	3.75	300	342.31	324.82	413.56	324.91
SPACE8-16way	3.75	300	**116.84**	**115.26**	**79.06**	**64.88**
SPACE8-Hway	3.75	300	303.60	266.45	122.91	93.26
SPACE16	896	128	1486.39	290.43	371.26	373.83
SPACE16-16way	896	128	**1366.51**	**186.13**	**85.77**	123.81
SPACE16-Hway	896	128	1521.12	304.30	106.11	**106.19**
SPNbox8	0.25	160	90.30	86.85	94.51	97.30
SPNbox8-16way	0.25	160	109.17	103.53	72.15	66.35
SPNbox8-Hway[a]	0.25	160	83.03	81.67	83.28	78.36
SPNbox8-LUT	4	160	**70.42**	59.41	44.67	43.28
SPNbox8-LUT-Hway	4	160	81.24	**56.56**	**42.19**	**30.54**
SPNbox16	128	80	**86.07**	**71.42**	73.02	62.62
SPNbox16-8way	128	80	100.33	77.67	**38.97**	**32.38**
SPNbox16-Hway	128	80	111.02	87.98	45.58	36.98
SPNbox16-LUT-Hway	1024	80	746.13	136.35	43.79	64.08
WEM16	13312	104	1045.30	278.21	330.54	138.53
WEM16-8way-Half	13312	104	**262.27**	**125.95**	133.84	**54.73**
WEM16-Hway	13312	104	856.82	173.57	**89.62**	109.93

[a]Refers to the constant time implementation (see Sect. 4.3).

Additional builds using `gcc` 4.9 were also evaluated, but, in exception of the SPNbox16 and single block SPACE8 and WEM16 experiments on the Cortex-A53 and A55 (ranging from 9.38% to 39.56% speedup favoring `gcc`), `clang` generated faster binaries, with speedups ranging from 3% (SPACE16 binaries) to 43.45% (16-way SPNbox8); see Appendix A for the complete results. Finally, we also show a comparison with an optimized black-box AES-128 in CTR mode implemented with and without AES instructions present on the Cryptographic extensions of the ARMv8-A ISA. The AES implementation is similar to the one found in the Linux Kernel (see Footnote 1).

5.2   Analysis

The results in Table 1 show that both n-way and H-way strategies are generally competitive with one another, with both usually improving the versions optimized for a single block. One exception is SPNbox-16 in the simpler Cortex-A53 and A55 cores. This might be explained by the smaller pipelines on these CPUs being already properly maximized by the single block version, due to the amount of NEON instructions in its diffusion layer.

The WEM proposal, with the need for a publicly known permutation layer, can be efficiently implemented in ARM processors if the AES algorithm is used and hardware support is available to speed it up. However, most of its performance depends on the table lookup layer: since each 16-bit word of the state must be substituted using *different* lookup tables, CPUs without enough cache memory to store these tables will have timings penalized by the requirement of accessing slower memory in order to load them. While processing a single 16-byte block requires a large portion of fast memory, doing the same operation on multiple blocks allows a large part of a single table to be stored in local cache, avoiding main memory latencies. This is better explored when smaller tables are used to compose a bigger one, such as in the "half-word" tables strategy. Since the Cortex-A57 has a large L2 cache, its possible that the horizontal implementation better uses this cache by keeping multiple tables in them, which could help explain its performance over the other versions on this CPU.

In Table 2, we compare the performance of SPACE and SPNbox on similar hardware (though measurement methods may differ) with results already present in the literature. For SPACE-8 and 16, even though it uses a large lookup table which does not completely fit into cache memory, their performance can be greatly improved in cases where multiple blocks are processed at a time, such as in encrypting long messages using the CTR mode of operation. Previous work [8] did not account for this, reporting an average of 409.57 and 377.51 cycles per byte using the A57 core of a Samsung Exynos7420 CPU, respectively on SPACE-8 and 16.

Table 2. Comparison of best performing implementations of SPACE and SPNbox in Cortex-A57 with reported literature.

Cipher	Average performance (cpb)	
	This work (version)	Bogdanov et al. [8]
SPACE-8	**79.06** (16way)	409.57
SPACE-16	**85.77** (16way)	377.51
SPNbox-8	**42.19** (LUT-Hway)	42.66
SPNbox-16	38.97 (8way)	**27.37**

SPNbox Analysis. SPNbox implementations can be optimized by exploring its θ layer, in which $GF(2^n)$ arithmetic is thoroughly used. Rearrangement of input data can speed up this step by eliminating permutations and allowing further binary field optimizations. While SPNbox-16 clearly benefited from these optimizations, the same is not true for SPNbox-8. In SPNbox-8, the fact that it has a more intricate diffusion layer combined with the smaller S-boxes lends incredibly well for implementing both γ and θ layers as lookup tables, when a constant time implementation is not a prerequisite. When it is a requirement, one can still use SPNbox8-Hway at a price on the best possible performance.

Our experiments do not match reported numbers [8], particularly for the SPNbox-16 implementation, which reports an average performance of 27.37 cycles per byte. This can be due to differences in experimental methodology to capture timings or unknown memory optimizations. To further investigate this, we did two additional tests on the Cortex-A57 core, using the SPNbox16-16way implementation, with their results shown in Fig. 5.

First, we performed a test aimed at removing the impact of cache hit ratio, by encrypting a single 128 byte message in ECB mode for 1024 iterations and taking their average cost. In this test, we obtained an average encryption time of 26.48 cycles per byte, which matches the one reported by Bogdanov et al. [8].

As for the second test, to have a notion of the impact each layer has on the performance of the SPNbox-16 cipher implementation, we implemented and tested two "partial" ciphers, where either only the γ layer (memory dependent) or the θ and σ layers (NEON dependent) were executed, this time using the same parameters as the general test, only now using ECB mode. Note that these give only an approximation on the performance of each layer since different compiling optimizations may apply. Furthermore, the γ and θ layers may partially execute simultaneously in the full cipher implementation when processing multiple blocks.

In these tests, the cipher had an average performance of 34.42 cycles per byte. Its γ layer had the heaviest cost, with an average of 26.99 cycles per byte, while the rest of the

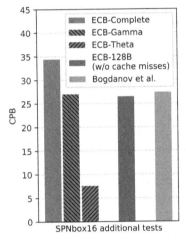

Fig. 5. Exploratory experiments regarding SPNbox16 performance.

cipher had an average of 7.55 cycles per byte. This shows the large dependence on memory performance, and perhaps surprisingly, shows that even when executing only the memory operations, the time reported by Bogdanov et al. [8] already matches our measurements.

6   Conclusions

In this work we implemented three recently proposed dedicated white-box ciphers: the WEM cipher [9], the SPACE cipher [7] and the SPNbox cipher [8]. Each cipher has the key extraction security of its proposed implementations dependent on the security of standard block ciphers such as the AES in the black-box context. Additionally, these ciphers focus on related security concerns such as code lifting by including in their design incompressible lookup tables. While some efficiency comparisons exist in the literature among dedicated ciphers, no direct comparisons between several implementations, as we have done here, had been done up to now. Our results show that, while still far from the performance of hardware-assisted black-box implementations of standard ciphers such as the AES, dedicated white-box ciphers can be competitive when considering software implementations of the AES cipher. With the possibility of new instructions, and an increase in cache size and performance, it is likely that these ciphers may reach an acceptable performance for most applications for which black-box implementations of the AES cipher are used currently, particularly for the SPNbox family of ciphers.

As a final remark, we note that none of the proposed dedicated ciphers were subject to relevant cryptanalysis effort regarding recent implementation attacks such as differential computation analysis, since most available tools for tracing and statistical analysis focus on standard ciphers. Thus, an interesting avenue of research might be in developing techniques to attack some of these implementations in this manner.

Appendix A: Comparison of clang and gcc Compilers

In this Appendix we present our complete performance measurements, shown in Table 3.

Table 3. Measured performance of dedicated ciphers in CTR mode of operation for messages of 2048 bytes, using both gcc and clang compilers. Grey cells indicate a speedup of over ten percent between compilers.

Implementation	Average Performance (cpb)							
	A53		A55		A57		A75	
	clang	gcc	clang	gcc	clang	gcc	clang	gcc
AES128-Crypto	1.21	1.23	1.2	1.23	0.95	1.03	0.91	0.90
AES128-Asm	21.95	21.95	21.94	21.94	24.31	24.31	21.59	21.59
SPACE8	342.31	270.26	324.82	250.73	413.56	419.01	324.91	316.19
SPACE8-16way	116.84	131.14	115.26	129.77	79.06	82.43	64.88	70.57
SPACE8-Hway	303.6	359.46	266.45	322.47	122.91	139.16	93.26	107.99
SPACE16	1486.39	1531.5	290.43	299.07	371.26	353.06	373.83	364.18
SPACE16-16way	1366.51	1370.22	186.13	192.97	85.77	96.34	123.84	118.63
SPACE16-Hway	1521.12	1565.59	304.3	326.13	106.11	107.76	106.19	121.9
SPNbox8	90.3	116.85	86.85	115.45	94.51	130.65	97.3	127.97
SPNbox8-16way	109.17	185.7	103.53	177.49	72.15	127.58	66.35	84.48
SPNbox8-Hway	83.03	92.94	81.67	91.05	83.28	101.41	78.36	98.4
SPNbox8-LUT	70.42	71.79	59.41	69.48	44.67	49.03	43.28	46.93
SPNbox8-LUT-H	81.24	88.06	56.56	72.54	42.19	43.41	30.54	37.99
SPNbox16	86.07	92.13	71.42	74.97	73.02	84.16	62.62	72.08
SPNbox16-8way	100.33	71.89	77.67	57.85	38.97	44.11	32.38	37.53
SPNbox16-Hway	111.02	85.15	87.98	71.74	45.58	50.52	36.98	44.7
SPNbox16-LUT-H	746.13	755.02	136.35	130.85	43.79	46.08	64.08	64.07
WEM16	1045.3	872.51	278.21	254.36	330.54	324.72	138.53	122.95
WEM16-8way-Half	262.27	242.32	125.95	142.31	133.84	127.97	54.73	81.85
WEM16-Hway	856.82	1710.67	173.57	276.1	89.62	93.63	109.93	117.72

References

1. Alpirez Bock, E., Bos, J.W., Brzuska, C., et al.: White-box cryptography: don't forget about grey-box attacks. J. Cryptol. 1–49 (2019). https://doi.org/10.1007/s00145-019-09315-1

2. Bernstein, D.J., Schwabe, P.: NEON crypto. In: Prouff, E., Schaumont, P. (eds.) CHES 2012. LNCS, vol. 7428, pp. 320–339. Springer, Heidelberg (2012). https://doi.org/10.1007/978-3-642-33027-8_19

3. Billet, O., Gilbert, H., Ech-Chatbi, C.: Cryptanalysis of a white box AES implementation. In: Handschuh, H., Hasan, M.A. (eds.) SAC 2004. LNCS, vol. 3357, pp. 227–240. Springer, Heidelberg (2004). https://doi.org/10.1007/978-3-540-30564-4_16

4. Biryukov, A., Bouillaguet, C., Khovratovich, D.: Cryptographic schemes based on the ASASA structure: black-box, white-box, and public-key (extended abstract). In: Sarkar, P., Iwata, T. (eds.) ASIACRYPT 2014. LNCS, vol. 8873, pp. 63–84. Springer, Heidelberg (2014). https://doi.org/10.1007/978-3-662-45611-8_4

5. Biryukov, A., Khovratovich, D.: Decomposition attack on SASASASAS. Cryptology ePrint Archive, Report 2015/646 (2015). https://eprint.iacr.org/2015/646

6. Bock, E.A., Amadori, A., Bos, J.W., Brzuska, C., Michiels, W.: Doubly half-injective PRGs for incompressible white-box cryptography. In: Matsui, M. (ed.) CT-RSA 2019. LNCS, vol. 11405, pp. 189–209. Springer, Cham (2019). https://doi.org/10.1007/978-3-030-12612-4_10

7. Bogdanov, A., Isobe, T.: White-box cryptography revisited: space-hard ciphers. In: Proceedings of the 22nd ACM SIGSAC Conference on Computer and Communications Security, CCS 2015, pp. 1058–1069. ACM, New York (2015)

8. Bogdanov, A., Isobe, T., Tischhauser, E.: Towards practical whitebox cryptography: optimizing efficiency and space hardness. In: Cheon, J.H., Takagi, T. (eds.) ASIACRYPT 2016. LNCS, vol. 10031, pp. 126–158. Springer, Heidelberg (2016). https://doi.org/10.1007/978-3-662-53887-6_5

9. Cho, J., et al.: WEM: a new family of white-box block ciphers based on the even-mansour construction. In: Handschuh, H. (ed.) CT-RSA 2017. LNCS, vol. 10159, pp. 293–308. Springer, Cham (2017). https://doi.org/10.1007/978-3-319-52153-4_17

10. Chow, S., Eisen, P., Johnson, H., Van Oorschot, P.C.: White-box cryptography and an AES implementation. In: Nyberg, K., Heys, H. (eds.) SAC 2002. LNCS, vol. 2595, pp. 250–270. Springer, Heidelberg (2003). https://doi.org/10.1007/3-540-36492-7_17

11. Cioschi, F., Fornari, N., Visconti, A.: White-box cryptography: a time-security trade-off for the SPNbox family. In: Woungang, I., Dhurandher, S.K. (eds.) WIDECOM 2018. LNDECT, vol. 27, pp. 153–166. Springer, Cham (2019). https://doi.org/10.1007/978-3-030-11437-4_12

12. Dunkelman, O., Keller, N., Shamir, A.: Minimalism in cryptography: the even-mansour scheme revisited. In: Pointcheval, D., Johansson, T. (eds.) EUROCRYPT 2012. LNCS, vol. 7237, pp. 336–354. Springer, Heidelberg (2012). https://doi.org/10.1007/978-3-642-29011-4_21

13. Fouque, P.-A., Karpman, P., Kirchner, P., Minaud, B.: Efficient and provable white-box primitives. In: Cheon, J.H., Takagi, T. (eds.) ASIACRYPT 2016. LNCS, vol. 10031, pp. 159–188. Springer, Heidelberg (2016). https://doi.org/10.1007/978-3-662-53887-6_6

14. Gouvêa, C.P.L., López, J.: Implementing GCM on ARMv8. In: Nyberg, K. (ed.) CT-RSA 2015. LNCS, vol. 9048, pp. 167–180. Springer, Cham (2015). https://doi.org/10.1007/978-3-319-16715-2_9

15. Junod, P., Vaudenay, S.: Perfect diffusion primitives for block ciphers. In: Handschuh, H., Hasan, M.A. (eds.) SAC 2004. LNCS, vol. 3357, pp. 84–99. Springer, Heidelberg (2004). https://doi.org/10.1007/978-3-540-30564-4_6

16. Knuth, D.E.: The Art of Computer Programming: Seminumerical Algorithms, vol. II, 3rd edn. Addison-Wesley, Boston (1998)

17. Krovetz, T., Rogaway, P.: The software performance of authenticated-encryption modes. In: Joux, A. (ed.) FSE 2011. LNCS, vol. 6733, pp. 306–327. Springer, Heidelberg (2011). https://doi.org/10.1007/978-3-642-21702-9_18

18. Lepoint, T., Rivain, M., De Mulder, Y., Roelse, P., Preneel, B.: Two attacks on a white-box AES implementation. In: Lange, T., Lauter, K., Lisoněk, P. (eds.) SAC 2013. LNCS, vol. 8282, pp. 265–285. Springer, Heidelberg (2014). https://doi.org/10.1007/978-3-662-43414-7_14

19. Saxena, A., Wyseur, B., Preneel, B.: Towards security notions for white-box cryptography. In: Samarati, P., Yung, M., Martinelli, F., Ardagna, C.A. (eds.) ISC 2009. LNCS, vol. 5735, pp. 49–58. Springer, Heidelberg (2009). https://doi.org/10.1007/978-3-642-04474-8_4

Batch Binary Weierstrass

Billy Bob Brumley$^{(\boxtimes)}$ ⓘ, Sohaib ul Hassan, Alex Shaindlinⓘ, Nicola Tuveriⓘ, and Kide Vuojärviⓘ

Tampere University, Tampere, Finland
{billy.brumley,n.sohaibulhassan,chloenatasha.shaindlin,
nicola.tuveri,kide.vuojarvi}@tuni.fi

Abstract. Bitslicing is a programming technique that offers several attractive features, such as timing attack resistance, high amortized performance in batch computation, and architecture independence. On the symmetric crypto side, this technique sees wide real-world deployment, in particular for block ciphers with naturally parallel modes. However, the asymmetric side lags in application, seemingly due to the rigidity of the batch computation requirement. In this paper, we build on existing bitsliced binary field arithmetic results to develop a tool that optimizes performance of binary fields at any size on a given architecture. We then provide an ECC layer, with support for arbitrary binary curves. Finally, we integrate into our novel dynamic OpenSSL engine, transparently exposing the batch results to the OpenSSL library and linking applications to achieve significant performance and security gains for key pair generation, ECDSA signing, and (half of) ECDH across a wide range of curves, both standardized and non-standard.

Keywords: Applied cryptography · Public key cryptography · Elliptic Curve Cryptography · Software implementation · Batching · Bitslicing · OpenSSL

1 Introduction

The use of Elliptic Curve Cryptography (ECC) was first suggested in 1985, independently by Miller [23] and Koblitz [19]. Due to the fast group law on elliptic curves and the absence of known sub-exponential attacks, ECC has since gathered momentum as an alternative to popular asymmetric cryptosystems like RSA and DSA, as it can provide the same security level with keys that are much shorter, gaining both in computational efficiency and bandwidth consumption.

A prevalent assumption is that for software implementations, curves over large characteristic prime fields are generally more efficient than their binary field counterparts, and that, vice versa, the opposite applies for hardware implementations, i.e., that ECC scalar point multiplication (usually the most costly operation in ECC cryptosystems) is much faster over binary extension fields.

As we will detail in the following sections, the first half of the above assumption has been repeatedly challenged, especially considering the effect of alternative coordinate representations and the advances in the manufacturing processes

© Springer Nature Switzerland AG 2019
P. Schwabe and N. Thériault (Eds.): LATINCRYPT 2019, LNCS 11774, pp. 364–384, 2019.
https://doi.org/10.1007/978-3-030-30530-7_18

and design of general purpose CPUs, e.g. with the introduction of dedicated units for carry-less multiplication and the widespread adoption of vector processing (a.k.a. SIMD: Single Instruction, Multiple Data) in popular Instruction Set Architectures (ISA).

In this work, we focus on bitsliced binary field arithmetic as a strategy to take advantage of the characteristics of modern processors and provide fast batch "fixed point"[1] scalar multiplication for binary ECC.

Our Contribution. We propose a set of three tools

1. to optimize bitsliced binary field arithmetic, potentially supporting any architecture, by selecting the performance-optimal configuration of the underlying finite field layer for a given platform;
2. to implement an ECC layer for any given binary curve, building on the layer provided by the first tool, and providing constant-time fixed point scalar multiplications that performs very competitively with existing state-of-the-art results;
3. to integrate the generated ECC implementations in OpenSSL, overcoming the restriction of batch computation at the application level.

The combined output of these tools transparently provides constant-time and efficient implementations of bitsliced binary ECC for real-world applications built on top of OpenSSL. This challenges once again the notion that binary ECC are not well suited for software implementations, and at the same time overcomes the main drawback of similar techniques, proving it is also practical for real-world deployment.

Overview. In Sect. 2 we discuss the background for this work, recalling related works on top of which we build our contribution or that pursued similar goals. In Sects. 3 and 4 we discuss definitions, challenges, the design, and the analysis of our results related with the binary field and elliptic curve arithmetic layers. Section 5 describes the third and last of our contributions, integrating our implementations in OpenSSL to provide seamless support of constant-time and fast bitsliced binary ECC to real-world applications. Finally, we conclude in Sect. 6, with a discussion of the limits of our current contribution and future work directions for this research.

2   Background

2.1   Bitslicing

SIMD is a data parallelism technique that facilitates parallel computation on multiple values. For example, processors featuring AVX2 contain 256-bit registers

---

[1] In this paper we refer to scalar multiplication by the conventional generator point for a given curve as *"fixed point" scalar multiplication*. In real world applications, this is the fundamental operation for ECDH and ECDSA key generation, and for ECDSA signature generation. This operation is opposed to *"generic point" scalar multiplication*, intended as a scalar multiplication by any other point on the curve: the latter is used in ECDH key derivation and ECDSA signature verification.

ymm0 through ymm15. Viewing these as four 64-bit *lanes*, the instruction vpaddq
%ymm0, %ymm1, %ymm2 takes ymm0 $= (a_0, a_1, a_2, a_3)$ and ymm1 $= (b_0, b_1, b_2, b_3)$ then
produces their integer vector sum ymm2 $= (a_0 + b_0, \ldots, a_3 + b_3)$ where all sums
are modulo 2^{64}. There are several ways to split the register; e.g. as 8-bit, 16-
bit, etc. lanes, each requiring dedicated microarchitecture support and distinct
instructions for the register-size variants (e.g. add, subtract, multiply, etc.). Put
briefly, *bitslicing* takes this to the extreme and views any w-bit register as w
1-bit lanes. This lightens the microarchitecture requirements, as 1-bit addition
(or subtraction) is simply bitwise-XOR; 1-bit multiplication is bitwise-AND.
Bitwise operations are a fundamental feature in ISAs, and are in fact independent
of explicit SIMD support: any generic, non-SIMD w-bit architecture natively
supports 1-bit lane SIMD, i.e. bitslicing.

Deployments. Outside of primitives that integrate bitslicing into the design
such as Serpent, SHA-3, and Ascon, we are aware of two large-scale deployments of bitsliced software: one defensive and the other offensive. Käsper and
Schwabe [18] provide a bitsliced implementation for AES, mainlined by OpenSSL
in 2011. In the pre-AES-NI era and with only SSE2 as a prerequisite, this was
groundbreaking work that exceeded the performance of traditional table-based
AES software, yet additionally provided timing attack resistance. *John the Rip-
per*[2] is a security audit tool that bitslices DES to batch password hashing. The
main application is to hashes utilizing the crypt portion of the standard library.

Obstacles. The ability to batch public key operations is the largest restriction
for bitsliced software. Real-world APIs (e.g. OpenSSL) do not support such a
seemingly narrow use case, as e.g. in ECC the most common operations are
single or double scalar multiplications, not w in parallel. Even research-oriented
APIs such as SUPERCOP do not have this feature. And for key agreement
on a typical single threaded application, there is no clear way how to utilize
such an implementation. On the engineering side, it is very tempting to directly
leverage academic results on minimizing gate count for bitsliced software, since
each gate will map to an instruction. However, this is only part of the story
since register and memory pressure impose constraints, as well as instruction
level parallelism, scheduling, and binary size. Indeed, both [8, 34] note the latter
disconnect. Binary finite field multipliers with low gate count [5] do not directly
map to efficient bitsliced multipliers, since arithmetic instruction count is only
a small part of overall performance on a platform.

2.2 OpenSSL and ENGINEs

As already mentioned, arguably the main drawback of batch operations for cryptographic implementations is that they are generally seen as not practical: this
comes in part by the lack of support for batch public key operations in mainstream cryptographic libraries. Among many others, one example supporting
this argument is BBE251 by Bernstein [5]: despite the high performance, we are

---

[2] https://www.openwall.com/john/.

not aware of any deployments or standardization efforts supporting this curve in the past decade. We hypothesize this is because it seemingly does not meet the characteristics for mainstream cryptography software.

To counter this argument and to evaluate our work in a real-world scenario, we decided to target OpenSSL, an open source project consisting of a general-purpose cryptographic library, an SSL/TLS library and toolkit, and a collection of command line tools to generate and handle cryptographic keys and execute cryptographic operations. The project is arguably ubiquitous, providing the cryptographic backend and TLS stack of a considerable portion of web servers, network appliances, client softwares, and IoT devices. Thanks to the wide range of supported platforms and more than twenty years of history, it has become a de facto standard for Internet Security.

In the literature, a common pattern to integrate alternative implementations in OpenSSL consists in forking the upstream project to apply the required patches. This then requires maintaining the fork to include, alongside the research-driven changes, patches from upstream to fix vulnerabilities, bugs, or provide new features. As an example of this methodology, the Open Quantum Safe project [30] maintains a fork[3] of OpenSSL to evaluate candidates of the NIST Post Quantum Project. The history of the repository shows the level of effort required to maintain a fork of OpenSSL up to date with both research work and upstream releases.

Considering how demanding this approach can be, it is not surprising that most of the academic results often prefer to evaluate their results with ad-hoc software or toolkits like SUPERCOP[4], which generally operate in isolation and are not necessarily representative of the performance or features of the applications of the research work in real-world use cases.

As an alternative to these two approaches, we build on top of the framework proposed by Tuveri and Brumley [33], instantiated in `libsuola`[5]. This framework allows to provide alternative implementations of cryptosystems to OpenSSL applications, by using ENGINEs: OpenSSL objects that act as "containers for implementations of cryptographic algorithms". Originally introduced to support hardware cryptographic accelerators, the same construct can be used to provide alternative software implementations. It offers a mechanism to configure a whole system or individual applications to load ENGINEs at runtime, transparently providing their functionality to existing applications, without recompiling them.

While we defer to Sect. 5 for a description of the ENGINE instantiated as part of our contribution, we further motivate here our choice remarking that this approach, on top of lowering maintenance costs, allows to reuse existing applications with no effort, providing multiple and diverse ways to validate the correctness and interoperability of our implementation. This also allows us to

---

[3] https://github.com/open-quantum-safe/openssl.

[4] https://bench.cr.yp.to/supercop.html.

[5] https://github.com/romen/libsuola.

use existing projects to benchmark and evaluate our contribution in comparison with state-of-the-art real-world implementations.

3   Binary Field Arithmetic

A binary extension field is a finite field of the form $\mathbb{F}_{2^m}$, where m is an integer called the dimension of the field and $m \geq 2$. Elements of the field $\mathbb{F}_{2^m}$ can be expressed as polynomials of degree less than m with coefficients in $\mathbb{F}_2$, which have an underlying set of $\{0, 1\}$ and in which addition corresponds to binary XOR and multiplication corresponds to binary AND. Any two finite fields with the same number of elements are isomorphic to each other, but calculations in a particular finite field are performed modulo an irreducible polynomial P of degree m, and different choices of P produce different results. Since the underlying set of $\mathbb{F}_2$ is $\{0, 1\}$, elements of $\mathbb{F}_{2^m}$ can also be represented as binary strings; for example, with $m = 8$, the element $x^6 + x^3 + x + 1$ can be written 01001011_2.

The simplest method of multiplying elements of $\mathbb{F}_{2^m}$ is to multiply them as polynomials using schoolbook multiplication and then reduce the result modulo the field polynomial P by polynomial long division. Bernstein [5, Sect. 2] collects many asymptotic improvements on $M(n)$, the number of bit operations required to multiply two n-bit polynomials, over this method: $M(n) \leq \Theta(n^{\lg 3})$ due to Karatsuba, $M(n) \leq n2^{\Theta(\sqrt{\lg n})}$ due to Toom, and $M(n) \leq \Theta(n \lg n \lg \lg n)$ due to Schönhage and Strassen. Bernstein also establishes tighter explicit upper bounds on $M(n)$ for $n \in \{128, 163, 193, 194, 512\}$, and provides[6] straight-line code for cases from $n = 1$ to $n = 1000$, and verified upper bounds on the number of bit operations required in each case.

3.1   Splitting Strategies

For small n, the straight-line code can be very efficient, but for large n, it becomes inefficient, partly because the compiled code becomes too large to fit in the cache. Additionally, the algorithm that uses the fewest bit operations will not necessarily take the fewest cycles to run when implemented, because in bitsliced batch computations a nontrivial number of cycles are spent performing load and store instructions, which is not accounted for in the bit operation count. There are several conventional concerns about the correlation of bit operation count and software performance, and while bitslicing relieves some of these concerns [5, Sect. 1], the overhead incurred by loads and stores remains relevant. This is a gap in the existing literature, which mostly reports results in terms of bit operations [10, 11, 16].

Recursive algorithms for polynomial multiplication, such as Karatsuba and Toom, have better asymptotic performance than straight-line multiplication, but they incur more overhead, so for sufficiently small inputs, straight-line multiplication is faster in practice. Due to these considerations, the fastest way (in terms

---

[6] https://binary.cr.yp.to/m.html.

of cycle count) to batch multiply polynomials of cryptographic sizes in $\mathbb{F}_{2^m}$ is usually to begin with recursive splits, and then switch to straight-line multiplication when the subproblem size becomes small enough for this trade-off to occur. The exact size at which this threshold is located may depend on both the architecture and the field dimension.

For larger subproblems, there are many different recursive algorithms for polynomial multiplication. Of the recursive multiplication strategies described in [5], we use two: the one called "five-way recursion", which corresponds to the WAY3 macros in our implementation, and the one called "two-level seven-way recursion", which corresponds to the WAY4 macros. (There is also "three-way recursion", corresponding to WAY2 macros, but we omit them; since WAY4 splits the current problem into four subproblems of roughly equal size, and WAY2 splits it into two subproblems of roughly equal size, we expect that WAY4 is a more efficient version of back-to-back WAY2 splits.) For simplicity, and in keeping with the names of the macros, in this paper we refer to the WAY3 macros as "three-way recursion" and to the WAY4 macros as "four-way recursion". Different subproblem sizes may have different optimal choices of recursion strategy (and again, these can be architecture-dependent), so the complete collection of recursive multiplication steps taken before dropping down to straight-line multiplication may be both architecture- and dimension-dependent.

For a given field size, on a given architecture, a strategy to choose whether to use a recursive algorithm or switch to a straight-line multiplication at each intermediate step needs to be created. Said strategy aims to minimize the total number of cycles required to multiply a batch of w polynomials of the given degree. We refer to this result as the optimal *splitting strategy* for that size. The strategy is generated for the library and necessary straight-line multiplication files are included.

The functions for straight-line multiplication are called gf2_mul_M and the functions for recursive multiplication are called karatmultM, where M is the size of the input. Reading Fig. 1 from the bottom line up, this code splits 251 four ways with a WAY4 macro (specifically WAY43 because $251 \equiv 3 \mod 4$) and performs recursive multiplication on subproblems of size 62 and 63; 63 is split four ways with a remainder of 3 and 62 is split four ways with a remainder of 2; both 62 and 63 are split into subproblems of size 15 and 16, which are handled with straight-line code.

```
/* (43K251, 43K63, 42K62, G16, G15) */
WAY42(62, gf2_mul_15, gf2_mul_16)
WAY43(63, gf2_mul_15, gf2_mul_16)
WAY43(251, karatmult62, karatmult63)
```

Fig. 1. Optimal splitting strategy on Skylake for $m = 251$.

When reporting benchmarking results, we display the splitting strategy in a concise format: a list of multipliers in descending order of subproblem size, with recursive multipliers represented by the numbers after the WAY macro + K + the input size, and straight-line multipliers represented by G + the input size.

Architectures. The purpose of the free and open-source software (FOSS) benchmarking tool we developed[7] is to experimentally determine the best splitting strategy for a particular field size running on a particular architecture. The tooling currently supports AVX2, AVX-512, and NEON, but is easily extendable to other ISAs. The bulk of our code utilizes macros for C compiler intrinsics to emit architecture-specific instructions, so adding an ISA consists mainly of internally defining these macros for the target architecture. We used the following environments for the benchmarking: *AVX-512*, a 2.1 GHz Xeon Silver 4116 Skylake (24 cores, 48 threads across 2 CPUs) and 256 GB RAM running 64-bit Ubuntu 16.04 Xenial (clang-8, $w = 512$); *AVX2*, a 3.2 GHz i5-6500 Skylake (4 cores) and 16 GB RAM running 64-bit Ubuntu 18.04 Bionic (clang-8, $w = 256$); *AVX2-AMD*, a 3.7 GHz Ryzen 7 2700X (8 cores, 16 threads) and 16 GB RAM running 64-bit Ubuntu 18.04 Bionic (clang-8, $w = 256$); *NEON*, a Raspberry Pi 3 Model B+, 1.4 GHz Broadcom BCM2837B0 ARMv8 Cortex-A53 (4 cores) and 1 GB RAM running 64-bit Ubuntu 18.04 Bionic (clang-7, $w = 128$).

3.2 Benchmarking

The benchmarking for the new software was done by recursively generating different splitting strategies for the multiplication of the polynomials. The dimension of the original field is recursively split three-ways and four-ways until the limits for straight-line multiplication are reached. While within the limits, strategies are generated for both recursive and straight-line multiplication, because we found that using straight-line multiplication was not always the optimal solution even when they were available. Thus we also generate many strategies that still use the recursive split while within the limits of straight-line multiplication. While Bernstein [5] has straight-line multiplications defined in a larger range, we decided to limit it between polynomials of degree $[5, \ldots, 99]$ for the scope of this paper.

We divided the generated splitting strategies into three categories, two of which were eliminated from this paper. The two eliminated categories consisted of *mixed multiplication* and *non-strict recursion threshold*. The nature of these categories and the reasons for elimination is discussed below.

The *mixed multiplication* category includes all the strategies where at least one subproblem of the recursive call is not handled like the others. An example of this would be WAY43(251, karatmult62, gf2_mul_63), where one subproblem is handled with a recursive call, and another with straight-line multiplication. The benchmarking tool still supports this option, but our preliminary testing showed no benefits for allowing mixed multiplication. The number of possible strategies is also vastly larger (6 vs. 11 with degree 63, 14 vs. 62 with degree 127 and 193 vs. 4546 with degree 251), rendering the tool prohibitively slow with

---

[7] https://gitlab.com/nisec/gf2sliced.

higher values. Though there may be some edge cases where using a recursive call for the higher value and straight-line for the lower value subproblem would yield a more optimal result, we found none.

The *non-strict recursion threshold* category includes all the strategies where the greatest value of straight-line multiplication is greater or equal to the least value of a recursive multiplication. An example of this would be the strategy (43K251, 30K63, 32K62, G23, 42K22, 41K21, G21, 40K20, G6, G5), where we see both a G23 which has a greater value than K22, and K21 which is equal in value to G21. Our assumption is that once we cross the threshold on straight-line multiplication, using recursive multiplication will be slower. As is the case with mixed multiplication, limiting the search space by excluding this category considerably increases the efficiency of the benchmarking tool. We believe that this elimination does not significantly reduce the chances of finding the optimal strategy. If straight-line and recursive multiplication of the same subproblem size, such as G21 and K21, is wanted inside one strategy, the current version of the benchmarking software needs to be modified.

Unlike the mixed multiplication strategies, the strategies with non-strict recursion threshold are only eliminated after all the strategies have been generated. The final search space includes all the strategies that did not meet the criteria for elimination in the previous two steps.

After the paths have been generated, the benchmarking tool takes one strategy at a time, creates a configuration header file for the binary field arithmetic C program, and compiles and runs the test harness, which outputs the number of processor cycles it takes for a batch of polynomials to be multiplied. When all the strategies for that field size have been tested, the program outputs a file containing the strategies in ascending order of cycles, as well as the configuration file for the best found strategy for a given platform. Our ECC layer (Sect. 4) uses this configuration at build time to produce the most efficient solution.

Figure 2 shows the results of the best strategy in benchmarking on three different processor architectures, and Table 1 selective data points on four different processor architectures. NEON has a register width of 128 bits, AVX2 has a register width of 256 bits, and AVX-512 has a register width of 512 bits; these are the denominators by which the total cycle counts are scaled.

In theory, AVX-512 should perform twice as fast as AVX2 in terms of scaled cycle counts, because AVX-512 processes twice as many elements in one batch. Performing linear regression on the data sets in Fig. 2 with `gnuplot` indicated that AVX-512 is faster than AVX2 by a factor of approximately 2.17 in practice.

We disabled Simultaneous multithreading (SMT) for all experiments in this paper. While we used multiple cores during benchmarking to find the best splitting strategy, the results in Table 1 (and later in Table 2) were ran on a single core.

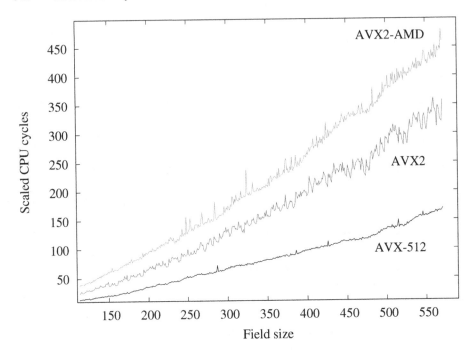

Fig. 2. Binary field multiplication performance in scaled CPU cycles.

Table 1. Selective binary field multiplication performance in scaled CPU cycles.

m	113	131	163	191	193	233	239	251	283	359	409	431	571
AVX-512	13	16	22	30	31	44	44	51	59	82	99	104	170
AVX2	24	30	43	54	55	84	77	91	121	166	216	214	351
AVX2-AMD	37	47	67	83	89	114	116	132	153	224	274	300	459
NEON	228	290	425	523	534	708	724	805	928	1340	1659	1819	2953

3.3   Related Work

The cycle counts in this subsection are reported for $m = 251$ unless otherwise noted, since it is a common field size in the literature to approach the 128-bit security level and therefore provides the best basis for comparison. We first note that the comparison here (and later in Sect. 4.5) to previous work is not without caveats, due to different computation models (i.e. parallel vs. serial) and ISA availability over time.

Aranha et al. [4] benchmarked several field operations on three different Intel platforms (Core 2 65 nm, Core 2 45 nm, and Core i7 45 nm) Their best multiplication result was 323 cycles, achieved on the Core i7 platform with López-Dahab multiplication.

Taverne et al. [31,32] benchmarked López-Dahab multiplication on an Intel Westmere Core i5 32 nm processor, reporting 338 cycles for code compiled with GCC and 429 cycles for code compiled with ICC (the Intel C++ Compiler), and achieved a speedup to 161 cycles (GCC) and 159 cycles (ICC) by performing Karatsuba multiplication with the new carry-less multiplication instruction.

Câmara et al. [9] report timings for an ARM Cortex-A8, Cortex-A9, and Cortex-A15 processor, with code compiled with GCC. López-Dahab multiplication takes 671 cycles on A8, 774 on A9, and 412 on A15; their contribution is the Karatsuba/NEON/VMULL multiplication algorithm, which takes 385 cycles on A8, 491 on A9, and 317 on A15.

Oliveira et al. [25] benchmarked Karatsuba multiplication with carry-less multiplication on Intel Sandy Bridge for field size $m = 254$ and achieved 94 cycles with GCC (and report similar results for ICC).

Seo et al. [27] achieve 57 cycles for $m = 251$ and 153 cycles for $m = 571$ on ARMv8 by using the 64-bit polynomial multiplication instruction PMULL instead of the 8-bit polynomial multiplication instruction VMULL used in [9].

4   Elliptic Curve Arithmetic

A non-supersingular elliptic curve E over the binary finite field $\mathbb{F}_{2^m}$ is a set of points $(x, y) \in \mathbb{F}_{2^m}$ satisfying the short Weierstrass equation:

$$E(\mathbb{F}_{2^m}) : y^2 + xy = x^3 + ax^2 + b$$

where the parameters $a, b \in \mathbb{F}_{2^m}$ and the set of points in $E(\mathbb{F}_{2^m})$ is an additive Abelian group with identity element as the point at infinity $\mathcal{O}$ i.e. $P + \mathcal{O} = \mathcal{O} + P = P$ and the inverse element at $-P = (x_1, x_1 + y_1)$. For the sake of simplicity, the remainder of this paper will refer to this curve form as *short curves*.

4.1   Scalar Multiplication

The elliptic curve point multiplication is seen as the most critical and compute-intensive task, therefore a lot of emphasis is given on improving the algorithms for efficiency and security. For a given ℓ-bit scalar $k \in \mathbb{Z}$ and point $P \in E$, the point multiplication can be formulated as:

$$kP = \sum_{i=0}^{\ell-1} k_i 2^i P$$

where k_i is the i_{th} bit of the scalar. This naive method, a.k.a. binary method, scans the bits of the scalar one at a time, performing double operations for each $\ell - 1$ bits in addition to the add operation where $k_i \neq 0$.

An alternate approach was proposed by Montgomery [24]: where the same number of double-and-add operations are repeated in each step. Although—in terms of computational time—it seems more expensive as compared to the naive method. However, the advantage is the resistance against side-channel analysis by removing the conditional branches depending on the weight of scalar bits.

For performing fast ladder multiplication, differential addition and doubling is applied, which computes $P_1 + P_2$ from P_1, P_2 and $P_2 - P_1$ and similarly $2P_1$ from P_1 for the doubling. The relation $P_2 - P_1 = P$ here is the invariant, i.e. the difference of these two points is known and constant throughout the ladder step. Short curves have a nice property, by applying suitable coordinate transformation, the knowledge of only x-coordinate is sufficient to perform the entire ladder step. This considerably improves the performance, since there is no need to evaluate the intermediate results of the y-coordinate at each ladder step.

An important consideration—for the performance optimization of EC double and add operations—is the representation of point coordinate system. The use of projective coordinates in most cases is preferred over the affine coordinates, due to the heavy inversion operations involved in the later. A number of coordinate systems, in the context of binary curves, have been studied such as lambda [25], Jacobian [12], and homogeneous projective [1]. Among them, López and Dahab [21] is a popular choice in binary elliptic curves, with various performance improvements proposed [2,7,20]. For a projective form of the short curves equation defined as:

$$E(\mathbb{F}_{2^m}) : Y^2 + XYZ = X^3Z + aX^2Z^2 + bZ^4$$

the LD-projective point $(X_1 : Y_1 : Z_1)$ is equivalent to the affine point $(X_1/Z_1 : Y_1/Z_1^2)$, where the inverse is $(X_1 : X_1Z_1 + Y_1 : Z_1)$. It is further assumed that $Z_1 \neq 0$ and $\mathcal{O}$ is not among the points.

4.2   Differential Montgomery Ladder

For short curves, Bernstein and Lange[8] provide a very efficient differential addition and doubling (ladder step) formulas, originally derived from [29]. The representation, known as XZ, is a variant of the original LD coordinates. For each scalar bit k_i—assuming the invariant $P_2 - P_1 = P$ is known—the fast differential addition and doubling takes 5 multiplications, 4 squares and 1 multiplication by the constant $\sqrt{b}$. As mentioned by [14], this is the best case bound achieved for Montgomery ladder also on other forms of curves, such as Hessian [15], Huff [13], and Edwards [7], which means that choice of curve form is mostly irrelevant in terms of the computational cost. It is still possible to achieve slight performance gains over this bound by leveraging efficient forms of subfield curve constants [3].

Given $P_1 \neq \pm P_2$, to compute the differential point addition $P_3 = P_1 + P_2 = (X_3 : Y_3 : Z_3)$ where $P_1 = (X_1 : Y_1 : Z_1)$, $P_2 = (X_2 : Y_2 : Z_2)$ and, point

---

[8] https://hyperelliptic.org/EFD/g12o/auto-shortw-xz.html.

doubling $P_4 = 2P_2 = (X_4 : Y_4 : Z_4)$, the formulas are defined as follows.

$$A = X_1 Z_2, B = X_2 Z_1, C = X_1^2, D = Z_1^2$$
$$Z_3 = (A + B)^2$$
$$X_3 = X Z_3 + AB$$
$$X_4 = (C + \sqrt{b}D)$$
$$Z_4 = CD$$

As previously mentioned, the Montgomery ladder differential addition and double method does not take into account the y-coordinate during the computation, however to get back to the affine coordinates we need to recover the y-coordinate. López and Dahab [22] presented a formula to retrieve the y-coordinate, which enabled the complete point multiplication using the Montgomery ladder method, i.e. also compute the resulting affine point. In our case we applied a further optimization to the original formula by setting $Z = 1$ since the invariant $P_2 - P_1 = P = (X : Y : Z)$ is fixed, the resulting simplified version is formulated as:

$$x_1 = \frac{x Z_2 X_1}{x Z_2 Z_1}$$
$$y_1 = y + \frac{(X_2 + x Z_2)((X_1 + x Z_1)(X_2 + x Z_2) + Z_1 Z_2 x^2 + Z_1 Z_2 y)}{Z_1 Z_2 x}$$

The cost of recovering y is 10 multiplications and 1 inversion, which is small, considering that it is performed just once at the end of the ladder.

4.3   Linear Maps

As a further optimization, we also considered replacing the multiplication by the curve constants, and x-coordinate of the generator point during the ladder step by a linear map. For a finite field $\mathbb{F}_{2^m}$ represented as m-dimensional vector space $(\mathbb{F}_2)^m$, the linear map $T : \mathbb{F}_{2^m} \mapsto \mathbb{F}_{2^m}$ for multiplication by a constant b is an $(m \times m)$ matrix B with entries in $\mathbb{F}_2$. The elements b_i in B can be pre-computed: for a basis α of degree m, $b_i = \alpha^i b$ for $0 \le i < m$, where b is the element of vector space $(\mathbb{F}_2)^m$. The multiplication by an element $a \in \mathbb{F}_{2^m}$ can then be replaced by $b \cdot a = Ba$, where each bit in the product can be written as $\sum_{i:b_{i,j}=1} a_i$.

This essentially means that if there are l non-zero bits for each row of the matrix B, in total we need $(l-1)m$ XOR gates for the entire matrix. This is not the optimal number of gates, since common sub-expression elimination is not accounted for. For this purpose we tried optimization as suggested by Bernstein [6] which produces approximately $ml/(\log l - \log\log(l))$ XORs, in addition to m number of copies of the intermediate results.

For hardware implementations, this straight-line optimization makes sense. However, in the software case this also increases both register pressure and, more importantly, binary size. For the above ladder step formula, we applied the tooling from [6] to replace multiplications by both the curve constant and fixed generator x-coordinate by the straight-line code. The resulting binary far exceeded the L1 cache size, and benchmark results showed it takes away any performance gains when compared to generic finite field multiplication in the ladder step.

4.4 Implementation

Our bitsliced ECC layer builds on our finite field layer from Sect. 3. As a FOSS library[9], it exposes a single function EC2_batch_keygen that takes four arguments: (1) EC2_CURVE pointer to an opaque object provided by the library to represent a specific curve; (2) unsigned char pointer k, where it is assumed the caller has filled this input with enough randomness for w scalars, and from which the caller will retrieve the scalars as an output; (3) unsigned char pointer x storing the resulting x-coordinate of the scalar multiplication by G; and similarly (4) unsigned char pointer y for the y-coordinate. Geared to ease real-world deployment discussed further in Sect. 5, since our application is *only* to fixed (generator) point scalar multiplication, EC2_batch_keygen internally makes a number of optimizations.

We assume the scalars are provided in bitsliced form, simply viewing the first w bits at k as bit 0 of the scalars, and so on for the rest of the bits. This imposes no practical requirement on the caller—they are just random bytes, only viewed differently.

As previously discussed, for the range of standardized curves under consideration in this work, the linear maps for constant multiplications are not efficient when bitslicing, hence we implement them as generic finite field multiplications with fixed pre-bitsliced form stored in the binary. The *exception* to this case is curve2251, which has small and sparse curve coefficients. Here we implemented a dedicated ladder step using a slightly different formula involving the curve coefficient b and replace the multiplication with a straight-line linear map. Since this curve is not fixed by a standard, we found the lexicographically smallest x such that the resulting generator satisfies ord$(G) = n$, the large prime subgroup order. We then replaced this multiplication (by x-coordinate e) in the ladder step with a straight-line linear map. Of course we could do the same for standardized curves, but this would violate interoperability.

After scalar multiplication, EC2_batch_keygen recovers the y-coordinate, since key generation is our motivating use case and not simply key agreement where the x-coordinate is sufficient. Our finite field layer uses Itoh-Tsujii [17] in the inversion step, where the addition chain for exponentiation is efficient and fixed based on the finite field degree. Our finite field layer also supplies efficient finite field squaring with a straight-line linear map.

Finally, EC2_batch_keygen converts the outputs for k, x, and y from bitsliced form to canonical form for consumption by linking applications. Note for our use

---

[9] https://gitlab.com/nisec/ec2sliced.

case of key generation, there are no exceptions in the ladder step, the y recovery, or scalar corner cases. We completely control all scalars and points.

4.5 Benchmarking

Our tooling for the ECC layer generates and exposes an EC2_CURVE object for each fixed curve. We restrict to short curves with (1) no efficient endomorphism and (2) field degrees that are prime. Table 2 reports the performance across our four target architectures. Each curve was benchmarked using the best splitting strategy for its respective underlying field, as measured by the benchmarking process described in Sect. 3. Similar to Sect. 3, the reported cycle counts are scaled, dividing by w.

Table 2. ECC performance on four architectures in scaled CPU cycles.

Curve	AVX-512	AVX2	AVX2-AMD	NEON
sect113r1	9547	18074	27470	153944
sect113r2	9540	17962	27487	153948
sect131r1	13684	26821	40478	227765
sect131r2	13639	26856	40466	228168
sect163r1	22849	45231	70046	427274
sect163r2	23175	46826	70413	448744
c2pnb163v1	23005	45017	74888	435651
c2pnb163v2	22881	45490	74413	426473
c2pnb163v3	22805	45380	74422	429631
c2tnb191v1	36094	66799	102005	632907
c2tnb191v2	36262	64963	101235	617958
c2tnb191v3	35680	64454	101325	629464
sect193r1	37899	67325	109376	639270
sect193r2	37936	67730	109434	640406
sect233r1	65491	125804	167761	1013458
c2tnb239v1	67144	119490	175914	1079930
c2tnb239v2	67105	117703	174388	1085560
c2tnb239v3	67181	120304	175676	1063116
curve2251	57756	106391	146031	870376
sect283r1	105304	218130	272544	1595423
c2tnb359v1	186680	362665	504219	2961857
sect409r1	260619	546690	697021	4229741
c2tnb431r1	283319	567608	780886	4812995
sect571r1	627668	1303759	1629335	10676160

For the sake of discussion, our results show it is more efficient to use canonical representations of the curve constants, including curve coefficients and x-coordinate of the generator point. This saves in terms of computational cost during the differential addition step, allowing curve2251 to significantly outperform curves at comparable field sizes.

Finally, we briefly compare with selective results from the literature. Bernstein [5] reports 314K (scaled, SSE2, $w = 128$) Core 2 cycles for the binary Edwards curve BBE251. Aranha et al. [4] report 537K, 793K, and 4.4M Core i7 cycles for curves curve2251, B-283, and B-571. Taverne et al. [32] report 225K Sandy Bridge cycles for curve2251 in constant time, 100K cycles for B-233 in non constant time, and 349K cycles for B-409 in non constant time. Oliveira et al. [25] report 114K Sandy Bridge cycles for a 254-bit curve in constant time, yet with a non-standard composite extension. Câmara et al. [9] report 511K, 866K, and 4.2M ARM Cortex-A15 cycles for constant time curve2251, B-283, and B-571. Oliveira et al. [26] report 46K Skylake cycles for a 254-bit curve in constant time, yet again with a non-standard composite extension.

Generally, even without focusing on a single curve yet imposing the batch computation requirement, the results in Table 2 compare very favorably with the existing literature. Considering it is automated tooling that generates the finite field layer, and the ECC layer utilizes a stock ladder with no fast endomorphisms or precomputation, this demonstrates the tooling has wide applicability and can provide a strong baseline for performance comparison.

5   ENGINE Implementation

As mentioned in Sect. 2, we integrate our bitsliced implementation in OpenSSL through an ENGINE modeled after libsuola [33]. In the spirit of open science, our contribution, dubbed libbecc, is released[10] as open source: technical implementation details can be inspected in the project repository, which also includes documentation about the building process and usage.

We defer to [33] for a detailed description of the ENGINE framework and how it integrates with the OpenSSL architecture, while in this section we provide an overview of the design of libbecc in comparison to libsuola.

Our ENGINE provides implementations for most of the named[11] binary curves defined in OpenSSL and adds dedicated support to curve2251; this is achieved building on top of the work described in Sects. 3 and 4, which provide the actual batch implementation for elliptic curve and binary field operations. The libbecc code mainly provides an interface to query the underlying layers and to dispatch

---

[10] https://gitlab.com/nisec/libbecc.

[11] The term "named" here is used in contrast with curves described by arbitrary parameters: usage in real-world applications is dominated by curves that have been assigned code points as part of standards, delivering both security assurances on the cryptographic features and security evaluation of the group defined by the specified set of parameters, and saving the users from the need of performing expensive validation of the group parameters during curve negotiation.

to the relevant codepath when, through the OpenSSL library, an application requests a cryptographic operation that requires computation over a supported curve and field.

5.1 Providers

The other fundamental function of `libbecc` is to implement the logic to maintain a state for each performed batch operation, so that following requests can be served from the precomputed results rather than issuing a new batch operation.

We achieve support for batch ECC operations using the `ENGINE` API to register `libbecc` as the default `EC_KEY_METHOD`: by doing so our `ENGINE` is activated for any operation involving an `EC_KEY` object, including ECDH and ECDSA key generation, ECDH shared secret derivation and ECDSA signature generation and verification. `libbecc` retains a reference to the default OpenSSL `EC_KEY_METHOD`, which is used to bypass our `ENGINE` for unsupported curves or for operations such as ECDH derivation or ECDSA verification: these operations are not supported by our bitsliced code, limited to "fixed point" scalar multiplications, i.e., limited to scalar multiplications by the conventional generator point for a given curve.

Following `libsuola` approach and terminology, `libbecc` supports the notion of multiple providers to interface with the OpenSSL API, by providing a minimum set of functions to:

- match an **EC** object with any of the supported curves, returning either *unsupported* or a provider specific integer identifier for the specific curve;
- generate one key for a given curve identifier, returning a secret random scalar and the corresponding public point;
- perform the setup step of ECDSA signature generation for a curve identifier, returning the modular inverse of a secret nonce scalar and the corresponding **r** component of a (**r**,**s**) ECDSA signature.

Providers can then internally differ on the way the batch logic is implemented to support a bitsliced scalar multiplication.

Provider: serial. Specifically, we instantiate one provider, dubbed `serial`, that stores the internal state and buffers for key generation and signature setup with a thread local model. In this model, each thread of an OpenSSL application loading our `ENGINE` stores its own local state and buffers, and the batch results are not shared across separate threads.

In our design, we opted to perform all the operations required by a specific cryptosystem operation during the batch computation, including the conversion of raw binary buffers in OpenSSL `BIGNUM` objects, and, during the batch computation for `sign_setup`, also the batch inversion of the original nonces. To improve performance, we implemented the batch inversion using the so-called Montgomery trick [24, Sect. 10.3.1] which allows to compute simultaneously the inverses of n elements at the cost of 1 inversion and $(3n - 1)$ multiplications [28, Sect. 3.1].

The design of the `serial` provider is the most straightforward strategy to implement batch operations in OpenSSL. It avoids synchronization issues and allows us to evaluate the performance of our implementation compared to the baseline upstream implementation with classic benchmarking tools, as they usually consist of a serial loop of repeated operations.

On the other hand, we acknowledge that this is not the optimal implementation for real-world high-load multi-threaded or multi-process applications, which would actually benefit the most from bitsliced operations, saving memory resources and minimizing the number of batch operations to run, if a more clever logic to share the results of batch operations were implemented. In particular, although of limited academic value for this paper, it would be interesting to add a provider supporting inter-process communication, to have a separate system-wide *singleton* service in charge of running the batch operations and storing the results, while applications using `libbecc` would simply request a fresh result from the service. Such design would minimize memory consumption and the number of batch operations across the whole system, and it would also provide a stronger security model to protect the state and buffers in memory, as they would be stored in a separate process space. Leveraging the access control capabilities of the underlying operating system, this would be inaccessible from a compromised application.

5.2   Benchmarking

To evaluate the actual practical impact of the presented improvements, we instantiated a benchmarking application built on top of OpenSSL 1.1.1. Table 3 reports the average number of CPU clock cycles to compute a single ECDH/ECDSA key generation and ECDSA signature generation. We compare the results recorded against the default implementation with a run of the same application after loading `libbecc` at runtime; due to space constraints we limit this analysis to the AVX2 platform. For comparison, we also include measurements relative to operations on top of popular prime curves, namely ECDH/ECDSA over `secp256r1` (a.k.a. NIST `P-256`), and EDDSA over `ED25519` and `ED448`.

The benchmarking application consecutively runs 2^{16} operations for each curve, recording the number of elapsed CPU cycles after each operation; Table 3 reports the average of such measurements. It should be noted that, for the default implementation, each measure for a given operation on a given curve is relatively close to the average reported on the table; for the `libbecc` implementation instead, due to the nature of batch operations, we record execution time spikes when a new batch is computed followed by a relatively low (between nine and sixteen thousands of CPU cycles, depending on the field size of the curve) plateau for each following operation until the batch is consumed.

Table 3. OpenSSL performance on AVX2: average CPU cycles for operations on selected curves.

Curve	Average CPU cycles per operation			
	Key generation		Signature generation	
	default	libbecc	default	libbecc
sect113r1	309998	26758 (11.6x)	323163	25049 (12.9x)
sect113r2	309892	26810 (11.6x)	323586	25043 (12.9x)
sect131r1	515314	37617 (13.7x)	533484	35950 (14.8x)
sect131r2	519635	37293 (13.9x)	540221	35711 (15.1x)
c2pnb163v1	699094	54717 (12.8x)	718671	52785 (13.6x)
c2pnb163v2	690930	54603 (12.7x)	710865	52653 (13.5x)
c2pnb163v3	700345	54432 (12.9x)	722117	52709 (13.7x)
sect163r1	690258	53996 (12.8x)	719847	52548 (13.7x)
sect163r2	697992	54875 (12.7x)	725706	52635 (13.8x)
c2tnb191v1	673839	74407 (9.1x)	694368	72989 (9.5x)
c2tnb191v2	668479	74308 (9.0x)	695895	72811 (9.6x)
c2tnb191v3	669240	73836 (9.1x)	697687	73037 (9.6x)
sect193r1	762628	77378 (9.9x)	803603	76853 (10.5x)
sect193r2	758937	77109 (9.8x)	800200	76908 (10.4x)
sect233r1	940852	133436 (7.1x)	985741	133941 (7.4x)
c2tnb239v1	966659	127149 (7.6x)	1008116	126843 (7.9x)
c2tnb239v2	960048	126222 (7.6x)	1004913	126053 (8.0x)
c2tnb239v3	961976	125478 (7.7x)	1008270	125681 (8.0x)
curve2251	1139439	118368 (9.6x)	1198634	118661 (10.1x)
ED25519	130295	130254 (1.0x)	131174	129597 (1.0x)
secp256r1	35805	36741 (1.0x)	69228	68921 (1.0x)
sect283r1	1631437	226075 (7.2x)	1700907	225973 (7.5x)
c2tnb359v1	2016295	377226 (5.3x)	2126677	374781 (5.7x)
sect409r1	2731705	552476 (4.9x)	2880190	551485 (5.2x)
c2tnb431r1	2968140	587026 (5.1x)	3125245	579913 (5.4x)
ED448	960595	957772 (1.0x)	969825	969300 (1.0x)
sect571r1	6283098	1359731 (4.6x)	6624862	1311432 (5.1x)

6   Conclusion

In this paper, we developed a tool to optimize bitsliced binary field arithmetic that can potentially support any architecture. Guided by benchmarking statistics, at the finite field layer the tool tries different polynomial splitting strategies to arrive at the performance-optimal configuration on a given platform. Building on this layer, we developed a second tool that implements an ECC layer for a given binary curve, and performs very competitively; e.g. 58K AVX-512 (scaled) cycles for constant-time fixed point scalar multiplication on curve2251. Building on both these results, our last layer links OpenSSL with the output, overcoming the restriction of batch computation at the application level. Our approach in libbecc seamlessly couples applications with the batch computation results, facilitating real-world deployment of bitsliced public key cryptography software.

Future Work. Our ECC layer is specific to short curves; a natural direction is to extend with support for other binary curve forms, even using the birational equivalence with short curves where applicable to maintain compatibility with existing (legacy, X9.62) standards exposed by OpenSSL through libbecc. Lastly, the architecture of libbecc has several applications outside binary ECC. Exploring similar functionality for traditional SIMD instead of bitslicing is another research direction, providing batch computation for curves over prime fields. Such an implementation would have much lower batch sizes, but potentially far greater performance since it relaxes register and memory pressure.

Acknowledgments. This project has received funding from the European Research Council (ERC) under the European Union's Horizon 2020 research and innovation programme (grant agreement No. 804476). The second author was supported in part by the Tuula and Yrjö Neuvo Fund through the Industrial Research Fund at Tampere University of Technology.

References

1. Agnew, G.B., Mullin, R.C., Vanstone, S.A.: An implementation of elliptic curve cryptosystems over $F_{2^{155}}$. IEEE J. Sel. Areas Commun. **11**(5), 804–813 (1993). https://doi.org/10.1109/49.223883
2. Al-Daoud, E., Mahmod, R., Rushdan, M., Kiliçman, A.: A new addition formula for elliptic curves over GF(2^n). IEEE Trans. Comput. **51**(8), 972–975 (2002). https://doi.org/10.1109/TC.2002.1024743
3. Aranha, D.F., Azarderakhsh, R., Karabina, K.: Efficient software implementation of laddering algorithms over binary elliptic curves. In: Ali, S.S., Danger, J.-L., Eisenbarth, T. (eds.) SPACE 2017. LNCS, vol. 10662, pp. 74–92. Springer, Cham (2017). https://doi.org/10.1007/978-3-319-71501-8_5
4. Aranha, D.F., López, J., Hankerson, D.: Efficient software implementation of binary field arithmetic using vector instruction sets. In: Abdalla, M., Barreto, P.S.L.M. (eds.) LATINCRYPT 2010. LNCS, vol. 6212, pp. 144–161. Springer, Heidelberg (2010). https://doi.org/10.1007/978-3-642-14712-8_9
5. Bernstein, D.J.: Batch binary Edwards. In: Halevi, S. (ed.) CRYPTO 2009. LNCS, vol. 5677, pp. 317–336. Springer, Heidelberg (2009). https://doi.org/10.1007/978-3-642-03356-8_19
6. Bernstein, D.J.: Optimizing linear maps modulo 2. In: SPEED-CC: Software Performance Enhancement for Encryption and Decryption and Cryptographic Compilers, Workshop Record, pp. 3–18 (2009). http://cr.yp.to/papers.html#linearmod2
7. Bernstein, D.J., Lange, T., Rezaeian Farashahi, R.: Binary Edwards curves. In: Oswald, E., Rohatgi, P. (eds.) CHES 2008. LNCS, vol. 5154, pp. 244–265. Springer, Heidelberg (2008). https://doi.org/10.1007/978-3-540-85053-3_16

8. Brumley, B.B., Page, D.: Bit-sliced binary normal basis multiplication. In: Antelo, E., Hough, D., Ienne, P. (eds.) 20th IEEE Symposium on Computer Arithmetic, ARITH 2011, Tübingen, Germany, 25–27 July 2011, pp. 205–212. IEEE Computer Society (2011). https://doi.org/10.1109/ARITH.2011.36

9. Câmara, D., Gouvêa, C.P.L., López, J., Dahab, R.: Fast software polynomial multiplication on ARM processors using the NEON engine. In: Cuzzocrea, A., Kittl, C., Simos, D.E., Weippl, E., Xu, L. (eds.) CD-ARES 2013. LNCS, vol. 8128, pp. 137–154. Springer, Heidelberg (2013). https://doi.org/10.1007/978-3-642-40588-4_10

10. Cenk, M.: Karatsuba-like formulae and their associated techniques. J. Cryptogr. Eng. **8**(3), 259–269 (2018). https://doi.org/10.1007/s13389-017-0155-8

11. Cenk, M., Hasan, M.A.: Some new results on binary polynomial multiplication. J. Cryptogr. Eng. **5**(4), 289–303 (2015). https://doi.org/10.1007/s13389-015-0101-6

12. Chudnovsky, D., Chudnovsky, G.: Sequences of numbers generated by addition in formal groups and new primality and factorization tests. Adv. Appl. Math. **7**(4), 385–434 (1986). https://doi.org/10.1016/0196-8858(86)90023-0

13. Devigne, J., Joye, M.: Binary Huff curves. In: Kiayias, A. (ed.) CT-RSA 2011. LNCS, vol. 6558, pp. 340–355. Springer, Heidelberg (2011). https://doi.org/10.1007/978-3-642-19074-2_22

14. Farashahi, R.R., Hosseini, S.G.: Differential addition on binary elliptic curves. In: Duquesne, S., Petkova-Nikova, S. (eds.) WAIFI 2016. LNCS, vol. 10064, pp. 21–35. Springer, Cham (2016). https://doi.org/10.1007/978-3-319-55227-9_2

15. Farashahi, R.R., Joye, M.: Efficient arithmetic on Hessian curves. In: Nguyen, P.Q., Pointcheval, D. (eds.) PKC 2010. LNCS, vol. 6056, pp. 243–260. Springer, Heidelberg (2010). https://doi.org/10.1007/978-3-642-13013-7_15

16. Find, M.G., Peralta, R.: Better circuits for binary polynomial multiplication. IEEE Trans. Comput. **68**(4), 624–630 (2019). https://doi.org/10.1109/TC.2018.2874662

17. Itoh, T., Tsujii, S.: A fast algorithm for computing multiplicative inverses in $GF(2^m)$ using normal bases. Inf. Comput. **78**(3), 171–177 (1988). https://doi.org/10.1016/0890-5401(88)90024-7

18. Käsper, E., Schwabe, P.: Faster and timing-attack resistant AES-GCM. In: Clavier, C., Gaj, K. (eds.) CHES 2009. LNCS, vol. 5747, pp. 1–17. Springer, Heidelberg (2009). https://doi.org/10.1007/978-3-642-04138-9_1

19. Koblitz, N.: Elliptic curve cryptosystems. Math. Comput. **48**(177), 203–209 (1987)

20. Lange, T.: A note on López-Dahab coordinates. IACR Cryptology ePrint Archive 2004, 323 (2004). http://eprint.iacr.org/2004/323

21. López, J., Dahab, R.: Improved algorithms for elliptic curve arithmetic in $GF(2^n)$. In: Tavares, S., Meijer, H. (eds.) SAC 1998. LNCS, vol. 1556, pp. 201–212. Springer, Heidelberg (1999). https://doi.org/10.1007/3-540-48892-8_16

22. López, J., Dahab, R.: Fast multiplication on elliptic curves over $GF(2^m)$ without precomputation. In: Koç, Ç.K., Paar, C. (eds.) CHES 1999. LNCS, vol. 1717, pp. 316–327. Springer, Heidelberg (1999). https://doi.org/10.1007/3-540-48059-5_27

23. Miller, V.S.: Use of elliptic curves in cryptography. In: Williams, H.C. (ed.) CRYPTO 1985. LNCS, vol. 218, pp. 417–426. Springer, Heidelberg (1986). https://doi.org/10.1007/3-540-39799-X_31

24. Montgomery, P.L.: Speeding the pollard and elliptic curve methods of factorization. Math. Comput. **48**(177), 243–264 (1987). https://doi.org/10.2307/2007888

25. Oliveira, T., López, J., Aranha, D.F., Rodríguez-Henríquez, F.: Two is the fastest prime: lambda coordinates for binary elliptic curves. J. Cryptogr. Eng. **4**(1), 3–17 (2014). https://doi.org/10.1007/s13389-013-0069-z

26. Oliveira, T., López, J., Rodríguez-Henríquez, F.: The Montgomery ladder on binary elliptic curves. J. Cryptogr. Eng. **8**(3), 241–258 (2018). https://doi.org/10.1007/s13389-017-0163-8

27. Seo, H., Liu, Z., Nogami, Y., Choi, J., Kim, H.: Binary field multiplication on ARMv8. Secur. Commun. Netw. **9**(13), 2051–2058 (2016). https://doi.org/10.1002/sec.1462

28. Shacham, H., Boneh, D.: Improving SSL handshake performance via batching. In: Naccache, D. (ed.) CT-RSA 2001. LNCS, vol. 2020, pp. 28–43. Springer, Heidelberg (2001). https://doi.org/10.1007/3-540-45353-9_3

29. Stam, M.: On Montgomery-like representations for elliptic curves over $GF(2^k)$. In: Desmedt, Y.G. (ed.) PKC 2003. LNCS, vol. 2567, pp. 240–254. Springer, Heidelberg (2003). https://doi.org/10.1007/3-540-36288-6_18

30. Stebila, D., Mosca, M.: Post-quantum key exchange for the internet and the open quantum safe project. In: Avanzi, R., Heys, H. (eds.) SAC 2016. LNCS, vol. 10532, pp. 14–37. Springer, Cham (2017). https://doi.org/10.1007/978-3-319-69453-5_2

31. Taverne, J., Faz-Hernández, A., Aranha, D.F., Rodríguez-Henríquez, F., Hankerson, D., López, J.: Software implementation of binary elliptic curves: impact of the carry-less multiplier on scalar multiplication. In: Preneel, B., Takagi, T. (eds.) CHES 2011. LNCS, vol. 6917, pp. 108–123. Springer, Heidelberg (2011). https://doi.org/10.1007/978-3-642-23951-9_8

32. Taverne, J., Faz-Hernández, A., Aranha, D.F., Rodríguez-Henríquez, F., Hankerson, D., López, J.: Speeding scalar multiplication over binary elliptic curves using the new carry-less multiplication instruction. J. Cryptogr. Eng. **1**(3), 187–199 (2011). https://doi.org/10.1007/s13389-011-0017-8

33. Tuveri, N., Brumley, B.B.: Start your ENGINEs: dynamically loadable contemporary crypto. In: IEEE Secure Development Conference, SecDev 2019, McLean, VA, USA, 25–27 September 2019. IEEE Computer Society (2019). https://eprint.iacr.org/2018/354

34. Wiggers, T.: Energy-efficient ARM64 cluster with cryptanalytic applications. In: Lange, T., Dunkelman, O. (eds.) LATINCRYPT 2017. LNCS, vol. 11368, pp. 175–188. Springer, Cham (2019). https://doi.org/10.1007/978-3-030-25283-0_10

Author Index

Printed in the United States
By Bookmasters